MW01258992

Bach's *Well-tempered Clavier*

Bach's *Well-tempered Clavier*

THE 48 PRELUDES AND FUGUES

David Ledbetter

YALE UNIVERSITY PRESS
NEW HAVEN AND LONDON

For information about this and other Yale University Press publications, please contact
U.S. Office: sales.press@yale.edu www.yale.edu/yup
Europe Office: sales@yaleup.co.uk www.yaleup.co.uk

Set in Bembo by Northern Phototypesetting Co. Ltd, Bolton
Printed in the United States of America

ISBN 0–300–09707–7

Library of Congress Control Number 20021099926

A catalogue record for this book is available from the British Library

10 9 8 7 6 5 4 3 2

Published with assistance from the Annie Burr Lewis Fund.

Frontispiece: Bach's original title-page (1722) for Book I.

In memory of
Stanislav Heller

Contents

Part Two: Commentaries

Illustrations

Preface

The two Books of *The Well-tempered Clavier* of J.S. Bach, commonly known in English as The 48 Preludes and Fugues, are at the centre of European civilisation, and are the beloved property of generations of people all over the world. If all of western art music were to be lost and only one work survive, this would be the first choice of many. The achievement of the music at an intellectual level alone puts Bach among the leading intellects of European history. Yet his ability to explore and develop musical materials is fully matched by the scope and power with which he explores moods, emotions and characters, and this is what has made his music so beloved by so many. His own contemporaries remarked how, in spite of formidable complexity, his mastery of ordering materials and of the arts of rhetoric was such that he could reach out and touch the hearts even of those with no special knowledge of musical techniques. The music of Bach transcends the techniques, styles and types of his time and can communicate directly with people who know nothing except the notes he wrote. Why, then, should anybody want to read, let alone write, a book about the very musical traditions he transcends?

The 48 grew out of Bach's teaching activity and, like other great educators in his tradition such as Lassus and Schütz, his teaching was by musical example rather than verbal pretext. He dealt almost uniquely with talented pupils intending to be professional musicians, and they provided him with a knowledgeable audience who could appreciate and encourage him in the speculative aspects of composition. He took virtually every ingredient of music available to him and treated it in the most inventive and original way, finding new possibilities and exploiting the tensions of new combinations, not only of materials, but also of styles, types, genres. All of these he transmuted in the alembic of a powerful intellect and personality, making something great from even humble materials so that they have endured beyond their time. To ignore the context means that we can see only the finished pieces, and have to invent some way of our own to try to penetrate the surface of the music. This was not Bach's idea at all. His aim was to draw people into sharing his own competence and standards, through application and knowledge. If we are not drawn into this process we turn our backs on the most thrilling artistic training that music has to offer.

To write about music of such quality, so well known, and with such an enormous amount written about it already is a daunting prospect. I came to it through giving music college courses essentially for performers. The 48 Preludes and Fugues are the very sophisticated end product of many strands of a rich tradition, and an ideal vantage point from which to survey virtually all aspects of Baroque keyboard music. Players who are unaware of the stylistic variety in the background tend to make Bach's music sound all the same. But they are also naturally curious about music which so obviously does not reveal all its secrets on first acquaintance. Unlike more recent composers who were inspired by the 48 to produce works demonstrating personal systems of their own, Bach dealt entirely in traditional materials that were readily understood by (at least the better educated of) his contemporaries, and this is a fundamental difference. Awareness of the richness and variety of the tradition gives richness and variety to the performance.

For music analysis too a knowledge of context is vital, otherwise false conclusions can be drawn. In looking for recommendable literature I found much traditional analysis too narrowly focussed on pitch events. Bach lived at a time when prototypes of dance, sonata, concerto and aria were being fused, a process to which he contributed with great cogency and resourcefulness in his suites, partitas, sonatas, and preludes and fugues. An analysis that ignores elements of compositional prototype, style and genre is not telling us much about why Bach wrote the notes the way he did. Another reason why his music speaks is Bach's essential practicality as a musician: for him writing a fugue was as practical a matter as tuning a harpsichord. Yet even something so obvious as the very resourceful way in which he exploits pitch levels on the four-octave keyboard for the structural and emotional projection of a piece hardly figures in any analyses I have seen. Fugues in particular tend to be treated as abstract entities when for Bach they were rooted in improvisation, sonority, character and expression.

The literature about Bach stretches back one quarter of a millennium to his own time. This book reflects the period of the late twentieth-century early music revival, when the interest and dedication of a generation of instrument makers and players combined to make possible once more direct practical knowledge of the instruments and repertories of Bach's time. Like others of my generation I started with Bach, but then went away to explore these other fields before returning. There has been a vast amount of research and new thinking about Bach in the last quarter-century. My intention is to make at least some of this available in a monograph which people can use to nourish and deepen their understanding of the 48; not to present finished analyses and conclusions, but to sketch background concepts and techniques in the commentaries and thereby equip readers to make their own journeys of discovery in contemplating the music for themselves. This is only one of many possible approaches and I am very conscious of its limitations. Even in terms of context much more is now becoming known in detail about Bach's immediate environment. All I can say is that I have made a start, and I look forward to the refinements that others will assuredly bring. I have not addressed the vast issue of reception history. The 48 has been at the centre of music training and analysis since Bach's time, and his general influence on composers is immeasurable. This is the area where most new work is currently being done and much needs to be defined before a general summary can be attempted.

I originally aimed to deal with issues at the level where they interested me, while at the same time trying not to leave behind readers lacking the requisite technical knowledge. I found this ultimately too cumbersome, and the interesting points were swamped in basic explanations such as could be found in many other books. I have therefore necessarily had to concentrate on what is new. Explanations of basic concepts are readily available in the *New Harvard* and *New Grove* dictionaries of music. I have, however, included a Glossary of technical terms, and for the very technical business of tuning and temperament an Appendix that aims to put the first principles in a concise and straightforward way.

I wish to express my thanks to all who have assisted me in this project. Special thanks are due to the Leverhulme Trust, who provided me with a research year, and to the Research Committee and Library of the Royal Northern College of Music. I wish to thank particularly the music librarians of the British Library, Cambridge University Library, the Staatsbibliothek zu Berlin and the Leipziger Städtische Bibliotheken; also Bärenreiter Verlag for permission to reprint the extract in Ex.8.1b. Many individuals have contributed to my work, in particular Lothar Bemmann, John Caldwell, David Fuller, Hubert Henkel, Francis Knights, Dieter Krickeberg, Grant O'Brien, Winfried Schrammek and Lance Whitehead; Jon Baxendale has set the music examples. Of Bach scholars, I am particularly grateful to Alfred Dürr for his encouragement and for very kindly allowing me to see materials for the Neue Bach-Ausgabe edition of Book II before it was published, and to Yo Tomita, whose generosity with time and information is seemingly inexhaustible. Finally I would like to express personal gratitude to the memory of Joseph Groocock, who was an inspiring and unstinting teacher of fugue at an early stage of my career and whose own book on the 48 is due for publication at the same time as this; and to Brigitte von Ungern-Sternberg for much fun, support and assistance in Berlin.

Abbreviations

A large number of sources for *The Well-tempered Clavier* are mentioned in this book. It is not possible to give full details for all of them: for further information the reader is referred to the Critical Notes in AB I and II, and to KB V/5, and V/6.1 and 2.

AB I, II	*J.S. Bach: The Well-tempered Clavier, Part I, Part II*, ed. R. Jones (London: The Associated Board of the Royal Schools of Music, 1994)
BA I, II	*Johann Sebastian Bach: The Well-tempered Clavier I, II*, ed. A. Dürr (Kassel: Bärenreiter, 1989, 1996)
BG XIV	*Das wohltemperirte Clavier, erster Teil, zweiter Teil*, ed. F. Kroll, Gesamtausgabe der Bach-Gesellschaft, Jahrgang XIV (Leipzig: Bach-Gesellschaft, [1866])
BR	*The Bach Reader*, ed. H.T. David and A. Mendel (New York: Norton, 2/1966)
BWV	*Bach-Werke-Verzeichnis*, ed. W. Schmieder (Wiesbaden: Breitkopf & Härtel, 2/1990)
D-B	Staatsbibliothek zu Berlin
D-Dl	Dresden, Sächsische Landesbibliothek, Musikabteilung
DdT	*Denkmäler deutscher Tonkunst*
Dok.I, II, III	*Bach-Dokumente*, ed. W. Neumann and H.-J. Schulze (Kassel: Bärenreiter, 1963–78)
DTÖ	*Denkmäler der Tonkunst in Österreich*
GB-Lbl	London, The British Library
I-Bc	Bologna, Civico Museo Bibliografico-Musicale
KB V/5	Plath, Wolfgang, *Johann Sebastian Bach: Neue Ausgabe sämtlicher Werke Serie V. Band 5 Klavierbüchlein für Wilhelm Friedemann Bach. Kritischer Bericht* (Kassel: Bärenreiter, 1963)
KB V/6.1	Dürr, Alfred, *Johann Sebastian Bach: Neue Ausgabe sämtlicher Werke Serie V. Band 6.1 Das wohltemperierte Klavier I. Kritischer Bericht* (Kassel: Bärenreiter, 1989)
KB V/6.2	Dürr, Alfred and Bettina Faulstich, *Johann Sebastian Bach: Neue Ausgabe sämtlicher Werke Serie V. Band 6.2 Das wohltemperierte Klavier II. Kritischer Bericht* (Kassel: Bärenreiter, 1996)
MB	*Musica britannica*
MGG	*Die Musik in Geschichte und Gegenwart*, ed. F. Blume (Kassel: Bärenreiter, 1949–79); ed. L. Finscher (2/1994–)

NBA V/6.1, 2	*Johann Sebastian Bach: Das wohltemperierte Klavier I, II*, ed. A. Dürr, Neue Ausgabe sämtlicher Werke Serie V. Band 6.1, 2 (Kassel: Bärenreiter, 1989, 1995)
NBR	*The New Bach Reader*, ed. H.T. David and A. Mendel, revised C. Wolff (New York: Norton, 1998)
New Grove 2	*The New Grove Dictionary of Music and Musicians*, ed. S. Sadie (London: Macmillan, 2/2001)
NL-DHgm	The Hague, Gemeente Museum
PF	*Preludes Fughettas composed in conjunction with the Well-tempered Clavier II*, ed. A. Dürr (Kassel: Bärenreiter, 1995)
Schweitzer I, II	*J.S. Bach: Le musicien poète* (Paris 1905; enlarged German edition Leipzig 1908); translated E. Newman (London: A. & C. Black, 1911)
Spitta I, II, III	Spitta, Philipp, *Johann Sebastian Bach* (Leipzig 1873–80); translated C. Bell and J.A. Fuller-Maitland (London: Novello, 1883–5)
US-NH	New Haven, Yale University, The Library of the School of Music
US-Wc	Washington, Library of Congress
VBN	Beißwenger, Kirsten, *Johann Sebastian Bachs Notenbibliothek* (Kassel: Bärenreiter, 1992)
Wegweiser	Anon., *Kurtzer jedoch gründlicher Wegweiser* (Augsburg, 4/1708, 5/1718); partial ed. R. Walter (Altötting: Coppenrath, 3/1964)

Introduction

Bach had little patience with expressing his artistic purposes in words, at least in written form. The first volume of the *Bach-Dokumente*, in which his writings are collected, is by far the slimmest of the three, and the writings consist mainly of business letters and references. The one place where he did express his musical intentions verbally is in title-pages, whether of publications or of fair-copy manuscript collections such as the *Orgel-Büchlein*, the Inventions and Sinfonias, and *The Well-tempered Clavier*. In these the terms he used and the intentions he expressed are very revealing if read with a sense of their use in his environment. This book therefore has a series of six introductory chapters aiming to give a context for each of the principal terms of the 1722 title-page of *The Well-tempered Clavier* (Book I). Then, since both Books contain groups of pieces that work systematically through possibilities, details of which are vital for understanding the 48, not least for performers, and since people playing individual preludes and fugues will want some particular comment for the pieces they are working on, there are two chapters (one for each Book) giving more detailed information about each of the 96 pieces.

1. *The 1722 title-page*

The formulation of a title-page should ideally be brief and to the point, and in Bach's day took a standard form of: (1) motto, (2) statement of genre, (3) details of use, (4) author, (5) author's professional position, and (6) details of publication, where relevant.[1]

The 1722 title-page may therefore be analysed as follows (with the principal terms in bold):

(1) Das **Wohl*temperirte Clavier***.	*The* ***Well-tempered Clavier***.
(2) oder ***Præludia***, und ***Fugen*** durch **alle Tone und Semitonia**, So Wohl *tertiam majorem* oder *Ut Re Mi* anlangend, als auch *tertiam minorem* oder *Re Mi Fa* betreffend.	or **Preludes** and **Fugues** through **all the tones and semitones**, both with the major 3rd, or Ut Re Mi and with the minor 3rd, or Re Mi Fa.
(3) **Zum Nutzen und Gebrauch der Lehr-begierigen *Musical*ischen Jugend**, als auch derer in diesem *studio* schon *habil* seyenden besonderem ZeitVertreib	**For the use and improvement of musical youth eager to learn**, and for the particular delight of those already skilled in this discipline
(4) auffgesetzet und verfertiget von Johann Sebastian Bach	composed and presented by Johann Sebastian Bach
(5) *p.t.* HochFürstlich Anhalt-Cöthenischen Capel-Meistern und Directore derer Cammer *Musiquen*.	while capellmeister to the Prince of Anhalt-Cöthen, and director of his chamber music.[2]
(6) *Anno* 1722.	in the year 1722.

In taking these terms as chapter headings I have put the noun *Clavier* first and the qualifier *Well-tempered* second in order not to begin with what is probably the most abstruse discussion for the non-expert reader. There follow chapters on the prelude, the fugue, tonality, and the place of the 48 in Bach's educational programme.

Reference is made in the text to individual sources where they are relevant to the argument of this book. Full details of the very complex source situation are readily available in the Critical Notes of AB I and II, and in KB V/6.1 and 2. I have therefore not reproduced the details here, and have included only brief information in this Introduction in order to sketch the background to the genesis of the two collections.

2. Genesis and sources

Book I The origins of both Books probably go back to Bach's teaching at Weimar. Heterogeneous origins are more obvious for Book II, but Book I also is a composite collection. The only documentary evidence for the composition of (presumably) Book I is a section of E.L. Gerber's life of Bach in his *Lexicon der Tonkünstler* (Leipzig 1790). Gerber's father, H.N. Gerber, had studied with Bach in the mid-1720s, including *The Well-tempered Clavier* (Book I) which Bach played through to him no less than three times, so Gerber's 'certain tradition' may be a family one.[3] The whole passage is worth quoting:

> . . . And this astonishing facility, this fingering never used before him, he owed to his own works; for often, he said, he had found himself compelled

> to make use of the night in order to be able to bring to realisation what he had written during the day. This is all the easier to believe since it was never his habit in composing to ask advice of his clavier. Thus, according to a certain tradition, he wrote his *Tempered Clavier* (consisting of fugues and preludes, some of them very intricate, in all 24 keys) in a place where ennui, boredom, and the absence of any kind of musical instrument forced him to resort to this pastime. (Dok.III p.468, NBR p.372)

Speculation has attempted to identify the 'place': perhaps the prison at Weimar where Bach was detained for a month just before he left Weimar for Cöthen at the end of 1717, or Karlsbad (Karlovy Vary in Bohemia), a spa town where he went in the suite of Prince Leopold of Cöthen on several occasions. The latter is unlikely since the purpose of his presence there was to demonstrate his own ability and to direct the other musicians the Prince took with him. The passage is based on things that are certainly true of Bach, but it is also tainted with decorative myth-making aimed at presenting Bach as extraordinary and unique in all respects, a feature common to many later anecdotes. The 'fingering' concerns Bach's use of the thumb (a point also mentioned by C.P.E. Bach). Bach certainly seems to have developed a technique based on pivoting over the thumb, more advanced than what had been general in his youth, and the Book I preludes that appear in Wilhelm Friedemann Bach's *Clavier-Büchlein* show the sort of exercise he developed for this. But he was by no means alone, and the technique he developed was no different from that described by Rameau in his *Méthode* of 1724. That Bach composed away from the keyboard will impress those unaccustomed to writing music, and of course he could never have produced the prodigious amount of concerted church music of his early Leipzig years had this not been so. But for keyboard music Gerber's assertion is contradicted by C.P.E. Bach, who tells us that Bach tended to base his clavier works on improvisation ('Fantasiren'; Dok.III p.289, NBR p.399). The 'place of ennui and boredom' also has generic associations, particularly with learned counterpoint ('very intricate fugues'), just as the famous descriptions of the impassioned playing on the violin by Corelli (in the 1709 English translation of Raguenet), or on the clavichord by C.P.E. Bach (Burney) resonate with classic descriptions of the lyre playing of Orpheus. Luigi Battiferri, in the Letter to the Reader of his collection of learned keyboard *Ricercari* (Bologna 1669, a work which may be in the background to Bach's learned counterpoint), claims to have written them 'more to avoid idleness than for any other purpose'.[4] There is a note of disparagement and apology here for such an uningratiating pursuit, shared by Gerber's 'Zeitvertreib' (pastime), which is most definitely not shared by Bach's 'besonderem Zeitvertreib' in the 1722 title-page. If there is a grain of truth behind Gerber's story, it may apply to the more schematically planned fugues of Book I, though even these have a strongly tactile keyboard quality not found in Battiferri's ricercars.

The sources of Book I give a more suggestive impression.[5] The central, and by far the most important, source is the autograph fair copy (Staatsbibliothek zu Berlin, Mus.Ms.Bach P 415) whose title-page is analysed above.[6] But there are also around half a dozen sources containing early versions of pieces. Of these the best known is the *Clavier-Büchlein* for Wilhelm Friedemann Bach, begun by Bach on 22 January 1720. Into this Friedemann, around 1721 and with assistance from his father, copied early versions of 11 of the first 12 preludes of Book I (there is no prelude in E flat major).[7] The interest of this particular source, apart from its very direct connexion with Bach, is what it seems to reveal about Bach's educational programme and the place of the Book I preludes in it (this is discussed in Chapters Three and Six below). It also raises several questions. Was there originally a series of educational preludes without fugues? To what extent do the fugues really belong to the preludes, or were they originally two different collections, probably not covering all keys?

Suggestive as the *Clavier-Büchlein* is, it does not contain the very earliest known versions. These are in a manuscript (currently unlocated but there is a microfilm of it) copied around 1800 for J.N. Forkel (Bach's first biographer), who edited one of the very first printed editions of the 48 (Vienna: Hoffmeister, 1801).[8] The copy was made from a (now lost) original that Forkel presumably had acquired from W.F. or C.P.E. Bach, both of whom he knew personally. Since this is already a complete copy of Book I it unfortunately tells us little about how the concept of a collection of preludes and fugues in all keys originally germinated in Bach's mind. For that we can only speculate, considering the nature of the pieces and the circumstances of Bach's career around 1720. In assessing the relationship between prelude and fugue, it should be remembered that fugue for Bach was not an abstract exercise. The ability to project complex counterpoint was for him the touchstone of good keyboard playing, so the fugues are no less an exercise in practical keyboard skill than the preludes (Dok.III p.476, NBR p.322).

Signs that a number of the pieces were originally written with the old 'Dorian' key signatures suggest that they were not conceived as part of a collection covering all keys. Also, some pieces show signs of having been transposed into the remoter keys (D sharp minor, G sharp minor), implying a mixed origin for the collection, with some pieces newly composed for the purpose and others brought in from older stocks. Some pieces may even have originally been notated in the old keyboard tablature (KB V/6.1 p.357). Judging by the early sources it looks as if Bach gradually built up the collection in the same way as he was later to assemble Book II, by having individual preludes and fugues on separate leaves, generally with the prelude on one side and the fugue on the other. These could be kept together in a box and corrected, jettisoned, or added to as Bach refined the pieces, until he was finally ready to make the

1722 fair copy.[9] It was during this process that Bach got round to using the modern system of key signatures.[10]

The move towards using every note on the keyboard as a tonic was very much in the air at the time (fully discussed in Chapters Two and Five), so Bach may well have been working around to it anyway. As far as a proximate stimulus is concerned, this may have been provided by the Hamburg composer and writer on matters musical Johann Mattheson, who also seems to have been in the background to Book II. Mattheson is perhaps best known for his youthful escapades with Handel who, like many others, seems later to have wanted to keep him at arm's length (Burrows 1994 pp.16–18). Mattheson abandoned a career as singer and opera composer when he started to go deaf, and took to writing about music, particularly for a new type of elegant and lettered audience that had little patience with what they considered the pedantry and obscurity of traditional German writing. In 1713 he published his first book presenting his new view, replacing old cantoral tradition with current French fashion as implied by the word *Orchestre* in its title. His strictures on tradition raised hackles, most notably those of Johann Heinrich Buttstett, a distant relative of Bach's and organist at Erfurt, who in 1716 published a reply.[11] In it he defended technical aspects of the tradition such as the modes and solmisation (the system of hexachords based on calling the notes Ut Re Mi etc. rather than letters of the alphabet) by appealing to the old Renaissance neo-Platonist tradition of the heavenly harmony which, after all, had been subscribed to by Martin Luther himself and was the basis for the value placed on music in the Lutheran Church (see Chapter Five).

Bach himself deeply valued this tradition, not just as a large part of his connoisseurship of musical styles and materials, but also as the basis of the livelihood of generations of his family. In 1717 Mattheson published a second *Orchestre* defending the first and viciously attacking Buttstett. Whatever Bach thought of Buttstett, he could hardly overlook the fact that Mattheson had seen fit to include in this a quite gratuitous and obscene criticism of Bach's father-in-law, Johann Michael Bach, a good composer whom Bach respected, painting him as a provincial booby with inadequate grasp of fashionable French style.[12] In the midst of this Mattheson had the impudence to insert a patronising footnote addressed to J.S. Bach in Weimar, asking him to provide biographical information towards a projected Triumphal Arch (*Ehrenpforte*) of 100 German musicians, not in the event published till 1740 (Dok.II p.65, BR pp.228–9). It can hardly be wondered at that Bach failed to respond to this invitation. Further circumstances that may have a bearing are that Mattheson published in Hamburg in 1719 a collection of figured-bass exercises in all 24 keys, the first publication to do this; and that Bach was in Hamburg in November 1720 playing for the post of organist at the Jakobikirche. Bach rarely expressed himself in written words, but his 1722 title-page makes a point of describing major and minor keys in old-fashioned terms of the hexachord (Ut Re Mi), and the very first prelude and fugue could be read as a supportive commentary on Buttstett's frontispiece (see Chapter Five and the commentaries on the C major and D minor pairs in Chapter Seven). There could be no finer irony than that Bach, the firm supporter of tradition, should have written the first collection of fully composed pieces to use every key as a tonic, amply demonstrating an advanced connoisseurship of the latest French styles and how they might be given depth by traditional techniques.

It is most unlikely that Bach intended printed publication of *The Well-tempered Clavier* of 1722. The cost of engraving such a quantity of complex music in keyboard score would have put copies way beyond the reach of its intended market.[13] In any case, the prevalence of printed over manuscript copies of music did not begin to establish itself until the 1780s. Copying music was in Bach's day considered one of the principal ways of learning to compose, involving humility, effort and close observation. The 1722 fair copy was made by Bach as an exemplar for students to copy from. The success of his achievement may be gauged by the fact that more copies were made of it than of any other Bach work.[14] From corrections made in P 415, and how these are reflected in copies, we may distinguish an original state and three stages of revision, commonly assessed as A1 (1722), A2 (perhaps 1732, the date at the end of the MS), A3 (probably after 1736), and A4 (probably in the 1740s; NBA V/6.1 p.X). The later revisions of Book I therefore overlapped with the preparation of Book II.

After Bach's death it is not known what happened to the autograph. It is not listed in C.P.E. Bach's estate in 1790. Robert Volkmann (composer) acquired it some time after 1840, and there is a tradition that it suffered flood damage from the Danube in Budapest where Volkmann lived from 1842. Volkmann gave it during his lifetime to Richard Wagener, professor of anatomy at Marburg, who presented it to the Royal Library, Berlin, in 1874. With time the MS deteriorated, particularly because the ferrous content of Bach's (home-made) ink oxidised and ate through the paper, meaning that note-heads would fall out like confetti when you opened a page. In order to counteract this a number of pages were covered with chiffon silk in 1941/2 (this is visible in the facsimile edition). It then turned out that the adhesive keeping the chiffon in place was in turn degrading the paper, so in 1986 the chiffon was removed and each page split (like Melba toast) and given a new paper core. Now it lives in a box containing the old binding (dating from the mid-nineteenth century), the bits of chiffon silk, and the MS itself in a linen folder (KB V/6.1 pp.19–20).

Of the copies, of special interest for performance indications are that by Bach's pupil C.G. Meißner (*NL-DHgm* 69.D.14, formerly known as the 'Zurich Autograph'; see NBA V/6.1 Anhang 3); Anna Magdalena Bach's (P 202), with many ornaments added by Wilhelm Friedemann Bach; and the personal copy of Bach's pupil Kirnberger (not copied by him: *D-B* Am.B.57 (1)), with fingerings presumably by Kirnberger (see the commentary on the B flat major prelude).

Book II During the decade 1735–45 Bach produced a phenomenal amount of keyboard music, both new works and revisions of old ones. Part II of the *Clavier-Übung* was published in 1735, Part III in 1739, and the Goldberg Variations in 1741. From 1738 to 1742 he put together Book II and at the same time prepared the manuscript of the so-called 'Eighteen' chorale preludes for organ (P 271). As these were finished he went straight into *The Art of Fugue* and prepared the first version of that (P 200) around 1742. Bach's preoccupations of the 1730s are most clearly seen in *Clavier-Übung* III. They are an interest in the most traditional (*stile antico*) and the most 'modern' (galant style), sometimes kept separate, but sometimes combined as opposite manners in the same piece. These are also worked in Book II, together with Bach's renewed interest in genera of counterpoint, an interest he was to develop systematically in *The Art of Fugue.*

There are several reasons why Bach may have wished to provide a counterpart to *The Well-tempered Clavier* of 1722. He had been using that as teaching material for fifteen years and very probably wanted variety, and also pieces in the latest styles. The late 1720s and 1730s are the time when he had the greatest number of pupils, with further talented children born in 1732 (Johann Christoph Friedrich) and 1735 (Johann Christian) who would eventually need to be catered for. The style issue was very important in the 1730s because of the criticism of him published in 1737 by Johann Adolph Scheibe, accusing him of a heavy, outmoded style, overloaded with counterpoint. The controversy over this was to plague Bach for the best part of a decade (NBR pp.337–53). In 1738 defences of him were published by a university friend, J.A. Birnbaum, and a learned friend and pupil, L. Mizler. On a day-to-day level it was shortly before this that Bach's relations with the Rector of the Thomasschule had reached their lowest ebb (1736–7). It is therefore not surprising that he retreated into the more speculative area of his composition (keyboard music) where he had the largest and most appreciative following, and where he could deal with the most enduring artistic principles. In addition, it was around 1738 that his colleague at the Frauenkirche at Halle, Gottfried Kirchhoff (who took the post there in 1714 when Bach turned it down), published his (now lost) *L'ABC musical: Präludia und Fugen aus allen Tönen*, expressed as *partimenti.* And in 1737–9 Johann Mattheson impinged again with his largest and most prestigious book, *Der vollkommene Capellmeister*, explaining, among much else, genera of counterpoint, and following on from two publications (1735, 1737) of keyboard fugues of his own on several subjects.[15] *Der vollkommene Capellmeister* contains another invitation to Bach, to write fugues on three subjects, which could join Mattheson's own (Dok.II p.378). Bach commented on the invitation in his own way in Book II; to have responded in any other way would have been to lend his weight to Mattheson's opportunistic persecution of others.

The source situation for Book II is considerably more complex than for Book I, as is the literature.[16] There is no single authoritative autograph source to compare with P 415. What we have is a collection of individual leaves known as the London autograph (roughly ⅜ is in the hand of Anna Magdalena Bach), begun in 1739;[17] and a fair copy dated 1744 made by Bach's eventual son-in-law Johann Christoph Altnickol, whose first duty as a pupil of Bach's was evidently to make the copy (P 430). He must have been bright because Bach seemingly asked him to make alterations on his own initiative. The problem is that what Altnickol copied from was not the London autograph but another original (probably begun around 1738; now lost) which seems to have contained to some extent earlier states of pieces. In other words, Bach seems to have had two boxes with individual preludes and fugues on separate leaves and to have worked on both of them, but unsystematically. Before he gave Altnickol the older one to copy from he went through it again (around 1742–4), so that it ended up with a mixture of partly earlier, but also partly later, readings than the London autograph. This creates problems for editors in deciding on a final version, solved by Alfred Dürr in NBA V/6.2 by giving two complete versions of Book II, one from the London autograph and one from P 430.[18]

The sources for Book II reveal much more about the anthology nature of the collection than do those of Book I. There are some thirteen sources containing early versions. The earliest of these (none autograph) date from the 1720s, though since they are copies the originals must have been older and some items may well go back to Weimar days, even before Bach started compiling Book I. In assessing the original date of a piece it has to be borne in mind that relative simplicity does not necessarily imply a very early date. It could be that a piece was sketched by Bach during a lesson, and that could have happened at any time. Also, a piece may seem simple in comparison with what Bach ultimately made of it, but sophisticated in comparison with the sort of prototype it relates to (see the commentary on the C sharp major fugue in Chapter Eight).[19]

Two sources show us how Bach began assembling materials for Book II around 1738. One, copied by his pupil J.F. Agricola (P 595), has four fughettas, in C major and minor and D major and minor, beginning a series in the commoner keys. The major-key fughettas were transposed up a semitone to C sharp and E flat when they went as fugues into Book II. The other source was copied by Anna Magdalena Bach (P 226), and has a prelude in C major (transposed up to C sharp in Book II) and the D minor pair. Thereafter we can see in the London autograph two campaigns for covering the chromatic octave.

The first (*c.*1739–40) has the commoner keys, the preludes are headed 'Praeludium', and the pieces are copied either by Bach or Anna Magdalena or a combination of both. The keys are c, d, E flat, E, e, F, f sharp, G, g, A, a, b. The second campaign (*c.*1740–41) has the advanced keys, with preludes headed 'Prelude', copied by Bach. The keys are C sharp, d sharp, F sharp, g sharp, B flat, b flat, B. The last pieces added are the A flat prelude (*c.*1741) and the C major pair and the A flat fugue (*c.*1742, worked up from earlier pieces). The pairs in C sharp minor, D major, and F minor are now missing, but evidently came in the second campaign since Bach's most literal copyist heads them 'Prelude' in his copy (KB V/6.2 p.33).

We have no autograph title-page for Book II, but most copies have something like that of Altnickol's 1744 copy (P 430) which is a cut-down version of the 1722 one:

> Des Wohltemperirten Claviers Zweyter Theil,
> besthehend in Praeludien und Fugen durch all Tone und Semitonien
> verfertiget von Johann Sebastian Bach,
> Königlich Pohlnisch und Churfürstl. Sächs. Hoff Compositeur, Capell-meister, und Directore Chori Musici In Leipzig.
> [Altnickols signature and the date are after the last fugue.][20]

Strictly speaking, each Book is a *Well-tempered Clavier* in itself, and to call it Part I or Part II implies that the part is incomplete. But judging by the prevalence of 'Zweiter Teil' on the title-pages of copies of Book II, at least Bach's pupils regarded this Book as Part II. There is no totally satisfactory solution so I have followed traditional English usage, with 'the 48' as a collective title, and Book I and Book II for the individual components.

Judging by the number of copies made it looks as if after 1740 every one of Bach's pupils had to make a copy. Of interest to performers is, again, Kirnberger's copy for its fingerings (*D-B* Am.B.57 (2); see the commentary on the G major fugue in Chapter Eight).

PART ONE

Concepts

CHAPTER ONE

Clavier

The unspecific nature of the word *Clavier* in early eighteenth-century Germany has left the question of Bach's preferred instrument for *The Well-tempered Clavier* open to much argumentation and assumptions based on personal prejudice. The main arguments for harpsichord and clavichord respectively were set out in a debate which ran through the first decade of the twentieth century: those on the harpsichord side by Karl Nef in two well-informed and rational articles (1903, 1909); those on the clavichord side by Richard Buchmayer (1908). Nef's arguments provided the substantive element in further articles by the arch-champion of the harpsichord, Wanda Landowska (1907, 1911), who added an element of her own hysterical prejudice against the clavichord. In spite of her knowledge of seventeenth- and eighteenth-century instruments, and even occasional public performances on them, her dislike of the clavichord was lifelong and passed on to generations of students. When Ralph Kirkpatrick broadcast Book I of the 48 on the clavichord in New York in 1945/6 Landowska is said to have remarked that it was a pity he could not afford a harpsichord.[1]

The clavichord side was championed in the early part of the century by Arnold Dolmetsch, who recorded eight preludes and fugues as well as the Chromatic Fantasia in 1932, and later by Ralph Kirkpatrick, who recorded the entire 48 in 1967.[2] Few recent recordings have been on the clavichord, and none on the sort of clavichord Bach might have used before 1740.

The articles of Nef and Buchmayer are refreshingly sensitive and objective, even if Buchmayer's repetition of Forkel's opinion that Bach would have found the harpsichord 'soul-less' does not necessarily reflect Bach's attitude. Later German writers suffered from a misapprehension of the nature of the harpsichord: Erwin Bodky (1960, but summarising writings going back to the 1930s) considered that the essence of harpsichord expression was in changing stops and manuals; Karl Geiringer (1967 p.259) thought that pieces without rests cannot be for harpsichord because manual changes are not possible. Such attitudes are difficult to understand now unless one remembers that from the 1930s to the 1960s the great majority of harpsichords made in Germany were of an 'improved' modern type which had neither the quality of sound nor the responsiveness of instruments of historical construction. Our knowledge of all keyboard instruments in Bach's environment, and particularly the harpsichord, clavichord, pianoforte, and even the Lautenwerk, has increased immeasurably since then.

1. *Clavier*

The most straightforward meaning of the term clavier is simply a keyboard. It is used when different types of keyboard are described, as for example by Johann Baptist Samber in his important organ tutor of 1704,[3] who lists the possibilities as (1) fully chromatic; (2) with short octave; and (3) with split keys (*subsemitonia*) (p.89). Bach's Weimar cousin J.G. Walther, in his educational treatise for Prince Johann Ernst of Sachsen-Weimar, gives the same basic definition, adding that it may be for the hands (*Manuale*) or the feet (*Pedale*; 1708 pp.44, 55). Various contemporary dictionaries define the word clavier as the keyboard of clavichord, harpsichord, or organ. This is precisely the usage of Werckmeister in his 1681 title-page 'Wie . . . ein *Clavier* wohl zu *temperiren* . . . sey', and in his numerous tirades against split keys. In view of other similarities of terminology between Bach and Werckmeister, this is the most likely definition of the term in the *Well-tempered Clavier* title: linked to the term 'wohltemperirt', a fully chromatic keyboard, without split keys, tuned so that all 24 keys are usable as tonics.

Although towards the end of Bach's life the term clavier came sometimes to be used specifically for the clavichord, for most of his life it meant keyboard instruments in general.[4] Usage was however variable, depending on context and phraseology. Mattheson in 1713 (pp.256, 262) expands on a distinction going back to Praetorius (1619) between organ, clavier (by which Mattheson means harpsichord) and *Instrument* (which includes other keyboards such as virginals, spinets, regals, positives, and clavichords). The use of the term *Instrument* for virginals or spinet stretches from Praetorius to Türk (1789), but the restriction of *Clavier* to harpsichord is unusual, perhaps because Mattheson was looking for an elegant German equivalent for the French *clavecin*. Clavier was also used in this sense in Bach's environment. In documents and title-pages having versions in both French and German, the German *Clavier* is commonly rendered by the French *clavecin*, though this is probably only because the harpsichord and spinet were the only two keyboard instruments in common use in France other than the organ. In the earliest account of the famous contest arranged between Bach and the French organist and harpsichordist

Louis Marchand in Dresden in September 1717, J.A. Birnbaum, who was probably writing with Bach's assistance, many times talks of Bach's prowess on 'organ and clavier'. Marchand was 'the greatest man in all France on the clavier and the organ' and the contest was to have taken place on the clavier (1739; Dok.II p.348, NBR p.79). Jakob Adlung, who claims to have had the same story from Bach himself, uses the same terminology (1758; Dok.III p.121, BR p.445). It is most unlikely in this instance that clavier can mean anything other than harpsichord.

In its general sense the main question is to what extent the term clavier included the organ. In general descriptions of keyboard instruments it could include the organ, as in Adlung's list (1768 I p.3) where it covers organ, clavichord, harpsichord, clavicytherium, spinet, Lautenwerk, Violdigambenwerk 'etc.', which is obviously meant to cover every available keyboard instrument. This is the range of the term also in various *Clavier-Übung* collections,[5] including Bach's own, which embrace organ (III), two-manual harpsichord (II and IV), and unspecified clavier (I). This inclusive usage was common in the titles of published collections of keyboard music, for obvious reasons.

There is however a distinction in the locution 'Orgel und Clavier' which is very common in describing people's accomplishments. This distinction is made in Bach's obituary, written mainly by C.P.E. Bach, and in Forkel's biography, where Bach as organist and as clavier player is the subject of two separate chapters. Bach himself made the distinction on occasion. For example in recommending G.G. Wagner for the post of cantor at Plauen in 1726, he lists among his accomplishments 'fernehin spielet er eine gute Orgel und *Clavier*' (Dok.I p.48). The same distinction is in the title-pages written around 1720, when Bach was rationalising and extending his teaching material, of the *Orgel-Büchlein*, and the *Clavier-Büchlein* for Wilhelm Friedemann Bach (Dok.I pp.214–15). Exclusion of the organ is implicit in the advertisement for the second and third Partitas in 1727, which is addressed 'denen Liebhabern des *Clavieres*' (Dok.II p.169), recalling the identical formulation in the title-page of the 1723 fair copy of the Inventions and Sinfonias (Dok.I p.220).

'Liebhaber' do not come into the 1722 title-page for Book I of the 48, their place being taken by 'those who are already skilled in this discipline', i.e. playing in all keys: Bach intended this collection primarily as the apex of his system of professional keyboard training, rather than for the delectation of amateurs. It is therefore more relevant to the 48 to consider the use of the term clavier in its educational sense, an equally common usage in the first half of the eighteenth century. It is a striking fact that during Bach's time at Weimar and Cöthen all documentary references to him having to do with a keyboard instrument other than the organ are explicitly to the harpsichord (*clavecin, Clavicymbel* etc.).[6] But for his pupils the term is always clavier. P.D. Kräuter, for example, had a grant in 1712 'for learning clavier and composition' with Bach

(Dok.II p.47), and formulations similar to this are common in accounts of pupils' activities throughout his career. With this instructional usage we are back to the keyboard itself, and only by extension to particular keyboard instruments. This is what was meant in the report of the committee responsible for appointing a new cantor for St Thomas's Leipzig in 1723, when they said Bach 'excelled in the clavier' (Dok.II p.94). He was a master of the keyboard. The crowning skill in that mastery was the ability to play with equal facility in all keys on the well-tempered keyboard.

2. *Harpsichord*

The only keyboard instruments, other than the organ, with which Bach is associated in references dating from his lifetime are the harpsichord, the Lautenwerk, the pianoforte, and the non-specific clavier. In works that have got a specific designation it is for harpsichord.[7] From 1708 Bach was court organist at Weimar, but also court harpsichordist, and had to apply himself to harpsichord repertoire (C. Wolff 1991 p.27). Both here and at Cöthen he had responsibility for the maintenance of harpsichords (Dok.II pp.41, 70, 86), a task at which he excelled according to C.P.E. Bach (Dok.III p.88). His prowess as a harpsichordist must have been as notable as that as organist, if the story of the Marchand competition is anything to go by, and the fact that Prince Leopold appreciated this is reflected by the stream of ensemble works with virtuoso harpsichord participation that Bach produced at Cöthen, when his involvement with the organ lessened, works that include the Fifth Brandenburg Concerto and sonatas with obbligato harpsichord. This continued in Leipzig, with the second part of the *Clavier-Übung* (1735) and the harpsichord concertos in the late 1730s. Bach's continuing interest in the development of virtuoso harpsichord technique is well attested in such works as the C minor Fantasia 'per il Cembalo' BWV 906 (*c.*1726–31) and the Goldberg Variations (1741), and there are some mild evidences of it in Book II of the 48 (*c.*1740).

One of the implications of the word clavier is that circumstances may well dictate which keyboard instrument to use. There can be no doubt that for Bach the harpsichord was the instrument for public performance. Even Forkel says that he regarded the clavichord as for study and private entertainment (1802 p.17, NBR p.436). It would therefore be natural to see pieces which use figurations and textures associated with public genres such as the concerto as more probably conceived for harpsichord. The aggressive virtuosity of the fugues in G major and A minor from Book I, the former with figurations strongly recalling the Fifth Brandenburg Concerto, the latter with its Vivaldian drive and grand expansion of texture towards the end, requires the brilliance of the harpsichord to make its full effect. The 'concert' endings that Bach added to some of the preludes from W.F. Bach's *Clavier-Büchlein* as he assembled Book I may indicate a change from one instrument to another, or at least a dual usability: the étude for study, the virtuoso piece for performance. Both C.P.E. Bach and Marpurg recommend students of the keyboard to play pieces on both harpsichord and clavichord: the clavichord for expression, and the harpsichord for strength (C.P.E. Bach 1753 p.9; Marpurg 1765 p.4).

The conscious restriction of compass to four octaves (C–c''') in Book I in itself argues for a general usability in line with the educational dimension of the word clavier. Although this compass is the commonest one in Bach's keyboard works generally up to around 1726, there are numerous cases of its being exceeded in works either specifically for harpsichord (such as the Fifth Brandenburg Concerto, which in the 1721 version requires BB–c''') or more likely to be for harpsichord. There is as little standardisation in pieces as there is in surviving instruments. While the Weimar manual concerto transcriptions taken as a whole require a compass of BB flat–d''', there are within them cases of transposition to keep within the four-octave compass (for a summary see Schulenberg 1992 p.401). Most relevant to Book I is the *Clavier-Büchlein* for Wilhelm Friedemann. The Book I preludes there (entered over the period 1720–2) stay within the four-octave compass, but the Menuet BWV 843 immediately before them (entered 1720–1) requires GG. Both the two-part Invention and the three-part Sinfonia in E major (BWV 777 and 792) require BB. At the other end of the compass, the *Clavier-Büchlein* does not exceed c'''. Alfred Dürr, in his survey of keyboard compass in the clavier works, concludes that Bach around 1720 must have had an instrument which went down chromatically to AA, but without GG since it is often avoided (1978a p.81), the GG in BWV 843 being unique in this respect. A clavichord with this keyboard would have been a rarity indeed, but harpsichords in Bach's area commonly extended to AA, GG or even FF (Henkel 1977, 1989). The fact that this compass is not exceeded does not of course preclude a number of pieces having been primarily or exclusively designed for harpsichord. As Dürr says, Bach's sons would hardly have been given the newest or most expensive instruments to practise on, and his other pupils must have had to make do with whatever instruments they owned or could get access to (1978a p.77). Even so, the inclusive educational meaning of the word clavier need not also mean an inclusive intention in composing individual pieces.

Over the last two decades much has been learnt about harpsichord types in Bach's environment. The two instruments at Charlottenburg have been identified through their decoration as the work of Michael Mietke, from whom Bach collected a harpsichord for the Cöthen court in 1719 (Krickeberg 1985, Germann 1985). More surprising has been the reinstatement of the so-called 'Bach-Flügel',[8] long thought to have belonged to Bach, but whose connexion with him and even with eighteenth-century tradition was doubted by Friedrich Ernst (1955), who had been involved in restoring it for the 1950 bicentenary.[9] From having been a jewel of the collection it languished for several decades in a semi-dismantled state in a cellar of the Berlin Instrument Museum until it was recognised by Dieter Krickeberg as the work of Johann Heinrich Harrass (d.1714) of Gross-Breitenbach in Thuringia. It had belonged in the late eighteenth century to Count Voss-Buch, who bought Bach manuscripts from Wilhelm Friedemann Bach in the 1770s. Wilhelm Rust, who knew members of the Voss-Buch family, reported in 1890 that by family tradition the harpsichord also had come from Wilhelm Friedemann, and indeed it is difficult to see how otherwise an instrument from a small town in Thuringia would have ended up with a well-to-do family in Berlin, which had its own flourishing harpsichord building tradition of Mietke and Rost. The connexion with Bach is by no means proved, but the possibility is intriguing given the unusual nature of the instrument. It has a five-octave compass (FF-f'''), rare even in French harpsichords before 1714, and an original disposition of 1 × 16' and 1 × 4' stops on the lower manual, and 1 × 8' (with buff) on the upper.[10] Later the 4' was moved to the upper manual and another 8' added to the lower, an alteration that could have been made before 1714.[11] So Wilhelm Friedemann may after all have grown up with a harpsichord of the celebrated 'Bach disposition', so long discredited. What is clear is that there was a strongly individual Thuringian tradition of harpsichord building, with 16' and even 2' stops not uncommon, perhaps because many harpsichord makers were also organ builders. This contrasts with the more cosmopolitan and Francophile centres of Berlin, Hamburg and Hanover, although Michael Mietke, or his sons, made at least two harpsichords with 16' stops.[12] None of these types accords with the old view that German makers were indebted mainly to Italian models.

3. *Clavichord*

The statement that Bach's favourite clavier was the clavichord goes back no further than Forkel (1802 p.17; NBR p.436). There are no references to Bach playing the clavichord which date from his lifetime. The earliest dates from 1775, when Johann Friedrich Agricola, who had studied with Bach between 1738 and 1741, remembered Bach 'often' playing the Sonatas and Partitas for unaccompanied violin on the clavichord, adding as much extra harmony as he considered necessary (Dok.III p.293, BR p.447). Although Forkel is a valuable witness in that he knew both C.P.E. and W.F. Bach personally, he was also writing at a time of rising German nationalism and reaction against things French. His expressed purpose was to present the music of Bach as 'an inestimable national inheritance, against which no other people can set up anything comparable'.[13] The clavichord was the German keyboard instrument because it could express the soul, unlike the 'soul-less' harpsichord suitable only for the 'empty and effete' music of Louis Marchand and François Couperin (1802 p.7; NBR p.427). Other evidence suggests that Bach's own attitude to the French harpsichord school was very different from this.

The clavichord was nonetheless the commonest keyboard instrument in Bach's environment.[14] It is the one recommended as an instrument of study for beginners in German writings from Virdung (1511) to F.C. Griepenkerl (1820), though that in itself may have made it less than attractive to Bach as a virtuoso performer, however much he occupied himself with it as a teacher. The vogue of the clavichord as the vehicle of *Empfindsamkeit*, with instrument-specific effects such as *Bebung* and *Tragen der Töne*, began only towards the end of Bach's life and there is no evidence of them in his clavier works.[15] In addition, the instrument as he would have known it up to the 1740s had technical limitations which would have ruled out some at least of the 48. Yet Forkel's words deserve consideration. Taken with other remarks of his about the clavichord, they give a subtler and more believable picture than just crude partisanship.

Forkel certainly knew the best of late eighteenth-century clavichord playing. He had been a friend and pupil of W.F. Bach, and praised him for his 'extraordinary *Delicatesse*' (1782 p.114). The clavichord was the ideal vehicle for the oratorical manner of the Enlightenment: 'A pleasant, gentle, ingratiating and captivating tone is not enough. It must in addition be, like the various passions, now gentle, now livelier, now wild and vehement; it must be able to assume all these different qualities and be so flexible that it can be drawn, dragged, enlivened, struck, held, not to mention the endless gradations of loud and soft and the Bebung.'[16] This strongly recalls Burney's celebrated description of C.P.E. Bach's playing, and the *Probestücke* C.P.E. Bach provided to illustrate the first part of his *Versuch* (1753), with their mercurial changes of mood and style, multiple dynamics, and clavichord-specific effects. But where in J.S. Bach's clavier works would such overtly emotional performance be in place outside the Chromatic Fantasia, significantly one of Bach's best-known keyboard pieces in the later eighteenth century, yet awkward to play on the sort of clavichord Bach might have had around 1720? Both W.F. and C.P.E. Bach admitted to Forkel that they had had to choose a style of their own since they could never have competed with their father in his (1802 p.44; NBR p.458). Their style was particularly associated with the clavichord as a 'new' instrument. In any case it was evidently only on the very finest Silbermann clavichords that C.P.E. Bach was able to produce all his effects.[17] Forkel was under no illusion that the clavichord in Bach's day was suitable for this type of expression: it reached its first perfection only with Fritz of Brunswick and Hass of Hamburg (i.e. in the 1740s). Before that it had lacked sufficient volume and compass (1782 p.5), and the fact that it was fretted prevented it playing in all keys since 'it could not yet be tempered pure' (1802 p.14, NBR p.433). His description of Bach's attitude to it is correspondingly more modest: Bach considered it the best instrument for study and for private entertainment, and for the expression of his most refined ideas, 'and did not think any harpsichord or pianoforte could produce such a variety of shadings of tone as this admittedly quiet yet on a small scale extraordinarily pliable instrument' (1802 p.17, NBR p.436).[18]

There is nothing here that we cannot readily believe of Bach. Certainly it was the common practice instrument of organists, most often made by organ builders, up to around 1740 with the common organ short-octave keyboard compass C/E–c''' (Meer 1975 p.102), the short octave being an economy that made more sense on the organ than on a stringed keyboard instrument. Praetorius extols the advantages of the clavichord for beginners in being easy to maintain, because there are no troublesome quills, and to tune, because it is fretted (1619 p.61). J.G. Walther (1732 article 'Clavicordo') describes it as the 'first grammar' of all keyboard players. The word grammar has a pejorative ring, at a great distance from the fully developed artist's concerns of rhetoric and declamation, just as the basics of notation are at an infinite distance from the art of playing well (François Couperin 1717 Preface). Yet many Germans regarded the clavichord as having virtues in the formation of sensitivity of finger and ear beyond those of a mere functional keyboard. Handel, from a similar background to Bach's, said as much to Mrs Delany.[19]

Particularly after around 1700 there was a growing interest in it as an instrument in its own right. Clavichords were being made with a fully chromatic C–c''' compass, with double rather than triple or quadruple fretting, and with luxurious finishes implying elegant, upmarket destinations. They figured at courts: the organ builder H.G. Trost in the 1720s looked after clavichords as well as harpsichords and spinets at Altenburg, as well as three clavichords in addition to a harpsichord that had been brought over from Friedenstein in Gotha (Friedrich 1989 p.55); J.C.F. Fischer's grandly titled *Les pieces de clavessin* (1696) were republished as the more homely *Musicalisches Blumen-Büschlein* in 1698. In the dedication to Princess Francisca Sybilla Augusta of Baden he says he will not disturb the boudoir of the new mother with the noise of violins and trumpets, but play these suites with the quiet reverence due to the new-born child on the clavichord or spinet ('Instrument'). Mattheson was merely reflecting the trend when in 1713 he told the 'Galant Homme' that the clavichord was the 'most beloved of all claviers' (p.262). 'Hand- und *Galanterie*-Sachen' such as overtures, sonatas, toccatas, suites etc. are best played on the clavichord, where one can express the singing manner with overholding and softening (a reference to French harpsichord style) much better than on the spinet and harpsichord (p.264). It is probably no accident that this is virtually identical to the list of genres on the title-page of his own *Harmonisches Denckmal* (1714).[20] There is no reason to regard certain types of repertory as the exclusive preserve of any one instrument.

It must be borne in mind, however, that unfretted clavichords were extremely uncommon before 1740. Only three German examples are known to survive, of which the most important is by Johann Michael Heinitz, made possibly in Berlin and dated 1716.[21] Unfretted instruments must have existed at least by the 1690s, since in the introduction to a collection of organ toccatas and Magnificat versets the Augsburg Cathedral organist Johannes Speth (1664–c.1720) says his pieces will need 'a well set up and properly tuned spinet or clavichord, and the latter will have to be arranged so that every key has its own choir of strings and not that 2, 3, or 4 keys strike one choir' (1693 *Vor-Bericht*).[22] The main issue here is tuning, and the usual fretting for ¼-comma meantone would not cope with his pieces which demand E flat as well as D sharp, A flat and G sharp, A sharp and B flat, and E sharp. Fretting for anything other than ¼-comma meantone would have been unusual before around 1720 (Hellwig 1973).[23] The rough and ready solution of bending tangents is unlikely to have produced satisfactory results (Petri 1782 p.374). More satisfactory would be to temper the basic 5ths ⅙ comma or less (Barbour 1951 p.148). This is the principle behind the 'well-tempered' tunings described (imprecisely) by Werckmeister (1698b pp.64–5) for triple-quadruple-fretted ('gebunden') and double-fretted ('bundfrey') clavichords. His tract is important for showing that the term 'wohltemperirtes Clavier' was applicable to the fretted clavichord in Bach's environment.

Werckmeister here says that tangents really need to be arranged for a 'good temperament', and from the 1720s some were set up for well-tempered tunings, or even approached equal temperament (Hellwig 1973 p.65; Henkel 1981 p.17). Significantly, though, writers who advocated equal-tempered or similar tunings, such as Bendeler (c.1690) and Neidhardt (1706), list spinet, harpsichord and regal as candidates for their tunings, but not the clavichord. It is noticeable that in his obituary, C.P.E. Bach switches from the general clavier to the specific 'Clavicymbal' when he comes to Bach's skill at tuning (Dok.III p.88).

A further technical difficulty of playing the 48 on the usual German clavichord of before 1740 is the short-octave (C/E–c''') organ compass. This would exclude all 96 pieces in the two books of the 48 with the exception of a few early versions (such as those of the preludes in C major, D minor, and E minor of Book I, given in NBA V/6.1 Anhang 1). Some instruments had split keys for D/F♯ and E/G♯, which increases possibilities but they still lack C♯ and E♭, and some rapid figurations would be very awkward to negotiate. Instruments with fully chromatic keyboards were not common, and even those without the short octave often lacked the C♯, which would rule out 17 pieces of Book I and 16 pieces of Book II.[24] There is no evidence in copies of figurations being adapted to accommodate the short octave, though players may have adapted as they played on particular instruments. Book II requires AA–d‴♭, though C–c‴ is only rarely exceeded and the two cases that go beyond c‴ are in pieces which have been transposed upwards (the C sharp major Fugue, to c‴♯; and the A flat major fugue, to d‴♭). The five-octave (FF–f‴) keyboard, common from the 1760s, survives first in an instrument by H.A. Hass (Hamburg 1742), but the compass AA–f‴ is given by Henkel for a German instrument (double-fretted) from the second quarter of the 18th century (1981 p.50, No.21). But given the mixed origins of the pieces in either Book of the 48 it is somewhat artificial to posit a single instrument that could play them all.

The technical difficulties of playing pieces in complex textures and advanced keys on the fretted clavichord have been variously exaggerated by proponents of the harpsichord, and minimised by those of the clavichord. Erwin Bodky considered that they ruled out the clavichord entirely; Arnold Dolmetsch and Edwin Ripin considered that there are surprisingly few passages which they make unplayable. The main problem is the great variety of fretting patterns, particularly in the late seventeenth century.[25] We may eliminate instruments with triple and quadruple fretting in the upper part of the keyboard. These are quite suitable for 17th-century modal music with a decorated melody or running passagework in the right hand and a two-part or chordal accompaniment in the left, but are quite unsuitable for the keys and textures of the 48. From around 1700, however, there is a fair degree of standardisation, with double fretting generally starting around c, and all the d's and a's free.[26] The typical octave is therefore as follows:

c/c♯, d, e♭/e, f/f♯, g/g♯, a, b♭/b

Henkel gives semitone values for eleven relevant clavichords, showing that in the great majority of cases these are the actual notes (i.e. e♭, not d♯ etc.). In fact chromatic semitones tend to be rather smaller than they need be. It can easily be seen that a place such as bar 45 of the C sharp minor Fugue of Book I, where the counterpoint requires a d″♯ to be held through an e″, cannot be literally rendered on this instrument; a more serious conflict is at bar 94, where the same two notes are required as part of two of the subjects of the fugue. By far the most thorough and scientific investigation of this problem has been made by Richard Loucks (1992), who has graded simultaneous semitones into five types, in ascending order of awkwardness: (a) which involve no fretting conflict; (b) where the lower note is sounded first: this means losing a held note (as in bar 45 of the C sharp minor Fugue), and in many cases could slip past without notice; (c) where the upper note is sounded first: this can create a serious problem in losing an important thematic note; (d) rare cases where both notes of a fretted minor 2nd are required to be struck simultaneously (as in bar 94 of the C sharp minor Fugue): this has to be got around by some expedient such as arpeggiation, or altering the music; (e) when this occurs in the course of important thematic material and there is no possibility of fudging it.

All in all, Loucks finds only seven instances of types (d) and (e) in all 96 pieces. There is of course the extra degree of care needed in many places to ensure that notes sound properly, particularly in intricate textures in advanced keys but, as Loucks very reasonably points out, that is part of the art of playing the clavier.

The fretted clavichord is therefore an important instrument for the 48. Given the mixed origins of the two collections, and the general educational intention, the instrument is ideal for students in terms of economy, the necessity for a clean finger action, and ease of tuning and maintenance. The great educative value of the clavichord is that it takes a positive effort of hand and ear to make a singing sound on every note. The problem of blocking, its main bugbear, seems much less on 18th-century instruments in good condition than on some modern versions.

4. *Spinet*

The spinet has been curiously neglected in discussions of possible instruments for the 48, possibly because it was impossible for Germans of the Wilhelmine era to envisage this 'Tonheld deutscher Nation' seated at such a thing. But as an instrument readily available to 'lehrbegierige Jugend' it comes very much into the frame.[27] In fact it is as probable as the clavichord, if not more so. In the 17th century it was so common that it was known simply as 'Instrument', a fact lamented by Praetorius as a vulgar particular use of a general term. In Praetorius's time 'Instrument' covered 'Clavicymbel, Symphony, Spinet, Virginal und dergleichen' (i.e. quilled keyboard instruments; from the reference to his illustrations it is clear that Symphony is another term for spinet/virginal-type instruments; 1619 p.11, p.62, Plate XIV). This is the meaning in the title of Ammerbach's *Orgel oder Instrument Tabulatur* (1571/1583) of which Bach possessed no less than three copies, Ammerbach being one of his predecessors as Thomascantor in Leipzig. By Adlung's time the word spinet meant a small 2'- or 4'-pitched instrument, a large one at 8' pitch being called 'Instrument in the narrower sense' of the word; it could also be called Virginal (1758 p.558). Türk reflects this continued usage into the late eighteenth century (1789 p.3).

Harpsichords were not common in seventeenth-century Germany, the spinet in its various forms being the standard plucked-string keyboard instrument. Such title-pages of keyboard works as go beyond the word clavier virtually always mention the spinet, in formulations such as 'allen Liebhabern des Claviers auf einem Spinet oder Clavichordio zu spielen' (Johann Krieger, *Sechs musicalische Partien*, Nuremberg 1697); the clavichord is never mentioned on its own. The spinet is generally listed as one of the instruments beginners graduate to after having started on the clavichord (e.g. Walther 1732 'Clavicordio'). It is also an instrument mentioned, rather than the clavichord for obvious reasons, when advanced tunings are proposed, as in Werckmeister's *Musicalische Temperatur* (1691), where it is the only stringed keyboard instrument (title-page and p.2). In fact with its one 8' set of strings, and a separate string for each note, it is an ideal instrument for learning to tune or to experiment with tunings.

The word 'Spinett' in late seventeenth-century Germany covered all plucked stringed keyboard instruments other than the harpsichord. It existed in a variety of shapes, but generally was rectangular or trapezoid with a single set of strings at 8' pitch and a keyboard compass of C/E–c'''. Its various forms had different qualities of their own and it was not just a cheap alternative to the harpsichord.[28] Fewer survive than clavichords since this homely instrument went out of fashion before the harpsichord did. Adlung, writing probably in the late 1720s, says that, although it had gone out of fashion, it could still be as usable as a harpsichord if well made. He says it has four octaves and as many keys as the harpsichord (therefore a chromatic compass C–c'''; 1768 II p.123).[29] A mid-eighteenth-century German pentagonal spinet with this keyboard was in the Leipzig collection (Henkel 1979 No.58), so possibly instruments of that sort were being made through the first half of the century. Ones with the common C/E short octave (therefore lacking C♯ and E♭, and also F♯ and G♯ if there were no split keys) would be virtually useless for the 48.

After around 1700 the place of the rectangular instrument was taken by the newly fashionable bentside spinet ('Querspinett') which genuinely was a cheaper and space-saving alternative to the harpsichord. It could have a similar range and registration to the harpsichord, as has the instrument by Christoph Heinrich Bohr (Dresden, probably 1713), No.56 in Henkel 1979. This has two manuals, with two 8' and one 4' stops, and a compass of GG/BB–c''', with split E♭/BB. It thus descends diatonically from C to GG, but lacks C♯, which cuts out over one third of the pieces in Book I, including most of those in the advanced keys which were the main point of the collection. It could, however, play up-to-date repertory in keys from C minor to A major such as François Couperin's first book (1713).[30] This is the type of instrument J.G. Walther meant in describing the spinet as a small harpsichord (1732 'Spinetta'). Many German makers produced them, including Michael Mietke (Krickeberg and Rase 1987 p.310).

The 'Spinettgen' in the list of Bach's effects at his death was probably at quint or 4' pitch, hence the diminutive. Its valuation of three thalers was near the bottom for a usable instrument. The rubbish valuation was 16 Groschen (a viola and a cello in the inventory): Werckmeister says that instruments at this price are only good for cooking fish (1698b p.67; Dok.II p.493). It has been thought that the '3. Clavire nebst Pedal' given to the fifteen-year-old Johann Christian by Bach before his death may have been a complete set of stringed keyboard instruments: harpsichord, clavichord, spinet and pedal-clavier.[31] This is an attractive idea, but it is very noticeable how precise the terminology is in the inventory, with three grades of 'Clavesin', and also 'Lauten Werck' and 'Spinettgen', apart from various other instruments carefully graded in quality. The two older brothers from Bach's first marriage were already making disapproving noises that Johann Christian should be taking an equal share in the estate having received this gift; it is unlikely that they would have acquiesced had there been anything as valuable as a harpsichord involved. The very portable clavichord is conspicuous by its absence from the list, and this was the time when the word clavier was coming to mean it particularly.[32]

5. *Organ*

Whatever Bach's original intention, there was certainly a tradition in the later eighteenth century of playing the 48 on the organ. In England particularly, where pedal technique was rudimentary, they were thought of as organ repertory, from Johann Caspar Heck (1775; Dok.III p.299) through Samuel Wesley to Mendelssohn and beyond. A.F.C. Kollmann thought this due to lack of knowledge of Bach's large organ works:

> . . . it must be observed; that though many of Bach's pieces composed for the harpsichord, also have a fine effect on a manual organ, particularly most of his forty-eight fugues in the Well Temper'd Clavier . . . the list of his works will shew, that they do not come under the denomination of his *organ* pieces; because they are deficient in *his* principal requisite for such pieces, being a part for obligato *pedals*. And consequently their effect cannot give an idea of his organ playing; unless an obligato part for the *pedals* be still selected from their bass part, and performed on a double bass stop. (1812 p.35)

The custom of playing them on the organ was merely transplanted from Germany. Rellstab in 1790, announcing an edition of the 48, said that corrupt versions of the pieces were circulating among clavierists and organists (Dok.III p.487). We still have many of these 'corrupt' versions in manuscript collections where items from the 48, particularly early versions of pieces from Book II, are mixed in with undoubted organ works. Some sources include pedal indications, notably for the E and E flat major Fugues of Book II, and many pieces have the heading 'manualiter', including a source of Book I very close to Bach

(P 401) which has it on each folio. If these two fugues from Book II seem suitable candidates, performance on the organ seems to have been by no means limited to *alla breve* fugues. One of Bach's last pupils, Johann Christian Kittel, who studied with him between 1748 and 1750 and was one of the most important transmitters of the Bach tradition into the 19th century, envisages what many would regard as quintessentially stringed-keyboard textures as examples of the harmonic type of prelude for organ:

> Pieces in this style demand a very fine harmonic instinct and insight. Since the organ is almost the only instrument on which their effect measures up to expectation, so this manner of writing deserves particular attention from organists . . . . Bach also left the best models of [it]. I shall only mention the well known preludes in C major from the first part of the Well-tempered Clavier, and C sharp major from the second. The latter in particular is to be played slowly on the organ (many falsely believe that Bach's pieces cannot be played quickly enough) with well chosen, gentle registration, like a fervent, devotional prayer in which desires and sighs break free from the oppressed heart, and the lively fugal conclusion like an Amen full of joyful trust. (1803 pp.64–5)[33]

Admittedly Kittel's own examples of the harmonic type of prelude are in the 'gebunden' style with tied notes and suspensions, and are much more in keeping with the late eighteenth-century ideal of solemn organ style.

In the twentieth century the organ has found convinced advocates for the 48. Hans Brandts Buys thought that all Bach's works with the C–c''' compass restriction were for organ since works designated for harpsichord exceed this range (1955 p.110–11). Bernard Bartelinck, who had performed both Books on the organ of the Oude Kerk, Amsterdam, found the big, late-Baroque type of organ ideal for them, particularly the fugues in five parts; the three-part fugues he played as trios (1957 pp.153–4). Elinor von der Heyde-Dohrn has made an elaborate subjective case for the organ, with good points (1978). Unfortunately the instances she cites point up the distinctiveness of Bach's organ writing as opposed to the 48. For instance, the D sharp minor Fugue of Book II has in common with the D minor Fugue BWV 538/2 (the so-called 'Dorian' fugue) a D tonality, and a scalar ascent with syncopations in its subject, but there the similarity ends. The quality of intense personal meditation, with a very sensitive and detailed manipulation of texture, in the D sharp minor fugue has little in common with the broad achitectural paragraphing and public rhetoric of the 'Dorian'. The most convincing and best documented case was made by Robert L. Marshall (1986). His conclusion is that, on account of the C–c''' compass restriction, the organ cannot be ruled out as an instrument for the 48. Even in Book II this compass is exceeded only occasionally, and some earlier versions keep within it. Such descriptions as we have of Bach's public performances were all on the organ, though the Marchand contest was to have been on the harpsichord. Unfortunately the one description of Bach playing the 48 (Book I), by E.L. Gerber, says Bach played them to his father, H.N. Gerber, during lessons 'an eines seiner vortreflichen Instrumente' (Dok.III p.472). Since Türk (1789) still uses the word 'Instrument' in the narrow meaning of a plucked-string keyboard instrument, it looks as if that is what Gerber (1790) meant.

Some of the limitations of the clavichord also apply to the organ. Fully chromatic four-octave keyboards were not unknown in church organs before 1720, but they were not common.[34] Normally, like the clavichord, they lacked the low C♯, which therefore rules out such seeming organ candidates as the C sharp minor fugue of Book I. Positive organs must have been common in homes, judging by the number of references to them in works dealing with keyboard instruments. Adlung (1758 p.551) describes positive organs in private houses, with stops up to 2' maximum and without pedalboards but sometimes with pulldowns. He also mentions claviorgana (p.563) but says these were more common in his youth (i.e. 1710s and 1720s).

The tuning problem is also in common with clavichords. Organ builders were very conservative and many church organs must still have been tuned in something very like ¼-comma meantone, though more sophisticated places seem to have used more modern tunings. Bach's *Orgel-Büchlein* (1708–17) has a range of tonics from A major to F minor, and visits all twelve major triads. A much wider range of tonics is in Fischer's *Ariadne Musica Neo-Organoedum* (1702), which has all but C sharp and F sharp majors, and their relative minors, and G sharp minor. Circulating tunings were more practicable on positive organs and must have been quite widely practised judging by the number of references in the writings of Werckmeister, Neidhardt, Mattheson etc.[35]

The verset tradition from which *Ariadne Musica* sprang is on the face of it the most convincing link between the 48 and the organ. Bach's organ students at Weimar had to contemplate the possibility that they might have to function in a Catholic church. Some German towns had both Catholic and Lutheran churches, such as Erfurt where Bach's relative Johann Heinrich Buttstett played the organ in churches of both persuasions.[36] Some early sources of preludes and fughettas subsequently used in Book II suggest that Bach at Weimar may have been compiling a teaching collection similar to *Ariadne* (see Chapter Three section 1). But in spite of the organ environment of the composition prototype the pieces are by no means clearly in an organ style. Accounts of Bach's teaching are all to do with the clavier. His organ teaching probably consisted of thoroughbass and improvisation, the skills required in tests for organ posts (Stauffer 1994 pp.36–7). Pedal technique could have been taught on the pedal harpsichord or clavichord, the usual instruments for organ teaching and practice (Ford 1997). The revisions to the C major prelude BWV

870a, in its original form so like an organ improvisation, seem designed to convert it into an effective harpsichord piece.[37] Peter Williams (1980 I pp.141–2), in assessing the often-remarked similarity of this prelude to the organ Prelude in the same key BWV 545/1, concludes that BWV 870/1 is as idiomatic for the harpsichord as 545/1 is for the organ. The issue is further complicated by Bach's liking for writing for one instrument in the style of another, particularly in Book II. The residual organ nature of BWV 870/1 is more effective as a dimension of reference on the harpsichord, particularly as the C major opening work of a collection, than it would ever be if actually played on the organ.

In summary, there is nothing in either Book that demands the organ. None of the pieces has the kind of bass-line strategy which is so noticeable in Bach's large-scale *pedaliter* organ works.[38] No special meaning can be attached to the word *manualiter,* which is applied to all sorts of pieces in many different sources. Some pieces may be closer to prototypes associated primarily with the organ and may therefore be effective as organ pieces,[39] but the sort of publications these prototypes appear in usually give a clavier alternative to the organ. In the list of Bach's works given by C.P.E. Bach in his obituary (Dok.III pp.85–6) the organ works are given as 'für die Orgel', but both Books of the 48 as 'fürs Clavier', which looks as if we are left with the distinction between organ and clavier.

6. *Lautenwerk*

Unlike the clavichord, Bach's use of the Lautenwerk (lute-harpsichord) is well attested.[40] There were two (termed 'Lauten Werck') among his effects at his death, as well as one good lute (Dok.II pp.492–3). There is also a description by J.F. Agricola (who studied with Bach at the time when he was putting together Book II) of a Lautenclavicymbel made for Bach by the organ builder Zacharias Hildebrandt around 1740. But Bach's involvement with the instrument evidently went back much earlier than this. A document is reported that records his having a Lautenclavier made by a cabinet maker in Cöthen around 1720.[41] The earliest unambiguous German reference to this type of instrument is from Augsburg in 1713.[42] Certainly they were being made in Hamburg by 1718 by Johann Christoph Fleischer, who also made lute-type instruments; at Ilmenau (just south of Arnstadt) by 1722 by Johann Georg Gleichmann; and by Bach's cousin Johann Nicolaus Bach by the early 1720s in Jena, where Jakob Adlung knew them.[43]

In spite of all this there is much about the instrument we do not know (there are no surviving examples), and it is by no means clear exactly what Bach played on it. For the instrument we have as much as Agricola tells us: it had a shorter scaling but in all other respects was like an ordinary harpsichord; it had two sets of gut strings and a 'little octave' (presumably 4') of brass; in its normal setting, when only one stop was engaged, it sounded more like a theorbo than a lute, but with the 'lute stop' (i.e. buff stop) and 'cornet stop' (4'?) together even professional lutenists could almost mistake it for a lute (Dok.III p.195; NBR p.366). Taking this with the much more detailed description of the Lautenwerk given by Adlung (1768 II pp.133ff) it is clear that the aim of the instrument was to reproduce as closely as possible the characteristic sound of the lute, with its highly prized expressive delicacy of nuance, but at the same time getting around its technical difficulty. Even details such as wooden tuning pegs were copied by J.N. Bach, and Adlung makes it clear that the stringing was modelled on the stringing pattern of the lute. In other words it was intended to be a mechanised lute rather than a gut-strung harpsichord.[44]

Taking as a model the largest type of lute (14-course) of around 1740, such as might have been made by Bach's Leipzig friend and contemporary Johann Christian Hoffmann (1683–1750),[45] one may propose the following interpretation of Agricola's description of Bach's Lautenclavicymbel:

(1) it would be double strung at the octave (one set of strings at 8', one at 4' pitch) from GG to c♯; double strung at the unison (two 8' sets) from d to c', and single strung (one 8' set) above that. The most likely use for the 4' brass set is as the octave doubling in the bass (which perhaps explains why the gut strings alone sounded more like a theorbo: it is not known exactly how German theorbos of this time were strung, but it is likely that they were single-strung in the bass). Metal octave strings on this sort of lute would have been very rare, but on the Lautenwerk they would be easier to keep in tune than short gut ones;

(2) the whole instrument would have been undamped, so a lightly applied buff stop would have mitigated the over-resonance, not a problem on the lute where courses are constantly refingered or damped with the right-hand thumb in descending scales on the diapason courses. It would also help to give something of the fingered effect of the lute sound, rather than the effect of constant open strings;

(3) J.N. Bach carried imitation of the lute as far as having three manuals, not with different stops, but activating three different sets of jacks on the same strings, each set being successively further from the nut. Adlung says this was to give dynamic nuance, but it also reproduces the effect of lutenists moving their plucking point away from the bridge with consequent change of tone colour. With all this expenditure of skill and effort it would be surprising if the end result had not been sufficiently close to the lute to satisfy a lutenist. It is possible that Bach's instruments may have had more than one manual.

We cannot know how much Agricola meant by 'in all other respects like an ordinary harpsichord'. If this includes compass then it would have a minimum of four octaves (C–c''') rather than the GG–e'' which is the total range required by Bach's works associated with the lute.[46] In assessing the valuation (30 thalers) of the instruments in Bach's estate, possible compass and number of manuals have to be set against the objective value of materials and craftsmanship in a curiosity instrument that was going out of fashion. The lute in the inventory was valued at 21 thalers, and three ordinary harpsichords at 50 thalers each.

Which of Bach's works may have been conceived for the Lautenwerk is also very uncertain. He may have used it only for improvisation, or have played works by lutenists: there is no great difficulty in playing on the keyboard from lute tablature. Much has been made of the technical awkwardness on the lute of Bach's supposed lute works, but while they are difficult they are not unplayable using scordaturas current in German lute music at the time, so they need not be regarded as necessarily for Lautenwerk. The strongest candidate is the Suite in E minor BWV 996, which is the only piece designated for it. The main source for this has strong Weimar connexions in that it was copied by J.G. Walther and belonged ultimately to Johann Tobias Krebs. The designation 'Aufs Lauten Werk' was added subsequently to Walther's copying, in another hand. It uses the range C–c'' (that of an 11-course lute) which tallies with Adlung's description, and is generally the most problematic of Bach's ostensibly lute works to play on the lute. If this was the compass of an instrument Bach possessed at Cöthen it would exclude all of Book I of the 48. Nor are there any of the characteristic textures of Bach's lute works in that Book.

Book II is a more tempting candidate. It was compiled around the time when Hildebrandt made his Lautenwerk for Bach, and there is the famous visit of the Dresden lutenists Silvius Leopold Weiss and Johann Kropffgans to Bach in August 1739 (Dok.II p.366; NBR p.204). On the strength of this Don Franklin has proposed as possibilities the pieces in C sharp minor, F minor, G sharp minor and B major, all from the layer of the London autograph copied around 1740 (1987 p.459). This is presumably on account of features of galant style in these pieces. But they have nothing of a lute texture and would be more at home on the unfretted clavichord or pianoforte if a keyboard instrument with dynamic nuance is desired.

A more convincing candidate is the E flat prelude, which has striking similarities to the prelude in the same key 'pour la Luth. ò Cembal.' BWV 998/1. The Book II prelude was entered slightly earlier than the ones Franklin proposes (probably 1739), while BWV 998 dates from the early 1740s. Although the Book II prelude is in an unusual keyboard texture, more like a keyboard adaptation of a piece for solo instrument, it is not playable on the lute, and its range (to c''') puts it outside the probable range of the Lautenwerk. It is combined with a fugue in the sustained ('gebunden') organ style, found also in D major with pedal indications in an early version copied around 1738/9 by J.F. Agricola (P 595; the pedal indications were added later in different inks). It is thus unlikely that the prelude was conceived for Lautenwerk. It is more likely to be a development of the textures of the lute and Lautenwerk for harpsichord, which Bach (with his usual liking for combining opposites) thought would contrast well with a fugue written in the opposite, organ style.

7. *Pianoforte*

Bach's knowledge of the pianoforte is as well documented as that of the Lautenwerk, though which of his works he may have conceived for it is hardly less a matter for conjecture. Forkel's statement that the new pianofortes were as yet 'much too coarse' to satisfy Bach has to be taken along with his view that the harpsichord was 'too soul-less' and his patriotic German view of the clavichord. The two surviving instruments at Potsdam show that, at least in the last decade of Bach's life, excellent instruments were being made.[47]

There are three occasions on which Bach is said to have played the pianoforte. The best documented is his visit to Potsdam in May 1747, described in a contemporary newspaper account (Dok.II pp.434–5, NBR p.224) and also by C.P.E. Bach and Agricola in the 1754 obituary (Dok.III p.85, NBR pp.202–3).[48] Taking these two together, it seems that Frederick II played his theme over to Bach on a pianoforte, and that Bach thereupon improvised a fugue on this theme, also on a pianoforte. Later Bach, at Frederick's request, improvised a six-part fugue, but on a subject of his own, and it is not clear on what instrument he played it. Forkel, who says that he got his information about the occasion from W.F. Bach, has Bach going round the Sanssouci palace with the king and all his musicians, trying and improvising on many of Frederick's fifteen pianofortes (1802 p.11, NBR pp.429–30). By October 1747 Bach had the *Musical Offering* completed and printed, with a presentation copy on special paper for the king. The six-part Ricercar on the royal theme was not played at Potsdam, but it is likely that the three-part Ricercar as printed is a worked-up version of what Bach improvised on the occasion (C. Wolff 1987 p.206, 1991 pp.324ff).

The other two occasions come from another of Agricola's footnotes to Adlung 1768 (Dok.III p.194, partial translation in NBR pp.365–6). At an unspecified date Gottfried Silbermann made his first two pianofortes, on one of which Bach played. He admired the sound greatly but found it weak in the treble, and the action too heavy. Silbermann was incensed by this criticism, but out of regard for Bach worked on these problems for 'many years'. Eventually, when he had made considerable improvements, particularly with regard to the action, he sold one to the princely court at Rudolstadt. Then the King of Prussia (Frederick II) ordered one and, having approved it, several others. All who had seen the two original pianofortes, including Agricola, realised how much work Silbermann had put into the improvements. Silbermann then showed one of his new models to Bach, who played it and gave it his 'complete approval'. Agricola had all this from Silbermann himself, but did not write it until twenty or more years after the events it describes.

In trying to assess at what stage Bach would have had available pianofortes which he found satisfactory, much depends on the date of his first trial of them, and estimates of this have varied wildly. The first mention of a Silbermann pianoforte is in the 1733 edition of Zedler's *Universal Lexicon*, which says that Silbermann had 'recently' invented a new instrument called 'Piano-Fort' and supplied one the year before (1732?) to the Crown Prince of Saxony (to whom in 1733, on his accession as the Elector Friedrich August II of Saxony and King August III of Poland, Bach dedicated the Kyrie and Gloria of his B minor *Missa*). This has been read in conjunction with the account of a new type of *Clavicymbel* used at one of Bach's concerts at the Leipzig Collegium Musicum in June 1733 (Dok.II p.238) to mean that Bach had been fully satisfied by that stage, and that therefore the first trial could be put back perhaps as far as 1725.[49] At the other extreme, he may not have been fully satisfied until his Potsdam visit in 1747 (Ernst 1963 p.4).

Looking at the chronological clues in Agricola's description, the most likely time for a new instrument at Rudolstadt is 1737 or after, when the Schwarzburg-Rudolstadts embarked on a lavish rebuilding programme designed to convert Heidecksburg, burnt out in 1735, into a magnificent late-Baroque palace. Frederick II of Prussia may have seen his first instrument while he was still in waiting at Rheinsberg, but if it was when he was king it must have been 1740 or later. The balance of probabilities for Bach's finding a satisfactory pianoforte is therefore around 1740. On the basis of documents in the Prussian archives and Silbermann's contracts, John Koster has suggested 1743 for the earliest that Bach could have found a satisfactory pianoforte, with 1736 as his first trial.[50] He certainly had an interest in them, as in all new instruments, since he sold one, whether of his own or as an agent is not known, in 1749 (Dok.III p.633). The designation of this 'Piano et Forte' tallies with terminology used by Silbermann.[51] Terminology remained fluid throughout the eighteenth century and until after 1800 the terms *clavecin* (*à maillets*) and *clavicembalo* (*a martelletti*) could include the pianoforte. It has even been proposed that the prized veneered 'Claveçin' in Bach's estate, which he particularly wished to remain in the family, was a Silbermann pianoforte (E. Badura-Skoda 1991 p.166).

While there was sporadic experimentation in the early 1720s, it was the publication in 1725 of a German translation of Maffei's 1711 article on

Cristofori's pianofortes that gave the impetus to Saxon makers (Schott 1985 p.29). We may therefore rule out the pianoforte as a usable instrument available at the time of Book I.

With Book II we can only guess on grounds of style what might have been thought suitable for the new instrument. On the assumption that the three-part Ricercar from the *Musical Offering* has a relation to Bach's pianoforte improvisation at Potsdam, Christoph Wolff has listed features which it has in common with the Berlin style: spare three-part texture and intimate manner, careful articulation of staccato and legato for countersubject-type motifs of different characters, figures implying a crescendo and diminuendo (bb.38ff), affective sigh figures (bb.108ff; C. Wolff 1987 p.206). These features are part of the characteristic language of C.P.E. Bach's Prussian sonatas of 1742, from which one might add off-beat right-hand chords separated by rests, and the sophisticated mixture of duple and triple groups. Admittedly the three-part Ricercar lacks the dynamic markings of the Prussian sonatas, but even there they are relatively sparse, and Bach himself seems to have used dynamic markings in keyboard music only to indicate manual changes.

The most directly comparable piece in Book II to the three-part Ricercar is the D minor Fugue. Not only has it a very similar chromatic descent in the second half of its subject, but bb.123ff of the Ricercar seem to contain a reminiscence of it, perhaps unconsciously. The D minor Fugue, however, lacks the dynamically sensitive features noted in the Ricercar, and it is combined with a prelude whose origins can be traced back to the 1720s. Casting a subjective eye on the rest of the book, one might think of the preludes in D major, whose character contrasts in the opening bars seem to imply dynamic contrasts; F minor, another binary piece in a sonata idiom; G sharp minor, which has often been thought of as a candidate; and perhaps also the F sharp major Prelude and Fugue, whose prelude particularly has stretches of harmonic wash based on a quasi-Alberti figure which would respond very well to dynamic nuancing. It would be wrong, though, to cry pianoforte, or clavichord for that matter, at every piece featuring sensitive textures and appoggiaturas. The highly sensitive, appoggiatura laden Sarabande of the G major Partita BWV 829 (1730) has perfectly idiomatic harpsichord antecedents in such pieces as *Les langueurs tendres* from François Couperin's Second Book (1717).

8. Summary

Bach's lifetime was a period of great change and experimentation in musical instruments as well as musical styles, and other instruments such as the Hammerpantaleon, which had a certain vogue in the 1720s, the Cembal d'amour, invented by Gottfried Silbermann, and the Bogenclavier, praised by C.P.E. Bach and Marpurg, were available. Magical as they must have sounded, they are somewhat limited in their range of effects and, while this or that piece may work very well on one or the other, there is little evidence of specially targeted textures in the 48. Individual pieces may recall the style of this or that instrument: organ, Lautenwerk, perhaps pianoforte. But the only instrument which was available through the whole period 1720–40 which can cope satisfactorily with everything is the harpsichord. According to C.P.E. Bach, the particular instrument that Bach was able to tune 'so consonantly and suitably that all keys sounded fine and agreeable' was the harpsichord (Dok.III p.88, NBR p.307). This is not to say that, given the mixed origins of the two collections, other instruments were not also envisaged. But to think of the 48 as essentially for one optimum instrument need not necessarily be an impoverishment. Part of the richness of these collections is their range of stylistic and instrumental reference, and that richness may be concentrated by being seen in the spectrum of a single instrument.

Subjective assessments are really neither here nor there. The common view has been that the clavichord is more suitable for the first book and the harpsichord for the second. But from the point of view of instruments available to Bach and his pupils the clavichord is more appropriate to the second book; the only instruments that can be said without reservation to be able to cope with all of Book I are the harpsichord and spinet. To say that the first Book is best suited to a late eighteenth-century German clavichord is no different from saying that it works best on a modern grand piano. It may be that it can be performed magnificently on either of these instruments, but there is no more historic justification for one than for the other.

The argument about instruments is really a product of modern concert life and is remote from Bach's way of thinking. The purpose of the collections was not to provide repertory for this or that instrument, but for young people wishing to study composition and performance, and for the more advanced to refresh their spirits, a concept deeply rooted in the Lutheran tradition as the purifying function of music. The very vagueness of the word clavier reveals a generalised purpose, borne out by the retraction of compass to a minimum standard in the first book and in some sources of the second, and by the lack of anything that absolutely requires more than one manual. From this central point they range out to explore the rich late Baroque tradition, with its many roots in diverse nations, instruments, and types of composition.

CHAPTER TWO

Well-tempered

For Bach the issue of tuning was important, or he would not have put it in the title. But it would be a mistake to see it as the main issue, as Marpurg does in calling the collection *The Art of Temperament*.[1] The function of *The Well-tempered Clavier* is, according to the title-page, to demonstrate the possibility of writing and playing in all 24 major and minor keys. The tuning of the instrument was a means to that end.[2]

The term 'well-tempered' does not in itself imply a specific tuning, any more than 'clavier' implies a specific instrument. It means no more than a tuning in which it is possible to play tolerably in all keys. Much hangs on the word 'tolerably' since a variety of tunings have been associated with the term. In the older modern literature it is taken for granted that it meant equal tempered, and that the function of the collection was to demonstrate the possibilities of equal temperament, which was thought to have been 'discovered' at the end of the seventeenth century. Because few people in the earlier part of the twentieth century had direct experience of tuning different temperaments, the debate about them in the seventeenth- and eighteenth-century literature seemed unreal. As devoted a scholar as C.S. Terry found it 'strange that a technical controversy should have been resolved by a volume of genius so alien in feeling to the academic debate which invited them!'[3] This misses the real point of the debate and its relevance to Bach. Even Murray Barbour, who published (1951) the first comprehensive twentieth-century discussion of historical keyboard temperaments in English, evidently had little direct practical experience of the temperaments he discussed, and his argument is slanted towards the view that equal temperament was the logical goal of historical progress.

This situation began to change drastically during the 1960s as keyboard instruments of historical construction became general and players came to realise the startlingly different colours and effects of different tunings. In 1960 Herbert Kelletat published an elaborate argument that Bach's tuning was one of those proposed in the 1770s by Johann Philipp Kirnberger, a former pupil of Bach's and one of the principal musicians in the later eighteenth century to preserve and promote his music. Other circulating but unequal temperaments for *The Well-tempered Clavier* have been proposed by Herbert Kellner (1977 etc.) and John Barnes (1979). These tunings were fully worked out mathematically and appeared in print, but good players have their own continually evolving preferences. The 1960s and 70s were exciting times of rediscovery and experimentation when much received wisdom was overthrown. After experiencing the purity and sonorousness of unequal temperaments, players turned with disgust from the hectic, fast-beating major 3rds of equal temperament and the characterless, commonplace sound it can give to an instrument. This experience was then projected on to Bach. Bernhard Billeter, for example, in 1970 said that, although the precise way in which Bach tuned his keyboard instruments is and will remain a mystery, 'we know that' he did not use equal temperament.[4] However understandable the reaction, this merely replaces one dogma with another, neither adequately based on historical evidence.

In the 1980s the dialectic began to find its equilibrium, and the centenary year 1985 saw the publication of the two most balanced, historically based assessments. Rudolf Rasch gave a survey of the many writings of the organ builder Andreas Werckmeister (1645–1706). Werckmeister worked in the part of Germany just north of Bach's native Thuringia and there are many ways in which he was connected with the world in which Bach grew up. In the pre-1960 era Werckmeister had often been cited as the man who 'discovered' equal temperament in 1691. Anybody who had read the *Musicalische Temperatur* realised that it principally recommended two unequal temperaments, of which the most influential has been the one known as Werckmeister III. Since this temperament has a strongly different character from equal temperament, added to which the word 'wohltemperirt' itself seems peculiarly associated with Werckmeister, it was enthusiastically taken up in the 1970s as the Bach tuning and the proposals of Kellner and Barnes are in fact adaptations of it. Rasch showed, however, that Werckmeister's views changed gradually over the span of his writings from 1681 to his last, posthumously published work of 1707, finally recommending a form of equal temperament from around 1698.

The other 1985 publication was Mark Lindley's consideration of Bach's tunings (rightly in the plural), which is the most convincing discussion of this thorny problem in print.[5] Older writers had been puzzled by the sheer volume of late seventeenth- and early eighteenth-century writing devoted to unequal or nearly equal temperaments, when the option of equal temperament was available. Lindley showed that reconciling these two types of temperament into something which would have something of the advantages of both was in fact the object of the debate, and sensitively suggested its specific relevance to

Bach. After 1985 equal temperament was back in business, though now what is meant is something more subtle and musical than strict mathematical equal temperament, and which would certainly have been adjusted to suit the instrument and repertory to be played.

1. The background to Bach's tunings

The term 'wohltemperirt' is particularly associated with Werckmeister. Through his activities as organist, organ expert, and his publications Werckmeister was by far the most influential writer on tuning in Bach's area at the end of the seventeenth century, and his writings continued to be a point of reference and recommendation until well into the eighteenth. Far from being the work of an ivory-tower theoretician, they are marked by strong practical sense, and his proposals for circulating tunings continue the tradition of adjustments to ¼-comma meantone practised by German organ builders of the mid-seventeenth century.[6] By the 1670s builders such as Christian Förner and Zacharias Thayssner, and the organist Johann Caspar Trost the younger, were moving towards a more radical solution to the problem of circulating through all keys, and Werckmeister's first publication of 1681 sums up this phase.[7]

The title-page has the first use of our term. It states that the purpose of the tract is to explain how, with the help of the monochord, 'ein *Clavier* wohl zu *temperiren* und zu stimmen sey'. Taking Werckmeister's writings from 1681 to 1691 as a whole, the term does not necessarily mean a specific temperament, but one which answers the following criteria: (1) one can go around the entire circle of keys without encountering any impossible sonorities ('damit man nach heutiger Manier alle *modos fictos* [i.e. transposed modes] in einer erträglichen und angenehmen *harmoni* vernehme', 1681 title-page); (2) this is to be enabled by adjusting the temperament, without recourse to split keys (*subsemitonia*). Werckmeister was struck by the novel beauty of enharmonic change ('Veränderungen': 'Wenn wir hingegen ein wohl *temperirtes* Clavier haben/ können wir aus jeglichen *Clave* alle *modos* haben/ und dieselben versetzen wie wir wollen/ welches einem/ so im Clavier *circulariter* bewandert ist/ seine Veränderungen giebet/ und sehr angenehm ins Gehör fället', 1687 p.120). Split keys, though commonly used in the seventeenth century, land you on a tonal flat earth where notes of different function cannot be exchanged enharmonically since they are different pitches;[8] (3) it is a single tuning. This is inevitably so on the organ, but in his many references to stringed keyboard instruments Werckmeister makes no mention of retuning between pieces on the analogy of the lute; some temperaments do, however, favour certain types of repertory, such as his Temperament IV (1691) which is designed to favour the seventeenth-century church modes.

Of the six temperaments described in 1691, No.III is clearly Werckmeister's preference among the ones he considers correct. He had good reason to be proud of it, since it is the first unequal temperament to allow satisfactory musical performance of all possible tonalities.[9] It builds logically on tradition in that it uses the familiar tempering of ¼-comma meantone. In this it follows a different avenue from the equally logical meantone adjustment common in France, for harpsichords at least, where the 5ths were expanded to –⅙ comma and the major 3rds to +⅓ comma, thus narrowing the wolf 5th from +1¾ commas to +⅚ comma, and the four unsociable major 3rds from +2 whole commas to +1⅓ commas.[10] It is not clear how much ⅙-comma meantone was used in Germany since it is hardly mentioned in the contemporary German literature. But many French musicians were employed at German courts, and it was the temperament particularly associated with Gottfried Silbermann. Werckmeister III, by its cunning placement of the fourth ¼ comma 5th, has no major 3rd wider than 1 comma (and only three of those), and no 5th tempered more than ¼ comma. It also has the least consonant major 3rds on the traditional notes C sharp, F sharp and G sharp, thus keeping the extreme keys in the usual places while giving them a usable form.

Werckmester says that he first considered equal temperament around 1675.[11] He mentions it in 1691 as the temperament to use if you wish to play equally frequently in every key, not making a distinction between usual and rare keys.[12] It had been part of the German keyboard tradition via Froberger who studied with Frescobaldi, a known advocate of equal temperament on the keyboard,[13] and Werckmeister mentions a canzona by Froberger (d.1677), written in the 1660s, which transposes its subject around the entire circle of 5ths.[14] In 1697 he recounts (p.36) that advocates of equal temperament say that it will have to be the temperament of the future when people will wish to exploit the key of C sharp as much as C, but that he himself has resisted it hitherto in order to preserve the purity of the more usual keys.

It says much about the Lutheran mentality of the time that what finally convinced him of the validity of equal temperament was an unnamed theologian deriving its proportions from the biblical description of the construction of Solomon's palace.[15] This type of numerological speculation played an important part in Werckmeister's thought. His Temperament VI of 1691 was supposedly based on a Keplerian notion of the harmony of the universe, and the mystical interpretation of equal temperament was much developed in the posthumously published *Paradoxal-Discourse* of 1707. In this he was by no means alone. In 1717 the mathematician and mining engineer Christoph Albert Sinn published a tract ostensibly to present the proportions of equal temperament for organ builders (who need exact measurements for casting pipes). He spends the first 112 pages discoursing on the 'secret cosmic harpsichord' ('das geheime Welt-Clavicymbel') in a tradition going back through Kircher to Kepler and Robert Fludd at the beginning of the seventeenth century. This may seem curious to us, but it was important to counter opponents of equal temperament who held it to be unnatural, if not diabolically inspired.[16]

By the time of his little thoroughbass treatise (1698b) Werckmeister was using the term 'wohl temperiren' to include equal temperament, though among others. Practical sense indicates that the temperament should suit local circumstances and requirements – a plurality of approach taken further in the next generation by Neidhardt. In the same spirit of practical sense he does not give monochord measurements for equal temperament ('ich . . . binde mich an kein *Mod*el'): it is a matter of sharpening all the major 3rds and flattening all the 5ths, everyone can adjust it as he will: 'Da ist das temperament getroffen' (1702 p.17).

Johann Georg Neidhardt (*c.*1685–1739) took over where Werckmeister left off. He was a good practical musician (capellmeister at Königsberg from 1720) as well as an expert mathematician, and his three books on keyboard tuning (1706, 1724, 1732) give a lucid picture of the reception of equal temperament in early eighteenth-century Germany. His writings on temperaments, together with Werckmeister's, are repeatedly mentioned by writers such as Mattheson, Sorge and Marpurg as the foundation literature of temperaments for modern music.

His first book, written while he was still a theology student at Jena, aims to present the mathematical proportions of equal temperament which Werckmeister had omitted. Neidhardt was in correspondence with Werckmeister[17] and clearly knew his writings well since his rationale for circulating temperaments and many of his formulations are strikingly similar.

His criticisms of Werckmeister III (p.39) give a good idea of how advanced opinion was moving in the early 1700s: (1) major 3rds a whole comma wide are unbearable; (2) as a result the major keys with the three worst 3rds on the tonic or nearly related triads remain unrefined ('un*excoli*ret'): he lists C sharp, E flat, F sharp, A flat and B majors; and C sharp, D sharp, F, F sharp, G sharp, B flat and B minors; (3) it is a torment to accompany when *chorton* and *cammerton* instruments are mixed. These points continued to be made by advocates of equal temperament into the second half of the century.

Neidhardt made his theoretical calculations when he was still very young and only later refined his practical skills.[18] The Erfurt organist Jakob Adlung (1699–1762), another advocate of equal temperament, reports Neidhardt's unsuccessful attempt to tune a Gedackt with the aid of a monochord.[19] Adlung's point is that there is no substitute for ear and instinct in tuning, and tells a similar story about the unsuccessful efforts of the Quedlinburg organist and mathematician Johann Georg Meckenheuser, who published another apologia for equal temperament in 1727.[20] Neidhardt's experiment was probably a year or two before 1706 and was made in competition with the organist of the Jena Stadtkirche, Johann Nicolaus Bach, a second cousin of Bach's. J.N. Bach, being an experienced musician and a resourceful instrument maker, tuned his Gedackt by ear and found the temperament perfectly. Clearly such dyed-in-the-wool musicians with generations of tradition behind them spurned gadgetry and relied on their ear and experience.[21] Neidhardt had evidently acquired practical experience by 1706 since he says (p.103) that there is no difficulty in tuning equal temperament when one is familiar with the beats ('wenn man die Schwebungen im Kopfe hat') and gives a straightforward recipe. Clearly there were good and experienced organ tuners who were perfectly capable of tuning equal temperament in the early years of the eighteenth century, even if many chose not to.

The supposed difficulty of tuning equal temperament was one of the things frequently held against it by conservatives. Adlung gives various recipes of which the easiest is based on the tuning of 3rds (1758 p.313). You tune c to c' pure, then divide the enharmonic diesis equally so that the three major 3rds c–e–g♯/a♭–c' beat at the same speed. Having tuned e–e' pure, you tune the four 5ths c–e' to beat equally, and so on.[22] Tuning by this method it is very easy to colour the 3rds so that, for example, e–g♯ beats as in equal temperament, with c–e a touch slower and g♯/a♭–c' a touch quicker, thus preserving something of the nuance between front and back keys of unequal temperaments. Lack of this nuance was one of the principal objections to equal temperament. Most people, says Neidhardt, miss the variety of major 3rds and consequently of affects.[23] He therefore in 1724 and 1732 suggests a number of coloured tunings for different circumstances. The spectrum runs in 1724 from the most unequal for a village, through progressively more equal temperaments for a small town and a large town, and with regular equal temperament for a court. In 1732 he adjusts this so as to have a slightly nuanced equal temperament even for the court.[24]

Similar nuanced tunings were proposed by Georg Andreas Sorge (1703–78). Sorge was organist at Lobenstein in Thuringia, a composer of some originality, and a theorist who combined excellent mathematical skills with a very keen ear.[25] Like Neidhardt's, his writings on tuning are very clear and straightforward, and we owe to him some of the very few evidences of Bach's attitude to tuning. Finally, even the ardent Berlin proponent of equal temperament Friedrich Wilhelm Marpurg (1718–95), described a modified equal temperament (a 'Mitteltemperatur' that is 'fast gleichschwebend') as perhaps the most useful of all ('Vieleicht ist diese die schicklichste', 1757 p.119).

Looking at German writings on tuning as a whole in the period of Bach's lifetime, there was a strong tradition of very competent theorists and musicians who described temperaments sensitively and with mathematical care, but always with the ear and instinct of the practical musician paramount. A wide variety of tunings must in practice have been used (every keyboard player has their own preferences) but the consensus of the best informed and most advanced thinking is clear and, whatever Bach's own preferences, this was the climate in which he worked.

2. *Bach and tuning to 1722*

We have no way of knowing what Bach's exact tuning preferences were, but we can at least assess likelihoods. There are a few general points about which we can be reasonably certain:

(1) His views changed and developed during the course of his career: he began in the context of the late seventeenth century and lived on into the age of *Empfindsamkeit.* Ideas of temperament, tonality, style, and keyboard technique are in reality inseparable aspects of a single development. (2) Tuning was an important issue to him, as were all other aspects of music. C.P.E. Bach reports: 'The exact tuning of his instruments as well as of the whole orchestra had his greatest attention. No one could tune and quill his instruments to please him. He did everything himself . . . .'[26] (3) His approach was practical and intuitive; it is most unlikely that he engaged in mathematical computations, or worked out temperaments with a monochord. He did not 'occupy himself with deep theoretical speculations on music, but was all the stronger in the practice of the art';[27] 'in these questions [tuning] he went by the light of nature, and not according to rule'.[28] (4) His views and practice were in general accord with the tradition of his time and place, and probably at the advanced end of the spectrum. Had he had some highly personal and idiosyncratic views they would surely be reflected somewhere in the literature.[29]

Bach's early years were spent in an environment of transition where there was much experimentation, but where there were three main types of tuning in practice: ¼-comma meantone, something like Werckmeister III, and something like equal temperament.[30] Of these the Werckmeister III type was used not only in and around Thuringia, but also in some parts of north Germany. It seems likely that Buxtehude had the organs of the Marienkirche, Lübeck, retuned to it in 1683.[31] After Bach had returned from this three-month visit to Lübeck in 1705–6 he confounded the Arnstadt congregation by mixing strange notes with the chorales. Buxtehude was known for his richly harmonised improvisations on chorales, and if Bach used the same vein on an organ nearer ¼-comma meantone the result would have been indeed strange. It was perhaps to facilitate this that he arranged two years later for the Blasiuskirche organ at Mühlhausen to be completely retuned, possibly in a temperament à la Lübeck.[32]

Apart from the organs at Lübeck, there were organs nearer home in the Harz area, just north of Thuringia, using Werckmeister temperaments. Works of Werckmeister's were in the library of the Michaelisschule at Lüneburg, where Bach could have got to know them.[33] Peter Williams has noted strikingly similar formulations to Werckmeister's in Bach's reports on organs.[34] Bach's relative and organ colleague at Weimar, Johann Gottfried Walther, went to Halberstadt and Magdeburg in 1704 to get to know Werckmeister, for whom he had a high regard. He remained in correspondence with him and obtained from him copies of many organ works of Buxtehude.[35] The article '*Temperamento*' in Walther's *Lexicon* (1732) cites Werckmeister 1691. Whether or not Bach ever used straight Werckmeister III tuning is open to question. As it stands it is obviously designed for ease of tuning, and to be acceptable to conservative-minded organ builders in its very straightforward tempering of the 5ths. Sophisticated musicians must have used something more subtle.[36] But a highly coloured tuning of that sort does suit Bach's earlier clavier works, such as the F sharp minor Toccata (BWV 910), with its very long sequences, and the D minor Toccata (BWV 913), whose third, improvisatory, section uses a repeated rhythmic figure to explore remote sonorities such as A flat major and E flat minor. This section loses much of its sense of adventure in an equal tuning.[37]

It is likely that the development of Bach's style in his later Weimar days, which entailed not only changing concepts of structure and tonality under Italian, particularly Vivaldi's, influence, but a development of keyboard technique as well, was accompanied by a change of tuning along the lines of the later works of Werckmeister, and of Neidhardt. A work of Werckmeister's which is particularly intriguing from the point of view of *The Well-tempered Clavier* is the thoroughbass tutor of 1698. This had a certain popularity, being reprinted in 1715, and reissued in 1737 by Bach's friend and pupil the theorist Lorenz Mizler. It ends with a short lesson, 'Wie man ein Clavier stimmen und wohl temperiren könne', which is as straightforward and practical an instruction as one is likely to find in print. After an explanation of beats and of the intervals that have to be divided to make a temperament, he gives, without any quantities, a recipe for tuning a sort of equal temperament by 5ths up from c, all very slightly narrow except for the last few (from e♭) which may be very slightly wide or, in the case of f–c, pure, depending on how one wants the 3rds on b, e♭, e, a♭, and f to be. He then gives recipes for tuning triple-fretted and double-fretted clavichords into some semblance of a circulating temperament. All this is pitched at a fairly homely level, but it does correspond to two remarks from the Bach tuning lore: (1) that he tuned all major 3rds wide;[38] and (2) C.P.E. Bach's statement that almost all 5ths should be tuned narrow.[39] Bach himself assuredly did not need this sort of low-level instruction, and these two points could apply to a number of tunings, but he may have recommended this little treatise to Mizler, who says it is the best instruction before Neidhardt.[40] It is tempting to think that Bach may have used it to recommend to pupils who asked for something straightforward and concise to read about tuning, in the same way that he apparently used F.E. Niedt's *Musicalische Handleitung* for instruction in thoroughbass and improvisation.

Something of Bach's attitude to the Werckmeister III-type tuning at this stage may be reflected in the report of the inspection he made in 1716 together with Johann Kuhnau (his predecessor as Thomascantor at Leipzig) and C.F. Rolle (organist at Quedlinburg) of the new organ by Christoph Kuntz (Cuncius) at the Liebfrauenkirche, Halle.[41] They had previously found fault with Kuntz's temperament on certain notes of all three manuals and he had undertaken to retune them in accordance with a 'noch passablen guten Temperatur' he had shown them. According to Sinn, Kuntz used the Werckmeister III tuning[42] and the 'passably good temperament' may have been something that reduced the whole-comma major 3rds of that. Kuhnau himself said in 1717 that he was prepared to accept equal temperament on instruments whose sound dies quickly such as the clavichord and harpsichord, though he had never tried it with the rigorous exactness of the monochord.[43]

On the face of it, it might seem significant that Bach elected to arrange the key scheme of *The Well-tempered Clavier* of 1722 to go up the chromatic scale from C, with tonic major and minor alternating, rather than in a scheme going round the circle of 5ths from C, with major keys alternating with their relative minors, as Heinichen had pictured in 1711.[44] Bach's ordering, putting C major and C sharp major in close proximity, would seem to be the fulfilment of Werckmeister's prophecy (1697 p.36) that in the future people would tune all consonances equally and play an air indifferently in C or in C sharp. This assumption holds good, though, only if Bach had conceived the scheme fully formed from the beginning. The early sources for the collection show that the concept only gradually assumed its final shape. The original idea seems to have been to provide pieces for the notes of the hexachord, along the lines of seventeenth-century verset collections, or perhaps for the complete white-note scale, as with the first seven Praeambula (later called Inventions) in Wilhelm Friedemann Bach's *Clavier-Büchlein*. The filling in of chromatic steps was an extension of this essentially conservative plan. Different orderings in two of the early sources of *The Well-tempered Clavier* are relics of this stage.[45]

Other features show how Bach evolved towards the final state in the early 1720s. Early versions of some minor-key pieces have 'Dorian' key signatures, and some major-key pieces may originally have been notated 'Mixolydian'. These signatures would be illogical in a fully chromatic context.[46] They hark back to styles and a world where unequal temperaments prevailed.

Impressions from the music are dangerously subjective, yet there are striking instances of appropriate colours in an unequal temperament. Taking those preludes which have early versions in W.F. Bach's *Clavier-Büchlein* one could mention the character difference between the Preludes in C and C sharp major; the bleak, wintry character of the E flat minor triad with a wide major 3rd on g; the colours of variable major 3rds and 7ths in the A flat major scale in bars 6–8 of the F minor Prelude; many will have their own observations.[47] Yet only if it could be shown that these pieces were composed into the *Clavier-Büchlein* could we be sure that they were not transposed from other keys, and that cannot be certain.[48] In Book I the D sharp minor fugue, and the G sharp minor prelude and fugue possibly, seem each to have been transposed up a semitone to fill gaps in the chromatic scheme.[49]

It is instructive to look at the views of another composer with a strong speculative bent who was moving in the same direction, Bach's near-contemporary in Hamburg, Johann Mattheson (1681–1764). It is by no means clear what connexions there may have been between Bach and Mattheson, or what Bach thought of him,[50] but Mattheson's publication in 1719 of figured-bass exercises in all 24 major and minor keys, the most significant step in the direction of *The Well-tempered Clavier* since Fischer's *Ariadne Musica* (1702), may have had an influence on Bach's developing concept. Bach visited Hamburg in 1720 to audition for the post of organist at the Jakobikirche, where Mattheson evidently heard him play but did not meet him.[51] Mattheson's book had been published three months before.

Unlike Bach, Mattheson keeps us copiously informed in theoretical publications about the development of his ideas. Being a contentious spirit he is not above taking sides variously in the same argument, so it is sometimes difficult to tell in what direction, if any, his real opinions lie. In his first publication (1713) he gives his famous list of key characters, but omits C sharp, F sharp, A flat and B majors, and C sharp, E flat, G sharp and B flat minors as being very seldom used (p.252). This recalls Neidhardt's (1706) remark about such keys being unrefined in unequal tunings, and Werckmeister's similar remarks that equal temperament is not needed if such keys are rarely used. By 1717 Mattheson was working towards his scheme of providing exercises in all keys, and his views had moved on, in theory at any rate.[52] He recommends both Werckmeister and Neidhardt, but says that Neidhardt (1706) has given the best description (1717 p.85). Most organ builders are unable to tune it, but although Mattheson says that it may be done on the harpsichord (p.87), it seems unlikely that he had achieved it himself since he says two years later that he had never found it outside Neidhardt's book (1719 p.99).

The object of Mattheson's continuo exercises in all keys is not to demonstrate any particular temperament, but to provide practice for learning the handshapes ('die Griffe') for chords in unusual keys so as to have total fluency in continuo playing (1719 Erster Theil pp.56–7). He does nonetheless considerably refine on his brief remarks on tuning of 1717. One of his concerns is to preserve the distinction of key characters. For this he proposes a temperament of his own, based on just intonation, but which he must have regarded as somewhat theoretical in view of his later remarks.[53] But in order to play in all keys the real issue is whether or not equal temperament is the solution. He finds pure equal temperament, as proposed by mathematicians, musically insensitive. Having all 12 semitones the same size is not the aim of music, but that they should all sound pure and agreeable. If they are all the same size they sound wrong, so why take the trouble?[54] The practical temperament of a musician may not agree with mathematical calculations, but it will be better in giving more accurately the pleasurable variety of keys. This does not reduce the diversity of keys, but quadruples them.[55]

If the exact proportions of equal temperament are one side of the definition, the other is intervals tempered by a whole comma, which are unbearable (p.55), a view shared by many from the 1720s.[56] This rules out those temperaments which have one or more Pythagorean 3rds. The views expressed by Mattheson must have been widespread, since it was precisely to satisfy this definition that Neidhardt, Sorge and Marpurg devised their subtly shaded, non-equal temperaments. As far as Bach's tuning in 1722 is concerned, it would seem reasonable to suppose that he had something in which every key could be used equally as a tonic (i.e. no Pythagorean 3rds), but at the same time preserved something of the evolutionary nature of the collection in a subtly shaded inequality.

3. *Bach and tuning* c.*1740*

Such leads as we do have for Bach's tuning apply to the 1730s and 40s and have to do with organs he is known to have played, or with the views of people in his circle, and the evidence points overwhelmingly to equal or near-equal temperament. In September 1739 Bach visited and tested the organ in the Hofkapelle, Altenburg, which had recently been completed by Heinrich Gottfried Trost. The tuning of this organ had been the subject of much debate, involving not only the commissioners and the builder but also the Gotha Capellmeister Gottfried Heinrich Stölzel, well known to Bach, and possibly Bach himself.[57] The records of the debate, in which five different temperaments were proposed (including a version of ¼-comma meantone, equal temperament, and two of Neidhardt's) are unique in Bach's area for discussing a tuning issue in such detail.[58] The tuning decided upon was equal temperament ('the newest and the best' according to the court organist Lorenz), but Trost's effort at it had noticeably, some said objectionably, sharp D sharps and B flats, giving perhaps the +11⁄12-comma major 3rds of one of Neidhardt's more rustic temperaments. The specification given to Trost was that it should be playable satisfactorily in all keys, and Bach is said to have accompanied the Creed on it, transposing each verse up a semitone from D minor to E flat minor to E minor.[59]

The organ builder closest to Bach was the Leipzig builder Zacharias Hildebrandt, who made Bach a 'lute-harpsichord' around 1739. In 1748, Bach's pupil Johann Friedrich Agricola was chosen with Bach's recommendation to be organist of the Wenzelkirche, Naumburg, where the organ had recently been rebuilt by Hildebrandt and inspected by Bach to ratify that the contract had been properly fulfilled. In 1753 Agricola said of Hildebrandt: 'in the temperament he follows Neidhardt, and one can modulate very nicely into all keys, without giving the ear anything unpleasant to hear, which for today's taste in music is the most beautiful.'[60] In a survey of Hildebrandt organs, Ulrich Dähnert concludes that both Hildebrandts used one of Neidhardt's near-equal temperaments rather than equal temperament itself.[61]

A number of people in Bach's immediate environment in the 1730s and 40s were concerned with the issue of tuning, which continued to be a lively topic of debate. Many were involved in the Corresponding Society of Musical Sciences founded by Lorenz Christoph Mizler together with Count Lucchesini and Bümler in 1738. We have already met Bümler as one of the earliest in the eighteenth century to calculate equal temperament. Mizler was a figure of the Enlightenment, a student of Gottsched and Christian Wolff, with interests in theology, natural sciences and mathematics apart from the history and theory of music. Bach was a 'good friend' of his, joining the Society as its fourteenth member in 1747, and in all probability finding in him a stimulating way of keeping up with current developments.[62]

In 1737 Mizler published (pp.56–8) his explanation of the theory and tuning of equal temperament, followed by the rather homespun recipe for a slightly unequal temperament from Werckmeister 1698b discussed above. Werckmeister was not to be despised, says Mizler, being in his time one of the best and most learned writers on music. Even though times have changed many may find this tuning both pleasant and useful (p.58). The instruction is clearly aimed at students and amateurs, and Mizler's remarks are typical of the move away from Werckmeister to Neidhardt. In 1742 Mizler published another work of interest to Bach, an annotated German translation of Fux's *Gradus ad Parnassum* (1725) of which Bach owned a copy of the Latin first edition.[63] Curiously for a champion of the church modes, Fux says that in the modern system the inequality of tones and semitones is removed. Mizler, in a footnote, finds nothing unusual about this, and directs practical musicians who wish to know more about temperaments to the *Musicalische Bibliothek*, where he had published his own description of equal temperament in 1737.[64]

Apart from Stölzel, who had recommended equal temperament for the Altenburg organ, and who became a member of the Society in 1739, the

Nordhausen organist and composer Christoph Gottlieb Schröter became the fourth member in the same year. Schröter was somebody whose judgment Bach respected, and Mizler later (1747) published his description of equal temperament.[65] Others in Bach's orbit, though not in Mizler's Society, were Conrad Friedrich Hurlebusch and Johann Georg Hille. Hurlebusch's contacts with Bach are well documented, and Bach may have modelled the E flat Praeludium and Fuga (BWV 552) from *Clavier-Übung* III on a keyboard *Ouverture* of his.[66] In 1756 he is mentioned by Barthold Fritz in the dedication to his dissertation on equal temperament as one who endorsed Fritz's tuning, the other being C.P.E. Bach. Hille, cantor at Glaucha near Halle, knew Bach, whom he visited in Leipzig in 1739. In 1740 Bach returned the visit, and particularly admired a linnet that Hille had trained to sing beautifully.[67] After these friendly contacts with the greatly admired Bach, Hille published a short treatise on musical intervals, writing that in the best temperament all 5ths should beat ¹⁄₁₂-comma narrow ('weil er aber nach der besten Temperatur ein zwölftel Comma unterwärts schweben mu*ss* . . .' 1740 p.11).

The member of Mizler's Society who wrote most comprehensively about tuning was Georg Andreas Sorge, who joined as fifteenth member one month after Bach in 1747. Sorge has left us the only direct and precise statements about tuning attributed to Bach during his lifetime. How well he knew Bach is not clear, but he was certainly a great admirer and seems to have enjoyed friendly relations with him. His *Drittes halbes Dutzend Sonatinen vors Clavier* (pre-1745) are dedicated to Bach as 'prince of clavier players', and the dedication addresses Bach in a manner that implies at least one genial meeting.[68] In subtlety of approach combined with strong practical sense, Sorge continued the Neidhardt tradition. He himself said his aim was to popularise the ideas of Neidhardt, whose books many owned but few understood (1749 p.18).

Of his six essays on tuning, the *Gespräch* of 1748, which contains his comments on Bach, also gives the best picture of the general context. Modern music demands that one 3rd should sound as good as another: all reasonable composers understand this since they write a♭–c as often as they write e–g♯. It follows that if all 3rds are to sound equally good, then all major 3rds should be equally ⅓-diesis (= ⅔-comma) wide. Yet many resist this logic, finding these major 3rds too harsh ('scharff'), not beautiful and agreeable ('schön und lieblich', 1748 dedicatory letter). In order to take account of this reality Sorge proposes elsewhere in his writings various near-equal temperaments, some of which are Neidhardt's and some his own. Here he singles out as an example of a temperament unsuited to modern music the ⅙-comma meantone apparently used by Gottfried Silbermann, which leaves half of the 24 keys all but unusable ('fast unbrauchbar' p.11). Sorge invokes all experienced practical musicians ('erfahrene Musicos') and in particular Bach to witness that this is so (p.21). In terms of a consensus that found major 3rds a whole comma wide too harsh, and 5ths more than ¼-comma narrow unacceptable, the four major 3rds well over a whole comma wide (+1⅓) and one 5th almost a whole comma wide (+⅚) severely restricts the usability of keys. Bach, says Sorge, found the four major 3rds 'barbaric' (p.28), a word Sorge himself later used to describe major 3rds no more than one whole comma wide (1773 p.57). Whether or not the 63-year-old Bach, who seems to have had good relations with Silbermann, gave permission for the use of his name in this diatribe is not clear.[69]

All that can be deduced from this directly is that Bach found Silbermann's temperament too crudely differentiated. In view of the fact that he of all composers was particularly associated with the full use of all 24 keys this is hardly surprising. In the obituary written by C.P.E. Bach and Johann Friedrich Agricola, Bach's tuning of harpsichords is described as so pure and correct ('so rein und richtig') that all tonalities sounded handsome and agreeable ('schön und gefällig'), and there were none that had to be avoided because of impure intonation.[70] Both of them must have used something like equal temperament, since C.P.E. Bach recommended Barthold Fritz's *Anweisung* (1756), and Agricola was involved in the publication of Adlung's *Musica mechanica* (1768), which recommends only equal temperament, and himself recommended Sorge's *Anweisung zur Rational-Rechnung* (1749; Agricola 1757 p.20).

Johann Philipp Kirnberger was a pupil of Bach's at roughly the same time as Agricola (1739–41). Estimates of the actual duration of his studies vary from a few months to two years, but there is no doubt about his enormous admiration for Bach as performer, composer and teacher, and he was to be one of the main preservers and promoters of Bach's music in the second half of the eighteenth century. At the beginning of his most important work, *Die Kunst des reinen Satzes in der Musik* (1771ff), Kirnberger gives a fair summary of developments in the early eighteenth century. After a period of experimentation, some writers came to the conclusion that the simplest way out of the problem was to divide the octave into twelve equal steps. Many considered this equal temperament to be very advantageous since it is possible to play with almost complete purity in all the major and minor keys.[71] This represented the situation in the 1730s and 1740s, and Kirnberger's first theoretical work (*c.*1760) was a geometric presentation of equal temperament, without any aesthetic judgment of it. It was presumably around this time, when he was on good terms with his later sparring partner Friedrich Wilhelm Marpurg, that he discussed with Marpurg what Bach had told him about tuning. The one element of this to have come down to us is that Bach 'expressly required of him that he tune all the [major] 3rds sharp'.[72]

Kirnberger later had two objections to equal temperament, which in themselves are common enough in the literature going back to Werckmeister and may conceivably have been expressed by Bach: (1) that it cannot be tuned with absolute mathematical accuracy by ear; and (2) that it eliminates the diversity of keys.[73] But his solution, first proposed in his fourth collection of *Clavierübungen* (1766), is very wide of the consensus outlined above. His basic temperament (I) is Pythagorean, with a whole syntonic comma on the 5th d–a, and the remaining 1/12 of the ditonic comma on f♯–c'♯. Since people find the whole-comma 5th intolerable he is prepared to divide it over d–a–e', giving two ½-comma 5ths (temperament II). It is quite plain from his instruction that this is a tuning for amateurs who have difficulty hearing beats, and the object is to find a tuning which can be achieved with as many pure intervals as possible. If they want to know more, he directs them to Fux's *Gradus* and Marpurg's *Anfangsgründe* (1757). Inasmuch as Fux discusses temperament it is equal temperament, and Marpurg discusses a range of temperaments with near-equal ('fast gleichschwebend') as perhaps the most usable, continuing the traditional consensus of Werckmeister–Neidhardt–Sorge.

Apart from its aesthetic unsuitability (the ½-comma fifths can only work as special effects in their Pythagorean surroundings) Kirnberger nowhere attributes his temperament II to Bach. He describes it in *Die Kunst des reinen Satzes*, which is an attempt to present systematically Bach's 'method' of teaching composition, but inasmuch as Bach is mentioned in this context, he is dragged in as a red herring in Kirnberger's subsequent dispute with Marpurg. Kirnberger's temperament III, dividing the syntonic comma over four 5ths c–g–d–a–e, which has been proposed as the Bach tuning by several twentieth-century writers,[74] cannot logically be Kirnberger's Bach tuning since it was formulated later in response to criticisms of the ½-comma 5ths by writers such as Sorge and Marpurg. It is in any case a crude version of the temperaments of Werckmeister and Bendeler of the 1680s and 1690s, with no less than five whole-comma major 3rds as opposed to Werckmeister's three, and was criticised as such by Sorge long before Kirnberger proposed it (Sorge 1744 pp.26–7). Even so knowledgeable and dispassionate an observer as Daniel Gottlob Türk found some of the triads so much less pure than in equal or near-equal temperaments that they vitiated the supposed gain of key colour, and regretted the influence it had since its inclusion in Sulzer's *Allgemeine Theorie* (Türk 1787 p.201).

4. *Summary*

With so much writing about temperaments in Bach's immediate environment, much of it by people with whom he was directly connected, it is not difficult to form a general impression of his probable views. Starting with some version of Werckmeister III, he seems to have moved towards something more evenly circulating by 1722. He may have paid lip-service to equal temperament at that stage, but the feeling of the music is that there is still a sensitivity to intervals and keys based on unequal tuning. By 1744 equal temperament was well established, though in practice what was used was humanised to retain a nuance of traditional key character. The C sharp major Prelude of Book I contrasts vividly with the C major one in a way which suggests the old key distinction, and exists only in that key. The C sharp major Prelude of Book II is a prelude in C major of similar character to that of Book I, transposed.

CHAPTER THREE

Preludes

1. The Prelude and Fugue as a genre

Traditionally the separate prelude and fugue combination in Bach's mature work has been seen as the result of a loosening, and eventually separation, of the elements of the composite, sectional form of the seventeenth-century toccata/praeludium/canzona into its component parts. There is much truth in this view, and it is a readily observable phenomenon in the works of Bach's immediate predecessors. Already in Kuhnau's second *Clavier Übung* (1692) the Praeludia which refer to this seventeenth-century sectional model tend to be in a clear bipartite form with a break between sections. Openings have a more motivically worked, concertante character than the improvisatory flourish and decorated chords of the earlier type, and the following fugues are more elaborately developed, with longer and more characterful subjects. George Stauffer has charted a similar break-up of the sectional praeludium into two distinct entities in Bach's early organ works (1980 pp.129–30). Fugue as a manner of composition was one of Bach's primary interests, and his elaboration of this element necessitated a corresponding expansion of the prelude to form a matching element in a contrasting manner. Yet Bach was by no means alone in moving away from the old rhetorical, sectional framework to separate movements unified in character and material, developed around a tonal structure. It is a general trend of the Italian genres of sonata, concerto and cantata from the 1680s.

By the beginning of the eighteenth century the sectional praeludium could encompass a variety of different compositional types ranging from free improvisation, to dance elements, to the strictly contrapuntal canzona. Sophisticated, cosmopolitan examples such as the Toccatas of Georg Muffat's *Apparatus Musico-organisticus* (Salzburg 1690) could include a variety of current French and Italian manners as well. If the prelude could include such a range of styles and techniques, then it could simply concentrate on one of them, following the late seventeenth-century trend, most conspicuously represented in the sonatas of Corelli, away from multi-sectioned pieces towards separate movements, each with its own internal economy of material and character, developed around a tonal structure. Progressive composers of the late seventeenth century in Bach's area were moving towards more unified pieces, notably Johann Pachelbel who was probably the single most influential figure in Bach's immediate background.

A genre of separate prelude and fugue that reaches far back into the seventeenth century is the verset collection, cultivated as much in Lutheran areas (Pachelbel) as in Catholic ones (Kerll). The verset tradition has many reflexions in the 48, not least in the objective of covering all the modes (Constantini 1969). In this tradition the opening and concluding flourishes are necessarily separated from the intervening fugues by chanted verses of the Magnificat or the Mass Ordinary. It is of course possible to cut up a sectional piece such as a canzona or toccata and use it for this purpose. The idea of the verset appears to go deeper into Bach's teaching practice than the Lutheran chorale prelude. The title-page of the *Orgel-Büchlein*, with its educational agenda, was the last thing he added to it (after *c.*1720), at the time when he was writing similar title-pages for other, more ostensibly educational works such as the Inventions and Sinfonias (1723) and *The Well-tempered Clavier* (1722). He does not seem to have routinely handed out the *Orgel-Büchlein* chorales to students, since few of them made copies from it (Stauffer 1994 p.32). On the other hand he seems to have had a substantial stock of clavier teaching material prior to 1720, some of which eventually found its way into Book II, and this relates to the verset tradition. One source of the five preludes and fughettas which Bach was eventually to use as an initial quarry of material for Book II has the heading 'Praeludia, und Fugen./ Zum Nutzen und Gebrauch/ der Lehrbegieringen Musicalischen/ Jugend, als auch derer in diesem Studio schon habil seyenden/ Besondern Zeit Vertreib/ aufgesetzet und verfertiget/ Von/ Johann Sebastian Bachen.' (P 804). The source from which this was copied may antedate the 1722 title-page. Constantini has shown that this formulation is a verset-tradition topos, expressed for example by Fischer in *Ariadne Musica* (1702) as 'Magistris aeque ac Discipulis virtute et utilitate maxime commendendam'.[1] These early teaching pieces were not worked systematically enough to be usable in the Inventions or Book I, but remained to be adapted for Book II. In other words, Bach at some time before 1720 began putting together as teaching material a group of verset-type prelude and fugue pairs, the very nature of which was for demonstration and teaching purposes. Magnificat versets were as much a Lutheran tradition as a Catholic one. In the preludes and fughettas the early version of the C major prelude (BWV 870a/1) and the Praeludium in D minor BWV 899/1 are in a noticeably organ style, though others seem more suitable for clavier than for organ.

BOOK I

2. Prelude traditions

By Bach's time the concept of the prelude could draw on a rich array of prototypes. He himself had a connoisseur's knowledge of the keyboard tradition back to the early seventeenth century. From his earliest years he had a voracious appetite for new music, quickly assimilating new styles and techniques and exploiting them in his own compositions. His first teaching in clavier playing was from his eldest brother Johann Christoph Bach, a pupil of Pachelbel who in turn had learnt from Kerll. According to C.P.E. Bach, works in the south German tradition of Kerll, Pachelbel and also Froberger were contained in the book that Johann Christoph kept locked in a cupboard with a grille, through which young Bach fished it out to make illicit copies by moonlight (Dok.III p.81, NBR p.299). He retained a lifelong admiration for Froberger and may have possessed the collection of canzonas and capriccios published in Mainz (1696) and Frankfurt (1714; Dok.III p.124, BR p.445). He went from Lüneburg, where he was at school, to Hamburg to hear the aged Reinken, who had studied with a pupil of Sweelinck's, play the organ. The north German tradition of Reinken, Bruhns and Buxtehude was equally familiar to him at first hand (Dok.III p.82, NBR p.300). Apart from these leading figures we can get an idea of the sort of repertoire Johann Christoph played from two manuscript collections he compiled, now known as the Andreas Bach Book and the Möller manuscript, and more generally from other collections such as the Eckelt tablature, compiled by another pupil of Pachelbel's.[2]

We cannot be sure of the details of the teaching tradition in which Bach received his first instruction, but it is likely to be reflected in a general way in the *Musicalische Handleitung* of Friedrich Erhard Niedt (1674–1708). Niedt had studied from 1695 with Bach's gifted and enterprising Jena cousin Johann Nicolaus Bach, whom we have already met competing with Neidhardt in tuning an organ in equal temperament and building elaborate and ingenious Lautenwerke, and whom Bach later respected as the senior member of the family. The *Musicalische Handleitung* may well represent something of the instruction traditional in the Bach family. Not only is Niedt's method of building up to composition from figured-bass playing the same as what we know of Bach's own method, but Bach seems later to have used at least Part I (1700) of the *Musicalische Handleitung* in his own teaching.[3] The idea of basing composition on thoroughbass was in any case the current one in Lutheran Germany, as testified by Heinichen (1711, 1728, for whom Bach acted as agent) and Mattheson (1719 etc.).

These were the traditions Bach started with. By 1720 he could draw on cosmopolitan prototypes from sonata, dance, and aria, as well as his own development of the invention principle. All these the non-specific title of prelude allowed him to treat with some freedom. Book I has every sign of being a systematic demonstration of the variety of the prelude as a genre, designed to give a comprehensive educational scheme covering both playing technique and composition.

3. *The traditional sectional Praeludium*

There are two respects in which Niedt's instructions have a bearing on the preludes of Book I. One relates to improvising in different textures over a given figured bass; the other to improvising more elaborate preludes in sections of different character. The commonest meaning of the term prelude in the seventeenth-century German tradition is of an improvisation to introduce some more premeditated type of piece. This meaning goes back to Praetorius (1619), who uses the terms Toccata, Praeambulum and Praeludium for a piece consisting of plain chords and runs, improvised ('fantasirt') on the organ or harpsichord before a motet or fugues (III p.23). Apart from alerting listeners that music was about to begin, it had a number of purely practical functions in that it gave singers their pitch, and also allowed instruments, if present, to check their tuning. Out of this simple improvisation the large-scale north German Praeludium *pedaliter* for organ began its development, the most elaborate of the prelude genre in the Baroque, in the generation of Sweelinck's pupils. The Praeambula of Scheidemann typically have a free opening section, an imitative or fugal middle section, and a free closing section. Into this sectional structure Weckmann and others introduced more stylistically diverse elements from the south German Toccatas and Canzonas of Froberger. The apex of this development is in the large multi-sectioned Praeludia of Buxtehude. These contrast free virtuoso flourishes with elaborately worked fugal sections, and the traditional rhetorical style with the motor energy of the new Italian manner, and often have subtle motivic and other links between sections.

Niedt's recipe for improvising this type of prelude (given in Chapter XI of Part II) is of particular interest since it uses the formal model of the commonest type of late seventeenth-century Praeludium, and must have been a common formula for improvising such things. It also uses a given figured-bass structure. Niedt's sections are as follows: (1) a semiquaver flourish decorating the tonic chord (this is divided between the hands and Niedt gives a number of specimen patterns); (2) a section of chords decorated by runs (as Praetorius) and some imitative figures (this all decorates the given figured-bass structure); (3) Niedt has a chaconne next, rather than an imitative section, a useful exercise for learning improvisers; and (4) a final section with more chords and flourishes, again decorating the given figured bass.

Praeludia of this type are exceedingly common in late seventeenth-century German organ and clavier music. Very straightforward examples are in Kuhnau's first *Clavier-Übung* (1689). These are pretty well exactly according to Niedt's recipe, only substituting a lightly contrapuntal, and easily improvisable, fugato for the chaconne. Sophisticated peaks of the repertory such as the toccatas of Froberger or the organ praeludia of Böhm and Buxtehude are worked-up versions of improvisations on this general model, as are a number of Bach's clavier toccatas. Among the most sophisticated examples is the E flat major prelude from Book I. This is a type of composition which Bach had abandoned by his later Weimar years and the E flat stands apart from the other preludes in the book. Judging by other early Weimar keyboard works, Bach was fully capable of writing a piece of this accomplishment at that stage; or he may for the purposes of Book I have reworked an old piece. He may even have composed this piece specially to fill a gap as the compendium nature of *The Well-tempered Clavier* evolved, since it is surely included to represent what was traditionally the archetypal German keyboard praeludium.

A further stage of integration of contrasting sections is in the B flat major prelude. This is based on the type of materials used in the D major Praeludium VI of Fischer's *Les pieces de clavessin* (1696), which is a late seventeenth-century version of Praetorius's alternation of sustained chords ('schlicht') and florid passages ('colorirt'), a formula that goes back ultimately to Conrad Paumann and the Buxheim Organ Book. In the B flat prelude Bach has unified these opposite ingredients on the principle of the sonata moto perpetuo, used by Corelli to link successive ideas by means of a constant motor energy.

4. *Figuration Preludes*

The other respect in which Niedt's instructions are relevant to Bach's preludes is in the elaboration of figured basses. The given figured basses provide the structures around which preludes can be developed by means of improvised figurations, a process of elaboration Niedt calls *Invention* (Part II Chapter XI). Chapter VII of Niedt's Part I and much of Part II (*Handleitung zur Variation*) is concerned with ways of building variations on given harmonic plans using a number of standard techniques such as decorations of the bass, or varieties of broken-chord patterns in the right hand, or developing a motive, or what he calls sonata style (i.e. the style of an ensemble string sonata: in his example a texture of repeated chords).[4] All of these manners may be found in contemporary praeludia.

The type of figure variation that uses a single broken-chord pattern throughout the piece has long been seen to lie behind some of the preludes of Book I, notably those which are in the first group of entries in Wilhelm

Friedemann's *Clavier-Büchlein.* It would be pointless to pursue the similarities between Niedt's examples, or pieces of this type by Bach's immediate predecessors, and Bach's own preludes into too much detail. But this is certainly another traditional form of prelude, used by Kuhnau in the G major Praeludium of his Partie V (1689) and by other figures from the environment of Bach's youth such as Handel's teacher F.W. Zachow, and J.C.F. Fischer. Zachow's Praeludia in this manner introduce fugues, and are on a par with Kuhnau's;[5] Fischer's introduce suites ('Clio' and 'Polymnia' from the *Musicalischer Parnassus*) and are on a level of sophistication nearer to Bach's.[6] The striking similarities of these two preludes to Bach's preludes in C major from Book I and C sharp major from Book II do not have to imply an imitation either way. More important is that they are the result of common aims and materials in a common tradition.

In Book I there are two main types of figuration prelude, both designed to cultivate the relation of hand to keyboard. The first type uses a consistent broken-chord pattern (C major, D minor) which one might call a hand-shape type (the German word 'Griffe' was used for chords); the second is based on a motive designed to cultivate equality of little finger and thumb with the other fingers (C minor, D major, E minor). The purpose of these preludes and the logic of Bach's method is best seen in the *Clavier-Büchlein.* In terms of the development of keyboard technique (*musica practica*), the C major prelude has right-hand broken chords with a still hand, the D minor has them with the hand moving round the keyboard. The C minor emphasises little finger and thumb with a still hand, the D major has the right hand moving round the keyboard. The E minor is an equivalent exercise for the left hand. As examples of composition (*musica poetica*), the C major and D minor preludes use just chord notes; the C minor, D major, and E minor preludes build on this by adding decorative notes in traditional patterns of *figurae*, explained by J.G. Walther in his composition tutor (1708).[7] These patterns involve use of dissonance on the third semiquaver of each beat: an auxiliary in the C minor prelude, a passing note in the D major, a more elaborate pattern with an accented auxiliary in the E minor. The same agenda of plain arpeggiation, then arpeggiation with dissonant decoration, may be seen continuing in the second half of Book I in the open-hand preludes in G major and F major.

The broken-chord type of prelude based on a regular pattern, of which there are numerous examples in Bach's clavier works outside *The Well-tempered Clavier*, has a seventeenth-century ancestry going back to the chitarrone toccatas of Kapsberger (1604)[8]. Arpeggiation is also recommended by Frescobaldi for the chordal sections of his toccatas when playing them on the harpsichord rather than the organ, in order 'not to let the instrument sound empty'.[9] It can in itself be, or be part of, a piece of concert music. In the later seventeenth century tonal direction was added to motivic concentration in pieces based from a single motif worked around a tonal structure, a development associated particularly with the Italian sonata moto perpetuo. This need not be done in the abstract, but can be the basis of a character piece. The little Prelude that opens the famous Frost Scene in the third act of Purcell's *King Arthur* (1691) is constructed entirely from a motif of three semiquavers followed by a crotchet, representing people shivering with cold. The reference to French character ballet is obvious, but this combines character with an extreme version of Italian motivic integration. A similar marriage of Italian motivic economy with French character, more immediately in Bach's world, may be found in harpsichord works of François Couperin such as *Les lis naissans* (13th *Ordre*, 1722).

The view presented so far is of three phases of central German clavier prelude around 1700: (1) a sectional, improvisatory type, traditionally associated with the organ; (2) a chordal type with its surface decorated by a consistent pattern, often used as a technical exercise; and (3) a character-piece type (Bergner 1986 p.10). From around 1710 the situation became considerably more complicated.

5. *The Invention principle*

Niedt's use of the term Invention for a pattern developed on a given harmonic formula has another resonance in Bach which draws further prototypes into the orbit of the prelude. The (two-part) Inventions and (three-part) Sinfonias, as they were called in the final version of 1723, had the headings Praeambulum and Fantasia in the *Clavier-Büchlein.*[10]

Although all the Inventions are constructed on standard late-Baroque harmonic progressions such as the circle of 5ths and so on, as in Niedt's figured basses, the first three (in the sequence in which they appear in the *Clavier-Büchlein*: C major, D minor, E minor) develop linear, scale-based motifs in an obviously contrapuntal way. But there follows a series using arpeggio-based motifs whose beginnings seem designed to demonstrate standard harmonic opening gambits:

No.4 (F major) decorates just the tonic chord;

No.5 (G major) opens with the next simplest progression, I V I;

No.6 (A minor) does the same, but with a suspension in the bass;

No.8 (B flat) uses the common four-chord formula, over a tonic pedal $\begin{smallmatrix}5\\3\end{smallmatrix}$, $\begin{smallmatrix}6\\4\end{smallmatrix}$, $\begin{smallmatrix}7\\4\\2\end{smallmatrix}$, $\begin{smallmatrix}5\\3\end{smallmatrix}$;

No.9 (A major) has a circle of falling 3rds;

No.10 (G minor) is based on the descending chromatic tetrachord (*lamento* bass) which in itself can imply a circle of 5ths.

Similar opening gambits are demonstrated in the Book I preludes: the progression noted in the B flat Invention (No.8) opens the preludes in C minor, D minor, F major, G major, and closely related ones open those in E minor and A minor; another very common four-chord progression (I II^2 V^6_5 I) opens the prelude in C major; and a further one (I I^6 II^7 V^7 I) that in D major.

The Inventions range from relatively straightforward harmonic decoration (F major, G major) to highly ingenious motivic explorations in double counterpoint (G minor, F minor) and finally canon (C minor), all under the heading Praeambulum. Judging by the first ten items in the *Clavier-Büchlein*, of which some are entitled Praeambulum, some Praeludium, Bach regarded the terms as interchangeable. Thereafter he probably used Praeambulum for what were later to become the Inventions simply to distinguish them as a different series from the Praeludia which later became part of Book I, rather than because he intended some particular nuance of difference between the terms. The Inventions were to demonstrate techniques of motivic development strictly in two parts; the Praeludia began as finger-technical exercises. That Bach had no particular attachment to Praeambulum as a genre title is evident from his dropping it in favour of a term which more exactly expressed his intention, that is of demonstrating how to discover and develop good 'inventions' in Niedt's sense. Likewise the term Fantasia could cover a very wide spectrum, from highly premeditated and ingenious examples of *stile antico* counterpoint, for which it was used by seventeenth-century composers such as Frescobaldi and Froberger, to pieces in the tradition of *fantasiren* (improvising in a free and unpredictable style) such as Bach's own Chromatic Fantasia (Schleuning 1971 I p.13). This ambiguity probably made it seem suitable for the three-part series: contrapuntal pieces that were obviously neither fugues, ricercars, nor canzonas.[11] The switch to Sinfonia, with its implications of instrumental ensemble music, underlined their function of cultivating playing in three obbligato parts.

Bach was here grappling with problems of terminology in the context of a long and complex tradition, comprehending a wide range of instrumental forms and techniques, and drawing on different national styles and local usages. In addition, the development of tonal harmony, with its radically different concepts of musical structure from what had prevailed for much of the seventeenth century, had undermined the neatness of the old categories. The fact that he sought exact classification for different types of piece, and changed his terminology accordingly, indicates the scientific fastidiousness of Bach's mentality. But, significantly, there were in reality no exact terms for what he intended so that it was the function, not the form, of a type that became its definer (Stauffer 1980 p.2).

The terms Praeludium and Fuga, used in Book I, were convenient in implying a contrasting pair of pieces, one free in the sense of being undefined in genre, the other strict in observing the conventions of fugal exposition and generally staying in a set number of parts. Bach's changes in terminology in the Inventions imply that the term Prelude could cover ingredients of fantasia, sinfonia, or sonata, as well as freely improvised pieces, or ones figured out over standard bass progressions, and this freedom suited his purpose ideally.

Of the preludes in Book I that are similar to the Inventions and Sinfonias, only the A major (in 3 parts) would be able to take its place among them. The preludes in F sharp major and G major have the qualification of being strictly in two parts but there is no real inversion of material, a fundamental characteristic of the Inventions. The two-part preludes in C sharp major and F major and the three-part ones in G sharp minor and B major have freedoms of texture which would exclude them. In the Book I preludes Bach therefore seems to have had similar practical and compositional objectives to those worked out in the Inventions, but in a freer framework than he allowed himself there. The preludes in F sharp minor and B major are built up from the sort of finger-exercise patterns used in the inventions in C major, D minor, and E minor; the prelude in A flat major is in the same violin-sonata manner as the B minor invention.

6. Sonata, Dance, and Ritornello principles

The undefined nature of the prelude as a genre allows Bach freedom to experiment in other respects as well. The leading vehicle for secular keyboard music in the early years of the eighteenth century was the dance suite. But from the middle of the seventeenth century Italian composers had developed versions of the standard dances that were abstracted from the phrase structure and melodic characters of the original dances into a sonata style, a process which can be observed in Corelli's trio sonatas and which reached its most influential form in his violin sonatas Op.5 (Rome 1700). Thus a sonata Allemanda, for example, came to have in common with the dance only a **c** time signature, a predominant semiquaver note value, and a binary structure. In all other respects it was a sonata Allegro. One can compare traditional and abstracted treatments in the Allemanda of Bach's B minor violin partita BWV 1002. The primary version has the traditional rhythmic characteristics of a French Allemande, with fully notated rhythmic inequality and phrases clearly marked out by cadences; the Double reworks it in the abstracted Corellian sonata manner of a moto perpetuo of semiquavers.

The generation after Corelli moved away from dance titles to sonata movements entitled Allegro and so on, and commonly employed the sort of structure that is typically represented in the Courante of Bach's cello Suite in G major (BWV 1007). The origin of this structure goes back to the development of tonal patterns by Italian sonata composers in the second half of the seventeenth century. Ex.3.1 gives the *soggetto* of the opening Allegro of G.M. Bononcini's sonata Op.6 No.8 (1672). This has one of the commonest patterns, consisting of three ingredients: (1) character head-motif; (2) sequential continuation (based on the circle of 5ths); and (3) cadence. This particular example modulates to the dominant, which is unusual, and it mixes modes in a charming and idiosyncratic way, typical of Corelli's precursors, but which Corelli ironed out into a more balanced and 'classical' style. Corelli tended to reserve a chromatic tinge for the ends of sections, a feature that Bach and others were to develop further.

Bach used this pattern in longer fugue subjects such as those of the organ fugues in A minor BWV 543/2 and G minor BWV 542/2, or with dramatic separation of its elements in the fugues in D major BWV 532/2 or C major BWV 564/3. In the 48 it occurs as a fugue subject only in some of the earliest ones, the G major and A flat major fugues of Book II. Nonetheless this shape, with its potential for thematically unified development, permeated other genres. The most notable is the Italian cantata from the 1680s, when it could be used as an instrumental ritornello to open an aria. By Bach's time the three elements had been expanded so that the character head-motif became a pair of balancing four-bar phrases (antecedent and consequent), and the sequential continuation was followed by a closing idea, often with a chromatic tinge or a pedal, before the cadence.[12] A classic example of this is the ritornello of the aria 'Bereite dich Zion' from Part I of the *Christmas Oratorio* (Ex.3.2). Here the character is of the passepied, so it starts with two balancing four-bar phrases (1). There is the usual sequential continuation (2), but now there is a closing idea, in this case with a chromatic tinge (3) before the cadence (4).

This formula gives a very satisfactory balance of elements, with a static, closed phase; a dynamic open-ended phase; and a characteristic concluding

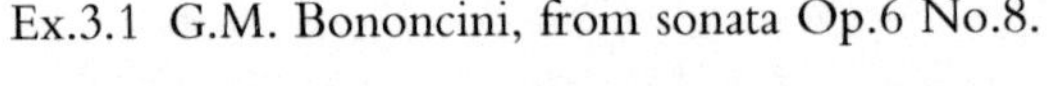
Ex.3.1 G.M. Bononcini, from sonata Op.6 No.8.

Ex.3.2 Bach: aria ritornello from 'Bereite dich Zion' (*Christmas Oratorio*).

figure to mark section endings. As such it is one of the commonest structures in Bach's music.[13] By the simple expedient of making the sequential continuation (2) modulate to the dominant, this aria ritornello shape can be converted into the first half of a sonata movement, as in the Courante of the G major cello Suite (Ex.3.3). This in itself demonstrates how dance genres had merged into the binary sonata, the suite becoming a way of stringing together what are in effect sonata movements or, at best, concertante dances. Here element 1 has two balancing four-bar phrases, with a half close at b.4 answered by a full close at b.8; element 2 modulates to the dominant; and element 3 has a pedal. The formula is clear, but Bach rarely uses a standard formula without playing on it in some novel and striking way. In this instance he makes the second four-bar phrase of element 1 contain a sequence (X), which he uses again in the continuation (element 2) where it naturally belongs. He also interrupts the cadence (element 4) of the first strain. At the end of the second strain he plays magnificently on this feature by inserting the sequence (X) again before the final cadence. The sequence therefore, normally the material of the continuation (2), becomes part also of the character head (1) and the cadence (4), where it points to the fact that the closing pedal (3) is in fact its inversion. One element

Ex.3.3 Courante from G major Cello Suite BWV 1007.

Ex.3.3 (Continued)

has thus come to permeate all other elements of the scheme. Bach's ingenuity and resourcefulness in the handling of this structural formula is richly represented in both Books of the 48.

Given this aria ritornello structure, there are various ways in which it can be handled to make a complete piece. In a da capo aria the usual procedure for the first section is to re-run it several times around related key centres (established by cadences), expanded to accommodate the voice both from the point of view of expressing particular words and also with each successive vocal break becoming more elaborate, with longer florid passages, long notes, wider pitch range, and so on. Bach's Weimar cantata arias offer a great variety of versions of this model. The most straightforward way of dealing with it in a binary sonata movement is to re-run the events of the first strain, which ended in the dominant, back from the dominant to the tonic in the second strain, with extensions and developments of individual elements, as Bach does in the G major cello Courante. For this there are two standard tonal schemes used by Bach, one for major-mode and one for minor-mode pieces. The scheme for the major mode is:

Tonic – Dominant :|: Dominant – relative – Subdominant – Tonic :|

The peak of harmonic density and dissonance tends to be at the relative-minor phase (see Ex.3.3, bb.24–8).

The scheme for the minor mode is:

tonic – Relative – dominant :|: dominant – subdominant – tonic :|

Minor-mode pieces therefore tend to have more complex first strains since they visit an extra key centre before the double bar.

Bach does use this binary scheme in Book I, but not in preludes. It comes, without the double bar, in fugues such as the C minor, which has exactly the minor-mode scheme in the first half, then re-runs the events of the first half back to the tonic in the second half, with developments and extensions. In preludes Bach prefers to have more than one re-run of the ritornello shape, though using the same harmonic schemes. The obvious example is the E major prelude, with three statements of the ritornello shape: from Tonic to Dominant, from Dominant to Subdominant; and from Subdominant to Tonic. This has the very neat feature that the first statement, which modulates up a 5th from Tonic to Dominant, can simply be transposed in the third section to modulate up the 5th from the Subdominant back to the Tonic, thus fulfilling the requirements of unity and variety and having the effect of a reprise. A more complex example is the F sharp major prelude, with no less than five statements of the ritornello shape. The potential of this very fruitful and flexible shape for variety of treatment and development is seemingly limitless, and Bach was to exploit it in much more elaborate and extended ways in the preludes of Book II.

One less-than-typical feature of the E major Prelude of Book I is that the first section is somewhat short for a sonata first section, and makes up only one third of the piece (8½ of 24 bars). A more typical proportion would be of ⅖ : ⅗. This is the proportion Bach aimed for in his revisions of several preludes (the early versions are given in NBA V/6.1). The preludes in C sharp minor, E flat minor, and F minor had a 1:1 proportion in their earliest known versions. In his reworking Bach adjusted this to make the first section ⅖ of the piece. The proportion is virtually exact in the case of the preludes in E flat minor (16 of 32 became 16 of 40 bars) and F minor (9 of 17 became 9 of 22 bars); it is less so in the C sharp minor (14 of 33 became 14 of 39 bars), but in this case the enlargement of the prelude was done by improving the balance within existing sections rather than by adding a new one.[14]

7. *Other types*

If the first group of Praeludia entered in the *Clavier-Büchlein* are mainly concerned with finger action, of the second (C sharp major and minor, E flat minor and F minor) only the C sharp major belongs to the technical study type: in its earliest known version it is a highly ingenious demonstration of how to get the most brilliant effect in the most advanced key with the simplest means. The others are more concerned with cantabile projection and the moulding of melodic and harmonic shapes, all in advanced keys. It has been noted in connexion with the E flat major prelude that Bach seems to have brought in more prelude types as the compendium nature of Book I evolved. For this he had models in the clavier suites of Kuhnau and J.C.F. Fischer. Kuhnau in his two *Clavier-Übungen* (1689, 1692) has examples of the sectional type of prelude, the patterned chordal type, and the sonata type in the Niedtian sense of the seventeenth-century string ensemble sonata, not the later galant type cultivated by Bach. In his Partie IV (1692) he also uses the ciacona as a prelude possibility, an element recommended by Niedt. Bach explored this possibility in the Passacaglia in C minor for organ BWV 582, but not in the 48.

Fischer in his *Pieces de clavessin* (1696) has a number of preludes of varying degrees of elaboration that correspond to the first two sections of Niedt's sectional recipe. He also has two Praeludia which have long been seen as prototypes for Book I.[15] We have noted that his Praeludium VI in D major uses in various sections ingredients which Bach integrated into a single sweep in the B flat major prelude. Fischer's Praeludium II in F major uses a pattern of repeated chords which Bach enriched and made more cogent in the B flat minor prelude of Book I. This pattern was a favourite of Fischer's, which he used again in several of the *Musicalischer Parnassus* suites with the titles Toccata, Toccatina, Tastada.

Finally there are two Italian prototypes. The first is the Vivaldian concerto, whose thoroughgoing influence on all aspects of Bach's composition technique and style from around 1713 it would be difficult to overestimate. Most obvious is the ritornello principle of the concerto Allegro, a procedure that has been seen as leading to the Invention principle via the preludes of the English Suites (Hermelink 1976 pp.69–70). This Invention principle, as opposed to Niedt's, is best described by Forkel as 'A musical subject . . . so contrived that by imitation of the parts the whole of a composition might be unfolded from it. . . . The rest was only elaboration, and if one but knew properly the means of development, did not need to be invented.'[16] It lies at the basis of many of the preludes. Less obvious is the influence of Vivaldi's slow movements. The prelude in E flat minor combines a number of Vivaldi slow movement features, most obviously the texture of solo melody over a cushion of repeated chords in the upper strings, as in the Larghetto of Vivaldi's Op.3 No.7, arranged for harpsichord by Bach in BWV 972. A second, less obvious one, noted by Christoph Wolff (1991 pp.75–8), is in the Largo of Op.3 No.3, arranged by Bach in BWV 978, which has orchestral chords alternating with solo arpeggios, the two elements gradually becoming more intermingled as the piece proceeds. The E flat minor prelude builds on and greatly extends these ideas.

The other Italian element is in the B minor prelude. This uses an archetypal preludio texture and movement associated with Corelli's *Sonate da camera*, the closest example in its figurations being that of Op.4 No.2 (Bologna 1694). François Couperin mentions the practice of playing Italian string music on the harpsichord (1717 pp.35–6), and there is no reason to believe that this was unique to Paris.[17] This final example of a prelude type neatly refers back at the end of the collection to the Corellian aspects of the C major fugue, while in its course it moves away from the serene diatonic harmony of Corelli to prepare the thorny chromaticism of the final fugue subject.

In spite of its compendium nature, a number of current prelude types are not represented in Book I. One is the Corelli concerto allegro, used by, for example, Mattheson in the 7th and 10th suites of his *Pieces de Clavecin* (1714). The quality of these suites is unlikely to have inspired Bach, or made him think kindly of Mattheson's writings, but the prototype was there for use. Another is the free arpeggio type, also used by Mattheson, and notably by Handel (1720). Of French types, the overture does not figure. This must be because its second section is traditionally fugal. It is therefore more suitable to introduce a suite, as in the D major Partita BWV 828 or the B minor Overture BWV 831, than a fugue. Although many of the preludes are strongly characterised rhythmically, there are very few in which one can pinpoint an actual dance rhythm. It would be quite wrong to force, for example, the E major prelude into the character of a gigue. Only the C sharp minor prelude is reasonably close, in this case to a siciliano. But even here the character of the piece is not straightforward, and the siciliano reference is only one element in it. It is the subtlety and complexity of reference that gives these pieces much of their fascination.

One might also have expected to find representatives of the recent and prestigious prototypes included by François Couperin in *L'art de toucher le clavecin* (1717). These should have been of interest since they equally had an educational function.[18] What Couperin's preludes do superbly is cultivate the sensuous sonority of the harpsichord, whether in the *brisé* manner or in a line that sets out to recreate the expressiveness of the viol on the inherently inexpressive harpsichord (prelude in B flat). Only Couperin's preludes in B minor and E minor have something of the invention about them. In Book I only the prelude in F minor could be said to cultivate instrumental sonority for its own sake, since there is no other reason for notating the holding on of broken-chord notes. If he did know them, Bach may not have wished to include Couperin's type of prelude since they are models of improvisation rather than composition. Although some of the Book I preludes undoubtedly began life as improvisations (notably the prelude in C major) the history of their reworking, polishing, and refinement shows that Bach went for a finished effect. Couperin's preludes are no less full of art, but they never lose the sense of relaxation and freedom of improvisation.

BOOK II

8. Types in common with Book I

The most striking difference from Book I is the high proportion of binary preludes: ten in Book II, but only one in Book I. This has been attributed to Bach's preoccupation with binary structures in the Partitas published from 1726 on (Hermelink 1976 p.74). But this point could be made with even more force about Book I, put together at roughly the same time as the Suites for unaccompanied cello and the Partitas for unaccompanied violin, quite apart from the English and French Suites for clavier. In Book I Bach seems to have welcomed the unspecific nature of the prelude as a genre for allowing him to experiment with structures that were not those of the binary dance. By the later 1730s he was no longer so involved with dance structures and this may partly account for the increase in binary preludes. There is also undoubtedly an element of keeping up to date with the sonata style of his eldest sons: having a stock of material in more recent styles was assuredly one of the motives for assembling Book II in the first place. Even so, there is little that is radically new in the actual structures of Book II, even among the binary pieces. Some are no different in general plan from dance structures of around 1720, and Bach is still as fond of the aria ritornello shape. What is new is the great expansion in scale of the pieces, and increase in expressive power.

Most of the types noted in Book I continue to be represented, though in smaller numbers. The arpeggiated pattern of the first prelude there is represented in the C sharp major prelude (also in C originally) here. The Invention type, based on a finger exercise pattern, as in the F sharp minor and B major preludes in Book I, can be seen in the C minor prelude of Book II. The type that demonstrates complex invertible counterpoint is in the A minor prelude, which shares the same chromatic topic as the G minor Invention. Freely treated three-part Sinfonias are in the preludes in A major, which uses melodic inversion, and B flat minor, with triple invertible counterpoint. As in Book I, however, both of these have features which take them out of the strict Invention/Sinfonia category. The early version of the D minor prelude is in the manner of the little preludes of the Cöthen period. Like the first version of the C sharp major prelude of Book I, this seems designed to allow a brilliant effect from technically undemanding means. This no doubt explains the popularity of both of these pieces, to judge by the number of copies made of them.

As with Book I, the verset Praeludium lies behind several of these pieces. A common type in Fischer's *Ariadne Musica*, as in many other collections, is for several voices to unfold over a pedal, the pedal being initially on the tonic, then moving to the dominant. This gambit was used in the E major prelude of Book I, where it is treated in the manner of a pastorale and woven into the aria ritornello structure. Bach seems to have been particularly fond of it, and of building it into sonata structures where he can combine the opposites of free organ improvisation and composed clavier sonata. It reappears in the E major prelude of Book II, paired with a *stile antico* fugue on the same subject as the E major fugue in *Ariadne Musica.* In the five preludes and fughettas, one of the early groups Bach drew on initially for Book II and which themselves have roots in the verset tradition (discussed above in section 1 of this chapter), this type of opening can be seen worked in a rather free, improvisatory style in the D minor Praeludium BWV 899/1, and then used as the basis for an expanded binary sonata structure in the G major one BWV 902/1. This fine prelude was not used in Book II, but the one Bach finally chose (BWV884/1) has a further sonatification of this basically organ opening. Here it forms the first of the usual three-element sonata first section, but worked in an utterly clavier style, with close similarities in its figurations and in the chromatic tinge of the third element to the Allemande of the G major French Suite.

9. Newer types

If the high proportion of binary preludes is the most notable surface feature of Book II, pointing to the influence of the sonata, it is less remarkable in itself than as a symptom of a radical new integration of elements. We have noted the move from binary dance to binary sonata in the works of Corelli, a process which was to reach completion in the 1720s. Corelli used two very influential principles. One was to link a number of different, not necessarily related, ideas together in a moto perpetuo of a single predominant note value, best seen in the Allegro second movements of his Op.5 violin sonatas. This principle was at work, linking disparate ideas together, in the B flat major prelude of Book I. The other principle, described by Georg Muffat (1701) as the main reason for Corelli's vogue, is the combination of the gracefulness of French dance metre with the brilliance of the Italian concerto style in a concertante treatment of dance genres. Bach used this type of dance with concertante elements in, for example, the smaller dances (minuets, gavottes etc.) of his unaccompanied string music and in the orchestral overtures. Around 1720 Bach was using a sonata structure based on the aria ritornello, as in the allemandes and courantes of the cello suites. From the later 1720s this structure continued to be used, but with much greater character contrast between elements, as can be seen, for example, in Telemann's Fantasias for harpsichord (Hamburg 1733). This is all part of the move from the binary dance, where the genre is the character of the piece, to the character piece proper. At the same time the Corellian type with a succession of different ideas became more highly characterised, a process which may be seen in the violin teacher–pupil line Corelli–Somis–Leclair. The keyboard equivalent is in the sonatas of Domenico Scarlatti, which run a number of highly characterised ideas, often involving strong contrasts and surprises, from tonic to dominant in the first strain, and the same series with extensions and developments back to the tonic in the second strain. This is the common model, which Scarlatti treated with infinite originality. One way of avoiding predictability is to shuffle the order of ideas in the second strain. Nearer to Bach, this model was worked in a very different style, but with equal originality, by C.P.E. Bach in the Prussian and Württemberg sonatas (1742, 1744).

The nearest Bach comes to this new type of sonata in Book II is in the B flat major prelude, with a series of no less than seven related ideas in the first strain, which are then shuffled into a different pattern in the second. The sonata principles of a succession of different ideas and of contrast were taken on by Bach and worked into his existing formal principles in very fruitful ways. One is the way in which it affected the invention type. In the 1723 Inventions the material is highly unified, everything developing from the opening. In the preludes in D sharp minor, E minor and B minor of Book II Bach incorporates the sonata principle of successive ideas into this by combining his initial *inventio* with a series of new counterpoints at each appearance during the first strain. These may then be treated as a series of sonata character ideas, and the series be re-run from dominant back to tonic after the double bar. Bach's mind is remorselessly integrative, and in this case all the ideas are linked by being counterpoints to the same initial theme. Another type of prelude takes the principle of contrast and presents two clearly contrasted character ideas at the opening, as in the D major and F minor preludes. But rather than moving on to further contrasting ideas, Bach spends the rest of the piece integrating them in various ways, and demonstrating their fundamental relationship. These two preludes are very obvious examples of this. The principle of two contrasting ideas at the opening is nonetheless present in a more subtle guise in the preludes in F sharp major, A flat major, G sharp minor and B major, where the argument of the piece is worked out on his favourite structural principle of successive re-runnings of the aria ritornello shape in a non-binary context.

In this new sonata-influenced manner, the subdominant reprise noted as a standard in Book I now survives only in older pieces worked up for Book II such as the C major prelude. More common now in the large preludes of the late 1730s is a tonic reprise (as in the preludes in D major, E flat major, F major, F sharp major and minor, and G sharp minor). Too much should not be made of this as pointing towards the Viennese Classical sonata form: C.P.E. Bach was a far greater influence there. The preludes lack the crucial Classical element of tonal duality reconciled in the reprise. But the fact that the final section must stay in the tonic rather than modulate to another key means that Bach cannot simply transpose his initial section but must recast it to stay in the tonic, an opportunity for further moulding and development of material in which Bach excelled as much as the Viennese masters.

In all this Bach is combining new elements with principles he had developed in the Inventions and Book I. The combination of old and new, of updating the tradition, is a fundamental objective of both books. The desire to do this was if anything more acute in the 1730s since he was coming under fire for being outmoded. *Clavier-Übung* III (1739) has some of his most remarkable combinations of old and new, and Mizler's announcement of its publication makes it look as if at least part of Bach's aim was to refute his critics (Dok.II p.387, NBR p.333). But the objective was a constant one with him and he would have continued it anyway.

If compositional elements combine old and new, Bach shows an interest too in practical matters such as keyboard technique and figurations. Devices which Rameau had described in his harpsichord Method of 1724 appear in the reversed-hand technique in the new ending of the C major fugue, and the little *batterie* with one hand enclosing the other which is the second of the two contrasting ideas at the beginning of the F minor prelude. There is also some modest hand-crossing in the B flat major prelude.[19] These are very tame compared with the technical explorations of the Goldberg Variations. But old and new are combined with great sophistication in less obvious ways. The B major prelude has a 'modern' scale of B, pivoted over the thumb, contrasted with the old seventeenth-century *roulade* technique of dividing scales between the hands. The B major also has a kind of Alberti broken-chord pattern, shared with the preludes in D sharp minor and F sharp minor. This can be nothing to do with Domenico Alberti (*c.*1710–40) since the pattern did not become at all common in Italian keyboard music before the 1750s (Freeman 1994 pp.236–7). Bach would in any case probably have found the effect crude, like the *Murky* bass, and the idea of writing many notes to little purpose is unlikely to have appealed to him. The pattern in itself is not hard to find in German keyboard sources of around 1700. The Intonatio primi toni of Murschhauser's *Prototypon* (Nuremberg 1703) could have been written to demonstrate how it evolved from standard seventeenth-century keyboard patterns, and more nearly in Bach's area it appears in works of Nikolaus Vetter in the Mylau tablature. The origin of the pattern in Bach's own work is not far to seek since it occurs in his concerto arrangements of around 1713, notably in the organ arrangement of Vivaldi's Op.3 No.8 BWV 593 where it literally reproduces a violin figuration. Bach's patterns of this sort are best seen as concerto-type figurations deriving ultimately from the violin, and designed to provide a lively texture to passages of harmonic movement from one key centre to another. Bach's interest in concerto effects seems to have revived in the 1730s when he was arranging harpsichord concertos for the Collegium Musicum, and concerto figurations crop up in keyboard works such as the so-called 'Wedge' fugue for organ BWV 548/2 and the last movement of the D major gamba Sonata BWV 1028.

Making the concerto arrangements at Weimar must have introduced Bach to the fascination of alluding to one medium in terms of another, something he worked out powerfully in the unaccompanied violin music, and which is one of the things Book II seems designed to demonstrate. The fascination lies in the fact that in some ways the evocation is more powerful than the real thing. Imitating new orchestral sonorities was a feature of harpsichord writing in the 1730s and 1740s, in the sonatas of Domenico Scarlatti and such works as the second *Livre* of Jacques Duphly (Paris 1748), and Bach provides an example in the D major prelude. Other evocations are of the organ praeludium (C major), the Lautenwerk (E flat major), and various instrumental trios (C sharp minor, A major, B flat minor). The G sharp minor prelude oscillates between the manners of keyboard sonata, invention, and violin sonata. In addition to this Book II is remarkable for some entirely novel keyboard textures and effects, such as in the preludes in F major (whose highly original texture probably derives ultimately from a type of French organ prelude), F sharp major and A flat major.

CHAPTER FOUR

Fugues

1. Definition

There are many modern misconceptions about the nature of fugue as practised by Bach, and many definitions have been attempted. Most of these suffer from being at once too precise and too vague. Vaughan Williams, for example, in an otherwise sympathetic article in the 5th edition of *Grove's Dictionary* (1954, 'Fugue') defines it as 'A musical movement in which a definite number of parts or voices combine in starting and developing a single theme, the interest being cumulative'. This is a perfectly good general definition for a concept of fugue which developed after Bach's time, represented most typically in the *Cours de contrepoint et de fugue* put together by J.F. Halévy from Cherubini's instruction (*c.*1837; English translation 1838). Cherubini quite rightly says that the fugue offers excellent opportunities for practising many techniques of composition in a tonal framework (1838 p.286), and it was for this training purpose that the theory of the nineteenth-century academic fugue was evolved. Its fruitfulness as a means for understanding Bach's concept of fugue is limited, but the irony is that it was Bach's fugues, and the prestige they acquired in Berlin, Vienna and Paris in the late eighteenth and early nineteenth centuries, which gave the impetus to the development of this theory. The process of codification of 'rules' based on Bach's practice, and consequent ossification of the genre, began immediately after his death with Marpurg's *Abhandlung von der Fuge* of 1753–4, the forebear of subsequent academic treatises.

Since the essence of fugue is so difficult to pin down, Vaughan Williams was careful not to say too much. Even so, neither of the two points he makes hold good for the late Baroque keyboard fugue. Fugues with a background in keyboard improvisation, such as some of Handel's or the fugue-type sonatas of Domenico Scarlatti, cannot be said to be in a set number of parts, nor can some pieces entitled Fugue in French Baroque organ repertory. A number of fugues in the 48 increase the number of parts towards the end, and this is so even in

Bach's strictest work, *The Art of Fugue*. Cherubini considered that a fugue could properly be said to have only one subject, any subsequent themes introduced being countersubjects (pp.302–3). This was certainly not the way of looking at it in Bach's time and earlier, where designations such as '*a due soggetti*', '*a tre soggetti*' and so on were common. The notion that the first voice enters unaccompanied, supposedly the reason why the three-part Sinfonias were not called fugues, is plainly not true of many of Bach's choral or instrumental fugues.

This very difficulty of definition results from the complexity of the tradition as it had developed by the early eighteenth century, with the term fugue meaning a number of different, sometimes conflicting, things. In order to appreciate Bach's achievement it is more fruitful to look at the concepts and materials of the tradition in which he operated, and to see with what enterprise and originality he built on them, than to approach his works as a closed and normative corpus that defines all the available options. Had he lived longer he would no doubt have written further fugal works which would then have to be taken into account in this definition. The extent and quality of his achievement can be assessed only in the light of his context.

2. *The theoretical background*

The theoretical concepts of fugue in Bach's background are best represented in the composition tutor written by J.G. Walther for Prince Johann Ernst of Sachsen-Weimar in 1708. This was the year of Bach's move to Weimar as organist of the court chapel, and Prince Johann Ernst was subsequently his composition pupil there. Walther's 'Praecepta der musicalischen Composition' does not set out to present a new and original view, but the central tradition. As such, it draws on the classic German theoretical treatises by Christoph Bernhard ('Tractatus compositionis augmentatus', MS *c*.1660) and Tomáš Baltazar Janovka (*Clavis ad thesaurum magnae artis musicae*, Prague 1701), and the equally influential Italian Giovanni Maria Bononcini (*Musico prattico*, Bologna 1688).

Walther's basic definition of the term *fuga* is simply as imitation: that is, a repetition in subsequent voices of some or all of the motifs (*Figuren*) and notes of the first voice (ed. Benary p.183). Otherwise it may just refer to the subject itself ('*Subjectum* oder *Thema*'), so called because in choosing it one is choosing a particular topic for discussion ('einen gewissen Satz . . . welchen man *tractiren* und abhandeln will'). This is the terminology for describing the discussion of a subject in an essay or a debate, and refers to a very important part of the Baroque concept of fugue, to which we shall return in section 4. But there are some important additional distinctions in defining the term *fuga*.

The 'some or all' in the imitation refers to a distinction between types of *fuga* that goes back the Renaissance. If 'all' is repeated then the piece is a canon (*fuga totalis*), a definition that recalls the first use of the term *fuga*, by Jacobus of Liège who was looking for a Latin equivalent for the Italian 'caccia' in the age of Landini. If only 'some' (*fuga partialis*) then we are approaching a more limited concept of imitation. The distinction between strict fugue or canon (*fuga ligata*) and free fugue (*fuga sciolta*) was introduced in the sixteenth century by Zarlino to deal with the current technique of imitative polyphony. Here Walther introduces a most important distinction, going back to the later fifteenth century. Fugue proper (*fuga propria*) must have imitation at perfect intervals (unison, octave, 5th above or 4th below); mere imitation (*fuga impropria*) may be at the other diatonic intervals. This was at all stages a fundamental distinction in the definition of fugue as opposed to the more general term imitation. In *fuga propria* the tones and semitones of the imitation correspond exactly to those of the leading voice. Other terms listed by Walther are *fuga authentica* and *fuga plagalis*. These refer to the tessitura of the subject in relation to the tonic in modal melodies and have a limited bearing on the 48. They do, however, provide a case of the term *fuga* applying just to the subject. *Fuga contraria*, as opposed to *fuga recta*, is when the answer to the subject is inverted. Again Bach uses this in some chorale preludes and in *The Art of Fugue*, but not in the 48.

In his *Lexicon* of 1732 Walther adds further terms, having cast his net wider to include important sources such as Angelo Berardi's *Documenti armonici* (Bologna 1687) and Brossard's *Dictionnaire* (Paris 1705). Some of these terms apply only to canon, but some apply also to fugue. Some have to do with devices, such as *fuga cancrizans* where imitation is reverted, and *fuga doppia* which has more than one (up to four) subjects in invertible counterpoint; and some relate to specific, self-imposed technical constraints (*fuga obliga*) such as *fuga composta* (all steps) and *incomposta* (all leaps). The system of *oblighi* is an important and complex one and will be dealt with separately in section 8. The most important new feature in the discussion of the word *fuga* in 1732 is that it is no longer just a process of imitation, but may now refer to a piece of music as a whole ('ein künstlich Stücke'), with terms applying to the character or style of a total piece such as *fuga grave*, with long note values and slow tempo, and *fuga pathetica*, grave but expressing some special affect. The use of *fuga* as a genre title dates back to Praetorius (1619 III p.21) who uses it as equivalent to ricercar. In fact, whereas in Italy *fuga* continued in its meaning of point of imitation through most of the seventeenth century, in Germany it was also used as a genre title parallel to ricercar from Praetorius's time on (Walker 2000 pp.118–19).

The term *fuga* may thus apply to the subject only; the counterpoint to the subject; the combination of the two; or to the total piece. Its one defining feature is that the answer to the subject should be at a perfect interval.

3. *Bach and the term Fugue*

The traditional Latin terminology used by Walther is most probably also Bach's, at least up to Book I, with *Dux* (leader) and *Comes* (companion) for subject and answer. These were introduced into German theoretical terminology by Seth Calvisius (1556–1615), a predecessor of Bach's as Thomascantor, to translate Zarlino's terms *guida* and *consequente* (Walker 2000 p.79).[1] For fugal works as a whole he rarely used any term other than *Fuga* or *Fugetta*. The traditional terms canzona and capriccio he used only once each in the keyboard works (BWV 588, 993); the term ricercar in the *Musical Offering* was chosen for its acrostic possibilities.

The one major exception is *Die Kunst der Fuge*, a title in itself implying that fugue is both a principle and a type of piece, where individual items are termed Contrapunctus. This word had a dual resonance in Bach's tradition which suited his purpose very well: on one hand it applied to a demonstration of learned counterpoint, as in Buxtehude's two settings of the chorale 'Mit Fried und Freud ich fahr dahin' in invertible counterpoint, called Contrapunctus I and II (1674; Snyder 1987 pp.214–16, Butler 1983 p.303); otherwise it was generally used with a qualifier to denote a type of counterpoint, such as *contrapunto fiorito*. Walther's article '*Contrapunto*' (1732) defines it first as a counterpoint, or second melody, set against a subject generally of *cantus firmus* type, based on chant or chorale; he then lists a large number of traditional genera of counterpoint, as described by Italian theorists of the seventeenth century such as Berardi and Bononcini. Demonstrating the use of different genera of counterpoint against a single subject is one of Bach's main purposes in *Die Kunst der Fuge*. The 48, particularly Book II, shares this objective to some extent, though not worked so systematically in view of the piecemeal way in which the collection grew. Because the primary objective was to provide pieces in all 24 keys, variety of character and expression are more prominent elements.

Learned counterpoint was a lifelong obsession with Bach. C.P.E. Bach testifies that his father's temperament drew him to music that was elaborate ('arbeitsam'), serious, profound (Dok.III p.87, NBR p.305). It is not clear how much of a hand Bach's eldest brother Johann Christoph took in his musical education other than giving him his first keyboard lessons, but Bach's early studies in composition were based, as was common at the time, on copying music, primarily keyboard music of the south German tradition (Froberger, Kerll, Pachelbel, all strong contrapuntists), not surprisingly since Johann Christoph was a Pachelbel pupil. Bach was thus responsible for his own development in this respect, and like many self-taught he had a strong respect for traditional values (Dok.III p.288, NBR pp.398–9).

But this was only one side of Bach's temperament. Emanuel goes on to say that he had, particularly in playing, a lighter and wittier side, and that he normally took things very lively. He was a connoisseur of all aspects of music. One of these was dance, and the subtly different characters of dance metres; another was the possibilities of musical expression, richly explored in his vocal works. During his career taste moved away from the traditional Lutheran view of the function of music. In this, music was considered to be a reflection of the divine harmony and a God-given means of purifying the emotions by liberating them from the negative forces of tedium and melancholy in order to direct them to positive joy and virtue. Luther's views on this were the foundation of the great German musical tradition within which the Bach family had flourished for generations, and lie behind the term 'Gemüths Ergoetzung' on the title-pages of Bach's *Clavier-Übungen*. By the 1720s the Enlightenment view was growing that the function of music was to express emotions as an end in itself, and fashion was moving away from traditional techniques associated with old-fashioned church music. This consensus is well represented by Bach's Leipzig and Dresden contemporary Johann David Heinichen (1728), who devotes considerable space to the ways in which music can reinforce the topics of operatic arias, and also to disparaging elaborate counterpoint.

The tension between the old and the new, and the challenge of reconciling them, was a spur to Bach. Like many of his contemporaries he sought to amalgamate techniques and formal prototypes of diverse geographical origins, Italian, French, and German.[2] What is unusual about him is his wish also to unite styles and techniques of diverse temporal origin. The mind that could embed a modal *cantus firmus* in canon with itself, in a trio sonata of the most elaborate and sophisticated galant style, complete with the latest mannerisms of flute technique, as Bach does in the *pedaliter* prelude on 'Vater unser' BWV 682 in *Clavier-Übung* III, was carrying anything his organist contemporaries were doing in that line a great deal further than they were capable of. This obsession with updating traditional techniques is most clearly seen in the fugues of the 48.

4. *Rhetoric*

Fugue as a genre in the seventeenth and early eighteenth centuries was considered to be the musical counterpart of various types of rhetorical projection, with consequent implications for the concept of fugal structure.[3] If the prelude could be considered the equivalent of an oration, the fugue was a debate. Christopher Simpson expresses this in terms common to many seventeenth- and eighteenth-century writers (1667 pp.156–7). Consort music is the musical counterpart of conversation, in which individual voices repeat or renew 'the Fuge or point'. The traditional words 'subject' and 'point' in themselves have a meaning in discussion. When a voice re-enters after a rest, the effect is 'as of a man that begins to speak again, after some little time of silence'. Forkel uses very similar terms in describing Bach's attitude: 'He considered his parts as if they were persons who conversed together like a select company. If there were three, each could sometimes be silent and listen to the others till it again had something to the purpose to say' (1802 pp.40–1, NBR p.455).

Forkel was familiar with the theoretical literature through work on his *Allgemeine Geschichte der Musik* (1788–1801), but here he is merely expressing a general tradition which it would be surprising if Bach had not shared. Nearer to Bach's time, Mattheson adds the notion of imitation as opposition, necessary to give a competitive atmosphere ('angenehmen Wettstreit') which is part of the entertainment value of the piece (1739 Part III Chapter 15 para.4). Marpurg, who had discussed fugue with Bach in Leipzig (Dok.III p.144, NBR p.363), describes imitation as contest ('Streit') with reference to the D minor Fugue of Book II (1753 p.143; Dok.III p.144). These are general indications of a much more far-reaching concept of fugue as an extended rhetorical structure.

Fugue from the sixteenth century attracted, more than other types, analogies between verbal and musical rhetorical categories. Around 1600, notably in the writings of the Rostock humanist and rhetorician Joachim Burmeister, for whom music was part of a total system of humanistic learning, fugue was considered a manner of writing rather than any sort of structural principle. At that stage it was a matter of equating specific contrapuntal techniques with rhetorical ones, so that these categories related to points of imitation and their treatment in the context of the sectional motet rather than to general structural considerations. But as fugue came to be perceived as a genre in its own right, and particularly with the development of tonal harmony as a structuring principle, it came to be related also to the structuring principles of rhetoric. The tripartite speech structure of proposition–confirmation–conclusion had been a model for musical structures, particularly where this reflected the structure of a text as in a song, since the time of Caccini. The influential Angelo Berardi (*c.*1636–94) discussed fugue in terms of this structure and was the first to relate particular techniques to a particular section. He associated the intensifying devices of stretto and canon with the final section since that was where the most artifice was required (1689 p.179).

Increasing closeness of imitation as a piece progresses was a traditional way of enhancing impetus, or the heatedness of the argument. As such it was one of the basic features of fugal structure described by Fux (1725; Mann 1958 pp.83, 89), whose most basic recipe for fugue is of a three-section piece with cadences on the 5th, the 3rd, and the tonic of the mode, and with the same subject treated in successively closer imitation in each section (Ex.4.1).

Ex.4.1 Fux 1725: example of a three-section fugue.

Fux was not presenting a new method, but a summary of a tradition of teaching composition going back to Zarlino.[4] Logic also provided the model of a tripartite formal structure in the syllogism, consisting of two premisses (major and minor) and conclusion (or *consequenza*, the term borrowed by Zarlino for fugal answer). Both Mersenne (1636) and Berardi explore this relation (Butler 1977 p.68).

Eighttheenth-century writers took up Berardi's relation of techniques to structure and pursued the formal relationship in more detail. Principal among these are J.C. Schmidt, capellmeister in Dresden and mentioned by Marpurg (1753) together with Fux, Handel, Heinichen, Stölzel and Telemann as prominent recent fuguists after Bach (Dok.III p.46), and Mattheson. Schmidt wrote to Mattheson in 1718 an elaborate comparison of fugal to oratorical structure (Butler 1977 pp.69ff), and Mattheson himself discussed issues of fugue in many of his writings, most extendedly in *Der vollkommene Capellmeister* (1739). By taking terms from the disposition scheme of classical rhetoric they arrived at a structural scheme which is essentially an elaboration of an early eighteenth-century bipartite structure for fugue consisting of a first, expository, section using all sorts of contrapuntal devices, and a concluding canonic section (Butler 1977 p.96). Canon in this context can normally be taken to mean stretto.

This scheme was elaborated in different degrees, and with differences of detail, by various writers. Of them, Schmidt describes a scheme very close to the disposition of classical rhetoric in which he links specific fugal techniques to each of its sections and subsections (Butler 1977 p.71). The elements of the rhetorical scheme are broadly: a proposition, or initial statement of the case; a section of amplification, with subsections of confutation (*oppositum*, presentation and disposal of opposing arguments), comparisons (*similia*), examples (*exempla*), and confirmation (affirming of supporting arguments); and a conclusion (final clinching peroration). In musical terms, the proposition is narrowly defined as the subject (*dux*) by Schmidt, but others include the whole material of the exposition; Schmidt has fugal inversion for the confutation; alteration in duration of notes in the subject for the comparison; transposition of the subject with augmentation and diminution for the examples; stretto for the confirmation; and closer stretto over a pedal for the conclusion. Mattheson and others developed further correspondences.

Such structures can of course be considered only as general guidelines; it would be absurd to apply them universally as an analytical key. They may well have been considered as primarily useful for improvisation, parallel to the traditional frameworks for improvising given in practical tutors from Niedt (1700) to C.P.E. Bach (1762). Whether or not Bach knew of Schmidt's scheme, or what he made of it if he did, is not known.[5] But this way of thinking of fugue was common at the time. Bach's familiarity with the theory of musical rhetoric is well attested by his friend J.A. Birnbaum, lecturer in rhetoric at Leipzig University, who took Bach's part against the criticisms of J.A. Scheibe in 1737–9. One of Scheibe's criticisms was that Bach, as a purely practical musician, had no special knowledge of the theoretical sciences necessary for composition. Birnbaum replied that Bach had a complete knowledge of the sections and subsections that the structuring of a musical composition has in common with the art of rhetoric, and can talk about them just as convincingly as he can use them in his works, while his insight into the art of writing was everything one could expect from a great composer (Dok.II p.352). Nobody familiar with Bach's vocal works would doubt this. That he thought of his instrumental works in this way, particularly those designed to demonstrate composition, is clear from the 1723 title-page for the Inventions. This structures the stages of composition according to the traditional three stages of preparing a speech: an original idea or *inventio* ('gute *inventiones* zu bekommen'), its development or *dispositio* ('selbige wohl durchzuführen'), and its eloquent delivery or *elocutio* ('am allermeisten aber eine *cantable* Art im Spielen zu erlangen').[6] Given his lack of a university literary training and the store he set by the titles of Capellmeister and 'Hof-Compositeur' which put him at the top of his profession, Bach must have been particularly sensitive to Scheibe's criticism that only a truly educated composer, learned in the arts of oratory and poetry ('Redekunst und Dichtkunst'), can know how to communicate properly and to compose music that is moving and expressive ('rührend und ausdrückend'; Dok.II p.316). It is magnificently answered in a fugue such as the D sharp minor of Book II (see the discussion in Chapter 8). Marpurg may have had this criticism in mind when he commented on Bach's ability to communicate even with unmusical people in fugue, not through learned counterpoint but through his mastery of declamation (1760; NBR p.364). The function of a fugue was to make the subject compelling, even if it is made of the most ordinary commonplaces, and this Bach achieved by masterly arrangement (*dispositio*) and a powerful dramatic sense, demonstrated in pieces such as the B minor organ fugue BWV 544/2, or the C major fugue of Book I (Harrison 1990 pp.40–1).

Bach expressed himself almost exclusively in musical terms, but in a tradition in which the word was of the greatest importance. The very density of the fugues of the 48, and the richness with which he uses learned devices, are a further development and exploration of these possibilities.

5. *Expression and character*

The *inventio* of a fugue is its subject, and this provides a microcosm of the whole piece, not only in its technical ingredients but also in its expressive nature. Mattheson discusses the *thema* in terms of small fragments chosen for their associations (1739 Part II Chapter 4 para.15; Butler 1977 pp.72–5). Since the subject appears first, every slightest detail contributes vitally to its character. The intervals of which it consists are therefore of the greatest expressive importance. In fugues with one or more retained countersubjects, which complement and reinforce the expression of the subject, the whole block of invertible counterpoint may be considered the *inventio* (described by Dreyfus as 'fugal complex'; 1996 Chapter 6).

Musicians of Bach's time were very sensitive to the affective value of all musical ingredients, and there are many tables of intervals and their affects from which one may extract a general consensus (Wessel 1955 pp.87–8). The falling 3rd is melancholy and supplicative (Book II, C minor); the falling 4th is pathetic, doleful, grave and solemn (Book I, B flat minor); the rising 5th is bold and commanding (Book II, E flat major); the rising minor 6th is lamenting, mournful, suitable for exclamations (Book I, D minor). This last subject, which gradually unfolds the minor scale degrees, is in sharp contrast to that of the E flat major fugue of Book II which, after its bold rising 5th, thrusts the major 3rd and 6th immediately at the listener (Bent 1994 p.98). Even ornaments have affective weight, an important point since Bach, in common with other great masters of musical materials and expression such as Monteverdi and Purcell, frequently gives ornamental elements motivic significance. Various eighteenth-century writers discuss ornaments in terms of their affective value. According to Quantz, short trills express cheerfulness and happiness (Wessel 1955 p.99; F sharp major fugues of Books I and II) and most writers speak of the mordent as happy and cheerful (p.104; Book II, C major). As with all such simple equations, the interest is when ingredients of different affective value are mixed to give a subtle shade, as in the F minor fugue of Book II with its falling 5th, cheerful mordent, pathetic falling diminished 7th, and lively bourrée rhythm, all in the context of a strongly flavoured minor key.

The most obvious cases of expressive subjects are those with a chromatic element. In seventeenth-century fantasias such subjects tend to have a neutral quality, as demonstrations of the *genus chromaticum*. Bach gives them a strong element of personal expression. Even when he uses the commonest formula, the descending chromatic tetrachord (*lamento-bass* pattern), in a fairly straightforward form, as in the D minor fugue of Book II, it is set up with a rising figure of galant-style triplets which take away the stiffness of the formula and give it a floating quality, further emphasised by the supporting counterpoint. Less personal is the subject of the E minor fugue of Book I, but this is a speculative piece aiming to combine this traditional ingredient with the motoric manner of the Italian violin sonata, and the stiffness of the subject is worked out in the rigid symmetries of this fugue. The rising chromatic tetrachord is given the most subtle personal expression in the F sharp minor fugue of Book I by its hesitant, syncopated rhythm, an effect also worked out between the subject and countersubject of the D sharp minor fugue of Book II.

The other traditional chromatic shape used in the 48 is the *chiasmus* (cross shape).[7] Both the half-way point and the conclusion of Book I are marked by fugues with subjects of this type. The F minor fugue moves chromatically in two directions, as does the so-called 'Wedge' fugue for organ BWV 548/2; the B minor fugue is designed to cover all twelve semitones and is full of chiastic symmetries. In both cases the expression is a blend of the personal chromatic element and the traditional *dignitas* of a single note value and a final cadential trill.

Characteristic rhythms also play a part in the affect of a subject. Some have gone to great lengths to relate Bach's rhythms to the metres of ancient Greek verse (Westphal 1883, 1891; C.F.A. Williams 1893). This is not so far fetched as it might seem today since Greek learning was part of connoisseurship in the Baroque. Mersenne (1636) spent much time detailing Greek metres and their affects, particularly in relation to dance rhythms, and these were worked out in a most practical and influential way by Lully.[8] Mattheson gives the fullest summary for the late Baroque (1739 Part II Chapter 6), and some of his examples are strikingly similar to Bach's rhythmic patterns. But it would be as insensitive and pedantic to apply Mattheson's affects crudely in respect to rhythm as it would be to take his 1713 description of key characters as normative. Given the rich variety of stylistic prototypes Bach drew on, it cannot always be said that a particular rhythmic character was in the forefront of his mind. Some subjects do nonetheless have prominent rhythmic characteristics which may relate to these traditional affects.

Of verse feet with two syllables, the example of the spondee (two long syllables) relates to the subject of the B major fugue of Book II (Ex.4.2).[9] The Greek term spondee means a libation, or solemn offering; its affect is honourable and grave ('ehrbar und ernsthafft') and at the same time easily comprehensible (paras.6–8). Of feet with three syllables, the tribrach (three short syllables) relates to the G sharp minor fugue of Book II (Ex.4.3a). This is mainly associated with gigues, but may include serious expression, and may also appear as triplet groups in non-compound times (paras.27–8). To some feet Mattheson attributes very specific affects, such as the proceleusmaticus (four short syllables), from a word meaning to command, for a rousing sailors' shout ('ein befehlendes, aufmunterndes Geschrey der Schiffleute'). It would be absurd to see such specific meaning in the repeated notes of the B flat major fugue of Book I and the G minor fugue of Book II, but there is no denying their insistent effect. More puzzling is the affect of the bacchius (a short and two longs), since Mattheson's example is strikingly similar to the G minor fugue (Ex.4.3b).[10]

Ex.4.2 Mattheson 1739: Spondee

Ex.4.3 (a) Mattheson 1739: Tribrach
(b) Bacchius.

(a)

(b)

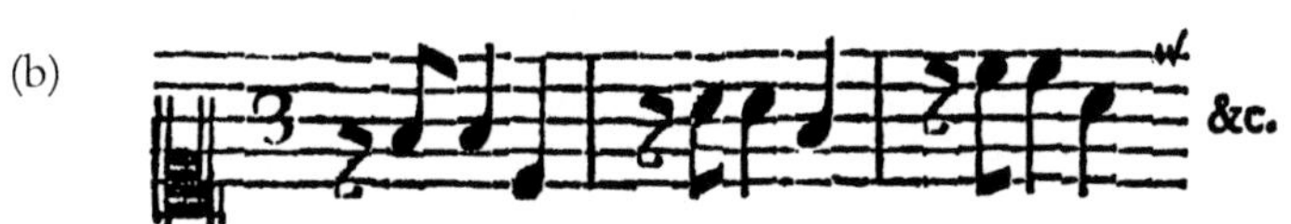

The hobbling and reeling ('hinckendes oder taumlendes') effect of this rhythm is associated with its ancient use by those making an offering to the god of wine. Mattheson adds that this rhythm was much used 'in der heutigen Melothesie', particularly in fugues with several subjects (para.29). Few would guess the affect of Bach's fugue as half-seas-over, and yet there is a curious lurching effect in the rhythm, emphasised by Bach in the off-beat beginning to his subject.

Mattheson was drawing on a common fund of lore, and he claimed to be doing no more than summarising common practice (Part II Chapter 13 para.142). There is no reason for Bach to have got his information from him, though part of *Der vollkommene Capellmeister* had already been published in 1737. But given Bach's demonstrative intentions with the 48 in other respects, it is not unlikely that he intended to demonstrate the technical and expressive possibilities of rhythmic characters. It can hardly be accidental that so many types of subject with a single note value are represented: all minims (B major of Book II), all crotchets (F minor of Book I), all quavers (B minor of Book I), all triplet quavers (G sharp minor of Book II), all triplet semiquavers (C sharp minor of Book II). Some characteristic rhythms, on the other hand, probably have to do with a different sort of association. The anapaest rhythm of the C minor and A minor fugues of Book I probably has less to do with its supposed character in prosody than the fact that it was used in the fugal movements of Benedetto Marcello's concerto Op.1 No.2 (arranged for harpsichord as BWV 981) and specially Vivaldi's D minor concerto Op.3 No.11 (arranged for organ as BWV 596). Vivaldi's lively, driving impetus, combined with the use of quadruple counterpoint and other fugal techniques, evidently appealed to Bach.[11]

Much has been made of Bach's use of dance metres, particularly in Book I, compiled at Cöthen when he was concerned almost exclusively with secular music and with the suite (Besseler 1950 etc.). Dance topics are as old as the concept of *fuga* itself, if the words to be set suggest them, and there is nothing new about them in themselves. Various dance metres appear as standard section types in contrapuntal works for keyboard by Frescobaldi and his followers, such as galliard rhythm in Frescobaldi's capriccios (1626) and gigue rhythm in Froberger's canzonas and capriccios. Gigue rhythm continues to be by far the most common dance metre in fugues in Bach's earlier keyboard works. Very few of the organ fugues in dance metre are other than gigues (they are listed in Little and Jenne 1991 Appendix B), though quite a number of fugal chorale preludes (not listed by Little and Jenne) are. Mattheson (1739 Part II Chapter 6) demonstrates how a chorale melody may be adapted to a variety of dance metres. In the fugues of the 48, as in the preludes, Bach was demonstrating variety of time signatures and metres, particularly the newer, lighter dance metres associated with French harpsichord and orchestral music.

All this is very well put by Kirnberger, who lamented the loss of variety of character in the later eighteenth century, both in the disappearance of the old modes, and in the range of metres. These are all aspects of expression and eloquence. One should learn to play dance pieces in order to learn how to project a melody, its variety of phrases, etc.: 'In particular it is impossible to write or play a fugue well without knowledge of all the variety of rhythms, and because study of these is neglected nowadays music has declined from its former dignity and fugues are no longer tolerated, since the type of impoverished performance that does not project phrase sections or accented beats leaves them no more than a chaos of notes.'[12]

Conservative as Kirnberger was, there is no doubt of the growing unpopularity of fugues, and this was specially so for the harpsichord. Niccolo Pasquali, writing in the mid-1750s, says that it is forty years since they were in vogue. Citing one of Handel's most effective keyboard fugues (from the E minor suite of 1720), he points out that in places not all the notes can be sustained, so the written four parts sound as only two. Music masters do not notice this because they can see the music, but to the listener it sounds as uninteresting as a thoroughbass. The Alberti-bass is much more suitable since it keeps the harpsichord in vibration (*c.*1758 pp.21–4). Pasquali has a point. One of the most striking things about Bach's keyboard counterpoint, and one generally ignored by analysts, is its lucid playability, an art not always mastered by even the best of his followers. It is instructive to compare the clarity and projectability of the counterpoint of, for example, the F minor Sinfonia BWV 794 or the A major prelude of Book I with the layout of similar material in the Andante of C.P.E. Bach's fourth Württemberg sonata (1744).

Clarity of projection is the essence of Bach's fugues, whether of rhythm, melody, or character. In Bach's day students learned character projection from dance suites, and Bach's contribution was to bring this liveliness and variety into the fugue. The traditional gigue is represented by the C sharp minor and F major fugues of Book II, but more recent types are also present, such as the bourrée (C sharp major of Book I, F minor of Book II, in metrical character if not in note values); the gavotte (F sharp major of Book II, which even has the characteristic gavotte four-quaver phrase ending, often in the form of a *tierce coulée*, at the end of the subject); the minuet (B flat major of Book II); and the passepied (F major of Book I, B minor of Book II; Little and Jenne 1991 Appendix B). None of these is in the form of the binary dance in the sense of a gigue with a double bar and the subject inverted thereafter. But Bach has explored with great subtlety the phrase structures of dances and how they can be wedded to the fugue (as in the F major fugue of Book I), and to the sonatafied binary dance (in the C minor fugue of Book I and the B flat major fugue of Book II; see Chapter Three section 6). Other fugues simply take a selection of genre markers, whether dance rhythms or the features of a French *entrée* (D major fugue of Book I), and work them in other formal terms. One might regard them to some extent as *en rondeau* in that the subject returns, though not always in the same key.

6. Stile antico

At the opposite pole from light character pieces and lively dances the *stile antico*, seemingly the essence of neutral *gravitas*, also has an expressive weight in that it represented for Bach the unchanging nature of fundamental values. Lorenz Mizler in announcing his German translation of Fux's *Gradus ad Parnassum* puts this in musical terms, referring to the Renaissance tradition in which the major triad is the perfect chord (because of the harmonic series), with dissonance as a decoration to enhance the beauty of consonance. The style of classic polyphony therefore is 'rooted in the unchangeable rules of harmony that have always existed, are existing, and will be so, as long as the edifice and the principles on which it rests do not change, may music as a phenomenon change as it will' (C. Wolff 1991 p.104).

Bach used it for just this symbolism in various places, such as representing the fundamental, unchanging nature of the sacrament of baptism in the Confiteor of the B minor Mass. He had a particular interest in it after the publication of Fux's *Gradus* in 1725, of which he probably bought his copy soon after publication (C. Wolff 1968 p.27). This interest was at its peak in the 1730s, perhaps connected with his desire to gain a title, if not a position, at the Catholic court at Dresden. More generally, he may have become more interested in the eternal verities of music as the unsatisfactory nature of his position in Leipzig deepened (Herz 1985 p.172). It bore fruit principally in parts of the B minor Mass, and in the third part of the *Clavier-Übung* (compiled 1735–9), where it involved not only features of style such as time signatures, note values and dissonance treatment, but also the use of modes. Mizler probably began his German translation of the *Gradus* in 1736, the year in which he renewed his contact with Bach, and most of it was done in 1739–42, just when Book II of the 48 was being assembled (C. Wolff 1968 p.28).

In fact Book II contains the clearest example of *stile antico* in the E major fugue. Not only is this based on one of Fux's demonstration subjects (see Ex.4.1) but it follows Fux's formal specifications, though with a degree of elaboration that Fux can hardly have envisaged. The stylistic focus of this fugue is emphasised by comparison with the looser treatment of *stile antico* features in the fugue in E flat major (probably an earlier piece, originally in D major). The E major fugue is a focussed demonstration of Fuxian *stile antico*, but the style came to Bach through various traditions and it would be wrong to reject other pieces as examples of it because of a too narrow definition. The irreducible features are the *alla breve* time signature; fundamental note values of semibreve and minim, with the crotchet as decorative; fluidly plastic lines which avoid regular periodicity; and the regular treatment of dissonance which gives the German term 'gebundener Stil' (tied style) since dissonances are normally suspended in tied notes. It was familiar to Bach throughout his life through collections of motets going back to the sixteenth century which were in use at the Michaelisschule in Lüneburg and were still being used by his choirs in Leipzig.

As far as keyboard repertory is concerned, it is represented in the seventeenth-century genres of fantasia and ricercar which retained the long note values (*fuga major*), as opposed to the madrigal style of the canzona which used the minim and crotchet as fundamental values (*fuga minor*). But ricercars in particular frequently introduced into themes a mannered element of chromaticism, or some other unorthodox and second-practice feature. Several of the ricercars in Frescobaldi's *Fiori musicali* (1635) do this, of which Bach acquired a manuscript copy in 1714 (Dok.I p.269).[13] Bach's subjects in this mannered vein have a powerful expressive grit because of the background orthodoxy of the style, just as Gesualdo's highly unorthodox dissonance treatment, from which this mannered style ultimately derives, gains its expressive force from a background reference to classic purity.

In the two fugues in Book I which relate most clearly to this tradition, Bach seems to have relished the feature of putting a highly expressive interval into a theme *in stile antico*: the C sharp minor with the leap of a diminished 4th, and the B flat minor with the leap of a minor 9th, complete with expressive *sospiro* (crotchet rest). Both are in five voices, exploiting the possibility of fuller texture in the context of slower, more stepwise movement. It is tempting to think that Bach's main interest was in this mannered element, were it not that the E flat major prelude of Book I combines in its third section old- and new-style subjects, but without any mannered pitch element. The D sharp minor fugue of Book I also has features of the style, if not the time signature and predominant note values. Its subject, however, far from being mannered, is a rare example in the 48 of a traditional modal-type subject.[14]

As with other aspects of composition, Bach liked to explore the possibilities of mixing styles into new composites. The C sharp minor fugue of Book I moves away from the old style after its first section into a sequential, quaver-based second subject, mixing elements of *fuga major* and *fuga minor.*[15] The only other fugue in the 48 with a *stile antico* element and with more than one subject is the B major of Book II, which brings together a very sophisticated amalgam of styles (see the commentary in Chapter 8).

A difficult performance issue is the question of ornamentation in *stile antico* fugues. A fugue of this type in the seventeenth century would have been played with a great number of ornaments, as described by Jean Denis (1643), and demonstrated by D'Anglebert (1689, from which Bach copied out the table of ornaments). A more modest level of ornamentation was used by John Blow (*c.*1700) in his copy of various Froberger contrapuntal pieces, including the Fantasia II which has been proposed as a model for the E major fugue of Book II.[16] J.G. Preller's copy of the G major Praeludium BWV 902/1 and some of W.F. Bach's copies of fugues from the 48 have more ornaments than most people now would care to play, and show that a tradition of rich ornamentation certainly existed in Bach's environment. It seems nonetheless that the profusion of ornaments common in the seventeenth century was somewhat toned down in the eighteenth. Sources which do aim to give a fairly complete ornamentation such as Gottlieb Muffat's *72 Versetl* (1726) are relatively restrained. Marpurg (1753 Tab.XXII Fig.I) quotes the opening bars of the first of D'Anglebert's fugues with only two of the original 23 ornaments, though this may have been to save engraving. Bach himself, in copying out (*c.*1714–16) Grigny's *Livre d'orgue*, tended to omit ornaments on the initial notes of fugue subjects (Kent 1992 p.54), though generally he made very little change to Grigny's notation. Sources of the E major fugue of Book II have slight differences of detail, but are very sparsely ornamented. The tradition was to notate pieces of this sort without ornaments, and we must envisage the possibility that Bach himself may have played quite a lot of them. It may be that Gottlieb Muffat's fugues in this style can give us some indication of the general density.

7. *Types of invertible counterpoint*

We cannot be sure exactly what terminology Bach used. J.G. Walther (1708 p.195) speaks of 'melodies' ('wenn 2, 3, oder vier Melodeyen also in einander geflochten werden'); later he uses the more usual 'themes', one of which is the *subjectum* and the other the *Contrapunct* (1732 '*Contrapunto doppio*'). Mattheson (1713 p.148) also speaks of double counterpoint having two 'themes' ('anstatt eines *Thematis* deren 2. haben'; also 1739 p.415). The term *Contra subjectum* is used by Kuhnau (1692) and Scheibe (*c.*1730), but not by Walther nor by the post-Bach fugal theorists Marpurg and Kirnberger.[17] Marpurg (1753) uses the terms 'Satz' and 'Gegensatz' for subject and countersubject, but he also uses 'Satz' both for a retained countersubject and for subjects with separate or later entries. In Bach's works, the Fantasia described as 'duobus subiectis' in the Möller MS is an early work in fact based on three themes in triple counterpoint announced at the beginning so that none has primacy (BWV 917). It is most likely that Bach used the same terminology as Walther 1732 since part of the function of the word Contrapunctus in *The Art of Fugue* is to describe the technique of setting different genera of counterpoint against a principal subject. Invertible counterpoint was generally 'doppelter Contrapunct' (as in Walther 1708 etc.) probably with some such locution as 'dreifach gedoppelter Contrapunct' for triple counterpoint, an illogicality also in Purcell's 'double descant in three parts'. The term used by Buxtehude and many others for the permutation of invertible counterpoint was 'evolutio' (Snyder 1987 p.214; Walther 1732, etc.), and this was used by Bach for both melodic and contrapuntal inversion in the fourteen canons BWV 1087.

Some have objected to the use of the term 'subject' for themes introduced after the initial exposition, either on the grounds that a fugue can have only one main subject, or that other subjects must have independent expositions of their own, otherwise they should be termed countersubjects. The stylistic reference to the seventeenth-century learned keyboard fantasia/ricercar, however, makes it plain that they would have been considered as subjects, according to the common designations 'sopra doi soggetti', 'sopra tre soggetti' and so on.[18] One can trace in the seventeenth century a progression from Frescobaldi's fantasias (1608), where various subjects may be introduced together at the beginning or successively during the piece; to the *Ricercari* (1669) of Frescobaldi's pupil Luigi Battiferri, who explores various combinations of from one to six subjects, either all introduced at the beginning, or each given a separate exposition of its own before being combined with the others; to the versets of Kerll's pupil Franz Xaver Murschhauser (1703, 1707) and the ricercars of Johann Pachelbel, both of whom used the procedure of a series of separate expositions.[19] This procedure relates to the structure of the motet, with a series of sections each based on its own point of imitation, as in the chorale fughetta where each section is based on a separate line of the chorale melody. Bach uses the scheme of separate expositions in the F sharp minor and G sharp minor fugues of Book II. Otherwise he seems to have found it too obvious, and preferred to combine the second subject with the first as soon as the second enters (as in the C sharp minor and A major fugues of Book I and the B major of Book II, the procedure favoured by Sweelinck and Froberger), or to work the new subject into his fugal fabric with subtlety and ingenuity, as in the C sharp minor fugue of Book II. The principle is variety of treatment and it is a pity to impose on it a rigid distinction of function and terminology.

The term 'double counterpoint' covered not only what we understand as invertible counterpoint, but also such techniques as augmentation canon and inversion canon (Walther 1708 pp.198–205; Mattheson 1713 pp.150–53), demonstrated ultimately by Bach in *The Art of Fugue*. There is also a curious type of augmentation in which the subject is aerated by rests (Walther 1708 ed. Benary pp.198–200; Mattheson 1713 p.151), but this does not seem to have appealed to Bach, who used it only in the initial subjects of Contrapunctus 10 and 11 of *The Art of Fugue*. Marpurg lists seven types of double counterpoint, invertible at intervals from the unison (octave) to the 7th (14th; 1753 pp.164–91). The most usual intervals for inversion, however, are the octave, 10th, and 12th. Explanations of these take a standard form, most classically formulated in Fux's *Gradus* (Mann 1958 pp.107–38). For a version closer to Bach we may take that in Walther 1708 (ed. Benary pp.195–208), which in turn is based on Giovanni Maria Bononcini's *Musico prattico* (Bologna 1688, German version Stuttgart 1701).[20]

Double counterpoint at the octave This is where the top part goes down an octave and the bottom part up an octave, the top part becoming the bass and vice versa. What the intervals will invert as is expressed in a simple table, the top line representing the intervals in the primary version, the bottom line what they will become in the *evolutio*:

1 2 3 4 5 6 7 8
8 7 6 5 4 3 2 1

Most intervals correspond well, with dissonances inverting as dissonances and parallel 3rds becoming parallel 6ths. Care must be taken in using the 5th since it will invert as a 4th, a dissonance in two parts which must move downwards by step in strict style. Walther gives various examples, of which the following uses all the intervals:

Ex.4.4 Walther 1708 para.389: double counterpoint at the octave.

Double counterpoint at the 10th Here the top part goes down a 10th to become the bass, and the bottom part up an octave (Inversion 1), or vice versa (Inversion 2), the intervals inverting as follows:

1 2 3 4 5 6 7 8 9 10
10 9 8 7 6 5 4 3 2 1

Parallel 3rds and 6ths are impossible since they will invert as parallel octaves and 5ths: these intervals must therefore be approached by contrary motion. Generally speaking dissonances should be avoided (Ex.4.5a). But if care is taken, the 2nd may go to the 3rd (inverting as 9–8) and the 7th to the 6th or 5th (inverting as 4–5 or 4–6; Ex.4.5b).

Ex.4.5 (a) Walther 1708 paras.408–9: double counterpoint at the 10th
(b) para.410.

Ex.4.5 (Continued)

Double counterpoint at the 12th Here the top part goes down a 12th to become the bass, and the bottom part up an octave, the intervals inverting as follows:

1 2 3 4 5 6 7 8 9 10 11 12
12 11 10 9 8 7 6 5 4 3 2 1

The crucial interval here is the 6th, which inverts as a 7th. Walther recommends avoiding it entirely except in the following type of situation where it can become a passing 7th (Ex.4.6).

Ex.4.6 Walther 1708 para.411.

The 7th and diminished 5th are not useful as tied notes, but the 2nd and 4th are good; otherwise the following progressions are good: 2–3, 4–3, 7–3, 7–5, 9–8, 9–3 (Ex.4.7).

Ex.4.7 Walther 1708 para.412.

An alternative inversion at the 12th is to put the top part down an octave and the bottom part up a 12th (Ex.4.8).

Ex.4.8 Walther 1708 para.413.

To all this Fux adds the possibility, richly exploited by Bach, of making four parts out of two-part counterpoint as follows (Ex.4.9).[21]

Ex.4.9 Fux 1725: 4 parts from 2.

Ex.4.9 (Continued)

8. *Genera of counterpoint*

An important part of the theory of counterpoint in the seventeenth century was the concept of the *obligo*; that is a technical constraint, or restriction of materials. This was educational in origin, and is explained as such by Zarlino (1558 Chapter 40). The principle is that, in order to gain technical skill, you take a subject (i.e. a *cantus firmus* in semibreves) and set a second part to it, restricting yourself to a certain type of materials. The restriction may concern note values, pitch, rhythm, or some combination of these. Beginners start with one note against each note of the subject, and this came to be known as the 'first species' of counterpoint. Zarlino also mentions syncopations, later called the 'fourth species'. Morley (1597) has both of these, and also a number of fixed rhythmic patterns. Later the system developed in a more mechanical way, with exercises of two minims to each note of the subject ('second species') and four crotchets ('third species'). A 'fifth species' uses all these materials in a freely composed line.

The best-known exposition of this system is in Fux's *Gradus*, but it was complete in Angelo Berardi's influential *Documenti armonici* (Bologna 1687, of which Bach apparently made a MS copy, VBN II/B/4), and Berardi also lists a great many other *oblighi*. Classic demonstrations of some of these are in Frescobaldi's contrapuntal keyboard works, but these are only one manifestation of a highly developed tradition (see Durante 1987).

Berardi begins the first book of the *Documenti* by listing the *oblighi* as follows. Restrictions may be rhythmic, as in *contrapunto alla zoppa* (limping rhythm, with a constant ♪♩♪), *contrapunto puntato* (with dotted rhythm), or *contrapunto perfidiato* (using a constant rhythmic pattern, of which Berardi gives a number); it may be a dance rhythm (*obligo in saltarello*), or be in a cross-rhythm with the subject (*in tempo ternario*); or the restriction may be of pitch, as in *contrapunto alla diritta* (using only steps), *di salto* (using only leaps, as in Frescobaldi's *Recercar ottavo, obligo di non uscir di grado*, 1626), *d'un sol passo* (repeating the same figure, but transposed), *contrapunto ostinato* (repeating the same notes but in different rhythms, as in Frescobaldi's *Recercar sesto, sopra fa, fa, sol, la, fa*); it may involve the omission of an interval (*contrapunto obligato*) as when one voice avoids fa and the other mi; or not using a certain interval (*contrapunto senza ottava, senza quinta*, etc.); a popular type was the device known as *inganno* where two different sets of pitches had the same solmisation syllables (see Newcomb 1987). One piece may combine a number of these (Berardi 1687 p.26).

On one level these restrictions may function as technical exercises, but on another they may be a dimension of wit in the seventeenth-century sense of a conceit. Their artificial, intellectual quality did not appeal to later writers on fugue such as Kirnberger (1782 p.3). In his treatise on double counterpoint he omits 'the hopping, limping, and dotted counterpoints', and he particularly dislikes those that avoid a melodic interval, 'because every composer will arrange his melody according to the character of the piece, be it in single or double counterpoint' (1777a p.168).[22] This may to a certain extent reflect Bach's view, since character and expression are fundamental priorities in his music and he made no distinction in this respect between fugue and any other genre. It is nonetheless striking how many of these devices he uses in Book II and in *The Art of Fugue*. Bach was clearly interested not only in the characterful use of them, as traditional techniques, but also in exploring the possibilities of the character they themselves give. Restriction of materials is after all fundamental to the definition of character.

Bach's use of these devices has been discussed by Christoph Wolff (1991) and Gregory Butler (1983). Butler makes a plausible case that the impetus to Bach's late fugal writing was the discussion of fugue in Mattheson's *Der vollkommene Capellmeister* (1739), of which Bach may have seen a draft towards the end of 1738. This would fit with the assembling of Book II in 1738–42 and the first version of *The Art of Fugue* thereafter. Mattheson certainly issued a challenge to Bach to write examples of fugues with three subjects (1739 Part III Chapter 23 para.66), and Bach provides a classic example in the F sharp minor fugue in Book II.[23] Mattheson also lists many of Berardi's genera of counterpoint (Part III Chapter 22), and adds some of his own. All this may well have spurred Bach to realise what in all probability had been a long-standing project. He did not need Mattheson to tell him about Berardi's techniques since they are listed by J.G. Walther (1732), and he may himself have made a copy of the *Documenti armonici* (VBN II/B/4). Bach also begins the incomplete fugue on three (or four) subjects from *The Art of Fugue* with the subject of Berardi's *Fuga reale* (1687 p.37), not given by Mattheson.

The Art of Fugue, since its subject is in minims and therefore has a *cantus firmus* quality, demonstrates a number of *oblighi* very clearly. Contrapunctus 2 has a countersubject in dotted rhythm (*contrapunto puntato*), Contrapunctus 3 uses only steps, and mainly chromatic ones (*alla diritta*),[24] and Contrapunctus 4 a reiterated figure (*d'un sol passo*). The first four fugues also provide examples of other *oblighi*, not mentioned by Berardi or Mattheson, such as the Chinese-puzzle type of figure with multiple overlapping rhythms that provides the episodes of Contrapunctus 1, a keyboard texture used by Frescobaldi and Froberger, and the cuckoo in Contrapunctus 4. Book II of the 48 has only two subjects of this sort: the E major and the B major. The E major develops ideas from Fux, but the B major countersubject uses a rhythmic *perfidia* à la Berardi, not exactly one he gives but which he might have expressed as *contrapunto perfidiato d'una minima con quatro crome congiunto con l'obligo della sincopa e quasi alla Zoppa*. Bach's ability to make such dry bones live is one of the principal delights of his fugues.

Other examples pointed out by Butler in the F sharp minor and B flat minor fugues of Book II are less obvious and better left to the discussions of those pieces. Elsewhere in his contrapuntal works Bach uses these devices, as in the countersubject of the three-part Ricercar from the *Musical Offering* (*di salto*). Nothing is too abstruse for him, even playing on solmisation syllables (*inganno*) in the seven-part canon BWV 1078.

9. *Verset fugues*

If the verset tradition was an important contributor to the development of the 48 both in the concept of the cyclic key scheme and in the combination of prelude and fugue, it was also an important factor in Bach's concept of fugue. A number of features in the fugues of the 48, which have been considered anomalous in terms of 'rules' developed from Bach's own general practice, are in fact common in this tradition.

Broadly there were two traditions of keyboard fugue in the seventeenth century: the *fuga major*, or extended fugue in the *stilus gravis*, with white note values, and often written in open score; and the *fuga minor* or short fughetta, generally in madrigal (black) note values, and written on two staves (Riedel 1980 pp.154–5). Groups of these were used in verset collections and, at least in the seventeenth century, were often based on motifs derived from the chant. But there were also various standard subject types, and later subjects included more modern styles such as the Italian trio-sonata type used in Murschhauser's *Prototypon Longo-Breve Organicum* (Nuremberg 1703, 1707). These short fugues often have the appearance of being isolated sections from the longer sectional genres of ricercar or canzona, and in fact extracts from longer Frescobaldi pieces are found copied into South German verset collections into the eighteenth century (Riedel 1960 p.120). Like such sections, they tend to concentrate on a particular effect, perhaps a dance or some other rhythm, a particular contrapuntal device, or a subject with a particular characteristic. They thus provide examples of fugues based on a single affect, albeit on a miniature scale. Their concise demonstration of devices and affects made them particularly suitable as models of composition.

Many of the fugues of the 48 show more or less signs of this influence. The most obvious case is the C sharp major fugue of Book II which we can see growing in three stages from a brief fughetta in C major on a standard verset figure used in the very popular *Wegweiser* (first published in Augsburg in 1668 and often reprinted), which Bach may have used for teaching purposes (Walker 1985 p.3). An even shorter figure is in the subject of the E major fugue of Book I: the step in iambic rhythm was a standard motif going back to Frescobaldi's *Fiori musicali*. It is possible that other brief subjects such as the A flat major of Book I should also be thought of in this context.

Bach was not interested in chant-based subjects as such in the 48 since his main object was to demonstrate tonal, not modal, harmony. Nonetheless, one of the derivations of the classic subject of the E major fugue of Book II is the outline of the Mode 3 Magnificat chant (normally beginning with the notes g a c: Murschhauser 1721 p.114; see Constantini 1969 p.45), which therefore relates to a Magnificat verset *fuga*. Character in the subject was particularly desirable so that a succession of versets contrast with each other, often with an increase in the speed of note values with each succeeding fughetta. Expressive, second-practice dissonances such as the diminished 3rd, 4th, or 5th, or the falling minor 6th are features of one type of subject, used notably in Johann Caspar Kerll's *Modulatio organica* (Munich 1686).[25] This is continued in the very seventeenth-century subject of the C sharp minor fugue of Book I, or with the more 18th-century intervals of minor 9th and diminished 7th in the B flat minor fugue of Book I and the A minor of Book II. A subject may have a particular characteristic such as dotted rhythm, as in the B major Fuga in Fischer's *Ariadne Musica* or the D major fugue of Book I. A type of subject using two motifs, the second of which harmonizes with the first so that the fugue can feature stretto, is used in the G minor fugue of Book I (which has often been compared to the E flat major Fuga of *Ariadne Musica*), based on the same principle; and the D major fugue of Book II, which uses two canzona motifs found in a similar conjunction in the *Wegweiser.*

Since many versets consist of no more than a single fugal exposition, there is the problem in four parts of ending, as it were, on the wrong foot. With the normal sequence of entries in the pattern subject–answer–subject–answer (*dux–comes–dux–comes*) the exposition will end on the dominant unless something is added to bring it back to the tonic. A common solution in versets is to have a different sequence of entries, such as *dux–comes–comes–dux*, so as to end in the tonic. This is the option adopted by Bach in the C major fugue of Book I, a fugue designed to demonstrate the utmost density and economy, so that he can finish the exposition and go straight into the first stretto without any distracting link. A similar procedure is in the F minor and F sharp minor fugues of Book I which have the sequence *dux–comes–dux–dux*, though in these fugues the fourth entry is separated from the first three by a substantial codetta based on countersubject material.[26]

A comparison of the fugues that build on the verset tradition (particularly the exhaustive treatment in the Book II fugues in D major and E major) with their verset prototypes is very instructive in demonstrating one of Bach's main intentions in the 48: to show how traditional materials could still have life and possibilities not yet explored. The irony is that, in proving this by example, he left others with the impression that there was little that they could do better. After 1750 it can hardly be said that composers built on Bach's achievements in the same vein; rather his achievements became finished objects for contemplation in theoretical writings.

10. Partimenti

According to C.P.E. Bach, writing to Forkel in 1775, Bach generally composed away from the keyboard except in some, though not all, of his clavier pieces, 'for which he took the material from improvisations on the clavier' (Dok.III p.289, NBR p.399). Fugues employing the more elaborate contrapuntal devices were most probably worked out on paper, but others may well be based on improvisation. Mattheson, following Kircher, ranks fugues as part of the *Stylus phantasticus* together with toccatas and sonatas (1717 p.121), and the ability to improvise them was a necessity for organists in Bach's environment, being one of the tests for appointment to the better organ posts (Dok.II p.344). Fugal sections in Bach's earlier clavier toccatas tend to have the feel of written-down improvisations, with their loose structure and stretches of decorated continuo harmony.

By the early eighteenth century, instruction in fugue in Bach's tradition grew out of the figured bass, rather than contrapuntal treatises, and so was approached as an improvised genre (Benary 1961 p.33). The technique of this was practised by using fugato movements expressed as figured basses, called in Italian *partimento* fugues and in German *Bassetgen*.[27] Niedt gives an example of one with a promise to say more about how fugues are to be improvised, which unfortunately he did not fulfil (1700 Chapter X). Heinichen also gives an example (1728 pp.515–20, trans. Buelow pp.208–10), and there are numerous ones in manuscript from Bach's environment. Bach evidently used this method himself for teaching fugue since there are five in the figured-bass instruction, based largely on Niedt, apparently taken down from his dictation at the Thomasschule (ed. Poulin 1994 pp.41–5).

This type of exercise derives from the seventeenth-century continuo practice of doubling the entries in ensemble fugues, the term *Bassetgen*, equivalent to the Italian *bassetto*, meaning that the lowest part is not in the bass clef. *Partimento* fugues have therefore the appearance of trio-sonata continuo parts without the other instruments. A similar procedure is in the French *partition réduite* of a five-part orchestral score to two parts, in which the entries of parts in, for example, the second section of an overture are copied as a single continuous line, often with changes of clef for each instrumental entry.[28] The common factor in all these instances is that the subject, where present, is always the lowest sounding part unless written out as a second part above it.

Some pieces strongly suggest that they have been worked up from this type of exercise, such as the Praeludium and Fuga in D minor by Johann Pachelbel in the Mylau tablature (ed. Shannon pp.7–10) in which the prelude is very like a figured-bass exercise and the fugue has all its entries in the lowest part except where there are only two upper voices. The fugues of the 48 are of course much more finished than this, but one may see a reference to it in the exposition of the A major fugue of Book I, on a subject which is in any case based on a continuo formula of rising 4ths and falling 3rds, and with the lowest part having all entries of the subject, including a feigned extra bass entry at b.6. The freedom of improvised fugue still survives residually in the occasional migration of the subject from one voice to another during its course, a feature particularly of French organ fugues, which survives in the C sharp minor and B minor fugues of Book I, and is used as a structural and developmental technique in the B flat minor prelude of Book II.

The most rewarding and systematically worked out exercises are those of Handel, the other most distinguished German improviser of fugues.[29] These are considerably more sophisticated in that they indicate entries of the subject over the given bass and so can demonstrate the use of double counterpoint and other devices. Alfred Mann has suggested that Handel's use of Latin for these voice-entry indicators, and tablature letters for pitch, implies that they are part of a cantoral tradition and that this is how Handel would have begun his study of fugue with his teacher in Halle, Friedrich Wilhelm Zachow.[30] They are therefore a series of lessons in fugue from one of the greatest practitioners in Bach's tradition. At a lesser level, but nonetheless of great interest, is the so-called Langloz manuscript, probably dating from around 1700 in Bach's area, consisting of a series of *partimento* fugues which show the relation of versets and *partimenti* in a common stock of subjects.[31]

The most interesting aspect of Handel's *partimenti* from the point of view of the 48 is what they reveal of the concept of fugal structure. The exercises develop more elaborate structures as they introduce more contrapuntal devices. They begin with a single exposition, very much in the verset manner, the four parts entering in the sequence *dux–comes–dux–comes*, with a few bars of continuo harmony at the end to bring the piece back to the tonic. For a longer piece a second exposition is added, balancing the first by reversing the order of entries in a device known as fugal inversion:

dux–comes–dux–comes | *comes–dux–comes–dux*

For further extension a third exposition may be added, taking in some entries in the relative key. In more elaborately worked fugues this structure of a series of expositions may be combined with unfolding the permutations of invertible counterpoint, as it commonly is in late seventeenth-century trio sonatas such as those of Purcell or, in Bach's environment, Reinken. Bach reworked three fugues from Reinken's *Hortus musicus* (Hamburg 1687) for harpsichord (BWV 954, 965, 966),[32] and the principle is one he liked to use in his earlier choral fugues.

Alternatively, successive expositions may explore various contrapuntal devices. This structure, without linking material, is particularly suitable for the C major fugue of Book I which explores increasing densities of stretto on a relatively compact scale. Three much larger fugues, among the most elaborate in the 48, also use it and for that reason have often been considered to be among the earlier compositions represented in Book I. Whether that is so, or whether Bach wished at Cöthen to provide examples of this standard fugal structure, it is difficult to imagine it being more powerfully used, with the density of contrapuntal argument contributing to an overwhelming expressive concentration. The double fugue in the E flat major prelude has expositions featuring double counterpoint at the octave, 10th and 12th, as well as stretti. The D sharp minor fugue has, among other features, a very elaborate scheme of normal exposition, followed by one with stretto; then normal exposition with the subject inverted, followed by one with stretto inverso; and finally one with the subject in augmentation. Most daunting of all is the A minor, with a normal exposition; one with the subject inverted; one with stretto recto; one with stretto inverso; and finally one with stretto recto and inverso at the octave and the 12th. Such a schematic tour de force, combined with the difficulty of performing the piece with its driving Vivaldian metre, must surely be the work of a young turk out to play the others into the ground, and may have been the sort of thing Bach had up his sleeve for the projected competition with Marchand in 1717.

11. *The Concerto principle*

Bach did not use this episodeless structure in quite such concentrated form again, though there is something of it in the D major, E major, and B flat minor fugues of Book II. For Marpurg this type of fugue, which he called strict fugue or *fuga obligata*, was specially characteristic of Bach, though he was probably thinking here of *The Art of Fugue*. But for most of the 48 Bach in fact turned decisively to a type of free fugue (*fuga libera*) which Marpurg associates more with Handel. In it the principal subject is not always present, and there are well-devised modulating episodes related thematically to the subject or countersubjects (1753 pp.19–20; NBR p.353). Bach's main concern in reworking Reinken's fugues was the addition of just such episodes, and the extension of tonal range: Reinken may have been the composer he criticised in conversation with Marpurg for not having 'enough fire to reanimate the theme by interludes' ('das Thema durch Zwischenspiele aufs neue zu beleben', Dok.III p.145, NBR p.363; C. Wolff 1991 pp.69–70).

This loosening of structure and separation of the incidences of the main material derives principally from Bach's use of the Vivaldian ritornello principle which he began to explore systematically from around 1713, though he had been well aware of it before then.[33] The amalgamation of formal and stylistic prototypes always held a fascination for Bach, and at Weimar he explored in vocal works various ways of integrating the orchestral sinfonia into the choral fugue (W. Neumann 1938 p.54). The combination of fugue and concerto is in its most classically condensed form in the C minor fugue of Book I, where blocks of triple counterpoint are separated by thematically derived episodes. A more expansive version of this combination, with broader concertante figurations, is in the G major fugue of Book I. At Cöthen Bach used in various works a combination of fugue and concerto ritornello with reprise, as in most of the preludes to the English Suites and several fugal allegros in the sonatas for obbligato harpsichord and violin. This is also the scheme used in the C sharp major fugue of Book I. In fact Bach had a number of favourite formal procedures which he could adapt to fugal materials as well as to any other ones.

The ritornello principle as used by Vivaldi in his Op.3 concertos was a very flexible and fruitful one. Some Allegros have non-thematic solo breaks based on harmonic figurations, such as that in Op.3 No.2, a charming movement which fades out unpredictably in a way that fully justifies the title 'Harmonic Caprice' (*L'estro armonico*). This type of relationship of episode to exposition is in the F sharp major fugue of Book I, in which the derivation of episode figures from the exposition is not obvious. Other Vivaldi movements develop motifs fairly logically during the solo breaks, as in Op.3 No.8 (arranged for organ as BWV 593). This type, which does something with the material, is the one that most appealed to Bach, judging by the concertos he chose to arrange for keyboard. Even when the episode material seems radically different from the exposition and in a relaxed concertante harmonic pattern, as in the E minor organ fugue BWV 548/2, the argument of the piece amalgamates and integrates the two types of material. A standard procedure with Vivaldi is to have the main ritornello, then a short solo break, then a repetition of all or part of the ritornello, then a longer solo break which eventually modulates to a new key. This pattern may be seen fairly straightforwardly reproduced in some of Bach's large concerto fugues such as the G minor fugue for organ BWV 542/2, which he may have played in Hamburg in 1720. In this the entire exposition is repeated in the tonic. In combining the concerto principle with the fugue, with the exposition corresponding to the tutti ritornello, Bach generally exploits the second tonic exposition in some way. In the G minor organ fugue the order of entries is adjusted so that the pedal entry is in the tonic the second time, in order to provide a suitable conclusion to this large opening tonic block. The equally concertante G major fugue of Book I uses the same pattern, but with the subject inverted in the second tonic exposition. Not many fugues of the 48 are on this expansive scale so the repetition normally amounts only to a single extra tonic entry after the end of the exposition (the E flat major and A flat major fugues of Book I).

The concerto principle may be used to aerate with episodes a fugue based on expositions such as the G major fugue of Book I, which in its main material follows a scheme of inversions and stretti comparable to the A minor fugue of Book I; or one based on blocks of invertible counterpoint (the C sharp major and C minor fugues of Book I). But the ritornello is more usually represented by only one or two entries of the subject. A condensation of the concerto idea that Bach likes to use as a basic model, though always with variety of detail, is to have an initial exposition, followed by an exposition in the sense that there is an entry in each voice, but in different keys and spaced out by thematically developmental interludes (the F sharp major, F sharp minor, and B major fugues of Book I). A similar procedure is used by Bach in arias, where the opening instrumental ritornello is re-run in expanded form when the voice enters. This allows Bach to make, as Marpurg says, ingenious transpositions of the principal subject into other keys and exploit a rich vein of subsidiary ideas

(Dok.III p.144, NBR p.363). It also has the no less important rhetorical function of 'reanimating the theme' by presenting it in different contexts and revealing all sorts of unsuspected aspects of it, so that finally even the most ordinary idea can, through accumulated experience, become utterly compelling. The Vivaldi experience helped Bach to consolidate, and dramatise, a tendency he had already developed in fugal writing. An important part of his interest in fugal structures was their dramatic potential, something relating to his own skill and spontaneity as a performer. In this Bach's grasp of *dispositio*, of arranging his materials based on his sense of a listener's expectations, is a crucial element of success.

CHAPTER FIVE

All the Tones and Semitones

'. . . through all the tones and semitones
both as regards the *tertia major* or *Ut Re Mi*
and as concerns the *tertia minor* or *Re Mi Fa*.'

We are so accustomed to the equal-tempered chromatic scale as a fundamental musical material that it takes some effort to appreciate the novelty and sophistication of the system reflected in Bach's terminology. The view that the traditional modal system was an antiquarian anachronism and a primitive step on the way to the clear light of tonal day does not do justice to the rich period at the beginning of the eighteenth century when several traditions overlapped and enmeshed, giving rise to a complex system in which composers were sensitive to the possibilities of different materials and the tensions between them.[1] Bach was in the forefront of the development of the tonal system, but he also regarded all current materials as useful and was prepared to use old ingredients when appropriate.

His primary work for demonstrating the full development of tonality is of course *The Well-tempered Clavier*, so that is not where we can most profitably look for modal ingredients.[2] The two essential elements of the tonal system are present in the title-page formulation: the possibility of using all 12 semitones as tonics, and of each scale having a major and minor form. But these are not expressed in what was even in 1722 the standard terminology. Later sources, copied when the fully developed tonal system had become a commonplace, expressed it in standard modern terms such as 'through all the major and minor keys' ('durch alle Dur und Moll-Töne').[3] Yet Bach avoided this simplicity in 1722, and none of these terms was unambiguous at that stage.

In their primary senses the terms *tone* and *semitonia* were purely geographical in relation to the keyboard, rather than reflecting a theoretical concept of key. Taking the modern piano keyboard as the norm, *tone* are the white notes and *semitonia* the black notes; *subsemitonia* are split black notes. This is not the result of a crude and ignorant outlook, but goes back to Renaissance theory where the tones (white notes) were the keynotes of the modes, and the black notes were the accidentals necessary for *musica ficta* (in France the black notes were still called 'les feintes' in Bach's time).[4]

By 'all the tones and semitones' Bach certainly did not mean 'every single major and minor key', since only 25 keys are represented in Book I and 24 in Book II. It was perfectly open to him to have done that had he wanted to: the Dutch organist and advocate of equal temperament Gerhard Havingha provided pieces in both B flat minor and A sharp minor in his keyboard suites of 1725. Bach's aim was primarily practical rather than theoretical, and his meaning is that each of the 12 notes of the keyboard is used as a tonic, including all the black ones. That this purely practical approach was the norm at the time is clear from the terminology for keys, which was based on the symbols used in the German keyboard tablature. All the black notes other than B flat were expressed as sharps (cis, dis, fis, gis, with tablature symbols associated with these particular notes on the keyboard) regardless of their tonal function or the way they were tuned, and they continued to be called these names even when used in keys such as E flat and A flat, and written in staff notation as flat notes. Thus the difference between E flat minor and D sharp minor in the Book I prelude and fugue was a theoretical one, obvious in the notation, but both would have been called 'dis'. This nomenclature may possibly be why Bach preferred sharp keys to enharmonically equivalent flat ones, even though the flat ones involve fewer accidentals and are therefore easier to read. Or it may simply be the convenience of transposing a piece up a chromatic semitone (from C to C sharp or D to D sharp etc.) without having to rethink the notation, when he needed a piece on a *semitonium*.

The practical element is also evident in the terminology used in conjunction with the earliest discussions of the necessity of being able to play in all keys. For example, in J.P. Treiber's *Der accurate Organist* (Arnstadt and Jena 1704), in which one major and one minor key chorale and their figured-bass accompaniments are transposed into all keys except F sharp major and D sharp minor, the aim of the exercise is expressed as follows: '. . . are taken thorough all tones and chords in such a way that in these two examples all chords ('Griffe') with the signatures of all keys and the most convenient position for the hand are demonstrated'.[5] The term 'Griffe' implies that chords are regarded in a purely practical way as hand-shapes, just as a guitarist or lutenist regards them. This is why it is not necessary to have every single possible key represented, since the hand-shapes will be the same in enharmonically equivalent keys and ability to 'grip' them depends only on the theoretical knowledge of key signatures.

Although not a professional musician, Treiber was closely involved in Bach's world in his Thuringian period, and lived in Arnstadt during Bach's time there. *Der accurate Organist* enjoyed a certain popularity, was reprinted in 1715, and

Bach's friend the distinguished organist C.G. Schröter (1699–1782) mentions it gratefully as his 'first teacher' (Arnold 1931 p.243). Those who wrote of the need to be able to play in all keys generally said that this arose in continuo accompaniment. Werckmeister, who mentions Treiber as one of the first to have circumnavigated the circle (1698b p.24), constantly makes the point that it was essential for the up-to-date professional to know how to play 'Lieder' in keys involving black notes and with black-note tonics.[6]

The same point is made by Heinichen in his continuo treatise of 1711, which contained the first published circle of 24 keys (again all the *semitonia* except for B flat are expressed as sharps), demonstrating not only the circle of 5ths but also the relation of major to minor keys. Heinichen says that knowledge of advanced keys is particularly necessary in recitatives: it is the recitative section of Bach's Chromatic Fantasia which uses advanced keys to strongly dramatic effect. Mattheson (1713 pp.64–5) took up these points from Heinichen, and in 1719 was the first to publish pieces, albeit figured-bass exercises, in 24 keys in the *Exemplarische Organisten-Probe*.[7] Mattheson associated advanced keys with secular music (few organs were tuned to cope with them) and particularly with recitatives, citing Handel's *Lucretia* cantata HWV 145 as an example where familiarity with advanced keys is needed if the accompanist is not to 'break out in a cold sweat of terror' (1719 Theoretische Vorbereitung pp.14–16). He also used the current terminology that playing in advanced keys involved familiarity with the 'Griffe' (Erster Theil p.56).

The model of pieces in 24 keys was there for Bach in 1719, the year before he visited Mattheson's home town of Hamburg to audition for the organist's post at the Jakobikirche. He approached it from a different direction, from the model of a *tonarium* of verset preludes and fugues represented at its most elaborate to date by the nineteen keys of Fischer's *Ariadne Musica* (1702). But the idea of completing the circle, and providing pieces ('Handsachen') in which his pupils (notably Wilhelm Friedemann) could get used to all the 'Griffe', was in this figured-bass tradition from Treiber to Mattheson.[8] Whether or not Bach needed Mattheson to tell him anything, it was clear what direction things were moving in, and that the next generation would need to be trained accordingly.

1. *Circles and labyrinths*

Discussions of *The Well-tempered Clavier* usually include listings of previous works which circumnavigate the 24 keys, some of which are more relevant to its background than others. Fretted instruments such as the lute and guitar provide examples dating back to the sixteenth century since, in theory at least, they were tuned in equal temperament (Lindley 1984). The first is evidently a manuscript collection by the blind Trieste lutenist Giacomo Gorzanis. It is dated 1567 and contains 24 passamezzo and saltarello pairs which are usually described as being in all the major and minor keys. In fact it would be fairer to say that they are in the Dorian and Mixolydian modes, transposed on to every degree of the chromatic scale. As with other examples for fretted instruments notated in tablature, this is a purely technical matter since the notation expresses only hand-shapes on the instrument, so there is no need to develop a system of key signatures which would show a theoretical understanding of keys. Since there were several sizes of lute in common use at the time, playing at nominally different pitches, we cannot know what Gorzanis would have notated had he written in staff notation. It is unlikely that he even thought in such terms: the object of the exercise must be to explore the unfamiliar hand-shapes involved with tonics that are unusual and uncomfortable on the lute. There is also in his case no perceptible difference in style or character between pieces with different finals other than that some will involve fewer open strings and therefore have a slightly different tone quality.

The same goes for the many Spanish guitar tutors explaining *rasgueado* (strummed) accompaniment (Christensen 1992). Among the first was that of the Catalonian physician and amateur guitarist Joan Carles y Amat whose *Guitarra espagnola* was first published in 1596. Amat tells the student that only two kinds of chords need be learnt: the major (*naturales*) and minor (*B mollados*) triads. But one must learn to play them in all twelve transpositions since the guitarist may need to adapt to the range of the singer. Simple as this is musically, it has profound implications in that it shows music taught and conceived as chordal entities that were self-sufficient and combinable in permutations independent of contrapuntal or modal control. But again, since this is all based on tablature and hand-shapes, it is a practical matter of pitch rather than the theoretical development of a key system.

The same conceptual difficulty applies to the much more sophisticated series of thirty prelude-type pieces by the Oxford lutenist John Wilson (Heather Professor of Music from 1656 and described by Anthony à Wood as the best lutenist of his day in England; Spring 1992). Probably written in the 1640s, there is at least one piece in every major and minor key, with some keys duplicated. At least here there is a nominal pitch since the same manuscript contains songs, and for most of these the voice implies a top-course pitch of g', the remaining courses being tuned in *vieil ton*. There is also a sense of exploration of the possibilities of the unfamiliar in that pieces in unusual keys such as what we would regard as E flat minor have a tortuous chromaticism which contrasts with the much more straightforward style in the usual home keys of the lute. It is likely that Wilson, unlike Gorzanis and Amat, did regard keys in our sense, since a mannered chromaticism had been a feature of English music since the 1620s. Contemporaneous viol consort repertory uses advanced keys such as

D flat major, unambiguously expressed as such in staff notation. These are essentially temporary excursions into a different colour, not only as regards pitch but instrumentally in that they involve higher positions with few or no open strings, and so do not make it necessary to develop a complete system of key signatures.[9]

More relevant to the extension of the key system and the development of the system of key signatures was the involvement of fixed-pitch instruments whose music was written in staff notation, primarily the organ, in accompanying or alternating with sung modal music, particularly psalm tones. This involvement became prevalent towards the end of the sixteenth century with the generally increasing use of instruments and the growing sophistication of instrumental technique. The problem is in the variable written pitch of the dominants of different modes. Since the dominant of a mode is also the reciting note of the psalm tone, and therefore the note to which most of the psalm is sung, it must be set at a comfortably singable pitch.[10] In church modes the dominant is not always the 5th degree in the authentic version of the mode, and is never the 5th degree in the plagal version. The written pitches of the dominants of the four basic authentic modes and their plagal (hypo-) versions are as follows:

Mode		*final*	*dominant*
I	Dorian	d	a
II	hypodorian	d	f
III	Phrygian	e	c'
IV	hypophrygian	e	a
V	Lydian	f	c'
VI	hypolydian	f	a
VII	Mixolydian	g	d'
VIII	hypomixolydian	g	c'

In the early sixteenth century two more authentic modes, with their plagal versions, were added:

IX	Aeolian	a	e'
X	hypoaeolian	a	c'
XI	Ionian	c	g
XII	hypoionian	c	e

These have little to do with 'foreshadowing' the keys of C major and A minor, but take account of the fact that composers used the notes C and A for perfect cadences (*clausulae finales*) since they were available in the natural hexachord. Bringing in these two notes as finals therefore was thought to bring the scheme to completion, with a pair of modes on each note of the hexachord. For this reason the numbers 8 and 12 became important symbols of completeness: eight for the original church modes, therefore used in verset collections for the Magnificat such as those by Kerll (Munich 1686), Murschhauser (Augsburg 1696) or Pachelbel (MS Nuremberg 1701–5); twelve for the complete modal system, as in Georg Muffat's *Apparatus musico-organisticus* (Salzburg 1690).[11] Twelve remained a symbol of completeness even in post-modal music, most notably in the highly influential publications of trios, solos, and concertos of Corelli and the concertos of Vivaldi. Alternatively it could be made up of two groups of six, or just in groups of six (as it were the authentic forms only), a number favoured by Froberger.[12]

It can be seen from the above list of modes that the written pitch of dominants in the 8 church modes ranges from f to d' (a major 6th). This presents no problem when the chant is unaccompanied and singers can choose a convenient pitch, but is impractically wide when tied to the fixed pitch of the organ. One possible solution was to put all dominants on a single pitch. This option was considered by, for example, Nivers (Paris 1683, see Howell 1958 pp.108–10). The chosen pitch should be slightly above the middle of the voice since melodic intervals are normally larger below the dominant than above it. Nivers suggests a (in low French pitch, which would be f♯ or g at a' = 440), though individual choirs will have their own preferred dominant pitch. But in spite of its logic this is not a workable solution since it gives awkward keys not available in the tuning of most organs: for example the Hypodorian mode with its dominant on the 3rd degree would have its final on f♯, and the Phrygian mode with its dominant on the 6th degree would have its final on c♯. The most commonly adopted solution was that described by Banchieri (Venice 1613–14), with dominants conveniently situated mostly on the notes g, a and b♭. This forms the basis of the system of 'church keys' generally used in seventeenth-century Germany (Riedel 1980 p.159):

Mode		*final*	*dominant*	*key signature*
I	Dorian	d	a	
II	hypodorian	g	b♭	1 flat
III	Phrygian	a	f	
IV	hypophrygian	e	a	
V	Lydian	c	g	
VI	hypolydian	f	a	
VII	Mixolydian	d	a	1 sharp
VIII	hypomixolydian	g	c'	

This is the bare bones of a very complex situation. It was by no means the only solution; the system was extended to include the remaining four newer modes; and it all became more and more mixed up with evolving tonality. The best composers dealt with its complexities and ambiguities with great connoisseurship and subtlety and this is what gives seventeenth-century repertory its fascination, not the notion that it is all primitive, groping steps towards tonal perfection.[13]

Although the basis of this is different from that of the tonal system, the principle of transposing modes around the keyboard was undoubtedly a contributory factor to the development of the concept of the 24 keys. Modes or keys involving *semitonia* were called transposed modes ('tons transposés') into the eighteenth century, and it was an important point of debate as to whether each key had its own integrity, as did each mode, or was merely a transposition of one of only two (major and minor) keys.

The earliest and most obvious cases of transposition around the whole keyboard are the so-called musical labyrinths. John Bull's famous *Ut, re, mi, fa, sol, la* (before 1619; MB XIV No.17) transposes the hexachord up in whole tones successively from G to F, then from A flat to F sharp before returning to G. It thus has the hexachord starting on every one of the 12 notes of the keyboard octave. There is no question of modulation from key to key in the tonal sense, but the cumulative effect of the ever rising pitch of the *cantus firmus* provides the logic of the piece. A closer approach to tonal logic was evidently in a similar piece by Froberger (d.1667) in the form of a canzona in which the subject was transposed through 12 keys around the circle of 5ths.[14] The piece is now lost, but sounds like a demonstration of the 5ths-circle diagram published in 1650 by Froberger's friend the Jesuit mathematician Athanasius Kircher. Kircher's circle is not yet the whole tonal story, since it includes only 12 major keys without their relative minors, a fact pointed out by Heinichen who was the first to publish a circle of all 24 keys, including minor ones, in 1711.

Generally, descriptions of the complete system begin around 1700. In that year in France J.-P. Freillon Poncein was the first to list 42 keys (i.e. 24 and enharmonic equivalents) in the fingering chart of his oboe tutor (Mattax 1991 p.31). One year later the organist and lexicographer Tomáš Baltazar Janovka listed 24 keys in chromatic order with modern key signatures in his influential *Clavis ad thesaurum magnae artis musicae* (Prague 1701).[15]

Other harmonic labyrinths of around this time include a canon given by Werckmeister (1702 p.99) whose *replique* is at the 4th below and so can go round the whole circle of 5ths/4ths. Werckmeister's terminology is again revealing in that he says the canon 'goes through the whole keyboard' ('gehet durchs gantze Clavier'), that is to say the theme is transposed to begin on every note of the keyboard octave, in precisely the same way as Bach meant with 'durch alle Tone und Semitonia'. Bach himself does not appear to have been interested in this sort of exercise. The *Kleines harmonisches Labyrinth* BWV 591 is probably not by him.[16] His pieces that wildly exceed the normal tonal ambitus do so for expressive reasons in a fantasia or recitative style, such as some of the early clavier toccatas, the G minor Organ Fantasia BWV 542/1, or the Chromatic Fantasia BWV 903/1. These are far from mere demonstrations of systematic modulation, but show how remote keys can be put to powerful expressive use. It is likely that Bach would have considered going through all 24 keys in a circle as mechanical and inartistic, which is what C.P.E. Bach says of it in his discussion of the free fantasia (1762 Chapter 41 para.9). A more important reason why Bach did not content himself with a labyrinth of this sort for his demonstration of the well-tempered clavier is that it could hardly demonstrate the quality of individual keys. Having an individual piece in each key means that the expressive world of that key can be explored within its own ambitus, just as in verset collections the qualities of the modes are successively demonstrated in individual pieces. There may nonetheless be a faint residual hint of the hexachord labyrinth in that a number of fugue subjects in Book I outline a 6th, in a pattern 1 6 5 4 3 (C major and minor, D major), or 1 6 5 (D minor, A flat major).

This is where Bach brought things further than Fischer had in his labyrinth of preludes and fugues, *Ariadne Musica* (1702). The key situation in that collection is more complex than it is generally described since the pieces have the character of further transpositions of the seventeenth-century 'church keys' rather than explorations of tonal keys on the given tonics. One pair (No.6) is archetypal Phrygian; of the rest, minor-mode pieces generally have a Dorian tinge, some majors such as A and B are Ionian, while A flat is Lydian. These modes are identifiable by key signature and by the location of cadences (*clausulae*) within the usual ambitus of the mode. So in spite of being an almost complete circle beginning and ending on C, Fischer is in many cases providing examples of transposed modes rather than 19 individual keys.

2. *Key integrity*

One of the most important debates of these decades was whether the new tonality was a real improvement over the modes, or in fact an impoverishment. Were there in reality only two keys, C major and A minor, which were transposed around like the modes, or did keys on different tonics have an integrity of their own? The answer to this was important if tonality was to be presentable as a richer system than the modes: twelve modes, with well attested expressive characters endorsed by the most prestigious philosophers of antiquity, reduced to two is an intolerable impoverishment; twenty-four 'new keys' each with its own expressive identity would be a great enrichment. The charm of the system is that it can be looked at in both ways and the answer cannot be clear-cut.

It is curious that, although many writers listed the supposed characters of modes, and later of keys, it does not seem to have been suggested that modes acquired different characters or identities when transposed. The traditional view is expressed by Johann Buttstett in his attack on Matthesons's 1713 listing of key characters: each mode has its own ambitus, dominant and affect, and this is not altered by the pitch at which it is sung.[17] If it could have been argued that each of the 12 modes acquired a new identity in each of 12 possible transpositions, then the modal system could provide 144 separate characters. The fact that this argument was not made leads Buttstett to ask why the two keys should be different when transposed. The answer to this is complex and many-faceted. The principal advantage of the tonal system, as then perceived, was that it offered the possibility of moving to a different key, rather than just cadencing on different degrees of a mode according to its traditional ambitus. As Rameau said, the strength of music to express emotions lies in the interlocking of keys rather than in the supposed quality of any key in itself.[18] This ability to journey from a point of departure to a series of ever more distant points, the distance being measurable in terms of the circle of 5ths, has been compared to the effect of depth of perspective in painting, as opposed to the two-dimensional set modal ambitus (Rubbra 1960 p.12).

Whatever the ultimate benefits of the system, it was certainly the desire to transpose that gave the main impetus for the development of new keys to complete the circle. Werckmeister proposed tempered tuning 'because nowadays people want to play all songs on all the keys'.[19] He could mean here chorales in modes, or modern arias in keys (see Lester 1989 p.90). The formulation is in a purely practical context, without implying that there is any expressive difference between keys, but individual players undoubtedly savoured differences of key colour. How they expressed this reveals both the subtle ways in which the systems interpenetrated one another and and the way in which even progressive thinkers liked to regard the development of 24 keys as a continuation and enrichment of the ancient system of modes.

In the early years of the eighteenth century keys were not considered to be simple transpositions, but were divided into types (*genera*) according to the number and type of accidentals involved. Usage varied, but J.G. Walther's (1708 pp.66–8) is probably closest to Bach.[20] Basically there are three types of note: diatonic (naturals); chromatic (with accidentals, and these are written values, not just black notes of the keyboard); and enharmonic (double sharps, Walther has no double flats). These form the basis of '3 types of scale which are used in modern compositions not in their pure form, but mixed'.[21] Keys involving more naturals than sharp/flat notes he classifies as diatonic-chromatic (*Genus Diatonico-Chromaticum*); keys with more sharp/flat notes than naturals are chromatic-diatonic (*Genus Chromatico-Diatonicum*); keys with more chromatic than enharmonic notes, and with few diatonic notes, are chromatic-diatonic-enharmonic (*Genus Chromatico-Diatonico-Enharmonicum*). In the following decades this complicated terminology fell out of use, but it shows an attitude that did not regard all keys as equal and equivalent, but banded in a spectrum from the ordinary to the rarefied.

This variable way of regarding keys was partly dependent on the use of unequal temperaments. Even at the time when Walther was writing this, the whole system of major and minor scales around the circle of 5ths was being termed simply the diatonic-chromatic genus as fundamentally one thing, in contradistinction to the old system of modes which may be transposed. Thus Neidhardt proposed in 1706 an equal temperament which would serve the whole 'diatonic-chromatic' system, as well as enabling transposition of the modes.[22]

This was the fundamental ambivalence of the tonal system which, in theory, can have all keys equal and equivalent, but which in practice is full of associations and sensitivities through having developed over a long period in complex historical surroundings. In keyboard music the first real appreciation of key colour was in the works of the French *clavecinistes* who, after the death of Frescobaldi in 1643, constituted the most progressive keyboard school in Europe. In the works of Louis Couperin (d.1661) the most strongly coloured keys are the then unusual ones of D major, C minor, and F sharp minor, keys more commonly explored on fretted instruments, and ones which are least like the traditional modes. Also highly progressive is Louis Couperin's technique in unmeasured preludes of spinning out long paragraphs of music by having one dominant 7th resolve on to another, keeping the movement from touching the ground tonally, a technique used much later in Classical sonata development sections. For François Couperin, in Bach's own time, key was an important aspect of the character piece. In Italian music, strong key colour was exploited by cantata composers of the generation of Carissimi, a tradition of dramatic key use notably exploited by Handel in his *Lucretia* cantata, already mentioned. One of the first listings of key, as opposed to mode, characters was by a French pupil of Carissimi, Marc-Antoine Charpentier (*c*.1690).[23]

The perception that less usual keys had the strongest individual characters is reflected in Mattheson's often-cited listing of 17 key characters (1713 pp.235–53; an English summary is in Buelow 1983 pp.401–2). Mattheson explicitly relates the commonest keys to the equivalent 'church keys', and he orders them as these were most commonly ordered, with D minor as '*Dorio*' first, G minor as '*Transpositus Dorius*' second, and so on. The characters he gives these keys also correspond broadly to their traditional modal affects. He was concerned to demonstrate the continuity of keys from modes, and also that by proceeding round the circle of 5ths beyond the natural tonics of the modes one comes to new keys which have their own character and integrity just as the traditional modes were supposed to do.[24]

Much has been made of these characters with regard to Bach, most notably by Rudolf Wustmann (1911), who attempted to relate them systematically to Bach's works in general and the 48 in particular. Yet Mattheson himself was very aware of their subjective nature. He begins by neatly summarising the wildly conflicting opinions of classical authors about the affects of the traditional modes, and introduces his characters for the newer keys modestly by saying that modern musicians are unlikely to be any more agreed about them than the ancients were about the modes (pp.233–5).

Wustmann, and others, found many of the characters relevant to the 48. One of the closest correlations was perceived for F sharp minor, characterised by Mattheson as 'leading straight to great affliction, yet it is more languishing and love-sick than deadly; otherwise it has in it something abandoned, singular, and misanthropic' (1713 p.251). Apart from the aria 'Buß und Reu' from the St Matthew Passion, Wustmann (p.70) cites the canonic Andante from the A major harpsichord and violin sonata BWV 1015, and the F sharp minor prelude from Book II of the 48. I personally find that a subtle mood of wistful melancholy more accurately describes the affect of these two movements than Mattheson's character, while the F sharp minor fugue of Book I, which Wustmann also mentions, is something more tragic. Mattheson's characters as he gives them are illustrative rather than prescriptive, and he seems to be thinking of particular pieces, probably his own.[25] His purpose was not to fix the character of keys, but to demonstrate that the newer keys could have an identity of their own just as the old modes did, rather than being no more than endless transpositions of C major and A minor. By 1719 he was giving an exactly opposite character for F sharp minor, as 'fresh, lively, and cheerful'.[26] Comparison of eighteenth-century key character listings generally confirms their subjective nature in that opposing characters are often associated with the same key, and it also to an extent confirms the effect of different tunings.[27]

What can one say of key character in the 48? Against the notion of definite characters is Bach's readiness to transpose pieces, often into what could be considered an opposing tonality. Book II has pieces which we know to have been transposed since there are earlier versions of them in different keys: the C sharp major prelude and fugue in C major (BWV 872a), and the A flat fugue in F major (BWV 901/2). The E flat major fugue was probably originally in D major (Tomita 1990 p.245). In addition, Don Franklin suggests that anomalies in the notation of the D sharp minor prelude may indicate an origin in D minor (1989a p.253), while Yo Tomita suggests E minor (1990 p.247). In all these cases Bach was transposing from a more usual to a less usual key to fill a gap in the chromatic sequence of keys. This hardly indicates an acute sensitivity to the special flavour of advanced keys. Particularly interesting is the transposition from C major to C sharp. This was probably in answer to a number of requirements: it is likely that Bach did not wish to begin Book II with a prelude of the same type as opens Book I; it may also reflect a more wholehearted acceptance of equal temperament as the normal tuning by the late 1730s in that identical music may be set on both front and back keys, and the view expressed by Werckmeister in 1697 that students should be trained to play as readily the same music in C sharp as in C.[28] But it may also be that having this type of piece in C had become too much of a cliché. Mattheson in 1731 said that C major had become the most crude and ordinary key so that one must do something unexpected with it, just as one can achieve a subtle effect by going against the usual affect of a more sophisticated key (pp.328–9). By transposing the very ordinary little prelude BWV 872a into C sharp, and refining considerably on its detail, Bach lifted it out of the ordinary onto another plane.

There are no variant versions in other keys for Book I, but it can be deduced that the D sharp minor fugue was almost certainly originally in D minor (KB V/6.1 p.188), the G sharp minor prelude was perhaps in G minor with a (hypo-) Dorian key signature (Dürr 1984 p.45); and there is a faint possibility that the F sharp major fugue was originally in F (KB V/6.1 p.351). If these are indeed transpositions it would again be a matter of filling vacancies in advanced keys. The case of the D sharp minor fugue is analagous to that of the C sharp major prelude of Book II in that its very traditional Dorian outlines are lifted onto a rarefied plane, matching the ingenuity and learning of the counterpoint, and no doubt enhancing the delight of those already practised in the art.

As regards key character in general, it is difficult to disentangle how much is due to the very strong characters that Bach projects, and how much to the key. Later composers who knew the 48 well seem to have been imprinted with Bach's characters for rarer keys, such as the brooding B flat minor canon in Brahms's Handel Variations Op.24, or the veiled bleakness of E flat minor in Fauré's song 'Prison' Op.83 No.1, which starts with repeated chords in the upper-middle part of the keyboard and builds up strong, Beethovenian dissonances. This bears out the main point in the most sensible summary of the problem of key character from Bach's environment, by Heinichen in *Der General-Bass in der Composition* (Dresden 1728).[29] It is that particular characters are the product of our associations with the works of good composers, rather than being inherent in the keys themselves, since very specific characters may be undermined by tuning or local pitch differences. He also makes the important point that pieces do not stay in the same key throughout, even though they may express the same affect throughout. Keys may have general characters, often based on instrumental associations such as the open strings of the violin, but famous composers have written sad and tender pieces in D major, A major, and B flat major, and conversely A minor, E minor, and C minor have had powerful and brilliant music written in them. In any case the tradition of the suite, and particularly the character *Ordres* of François Couperin, was to explore a number of different characters within the same key. Every single key is therefore suited to expressing many opposing affections. These contrasts are well borne out if one takes Bach's clavier works as a whole and compares pieces in any particular key.

In the 48 the degree to which character depends on key may be a product of the function of the piece. The finger-exercise preludes in Book I, for example, depend largely for such individual character as they have on key and metre. The character of the C sharp major prelude may reflect the key's restlessness in an unequal temperament, but Bach may equally just have wanted to provide a brilliant (and easy) piece in this then highly unusual key, or it may be a combination of both. Other functions may lie in traditions of composition. Modal outlines in a few fugue subjects have already been mentioned, and the hexachordal outline of the C major subject in Book I is historically associated with this key, as is therefore its learned and demonstrative character. B minor is a common key in Corelli's trio sonatas, which may account for the style and character of the Book I prelude.

Since key character is a largely personal matter, one naturally looks to Bach's texted works for guidance. Eric Chafe has given a useful digest of key associations in the vocal works, some of which are more relevant to the 48 than others (1991 pp.152–3). Even very obvious associations do not always seem relevant: the D major of trumpets and flutes has a clear reference in the prelude of Book II and perhaps the fugue of Book I with its festive rhythmic character, but the heroic/hunting (horn) or pastoral (recorder) quality of F major is not reflected. Bach may well have wished to avoid the obvious and explore other possibilities. Other keys occur so rarely that it is difficult to get a profile for them. G sharp minor is never used as a movement tonic, and B major almost never;[30] B flat minor and E flat minor are very rare as movement tonics, but B flat minor is used in recitatives for darkness, the cross, and suffering, and E flat minor for extreme torment. These are keys used in the Credo of the B minor Mass for the dead awaiting the resurrection ('Et expecto'). Some more usual keys have very steady associations. F minor is almost always for anxiety, tears, tribulation, sin, pain, sorrow, care, suffering and death, associations one may readily feel in Book I but hardly in Book II. C minor is a frequent key in the vocal works, overwhelmingly associated with death and burial and the sleep of death. More likely associations are F sharp minor and B minor with suffering and the cross, references it is not difficult to see in the fugues of Book I, particularly the B minor with its chiastic outlines, present also in the Adagio of the B minor harpsichord and violin sonata BWV 1014. E minor, the key of 'Aus tiefer Not', is similarly associated mostly with suffering, sorrow, doubt, pain, fear and the Passion, associations one may feel in Book I if not Book II. E major has a very common eighteenth-century association with blessedness, which may connect with the verset/Magnificat nature of the Book II pair (see Chapter Four section 9, and the commentary in Chapter Eight).

One would not expect more than a limited correlation of key character between the vocal and keyboard works since the vocal works are mainly tied to instruments and their capabilities (flutes hated G sharp minor: Hertel 1758 p.240), and being for the church they are generally concerned with a limited number of situations and expressions within a strong tradition of word setting. In chorale preludes for organ it is difficult to find any steady correlation, since the same chorale may be set in a number of different keys. Even keys that do seem to have some regular associations are used for quite opposite expressions: G major generally has either an extrovert concertante character, or a contemplative, even grieving, one; E flat major has a contemplative warmth but may also be agonised. There are many traditions which contribute to the 48.

Particularly in Book I, Bach seems to have a special feeling for the expressive possibilities of minor keys listed by Neidhardt as being unrefined ('unexcoliret') in the Werckmeister III tuning: C sharp, E flat, F, F sharp and B flat (1706 p.39). Most of these involve major 3rds on C sharp, F sharp and A flat, whole-comma-wide major 3rds in Werckmeister III, interesting as a transient effect but hardly usable as tonics. Bach in his way was creating these keys, almost certainly using a less unequal temperament that allowed for the subtle and suggestive individual character he gave them. The equivalent pieces in Mattheson 1719 show merely that it is possible to reproduce fairly standard affects in keys which had not hitherto been exploited. Bach's pieces are much more individual, yet it is undeniable that part of that individuality depends on the rarity of the key, as may be seen by comparing the B flat minor prelude with cognate ones by Fischer.

It has often been remarked that, in spite of the totally circulating nature of *The Well-tempered Clavier*, Bach has kept to the usual key relations within each key, and nowhere uses enharmonic modulations nor juxtaposes remote chords for dramatic purposes. The fact that he stays within the normal tonal ambitus of each key is part of the key's integrity. This is important for the pedagogical aim of the work, part of which has the purely practical object of gaining familiarity with the main chord-shapes ('Griffe') in each key on the keyboard. Also Bach was demonstrating types of composition, not free fantasia. Most pieces have a relation to sonata, aria or dance prototypes, so it is natural that they should use the tonal structures customary in these prototypes. And Bach was making the important point that since every key was capable of being used as a tonic, even the most unusual ones have their own integrity as tonal and expressive worlds, rather than being just places one might visit for special effect.

Bach's normal ambitus in a key is the balanced tonal one of tonic–dominant–relative–subdominant–tonic, most influentially used by Corelli, whose works provided models of tonal structure and balance in the late seventeenth century.[31] This contrasts with the seventeenth-century modal ambitus with cadences generally on the 5th and 3rd degrees. The classic tonal scheme was described by Heinichen in 1711 (p.269); others, however, clung to something of the modal ambitus. Mattheson in 1719 preferred to cadence on V, VI and III in major, and on III, V, VI and VII in minor, evidently disliking the subdominant (Schenkman 1981 p.19). Even Rameau in 1737 recommends the tonal goals of V and III, but rarely the subdominant (Seidel 1986 p.139). Bach set out in *The Well-tempered Clavier* to abandon modal elements in this respect, just as he changed modal to tonal key signatures as the plan of covering 24 keys developed.

3. Ut Re Mi

Apart from the succession of tonics around the circle of 5ths, the other aspect of tonality is the concept of the two modes, major and minor. Bach's manner of expressing this is of great interest, and has been the subject of much speculation.

The German terms used nowadays for major and minor, *dur* and *moll*, originally had a different implication, and it was precisely in the period 1690–1720 that they changed to have their modern meaning. Their origin is in the terms for the three hexachords of the Guidonian system, which was under severe attack during Bach's earlier life.[32] In their original context *dur* and *moll* meant primarily sharp and flat. In Lutheran Germany this terminology lasted up to the end of the seventeenth century, and occasionally beyond.[33]

The Guidonian system was first developed for melodic purposes, providing the basis for the old adage that all music is contained in the hexachord ('Ut, re, mi, fa, sol, la, sunt tota musica'; see for example Schmidt 1754 p.118). With the development of harmony, when it came to classifying triads according to the nature of their 3rds, terminology developed from this melodic concept to be expressed in terms of the first three notes of the modes, some of which stepped out a major 3rd and some a minor one. Thus the first three notes of the Ionian mode (ut re mi) step out a major 3rd, the first three of the Dorian mode (re mi fa) step out a minor 3rd. From this we get an abbreviated form of our adage, that all music is summed up in the notes mi and fa ('Mi et Fa sunt tota musica'). In one sense this can be taken melodically, that the hexachord and its mutations up from Gamma-Ut provide all the materials of music; in another it can have the more 'modern' meaning that all music is contained in the major and minor modes. It is in this 'modern' sense that it is cited by many writers in Bach's environment. Bach himself seems to have had all of these meanings in mind in the *Canon super Fa Mi, a* 7 of 1749 (BWV 1078; Dok.I pp.246–7, NBR pp.236–7).

Bach must have given some thought to the problem of formulation here since terminology was in the process of change. In his youth, keys in secular repertory were identified according to the late seventeenth-century system of keynote with indication of the quality of the third.[34] So, C major was expressed as C, or C♮, or Ce; C minor as C dis, or C♭, the signs ♮ and ♭ being synonymous with *dur* and *moll.* The C minor Passacaglia for organ BWV 582, for example, appears in the Andreas Bach Book as 'Passacalia ex C♭ con Pedale'. Similarly D♭ and E♭ are D minor and E minor respectively.

Things began to get untidy with increased use of keys on the *semitonia.* Here the basic principle that the 3rd, if not mentioned, is natural gives us 'ex Dis' for E flat major and 'ex Fis' for F sharp minor. But when the 3rd is not natural the bifocal nature of the terminology seems strained, with ♮ meaning sharp and ♭ meaning natural in the context of more elaborate key signatures, as well as in the more abstract sense of *dur* and *moll.* One solution was to adopt the French terminology for defining the nature of the 3rd. Since the French generally used the terms of the Guidonian pitch system, a key such as C sharp major would be 'C sol ut dièze, tierce majeure', terms which Mattheson found 'trop longs et embarrasans' compared with the simplicity of 'Cis dur' (1720, Avertissement). The French system is fundamentally the one Bach uses in his title-page, with the terms *tertiam majorem* and *minorem.*

Mattheson had spelt out virtually the whole modern system, of keynote name with 'dur' or 'moll', in 1713 (pp.60–3) as that which was used by 'modern' composers. The only feature which is less full than modern usage is the old tablature designation of black notes other than B flat all being expressed as sharps (cis, dis, fis, gis).[35] All of this was available to Bach and was in all probability the terminology he himself used as an up-to-date composer. It is significant here that it was in the course of putting together Book I that he went over to the complete modern system of key signatures (KB V/6.1 p.24). In 1722 he could have used, had he wished, a formulation such as that employed in the same year by the Dresden musical amateur Friedrich Suppig on the title-page of a labyrinth for harpsichord or organ: '*LABYRINTHUS MUSICUS* bestehend in einer *FANTASIA* durch alle *Tonos* nemlich durch 12 *duros* und 12 *molles*, zusammen 24 *Tonos*' (facsimile in Rasch 1990).

Instead Bach chose to use the terminology of Kuhnau's *Clavier-Übungen* of 1689/92, which was decidely antiquated by 1722. Kuhnau had published first 7 partitas in major keys 'aus dem Ut, Re, Mi, oder Tertia majore eines jedweden Toni' (i.e. C, D, E, F, G, A, B flat, majors), and then 7 partitas in minor keys 'aus dem Re, Mi, Fa, oder Tertia minore eines jedweden Toni' (C, D, E, F, G, A, B, minors).[36] Bach had long admired Kuhnau, and some of his early clavier works were modelled on Kuhnau's (Schulenberg 1992 pp.63, 65). He was personally acquainted with Kuhnau: in April 1716 they travelled to Halle as examiners of the new Cuncius organ at the Liebfrauenkirche there, and enjoyed 'ein besonderes Festessen' laid on for the examiners at the ensuing dedication festival (Dok.I pp.157–61, NBR p.77). As cantor of the Thomasschule Kuhnau enjoyed a distinguished reputation not only as musician, but also as scholar, linguist, philosopher, and teacher. So much so that his musical attainments appear to have been somewhat subsidiary: he boasted that he wrote the *Clavier-Früchte* sonatas of 1696 at the rate of one a day (Arbogast 1983 p.4). Bach nonetheless evidently found him congenial, and modelled his own first two sets of *Clavier-Übungen* on Kuhnau's. Bach wrote the 1722 title-page in the year that Kuhnau died and in which he applied to succeed Kuhnau as Thomas-cantor.

It was clearly important to Bach to present his work as the continuation of a tradition. Although he was a learned man and composer he expressed himself only with reluctance in writing (Dok.III pp.289–90, NBR p.400), and these title-pages are most of what we have of his views on music. He therefore used them to present his own assessment of himself in relation to the tradition. Kuhnau, in correspondence with Mattheson, said that one still had to use ut re mi fa to indicate the *tertiam majorem* and *minorem* when dealing with Catholics, i.e. south Germans, Austrians and Italians (Schenkman 1979/1 p.12). It is perhaps partly because of this, and the origin of the collection in the southern verset tradition, combined with Bach's very recent coming to explore systematically the 24 keys with their new key signatures, that decided him to use Kuhnau's terminology. It may also have been partly due to his wish to establish continuity with the cantoral tradition, which in Luther's view put music in a position second only to theology.[37] Any prospect of reducing this to the level of an elegant accomplishment, along the lines of Mattheson's *Orchestre* of 1713, spelt the end of the long-established high dignity of the composer.

4. *Solmisation and the Heavenly Harmony*

The issue of solmisation was hotly debated throughout Bach's life, and particularly between 1710 and 1720. It was therefore a matter on which musicians could be expected to have views.[38] The general situation, as reflected in instruction books, was that in Catholic areas Guidonian solmisation was accepted without question: an understanding of the system of mutations was essential for interpreting *musica ficta* in *stile antico* church music. Fux in particular was a staunch supporter of the system. In Lutheran areas many writers preferred the system of letter names, which was already being recommended by the Thuringian cantor Georg Quitschreiber in 1607 (Butt 1994 p.58). But they also described the Guidonian system and it seems to have been felt by most that an understanding of it was part of the equipment of a professional church musician. The Weimar poet laureate and writer on music Johann Christoph Lorber in his verse *Lob der edlen Music*, defending the orthodox Lutheran position in favour of music against pietist objections that it is a secular distraction, goes so far as to say that those who teach only A B C rather than Ut Re Mi are unskilled in music and should have their salaries withdrawn

(1696 p.80). The old solmisation was regarded by those who took a high Lutheran view of music as an important part of the cantoral tradition.

Bach certainly took this view. He was well versed in Lutheran theology as his library shows (Leaver 1983) and, during his later disputes with the Leipzig town authorities and the Thomasschule rector, went through the Bible marking up passages that emphasised the dignity of music and musicians (Trautmann 1969). On the title-page of Anna Magdalena Bach's *Clavier-Büchlein* of 1722 he jotted down the titles of several works of the Leipzig theologian August Pfeiffer (1640–89; Dok.I p.268). The title-pages of two of these books have interesting similarities in structure and wording to those of the fair copies of *The Well-tempered Clavier* (1722) and the Inventions (1723).[39] It is probable that he thought of these works as his musically equivalent contribution. Even if much of the wording consists of commonplaces such as may be found on the title-pages of many music publications in the Lutheran area at the time, it was still natural for Bach to take the orthodox Lutheran view of music both as the basis of his livelihood, and also as his support in professional disputes about status.[40]

This being the case, the use of the terms Ut Re Mi etc. on the title-page of *The Well-tempered Clavier* has provided the basis for some very elaborate constructions. The work that implies a large extra dimension in these seemingly innocuous terms is Johann Heinrich Buttstett's 1716 reply to Mattheson's *Das neu-eröffnete Orchestre* (Hamburg 1713) which had not only given what was, with Heinichen's *Anweisung . . . des General-Basses* (Hamburg 1711), the most important up-to-date view of music at the time in Germany, but had also been expressed in Mattheson's usual abrasive and provocative way. In his Introduction 'on the decline of music and its causes', Mattheson attributed the ill repute into which music had evidently fallen with people of refined taste to the pedantry and obscurantism of its practitioners. The modern '*galant homme*' was repelled by the horrendously obscure theory of music dating back a hundred and more years, with its outmoded complications that never in any case had much relevance to practice, purveyed by old-fashioned cantors.

Buttstett obviously identified fully with just the sort of person Mattheson had in mind. According to J.G. Walther, who studied with Buttstett in Erfurt, he was in his own teaching parsimonious in giving information and fond of obfuscation (Schünemann 1933 p.89). Buttstett's reply to Mattheson's *Orchestre*, and the subsequent debate, replicated similar confrontations elsewhere between the conservative approach of professional (trade) music teachers, based on tradition, authority, and rote learning, and the progressive one of the enlightened, philosophical amateur *cognoscento*, based on logical thought and the rational, dispassionate evaluation of evidence.[41] It also reflected a crisis moment when the traditional teaching of counterpoint, developed from the linear concepts of hexachords and modes, had come to seem irrelevant to

the practical reality of harmony as represented by the figured bass, using chord progressions of the tonal system of major and minor keys.

It would nonetheless be wrong to represent Buttstett solely as an obscurantist and ignorant victim of Mattheson's mordant wit. He was obviously incensed by Mattheson's needlessly provocative tone, but his reply is a well informed and articulate presentation of the conservative case and Mattheson's subsequent behaviour earned Buttstett as much sympathy as scorn.[42] The trouble was that the case Buttstett was putting was already a lost cause. His title *UT, MI, SOL,/ RE, FA, LA,/ tota Musica / et / Harmonia Aeterna* expresses the fundamentals of music as the major and minor triads in terms of Guidonian

(*facing page*) Johann Heinrich Buttstett: frontispiece from *Ut, Mi, Sol, Re, fa, La, tota Musica et Harmonia Æterna* (Erfurt [1716]), continuing the tradition of Kircher and the Renaissance neo-platonist conception of the heavenly harmony.

Johann Heinrich Buttstett: frontispiece from *Musikalische Clavier-Kunst und Vorraths-Cammer* (Leipzig [1713]); the figure with the hammer at the bottom left is Pythagoras, a reference to the frontispiece of Athanasius Kircher's *Musurgia Universalis* (Rome 1650).

syllables.[43] The illustration that goes with it (ill. 1) expresses two important things. First, the three flames enclosed in the six-pointed star link the three elements of the triad to the Trinity; and the star itself is composed of two interlocking triangles, the upward one representing the major triad (with the major 3rd below the minor 3rd), and the downward pointing one the minor triad (its inversion, with the major 3rd above the minor 3rd) (Blankenburg 1950 p.65). Buttstett had used a more explicit version of this symbolism in the frontispiece of his keyboard collection *Musicalische Clavier-Kunst* of three years earlier (Leipzig 1713; ill. 2). Second, the quotation from the Book of Job (Chapter 38.4–7) was the commonest Biblical reference for the Renaissance notion that measurement and mathematics represent the divine will, and that the major triad (*trias harmonica*), considered to be the perfect chord since it is the product of the first six elements of the harmonic series, was therefore the heavenly harmony sounding in perpetuity in the ear of God. It was also the classic citation for Lutherans wanting to justify the position of music in the church.

The mystical conception of number as the key to the mind of God was part of an integrated Renaissance philosophy where it was mixed with cabala and had received authorisation from the pseudo-Hermetic writings then thought by some to predate the Bible.[44] This system was crucially undermined in the early years of the seventeenth century by the redating of the Hermetic texts to the hellenistic period around 200 AD, and by the Cartesian view of number and mathematics as the key to a mechanistic universe. But the mystical tradition lived on, notably in Germany, and was influentially represented by Kircher's *Musurgia universalis* (1650) and by Werckmeister, who referred to it in many of his writings and gave the fullest late exposition of it in his last, the *Paradoxal-Discourse* of 1707. Buttstett's *Ut, Mi, Sol* was the last gasp of the tradition, and his dispute with Mattheson was a late and minor reflection of the famous dispute between Mersenne and the English Hermeticist Robert Fludd in the 1620s.[45]

Buttstett's illustration has a clear reference to the much more elaborate title-page of Kircher's *Musurgia*, but with some interesting differences.[46] Kircher has only the upright triangle representing the major triad. He also has 36 angels divided into nine choirs. The nine is comprehensible since it is the product of the three triads which form the eternal canon he gives to the words Sanctus Sanctus Sanctus. But 36 is a number traditionally associated with the 12 signs of the zodiac, each of which was thought to have two associated demons who could be invoked for the purposes of practical magic. This was set out in Cornelius Agrippa's *De occulta philosophia* (1533), and was naturally severely discountenanced by the Catholic Church, though it had its adherents among Lutherans (Yates 1964 Chapter VII). With the advent of scientific method in the seventeenth century such astrological numerology became the object of ridicule rather than fear, and this is the side Mattheson is on. He recounts how a gentleman had recently borrowed Kircher's *Musurgia* from him and while he was reading it felt he had constantly to look around the room in case the horrific technical terms ('die grausamen *terminos artis*') were raising evil spirits, as they might with Agrippa or some other magical author (1713 p.5). Mattheson gives the word 'art' here a very sinister dimension. It was bold indeed of Buttstett to leap to the defence of tradition in the way he did, even though he replaces Kircher's 36 angels by 14, presumably representing a major and a minor triad on each of the seven *tone*.

Has all this really any relevance to Bach's use of the terms Ut Re Mi on his 1722 title-page? The background to Buttstett's *Ut, Mi, Sol* and its possible relevance to Bach has been thoroughly explored by Walter Blankenburg.[47] Most of the evidence has to do with Bach's environment and the Lutheran cantoral tradition, and these were certainly factors in his world view. Even if he was not generally given to expressing himself in verbal form he was certainly not uninterested in speculative matters, as his extensive theological library shows. He had contact with deeply versed people such as J.G. Walther and L.C. Mizler, and we know that in conversation he was very well informed.[48] But it is ultimately not possible to say with any precision how much of the speculative dimension he was interested in, and such hard facts as we have about his views point to a musician whose concerns were primarily practical. The writer in his environment who most fully reflected the mystical cosmogony of the Kircher tradition was Werckmeister, but the only one of his writings we can definitely say Bach knew is the *Orgel-Probe* (P. Williams 1985), one of his least speculative works. The paragraphs of Niedt's *Musicalische Handleitung* (1700, evidently used by Bach to teach figured-bass playing), which touch on the heavenly harmony and the divine function of music are commonplaces of the time.[49] As Blankenburg himself says, it would have been more remarkable had Bach renounced them than accepted them (1942 p.75).

There is no doubt that Bach made a conscious decision to use Guidonian solmisation syllables, since the modern *dur/moll* terminology had been available for decades and would certainly have been known to him as a progressive composer. It is possible that he was expressing solidarity with his Erfurt relative in view of Mattheson's scathing attack on Buttstett in *Das Beschützte Orchestre* (Hamburg 1717), together with an insult to Bach's own father-in-law, and an invitation to Bach to send biographical information for Mattheson's projected *Ehrenpforte* (see section 2 of the Introduction). In 1717 Mattheson also laments that few musicians were capable of playing in all keys (p.368). But the likelihood is that Bach used the solmisation syllables to emphasise the continuity of modern composition with the tradition, since both old and new elements are represented in *The Well-tempered Clavier.* Buttstett himself in the introduction to his *Musicalische Clavier-Kunst* had defended the Guidonian solmisation as part of the noble tradition of Froberger, Kerll and his own teacher Pachelbel, all composers Bach is known to have admired. To these Bach would surely have added his elder colleague Kuhnau, whom he had admired and imitated in his youth, and whose formulation he adopted here. As Joel Lester suggests, Bach may also have been implying that he was not just continuing but completing the work of Kuhnau's *Clavier-Übungen* by having not only all the *tone* but all the *semitonia* as well (1989 p.90). And if the germ idea of *The Well-tempered Clavier* was to have a prelude and fugue on each note of the natural hexachord (springing from the 12 modes of Renaissance theory), by beginning on C as Ut Bach was able to demonstrate the continuity of the new system of 24 keys from the venerable tradition of Guido.

CHAPTER SIX

Bach as Teacher

'For the use and profit of musical youth, eager to learn'

The 48 is the apex of Bach's clavier teaching programme. In his formulation of the title-page he puts the educational intention first, before the 'rare entertainment of those already skilled in this discipline'. Here again Bach's wording has significant resonances in his tradition, which clarify and give focus to his intentions.[1]

Firstly, it is squarely in the tradition of verset collections of the previous half-century, where these two objectives had become commonplace (Constantini 1969 p.43). While Johann Caspar Kerll dedicated his *Modulatio organica* (Munich 1686) primarily to the Church, later ones were dedicated more typically to learning youth and for the pleasure of those more experienced. The title-page of the *Ars magna consoni et dissoni* (1693) of the Augsburg Cathedral organist Johann Speth is typical, with a wording close to Bach's:

> for the pleasure of advanced players; for the delight of tender ears; for the pastime of lovers of the noble art of music; for the benefit of teachers; and as useful practice for learners.[2]

But again Bach aims at the best by specifying that his youth is musically talented and eager to learn. Dedicated as he was as a teacher, he taught only those with a prospect of becoming professional musicians.[3]

A second resonance comes from the circle of composers fascinated by learned counterpoint, who were centred on Hamburg in the late seventeenth century: Buxtehude, Johann Adam Reinken, Johann Theile and Christoph Bernhard. This group drew together most strands of this tradition up to their time. The so-called Sweelinck theory manuscripts, actually compiled by Matthias Weckmann and Reinken in *c.*1655–70, draw on the first and classic discussion in Zarlino's *Le istitutioni armoniche* (Venice 1558 etc.), and also on later Italian theorists of the early seventeenth century as represented in

Germany by Marco Scacchi (Gehrmann 1901, Walker 1985/6). Both Bernhard and Theile were pupils of Schütz in Dresden, Theile being one of his youngest and last pupils and providing a link between Schütz and Bach (Benary 1961 p.76). Bach may thus be seen in a German tradition of great composers, going back through Schütz to Lassus, who were also influential teachers, but who taught by example rather than precept.

Theile (1646–1724) was considered the prime advocate of learned counterpoint in Bach's youth. In his later years Theile moved back to his native Thuringia (Naumburg), where he inspired many of the younger generation with his enthusiasm for learned counterpoint (canon, fugue, invertible counterpoint). J.G. Walther was a great admirer who copied out several of Theile's treatises, including the *Musikalisches Kunst-Buch*, of which he had already made a copy while he was a pupil of Buttstett in Erfurt in 1702 (Schünemann 1933 p.89). This, which in particular gives examples of permutation counterpoint, has been seen as a model for the *Musical Offering* as well as *The Art of Fugue* (Benary 1961, Walker 1989 pp.35–8). Theile's *Kunst-Buch* was directed to 'those eager to learn composition' ('Lehr-begierigen der Composition') and also to the 'amateurs of music' ('Liebhaber der Music') who wish to be 'enlivened and delighted' ('belustigt und ergetzt'; Dahlhaus 1965 p.vii).

The third resonance is in a book very close to Bach's teaching practice, the first part of Niedt's *Musicalische Handleitung* (Hamburg 1700, 2/1710; Poulin and Taylor 1989; Poulin 1994). Apart from providing the basis for Bach's own teaching of figured bass, Niedt gives examples of decorating figured-bass progressions in different patterns, a way which recalls not only the preludes of Book I in Wilhelm Friedemann's *Clavier-Büchlein*, but also many other similar types of piece in that tradition, for example in Kuhnau's *Clavier-Übungen* and Fischer's *Musicalischer Parnassus*.[4] Here again the work is for 'beginners eager to learn'.[5] All of these strands of tradition are present in *The Well-tempered Clavier.*

1. *Bach's educational tradition*

Of Bach's own musical education we know little in detail. According to J.G. Walther (1732) he 'learned the first principles on the clavier' from his eldest brother Johann Christoph Bach, with whom he lived in Ohrdruf from the death their father in 1695 until he went as a choral scholar to the Michaelisschule in Lüneburg in 1700.[6] C.P.E. Bach adds that Bach was not quite ten years of age when he began this instruction, and it was at just that age that Bach later began instructing Wilhelm Friedemann (Dok.III p.81; NBR p.299). There can be no doubt that the earlier lessons would have consisted substantially of the same elements as those that begin Friedemann's *Clavier-Büchlein*:

notes, clefs, the rudiments of keyboard tablature and staff notation, and a basic repertory of ornaments.[7] His first pieces would, however, probably have been learned aurally rather than from music, since that was the common way of teaching at the time, particularly when composers were teaching their own works. Bach himself apparently used this method to a certain extent.[8]

Playing from figured basses was part of the meaning of studying clavier, and again Niedt's *Musicalische Handleitung* may give us something of the method employed, since Niedt was a pupil of Johann Nicolaus Bach in Jena, and the *Handleitung* may well reflect a Bach family teaching tradition (Poulin and Taylor 1989 p.xiii). Certainly Niedt's progression from pure four-part figured-bass playing through more decorated realisation to improvisation and ultimately to contrapuntal composition was the common method of teaching composition of the time and coincides with what we know of Bach's own teaching.[9]

How far he had progressed as a keyboard virtuoso by the time he left Ohrdruf at the age of fifteen is difficult to assess. The story of Johann Christoph withholding pieces by Froberger, Kerll and Pachelbel from him, and his having to steal the manuscript from a cupboard and copy them out by moonlight, suggests that his brother was trying to hold him back. There is no reason to doubt the veracity of the story since it is told by C.P.E. Bach as a well-known piece of family lore (Dok.III p.81, NBR p.299). It has been suggested that Johann Christoph wished to deflect Sebastian from the keyboard, which would lead only to a cantorship, to the violin and other activities which would lead to the more prestigious and lucrative post of capellmeister, but this is unlikely. C.P.E. Bach was of the opinion that the instruction Bach received in Ohrdruf was probably designed to equip him as an organist and nothing more (Dok.III p.288, NBR p.398). It is much more likely that Johann Christoph did not want his precocious young brother playing all his best repertory. Certainly by the time Bach was eighteen the authorities of the Neukirche, Arnstadt, considered him a notable virtuoso and were prepared to pay him rather more than they had paid his predecessor.

This story underlines one of the main ways in which the young learned the trade of composition, by copying out repertory. At least from his Cöthen years onwards Bach was surrounded by family and pupils copying out music for performance, and the number of copies of the 48 testifies to its prestige as an educational work. For some, copying was no doubt a routine and unthinking activity. Bach himself, in his learning days, was alert to what he was copying and constantly making alterations.[10] He expected the same of his brighter pupils, such as Altnickol, who was given Book II to copy in 1744 as an educational exercise, and expected to use his intelligence and initiative in making certain alterations (Jones 1991 p.607). After 1740 virtually all Bach's pupils seem to have made copies of Book II (KB V/6.2 p.135).

If Bach relied on his own study and perceptions for the higher reaches of composition he was doing no more than what most composers of his day did. For keyboard composers, C.P.E. Bach lists (in addition to Froberger, Kerll and Pachelbel) Frescobaldi, J.C.F. Fischer, N.A. Strungk, Buxtehude, Reinken, Bruhns and Böhm, all of whom were, as he said, 'strong fugue writers' (Dok.III p.288, NBR p.399). Among them were also 'some good and old Frenchmen', though it is not clear which of these Bach would have known in his early years, since he is not known to have copied any French music before 1709 (VBN pp.190–5). French items in the manuscript collections of Johann Christoph are limited to harpsichord music of Marchand and Lebègue, and arrangements of orchestral dance music by Lully and Marais (Hill 1987 I pp.18–40). In addition to keyboard music, Bach had at Lüneburg access to one of the richest seventeenth-century collections of polyphonic and figural choral music in Germany, in the choir library of the Michaeliskirche, one of the chief sources of his later knowledge of older music (Heller 1989 p.8).

2. *Bach's teaching programme*

A great deal is known about Bach's way of teaching, from reports by his sons and pupils, from the title-pages to his educational works, and from the works themselves, particularly in sources such as Wilhelm Friedemann's *Clavier-Büchlein.* All of this can also be seen in the general context of teaching methods at the time, from which it is clear that Bach's method was typical in its outlines of contemporary teaching practice, the difference being in the quality of material and the level of musical stimulation provided.

Bach is known to have had pupils already at Arnstadt.[11] The first entries in the *Orgel-Büchlein* date from Mühlhausen (Stinson 1995a), though at that stage Bach can hardly have developed an elaborate teaching programme. A vivid picture of what it was like to study with Bach in his twenties is given by Philipp David Kräuter who studied with him at Weimar in 1712–13. Reporting to his funding body in his home town of Augsburg, he says that Bach wanted 100 thalers a year, but he talked him down to 80: 'for this he will give me board and instruction. He is an excellent, and also conscientious, man both for composition and clavier, and also for other instruments. He gives me at least 6 hours instruction a day, which I badly need particularly for composition and clavier, but also for other instruments. The remaining time I spend doing my own practice and copying, since he lets me have all the music I want.'[12]

Over the following ten years Bach gradually built up his stock of pieces, many of which began as repertory but which he later used for teaching. From 1720, when his eldest son began systematic instruction, he started to organise his teaching programme into a logical and comprehensive method. This is reflected in the title-page he added to the *Orgel-Büchlein* at Cöthen; in Friedemann's *Clavier-Büchlein* (begun 1720), which has early versions of 11 of the first 12 preludes of Book I, the Inventions and Sinfonias, as well as more elementary pieces very revealing of Bach's teaching; in Anna Magdalena Bach's first *Clavier-Büchlein* (1722), the surviving part of which contains mainly the French Suites; and in the fair copies of Book I of the 48 (1722) and the Inventions and Sinfonias (1723).

Given that Bach taught a relatively small number of pupils, and only talented ones, he was no doubt flexible in adapting material to their needs and abilities. He does nonetheless seem to have put his pupils through a certain progression of clavier pieces. C.P.E. Bach tells us that Sebastian's pupils had to begin straight off with his own 'not exactly easy' pieces (Dok.III p.23), but from other evidence it looks as if he put even quite advanced players back to basic things to begin with. Not many of his pupils left any detailed account of what they did. The most fruitful testimony is that of Heinrich Nicolaus Gerber (1702–75), published by his son Ernst Ludwig in the first part of his biographical *Lexicon* of musicians (Leipzig 1790; Dok.III pp.476–7, NBR pp.321–2). Gerber's early studies had been with, among others, Johann Friedrich Bach, Sebastian's successor at Mühlhausen. Gerber admired Johann Friedrich on account of his singing style of playing ('seiner cantabeln Spielart') but found him unsatisfactory as a teacher because he was permanently drunk. By the time he came to Sebastian in 1724 Gerber was already an experienced player and composer, having written, among other things, six clavier concertos (Landshoff 1933 p.10).

Bach's first question was if Gerber had industriously played fugues: he evidently considered the ability to mould several contrapuntal voices simultaneously to be the touchstone of good playing. 'At the first lesson he set his Inventions before him. When he had studied these to Bach's satisfaction, there followed a series of suites, then *The Well-tempered Clavier.*' The details of this are confirmed by the copies Gerber made: the Inventions, probably begun in 1724; then the French and some English Suites; then Book I of the 48 up to the D minor prelude and fugue, which he began copying in November 1725. The E minor Partita BWV 830 and the remainder of Book I were added some time later, after he had finished his studies with Bach probably by early 1726 (Dürr 1978b). Although E.L. Gerber says that his father began the study of figured bass after all this, the handwriting of Gerber's continuo exercise, a realisation of the bass of Albinoni's violin sonata Op.6 No.6, shows it to have been done after the Inventions, at the same time as the French Suites.[13] Normally the study of figured bass, the basis of composition, came after pieces ('Handsachen'), but in view of Gerber's advanced status and the short time he was with Bach the system was obviously telescoped somewhat.

A more detailed account of the early stages is given by Forkel who, although writing much later, was a personal friend of both Friedemann and Emanuel Bach and got his information from them. In any case what he says is corroborated by other writers and in the music sources, and the broad outlines are common to other instruction books of the time. In his chapter on Bach as teacher he describes the following elements (1802 pp.38–9, NBR pp.453–4): (1) Bach began by teaching his 'peculiar mode of touching the instrument'; this is the curious scratching touch first described by Quantz (1752) as special to Bach (Dok.III p.18, BR p.444). (2) 'For this purpose, he made them practice, for months together, nothing but isolated exercises for all the fingers of both hands, with constant regard to this clear and clean touch'; none were excused at least a few months of these exercises, and Bach thought that ideally they should be continued for at least six months to a year. (3) Short pieces based on these exercises, of which Forkel mentions the little preludes and the two-part Inventions. The system then proceeds as for Gerber.

3. *Keyboard technique*

The way in which Bach's teaching plan builds up to *The Well-tempered Clavier* may be seen in Wilhelm Friedemann Bach's *Clavier-Büchlein* (NBA V/5), begun on 22 January 1720, exactly two months after Friedemann's ninth birthday. The entries from Nos.1 to 24 (end of the Praeludia that later went into Book I) are successive, with Nos.1 to 20 (F major prelude of Book I) forming a single complex.[14] Friedemann was obviously a talented pupil since the material advances very rapidly.

The level of Bach's method is particularly clearly brought out when it is compared with other teaching methods of the time, which generally follow a very standard pattern. A useful comparison is with the teaching *Noten-Buch* of one of Bach's last pupils, J.C. Kittel, which may be taken as typical.[15] The method consists of the following elements: (1) explanation of pitch: clefs and notes, with both staff notation and German keyboard tablature systems; (2) note values and rests; (3) demonstration of time signatures; (4) explanation of ornaments ('Manieren'); (5) accidentals; (6) fingerings: scales, chords, interval patterns ('Application der Finger'); (7) exercises for common rhythmic situations; (8) short pieces with complete fingerings; (9) Minuet with variations: each variation concentrates on a particular keyboard-technical effect (systematic variations were a standard way of teaching divisions, improvisation, and composition).

This is an elementary textbook for pupils to copy out. With the intimate family relationship of Bach to Friedemann, much could be left to verbal explanation and initial items in the *Clavier-Büchlein* have only elements 1, 4 and 8.

Perhaps surprising in all these methods is the fact that ornaments come as one of the first elements, not as an embellishment to be added later. Trills and mordents were in fact the very first finger-exercises taught, which explains why the little fingering *Applicatio* No.1 in the *Clavier-Büchlein* already has complex ornaments. The alternation of two notes is the most basic step in developing technique, and as such was the first exercise for singers (for example, Printz 1678 pp.47ff) and thence instrumentalists. Patterns can then be introduced which involve progressively larger intervals. The primacy of trills in elementary keyboard teaching lasted throughout the eighteenth century. C.P.E. Bach says they are the most difficult ornament and must be practised industriously from the start (1753 Chapter 2 Part 3 para.7); his following paragraphs are probably the best lesson for this.[16] Marpurg (1760) puts them before any other finger exercises; G.F. Merbach (1782) began them at the second or third lesson (starting slowly); and even Rellstab (1790) begins with 'Manieren'. Trills remained an essential part of technique for Bach. Forkel tells us he devised exercises for single and double trills, and for combining a melody and a continuous trill in one hand (1802 p.14, NBR p.433), and these effects can be seen in the Gigue of the D minor English Suite and Variation 28 of the Goldberg Variations. Apart from odd moments such as the awkward left-hand trill in b.20 of the D minor fugue, Book I of the 48 has brilliant complex trills woven into an *étude* in the F major prelude, and melodic, cantabile trills in the final version of the E minor prelude.

Practice of trills (2nds) was then customarily extended, as in Printz's vocal tutor cited above, into figurations involving larger intervals, 3rds, 4ths, 5ths and so on.[17] These are probably the basis of the 'isolated exercises for all the fingers of both hands' that Forkel says Bach ideally liked to keep beginners on for six months to a year. Such exercises, which systematically pattern out intervals from the unison to the octave, are not only the basis of finger technique, but also of improvised divisions (variation technique), and thence of figural composition. On the keyboard this type of exercise has a German ancestry going back at least to around 1500 (Oswald Holtzach, 'Fundamentbuch', 1515; numerous patterns of this sort are given by Ammerbach, 1571).[18] In Bach's time the most notable example of it is in François Couperin's *L'art de toucher le clavecin* (Paris 1717 pp.28–34). Couperin calls these patterns *évolutions* and, as the best French instrumental tutors of the time tend to do, he makes elegant, rounded little musical sentences out of them, rather than giving them just as abstract mechanical patterns. This artistic approach from the beginning is one we can readily believe of Bach, who derived the little preludes and Inventions from such exercises. Couperin does not give fingerings for his *évolutions*, but Marpurg, who lived in Paris in the 1740s, gives in his extended German version of *L'art de toucher le clavecin* (Berlin 1755 etc., Tab.IX) fingerings for Couperin's patterns, and others of his own (Ex.6.1).

Ex.6.1 François Couperin (1717): *évolution* patterns with fingerings by Marpurg (1755) (a) progression of 3rds; (b) progression of 4ths.

What we have from Bach is not little exercises, but fully worked-out pieces, the end product of what was explained. It is not difficult to see the origin of some of the Inventions in these patterns, particularly when the opening figure is put end to end with itself and run around the keyboard in a sequence, as in the C major Invention. Ultimately Bach used this principle as an ingredient in very much more elaborate contexts such as in the D sharp minor and E minor preludes of Book II. The Book I Praeludia in the *Clavier-Büchlein* are generally concerned with more advanced technical matters than basic *évolutions*. One can nonetheless see *évolution* patterns in the background of other Book I preludes such as the F sharp minor (4ths), the G major from b.16 (7ths), and the B major (2nds), and in Book II the C minor (3rds).

The F sharp minor prelude raises an important issue of fingering in the 48. Fingered editions tend to give tortuous, non-sequential fingerings in advanced keys, designed to avoid at all costs having a thumb on a black note. This does not seem to match Bach's systematic treatment of figurations. From Bach himself we have only the two fingered pieces in the *Clavier-Büchlein*, plus a single fingering in the autograph of Book I (see the commentary on the C sharp minor prelude).[19] The *Applicatio* No.1 in the *Clavier-Büchlein*, very neatly constructed teaching piece as it is, must represent the type of exercise Bach himself began with since it has numerous antecedents in seventeenth-century instructional literature.[20] As C.P.E. Bach says, Bach started with the old, and had to work out the new for himself. The old is nonetheless indispensable, and its paired fingerings were still being recommended by C.P.E. Bach in 1753 (Chapter 1 paras.7, 12, 27, 30), along with seventeenth-century *roulade* fingering (groups of 1–4; already recommended by Ammerbach, 1571), and standard modern fingering.

The Praeambulum No.9 of the *Clavier-Büchlein*, with its more 'modern' violin-sonata arpeggio outlines, allows less choice of fingerings. The left hand, which traditionally used the thumb much more than the right hand did, has many uses of the thumb on black notes, though the tenor trill at b.13 involves crossing the second finger over the thumb to avoid it.[21] The right hand has a black-note thumb in b.5, where it involves an octave, but inconveniently avoids it in bb.21–2 where it involves a 7th. This has to be set against the C sharp major prelude of Book I which seems designed, in its basic material, to transfer the C major hand-shapes ('Griffe') to C sharp major. Forkel tells us that Bach used all the fingers in both hands 'in the most various positions', and made the thumb a main finger, since it was essential in advanced keys (1802 pp.14–15, NBR pp.433–4). Forkel's pupil F.C. Griepenkerl adds that Bach, unlike the normal practice of the early nineteenth century, used 1 and 5 on blacks 'as often as necessary', citing the E flat major two-part Invention as an exercise for this.[22] Chords will obviously require thumbs on black notes, but scales and scale-based patterns less obviously so. Mizler (1739 Tab.IV) gives the left-hand fingerings for a rising scale of C major as 54321321, and C sharp major as 54324321, as also A flat major, implying that there was no embargo on the little finger and thumb on black notes in Bach's circle.[23] This is notwithstanding Kirnberger's statement of Bach's general principle that the thumb is used after, rather than on, a *semitonium*, a principle borne out by the advanced-key fingerings given by C.P.E. Bach. Bach's variety of practice is evident in comparing the little *évolution* for the three middle fingers of the right hand at the opening of the B major prelude of Book I with the 'modern' B major scale, pivoted on the thumb (the only fingering given by C.P.E. Bach), that begins the B major prelude of Book II.

There are many contemporary scale fingerings, given in the abstract, but fewer for *évolutions* in advanced keys. The essence of the *évolution* is that the hand-shape is the motif shape. Does this mean that, for example, in the F sharp minor prelude of Book I the *évolution* of a 4th in the right hand at the opening should be consistently fingered 4321 regardless of where the thumb falls? There is very little evidence from Bach himself to decide this issue, and the fingered *Probestücke* that C.P.E. Bach provided with his 1753 *Versuch* are in such a different style that they are no help, though the sequential patterns he gives at the end of his chapter on fingering rigorously avoid the thumb on black notes. There is some slight evidence in the fingerings in J.C. Vogler's copy of the early version of the C major fugue of Book II (BWV 870a/2; NBA V/6.2 pp.311–13, PF pp.5–7): the left-hand semiquavers in b.8 are transposed up a tone in b.9 with the same fingering, giving a thumb on f♯. The relation of these fingerings to Bach is, however, uncertain. They are anything but consistent in their implications for articulation, and seem in places designed for a small hand. Given the key, they can provide little evidence for the more advanced keys.[24] There is too little evidence to come to any firm conclusion on the fingering of *évolutions* in advanced keys. The flexibility described by C.P.E. Bach and others is in keeping with what we know of Bach's practical mentality. As Forkel points out, equality of fingers, the tuning issue, and the move to using all 24 keys as tonics are all part of one development (1802 p.15, NBR p.434).

According to Forkel the purpose of the *évolutions* was to develop Bach's individual touch, in which 'the finger is not raised perpendicularly from the key, but that it glide off ('abgleitet') the forepart of the key, by gradually drawing back the tip of the finger towards the palm of the hand' (1802 p.13, NBR p.432). This is first described in very similar terms by Quantz (1752), who had personal experience of Bach's playing. Two points are clear from Quantz's description: he is talking of Bach's playing on the harpsichord ('Clavicymbel'), and the touch is used in rapid passages ('geschwinde Passagien').[25] It may tie in with Bach's preference for the French short and narrow keys on the harpsichord (Dok III. p.193, NBR p.365). For something that is described in so much detail as a fundamental aspect of Bach's keyboard technique by Quantz and Forkel, it is curious that C.P.E. Bach mentions it only for very rare and restricted situations: rapid repeated notes with two fingers, and the last upper note of rapid trills, and he says it is not for the pianoforte.[26] E.W. Wolf, one of the few to mention it ('abglitschen'), also has it for very restricted situations: again for very rapid notes, this time to prevent blocking on the clavichord, as 'the modern way of playing' Allegro scales if there is no slur; for very short dotted notes in Adagios, and for some ornaments; also for repeated bass notes in an Andante, and for Allegro crotchets to be played only half their value. Sliding the finger gives the effect of 't'nt' rather than 't't', i.e. with a singing effect on each note.[27] The fullest description is given by Forkel.[28] The true nature of this touch is mysterious in that the two people who had direct experience of Bach's playing (Quantz and C.P.E. Bach) are at variance.

In the sequence of the *Clavier-Büchlein*, after the *Applicatio*, there follow a couple of floridly decorated chorale preludes (for ornaments),[29] a few dances (for character), and a group of little preludes based on various broken-chord patterns, one of which (No.8) is another use of the so-called Alberti-bass pattern, actually a violin-based figuration in Bach's case (see Chapter Three section 9). These lead to the 11 Praeludia which, in extended form, were later incorporated into Book I. In the sequence of the *Clavier-Büchlein* there is a clear logic in these 'Handsachen' aimed at developing the relationship of hand to keyboard, and some may have originated in the 'particular pieces' Bach wrote for himself 'in which all the fingers of both hands must necessarily be employed in the most various positions in order to perform them properly and distinctly'.[30]

No.1 (C major) is for chord shapes, with a still hand, and for a particular cantabile touch (see the commentary in Chapter 7).
No.2 (C minor) is for bringing thumb and little finger into line with the middle three fingers, with a still hand.
No.3 (D minor) is for the same purposes as No.1, but with the right hand transferred around the keyboard.
No.4 (D major) is as for No.2, but with the right hand transferred around the keyboard, pivoted on the thumb.
No.5 (E minor) is a left-hand equivalent of No.4, concentrating on extension of the little finger, an important aspect of left-hand technique, particularly in continuo playing.
No.6 (E major) breaks the pattern, and may have originated with the E major French Suite; as an exercise it is for cantabile melodic projection in a standard keyboard texture of melodic right hand, with two accompanying parts in the left hand.
No.7 (F major) is for broken-chord shapes with an open hand covering an octave, extending the more restricted hand positions of Nos.1 and 3. This Praeludium ends the first complex of entries, on the *tone*; Bach then went back to fill in the *semitonia*. All of the advanced-key Praeludia have very strong characters and there is no reason to think they were not conceived in these rare keys.
No.8 (C sharp major) is a brilliantly playable *solfeggio* which transfers the hand-shapes ('Griffe') of C major up to C sharp, and neatly fulfils the often-repeated aspiration from Werckmeister (1697) to Mattheson (1720) that keyboard players should be able to play as readily in C sharp as in C.
No.9 (C sharp minor) seems designed for cantabile melodic projection (as its relative No.6), but now in a more complex texture of four parts; it also has the common rhythmic problem of reconciling the lilt of a dotted rhythm with constant quavers (see the commentary).
No.10 (E flat minor) is the most sophisticated essay in melodic projection in a freer, more recitative style.
No.11 (F minor) is the nearest to a French type of prelude, with sustained notes in broken chords (*tenues*), as in the F major prelude of Book II.

This coherent block of material, forming the core of Book I, is unique in the 48. As Book I developed one can see further technical features being explored: *évolutions* in the F sharp minor and G major preludes, perhaps trills for outside fingers in the A minor, and an amalgamation of old and new techniques in the B flat major, but there is no systematic progression. The preludes of the second half are more concerned with composition types, and also with demonstrating variety of time signatures (element 3 in Kittel's *Noten-Buch*).

Book II is less systematic, consisting of pieces of very diverse origins, from reworked early pieces to some of Bach's latest clavier creations. Only the C sharp major prelude is in the style of the *Clavier-Büchlein* Praeludia 1 and 3, with the continuum of a single note value and the implication of cantabile touch, as in the equivalent preludes of Fischer. The new feature in this prelude, and probably the reason why Bach worked it up, is the variation element between its two sections (see the commentary). *Évolutions* underlie the preludes in C minor, D sharp minor, and E minor, and the B major is another amalgamation of old and new techniques. There are some mild versions of newer technical devices, such as the reversed-hand *batterie* in the conclusion of the C major fugue (added around 1742), and the hand-crossing in the B flat major prelude. Bach was clearly not interested in exploring keyboard-technical devices as such in Book II: that came in the Goldberg Variations (1741), his contribution to the keyboard-technical Minuet and Variations tradition, represented by the final element in the *Lehrgang* of Kittel's *Noten-Buch*.[31]

The Praeludia were entered in the *Clavier-Büchlein* between 1720 and 1722. Chronologically the next entries were the Inventions and Sinfonias (here called Praeambulum and Fantasia), entered from late 1722 to early 1723. These are more advanced than the Praeludia in being more finished pieces, but also in that they represent a step on the way to fugue. Counterpoint was the supreme art of keyboard playing for Bach, as his initial remark to H.N. Gerber quoted above implies. In it the physical and intellectual aspects of music are in balance. The Inventions and Sinfonias therefore move beyond the decoration of chord patterns, based on improvisation traditions described by Niedt, to composition, as the title-page of the 1723 fair copy of the Inventions and Sinfonias says. It is significant that the performance element on that title-page uses terminology traditionally associated with obbligato counterpoint: to play cleanly in two and three parts, and to arrive at a singing style of playing ('eine *cantable* Art im spielen'; Dok.I pp.220–1, NBR pp.97–8). The term *cantabel* was traditionally used for music in obbligato parts, in which the individual lines formed logical, singable musical phrases. This is so of polyphonic vocal music and viol consort music, where all the parts are of equal interest, as opposed to violin-band dance music, where the inner parts are mere harmonic fillers without any integrity of their own. In keyboard improvisation the term is used in this sense by, for example, Georg Muffat, who in his thoroughbass tutor (MS 1699; ed. Federhofer 1961) gives specimen realisations first with plain chords, then with 'cantable Manieren', i.e. decorations and little imitations involving all the parts. In composition, 'cantabel setzen' was a standard term for composing in obbligato parts. J.H. Buttstett (1716), for example, says he learnt 'cantabel setzen' from Pachelbel in Nuremberg. This was considered the essence of compositional technique, and part of Bach's meaning is that learners can get a taste for it in playing the Inventions.

In playing, the term has many references. It was a commonplace of the time to say that the art of singing should be studied before playing the keyboard, and 'sangbar spielen' was what keyboard players should aim for. On a purely technical level, Forkel relates it to Bach's peculiar keyboard touch ('abgleiten') which enables us to play 'in a singing style and with proper connexion ('sangbar und zusammenhängend'), even on an instrument so poor in tone as the clavichord' (1802 p.13, NBR p.433). The possible ramifications of Bach's '*cantable* Art' are explored in the enormous modern literature on the term. Perhaps too much should not be read into it, and the essentials are summed up in François Couperin's happy phrase 'faire parler les touches' (1717 p.7). Bach left no dead wood or loose ends in his part writing, and he expected it to be played accordingly. The fugue subjects of the 48 offer rich scope for characterisation. To take just one example, the subjects of the G minor fugue of Book I and the D major of Book II have pairs of crotchets, one on the beat, one off. No good singer would sing these with equal emphasis if they involved a strong and a weak syllable.

4. *Composition*

It is artificial to separate the elements of training in Bach's time. The student went to a master and learnt everything from him: tuning and maintaining the instruments, notation and copying, technique, improvisation, and composition. These were all part of a unity. Even making a little musical sentence out of a finger exercise is an act of composition. In addition, the boundary between improvisation and composition was very imprecise: one of the objectives of writing fugues was to improve one's technique of improvising them. One often has the impression with pieces in the 48 that the early stages of a piece were improvised but that later, more intricate and less playable developments were worked out at the desk. Even then the practical elements of playability and sonority, as two aspects of the same thing, were at the forefront of Bach's mind.

Actual composition came late in Bach's teaching programme, after finger exercises, inventions, suites and *The Well-tempered Clavier*, and cannot have amounted to anything very advanced on the student's side since they were usually with him for only about two years or so. But the concerns of composition were there from the start. Copying music was then considered the main way of learning to compose, and for this the Inventions and *The Well-tempered Clavier* were the core works, judging by the number of student copies. Bach's teaching centred on the clavier: there are few surviving copies of the *Orgel-Büchlein* and none of *Clavier-Übung* III.[32] Many of Bach's pupils were aiming to be organists, and their main concern was to be able to meet the requirements of competitions for organists' posts. These are listed by J.A. Scheibe (1745) as follows:

> a complete understanding of thoroughbass, including how to transpose, and to accompany music outside the church;
> to know all the chorales, how to play and register for them, harmonize and match the words;
> to be able to improvise well ('geschickt präludiren'), for which he needs to have insight and practice in composing;
> to understand organs and how to maintain, test, and report on them.[33]

This agrees with the description of Bach's composition teaching given by C.P.E. Bach in answer to Forkel's enquiry (Dok.III p.289, NBR p.399). Pupils began with strict four-part writing by adding parts to a figured bass, then by harmonizing chorale melodies (which must have included modal harmonic language; Kirnberger 1776, Dok.III pp.221–3; Burns 1995). They then began figural counterpoint with two-part fugues, 'and so on'. Improvisation ('präludiren, fantasiren') was traditionally taught also on figured-bass outlines (Niedt 1706, C.P.E. Bach 1762). For more advanced composition there is evidence that the sonatas with obbligato harpsichord provided models, in addition to the more obvious items, in that they elaborate on the figured-bass tradition. The sonatas with violin were among the first of Bach's works to be published in the nineteenth-century revival, by Nägeli in 1802 as part of a group of learned works including *The Well-tempered Clavier* and *The Art of Fugue*. Some of the leading examples we have of pupils' work are along these lines; in the variant upper parts added to the bass of the G major violin sonata BWV 1021 (BWV 1022, 1038), and the collaborations in BWV 1020 and 1033. This points again to the artificiality of dividing Bach's teaching into categories. It all took place in the composer's workshop, and concert items could be drawn in as models, just as learner's études could be worked up into performable items, as happened with the *Clavier-Büchlein* Praeludia when they were incorporated into *The Well-tempered Clavier*. At the same time the demonstrative function was an essential spur to the speculative side of Bach's nature. The rigorous exploration of materials in the Inventions is a step on the way to the ultimate speculations of the Canonic Variations and *The Art of Fugue*.

Of Bach's students the one who claimed to give the most detailed account of his teaching 'method', at least for composition, was Kirnberger, in *Die Kunst des reinen Satzes in der Musik* (Berlin 1771–9).[34] This certainly contains the elements outlined by C.P.E. Bach in more or less that order, but it is difficult to imagine Bach explaining every step of the way in quite such circumstantial detail, particularly since he taught only pupils who had already showed some talent for composition in written work before he took them on. Most relevant to the 48 are parts 2 and 3 of Volume II ('Von dem doppelten Contrapunct'), which explain a great deal more than just invertible counterpoint (they include canon, augmentation, diminution, and many points of detail in counterpoint) but notably lack anything about the devices of seventeenth-century learned counterpoint and rhythmopoeia described by Mattheson (1739). Mattheson better sums up the rich traditions that Bach grew up with, and which are fully reflected in his fugal works. Significant, though, is the number of extended examples that Kirnberger gives, many of them from Bach's works, and part 3 consists almost entirely of examples. This certainly relates to what we know of Bach's teaching of both composition and performance, in which he preferred to demonstrate by example than by verbal explanation. Many details of this may derive from Bach, but as a whole it is far too discursive and theoretical to be believable as a method through which Bach would have put all his pupils except in its most general outlines, which in any case correspond to the normal teaching practice of the time. Marpurg is undoubtedly right that the practical Bach would have adapted his teaching to the needs of individual pupils (Dok.III p.305, BR pp.449–50).

The two books of the 48 are unique in Bach's keyboard collections in the sheer range and variety of styles, genres, techniques that they contain, as outlined in the other chapters of this book. The variety of treatment is constant, whether of ways of dealing with fugues on several subjects, of combining fugue and dance, of combining principles of aria and sonata of the 1710s or the 1730s with other genres, and exhaustive exploration of traditional materials. No wonder his sons felt it futile to continue on his terrain, and went off to do something entirely different of their own.

PART TWO

Commentaries

CHAPTER SEVEN

Book I

Prelude and Fugue in C major BWV 846

PRELUDE The traditions that contribute to this type of prelude are outlined in Chapter Three section 4. One is of the toccata arpeggiata, which goes back at least to Kapsberger's examples for chitarrone (Rome, 1604). These are a kind of harmonic *recherche*, exploring sonorities of ties and dissonances, and so provide a plucked-string equivalent to organ toccatas *di durezze e ligature*, just as passages of bow tremolo in seventeenth-century Italian sonatas and concertos provide the equivalent for bowed-string instruments.

The other tradition is of beginners' preludes, designed to develop a relationship between hand and keyboard in basic chord shapes. Purcell wrote a brilliant little prelude of this type for the beginner's suite which opens *A Choice Collection of Lessons* (London 1696). Closer to Bach are similar preludes in J.C.F. Fischer's *Musicalischer Parnassus* (Augsburg 1738). The purpose of the arpeggiation is to provide a continuum of sound on a stringed instrument, which can be manipulated for expressive purposes. The temporal placing of notes is virtually the only means of making the harpsichord expressive, a fact upon which seventeenth-century French harpsichordists built their highly expressive style in terms of the *style brisé*. Whereas they were concerned mainly with melodic expression, where asymmetry and unpredictability in the breaking of chords were important for pointing up individual melodic notes, the regular patterning of Bach's type of prelude means that it is the harmonic structure which the player has to point up by means of subtle rubato. Part of this is savouring the stronger dissonances, such as the last-inversion major 7th chords at b.8 and b.16, which themselves have a structural function in giving impetus to key changes.

After that, the main performance issue is whether or not the right-hand broken chords should be sustained. David Schulenberg suggests that since Bach has carefully written them out as separate notes, they are intended to be played as such (1992 p.167). Had Bach wanted them sustained he need not have resorted to complicated dots and ties, but could simply have used the conventional tenuto slurs, as he did in other arpeggiated harpsichord movements such as the Siciliano of the C minor Violin Sonata BWV 1017, or the Andante of the Torelli concerto arranged for keyboard as BWV 979. Against this view must be set the tradition of this sort of prelude. Part of the art of making the harpsichord sound is the ability to repeat notes seamlessly, without any gap between them, so that the instrument rings with continuous sound. This essential feature of harpsichord technique is a knack that must be mastered, but composers generally did not trouble with the intricacy of notation (dots, ties, etc.) needed to express it exactly since what was required was well understood.[1] Fischer's very similar arpeggio preludes from his 'Clio' and 'Polymnia' suites (Ex.7.1; for 'Polymnia' see Ex.8.7) relate to a seventeenth-century tradition of notating as 'dry' effects that are meant to sound 'wet' ('baigné' in Debussy's terminology).[2] Thus in the 'Clio' prelude there are two levels of repetition: crotchet in the left hand and semiquaver in the right; 'Polymnia' is more sophisticated, with a third level of repetition (dotted minim) in the bass. Bach's pattern, though seemingly simple, is in fact more sophisticated still, since the addition of a fifth part to the harmony yields constant cross-rhythms between the repeated notes in the right-hand figuration. In the earliest version of this prelude the second note of each left-hand bar was notated as a plain semiquaver.[3]

Because of the very complex nature of Bach's mind, and of *The Well-tempered Clavier* in particular, much significance has been read into the C major prelude, and it is difficult to know quite how much is justified. On one level it is simply an elaboration of the most elementary form of improvisation.

Ex.7.1 J.C.F. Fischer: opening of Praeludium harpeggiato from 'Clio' suite (*Musicalischer Parnassus*).

Ex.7.2 gives figured-bass skeletons of the early and the final versions of the prelude.[4] The opening four-bar harmonic formula is one used particularly by Italian cantata composers from Carissimi onwards to articulate the opening sentence of a recitative. The first version (Ex.7.2a) continues with what is probably the most basic of all improvisation shapes, a descending bass scale. This is articulated by a station on the dominant halfway down, and a visit to the subdominant at the end, but there is no attempt at making a satisfying rhetorical structure. The final version is an excellent example of Bach's preferred method of perfecting pieces by addition rather than recomposition. It has a much stronger and more controlled shape, through the use of sequential repetition (bb.8–11, cf. 16–19), and by having consonant points of arrival which mark off the sentences of the piece (marked by commas in Ex.7.2b).[5]

Ex.7.2 Figured-bass outlines of the C major prelude: (a) first version; (b) final version.

The dominant pedal from b.24 is dramatized by the strong chromatic progression in bb.22–3 which delays arrival on the note g.[6] The final version therefore is constructed on the two commonest improvisation formulas for preludes going back to the earliest examples in Adam Ileborgh's tablature (1448): a descending scale and a pedal.

If, on a practical level, this prelude is concerned with developing the relation of hand to keyboard, on a symbolic level the triadic nature of the prelude could be seen as springing from the heavenly harmony, represented by the major triad (the first six notes of the harmonic series) from which, in Renaissance theory, all music grows. This 'perfect chord' was used with identical symbolism by Monteverdi at the opening of *Orfeo* and the 1610 Vespers, and ultimately by Wagner in *Das Rheingold*.[7] The neo-platonist background to this concept, from the Renaissance via Werckmeister to Bach's Erfurt relative Johann Heinrich Buttstett, has been discussed in Chapter Five section 4. In Buttstett's title-page (ill. 1) the motto Ut, Mi, Sol is the major triad, Re, Fa, La the minor, and these are indeed the two first triads of Bach's prelude. On a practical level one might say that the layout of the first two chords of the prelude, with the 3rds on top, is simply the most effective melodically for that progression. On a symbolic level one might point to the two melodic notes e'' and f'', and view them in the light of Bach's canon BWV 1078 (1749) on the old summary of major and minor: 'Fa Mi, et Mi Fa sunt tota musica', which can also be made to yield the notes BACH (Chafe 1991 Chapter 2). Some have gone further and derived the subject of the first fugue from the prelude (notably Werker 1922, J.N. David 1962) in that the top notes of the chords in bb.3–7 of the prelude outline the 6th–10th notes of the subject of the fugue.[8] All that can be said about this is that many preludes and fugues did not originate together. In this case the melodic outline in the prelude was not there originally, but was introduced in the final version (Dürr 1984 p.15).

Number symbolism has also been considered to have a bearing on both notation and performance. The bass tie in b.33 seems to have been added later to the autograph P 415, and there is no tie in b.34. The arguments for a numerical significance here seem too abstruse.[9] Although the first version, notated mostly in semibreve chords, shows no difference, the final version changes the right-hand pattern from half-bar to whole-bar units in bb.33–4, and so the correspondingly slower rate of bass repetition is logical and effective.[10]

One small point: in b.23 it is uncertain whether b or c' is the essential harmony note. Heinrich Schenker thought the c' unessential, since it would otherwise be decorated by its own resolution.[11] But the traditional rule for unfigured basses was that, when the bass steps down a semitone to a dominant, the minor 6th degree takes a 6/4/3 chord,[12] in which case the b is unessential. In Bach's sophisticated and often ambiguous harmony the option of a diminished-7th chord is by no means to be ruled out and the ambiguity may well be intentional.

FUGUE If the prelude is a study of chordal harmony, with the minimum of passing dissonances, the fugue is a study of line, or perhaps melody. The elements of the subject correspond excellently to the traditional elements of melody ('melopoeia') as given in Brossard's dictionary, where they are principally steps ('di grado'), leaps ('di salto'), and ties ('distendimento').[13] In addition, the notes of the subject outline what every choirboy learned in his first singing lesson, the notes of the natural hexachord.

Traditionally composers began demonstrations of learned counterpoint with works based on the hexachord. The first of Frescobaldi's 12 *Capricci* (1624) is 'sopra Ut, Re, Mi, Fa, Sol, La', exhibiting many devices of counterpoint including augmentation, diminution, and stretto. The first of Froberger's Fantasias (1649) has the same title and similar intent.[14] The fact that Bach has chosen to use canzona (black) note values rather than *stile antico* (white) ones brings this fugue into the orbit of another tradition, the verset fugue.[15] Verset fugues by their nature relate to the eight church modes, and therefore to the *stile antico*. This has a bearing on the layout of the exposition, in which the sequence of entries (*dux–comes–comes–dux*) has often been commented on as exceptional in Bach's practice. The notion proposed by Schenker that fugues are essentially complete in three parts and that a fourth part is added simply to cater for four vocal ranges may be justified for the *stile moderno* fugue based on figural treatment of harmony. It is not so applicable in the old style, where the exposition depends on presenting two versions of the subject (*dux*) in the authentic version of the mode, and two of the answer (*comes*) in the plagal version. Normally the cantus and tenor have the authentic tessitura, and the alto and bass the plagal tessitura (see Ex.7.24).[16] The sequence of entries of *dux* and *comes* thus depends simply on the order in which the voices enter, rather than on the tonal concept of alternating tonic subject and dominant answer. In this particular fugue the alto and bass have the *dux* and the cantus and tenor the *comes*. The reason for the sequence *dux–comes–comes–dux* is therefore simply the result of the series of voice entries alto–cantus–tenor–bass. The old modal procedure is common enough in verset fugues of Kerll and Fischer,[17] and has the advantage of making a neatly rounded exposition after which Bach can go straight into his first stretto section.

Verset fugues are typically concise, continuously thematic without episodes, and explore techniques of thematic integration such as stretto or other devices, as for example in Fuga 11 of Fischer's *Ariadne Musica* where the countersubject is the inversion of the subject. In the C major fugue Bach carries this principle of integration to its extreme in a fugue where hardly a single note is non-thematic. This stems from the fact that the three ingredients presented in bb.1–2 all relate to the interval of a 4th: first stepped out, then as leaps, then decorated in a semiquaver division similar to François Couperin's *évolution* for the 4th (see Chapter Six section 3). After the hexachord, the tetrachord is another rich reference in this subject. In the early years of the eighteenth century, theorists were reinterpreting the old Greek genera (diatonic, chromatic, enharmonic), which had been read in a modal context by Vicentino and Frescobaldi a century before, in terms of the emerging tonal system based on the circle of 5ths (see Chapter Five section 2). These genera were based on tetrachords, as Neidhardt (1706 p.15) explains. The *genus diatonicum* has a tetrachord of two whole tones and one semitone, and Neidhardt repeats the tag 'Mi & Fa Sunt tota Musica', intervals as prominent and defining in Bach's subject as they are at the opening of the prelude.

Two of these tetrachords give the major scale, so it is possible to read Bach's subject as a unification of *antico* hexachord with *moderno* tetrachord, the sum yielding the totality of 24 keys. Corelli, whose works provided classic models of balanced tonal structures, equally showed an interest in combining the traditional hexachord with the modern key system, as demonstrated in his first published trio sonata (Op.1 No.1, Rome 1681).[18] It is not clear precisely which works of Corelli Bach knew, but he does seem to have known the trio sonatas Op.3 (Rome 1689), since he used subjects from the fourth sonata in the double fugue for organ BWV 579.[19] The very brilliant 12th sonata (Corelli's last 'church' trio sonata) contains in its final two sections two subjects which Bach used, whether by accident or design, in Book I: the one given as Ex.7.3a, and one which will be discussed later with reference to the A major fugue. Bach had already used similar material in the very early fugue on a theme of Albinoni BWV 946 (Ex.7.3b).[20] Albinoni was a Roman-influenced Venetian composer, and the counterpoints to the descending syncopated scale in his very Corellian subject show how closely all these ingredients hang together as part of one of the commonest formulas of invertible counterpoint.

The pattern of 4ths and 5ths, like the circle of 5ths, is a specifically tonal feature, yet it also figures in Fux's *stile antico* demonstrations of fugue (1725).[21] This being so, all elements of Bach's subject may be read as either *antico* or *moderno*. There could be no more fitting introduction to a collection whose purpose is to demonstrate how the venerable techniques of contrapuntal composition can be reinterpreted and brought to life again in terms of the *modi moderni*.

A 'modern' feature favoured by Bach is the indefinite ending of the subject. Smend (1947 p.12) saw the e' in the middle of b.2 as the official end, since it was the 14th note (therefore sum of the letters BACH).[22] He may be right, but the semiquavers run on seamlessly under the second entry without cadencing on the tonic note. The fugue pursues integration principally by means of stretto, but also by the possible combinations of the subject with its semiquaver

Ex.7.3 (a) Corelli: from Op.3 No.12, Allegro bars 1–2½;
(b) Albinoni: in BWV 946 bars 15–19.

continuation. These were listed by Kirnberger (1777a pp.192–3; Dok.III p.231) as in Ex.7.4. Of them Bach uses all but the inversion at the 12th.[23]

In formal structures Bach seems generally to have preferred the harmonic proportions ½, ⅓, and ¼, with sections clearly marked by cadences.[24] The fugue's 27 bars have a main division half-way (b.14). Each half is then divided roughly at the quarter mark, giving four expositions, each of six or seven bars and each with a clear and separate function.[25] This gives an episodeless exposition fugue of conservative design, but clearly related to the verset tradition. The functions of the sections are:

bb.1–7, exposition;

bb.7–14, close stretto at the 4th below (b.7) and 5th above (b.10); in addition, this section moves to the relative minor and explores more dissonant harmony, a necessary contrast to what could otherwise be a collection of bland diatonic combinations (as in Ex.7.4);

bb.14–19, triple stretto (bb.14–15), followed by quadruple stretto (bb.15ff);

bb.19–27, stretti over pedals: it has often been noted that this section is harmonically articulated by having a brief pedal on the supertonic at b.19, a

Ex.7.4 Kirnberger: combinations of the subject and its continuation.

longer one on the dominant at bb.21–2, and the longest on the tonic from b.24 to the end. This second half of the fugue has 14 entries, with one on each of the 7 *tone*. The final two bars, recalling the scale at the end of Froberger's Lament for Ferdinand IV, seem to be a *jeu d'esprit*, being the fulfilment of climbing steps, perhaps up to Parnassus, or to Buttstett's Shekinah. Or perhaps just because Bach likes to dissolve the intensity of dense contrapuntal argument into simple scale patterns at the end (as in the G major fugue, or the A major prelude).

The single most important revision Bach made to this fugue was the addition of a dot to the fourth note of the subject.[26] This greatly improves the clarity of the counterpoint, and also clarifies the upbeat nature of the first three notes of the subject: in the original version (given in NBA V/6.1 pp.128–9, BA I pp.6–7) it sounds as if the first six notes are all an upbeat to e'. Bach added the dot in the third round of revisions of P 415, probably after 1736. He then had to make changes in b.9, b.12, and b.15, which he did in this round and the final round (probably *c.*1740). Editors have bridled at some of Bach's final thoughts (given by Dürr and Jones), but they can be seen as genuine enhancements: the jagged cantus line at b.12 heightens the harmonic intensity of this passage; and the attractive variant of the subject in the bass at b.15 (designed to avoid the effect of a rising 7th in the cantus if the subject was in its normal form) is fully in the verset fugue tradition of fluid and free thematic moulding.

Prelude and Fugue in C minor BWV 847

PRELUDE This is second in the series of technical-exercise Praeludia in Wilhelm Friedemann's *Clavier-Büchlein*. The C major prelude practises chord shapes in their most basic form, with next to no dissonant decorative notes; the C minor brings thumb and fifth finger into equality with the three middle fingers, reflecting the move in the early decades of the 18th century towards treating all fingers as equal.[27] The prelude may also be seen as a model of improvisation along the lines of Niedt's *Handleitung zur Variation* (Hamburg 1706) in which the technique of improvised variations is practised by decorating a given figured bass with different figuration patterns (Chapter VI). Types of semiquaver figuration patterns (*figurae*) are discussed by J.G. Walther in his composition tutor (1708), the pattern used in this prelude being one with a dissonant third note (ed. Benary p.151).[28] More to the point, perhaps, are the patterns given by Niedt (Chapter II) for decorating simple intervals, starting with the unison and working up to the octave, a method for practising the technique of ornamentation that goes back to Ortiz and Ganassi in the mid-sixteenth century.

Attempts have been made to read the first five of the *Clavier-Büchlein* Praeludia as variations on a common harmonic basis in the sense of Niedt's instructions.[29] There is an element of validity in this, but the harmonic bases of the preludes relate to each other only in a general way. This prelude begins with a different formula from the C major's (Ex.7.5). In the two-part Inventions, where Bach worked systematically through standard opening gambits, this one occurs in the B flat major. Thereafter the C minor prelude has the same principle of scalic descent in the bass to a dominant pedal, but whereas the C major had a number of stations defined by root position triads, the C minor has only one, on the relative major (E flat, b.14). And whereas the C major uses a variety of chord types, the C minor concentrates on various uses of the last-inversion dominant 7th and the diminished 7th: the progression alternating 2 and 6 chords is a standard way of harmonising a descending bass scale.

In this, the variants for b.18 are instructive. Bach ultimately opted for c as the first bass note, and B♭ as the ninth, but the earlier versions show other thoughts about arranging these two notes in the left-hand figuration (NBA V/5 p.21; V/6.1 p.131, p.245). The trouble is that various copyists did not notice the B♭ half-way through the bar, and mechanically copied the figuration as it had been till then, with c also as the ninth note. This reading, adopted by Kroll on grounds of 'consistency', is the worst possible one. Bach went out of

Ex.7.5 Prelude in C minor: figured-bass abstract of the earliest version.

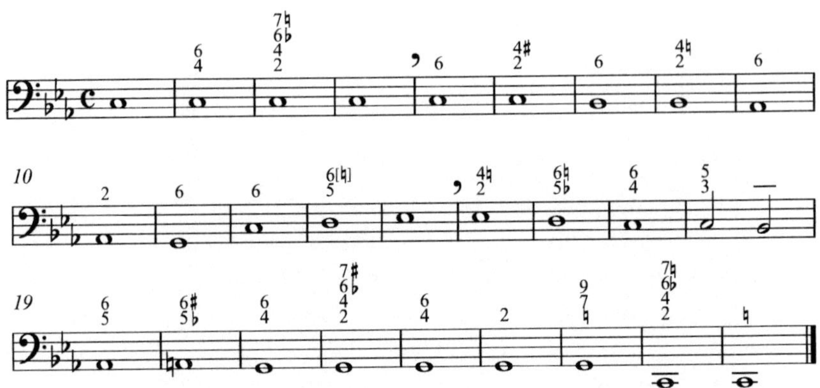

his way to emphasise the passing nature of this C minor chord, and particularly sought to avoid the effect of arrival on a root-position tonic at this point, since it would undermine the dramatic arrival on the dominant pedal at b.21.

Bach's conversion of this piece into something more than an étude was done with his usual economy, mainly by adding extra bars rather than recasting existing ones. The first version went straight from b.25 to b.35, and then ended with one bar of C major (totalling 27 bars). An intermediate stage (NBA V/6.1 pp.244–5) had the Presto/Adagio cadenza, but not quite the last three bars (37 bars). The P 415 version adjusts the right-hand figuration of the last bar to end on the 3rd of the chord on the weakest beat, giving a less final effect than an arpeggio going down to the bottom note of the keyboard. It seems another case of Bach's ultimate adjustments to the prelude being designed to allow the fugue to grow naturally from it, which it now does by having the first three notes of the subject sounded at the same pitch in the last bar of the prelude.

In adding the concert ending (bb.26 to the end) Bach has taken the dry finger-exercise figure and made of it a brilliant toccata figuration, as if this was the real-life situation for which the first was preparing. It expands on the change of figuration to cadenza style at b.25 and, as Siegfried Hermelink has well expressed it, the new ending enlarges the emotional scope of the piece by making a world of passion and rhetoric break in on the measured discipline ('Fleiß') of the original étude (1976 p.58).

One final point, Bach's original note values for b.34, last quaver, are , rather than the notationally more correct which dates from no earlier than Schwenke's copy. It is right that note values should add up, but equally the word Adagio implies the freedom of recitative. An accelerando was conventionally notated by reducing note values, and it would be wrong to treat these two bars with stiff, pedantic exactitude.

FUGUE This must be one of Bach's most written-about pieces. On one hand its triple counterpoint and developmental episodes made it a model for the 'examination fugue'. On the other it is something of an analysis warhorse, particularly since its harmonic scheme might be seen to prefigure the events of Classical sonata form. It is a tribute to the subtlety and flexibility of Bach's structures that so many different formal prototypes (sonata, concerto, dance, even the old German *Barform*[30]) can be read into it.

The subject has a strong feeling of rhythmic character, but there does not seem to be any particular traditional expression associated with it and it does not figure in the rhythmopoeia lists of Mattheson or Printz.[31] It has been compared to the anapaest phase (♬♩♪) of the Lullian chaconne/passacaille, as in the C minor organ passacaglia BWV 582,[32] but conventions of French style have no bearing on this fugue. More germane is a traditional seventeenth-century pattern used, for example, by Johann Krieger in Ex.7.6,[33] and also much used in Bach's early keyboard toccatas.

The point of the figure here is to engineer a series of interlocking imitations, a tradition going back to Frescobaldi. The general principle was used by Bach in, for example, Contrapunctus I of *The Art of Fugue*. That is not the case in the C minor fugue, but it is entirely in line with Bach's objective of modernising traditional techniques for this to be one strand feeding into this fugue.

The direct model is plainly a rhythm used in Venetian concertos, particularly the second movement of Benedetto Marcello's Op.1 No.2 in E minor (Venice 1708), arranged by Bach for clavier as BWV 981 in C minor; and in the fugal third section of Vivaldi's Op.3 No.11 (Amsterdam 1712), arranged by Bach for organ as BWV 596. The counterpoint in the Marcello movement is

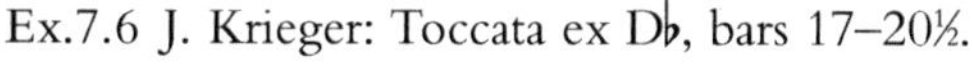

Ex.7.6 J. Krieger: Toccata ex D♭, bars 17–20½.

of the simplest, but the recurring pattern that rises chromatically from the dominant to the tonic may have a bearing on the pattern in bb.5–6 of the C minor fugue. Vivaldi provided a stronger model, and one that obviously appealed very much to Bach on account of its driving rhythmic energy, and its free and inventive, yet developmental, use of quadruple counterpoint. The driving energy is in the A minor fugue of Book I, and perhaps to a lesser extent here.[34] Bach was undoubtedly fond of this rhythm, at least around 1720, since he uses it also in the D major and F major Sinfonias, both of which feature triple counterpoint.[35]

In these uses of triple counterpoint, Bach is not at all concerned to demonstrate mechanically all six possible permutations. That had been done by Italian pioneers in the seventeenth century when the concept was new, and by seventeenth-century German figures such as Reinken, whose permutation trios Bach virtually recomposed when transferring them to clavier. Even Purcell's permutation trios, though much more inventive than Reinken's, share something of his stiffness. With Bach, a subtle and flexible treatment of form and a maturity in adjusting details for optimum sonority are the objectives, in order to show that traditional techniques which are intellectually satisfying need not be stiff and pedantic. The block of triple counterpoint (usefully described by Laurence Dreyfus as a 'fugal complex') is revealed in bb.7–8, and the sequence of composition is quite clear: idea 1 is in the bass, 2 (contrasting with it in regular quavers) in the cantus, and 3 (which mops up unused notes) in the middle. The block is harmonically satisfying in alternating the tonic with two chords using the note A flat, the second tenser than the first: in b.7 it is the 3rd of F minor, in b.8 the 7th of the diminished 7th. Bach emphasises this harmonic structure over the final pedal. The interest lies in what he does with idea 3, the filler part. At b.12 he changes its shape to give fuller sonority; at b.20 he transposes its first notes in the bass down an octave from the earlier version (NBA V/6.1 p.133) in order to lend weight to the return to the tonic. The best use is in the final appearance of the block at bb.27–8. He had used ideas 1 and 2 twice each as cantus, but idea 3 is weak in this position because of its upward 4th leap at the end, which is more like a cadential bass part. As always, Bach succeeds in making a shining virtue of necessity and turns this potential weakness to dramatic effect by adding a double appoggiatura and a rhetorical pause (b.28½).[36] Fugue in the 17th century was regarded as a play of wit, not pedantry, and as with Haydn, so with Bach, the tradition continued.

Structurally, Bach is concerned to show how the old technique of triple counterpoint need not be stiff, but can be treated in a free and inventive 'modern' way. A number of prototypes feed into this, which is why it can be looked at in a number of different ways and why the dogmatic exclusiveness of some approaches is too limiting. This is one of the clearest examples of the invention principle, in which all the material, including the countersubjects, grows from the subject. In this respect it is one of the most densely developmental fugues, much more so than, for example, the C sharp major fugue which is on a similar plan. The concerto ritornello principle also plays a part, with the block of triple counterpoint functioning as the ritornello, and with entries separated by 'interludes' (Bach's term).[37]

Heinrich Schenker perceives the sections of this fugue as based on three *Urlinie* descents, two of a 5th (bb.1–9 and 9–20) and one of an octave (bb.20–29).[38] This has the merit of underlining the central phase of increased harmonic tension, particularly from b.15, and bringing together the long tonic section from b.20, in which there is undoubtedly an element of reprise. In spite of Schenker's claim to be uncovering a hidden, organic form beneath the surface details, his analysis has a curious similarity to Riemann's ternary structures, just as Schenker's perception of the C major prelude as a series of four-bar phrases seems to impose a Classical model on a structure more fluid and varied than he allows for. There does seem a certain artificiality in reading back historically structural principles which override those of Bach's own time and his own clear signposts. Bach later favoured a sonata type with a reprise, but at this stage tended to use the standard procedure of running the same ideas from dominant back to tonic in the second half, with development and harmonic intensification, as he had from tonic to dominant in the first half (see Chapter Three section 6). This gives a binary shape in which events after the double bar correspond to those before it. The mirror-image relationship between the two sections is most rigorously explored by Bach in the E minor fugue of Book I; the C minor fugue treats it more freely.

In this key the tonic is both the top and bottom notes of the four-octave keyboard, and Bach as usual exploits keyboard range and pitch levels for structural articulation. The opening is in the middle c'–c" octave; the half-way point (b.15) is marked by the top c"', answered by the bottom C at the end. The second section (bb.15–31) is clearly conceived as a unit since it contains a complete exposition, with idea 1 in successively the middle (b.15), cantus (b.20), and bass (b.26) parts, just as in the first exposition. In addition, each event in this section corresponds to an event in the first section, generally with some intensification or reinterpretation. The entry at b.15 is the unstable, modulating version of the basic block, corresponding to bb.3–4; the little codetta of bb.5–6, which prepared the bass entry of the exposition, is greatly intensified in bb.17–20 by being inverted at the 12th, so raising the harmonic tension level by giving rise to cross-relations and other dissonances. Contributing to the raised dissonance level are the consecutive major 3rds in b.17, third beat, etc. These were frowned on in seventeenth-century *stile antico* since they outline the tritone, and were correspondingly 'corrected' in some sources (b♮ auxiliary in the bass at b.17, third beat; e'♮ in the alto in b.18, first beat). From b.20 the tension level subsides with the return of the tonic. The fact that the interlude from bb.22–5 does not modulate, as the corresponding phase at bb.9–10 did, gives a feeling of reprise. Bars 25–6 are effectively a dominant pedal whose irregular shape pleasingly delays the final bass entry to the second half of the bar. It is noteworthy that Bach in the second section, in addition to raising the harmonic tension level, also introduces unsymmetrical shapes at bb.17–20 and 25–6, getting away from the two-bar periodicity of the basic material.

Prelude and Fugue in C sharp major BWV 848

PRELUDE This prelude was twice revised. An early version of 68 bars (NBA V/6.1 pp.134–5) was expanded in the lost autograph draft (reflected in the *Clavier-Büchlein* version) to 104 bars. This version was also entered into P 415, where it was revised in details at two later stages.

In Book II the C sharp prelude exists in early versions in C major, but there is no evidence that the Book I prelude was composed other than in C sharp. Hermann Keller (1976 p.56) thought that its being in C sharp rather than D flat was evidence of a C major original, since it would be just a matter of adding the new key signature and adjusting the accidentals. Other pieces in Book I, such as the D sharp minor fugue and the G sharp minor prelude, show signs of having been transposed into advanced keys in this way. But there are no tell-tale signs here, as for example natural signs for B or E having been changed from flats. The normal name for the tonic note on the keyboard in Bach's time was cis, whether C♯ or D♭ was meant. In 1697 Werckmeister had prophesied a time when the art of music would be so advanced that players would be indifferent as to whether they played 'aus dem c. oder cis' (p.36). These two keys are expressed as opposites (all sharps as opposed to no sharps) and it is likely that Bach aimed at providing a piece to demonstrate this point. Its very lively character, in comparison with the C major prelude, is one of the factors in Book I that may point to a slightly unequal temperament.

The early version of this prelude, as that of the D minor prelude of Book II, shows Bach as a teacher providing a brilliant-sounding piece which is yet easy to play. The success of the final version as a brilliant Solfeggio in an extraordinary key is attested by a number of isolated copies of the prelude without the fugue, made by C.P.E. Bach and others (KB V/6.1 p.97). It is based on a common elementary exercise involving expanding broken intervals, suitable for singers, or keyboard or string players. The early version suggests this in its three versions of the opening figure. The original form may well have been that of b.9 (Ex.7.7a); it then became as in b.1 (b), perhaps in order to demonstrate the C sharp major handshape ('Griff') with the thumb on a raised note;

Ex.7.7 Prelude in C sharp major, versions of the opening figure in the early version at: (a) bar 9, (b) bar 1, (c) bar 25 (all given in C sharp major).

and ended as in b.25 (c) which follows more naturally from the preceding b♯ (see KB V/6.1 p.314).

Hugo Riemann (1890 I p.15), in accordance with his eight-bar phrase theory, puts an accent on the g''♯ in b.3, and that is one aspect of the opening phrase. But it does not do justice to the subtlety of Bach's phrase moulding in that the phrase also grows to the top a''♯, which will be the tensest third (apart from e''♯) in an unequal tuning. The left hand complements the right in having the same principle of interval contraction and expansion, worked in double counterpoint, with a hemiola to round off the phrase. The very elementary nature of this finger-exercise pattern goes well with the principle of playing everything as well in C sharp as in C, and with Bach's policy as a teacher to make 'little connected pieces' from such patterns.

The early version of the prelude fits very well the description of a 'little connected piece', being on a very simple scheme. An opening section presents four permutations of the opening eight-bar phrase, going up a sequence of rising 5ths (C♯ G♯ D♯ A♯); a middle section (from b.31), based on the hemiola figure, has more rapid harmonic change and contrapuntal interchange (4 bars); and a reprise (b.47) starts on the subdominant, whose answer is then in the tonic. The final six-bar dominant pedal of this version seems too short to end a piece consisting otherwise entirely of eight- or four-bar phrases, a feature which Bach rectified in the second version.

In the longer version Bach brilliantly expanded this study to a satisfying concert piece by means of a single insertion (bb.63–98). Essentially this is a long extension of the final dominant pedal, but it also takes the finger pattern of expanding intervals and turns it into a much more sophisticated and 'modern' *batterie* such as Rameau used in his 1724 *Pieces de clavessin*. In itself it has the same ternary shape as the original, with bb.63–72 reprised an octave lower at bb.87–96. The long-spun-out pedal and the brilliant style give the addition the effect of a cadenza, particularly since it breaks the eight- and four-bar phrase pattern with longer (ten-bar) and shorter (one- or two-bar) units. The adjustment of the final phrase from six bars to eight then gives a neat feeling of conclusion. Bach's later revisions to the prelude mainly involve conforming all appearances of the opening bar to the pattern of Ex.7.7c, and decorating the bass hemiola at b.8 with semiquavers on all its appearances.

One performance point: the cadential chords in the second last bar of this prelude are similar to those in the F major organ toccata BWV 540/1. Peter Williams (1984 p.203) notes staccato dashes over the quaver chords in one source of the toccata (P 290, from the C.P.E. Bach circle).

FUGUE This is one of Bach's sunniest fugues, without any of the hypertension one might expect from the extraordinary key.[39] Natalie Jenne (1974) convincingly analyses its rhythmic character, in accordance with Kirnberger's principles, as a bourrée. In which case its beginning on the second half of the bar is remarkable. It seems that Bach wished to emphasise the lightness of the subject, and also the fact that it ends firmly on the tonic on a main beat (b.3), an equivalent of a full stop which he usually sought to avoid in such *stile moderno* pieces, and a feature which he richly exploits in this fugue

Supposed thematic connexions between preludes and fugues are not always convincing, but there are in this case striking similarities between the opening of the prelude and the subject of the fugue, which have been noted by many commentators: both the early version of the prelude (Ex.7.7b) and the fugue subject open with a prominent rising 6th; the 3rd leap e"#–c"# comes next in both cases; and the 6th and 7th leaps in the left-hand part in bb.5–7 of the prelude are closely paralleled at the end of the subject. The subject is in fact very neatly constructed out of the basic materials of the prelude, which it shows to be all related in that the 3rd leap e"#–c"# in b.1 is answered by the 6th leaps in b.2. It is of course possible that the fugue came first, though this is unlikely in view of the elementary finger-exercise material on which the prelude is based. The fugue takes the handshapes of a technical study and converts them into a musical *jeu d'esprit.*

The first section of the fugue (bb.1–12) grows in the most natural and good-humoured way from the emphatic descending scale outline (notes 5–1) at the end of the subject. The answer (bb.4–5) continues it on down to g#, and the bass entry (bb.6–7) carries it down to c#. The principle of having a firm root-position chord at the beginning of each bar is then continued through an episode (bb.7–10) in which further scale steps continue on down to G# (b.10) for an entry of the subject in the dominant (Renwick 1995 p.15). This descending scale element defines and unifies a coherent section of varied events which is repeated da capo from b.42 to finish off the fugue. There the episode is adjusted to lead the bass down to the bottom C# of the keyboard (b.51) and a final entry in the tonic rather than the dominant. The fact that the subject ends firmly on the tonic note gives rise to this structural development. Bach equally exploits the feature dramatically by having the bass land on the root of a diminished 7th chord at b.13, swinging the harmony off into the first new direction of the central development of the fugue.

This is a good example of Bach's favourite combination of fugue with concerto da capo structure.[40] There has been much debate about the extent to which episodes may be seen as separate from expositions/ritornellos. The issue is not clear-cut, as anybody who has tried to work out manual changes for one of the concerto-form preludes of the English Suites, or organ fugues, will know. With a block of triple counterpoint, as in this fugue, the ritornello element does take an unusually definite form but, within the clearly defined sections, there are heirarchies in the structural independence of different episodes.

Prelude and Fugue in C sharp minor BWV 849

PRELUDE The last three of the group of four preludes in advanced keys in W.F. Bach's *Clavier-Büchlein* (C sharp, E flat and F minors) are of cantabile character, and are presumably meant for developing an expressive manner of playing after the earlier finger-exercise pieces. The C sharp minor prelude seems to build on the E major prelude (its relative major) in that the E major is an exercise in expressive melodic projection in a simple texture (one part in the right hand, two in the left). The C sharp minor is more sophisticated in demanding as much expressive sensitivity but in a more complex texture, often of four parts with two parts in the right hand. Bach's concern for expression and playability in this more complex texture is evident from the alterations to the detail of inner parts which he made in the later version, which allow a more natural shaping of the top part and also improve the profile of the inner parts.

Bach seems here to be providing an exercise for a problem of rhythm which is very common in his keyboard works. The siciliano rhythm ♩.♪♩ has a characteristic lilt that depends on slightly delaying the quaver; yet at the same time it has to combine with the six-quaver group ♫♫♫.[41] A quaver group such as this would not in any case be played absolutely evenly, with no rhythmic shaping. It needs a subtle combination of pairing with larger-scale projection of the whole group by lingering slightly on the first note of the six. This then coincides with the accented dotted crotchet of the siciliano rhythm. The rhythmic moulding of the quavers is the key to the expressive projection of this piece, particularly on the harpsichord which has little other expressive possibility than rhythmic placing.[42] This is an essential ingredient in the long and powerful build-up from b.19 to b.35. Most bars have the siciliano rhythm in the first half and only quavers in the second. The climax is worked on the old principle of putting one rhythmic unit end to end with itself continuously: the siciliano rhythm in the bass at bb.30–1, going down to the lowest note of the keyboard, then a long continuous shape of quavers in bb.32–4, falling into the final cadence. It was obviously to provide a satisfactory winding down from this extraordinary paragraph that Bach added bb.35–8 to the final version, by returning to the alternation of the two figures of the opening.

The additions Bach made to the final version do not radically change the shape of the piece, as they do in the C sharp major prelude, but are concerned with rounding out and setting off the fundamental sonata shape of an opening section of three phases, ending in the dominant (b.14), and a longer second section which visits other keys before returning to the tonic. Part of the highly unified and gripping character of the second section results from the unusual feature of so much of it being a prolonged dominant of C sharp minor. The subdominant at b.24, intensified by the Neapolitan d'♮, is part of the build-up to the top note of the keyboard in b.25, the b"♯ being part of the strong resolution of the Neapolitan 6th on to the diminished 7th. Not least of the glories of this piece is the masterly use of keyboard compass: the build-up to the highest note at bb.24–5 being matched by the long phrase down to the lowest note in bb.28–31. The alterations to b.11 cure a bar which previously was somewhat bald contrapuntally, and by transferring the quaver movement to the bass part set off more effectively the plunge to low C♯ at b.12. The addition of bb.14½–16½ introduces a moment of more relaxed two-bar periodicity (bb.15–18) before the long-spun-out development of the second section.

Alterations of detail seem mainly concerned with playability. Bar 25 has the distinction of containing the one and only fingering instruction in the autograph P 415: the number 5 on the third bass note, seemingly for a player with small hands. According to Dürr it was probably added at the A4 stage of revision, and there is no reason to suppose it was not added by Bach (KB V/6.1 p.218). On the other hand the tie a'♯–a'♯ in the cantus bb.11–12 was definitely not added by Bach, and was not entered into P 415 until 1861. It is, however, in many of the earlier copies (KB V/6.1 p.217). It is possible that Bach had various thoughts about this. In the early version the a' will be sounded since it is part of a sequence of right-hand quavers; on the other hand the first quaver in equivalent groups is tied, in the bass at b.12 and in the cantus at b.13, as well as at b.11 of the early version. It looks as if the omission of the tie may have been an oversight, particularly since it detracts from the importance of the low C♯: it is given by Dürr, but not by Kroll or Jones.

Bach entered the arpeggiation signs in bb.3, 8 and 34 when he first copied P 415; all the rest date from the A4 revision. It must be remembered that arpeggiation is a normal part of harpsichord technique when not notated, and when a positive indication is given, virtually all tables of ornaments explain it in terms of rhythmically notated chord spreads, not just a quick separation. The arpeggiations should therefore be treated sensitively as part of the expressive language of the piece. Hans Klotz's theory that Bach was careful to indicate the intended direction of chord spreads, using François Couperin's (1713) system of a hook at the top of the spread sign for a downward spread, and a hook at the bottom for an upward spread, will be discussed below with reference to the E flat minor prelude. The only seeming case for a downward spread is in b.29, though the effect is harmonically weak and it is by no means clear that a lower hook has not got mixed in with the ♯ sign for the b. One final point about ornaments: the cantus d''♯ at the beginning of b.16 seems to want an appoggiatura, being the lower note of a falling 3rd. There are appoggiaturas here in only two sources, of which the closest to Bach is Altnickol's 1755 copy P 402. Against an appoggiatura is the fact that the b.16 figure is thematic, and also is repeated in sequence at b.18. Nonetheless, a lack was evidently felt since some early sources add an e'' passing quaver to the last crotchet in the cantus of b.15 (KB V/6.1 p.218). All in all, it looks as if Bach ultimately intended this figure to be played as notated in P 415, with no appoggiatura or passing note.

FUGUE In this Book each group of four keys is rounded off by a substantial piece. This fugue is extraordinarily rich, not just in its musical working, but also in its range of stylistic and expressive reference. It belongs to the seventeenth-century tradition of mannered *stile antico* counterpoint for keyboard (ricercar/fantasia/capriccio), a genre dedicated to demonstrating learned devices such as the combination of several subjects, often with some mannered chromaticism, and sometimes with use of supposed Greek genera, or *oblighi*, or *inganni* (see Chapter Four section 8). Several of these feature in this fugue.

Most obviously, it has three subjects that combine in triple counterpoint. Bach was infinitely resourceful in dealing with fugues on several subjects (see Chapter Four section 7). In the Ricercar in G 'a 3 Suietti' by the Dresden capellmeister Nicolaus Adam Strungk (1640–1700), which has virtually the same first subject as Bach's albeit in the major mode, Strungk introduces his second and third subjects in a separate 'Stanza 2da' in the seventeenth-century sectional manner.[43] By contrast, Bach's fugue is extraordinarily organic and continuous, though with its phases clearly marked off by perfect cadences: Subject 1 has its own exposition; Subject 2, with running quavers, is introduced in b.35 and instantly combined with Subject 1; Subject 3, with emphatic repeated crotchets, enters at b.49, starting a long section that presents permutations of the triple counterpoint. The final section (from b.94) does not use Subject 2, but builds a climax from simultaneous stretti of Subjects 1 and 3.

The subjects admirably fulfil the requirement of triple counterpoint that each should have a distinct character. This is partly the result of Bach's combining here two styles of seventeenth-century fugue: the *fuga major*, in the *stylus gravis* with white note values, written in open score; and the *fuga minor*, the canzona or verset fugue, in black (*stile moderno*) note values, written in keyboard score (see Riedel 1980). The use of three different types of note value between the three subjects yields a dramatic contrast. The issue of keyboard score is important in this fugue, since it could not be written out satisfactorily in open score. In the autograph at b.96 the first cantus note is a semibreve f''♯, giving a theoretical six parts in the second half of that bar. This was 'corrected' by Kroll and Dürr to a minim, but is given as Bach intended by Jones. It is obviously necessary as part of the sequence of stretti of Subject 1 between the top three parts: the first two statements lack the last note of the subject (beginning on e" at b.94, and b' in the second half of b.95); the third entry (starting on f'♯ in the second half of b.96) is also incomplete, but this is not so noticeable since it goes straight into Subject 3. The semibreve f"♯ in b.96 is thus answered by the semibreve c"♯ in b.97, and this is an important part of the effect since the part-crossing proposed by Kroll will obscure the alto entry in b.95–6 by sounding as if the alto d"♮ in b.96 (third note of the subject) was a cantus note. This freedom is part of the keyboard-score fugue. Various efforts have been made (notably by Toch 1940–48) to torture the parts in bb.100–7 to yield entries of Subject 1. It is true that the first three notes are present in the tenor at bb.100–1, but the d'♯–c'♯ crotchets in the second alto at b.102 cannot realistically be a continuation of the same part. Similarly, the notes c'♯ | b♯ e' | d'♯ | c'♯ appear variously between the two alto parts in bb.104–7. Rather than requiring the parts to be rewritten, these should be seen as two cases of the subject migrating between parts, a procedure common enough in French organ fugues, as part of the build-up to the full and prominent entry in the cantus at b.107.

The freedoms in the treatment of Subject 1 apply equally to the other two subjects. Bach no doubt admired the living quality of Frescobaldi's contrapuntal parts, which interchange and develop shapes in a free and flexible way. It is in fact the non-thematic moments, where shapes are freely moulded, which are the development and the principal delight of such counterpoint. Frescobaldi's *Fiori musicali*, of which Bach possessed a manuscript copy, is perhaps the ultimate example of this mastery. One manifestation of this here is the way in which one subject flows into another, as the quavers of Subject 2 flow into the minims of Subject 1 in bb.48–9, or the head of Subject 3 leads off the quavers of Subject 2 in bb.65–6. Ultimately Bach took this principle of constant growth and development to a level and intensity not previously achieved, and which links the counterpoint of the late Renaissance to the techniques of development of the later 18th and 19th centuries. The countersubject in the bass at bb.4–7 takes the interval of the 4th in the subject and fills it in various ways. In fact, the crotchet and quaver shapes in this countersubject provide the material for the rest of this first section, and also for the essential ingredients of Subjects 2 and 3. In this way it can be said that all the variety and difference of the fugue unfold from the original subject, more subtly and remarkably in a long fugue in this style than in the more concise and obvious 'modern'-style fugues.

The subject, in *stile antico* note values and containing the interval of a diminished 4th, belongs to the type with some mannered chromaticism, whether by step or by leap (*passus* or *saltus duriusculus*). Of dissonant leaps in this type of piece the diminished 4th was in the seventeenth century probably the most common (Constantini 1967 p.179). It is the most starkly expressive interval of the *seconda pratica.* From the expressive point of view, many have pointed to the chiastic shape of the subject, and the fact that Bach used this shape to express the word 'crucify' ('kreuzigen') in the St. Matthew Passion, as it had been in the seventeenth century by composers such as Schütz and Kerll.[44] Other intervals have of course the same shape, such as the diminished 3rd in the second Kyrie of the B minor Mass, or the notes BACH themselves. The diminished 4th has the advantage of combining the cross motif with the notion of salvation ('Heil'),[45] a conjunction emphasised by the chorale 'Nun komm der Heiden Heiland', Luther's German simplification of the plainsong hymn 'Veni Redemptor gentium'. The chorale is normally in the 17th-century organist's Mode II, i.e. Hypodorian on G with a one-flat key signature (Ex.7.8a). Strictly, the 7th degree should be natural, but is sometimes given a *ficta* sharp (as in the opening chorus of BWV 61, and the organ chorale prelude BWV 660). Peter Williams has pointed out a connexion with the little organ fughetta BWV 699, which has this chorale's first phrase with the natural 7th, but goes on to combine it with Subject 3 of the C sharp minor fugue (Ex.7.8b).[46] This subject has a tie in the chorale-prelude version, which is present inconsistently in many early sources of the fugue, and some late ones (KB V/6.1 pp.221, 320). In the autograph the tie survives only at bb.71–2, perhaps as an oversight since there is no reason why this entry should be any different from the one in bb.67–8. The emphatic version of Subject 3, without

Ex.7.8 (a) chorale melody 'Nun komm der Heiden Heiland', opening phrase; (b) from the chorale fughetta BWV 699.

the tie, is clearly what Bach finally intended since the dramatic effect of the final accumulation of stretti (bb.94ff) depends on the crotchets being repeated into a dissonance. It is nonetheless interesting to see Bach at an earlier stage building up an equivalent series of stretti at the end of BWV 699. If we are fanciful we may see Bach, as an act of devotion, representing Christ on the cross ('Ave verum corpus') in Subject 1; the nails and the spear ('cujus latus perforatus') in Subject 3; and streams of healing ('unda fluxit sanguine') in Subject 2. After all, Biber used virtually the same symbols in his Crucifixion Sonata. Or it may be Bach, with his vast experience of dealing with these materials, stringing them together with supreme skill merely as a demonstration for the benefit of students and connoisseurs, as Purcell brings out his most harrowing effects in the demonstration aria 'Tis Nature's voice'.

The diminished 4th outline of this subject is a commonplace in seventeenth-century fantasias, verset fugues, hence fugues in ensemble pieces such as concertos.[47] A further seventeenth-century type, one which also derives from Italian mannerism of around 1600, is the Grave which is one of the very standardised movement types in Corelli's Op.6 concertos (Ex.7.9a). This is in the manner of the toccata/fantasia with tied notes and dissonances (*di durezze e ligature*) which was normally played on two unison 8' diapasons with tremulant at the Elevation in the Mass. The shape of this subject is the standard one for climbing sequences of suspensions, which Corelli exploits very effectively, building up the texture from the bass, with increasingly strong dissonances at higher pitches, and culminating in a minor 2nd between the top two parts in b.4. When Georg Muffat, in the concertos he dedicated to Corelli (*Armonico tributo*, 1682), used this type of movement he, typically for a German composer taking over Italian ideas, developed the principle more systematically, building up a more densely contrapuntal climax towards the end of the movement. Muffat also uses a five-part texture (Ex.7.9b).

The characteristic feature of building this type of movement up from the bass may be behind the organisation of Bach's exposition. A crucial difference, though, is the rhythmic organisation of Bach's subject, where the upper note of the diminished 4th is on an offbeat, therefore cannot be used for building up suspensions. That function is taken by Subject 3, which provides the climax of the fugue (bb.94ff) on just this principle. What may be in Bach's mind is another learned device of *artificioso* composition, the *inganno*. He does not use this device to generate new subjects, as Frescobaldi does.[48] Bach's *inganno* is palindromic (Re Mi Fa Mi Re), and this is reflected also in the palindromic rhythm of the subject. Whether by accident or design, the notes BACH (in the form a'♯ a'♮ | b'♯ b'♮ , i.e. Mi Fa Mi Fa, 'tota musica' etc.) are sounded in bb.70–1, the golden section point of the fugue.[49]

Bach ends the fugue with a wonderful summary of *stile antico* keyboard polyphonic effects for a final cadence, including the cross-relation between the major and minor 7th (bb.108–10) and the delay of the perfect cadence by having a 6th in the tonic chord (b.112). All this he decorates with a 'modern' diminished 7th (b.109).

Ex.7.9 (a) Corelli: Grave from Op.6 No.3;
(b) Georg Muffat: Grave of Sonata II (*Armonico tributo*, 1682).

Ex.7.9 (Continued)

Ex.7.9 (Continued)

One source of this fugue, dating from the early to mid-eighteenth century, and possibly coming from Bach's circle, has the marking 'Ped.' under the opening of the fugue. Dürr considers this an inauthentic later entry, and there is no other evidence that this fugue was conceived as pedaliter.[50]

Prelude and Fugue in D major BWV 850

PRELUDE This is Praeludium 4 in the sequence of preludes in the *Clavier-Büchlein*, following the prelude in D minor (see Chapter Six section 3). If the prelude in C minor is for practising equality of thumb and fifth finger without displacing the hand, this is a similar exercise for the right hand, but involving a lot of hand displacement, pivoted on the thumb. In expanding it for *The Well-tempered Clavier* Bach made it formally more significant by adding a subdominant reprise (bb.19–26), and a cadenza-like concert ending (bb.30–4) which, with its grand, florid style and demisemiquaver runs, prepares the manner of the fugue. Other than in the second half of b.29 (b.21 of the early version) Bach made no substantial changes to the notes: the additions were simply inserted into the existing piece and tailored to fit.

The principal crux is the bass note of the chord at the beginning of b.33. It is quite unambiguously A in the autograph, but appears in some not very close sources as B. According to Dürr this is probably a conjecture arrived at independently by several copyists. Jones cites Kreutz and Dehnhard who suggest that it may have been an alteration made for a small hand (AB I p.142). Tovey (1924) preferred the B reading, and he and Keller (1976 p.65) point to the resulting logical line from b.32: A | B | c'♯ d', which one might continue into the e' | f'♯ | of the final chords. Attractive as this is, it seems more likely that Bach intended the A. The more grindingly dissonant chord is in fact an extension of the 6/4 chord arrived at in b.32 and picked up again in the second half of b.34. Bach seems to be demonstrating the sort of thing one can do for a short cadenza at that point. With A, the final pedal pattern from b.27 is identical to that from b.105 of the C sharp minor fugue.

Some have noted the lack of an arpeggio sign for the second chord of b.34. There is one in copies by Anna Magdalena Bach (P 202) and Altnickol (P 402). There is very little room for one in the autograph. It is possible that the arpeggio sign at the beginning of b.34 was intended to apply to all the chords in the last two bars. The notation of the arpeggio signs in bb.33–4 seems to undermine Klotz's theory of Bach's arpeggiation (see the discussion of the E flat minor Prelude) since it is difficult to imagine that they could be intended to be spread downwards, yet the arpeggio signs lack the hook at the bottom which Bach is supposed to have used to indicate upward arpeggiation.

FUGUE Some writers have a tendency to see French overtures in every dotted rhythm, but there are many other references possible, a variety which David Fuller has explored (1985). The French overture is of course an important point of reference in this fugue, but there are other possible types in the background. It is tempting to see the *obligo* of *contrapunto puntato* (as in Contrapunctus 2 of *The Art of Fugue*), except that here there is no cantus firmus or cantus firmus-like subject for the dotted rhythms to play against. Dotted rhythms are nonetheless one manner of the verset fughetta, and part of the purpose of this fugue may be to demonstrate an extension and updating of that manner.[51] A more sophisticated, 'modern' type of dotted piece is the Lullian *entrée*, such as that in Telemann's E flat Overture, which is transcribed for keyboard in the Andreas Bach Book (ed. Hill 1991 p.177), or the fugue in the metre of an *entrée* in the Offertoire of Grigny's *Premier livre d'orgue*, copied out by Bach around 1709–12. The typical Lullian *entrée* is identical in character to the first section of one of his overtures. The D major fugue cannot in itself be a French overture, since that is in two sections, the first chordal, the second imitative or fugal, at least in its later-Baroque manifestation. What Bach has done is to take some features of the first section of the late Baroque French overture and work them as elements in the genre of fugue, thus making integral and thematic what had been ornamental. The elements are dotted rhythms, demisemiquaver tiratas, and equal semiquavers, an effect Bach liked to include, and which he marked to be played equal by means of dots in, for example, Variation 16 of the Goldberg Variations.

The character of the fugue is therefore that of the first section of an overture, that is, according to Mattheson, fresh and lively, yet in an elevated style.[52] This is not the place to rehearse the issue of what Kroll calls the 'somewhat brutal rule' of overdotting:[53] whatever approach is adopted should be one which supports the general character of the piece. Grammatical considerations are little help since there will be parallel octaves between cantus and bass in b.4 if you do overdot, and parallels which some have objected to between cantus and bass in the third beat of b.22 if you do not. Objections to clashes or parallels between ornamental notes often seem pedantic rather than convincing.

A further performance issue, which may be related, is the presence of ornaments in the subject and elsewhere in the same Breitkopf source which may originate from Bach's circle that had the decorated version of bb.42–3 of the C sharp minor fugue (the ornaments are given in AB I p.143).

Laurence Dreyfus has pointed to the underlying simplicity of this fugue, and the fact that the working of its stylistic surface is its principal aim. As an exploration of fugal art it is certainly a stark contrast to the C sharp minor fugue. Yet if we approach it from the verset fughetta, Bach has taken a simple enough idea and done an extraordinary amount with it in the way of building up a large-seeming, grand and dramatic piece. And, as J.N. David has remarked, if Handel had written it, it would be considered a marvel of consistent working.[54]

Analysts have sometimes been too rigid in their perception of its form. Czaczkes, for example, who is as doctrinaire about his theory of binary structures ('Zweiteiligkeit') as Riemann is about ternary ones ('Dreiteiligkeit'), sees four expositions arranged in two pairs (1982/I p.105). Such theories impose a stiffness on Bach which is the very thing he was so good at avoiding. Bach's art is to make one thing grow naturally from another. For instance, after the usual four entries ending on the dominant at b.6, he has a little link, then a bass tonic entry, answered by one which goes off most fluently into B minor (b.9), then moves seamlessly into another type of episode, and so on. There are no square corners in this. The main structural markers that Bach himself has put in are the perfect cadences, which in this case outline a sequence of falling 3rds, i.e. D major, then B minor (b.11), G major (b.15), E minor (b.17). This is one of the main Baroque alternatives to the circle of 5ths, with which one may ultimately circumnavigate the well-tempered keyboard, as demonstrated by Werckmeister in his continuo tutor (1698b p.21).[55]

Prelude and Fugue in D minor BWV 851

PRELUDE This is the third in the sequence of preludes in W.F. Bach's *Clavier-Büchlein.* It builds on the chord hand-shapes of the C major prelude, but where that involved a still hand position this adds shifting the hand around the keyboard.[56] The question is, does it demand a 'wet' legatissimo touch as the C major prelude does, or for example the Allemande of the E flat major French Suite, or an ordinary legato touch? Busoni prescribes non legato on the piano; Keller points to concealed inner lines which may be brought out by overholding. Certainly on the harpsichord the repeated left-hand notes at the beginning need to be glued together, as they would be in repeated-note or -chord accompaniments in the Vivaldi concerto arrangements, or in the Fischer preludes of this type. This prelude has the appearance of patterned-out figured-bass progressions, four-part chords with three notes in the right hand, in the manner of Niedt.[57] Similarly Mattheson, in his figured-bass exercises through 24 keys of 1719, suggests broken-chord patterns for realisation, and it might seem natural to play them in a sustained way since they are decorations of sustained chords.[58]

On the other hand, the little prelude in D minor BWV 926 which is No.4 in the *Clavier-Büchlein*, and which looks like a precursor of this prelude, has so much linear movement, and a bass line aerated by rests at the beginning, that legatissimo treatment seems inappropriate. This sort of moto perpetuo movement originates in the Corellian type of violin sonata, and it was coping with that style when transferred to the keyboard that spurred new developments in keyboard technique from the 1690s. The string nature of this writing may be seen in the violin obbligato of the aria 'Bereite dir, Jesu, noch itzo die Bahn' from Cantata 147, and it may be that decorations of figured basses are intended to sound in a string style. As far as tempo is concerned, this aria can hardly be a guide since the prelude ends in a stream of diminished triads in the brilliant style of the first-movement cadenza of the Fifth Brandenburg Concerto. There is probably no final answer to this: it can be used either way. The piece certainly feels like chords rather than separate notes, and that is how the anonymous analyst who added figurings in P 401, possibly guided by Bach, perceived it.[59] Legatissimo performance is more difficult, particularly when it involves changes of hand position, but it is undoubtedly very idiomatic and effective on the harpsichord, and it allows the expressive inner parts in the chords to tell.

The early version of the prelude has a masterly balance of even and uneven periods. For the final version Bach made a single 12–bar addition consisting essentially of a tonic pedal followed by a dominant pedal. Bar 23 neatly takes up the pattern of the beginning of the addition (b.15), now on the dominant, and continues it into the cadenza style of the final bars. There has been much discussion about the parallel octaves (b'♮ a' / B♮ A) in the chords in bb.25–6. Some sources omit the tie between the two d''s, perhaps in an attempt to mitigate the effect of parallels. There is no doubt about the tie in the autograph. Bach obviously wanted the chords to be as full as possible, and if they are arpeggiated, as was conventional for such chords, the question hardly arises.

FUGUE If the preludes in C major and D minor are related in their technical objectives, the fugues also show signs of being companion pieces. They are of practically identical length in the autograph (nine systems), and have complementary time signatures (𝄴 and $\frac{3}{4}$). Both subjects step out the lower tetrachord of their scale, then outline the 6th. The C major outlines the natural hexachord, which is also the major scale, or Ut Re Mi; the D minor outlines the minor scale, or Re Mi Fa. The terms of the title-page are thus embedded in these two subjects. But, whereas the natural hexachord is a neutral, traditional building block, the minor scale is 'modern', therefore containing strong affective potential. The major 6th in the C major fugue has no particular expressive force; the minor 6th here seems designed to demonstrate Brossard's character of that interval as expressing sadness, pain, or exclamations.[60] To emphasise the exclamatory quality Bach has put one of François Couperin's affective ornaments (the 'aspiration') on the b'♭ of the subject. Kroll gives this in Couperin's form of a small wedge shape; Bach in the autograph uses just a dot, as given by Dürr and Jones. Bach normally uses the dot not just for separation, but also for emphasis (see Klotz 1984 pp.175–80). Finally, the subject ends, unusually, on the 5th degree of the scale, giving a curiously questioning effect since it implies the Phrygian cadence.

Many have remarked on the family resemblance of Bach's D minor subjects (the D minor Invention, the prelude for this fugue), which tend to alternate the tonic with a diminished 7th. The diminished 7th is favourable to inversion, as demonstrated by the subject of *The Art of Fugue*, and this fugue. Perhaps the most interesting comparison is with the Allemande from the D minor violin partita BWV 1004, whose opening has just the expression of questioning exclamation of the subject of this fugue (Ex.7.10).

Ex.7.10 Allemanda from the D minor violin partita BWV 1004, opening.

From this develops a fugue which is unusually detailed in the notation of affective ornamentation and articulation, and therein lies the main problem of performance. The first question is whether the slur in b.2 applies to all four semiquavers, or just the last three (Ex.7.11). Dürr follows Kroll in reading it as a group of four, noting that Bach often wrote slurs slightly to the right of where they belong (KB V/6.1 p.228). However, a number of important sources have it applying to the last three only (notably the anonymous Breitkopf copy, and P 202, copied by Anna Magdalena Bach) and this is the reading preferred by Jones. One might add that a group of three semiquavers involving a lower auxiliary is one of the commonest situations in which Bach uses a slur (see Fuchs 1985 p.98, who gives various other examples). If this interpretation is adopted, care must be taken not to detract from the most emphatic note of the subject, which is the b'♭. It is this consideration that makes one suspicious of the extremely detailed, not to say fussy, articulation scheme in the anonymous Breitkopf copy (whose interesting readings are given in NBA V/6.1, Anhang 3; BA I Anhang).[61] But it does show that affective performance was expected in this piece. Tovey (ed. 1924 p.57) found the turns in bb.9–11 an anachronism from C.P.E. Bach's style, and pointed to the corresponding passage in the second half of the fugue (bb.30–2) where the left hand has dots, not turns, which he considered more appropriate. In view of other expressive details perhaps this hint of *empfindsam* style is not out of place. Turns would be awkward in bb.30–2, and if the turns were added in the last round of revisions (A4, probably *c*.1740), so were the dots (KB V/6.1 p.227).

Ex.7.11 D minor fugue, bars 1–22 in Bach's autograph P 415.

The slur in the countersubject in b.3 is also problematical. On the face of it, it looks like an instruction that these four semiquavers are not to be played with the usual pairing, as in the *tierce coulée*, but does it apply to all four semiquavers (as given by Dehnhard) or only to the last three (as given by Dürr and Jones; Kroll omits it)? Commentators from Spitta on have remarked on the extraordinary motivic economy of this fugue, where the countersubject is constructed entirely of motifs from the subject (the tetrachord, inverted in semiquavers; the 6th leap; and the auxiliary figure). From this point of view the slur seems most logically to apply to all four semiquavers since the motif is thematic. Similarly, the lower auxiliary figure at the end of the countersubject is also a turn figure, made explicit by Bach in the signs at b.9–11, and this may have a bearing on the performance of the trill in the subject. The notation '*tr*' which he uses for this trill is not in the *Explication* of ornaments in the *Clavier-Büchlein*, but it is written at b.29 with a turn, and adding a turn brings it within the motivic network of the piece.

This fugue carries further the symmetrical structure observed in the C major and C minor fugues. In the manner of the binary sonata, the second half (from b.21) runs the same events as the first half from the dominant back to the tonic. The main difference is that the exposition after bb.21 is of the inverted subject, just as in binary dances that traditionally have a contrapuntal component such as the allemande and gigue the principal motif is inverted after the double bar. As in the C minor fugue, the episodic material is all brought together to build up to the final tonic entries. These three fugues, taken together, leave the impression that, whatever their combinatorial cleverness, Bach was in them primarily concerned with reconciling the fugue with the binary dance/character piece/sonata.

Prelude and Fugue in E flat major BWV 852

PRELUDE This prelude is something of an enigma. Its sectional form reverts to the type of organ prelude that Bach had cultivated in his youth, but had abandoned in his later Weimar days in favour of the large-scale piece in a single span, using the principles of the Venetian concerto allegro. The key of E flat is missing from the sequence of preludes in the *Clavier-Büchlein*, which has led to speculation that this is an old piece which Bach kept in reserve and did not include there, probably because it was too long and difficult for the ten- to twelve-year-old Wilhelm Friedemann. It also does not fit in the keyboard-technical scheme of the other *Clavier-Büchlein* preludes, and it is unique among preludes in the 48 in including a fully developed fugue. It may originally have been conceived for organ (the early version has fewer semiquavers in the bass of the second section (bb.10–24) than the final one), in which case the key of E flat might seem to indicate that it could not be an early work. Mattheson (1719) said he knew of no toccatas or preludes in 'that fine, majestic key' because of the tuning of organs.[62] Nonetheless, in Bach's area there are organ pieces in E flat dating from his youth, by Johann Pachelbel (1653–1706), and in the so-called 'Mylau tablature' (compiled 1689–1700). He himself wrote for organ in E flat in the early layer of chorale preludes in the *Orgel-Büchlein* ('O Mensch bewein', see Stinson 1996 p.29). With its sophisticated French harmony, glorious spacing, and density of contrapuntal argument, the E flat prelude cannot be as early as the clavier toccatas. None of the early sectional preludes/toccatas is as integrated as this, and they tend to revert to the free style at the end.[63]

Bach may have composed it specially for *The Well-tempered Clavier* to represent one type of prelude: the sectional organ praeludium, with subtle thematic links between sections, as cultivated at its most sophisticated by Buxtehude (see Chapter Three section 3). It is nonetheless such a large and impressive concert item in itself, without the obvious didactic keyboard-technical function of the other preludes so far, that it may perhaps be more likely to have originated as a free-standing virtuoso piece in Weimar after around 1710. It certainly chimes in with the general policy of the collection in giving its elements a highly integrated treatment, and it may be seen as a step on the way from the early sectional preludes and toccatas to the more seamless integration of prelude and fugue elements in the C minor organ Praeludium BWV 546/1, dating from after Bach's arrival in Leipzig in 1723.

The E flat prelude is typical of Bach's maturity in creating a union of opposites. The opening uses an improvisation hand-shape figure, suitable for the feel ('Griffe') of the key, and developed over a pedal point. Although it is in the style of a free improvisation, it is not difficult to see the underlying pattern of rising 4ths and 5ths which provide the material for the next, strictly contrapuntal, section (from b.10). This fundamental unity is emphasised by an instruction pencilled in (not by Bach) to the autograph at b.10: 'not like an Alla breve, but continued as in the first bar'.[64] In other words, the player is not to imagine the time signature changing to ¢ and the tempo doubling, to what one might think suitable for the E flat fugue of Book II. It shows that this section was thought of as in *stile antico*, which it certainly is in its 'gebunden' (prepared and resolved) treatment of dissonance, and fluid metre. It is nonetheless a special effect, designed to contrast with the first section, and is untypical of true *stile antico* in being a solid, sustained block of counterpoint with no rests after the voices have entered. Bach made few alterations to the final version of this prelude, other than adding two bars to the first section (bb.3–4) and the decorative semiquavers in bb.20–1. The bass decoration in b.22 was originally in demisemiquavers. By converting it to semiquavers, and having it move down the parts in pitch, Bach makes this ornament quasi-thematic, brings out the glorious 9/7 chord at b.23, and links the 4th and 5th leaps of the second section to the semiquaver subject of the third.

Section 3 is a masterly double fugue in counterpoint at the octave, 10th and 12th which is yet a model of clarity and playability since it is based on the four-note handshape of Section 1. Inversions at the 12th are in b.47f (compare b.25) and b.49f; at the 10th in b.53f. The semiquaver subject also includes the emphatic repeated notes used in Subject 3 of the C sharp minor fugue for building up the final climax, and which here subtly prepare the cathartic bass entry at b.61.

FUGUE After such an imposing fugal creation, what can one possibly add under the heading of Fugue? Busoni's dreadful idea of following it with the E flat fugue from Book II, a less imposing piece in the same vein, only serves to emphasise the quality of Bach's artistic judgment and especially his demonstration that the genre of fugue is as capable of as great a range of style and expression as any other, except that it has an added dimension of intellectual delight rarely to be found in, for example, the operatic aria. This fugue contrasts strongly with its prelude in its much lighter style, with violin-sonata figurations and passages of what are in effect embroidered continuo harmony. Yet there are so many subtle allusions to the materials of the prelude that can hardly be accidental that the fugue seems designed to show how opposite expressions may derive from the same materials; or, in line with the policy of updating traditional techniques, that traditional solemn ingredients can be treated in a light and 'modern' way.

The subject in itself unites the E flat hand-shape of the opening of the prelude with the outline of the *stile antico* subject of the double fugue. It expands the hand from a 5th, to a 6th, to a 7th just as the prelude figure expanded it from a 5th to a 7th; and the relationship to the *stile antico* subject at b.25 of the prelude is clear from the answer in b.3 of the fugue (outlining b♭ e'♭ d' g' f'). However, this underlying *stile antico* outline is reinterpreted in a 'modern' tonal subject which modulates to the dominant. Modern too is the fact that the argument of the fugue is hardly contrapuntal (there is double, but not triple counterpoint), but harmonic in that it takes the chromatic step inherent in the subject and its continuation (a'♮ in b.1, a'♭ in b.2) as the principal point of interest, extends it in the linking passage at bb.4–5, and motivates such touches as the chromatic step in the countersubject at the beginning of b.6, which replaces what would otherwise be an octave leap (♫ d'–d"). The growth of this element, in the context of such a light style, into sequences of such richly chromatic and dissonant chords as in bb.14–16 is one of the principal delights of this fugue. Its relation to the prelude is made clear by the chromatic falling line in the Schumannesque final bar, recalling the corresponding chromatic line between cantus and alto in the last three bars of the prelude.

The fact that the subject modulates may explain the simplicity of the general harmonic plan. It is another version of the combination of fugue and binary sonata observed in previous fugues. In this case almost all of the first half (to b.17) is in the tonic, perhaps a reflexion of the fact that the answer is more in the tonic than the subject itself. The second half visits the relative minor, and has a long tonic reprise from b.26. Within this binary framework there is also a reference to a kind of ternary structure based on the Vivaldi concerto allegro plan. Thus, the cantus entry of the answer at b.11 has little to do with such anomalous terms as 'redundant entry', but a lot to do with Vivaldi's tendency in the Op.3 concertos to have, after the opening ritornello, a short solo break which stays in the tonic, then a repeat of all or part of the ritornello, again in the tonic; then to start the same solo break again, but extend it into a modulation (see Chapter 4 section 11). This is just what happens here, with the first solo break equivalent beginning at b.8, and beginning again in the second half of b.12, but continuing into a modulation to C minor.

The reprise in this case re-runs the events of the opening section in reverse: the bass entry of the answer at b.26 corresponds to the cantus entry at b.11; and the cantus entry of the subject at b.29 corresponds to the bass entry at b.6. In the exposition, the non-modulating alto answer at b.3 was a pale imitation of the modulating subject. Bach as usual makes a virtue of limitation, first by converting it into a curious, jokey, chromatically warped version in C minor at b.17, and finally in the alto entry at b.34, corresponding to b.3, by exploiting the rhetorical potential of the rest, together with the chromatic step, in a way which recalls the similar moment at the end of the C minor fugue. This mirror symmetry is enhanced by Bach's characteristic structural use of pitch levels and texture, with the concentration on the top octave of the keyboard at bb.4–5 balanced by the concentration on the bottom octave at bb.32–3.

Prelude and Fugue in E flat/D sharp minor BWV 853

In the same year as Bach dated the autograph copy of Book I (1722) Rameau published a listing of keys that demonstrates how keys on the *semitonia* were then regarded. For minor keys, the extreme sharp end is D sharp, and the extreme flat end is E flat. Both keys are given, and this is the interchange point. Major keys, on the other hand, go as far as A flat, then change to C sharp, F sharp, and so on. This is precisely the way Bach thought of these keys, on the evidence of *The Well-tempered Clavier*, and is no doubt based on the way the *semitonia* were thought of in traditional tuning systems. The policy in some old editions of transposing this fugue and other pieces in the sharpest keys into the equivalent flat ones is a historical falsification. Given the ambiguity of the keynote, there is a theoretical logic in having both keys represented. There is also a practical reason in that there is very strong evidence that the fugue was originally in D minor, and was transposed simply by altering the key signature.

PRELUDE There is no real evidence that the prelude was conceived in any other key than E flat minor. The only possible hint is in b.29, where Bach in the autograph used a sharp sign for the first g'♮, which might imply that he was transposing from an E minor original. But he reverted to the natural sign at the end of the bar, and in any case this bar comes from the additions in the final version, when the collection was being assembled in its present form, so it is unlikely that this piece was conceived other than in its present key (see KB V/6.1 p.188).

It certainly has the feeling of exploring a remote key, and therefore a rarefied expressive world, a feeling that has communicated itself to many.[65] It opens with another version of the harmonic formula used in the C major and minor and D minor preludes, but how different is the effect! There are also similarities to the prelude in the other remote flat key, B flat minor. In the *Clavier-Büchlein* the E flat minor continues the sequence of preludes in more advanced keys, following C sharp minor, and seems to share a similar technical aim, not in the sense of finger technique, but in the technique of expressive projection, which on the harpsichord is largely a matter of rhythm. The C sharp minor prelude was concerned with preserving the integrity of a characteristic rhythm in a complex texture, and with moulding the rhythm to project the expressive shape of the piece. The E flat minor is concerned with the freedom of projecting highly florid and expressive lines against a background of steady repeated chords in, as Landowska says, 'columns of arpeggios striking the three beats from the opening to the closing measures' (1965 p.186). The art is to find that subtle balance of discipline and freedom where rhetoric and expression can grip. The freedom of decorative line is represented graphically in the autograph by having long groups of semiquavers beamed together (reflected in the editions of Dürr and Jones; most older editions, including those of Kroll and Dehnhard, divide them into groups of four).

This is another place in Book I where a slightly unequal temperament makes a palpable contribution. The sour effect of a wide major 3rd on the g'♭ in the first chord, particularly in this part of the keyboard, adds a chilling bleakness to the sound world of the opening, resolved onto warm E flat major chords in a rich, low register from b.37.

This prelude is such a sophisticated working of its stylistic references that they are not immediately obvious. Sarabandes and French overtures hardly come into it. One rather romantic suggestion is that it is a lament for Bach's first wife, Maria Barbara, who died in July 1720 (P. Badura-Skoda 1993 p.215). Whatever one thinks of such biographical speculations, there is no doubt that this prelude has something of the character of a *tombeau*, whose features are very flat keys, dotted rhythms, and tiratas. The reference is, however, oblique: Arnold Dolmetsch's suggestion of overdotting would be ruinous to the expression of this piece; Badura-Skoda's interpretation of a slight swinging of the quavers in the manner of *notes inégales* is obviously what is required.[66] The cultivation of a convincing elasticity of rhythm is one of the objects of the piece. The primary references are to two manners in Venetian concerto slow movements. The first is of a cushion accompaniment of repeated chords in the upper strings, supporting a florid solo melody, of which there are several examples in Bach's concerto arrangements (BWV 972, 974). In adapting this prototype in an original keyboard piece Bach is not limited to a particular tessitura for the florid solo, so he makes it range expressively all over the keyboard. The other prototype is represented by the Largo of Vivaldi's Op.3 No.3 (arranged as BWV 978) where full chords alternate with solo flourishes (see C. Wolff 1991 p.77). This principle can be moulded expressively, as Vivaldi does, by varying the lengths of chord groups, or solo flourishes, and the climax is made by combining both elements. Bach uses these elements in this prelude, but simultaneously, and they are much more cogently extended and developed than by Vivaldi. It is particularly instructive to see how Bach extended the emotional range of the piece, and its range of significant pitches, in the final version. As in the C sharp minor prelude, the second page touches the extremes of the keyboard: the ornamental top c''' added in b.28 is answered by the dramatic descent to bottom D♮ added in bb.32–5.

Another improvement in the final version is the thinning out of some of the chords in bb.1–7, making a more subtle transition from melody to accompaniment. The difference must nonetheless be felt: the g''♭ on the second beat of b.4 was originally the top note of a chord and is therefore accompaniment, following a conventional *tierce coulée* melodic phrase-ending (compare b.8).[67] The placing of this note is therefore important. The ability to project on a single-manual harpsichord the subtleties of where functions merge and where they do not belongs to the more advanced reaches of performance. Details of notation are not always significant, but the notation of the turn in b.13 and the semiquavers in b.29 have given rise to comment. In b.13 Bach's intention is quite clear in the final revision of the autograph (♩. ♬♬♩) which is perfectly clear as a turn with a delay before it and a slight pause on the last note. Standard notation is not equal to this, and no edition reflects it accurately. In b.29 it has been asked why Bach wrote the semiquavers after a dot here, but after a tie in the next bar (Shedlock 1883 p.595). The answer is that the semiquavers in b.29 are a written-out ornament, often notated with a little 'u' sign, and should therefore be played as an ornament, as should the last two semiquavers of this bar which probably form the termination of an interrupted trill, as in the E minor prelude. The semiquavers in the following bar are thematic.

Bach was generally sparing of ornament signs in his manuscript keyboard works, and this piece is one of the most richly provided. There are, however, ornaments in other sources (notably P 202 and P 203) which could be added (Ex.7.12). The mordent on the first cantus note is particularly important since it shows that this note is the beginning of the melody, not just part of a chord.

Ex.7.12 Prelude in E flat minor with cantus ornaments from various sources, bars 1–4.

The most important ornament in this piece is the arpeggiation sign and, taking the most important sources as a whole, there is hardly a chord in the piece which does not have one. Information about the treatment of arpeggiation is both enigmatic and disturbing. Since arpeggiating chords is a normal part of harpsichord technique needing no special sign, an arpeggiation sign in itself generally means a deliberate, even rhythmic, effect, rather than just a quick spread, and is explained as such in virtually all tables of ornaments that deal with it. A refinement of this has been pointed out by Hans Klotz: that the direction of the spreads was carefully notated by French harpsichordists such as Chambonnières (*c.*1670) and especially François Couperin (1713). Couperin notated the direction of the spreads by means of a little hook at the top or bottom of the wavy line, depending on whether he wished the chord to be arpeggiated down or up. There is no denying that some of Bach's arpeggiation signs have a very definite right hook at the lower end indicating, according to Klotz, an upward spread. Where there is no such hook he supposes a downward spread (Klotz 1984 pp.169–71). Klotz cites a number of ornament tables, but not the one which is probably the most relevant, and which strongly supports his case, in the Andreas Bach Book (*c.*1707–*c.*1718; Ex.7.13).[68]

Ex.7.13 Arpeggiation as explained in the Andreas Bach Book.

The musicological evidence is impressive. No edition reflects Bach's notation in this respect and anybody wishing to investigate it will have to consult the facsimile of the autograph. Any assessment must involve a direct, personal feeling for Bach's handwriting that a printed interpretation can only falsify. Some interesting and plausible points emerge: for example that the second-beat chord in b.28 is to be spread down, and the third-beat chord up. On the other hand, the chord at the beginning of b.35 is by this token to be spread down, which detracts from the dramatic effect of the low D♮, and also from the importance of the c''♭ as leader into the right-hand cadenza passage in the rest of the bar. Players must decide for themselves. My own feeling is that, given the sensitivity to mood and effect in other aspects of the notation, the rigorous application of this principle introduces an illogical fussiness which is not supported by the cursory nature of Bach's ornament signs, and which undermines the concentrated mood of the Vivaldian slow movement, designed to contrast with the motoric outer ones.

FUGUE This fugue is in an earlier style than most in the collection on two counts: it is in the tradition of the seventeenth-century keyboard fantasia/ricercar which explores a subject in terms of learned counterpoint (it is the only fugue in Book I to use augmentation, a hallmark of that learned style); and in terms of Bach's fugal writing generally it is an exposition fugue, with brief links rather than episodes, each successive exposition introducing a new contrapuntal treatment. In this it resembles the A minor fugue, with which it is probably roughly contemporary. The rigorously maintained schemes of these two fugues contrast with the fugues of *c.*1720, which are concerned with refreshing fugal techniques in an up-to-date style. Comparing the rigidly schematic plan of this fugue with the very loosened-up style of the D sharp minor fugue of Book II is an instructive lesson in the difference between Bach's early and late styles.

The purpose of the collection in general is to demonstrate the tonal system in up-to-date styles. This is the only piece in Book I to have a substantial element of the modal tradition, and may have been included specifically to provide a representative of that. The subject has a traditional modal outline which has been compared to the chorale melody 'Aus tiefer Not', erroneously since that is a Mode III (Phrygian) melody (see Walther 1732 p.410), whereas this is a typical Mode I (Dorian) melody. One feature of this mode is the characteristic M shape of the subject, a commonplace of Renaissance polyphony and of learned seventeenth-century counterpoint. Its inversion is the subject of Froberger's Ricercar II (1656), and Bach used it in its most straightforward form in the first subject of the incomplete fugue of *The Art of Fugue.* The subject of the D sharp minor fugue adds to this the return to the 4th degree, typical of such archetypal Mode I melodies as Ave maris stella.[69] Bach used this outline in the early Canzona in D minor for organ BWV 588, and updated it in a galant context in the fugue of the B minor Flute Overture BWV 1067/1.

Other *antico* features are the strict, 'gebunden' treatment of dissonance, the rhythmic fluidity of line, and the subtle balance of curves and leaps. Very much in the Frescobaldi tradition is the constant remoulding of the subject, such as the bass entry of the inversion exposition (b.39), and the wonderfully dramatic bass entry in the inversion stretto (b.44) with its tolling 5ths, described by Landowska as 'stunning'. The principle of free moulding yields a new version of the subject in quasi-augmentation in the middle part of the triple stretto at b.24. It also allows for the climactic triple stretto at b.52, where none of the three entries is quite like the original subject. This is truly developmental counterpoint in the seventeenth-century learned tradition, where pleasure is taken in flexibility, wit and resourcefulness rather than in rigid, pedantic exactness. A less obvious antique feature is the outlining of the Dorian ambitus by perfect cadences on the 5th degree (b.19) and 3rd degree (b.30) which mark the ends of the first and second expositions respectively (see Meier 1992 p.181). The next perfect cadence is not until b.61, marking the beginning of the final section of augmentations.

The scheme of expositions is rigorously logical, as follows: b.1 exposition recto; b.19½ stretto recto; b.30 exposition inverso; b.44 stretto inverso; b.61½ augmentation exposition. Within this there are numerous felicities of counterpoint, such as the stretto recto at b.19½ being inverted at the 12th at b.27. Bach has compensated for the potential relaxation of tension of the augmentation entries by placing them rather high on the keyboard, and surrounding them with increasingly complex stretti, culminating in a stretto of all three versions of the subject (normal, semi-augmented, and augmented) at b.77.

The virtual certainty that this fugue was originally in D minor has long been known, and is confirmed in the sources. The most obvious pointer is the scale in b.15 which in D minor went up to c''' but now cannot go up to c'''♯ which is beyond the Book I keyboard. Of the control editions, Dehnhard alone gives c'''♯, following J.G. Walther (P 1074). Elsewhere accidentals from D minor have survived (B natural for B sharp, E flat for E natural; see KB V/6.1 p.188). Transposing modes around the keyboard in order to get convenient singing pitches was one of the ways in which advanced keys began to be explored in the early seventeenth century. By putting this fugue into such a sophisticated key Bach has lifted these very traditional, well-worn materials on to a rarefied plane, matching the exquisite ingenuity of the counterpoint.

There is always a problem of guessing how much ornamentation to add to pieces by Bach in this style. The Canzona BWV 588 exists in a highly ornamented version in the Mempell-Preller collection (edited in Faulkner 1984 pp.56–62). As an absolute minimum, the trill on the penultimate note of the subject (e'♯), which is given in copies by Anna Magdalena Bach (P 202) and J.G. Walther (P 1074) in b.3 and equivalent places, should surely be observed. It is possible also that the figure ♪. ♬ in the last beat of b.11 implies a trill.

Prelude and Fugue in E major BWV 854

PRELUDE In the *Clavier-Büchlein* this comes between the E minor and F major preludes. It therefore moves from five-finger, hand-shape preludes to shapes based on arpeggios: this in a cantabile style, the F major in an allegro style. This is in the typical keyboard texture for the projection of a right-hand melody, mainly with one melodic part in the right hand and two accompanying ones in the left. The C sharp minor prelude later builds on this by having similar cantabile effects in a more complex texture.

Bach's pupil H.N. Gerber gives this in his copy of *The Well-tempered Clavier*, but also in a very similar version as 'Prelude' to the sixth French Suite BWV 817 (P 1221, dated 1725). Hermelink has noted similarities between it and the Gigue of the suite, particularly when the main subject is inverted after the double bar (1976 p.52). It has to be said, though, that this prelude shares the same type of harmonic formula that opens many of the *Clavier-Büchlein* preludes.

The time signature and the prevalence of pedal points are part of the language of the pastorale, and in fact this prelude is a working of the aria ritornello shape in its sonata guise, with a pedal point substituted for the usual sequential modulation (see Chapter Three section 6). Bach runs this shape three times, each time modulating to a new key: the dominant at b.8½, the subdominant at b.15. Since the first section modulated up a 5th from tonic dominant, the last can be a literal reprise, modulating up a 5th from subdominant to tonic. Typically the ritornello shape has a characteristic closing idea, often with a chromatic twist, as here (bb.7–8), and this encourages Bach in a *jeu d'esprit* which is to make the modulation to the dominant minor, only ending the section in the major by means of a *tierce de Picardie*. This is more obvious in earlier versions of the prelude (including the *Clavier-Büchlein*) which have a d'♮ in the tenor in the last beat of b.7, and a d''♮ in the cantus in the second beat of b.8, with corresponding naturals in bb.21–2.

FUGUE This is one of Bach's lightest and wittiest fugues, combining the traditional and the 'modern' with extraordinary neatness. A subject with an iambic step is a commonplace in seventeenth-century verset collections, or for a section in other contrapuntal keyboard genres. It was used with great sophistication by Frescobaldi, who liked constructing Chinese-puzzle-type textures of interlocking rhythms from it: an example of this which Bach certainly knew is in the 'Alegro' section of the Epistle Canzona from the Messa della Domenica of the *Fiori musicali*. The texture survives in the numerous references to the iambic step throughout the E major fugue. At the same time this step is not just a figure in this fugue, but part of a subject, and the fact that the subject has no clearly defined ending, avoiding the clear cadentiality of, for example, Fischer's subjects, is part of Bach's 'modern' trend to continuity and integration. The many pedantic efforts to define the subject exactly really miss the point,[70] as does the debate about whether or not there is a 'proper' countersubject.

Of the many felicities of this fugue, one is that the subject neatly outlines a I–V–I progression, with the four semiquavers as an extension of the initial iambic step on the principle of division variations. It is a miniature version of the head-and-tail (*Vordersatz/Nachsatz*) shape. Bach extracts the essence from the harmonic shape of the subject by bringing it in over an important punctuating cadence at b.16. The answer (b.2) steps up to c"♯, which provides the one alternative tonal area (from b.16). Pedantic literalism would claim that the last entry (b.28) is on the dominant. The wit is in the fact that here the quaver step gives a questioning, interrupted cadence, answered by the good, strong perfect cadence of the semiquavers.

The structure of the fugue is of the simplest, with a kind of fugal inversion from the end of b.6 (expositions: 1 tonic–dominant–tonic; 2 tonic–dominant–dominant). After a brief excursion to C sharp minor there is a reprise with entries in closer stretto from b.19 (tonic–dominant (cantus, second beat of b.20) –tonic). Bach originally wanted to finish with the large and strong shape of a descending bass scale (the stages of his thought processes are given in NBA V/6.1 and provide an absorbing glimpse into his workshop). This would give parallel 5ths into the last beats of bb.24 and 27 between the bass and the turn figure, not very serious ones since they are the result of a decorative upper auxiliary. Bach nonetheless in his later revisions strove to eliminate the faintest hint of ungrammaticality, probably because of the educational intent of the collection.

Prelude and Fugue in E minor BWV 855

PRELUDE Bach made more alterations to this than to any other of the Praeludia in the *Clavier-Büchlein*, adding a florid melody which transforms the character of the original prelude, and a Presto second half which almost doubles its length. Substantial alteration was needed in order to convert it into a concert item. The added melody turns an obvious finger exercise into poetry, and the Presto gives it a brilliant and witty concertante development that also provides a bridge to the style of the fugue and, as Busoni points out, means that both prelude and fugue now have the same harmonic groundplan: the Presto addition begins in A minor and works back to the tonic, just as the second half of the fugue does.

In the *Clavier-Büchlein* sequence of preludes this comes as No.5, after the D major No.4. One may therefore see a technical progression from equality of all five fingers in both hands, without change of hand position (C minor); to right-hand equality, shifting the hand around the keyboard by pivoting on the thumb (D major); to left-hand equality with extension of the little finger (E minor), the only study specifically for the left hand. The left-hand moto perpetuo is, as such things of their nature are, an endurance test of accuracy with the necessity of shaping harmonic periods, in this case with the technical element of increasing the distance between the little finger and the others. The left hand is also the hand that needs most agility in continuo playing, which is why François Couperin recommends beginners to avoid accompaniment during their first years of playing (1717 pp.42–3). Here is an exercise for that and, as a left-hand companion for the D major right-hand study, it is presumably intended to share a similar tempo.

In addition to its keyboard-technical aspect it may also be taken as a model of improvisation. It uses the same type of opening harmonic formula as do most of the *Clavier-Büchlein* preludes, so links with Niedt's lesson for improvisation ('Fantasiren') through variations on a figured bass. In listing styles of improvisation, Mattheson ranges from *intonatio* (full chords) to *capricci* ('the more wonderful and extraordinary, the better'), and finishes with 'a kind of accompaniment . . . with full chords in one hand, and a regular pattern in the other' (1739 III 25/63; see P. Williams 1984 pp.102–3). Thus even the early version of this prelude builds on several functions and references. The final version provides a written memorial of J.F. Daube's description of Bach's 'intricate' style of continuo playing, when he would improvise something like a concertante part (NBR p.362). As Daube says, anybody who missed hearing him missed a great deal, but in this prelude his playing lives on.[71] The style of ornamentation is curiously similar to the ornaments attributed to Corelli in the *c.*1710 Amsterdam print of his Op.5 violin sonatas, where long notes are followed by extremely florid decorations concentrated at the end of the bar. Bach evidently continued to elaborate in performance, since most of the demisemiquavers date from the A4 revision (the plainer initial readings are given in NBA V/6.1 p.49).

In spite of its origin in improvisation the final version yet has a finished, composed appearance. In the early version the chords had varying numbers of parts, as in practical continuo playing; in the final version the accompanying chords are strictly in two parts. In them Bach has, as usual, taken the greatest care to avoid parallels, in this case by crossing parts at b.9 and b.15 (both part crossings are observed only in the Dürr and Jones editions). This is not pedantry, but simply that the piece must now be judged as a finished solo. Tovey suggests that the chords and the bass therefore belong together, and so the first bass note of each half bar should be sustained a quaver's length. The syllogistic logic of this may not be quite smooth, but the musical logic is sound and one can certainly imagine two continuo chords per bar accompanying the other parts.

For the trills in b.10 and b.12, where the trill fades out into a rest, Tovey sensitively envisages a diminuendo clavichord trill. This type of trill is in fact a French ornament, explained by André Raison (1688) with reference to the organ, and by Georg Muffat (1698) with reference to the Lully style of string playing.[72] Raison specifies that the finger should be lifted before the termination. This type of trill is also discussed by Bach's pupil J.F. Agricola, who provides evidence against the Berlin orthodoxy that the trill must always continue into its termination (see Agricola ed. Baird 1995 p.20). Nonetheless there may just conceivably be a clavichord dimension here. On the double-fretted clavichord the notes e"♭ and e"♮ are normally taken from the same string. An effect unique to this instrument is a trill where the main note (in this case d"♯) is held down while the e" is restruck several times, exactly in the manner of a lute trill. This effect is possible at b.12, a unique situation for a specifically clavichord effect in *The Well-tempered Clavier.*

FUGUE This is not one of the more popular fugues with performers, but is nonetheless one of those most referred to in the literature. There are two intriguing features: one is the nature of the subject, and the other is the fugue's extraordinarily precise binary structure. The fact that it works so exactly through a schematic concept puts it in a bracket with the fugues in D sharp minor and A minor, which equally work systematically through a logical framework. Like the A minor, it also has a fondness for phrases ending with an offbeat quaver.

This is the only fugue in the 48 in two parts. According to C.P.E. Bach (NBR p.399), Bach began his fugue instruction with fugue in two parts, of which there was once apparently a substantial collection.[73] It would be logical to see the E minor fugue as in some way related to the two-part Inventions were it not that the more fluid style and technique of the Inventions seems more 'mature' than the rigid scheme of this fugue.

In this fugue Bach has taken the idea of two parts and made the piece a thoroughgoing exploration of duality. The fugue has a two-bar subject, containing two elements, and spanning two keys. It is in double counterpoint throughout. It is divided in the 1:2 ratio: the second half begins at b.20 and is the mirror contrapuntal inversion of the first half. Bach has marked this very clearly for the listener by having both parts in octaves at the end of each section (b.19, b.38) in the Vivaldi concerto manner, a form of punctuation mark which he also uses in the first movement of the G minor gamba Sonata BWV 1029 and elsewhere, but very striking in such a strict fugue.[74] Yet in spite of being such an obvious part of the scheme, the idea of having the octaves at the end of the first half as well as the second occurred to Bach only in the final version of the fugue. Within this, each half is further subdivided as 1:2, this division being marked by less striking parallel 10ths at b.10 and b.29. In the fugue as a whole this subdivision is in the ratio 1:4. Another piece where Bach has a strict programme based on 2 and 4 is the first movement of Brandenburg Concerto No.2. There it is perhaps inspired by the harmonic series of the natural trumpet, where the octaves are partials 1, 2, 4, 8, 16. The octaves in the E minor fugue operate equally as a sound effect and a structural proportion. Finally, in the autograph Bach indulges in a little notational fiction in the last bar by writing what was a three-part chord in the right hand in the early version as three successive notes marked to be sustained by a tenuto slur, thus keeping his two-part texture to the end.[75]

There is added grit in the fact that the piece is not in duple, but in triple time. Bach plays on this structurally by introducing from b.15 a semiquaver figuration (inverted from b.34) that divides the bar in two, and when both parts go into octaves this duple division takes over entirely. The powerful possibilities of a subject that modulates to the dominant are realised by Bach in the sublime series of subject entries going up the cycle of rising 5ths in Cantata 50. In this fugue the fact that both subject and answer modulate up a 5th gives a dynamic which goes with the excited atmosphere of rapid chromatic movement. It also means that each quarter of the piece covers three keys.

The shape of the chromatic descending tetrachord is one which Bach seems to have associated particularly with E minor, as in the 'Wedge' fugue for organ BWV 548/2 and the Crucifixus of the B minor Mass (other examples are noted by P. Williams, 1997 p.95). Two fugues from Bach's background have been seen as contributing to this subject. The first is by Buxtehude (BuxWV 142; see Stauffer 1980 pp.127–8, and Snyder 1987 p.240), which has one subject modulating to the dominant, and another based on the falling chromatic 4th (Ex.7.14).

Ex.7.14 Buxtehude: subjects from the E minor Praeludium BuxWV 142.

In this large-scale sectional piece Buxtehude makes no systematic attempt to integrate these subjects. Equally pertinent is the E minor Praeludium of Bruhns, preserved in the Möller MS. In accordance with Niedt's prelude recipe, this opens with an improvised-type flourish in semiquavers (Ex.7.15a). This type of opening figure is generally based on handshapes natural to the key, and this example shows that Bruhns also felt E minor as an inherently chromatic key. The subject of the ensuing fugal section (Ex.7.15b) outlines the falling chromatic 4th in the lower half of the scale, before cadencing on the dominant.

Ex.7.15 Bruhns: E minor Praeludium, free and strict subjects.

Bach again appears to be going further than in the E flat major prelude, taking diverse ingredients from the tradition of sectional structure and amalgamating them into a single integrated concept, based partly on the Corellian principle of uniting diverse ingredients in a moto perpetuo based on a single note value, and partly on Bach's own concept of the invention, where everything is unified by developing from a small collection of elements at the opening.[76]

Prelude and Fugue in F major BWV 856

PRELUDE In the *Clavier-Büchlein* this is Praeludium 7, and comes after the E major. It is on the last note of the lower tetrachord of C and therefore finishes the bottom half of the scale. After this Bach went back to fill in the advanced keys, starting with C sharp major (Praeludium 8). The E major was the first to get away from finger exercises into the projection of a cantabile melody, and also from the **C** time signature. It uses $\frac{12}{8}$; the F major was originally $\frac{24}{16}$, then $\frac{24}{16}$ in the righ-hand stave and $\frac{12}{8}$ in the left (in the *Clavier-Büchlein*, cf. the G major

Prelude), and finally just $\frac{12}{8}$. Subsequent preludes extend the repertory of time signatures in a seemingly systematic way.

If the E major prelude introduces the arpeggio as a cantabile element, this treats it in an Allegro. Added to this is a study in the 'Doppelt-cadence' trill of the *Explication* of ornaments in the *Clavier-Büchlein*, the two ornaments ultimately deriving from D'Anglebert's table of ornaments of 1689. Just like other composers who were interested in thoroughly researching musical materials, back to Monteverdi, so Bach here takes what is essentially a melodic ornament and makes it a thematic element for development in its own right. Curiously, the *Clavier-Büchlein* version of this piece, hastily and untidily copied by W.F. Bach (KB V/5 p.89), does not notate these complex signs, but uses only *tr* or *tr*∼∼. The second of these implies a long trill, and long trills are written in early-version sources for bb.12–15. Since this is partly a study in trills, it would be logical to have to maintain them through complex activity in the other hand. In any case long trills contribute immeasurably to the prelude's bounding exuberance, culminating in the long left-hand one in bb.14–15.

FUGUE According to Kirnberger the most important way in which Bach updated the concept of fugue was in combining it with dance metre and structure. The highly individual and sophisticated way in which Bach combined fugue, dance, and the dance-based sonata principle is one of the main fascinations of these fugues.

The F major is one of the fugues that show most clearly Bach's indebtedness to Fischer's *Ariadne Musica*, and how he built on Fischer's work. Fischer's F major fugue is modern, in terms of the verset tradition, in that it is in a dance rhythm, the dance in this case being one of the traditional seventeenth-century French types of gigue (Ex.7.16). The underlying similarity of materials with

Ex.7.16 Fischer: F major Fuga from *Ariadne Musica*, bars 1–9: subject and countersubject.

Fischer's fugue have been neatly pointed out by David Schulenberg (1992 p.182). Fischer is not so much interested in researching dance metre and phraseology as in exploring combinations of his subject and countersubject, in stretto and in counterpoint at the 10th, in the tradition of the verset fugue.

Bach has taken this as a prototype and converted it to the metre of a recent type of passepied. This dance, like the gigue, goes back to the beginning of the seventeenth century, but the form that Bach uses was one of the dances popularised by Campra in *L'Europe galante* (1697).[77] Several new developments flow from this conversion of metre. Features of this type of passepied are: that it is in $\frac{3}{8}$-time, with a quaver upbeat, and has decorative groups of four semiquavers. The phrases are of four bars, and the first two phrases normally balance an offbeat ending with an onbeat ending (for examples see Little and Jenne 1991). In this phraseology the characteristic offbeat phrase ending with a falling 3rd (*tierce coulée*) at the beginning of b.4, which ends the subject, replaces the firm perfect cadence of dominant to tonic roots at the end of Fischer's subject, and allows Bach to integrate his subject with its continuation. We have already seen this policy of clouding the end of the subject and integrating it with what follows in the C major and E major fugues.

The ambiguity of where the subject ends then becomes a feature that Bach can play with. In this case the subject flows on into a second four-bar phrase with an onbeat ending into b.8. The whole tenor line from b.1 to b.8 therefore constitutes the two balancing phrases which normally make up the first section of a passepied. Bach's agenda in the first section of this fugue (to b.46) is to run this eight-bar passepied section several times: in the cantus from b.4, the bass from b.9, the cantus from b.17, and the bass from b.25. He then moves to D minor, with a dominant pedal in that key, and has the first strong perfect cadence into b.46. This agenda reveals the many-levelled subtlety of Bach's combination of fugue and dance.

The other prototype for this fugue is the sonata. This may be a continuous, rather than binary, structure as in the first half of Corelli's Op.5, but is essentially binary when combined with a dance genre. However, as with the genre of prelude, so the fugue allows Bach to treat elements with considerable freedom. He is not obliged to have a double bar and can, as here, capitalise on this freedom by being fluid in the treatment, number, and length of sections. There is no point in looking for an overall binary dance structure with a division at the half-way point (b.36), as most analyses have done, since the eight-bar phrase at the opening is in itself the first section of a passepied. As far as the overall structure of the fugue is concerned, Bach has as usual marked off his sections with absolute clarity by means of the traditional punctuation mark of a perfect cadence.

The specific sonata element here is not structural, but the moto perpetuo which he develops from the semiquaver group in the passepied metre, and which eventually supplants the metre. What one might regard as the involution of the plot arrives from b.46 (the golden section point) with the densest counterpoint (stretto) and the tensest harmony (numerous diminished 7ths in G minor). This section also intensifies the sonata element by adding a little decoration to the subject (the *échappée* B♭ as the second semiquaver in the bass at b.49), not just a little decoration Bach happens to have thought of, but structurally important in that it now makes the semiquaver movement continuous. After this tense, close-spaced and more active moment, the final section (from b.56) opens out into radiance with the bass striding up the scale from G minor to B flat, which becomes the bass note of a tightly spaced 6/4/2 chord at b.59; answered by a corresponding scale up to g'' in the cantus while the bass goes down to E as the bass of a wide open 6/5 chord (b.63), the other, balancing face of the dominant 7th. Finally, from b.68, the climbing scale is in both outside parts, the cantus scale formed by the little *échappée* put end to end with itself in sequence. Since this is the smallest thematic unit in the fugue, its rapid repetition is the most effective climaxing device. Just as in the prelude, Bach has taken something which is essentially an ornament and made it both thematic and structural, even making it the element that builds up the final climax of the piece.

Prelude and Fugue in F minor BWV 857

PRELUDE This is the last of the praeludia in the *Clavier-Büchlein* and returns to the time signature, but with a very different effect from the finger-exercise preludes since this is another cantabile piece. Some have seen dance character in it: Landowska points to the obvious similarity to the Allemande of the G major French Suite at the end of b.2 (1965 p.188), though the mood of that is so different as to make one wonder if there really is a similarity. More relevant is the Sarabande of the C minor Partita BWV 826 which also uses crotchet stems to indicate tenuti. In fact the F minor prelude is an exercise in harpsichord sonority through overholding, and the rich resulting harmonies make its nearest dance equivalent the Allemande of the E flat major French Suite. Here again one may mention Anna Magdalena Bach's copy of François Couperin's *Les bergeries*, which converts all Couperin's carefully notated tenuti into plain semiquavers.

What links all these pieces is not dance character but the sonata moto perpetuo, yet here with a very different effect from the allegro type. As in the C major prelude, the stream of notes of equal value creates a continuum which the player can mould expressively. Bach has therefore constructed this prelude out of delightfully fluid and variable phrase shapes: the first period (to b.9) is made up (in crotchets) of groups of 6+4+4+8+11. In other words, after an opening phrase of unusual cut, there are a few regular phrases where the left hand seems to make a false start with the opening idea, but succeeds finally by rising all the way up one of Bach's most glorious scales, from A♭ to a♭, decorated with 9–7 suspensions (bb.6–8). Nobody with any feeling for the harpsichord could bear not to sustain these chords. Here is another place in Book I where a slightly unequal temperament makes a contribution, giving an iridescence to the sequence, and particularly since the note d♭ makes an enhanced contribution if it supports a slightly wider than normal major 7th in b.7, and also in b.16. The strength of the scale as a shape diverts attention from the fact that its top note, which has to feel like a downbeat, is the second beat of b.8. Yet all has come right by the beginning of b.9.

In the very earliest version the prelude lacked bb.16½ to 21½. In adding these bars Bach rectified an imbalance in the piece. After the long and powerful opening period there were only two four-bar phrases. The addition makes a more satisfactory binary structure, with the top c''' in b.11 as the climax of the first half of the piece, and the dominant cadence in b.12 the half-way point. The addition adds a reprise, beautifully engineered over the highly expressive d♭ of the interrupted cadence of b.16. The dominant pedal gives a sense of traction to the long stream of dissonant semiquavers that rises to a climactic b''♭, again on the second beat of the bar, in b.20, before releasing the tension on the bottom C in b.21 (not in the early version) which now answers the top c''' in b.11 at the end of the first section.

FUGUE This key completes the lower half of the chromatic scale, and therefore has a substantial fugue with a chromatic subject; the B minor fugue, which completes the whole scale, then carries the chromaticism further at the end of the collection. In the first half of Book I (Nos. 1–12) the substantial fugues are Nos. 4, 8 and 12. Out of a total 24 this once again gives the harmonic proportions 2:1 (i.e. 24:12 or 8:4), the proportion of the octave; and 3:2 (12:8), or 3:1 (24:8 or 12:4), the proportion of the 5th.

In this fugue Bach gives a demonstration of quadruple counterpoint and, as always in the 48, it is not just a demonstration of a compositional technique for its own sake but of how to make it playable on the keyboard. Because it is so economical of materials quadruple counterpoint is particularly useful for choruses that have to be composed and rehearsed quickly, and Bach used it for a number of lively cantata movements (e.g. BWV 50 and 182, first chorus). Keyboard playability is more likely to be served by a contemplative style, as in this fugue, where the quadruple counterpoint is presented in full five times in the course of the piece. The economy of the technique, with the same materials being presented over and over again, means that there is a danger of monotony. But it also gives the possibility of a very focussed and concentrated expression, just as a song-writer can create a highly focussed expressive world through limitation of materials to just one or two ideas. In this case Bach has provided a rich web of varied ingredients.

The subject, like that of the C sharp minor fugue, is in the tradition of learned keyboard counterpoint as represented by the chromatic ricercars in Frescobaldi's *Fiori musicali*, with descendants by Froberger and Pachelbel. As in the Langloz *partimenti*, Bach treats the subject-type in black note values. This puts it in the *fuga minor*, verset tradition, albeit with a longer subject than most in that tradition.

Bach treats his traditional subject as a kind of cantus firmus, and surrounds it with expressive *figurae*, the anapaest rhythm (♬♩♬♪) and the 'suspirans' figure which begins with a rest ('sospiro': 𝄿♬♩) accompany it as the *pleurants* accompany a bier. The mourning quality of the subject comes from the fact that each pair of crotchets forms a semitone step, and there is the suggestion of the dissonant leap (*saltus duriusculus*) in the proximity of d'♭ and e'♮. This suggestion of dissonance is taken up in the counterpoints, which have a high level of incidental dissonance and cross-relations, contributing powerfully to the expressive sound world.

At first sight the structure of the first half of the fugue (to b.30) looks odd, with an exposition of *dux–comes–dux–dux*, and two further entries of the *dux* in the dominant (b.19) and tonic (b.27). Is this not a harmonically monotonous expanse? The scheme becomes plain, however, through the logic of the 'interludes'. Bach has subtly rounded off the quadruple squareness by crossing it with a triple scheme. Thus, there is a normal exposition procedure up to three voices, with entries in tonic–dominant–tonic from bb.1–12; then another triplet of entries tonic–dominant–tonic from bb.13–30, but relieved by interludes which have a clear developmental progression: bb.10–13 with the anapaest figure rising; bb.16–18 with it falling; and bb.22–26 with it both falling and rising. The tonic bass entry at b.27, which is the climax of the section, therefore corresponds to the tonic bass entry at b.7. But whereas that was only in three parts and as close-spaced and as low as possible on the keyboard, this has a wide and full texture with all four elements of the counterpoint. The harmonic scheme therefore is not monotonous, but a further concentration of mood.

The second half develops longer lines of semiquavers out of the materials of the counterpoint. There are two warm major-key entries, in A flat (b.34) and E flat (b.40), then a reprise of dominant and tonic entries from b.47. These entries have complex relations to the first section. Most obviously, the entries at bb.47 and 53 correspond to those at bb.19 and 27, so that the second section ends as did the first. Within that, the interlude from bb.50–52 is a transposition of the one from bb.16–18, and the three-part b.47 entry, placed as high as possible on the keyboard, answers the low entry at b.7. The three tonic bass entries at b.7, b.27, and b.53 far from creating monotony reveal three different structural faces of the same expression. There is no point in having quadruple counterpoint unless you display it, and Bach has shown how this technical device can be used to sustain a single concentrated mood over a long span.

Earlier sources of the fugue had a trill on the minim of the main subject, and the copy by Anna Magdalena Bach (P 202) also has it wherever playable (the places are listed in NBA V/6.1). Dürr suggests that this may be an unauthorised addition by W.F. Bach (KB V/6.1 p.254), but that Bach probably did not write a trill in the autograph since it would be taken for granted in this position (NBA V/6.1 p.VI). Learned keyboard counterpoint was customarily written without ornaments, though there are a number of sources which suggest that plenty of ornaments were played (see Chapter Four section 6). The trill which Bach did write (b.6) is not so obvious, particularly if the minim is already being trilled.

Prelude and Fugue in F sharp major BWV 858

PRELUDE It can be taken as certain that the time signature of this prelude was originally $\frac{12}{8}$. Several sources have it as that; the final bass note was changed from a dotted minim to a dotted crotchet only at the A3 stage of revision; and some sources consistently have ♪. ♪. instead of ♩. ♩., indicating a change from dotted crotchets (KB V/6.1 p.189). The change has been interpreted variously. Dürr (1986 p.266) thinks that it indicates a livelier tempo; Tovey (1924 p.105) says that the fact that it was originally $\frac{12}{8}$ should warn us against too lively a tempo. The lighter French character signature $\frac{12}{16}$ distinguishes this subtle and delicate prelude from the more cantabile E major one, or the G major Invention. It also fills out the comprehensive scheme of time signatures in Book I as a compound $\frac{2}{4}$, joining the compound **c** / $\frac{24}{16}$ of the G major Prelude.

The final time signature also underlines the similarity of the material of this prelude to that of the C sharp major: a triad hand-shape based on the raised keys. There is nothing in the sources or notation of either piece to indicate an origin other than in their present keys (KB V/6.1 p.109). This hand-shape is more obvious in the early version (NBA V/6.1 p.184; Ex.7.17) where the fifth finger would play d''♯, and after the repeated c''♯ the hand gradually opens out into the rest of the scale.[78]

The later version, particularly with the trill (which is not in the autograph but is in some closely associated sources), obscures this. A similar hand-shape is part of the materials of the prelude in the same key in Book II. The sequential continuation, which outlines a descending scale with 7–6 suspensions decorated by a variety of *échappée* effects, is a good example of Bach making a motif out of what is essentially an ornamental figure, as shown by Quantz for the same melodic situation (Ex.7.18).[79]

Ex.7.17 Prelude in F sharp major, early version, bars 1–2.

Ex.7.18 Quantz: decorations for the descending scale with 7–6 suspensions.

The character, with syncopations and demisemiquavers, cannot be as lively as the C sharp major, and there is nothing to suggest that Bach associated any hectic quality with this key. Rather it has a special radiance, most expressively worked in setting up the a''♯ in b.29 after a series of A naturals lower down the keyboard.

This prelude shares with the E major prelude Bach's favourite aria ritornello opening, with character head, sequential tail, and closing idea (bb.1–6½), which he re-runs with expansions and developments, adjusted to modulate to different keys. But whereas in the E major he used this principle to create a typical ternary structure, here he runs the ritornello a total of five times, creating a binary structure, with the division at b.15½, of a type unique in *The Well-tempered Clavier* but similar to that used on a much larger scale in, for example, the first movement of the Second Brandenburg Concerto. In the earlier version the second half ran a series of close-spaced entries of the head from b.15½, from A sharp minor via a sequence of rising 4ths (D sharp major, G sharp minor, C sharp major) back to F sharp major (NBA V/6.1 p.185; Ex.7.19).

Ex.7.19 Prelude in F sharp major, early version, bars 15–18.

The addition of the closing idea in bb.17–18 of the later version makes more of the fact that these are paired entries, imitated at the 5th whereas those in the first half had been imitated at the octave (bb.1, 7, 12). They thus make a more substantial development before the return of F sharp. It also makes the harmonic 2:1 division, observed in other pieces, more exact.

FUGUE This fugue is a prime example of Bach's ability to weave felicitous motivic relationships from standard shapes. The opening of the first countersubject (b.3 cantus, second beat) is a reversion, inversion, and diminution of the end of the subject. Much play is made with the cadential shape of the first four notes of the subject (cantus bb.7½–11, 18, 34–5). The subject as a whole, as Hermann Keller observes (1976 p.92), hangs on the first inversion of the tonic chord, but does touch the ground of the lower tonic at crucial points in the bass (b.7, b.22) and these points, together with the perfect cadences at b.11, b.23, and b.33, give the main structural articulation of the piece.

The subject outlines a series of descending 3rds (f"♯, d"♯, b', g'♯), and this is emphasised by the first countersubject (bb.3–4: e"♯, c"♯, a'♯), which also, as Spitta notes (III p.188), works in double counterpoint at the 12th with the subject, i.e. can form 3rds with the subject either above it or below it (see bb.15–16 and 32–3). After the first main cadence (b.7) the motif of 3rds is developed more explicitly in the second countersubject, with the pattern of falling 3rds becoming more extended until bb.23–5. This second countersubject in fact works as such only in its inverted version (bb.12f, 21f) which links it to the shape of the subject. In this form it is identical with the bass figure of the duet 'Wir eilen mit schwachen, doch emsigen Schritten' of Cantata 78, where it is used as the rhetorical device of *gradatio*, or moving up a scale to represent joyful progress from one place to another.

The fugue has an unusual structure, with an exposition of seven bars, then two sections, each roughly twice as long as the exposition (bb.7–23 and 23–35), the second of which is a kind of free contrapuntal inversion of the first (compare especially bb.11ff and 28ff). The changeover point is marked by the most decisive intermediary cadence in the piece, at bb.22–3.

Prelude and Fugue in F sharp minor BWV 859

PRELUDE This prelude is based on a standard finger exercise for 4ths, given by François Couperin as *progrès de quartes* ascending and descending (see Ex.6.1b). Marpurg fingers the rising 4ths in the right hand 1234, and falling 4321 consistently, with the left hand vice versa.[80] It would seem logical to suppose that what Bach had in mind was to use this fingering all around the keyboard in different keys, just as the preludes in C sharp and F sharp major demand the use of the same fingerings for raised keys (*Semitonia*) as for naturals (*Tone*). Intricate modern fingering designed to avoid the thumb on raised notes destroys this logic. The hand-shape is the motif shape, and the thumb will in any case have to be used on raised keys as the motif expands.[81]

As in other finger-exercise preludes, Bach has created from banal materials an extraordinarily ingenious character piece. From the constricted figure of the 4th, the hands gradually open to cover larger intervals, up to a 10th (b.8). The indefinite genre of prelude allows him to write what is essentially a two-part invention, but with freedoms of texture which he well exploits. The piece is in the common 2:1 binary shape, with a cadence on the dominant at the halfway point (b.12½). The first half is concerned with expanding the rising 3rd of the basic material in two parts. The second turns to the three-part texture of the opening with its isolated quavers, which give a skeletal form of countersubject (compare the right hand in b.2) similar to the bass quavers at the opening of the B minor two-part Invention. These are now expanded into chords (bb.14–15), and the feeling of expansion is further enhanced by having the 4ths motif inverted to its rising form. Finally (b.22), the dominant inversion of the opening given at bb.12–13 is repeated, but transposed down a 5th to the tonic, thus bringing back an intensified version of the constricted, overcast mood of the beginning. This is one of the most successful demonstrations in Bach's instructive works of how to develop the expressive possibilities of materials at the same time as developing their possibilities as shapes.

Part of the character is undoubtedly Bach's feeling for the subtle key of F sharp minor, with which he associates a mood of wistful melancholy here, in the equivalent pieces in Book II, and in the canonic third movement of the A major Sonata for harpsichord and violin BWV 1015.

FUGUE The union of materials and expression is as evident in the fugue, but with a much more powerfully expressive effect. Partly the power derives from the tension between objective, *stile antico* features (the $\frac{6}{4}$ metre, the cadential trill at the end of the subject, and the flexibly moulded lines recalling the D sharp minor fugue) and subjective, *stile moderno* personal affects (the rising chromatic line of the subject, used by Monteverdi and Schütz and by Bach in the subject of the first Kyrie of the B minor Mass to express supplication, and the 'sigh' motif of the countersubject). These are given great focus and intensity by extreme economy of material.

There is reason to think that the subject may be a reworking of the learned chromatic type used for example by Froberger in his Ricercar I (1656), a very influential piece published by Roberday (Paris 1650, Fugue 5ème) and Bourgeat (Mainz 1693), copied in the Eckelt tablature, and much imitated (Ex.7.20).[82] This is combined with a kind of diatonic modal outline such as is used in the first Kyrie *pedaliter* BWV 669 of *Clavier-Übung* III. Similarities with the G sharp minor fugue, apparently based on a verset of Kerll's (see the commentary), seem to imply that these two fugues are roughly contemporary and have largely the same objectives. In both cases Bach has managed to turn standard traditional ingredients into poetry in a way that is difficult to envisage from the originals.

The subject of the F sharp minor fugue is one of the most subtly expressive of Bach's, and a great test of the maturity of the player. In sensitive hands its pauses can be made to express an extraordinary depth of experience. With such a subject, contrast and alleviation are not what is needed. The countersubject merely intensifies it by continuing the developing quaver movement in a related affect, and by coming close to being its inversion. The episodic passages (b.7, bb.11–14 etc.) are closely woven from elements of the subject, and the one significant move to the relative major (bb.14–15) is instantly cancelled by a tonic minor entry. The constricted mood of the prelude is continued in that there are few leaps in either subject or countersubject. Many eighteenth-

Ex.7.20 Froberger: subject of Ricercar I (1656).

century writers mention progress by small intervals, and chromatic movement, as expressive of sorrow and doubt (Wessel 1955 p.86). This fugue is an extraordinary demonstration of how elementary materials such as scale segments can be made exceptionally expressive by means of rhythm, and the common vocabulary of decoration in suspensions, appoggiaturas, anticipations.

Like the prelude, the fugue is structured on the 2:1 proportion, with the half-way point marked by the dominant cadence at b.20. In the first half, pitch levels are kept low, and when the cantus finally enters (b.15) it is at the tonic pitch, and hardly rises above what the alto has reached before. The second half has the following scheme of entries: dominant inverso (alto b.15), dominant recto (cantus b.25); tonic recto (tenor b.29), tonic inverso (bass b.32). The purpose of this seems to be to reveal the consanguinity of subject and countersubject, and Bach has done this with great subtlety. The alto inversion entry in b.20 is quite unexpected. One might have expected something after the firm dominant cadence, but the inverted subject is combined with episode figures and itself consists of shapes which had formed the episode from bb.10 to 15. A further obfuscation is that it modulates back to the tonic via various other keys.[83] The subtlety of this entry should not be spoiled by the temptation to 'bring out the subject', if only to show that the player has noticed it. The soprano entry at b.25 is equally concealed initially by growing out of an arpeggio which contains the subject's first three notes, but it soon becomes more obvious. The remaining entries could not be more prominently placed. By putting the episode at b.7, which had prepared the bass entry of the exposition, up an octave Bach brings the pitch levels up to the top of the keyboard, and the void levels below are filled successively by the recto tenor entry at b.29 and the inverso bass entry at b.32, which could hardly be less ambiguous after the expectation created. The fugue is rounded off by an identical tonic soprano entry recto (b.37) to that which completed the first half (b.15). The fugue thus has the usual sonata shape of the second half re-running the events of the first from the dominant back to the tonic, with expansions and developments.

Riemann (1890 pp.93–4) comments that Bach makes no use of the possible inversion of both subject and countersubject, and that this demonstrates his immunity from the accusation of mechanical scholasticism. The problem with affective materials of this sort is that the aspiration of the subject and the lament of the countersubject may be, perhaps ridiculously, contradicted if they are inverted. In this case there is no reason expressively why the countersubject could not have been inverted, as the often-cited parallel with the chorale 'O Mensch bewein dein Sünde groß' which concludes Part 1 of the St Matthew Passion shows.[84] The F sharp minor fugue has only a moment of inversion of the countersubject at b.22. The inversion of the aspirational subject is perhaps more problematical, but two stylistic prototypes should be borne in mind. The first is the orchestral *passacaille* of Lully, in which the descending minor-key tetrachord from tonic to dominant notes is inverted in the course of the piece to rise five steps, giving the outline of the subject of this fugue. The other is the descending chromatic tetrachord of the operatic lament. The inverted version of the subject may be seen as a version of this, and so related in affect to its recto version. No more than any other great composer in writing a moving piece does Bach need to have been making a personal statement. He was merely demonstrating with ultimate mastery how both technical and expressive means can most effectively be developed and presented. A 'personal' note would be entirely inartistic and false and would undermine the universality of what he has achieved. This is not to say that a connoisseurship of emotions is not every bit as essential to the achievement as a connoisseurship of materials and technique.

Prelude and Fugue in G major BWV 860

PRELUDE This is the last of the finger-exercise preludes. It has a number of similarities with the D minor prelude, and both were the same length in their early versions (15 bars). While the D minor patterns out what are essentially continuo player's chords, the G major uses a more open hand position, and transfers the hand around the keyboard more rapidly. Bars 16½–18 use an *évolution* covering a 7th, given as such by Marpurg (1755 etc. Tab.X Fig.1).

The most intriguing point of comparison is the notation of the time signature (KB V/6.1 p.265). Originally the G major prelude gave both staves as **c**, exactly as the D minor though without the triplet indication. An intermediate version then gave both staves as **c**$^{24}_{16}$, a time signature he had already used in the *Orgel-Büchlein* chorale prelude 'Herr Gott nun schleuß den Himmel auf' BWV 617, probably dating from Weimar 1715–16 (Stinson 1996 p.17). That prelude well demonstrates Bach's fascination with, and connoisseurship of, complex metre, and is a notational tour de force in notating three distinct metres (one in each hand and one on the pedals) on only two staves, the upper of which has **c**$^{24}_{16}$, and the lower **c**$^{12}_{8}$. In the end, when he entered the G major prelude in P 415, Bach opted for another solution in separating the signatures between the staves, with **¢**$^{24}_{16}$ on the upper and **c** on the lower: a solution that avoids the pedantic appearance of having both together. It is clear to anyone familiar with the commonsense nature of eighteenth-century notation, when musical intelligence was relied on over mechanical consistency, that each signature applies to the motif it comes before rather than literally to the stave as such. Bach's solution is elegant and practical.

Bach clearly had his reasons for taking this option, rather than using the straightforward means by which the D minor prelude avoids the clutter of dotting every quaver. One is likely to have been his desire to include representatives of a wide range of time signatures: lists of time signatures were a standard item in teaching books of his time (see Chapter Six section 3). Another is that he may have wished for a subtly lighter metre than that of the D minor, as his pupil Kirnberger explains (Dok.III p.224).

In the final version Bach made two insertions that greatly improve the structure. The addition of bb.7½ – 8½ removes an awkward and premature gear-change of harmonic rhythm to two chords per bar, and keeps the figurations regularly alternating between the hands bar by bar until b.11. Then the switch to quarter-bar units is part of a logical build-up, culminating in simultaneous semiquaver movement in both hands from b.13. The additions in bb.14–17½ greatly expand this feature, with a better use of the top range of the keyboard, and a much more effective climax built from the earlier materials.

FUGUE Of the fugues that allude to the concerto principle in Book I, this is the one which in both form and manner conforms most closely to the concerto allegro scheme of Vivaldi's Op.3 and Op.4 from which Bach had arranged two concertos for organ and five for harpsichord at Weimar around 1713. As in other fugues using this principle, the G major fugue stays close to Vivaldi's practice of having a second ritornello statement in the tonic (see Chapter Four section 11). The second tonic exposition (bb.20–31) complements the first by presenting the subject in inversion, setting up what will be, with stretto, the main contrapuntal argument of the fugue. The device of inversion may have been suggested by the gigue metre, since gigues commonly invert their opening theme after the double bar. In showing the potential of the concerto principle for development and variety this fugue contrasts with the A minor fugue, an exposition fugue which also demonstrates inversion and stretto but without the concerto episodes. In the more expansive concerto manner of the G major Bach has loosened up the contrapuntal scheme, contenting himself with a few broad effects as opposed to the dense and remorseless logic of the A minor.

Further intriguing concerto connexions are in the style, with obvious similarity to figurations in the harpsichord part of the first movement of the Fifth Brandenburg Concerto, particularly when the fugue adds demisemiquavers from b.47. At its first introduction (b.9) this figure is immediately inverted (b.10), presaging the subsequent plot of the fugue. The figure is obviously related to the *bariolage* of the violin concerto style, such as Bach had used in his arrangements. An ingenious proposal has been made by Pieter Dirksen (1992) that the Fifth Brandenburg Concerto, notable as the first known keyboard concerto, was written by Bach, notable as the premier German keyboard virtuoso, to demonstrate that the harpsichord could rival the violin as a virtuoso solo instrument in the concerto. In particular there are similarities, primarily in the harpsichord cadenza, with Vivaldi's so-called 'Great Mogul' concerto Op.7/ii No.5 which Bach had arranged for organ (BWV 594). The G major fugue shows how all that can be combined with the intellectual rigour of the fugue.

Various points have been made about the subject as Bach has it. Hermann Keller sees its 7ths as related to the *évolution* passage that ends the prelude (1976 p.97). R.L. Marshall points to its rhythmic symmetry as specially characteristic, given that Bach's alterations to cantata parts show him aiming at this (1972 I p.188). This gives a more subtle shape than the more usual head-and-tail (*Vordersatz, Fortspinnung,* etc.) formula used, for example, in the fugues in concerto style for organ in A minor BWV 543/2 and C major BWV 564/3. In the G major fugue there are, as usual with Bach, various subtle correspondences. After the expositions recto and inverso in the tonic, there are two entries in E minor (a 3rd below the tonic, bb.38, 43), then a stretto recto in its dominant B minor (a 3rd above the tonic, b.51). Most of the inverso entries start on the 5th of the scale, but the E minor entry at b.43 begins on the 3rd, and this is matched by the final entry recto (b.79) on the 3rd of G major, yielding a striking and climactic reharmonization of the subject.

Prelude and Fugue in G minor BWV 861

PRELUDE The preludes of the second half of Book I are generally shorter than those, at least as revised, of the first, but this does not necessarily denote immaturity. This prelude has been criticised for abandoning the opening material after b.11 (Bergner 1986 pp.52–4). Yet the opening bar is in the manner of the opening of an Italian Adagio, rather than an invention, so the wonder is that Bach repeated it at all. The pattern in which the first half of the prelude (bb.1–11) is based on b.1 and continuations, and the second half (bb.12–19) on b.2 and continuations seems perfectly logical and typical of Bach around 1720.

The opening bar is in the manner of a sonata Adagio in which the solo instrument is given a long note, starting quietly and gradually establishing itself with a crescendo (*messa di voce*). This effect has here to be recreated on a stringed keyboard instrument, where the note dies away and crescendo on a held note is impossible. With a trill it is possible on the clavichord, and a gradually accelerating trill can give the effect on the harpsichord. There has been much discussion about the proper performance of the trill.[85] There are no direct instructions for this situation in the instructional literature for keyboard. Quantz recommends long trills for sad pieces, and a slower rate of repetition (1752 Chapter IX para.2). C.P.E. Bach in one place says that the trill, whether long or short, always begins on the upper note (1753 Chapter II Section 3 para.5), but later gives an example of the ribattuta, i.e. a trill beginning on the main note and getting gradually quicker (Tabula IV Fig.XXXVII). However, he mentions this in the context of a very particular situation, i.e. preceding what J.S. Bach in the *Clavier-Büchlein* describes as a 'doppelt-cadence' at a cadence (para.25). Another Berlin pupil of J.S. Bach's, J.F. Agricola, discusses the ribattuta only as an elementary singing exercise to practise trills: when singers are able they should start with an appoggiatura 'which is the true way of beginning the trill' (1757 III/(e)). The intended effect seems to be the singer's or instrumentalist's *messa di voce*, a dynamic ornament which may also include vibrato, as described in numerous tutors of the seventeenth and eighteenth centuries. Whatever best corresponds to that is what is required. It should be noted that Bach notated the first trill sign with a long tail (reproduced in the editions of Dürr and Jones) implying a long trill. There can be no significance in the fact that there is a crossbeam in the *tr* sign since both *tr* and *tr* are used as obvious equivalents in the F sharp minor prelude (b.12, b.18). The most likely solution is to use a version of the ribattuta, i.e. beginning on the main note and starting slowly, perhaps after a slight pause to let the main note tell, and get quicker. The prelude may have originally been conceived as an exercise for this effect. Whatever solution is adopted, the effect of an alarm clock is to be avoided, and it is as well to bear in mind C.P.E. Bach's thoughts about the performance of long trills in Adagios:

> On account of the dying away of the sound and the lack of increase or decrease of volume in a note, which is justly called by the painter's terms of light and shade, it is no small undertaking to play an Adagio in a singing manner, without either being too simple and leaving too many gaps, or giving a confused and ridiculous effect by putting in too many fancy notes. So, since singers and instrumentalists who do not feel this lack equally can seldom leave long notes without decoration . . . [stringed keyboards] can compensate for this lack by various means such as *style brisé* and the like. Also, the ear can put up with more movement on the keyboard than elsewhere. . . . The right balance is difficult to find, but not impossible; our means of sustaining (e.g. with trills and mordents) are as common for singers and instrumentalists as for us. But all these ornaments must be played so roundly that one could believe one heard just the written notes. This involves a freedom which cuts out everything slavish and mechanical. One must play from the soul, not like a trained songbird. A keyboard player deserves more praise for this manner of playing than any other class of musician. (C.P.E. Bach 1753 Chapter III para.7)

FUGUE The subject of this fugue has often been compared (since Seiffert 1899 p.230) with that of the E flat Fuga of Fischer's *Ariadne Musica*. David Schulenberg has shown that the similarities do not end with the subject, but extend to the structure as well (1992 p.187), so Fischer is very probably the proximate model. The subject is nonetheless a generic one in the verset tradition and used as such in the so-called Langloz *partimenti* (Ex.7.21a).[86] It thence was used in other contexts by W.F. Bach in his D minor Fantasia F.19 (noted by Riemann, 1890 I p.102). In these versions the cliché of the 7th leap is directly stated: without it the first four notes of the subject would simply be four notes of an ascending scale. Bach has made this more subtle, as did Telemann for the second point in an organ chorale probably dating from 1730–36; Ex.7.21b).

Ex.7.21 (a) Langloz MS, Fuga.14. Dis. dur, bars. 1–3; (b) Telemann, chorale trio 'Christ lag in Todesbanden', bars 9–10.

The essence of this verset subject is that it is in two halves, the second of which combines in counterpoint with the first, and therefore is designed for stretto. Fischer presents this very clearly (Ex.7.22) with a Fuga in two halves, the first being an ordinary exposition cadencing on B flat (b.5), and the second an exposition with first a double (bb.5–6), then a triple stretto (bb.7–8).

Bach has exploited the possibilities of this type of subject much more fully than his predecessors, both technically and expressively. As in the D major fugue of Book II he has separated the two elements of the subject dramatically with a rest, and lengthened the leading note (Sumikura 1977 p.236). Symmetry is enhanced by the pairs of crotchets at the end of each half. These are clearly meant to be performed as onbeat and offbeat, according to the principles of *quantitas intrinseca* as strong and weak syllables: very probably an ingredient of the 'singable manner' ('*cantable* Art') of playing referred to in the 1723 title-page of the Inventions and Sinfonias. It is also essential to convey the fact that the subject starts as an upbeat to a weak beat, with the strong beat on the leading note. By these means Bach has given a much stronger rhythmic and expressive profile to the original verset subject.

Ex.7.22 Fischer: Fuga in E flat from *Ariadne Musica.*

Bach has also greatly expanded Fischer's plan, again making the articulation of sections more subtle. The main cadences are at the 1:3 proportion points: on the relative major (b.12), and on the tonic (b.24 and b.34). The main structural argument, however, cuts across this in that the manipulation of texture, contrapuntal density, and pitch levels give the 1:2 proportion, with the halfway point at b.18½. Bach has taken Fischer's scheme and considerably expanded it, making much more of the stretti as a climaxing effect. The full four-part texture is reserved for the end of each half, where it is combined with stretto. Bach also refines on Fischer in having his two-part stretto (bb.17–18) in the less obvious counterpoint at the 12th. This inverts at the octave in the three-part stretto (bb.28–9) which forms the main climax of the fugue, again with the texture expanded to four parts. Bach also replaces Fischer's final tenor entry over a conventional pedal with a tenor entry over a bold descending scale, and with the texture further enriched to five parts. The scale was perhaps suggested by the descending outline of the cantus in Fischer's final bars and the fact that Fischer's subject, when straightened out, forms a scale.

Bach makes much more of the expressive possibilities of harmony. The major mode, that Fischer began with, Bach reserves for the radiant entries from b.12 which contrast so well with the tragic, minor-key opening. The upward-driving chromatic line in the bass at b.21½ contrasts with the relaxing diatonic descent in b.33.

Prelude and Fugue in A flat major BWV 862

PRELUDE The seeming mismatch between the key of this prelude and its violinistic style has prompted speculation about a possible origin in another key. Ulrich Siegele, in a brief but thought-provoking article that comments on several pieces from *The Well-tempered Clavier,* proposes it as a chromatically raised version of G major, pointing to similar concertante figurations in bb.39–40 here and the G major organ Praeludium BWV 541/1 (bb.66–7), the Praeludium of the G major clavier Partita BWV 829 (bb.88–9), and the G major prelude from Book II (bb.41–2) (1964 pp.162, 165). One might add the G major fugue from Book I, the only overtly concerto-style fugue in this book. Stauffer sees this type of figuration as a feature of concerto-type improvisation in the Weimar period, and further points to the rhythm 𝅘𝅥𝅯𝅘𝅥𝅯𝅘𝅥𝅮𝅘𝅥𝅮𝅘𝅥𝅮𝅘𝅥𝅮 as also common to this prelude and BWV 541/1 (1980 p.52). It has to be said, though, that the date of composition of the organ prelude is uncertain and could be as late as 1730, and Bach used this rhythm in many works.[87] In fact one could make an equally strong case for an A major original, which would give an open e'' string for the *bariolage* in bb.13–16. The second movement of the A major harpsichord and violin sonata BWV 1015 shares a number of these figurations, and it is perhaps significant that the seemingly idiomatic violin figurations noted by Siegele come in the sonata only in the harpsichord part. But there are plenty of similarities in other keys, and one could cite the Preludio of the E major violin Partita BWV 1006; the F major Invention which shares the same pattern of falling 3rds as the A flat prelude; or the B minor Invention, which shares the layout of character head and sequential tail in violin-sonata style, all in invertible counterpoint (noted by Schulenberg 1992 p.188).

There is nothing in the sources to suggest an origin in any key other than A flat, and the fact that some earlier sources lack a significant number of D naturals, implying an original in the old 'Lydian' three-flat key signature, argues for an original in A flat.[88] The opening has, like that of the C sharp prelude, the appearance of transferring common-key handshapes ('Griffe') on to a raised tonic (*semitonium*) in order to make players as conversant with one as with the other. This is particularly so since the first chord not only seems designed to demonstrate the A flat triad, but its placing on the keyboard also implies an interpretation of the term 'wohltemperirt' more subtle than anything with a Pythagorean 3rd on that note.[89]

Comparison of the earlier and later versions gives a good insight into how Bach was able to enhance greatly the significance of figurations (apart from NBA V/6.1, earlier variants are given by Busoni, in parallel with the later version, and in AB I p.155). In bb.9–13 Bach has kept the bass (which he had clearly thought of first), but recast the upper part, originally a rather ordinary pattern of parallel 6ths with the bass, by introducing a new and more characterful figure. This also works in double counterpoint, so its inversion can be used at bb.26–9. In bb.22–5 he has greatly enhanced and dramatized the move to the subdominant by replacing some routine figurations with long, highly directional scales.

Formally the prelude belongs not so much to the concerto allegro model as to the sonata structure derived from the aria ritornello, as described for the E major prelude.[90] The character head is a subtly worked, closed eight-bar period, and the sequential tail, which modulates down a 4th to the dominant, is in the semiquaver moto perpetuo manner of the Corellian violin sonata. The four-bar version of the character head in E flat (bb.18–21) introduces a new figure in the bass at b.20. This was already in the earlier version and may have something to do with the recasting of the upper-part figuration in b.9. It certainly chimes with the b.11 decoration of the plain crotchet on the first beat of b.10, and provides the motivation for the magnificent scales in bb.22–6. Bars 26–34 present the inversion of the original tail, which now modulates down the 4th from D flat back to A flat. The return in A flat from b.35 neatly recapitulates the main events of the prelude. All this subtlety and variety is achieved in a piece which uses no more than ten notes.[91]

FUGUE The triadic type of subject is a commonplace of verset fugues and canzonas. Schulenberg (1992 p.410) points to Canzon 1 of Frescobaldi's *Secondo libro di toccate* (1627). Nearer to Bach is the type of subject used by Pachelbel in Mode I Magnificat fugues (Ex.7.23a),[92] which clearly relates to the subjects of the D sharp minor fugue of Book I and of *The Art of Fugue*. The major-key equivalent is given in the Langloz *partimenti* (Ex.7.23b: connexions between the keys of F major and A flat major are discussed in the commentary on the A flat fugue of Book II).

Ex.7.23 (a) Pachelbel: Mode I subject of Magnificat verset; (b) Langloz MS: Fuga 23, subject.

It is also the outline of the chorale melody 'Wie schön leuchtet der Morgenstern', which may also have a bearing on the subject of *The Art of Fugue* since it was used by Mattheson (1739) to demonstrate genera of counterpoint.[93] Bach has given subtlety to this typically square canzona-type subject by beginning on a weak beat. In addition he offsets its squareness by combining it with a sinuous countersubject, of a type used with other square, triadic subjects such as that of the C minor organ fugue BWV 546/2, a Weimar work (particularly b.107f, see P. Williams 1980 I p.154), and the *manualiter* Fughetta on 'Allein Gott in der Höh' sei Ehr' in *Clavier-Übung* III (1739, but related to the C major organ fugue BWV 547/2, which may date from *c.*1717). Bach also exploits this triadic nature by expanding the 6th leap into a 7th for the entries at bb.23–4, giving a rising sequence, an expansion he used again to magnificent rhetorical effect in one of the greater fugues, Contrapunctus 4, of *The Art of Fugue* (bb.61ff; see Tovey 1931 p.9).

There have been various formal interpretations of this fugue (details of some are given by Czaczkes, 1982 I p.182), generally with the aim of inflicting a rigid sectionality where Bach plainly sought fluidity. It belongs to the pattern of the Vivaldian ritornello movement with full, tutti expositions at the beginning and end, and including Vivaldi's favourite procedure of having an extra tutti in the tonic (b.10) after the first, non-modulating solo break (bb.8–9). The fact that b.10 is intended as a tutti probably accounts for the addition in the later version of the alto quavers a♭ | a′♭ over the barline from b.10 to b.11, the logic of which is easier to see as Bach writes it in P 415 than it is in modern editions. The awkwardness of b.10 is untypical in a fugue designed to demonstrate playable counterpoint. Thereafter episodes are based on the sequential development of the tail of the subject in b.3, in triple counterpoint at the 12th and octave (bb.11–12, inverted at bb.14–15). These lead to 'tutti' entries in F minor (b.13), and further to B flat minor (bb.16–19). Thereafter the fugue is concerned only with developmental working of episodes until the final tonic exposition at b.27. A further inversion of the triple counterpoint based on the sequential tail of the subject (bb.19–20) is answered by a working of the head (bb.21–2); two versions of the subject with the rising 6th converted into a dominant 7th (bb.23–4) have the climaxing effect of climbing up in 4ths from E flat to D flat, giving rhetorical point to the subdominant emphasis one would expect at around this point (b.25). From here a long bass sequence, with some very ingenious working of shapes from the subject in the upper parts, leads down to the tonic reprise (b.27). The final broadly harmonized tonic entry in the last three bars gives a conclusion of rhetorical clarity rather than contrapuntal complexity to this 'Spielfuge', as it does to the fugue in C minor. As with the B minor organ fugue BWV 544/2, Bach has contrived through sophistication of art and rhetorical placing to make a most ordinary subject into a memorable and loveable theme (see Chapter Four section 4).

Prelude and Fugue in G sharp minor BWV 863

PRELUDE Hugo Riemann detected a kinship between this prelude and the prelude in C sharp minor 'metaphysically, transcendentally', and cited similarities in their openings, and in bb.3–4 here compared with bb.5ff in the C sharp minor (1890 I p.111). Schulenberg went further and proposed that the two pieces were composed in rapid succession to fill up the key scheme (1992 p.164). It is certainly tempting to speculate about the rare-key pieces. The preludes in C sharp major and F sharp major would work as two-part Inventions and could conceivably have grown out of a scheme for those. The three-part Sinfonias, on the other hand, are strictly in three parts so neither the C sharp minor nor the G sharp minor prelude could have been intended for a further development of those. There are, however, several good reasons for not regarding these two preludes as a pair. Firstly, the C sharp minor seems to have been written with some specific performance principles in mind (see the commentary), but the same is not apparent in the G sharp minor. And secondly, there is reason to suspect that both prelude and fugue in G sharp minor originated in G minor. The noticeably frequent lack of sharp signs to the E sharps in the earliest sources, and even occasionally in the autograph P 415, suggests an original with the 'Dorian' one-flat key signature. This would make more sense in terms of the common and traditional key of G minor (or Mode II) than for the advanced and 'modern' key of G sharp minor.[94] There are yet stronger reasons for supposing a G minor origin for the fugue. This prelude and fugue thus probably belong with the D sharp minor fugue as pieces Bach transposed to fill their place.

If this prelude cannot strictly be a three-part Sinfonia, it is nonetheless an excellent example of the Invention principle, fully deserving Spitta's description as 'a really inspired composition of the most subtle construction' (II p.174). The 'invention' in the upper part at b.1, based on a harmonic formula similar to that which opens the C major prelude and others, is present in over half of the bars of the piece, either recto or in inversion. The episodes based on it are expertly moulded. The original form (bb.3–4) has the semiquavers arranged to go round a circle of 5ths, with a chord change on every third quaver (as in the invention itself). The long episode beginning at b.19 has them at first in a more relaxed form with one chord only per beat; then more intensely with two chords per beat and simultaneous semiquavers in both hands; and finally yet more intensely with hemiola rhythm, leading to the climax diminished 7th on the first beat of b.25. The right-hand chords at b.24 are not restful violin double stops (as in the Adagio of the F minor harpsichord and violin sonata BWV 1018) but, in a milder way, are akin to the breathless excitement of trumpet *Bebung*, described by Altenburg (1795 p.118) and used most effectively by Bach in, for example, the B minor Mass. They should be played legatissimo to create the maximum sonority, and their effect in a contrapuntal piece is of stepping outside rational discourse in the heat of building to the climax.

One further performance detail is the slurred pairs of lower *échappées* at b.7. The same effect is in the C sharp minor prelude (b.36) and the E minor prelude (b.3). It is possible that Bach intended the usual French practice of overholding the first of each pair (C.P.E. Bach 1753 Chapter III para.18 may be describing this effect).

FUGUE Opinions of this fugue differ wildly, from immature 'Jugendarbeit' (Spitta) to 'one of the profoundest' in the 48 (Tovey).[95] In addition, it was Marpurg who started the red herring of the 'subdominant answer', oddly for somebody so well versed in traditional fugal literature (1753 p.46; Dok III p.30). The key to all of this lies again in the verset tradition. Just as the supposedly 'irregular' order of entries in the C major fugue has a perfectly ordinary explanation in the light of that tradition, so the supposed peculiarities of this fugue are explained, and Bach's objectives are illuminated.

If the F major fugue is a modernisation of Fischer's *Ariadne* fugue in the same key, and at the same time develops its elements in an infinitely more searching way, then the G sharp minor may find its origin in a verset fugue of Kerll's (1686).[96] Regarding the 'subdominant answer', this is quite normal for the Hypodorian mode where one expects the subject to lie in the octave d-g-d (soprano and tenor; Ex 7.24a), and the answer in the octave g-d-g (alto and bass; Ex.7.24b).[97] Ex.7.25 presents the exposition of Kerll's verset, aligned with Bach's, transposed into the 'Dorian' one-flat key signature.

Ex.7.24 (a) Authentic tessitura of Mode II; (b) plagal tessitura of Mode II; (c) Kerll's subject, adjusted to cadence on the dominant.

Ex.7.25 (a) Kerll: Magnificat secundi toni, Versus Et misericordia eius, bars 1–9; (b) Bach: G sharp minor fugue, transposed to 'Dorian' G minor, bars 1–9.

If he indeed based the fugue on this verset, Bach seems first to have imagined a more interesting and dramatic version of the subject that cadences on the dominant (Ex.7.24c). This converts a seventeenth-century model subject with mannered chromaticism into a tonally directed one, with a move to the dominant. By beginning on a weak beat he has, as in so many fugues originating in the verset tradition, given subtlety and flexibility to an otherwise rhythmically square subject type. In addition, he has decorated the subject with several other features common in that tradition. One is the overt cadentiality of the end of the subject, the very thing he avoided in adapting Fischer's F major Fuga. Having taken it on here, he makes it a pervasive element in the motivic working of the fugue. The other is the pattern of paired repeated notes, to be found in Kerll's *Modulatio organica* (1686, *passim*), Fischer's *Blumen-Strauß* (published 1732; see ed. Werra p.108), and many others. Bach took little else from Kerll's verset, except perhaps the entry starting on c" at the end of Kerll's exposition, and which may find an echo in b.15 and b.37 of Bach's fugue. There is no hint of Kerll's final stretto and pedal, perhaps because such clichéd finishing devices do not belong in a piece where Bach has reworked traditional materials in a newly subjective and expressive way. There is, on the other hand, no lack of contrapuntal sophistication since the exposition is worked in triple counterpoint, of which Bach uses five of the six permutations in the course of the fugue.

One of the features which Spitta considered to betray an early origin is the octave transposition of bb.7–8 at bb.11–12. This is also a feature of the F sharp minor fugue (bb.7–10 and 28–31), another fugue of extraordinary maturity, and is the main reason for thinking that these two fugues are roughly contemporary and have largely the same objectives. The F sharp minor subject may be a reworking of a traditional chromatic ricercar subject, with a similar intention of making it newly expressive to that of the G sharp minor (see the commentary).

Some old-fashioned features remain, such as the squareness of the exposition, with the subject entering regularly every two bars, demonstrated by the comparison with Kerll, and the fact that only half-way through the fugue (b.20) does it leave the tonic. At this point (b.21) a new motif is introduced, featuring the tritone leap of the subject, and the suspension which has provided the motivation for the episode beginning at b.13, and which rounds out the cadentiality of the end of the subject. The signs of a one-flat G minor origin are stronger than in the prelude and, as in the D sharp minor fugue, the transposition into a sophisticated key in itself rarefies and modernises the expression of the fugue.

Prelude and Fugue in A major BWV 864

PRELUDE In a collection designed to demonstrate the playability of keyboard counterpoint, this must be the most brilliant example of that objective (see Chapter Four section 5). The mere demonstration of triple counterpoint is not in itself the main point of the piece, since that is amply demonstrated elsewhere. Rather it is the art of laying it out in the most expressive, sonorous, and playable way on the keyboard.

Bach has graded the order of appearances of his block of triple counterpoint according to the degree of trickiness for playing of the different permutations. He has it in its most natural layout at the opening, with the crotchets in the bass, the most melodic line on top, and the harmonic filler part in the middle. On its second appearance (bb.4–5) the hands are reversed, with the running part in the left hand; and the third appearance (bb.9–10) has it in its trickiest form, with the running part in the middle, where it must migrate between the hands. That he was concerned more with playability than mechanical exactness is clear from adjustment to the left-hand part in the second beat of b.9. Some sources give the bass here in its usual form 𝄾 ♪ ♩ ♩, but this can only be pedantry.

Even the limitation of the four-octave compass is turned to expressive advantage by bending the opening of the semiquaver theme downwards on its first minor-key appearance (b.12). Bach has reserved to the end the very sonorous permutation of his counterpoint where the 7ths between middle part and bass in bb.1–2 are converted into the sharper dissonance of 2nds (bb.20–1). This, together with octave transposition, neatly gets around the potential flaw of having the same theme in the same part in the same key twice in succession (as the middle part has from bb.18 to 21). For these last two tonic appearances Bach obviously wished to have the liveliest themes in the outer parts.

Apart from the keyboard-technical aspect, the block of triple counterpoint is a very subtle major-key working of the cliché of the *lamento* bass. The subtlety is highlighted by comparing this with the much more conventional treatment in the little fughetta BWV 901/2, which later became the basis of the A flat major fugue in Book II, or the utterly conventional treatment in Ex.7.26 (see also Ex.8.24).

Here each element is consistently in the same part: the crotchet chromatic steps in the bass, the cliché of 7–6 appoggiaturas regularly resolved in the upper part, and the circle of 5ths patterned out in semiquavers in the middle.

Ex.7.26 Conventional triple counterpoint for the *lamento* bass (author).

Comparing this with the first two bars of the prelude, one can see how Bach plays deliciously on the ambiguity resulting from the translation to the bright key of A major. The first 7–6 appoggiatura is in the upper part, its resolution given special galant-style character by a chromatically decorated resolution. But the suspensions then migrate to the middle part, where they are given characterful second-practice resolution by leap. After only a couple of chromatic steps the bass strides cheerfully around the circle of 5ths in crotchets, while the running semiquavers take over the outline of the *lamento* bass. This skilful mixing of elements gives the piece its unique expressive colour and, like so many pieces in this Book, shows how traditional materials can be given new life.

The episodes are equally skilfully worked. The first (bb.6–8) is based on the appoggiaturas; the second (b.11) introduces a descending scale; and the third (bb.14–17) combines the two. These equally are arranged in graded order of playing trickiness. At the end the scales take over, and open out in the final bars to the widest pitch range, probably to prepare for the large fugue that is to follow.

Part of the point of the prelude is for the player to cultivate the art of characterizing three simultaneous lines of music, another meaning of the 'singable manner of playing'. The offbeat resolutions of the 7ths in the middle part at b.2 and elsewhere in the piece need to be faded out. The chromatic ornament in the upper part in the third beat of b.1, a kind of inverted *Anschlag*, features also in the equally sophisticated and expressive F minor three-part Sinfonia. Since this is a decorated appoggiatura it is possible that the first semiquaver should be held *coulé*-fashion through the second. In the Schübler chorale prelude on 'Wachet auf' BWV 645 this figure has a slur on the two semiquavers and a staccato dot on the quaver.

FUGUE Not the least part of the wit of this fugue is the combination of learned and free prototypes to which it refers. Learned are the use of two subjects (*a due soggetti*), and the reference to the *obligo* of proceeding only by leap, as described by Berardi and others, and demonstrated in Frescobaldi's *Recercar ottava, obligo di non uscir di grado* (*Ricercari e canzoni francese*, Rome 1615). This tradition is reflected in verset-type subjects such as Ex.7.27a from the *Wegweiser*. Versets are not as rigorous in keeping to the *obligo* as Frescobaldi is in his ricercar (it is merely a matter of a subject featuring leaps); nor is Bach either here or in the fugues that use *oblighi* in *The Art of Fugue*.

Also from the Frescobaldi tradition is a contrapuntal texture in compound time with multiple interlocking syncopations, creating a sort of rhythmic Chinese puzzle of one rhythmic figure inside another. Frescobaldi delighted in this texture, as in the *Cento partite sopra passacagli* (1637), variations 17–18, 105–6, etc., and Froberger in, for example, the final ($\frac{12}{8}$) section of his D minor

Toccata (1649 No.2; No.8 in Louis Bourgeat's Mainz publication of 1693). The effect was not limited to keyboard music, and one of its wittiest uses is in the final section of Corelli's trio sonata Op.3 No.12 (Rome 1689; also in A major: Ex.7.27b). This is the most spectacular sonata in a collection which Bach seems to have known (see the commentary on the C major fugue). The subject, with a pattern of falling 3rds and rising 4ths, has a strong resemblance to Bach's, as has the prevalence of witty cross-rhythms. Bach contrives a

Ex.7.27 (a) *Wegweiser*: Toccatina in B flat, bars 1–6; (b) Corelli: Op.3 No.12, opening of final section.

much more substantial and varied piece from these materials by introducing a second subject (bb.23ff) which complements the leaps of the first with running steps.

Bach's subject shares with that of the E major fugue the separation of head from tail and the ambiguity of identity of the subject. In the E major the character head is two notes; here it is only one, yet nobody could say it lacks character. It is as if Bach took an ordinary $\frac{6}{8}$ verset-type subject, separated the first note by adding a beat, and so demonstrates how a cliché can be made into something more interesting by sheer force of personality. This aspect evidently appealed to Beethoven who played it, according to Czerny's edition, with the first note of the subject *fortissimo staccato*, and the rest *piano legato*. The tail of the subject is based on the shape of one of the commonest scale progressions of the Baroque, a rising sequence in which the bass goes down a 3rd and up a 4th. Beethoven used the same interval pattern in the fugue of the A flat major piano sonata Op.110, and demonstrated the powerful rhetorical climaxing possibility of augmentation of the subject. That would be out of place in Bach's fugue, though he of course knew of the possibilities of the progression and used it in the powerful scalic gradation of the *pedaliter* chorale prelude on 'Wir glauben all an einen Gott' BWV 680 from *Clavier-Übung* III.[98]

Primarily this fugue relates to the freer traditions of verset fugue, and also of *partimento* or *partitura* (see Chapter Four section 10). Characteristic of the *partimento* is the number of entries in the lowest part in the first section (bb.1–20). This includes two successive bass entries (b.4 and b.6) in the manner of a *partitura*, i.e. a continuo part for a fugal instrumental piece where the continuo plays the lowest sounding part in the score. Equally characteristic of the *partimento* is freedom of voicing: for example, the middle voice becomes the top one at the end of the first entry of the second subject (b.25). One can think of an exchange of parts back at b.27 but that is hardly necessary since wit is the essence and this juggling is part of it. Dürr's complicated stemming (see Ex.7.28c), for which there is no precedent in the autograph, nor is it used by Kroll, Dehnhard or Jones, seems pedantic. The treatment of the subject is also very free. The alto entry at b.2 makes it seem that the subject consists of the first bar only, yet the soprano continuation in b.2 is subsequently revealed to be a constant part of it, in which case the opening seems to be a double fugue on one subject, as are some of Handel's *partimenti*.[99] The answer itself changes the intervals of the subject in order to combine at this point, and this freedom is gradually developed, notably in the bass entries at b.16 and b.33. Also characteristic of the *partimento* is the use of figured-bass clichés, as in the upper parts at bb.25–6 (in 3rds) and bb.42–3 (in 6ths). But because of the freedom of the genre, Bach has been able to give the most ordinary version (bb.25–6) the very felicitous effect of a triple stretto.

The overall shape of the piece is of a first section of 20 bars (bb.1–20); a two-bar link (bb.20–21); then a second section of 20 bars (bb.22–42) which introduces the second subject. Two short sections (bb.42–9 and 49–54) subtly recapitulate these events, all giving one of Bach's characteristically artful combinations of formal prototypes, in this case of binary and da capo structures. The interval alternation of the subject is given a strongly climaxing form at bb.49–50, where the falling 3rds are inverted to rising 6ths. This caused Spitta and others to propose that the cantus in the equivalent place at bb.29–31 should go up to d''' (i.e. from the last beat of b.30 into b.31, the cantus should be b'' e'' c'''♯ | d'''). This would give a pitch strategy typical in this collection of an opening in the middle of the keyboard, the highest note roughly half-way through, and the bass running down to the lowest note at the end (as for example in the C minor fugue). Having to avoid d''' spoils this crucial structural arrangement. Since Bach exceeded the four-octave C–c''' compass sooner in the bass than in the treble, Dürr suggests the possibility of a G major original (KB V/6.1 p.190), which would give the BB–c''' compass of, for example, the harpsichord in the Fifth Brandenburg Concerto (1721), but there is nothing in the sources to substantiate this.[100]

There are few significant differences between early and later versions other than at bb.4–5, which Bach seems to have reworked as he entered it into P 415 (KB V/6.1 p.29). Czaczkes (I p.195) proposes that the second subject derives from the original alto part in these bars: Ex.7.28 gives: (a) the original upper parts; (b) an outline of the second subject; and (c) both subjects as they appear at bb.23–4. In fact it seems that the second subject derives from a combination of both alto and cantus lines.

Ex.7.28 (a) A major fugue, bars 4–5, original upper parts; (b) outline of the second subject; (c) first and second subjects at bars 23–4 (as in NBA V/6.1).

The final version is a great improvement not only in avoiding the pitch stagnation of the cantus and giving a much better sense of direction to the upper parts, but also in avoiding anticipating the second subject.

Prelude and Fugue in A minor BWV 865

PRELUDE This prelude has been criticised on two counts. One, that it is out of proportion to the very large and powerful fugue, the other that it is lacking in structural finesse. The first, voiced by Spitta (II p.166), shows a lack of feeling for eighteenth-century variety and balance. As Mattheson says, if the chorale is long, the organist should play a short prelude in order to make sure that the service is the right length (1739 Part III Chapter 25 para.23). For the second, Hermelink, among others, has proposed it as an early work since it lacks transitions between sections (1976 p.66). The harmonic formula of the first four bars is the same as that of the finger-exercise preludes in C minor and D minor, and at 28 bars the prelude is similar in length to the earliest version of the C minor. But in comparison the A minor is a much more highly characterized and a more finished piece. It does nonetheless seem to have its origin in some keyboard-technical *évolution*, in this case mordents involving the thumb and the fifth finger. The result is a very attractive light and playful mood given subtlety by the mild minor key, and quite the opposite of the fugue, whose anapaest rhythm it inverts.

The final version makes no substantive additions to the early one, but various crudities are tidied up, and the performance implications of the notation are fully thought out. Dürr proposes that the A in the bass of the last bar of the early version was put up an octave in the final version for playability, and that this shows that the prelude had a separate origin from the fugue since the fugue ends with a long A which can only be played with a pedal (1984 p.64). It is more likely that Bach preferred the pattern of rising bass pitches from b.25. The last a is then taken up by the fugue subject, which also opens with the lower auxiliary we have just heard in the right-hand's final mordent figure. Given the prelude's appearance of being based on an elementary finger exercise, and the fugue's advanced virtuoso requirements, it is quite likely that they did originate separately. But in his adjustments Bach has contrived that the prelude introduces the fugue most felicitously, as indeed he did in the C minor prelude and fugue.

FUGUE This extraordinary fugue poses a number of riddles. It seems to belong with the D sharp minor fugue, and perhaps also the E flat major prelude, in an earlier layer of works, marked by a rigidly schematic agenda and a general lack of 'interludes' between expositions (see Chapter Four section

10). This relates to the traditional pattern of improvised fugue based on a series of expositions, or the A minor fugue from Reinken's *Hortus musicus* trio sonatas which Bach arranged for clavier (BWV 965/2) and which in its original state presents nothing but permutations of its triple counterpoint, without modulation or relieving episodes. Spitta (II p.163) placed it among very early (probably Arnstadt) works such as the sonatas in D major and A minor (BWV 963, 967) and the Capriccio 'in honour of Johann Christoph Bach' BWV 993, since these are the only other clavier works which require pedals.[101] He also perceived a close relationship between the scheme of this fugue and the fugal sections of Buxtehude's A minor Praeludium BuxWV 153. This similarity is not very compelling since Buxtehude's subject is of the old-fashioned canzona type and his scheme is nothing like as rigorous or elaborate as Bach's.

Such an early date seems unlikely for this monumental and highly accomplished piece. It could join clavier works written at Weimar before 1710 or so, but one of its most striking features is the driving anapaest rhythm of the subject, one which Bach often used in his mature concertos. This comes in two Venetian concertos which Bach arranged for keyboard around 1713–14: Benedetto Marcello's Op.1 No.2, arranged in C minor for harpsichord as BWV 981; and Vivaldi's Op.3 No.11 in D minor, arranged for organ as BWV 596. The Vivaldi fugue seems particularly relevant in that it uses four-part invertible counterpoint and inversion. It also features a descending scale in semiquavers which is prominent among the motifs of Bach's fugue. It may be that Bach was seeing what could be done in this manner in a solo virtuoso keyboard fugue. Certainly, if played with Vivaldian energy, the fugue has a stunning effect both for keyboard-technical and contrapuntal virtuosity. Peter Williams has proposed that it may be a demonstration fugue, not intended for performance, as he suggests that some of *The Art of Fugue* may be (1984 p.192), and that this may explain the difficulty of playing the ending, if it was just to demonstrate the device of a four-voice stretto over a pedal. From what we know of Bach it is unlikely that he ever intended anything as paper music, and the magnificent rhetorical ending of this fugue is plainly designed to be effective in performance. Rather than an abstract demonstration it seems more likely to have been intended as a competition piece, with which Bach in his twenties could play his opponent into the ground both as keyboard virtuoso and contrapuntist, if a pedal harpsichord was available for the occasion.

As with many of Bach's ingenious contrapuntal effects, the actual materials are simple, and therefore effective. In this case the subject is based on a scale outline which can be imitated at the unison/octave or the 5th/4th, recto or inverso (Ex.7.29). As in the D sharp minor fugue, the A minor works through a series of expositions which explore the possibilities with remorseless logic, and with clear marker cadences at the end of each exposition, as follows: (1) exposition recto bb.1–14½; (2) inverso bb.14½–27½; (3) stretto pairs recto at the

Ex.7.29 A minor fugue, stretto outlines: (a) unison recto, bar 27½; (b) octave inverso, bar 48½; (c) 5th recto, bar 64½; (d) 5th inverso, bar 67½.

octave bb.27½–48; (4) stretto pairs inverso at the octave (with an initial false entry at the 5th) bb.48–64½; (5) stretto pairs at the 5th recto b.64f, inverso b.66f; then stretto in two voices b.73f, in three voices b.76f, in four voices b.83f.

As Spitta points out, Bach worked a similar scheme in the B flat minor fugue of Book II with vastly more subtlety and maturity. Yet the A minor has an appealing grim doggedness and is not without its own subtleties. Marker cadences define the ends of expositions, but the second exposition (b.14f) has a stronger cadence at the end of the first inverso entry (bb.17–18); and trio-sonata-type relaxations (b.40f, b.70f) occur asymmetrically within expositions, in the manner of the D sharp minor fugue.

Prelude and Fugue in B flat major BWV 866

PRELUDE This prelude is similar to the B major prelude of Book II in its combination of traditional and new stylistic references and keyboard-technical devices, and shows Bach yet again updating traditional materials. The prototype is almost certainly the D major Praeludium of Fischer's *Les pieces de clavessin* (1696), a piece for pedal harpsichord/clavichord. Fischer's prelude is in five sections: (1) chords, presumably freely arpeggiated; (2) steady demisemiquavers in the pattern of the opening of Bach's prelude; (3) chords; (4) the demisemiquaver section transposed to the dominant; (5) a varied section with chords, including many dissonances, in dotted rhythm, and with demisemiquaver runs.

This gives a common late-seventeenth-century sectional structure with a pattern of section types. It alternates freely rhetorical sections with motoric patterned ones, in this case with a reprise element between sections 2 and 4, and with the rhetorical sections 1, 3 and 5 becoming progressively more elaborate. What Bach has done is to take Fischer's ingredients and build them into a two-section piece with a much higher degree of unity between the sections, rather as he did with the three sections of the E flat major prelude. One copy by an anonymous Bach pupil (P 401) adds the word *adagio* at the chords in b.11. It is unclear whether this is an initiative of the pupil's, or an instruction from Bach in a lesson (KB V/6.1 p.290). Either way, the word does not imply a slow tempo in these circumstances, but that the rest of the piece should be played in a freely rhetorical manner, as distinct from the motoric movement of bb.1–10. This is precisely the contrast between patterned and rhetorical sections in Fischer's prelude. But Bach has also linked the sections on the 'modern' principle of the Corellian moto perpetuo, where a number of events are unified by the motor energy derived from a single predominant note value, in this case the demisemiquaver. Unlike the Fischer prelude, where the final section stands somewhat apart from the others, Bach has the demisemiquavers predominate and the final bar returns to the opening figure.

The first section is based entirely on seventeenth-century keyboard technique, designed to produce brilliant effects without having to displace the hand or pivot on the thumb. The figure in b.1 was a particular favourite of Johann Pachelbel, Johann Christoph Bach's teacher. The scale passages in b.3 etc. are divided between the hands.[102] Scale passages seem generally to have been either divided between the hands in groups of four notes, or played in groups of eight using a *roulade* fingering of successive groups of four notes in one hand, both of which shapes occur in the final section of Fischer's prelude. In his second section it is possible that Bach is moving on to a new keyboard technique, with which a scale can cover the entire keyboard smoothly in one hand, pivoted on the thumb. In notating this he has been careful, unusually for Book I, to indicate which hand is to play which notes (KB V/6.1 p.289), so the scale in b.12 has the right hand run down to the bottom of the keyboard, and that in b.14 has the left hand running up almost to the top.[103]

FUGUE This is typical of the mature fugues of Book I in being as much a galant character piece as a demonstration of counterpoint. The repeated notes of the first countersubject have a strongly individual character, rather than being the cliché of the seventeenth-century canzona-type subject. In this respect this fugue looks forward to the G minor fugue of Book II. Bach offsets the static quality of the end of the subject by having a prominent step up at the beginning (the second bar is a decorated repetition of the first a tone higher), and the argument of the fugue consists of the artful and witty exploitation of these two characteristics. After the triple counterpoint has been exposed, a cantus entry (b.13) reminds us of the step up, followed by the static two bars, but which are then themselves transposed a step up (b.17). This is at the dynamic phase of the fugue where all is in development. In the equivalent place at the end (from b.43) Bach as a *jeu d'esprit* has the same effect but without the step up, giving as it were a repetition of the repetition.

With these shorter fugues one may expect correspondences between earlier and later stages of the piece. If the head of the subject is inverted it yields steps down, of which there are three at bb.19–21, extended to five at bb.30–4. The transposition up at b.17 takes the right hand to the top of the keyboard, and one might expect a corresponding point later in the piece where the left hand ran down to the low C. But this would not be in the nature of the material, so Bach has a different early/late correspondence: the first full statement of the triple counterpoint (from b.9) is in the closest possible spacing in the middle of the keyboard, while the last (from b.41) opens the spacing out. The fact that the full keyboard range is not exploited in Bach's usual dramatic way contributes to the very moderate character of the piece, and links again to the pitch restriction of the subject.

The fugue is in Bach's favoured version of the da capo structure, with the reprise (from b.35) beginning in the subdominant area, and the subdominant entry (b.37) answered by the final entry (b.41) in the tonic. The original ending had the top two elements of the triple counterpoint the other way up at bb.45–6. This meant that the running semiquaver motif came twice at the same pitch, albeit in a different part. Putting it down an octave in the same part gives better pitch variety and also uses a new permutation; and having the busiest parts close together at a lowish pitch at the end enhances the effect of winding down and fading out.

Prelude and Fugue in B flat minor BWV 867

PRELUDE Busoni in his commentary on this prelude speaks of the noble manner of the rare-key preludes in C sharp minor, E flat minor, and here. Bach certainly created very strong characters for these keys, which imprinted themselves on several later composers (see Chapter Five section 2).

A number of prototypes have been suggested for this prelude. The most likely is the type of prelude sometimes called Toccata, Tastada or Arpeggiata in the clavier suites of Fischer (1696, 1738; Ex.7.30c, see Appendix A) or the verset collections of the Munich organist and pupil of Kerll, F.X.A. Murschhauser (1703, 1707; Ex.7.30b, see Appendix A). The movement of these pieces (of rhythmicised chords) and the title Arpeggiata (how does one arpeggiate chords written in these rhythms?) are curious. It is therefore interesting to compare pieces of this type with the Phrygian Tastata from the *Wegweiser* (Ex.7.30a, see Appendix A).

The titles Praeludium, Toccata, Toccatina and Tastada are all applied to this type of piece by Fischer. Nonetheless the comparison suggests that this sort of repeated chord pattern may have been one of the ways in which movements which would have been played as chords or plain parts on the organ could be adapted for clavier. The *Wegweiser* Tastata comes out as something very similar to Murschhauser's Arpeggiata when played in this manner, and it shows that the pattern is in itself the arpeggiation, and does not need further elaborate spreading of chords. The sustained, organ origin accounts for the static nature of the bass. There are two pieces of this type in Fischer's *Les pieces de clavessin* of 1696; the piece that comes closest to Bach's prelude is the D minor Toccata of the 'Uranie' suite in the *Musicalischer Parnassus*. Characteristics are: plangent dissonances and multiple dissonances, the Neapolitan 6th, and a variable texture from few notes to very full chords. All of these feature in Bach's prelude, though used with a control and sense of dramatic effect that are unique in the tradition.

A further possible reference is the type of repeated chord pattern used by the Dresden lutenist and friend of Bach's Silvius Leopold Weiss at the opening of his *Tombeau sur la Mort de Mr Comte de Logy* (1721).[104] The opening harmonic formula and the key are the same and, though Weiss goes on to other textures and effects, the *lamento* character is borne out by the similarity of the movement of Bach's prelude to that of the opening Sonatina of the early funeral cantata BWV 106, a similarity noted by Keller (1976 p.118).[105]

As usual, Bach exploits the small change of the genre infinitely more purposefully than did his predecessors, particularly in adding an element of motivic development unusual in such pieces. The decoration of the chords at the opening becomes fundamental to the structure from b.3 where it moves into the bass, and the argument of the rest of the piece depends on the manipulation of this figure, notably in the long bass descent from b.16 to b.19. The prelude is divided by the cadence on the dominant at the exact mid-point (harmonic proportion). The manipulation of texture is remarkable, particularly so on the harpsichord where, as Quantz says, the number of notes in chords is the principal way of controlling dynamics. This prelude could be a demonstration of Quantz's comments on the relative weight and expressive voicing of dissonant chords (1752 Chapter XVII Section VI paras.9–16). The educational purpose of the type is to cultivate the legatissimo touch which will fill a stringed keyboard instrument with sound, and also by means of subtleties of touch and arpeggiation to project the expressive elements of the harmony.

FUGUE This fugue returns to the seventeenth-century version of *stile antico*, with a mannered dissonance in the subject, that we have already seen in the C sharp minor fugue. It comes at an equivalent place near the end of the collection as that had near the beginning, and these are the only two fugues in five parts. Whereas the C sharp minor began with entries built up from the bass in the manner of a Corellian *durezze e ligature* movement, this has entries from the top down in the manner of a motet.

Both fugues are brilliant examples of the genre, and clearly more mature works than the other *stile antico* fugue, the D sharp minor. Yet, as Busoni points out, one need only put the second note of the typically Mode I D sharp minor subject down an octave to have the same subject as this.[106] The upward minor 9th leap has had various expressive interpretations, not all of which are what one would expect in a post-Beethoven world. For Angelo Berardi it meant wisdom ('Sapientia'; 1689 p.33). An eighteenth-century consensus associated the interval with madness (Wessel 1955 pp.85–8), and Kirnberger (1782) cites it in this fugue as signifying despair. More relevant, perhaps, is Pirro's characterization as 'great distress', based on Bach's use of it in his vocal works (1907 pp.58–60). What appealed to Bach in this genre was the expressive tension possible between the objective control inherent in the *stile antico* and the tortured personal anguish of second-practice dissonance, enhanced by the weird key; a tension much appreciated and amplified by Beethoven in the fugue of the C sharp minor quartet Op.131, in which a passionately dissonant head contrasts with a serenely stepping tail.

As well as the C sharp minor fugue, the B flat minor is customarily compared to the opening chorus of BWV 64 (1723) and the organ fugue on the theme from Corelli's Op.3 No.4 trio sonata BWV 579 (probably an early Weimar work). Both of these feature stretto, and stretto is obviously the essence of this type of subject. Like the D sharp minor, this is an exposition fugue, with four expositions: the first (bb.1–25) cadences on D flat major; the second (bb.25–37) features stretto at two bars' distance and cadences on A flat minor; the third (bb.37–55) has a stretto at half a bar's distance (b.50) and cadences on E flat minor, with a stretto entry over the cadence; and the fourth (bb.55–75) features one simultaneous entry (b.55) with a sort of counterpoint at the 10th, and concludes with a complete five-part stretto.

Already in the first exposition the motet-style antiphonal pairing of voices gives the effect of double fugue on one subject, and the ambiguity of identity of the subject noted in several other fugues. Such ambiguity is typical of Bach's mature style, with its long-breathed paragraphs which reserve clear demarcations for important structural points. It is nonetheless clear that in this fugue he regarded all of the cantus in bb.1–3 as the subject.[107] Although in the early version the bass entry at b.32 lacked the rising crotchets of b.3 in bb.34–5, Bach eventually felt it to be inadequate to conclude a section in which all the other entries were complete, and also as too perfunctory a move to the very unusual modulation goal of A flat minor (of which more later). If four of the six entries in the third exposition use only the first two bars of the subject it is no doubt because most of the fourth exposition is based on the second two bars. The final five-part stretto (bb.67–72; Bach himself entered the diagonal voice indicators) is a *stretto maestrale* because all five entries have versions of all three bars of the subject complete.

Stretto is of course the most notable surface feature but, as with the learned contrapuntal works of Frescobaldi, it is not so much the entries of the set material which are the fascination of the genre as the constant free and fluid development of the living motivic contrapuntal tissue. Even though the effective arrangement of combinations involving the subject is a most important part of the art, it is the development of shapes in the contrapuntal fabric, and the subtle relationships which result, that show the quality of the composer's mind. Bach makes much play with the falling 4th or 5th of the head of the subject. This has an emphatic effect, shown by its use for setting an imperative in BWV 64/1 ('Sehet, welch'eine Liebe hat uns der Vater erzeiget'). In that motet-style chorus Bach enhances the rhetoric of this effect with off-beat entries. He uses this rhythmic device, called by Marpurg *per arsin et thesin*, only once in this fugue (b.46) and then not rhetorically, but to give point to the falling 4ths and 5ths of the rather routine medius part from b.43. Dürr's pedantic addition of rests in an effort to disentangle the voices, as if the fugue had been written in open score, undermines the felicity of this effect. Bach's simpler notation is quite adequate in a keyboard fugue where the voices have very unvocal tessituras. Very cogent use is also made of other non-thematic falling 5ths. The thematic 5ths of the stretto in bb.50–1 are immediately echoed by non-thematic ones in the bass in bb.51–2. This is not just a witty piece of imitation, but outlines the harmonic structure of the piece. It explains the unusual key of the flat 7th degree (A flat minor) at the half-way point as two 5ths down from the tonic. The second half of the fugue proceeds harmonically up these two 5ths back from A flat at b.37, via E flat at b.55, to B flat at b.75. The unity of surface detail and fundamental structure is what makes pieces of this sort so compelling and influential.

Unlike BWV 64/1 and BWV 579 the subject of this fugue has a minor 9th, rather than an octave, leap and is a good example of an instrumental piece using a poignant interval to gain a 'speaking' expression. The 9th is put to good dramatic use in the form of a rising minor 2nd in the bass at bb.63–4, the interrupted cadence that introduces the final tour de force of stretto, and a falling minor 9th at bb.72–3.[108] Finally, the stepping crotchets of the tail of the subject provide the main linking material and an important part of the argument of the fugue. The principle of parallel 3rds introduced at b.17 and b.19 is intensified at bb.34–5 and, after a section where they hardly appear, brought to ultimate fruition in the simultaneous entry from b.55 where they develop the chiastic outline inherent in the subject. Bach's final adjustments to this fugue were in the chromatic alterations in bb.58–9. Kroll gives d"♭ for the second crotchet in the alto of b.59. This is alluring in that it gives the chiastic BACH outline transposed up a semitone in that voice in bb.58–9. There is, however, no justification for this since the flat sign before the d" on the second crotchet of b.59 had been converted into a natural in the A3 stage of revision, before the ♭ was added to the c" at the end of b.58 in the A4 stage (KB V/6.1 pp.295–6). As with the syncopated entry at b.46, the double entry at b.55 is part of the art of making the ordinary significant. The maturity of this fugue is that it achieves this aim so economically and with such concentrated force of expression, in contrast to the D sharp minor whose set contrapuntal scheme is in the foreground.

Prelude and Fugue in B major BWV 868

PRELUDE This prelude and fugue have similarities to the G sharp minor pair. The prelude, although differing in expression from its relative, is based on similar keyboard hand-shapes. Where the G sharp minor used the whole hand, this seems based on a keyboard *évolution* involving the middle three fingers only, and is an excellent basic exercise for cantabile touch on the clavichord.[109] Given that the G sharp minor prelude shows signs of having been transposed from G minor, it is possible that the B major was originally in B flat, as Hermann Keller suggests, pointing to the rarity of Bach's use of B major as a keyboard tonic (1976 p.121). Otherwise there is only the second Passepied of the B minor French Overture BWV 831, itself originally in C major (BWV 831a). There is also a similarity of material to the Praeludium of the B flat clavier Partita BWV 825. But hard evidence is lacking, and Dürr notes various missing A naturals in both prelude and fugue which suggest an early version in the old-fashioned Mixolydian four-sharp key signature of B (KB V/6.1 pp.380–1).

The opening uses a favourite pattern of Bach's, of a rising scale that pauses on the leading note, then goes off in another direction (compare bb.4–5 of the F major three-part Sinfonia). The right-hand pattern is a particularly characterful and fruitful division of the plain crotchets of the left. Scale shapes are then important structurally in the piece: the modulation to the dominant (bb.3–6) outlines a descending scale shape in the bass, as does the modulation to the relative minor at the half-way point (bb.6–10). The alterations Bach made in the bass at bb.11–12 are important in emphasizing this feature. In the final version the 7th-leaps down emphasise the descending scale steps at bb.11 and 12, and reserve the low dominant F♯ for a more telling position at the end. Similarly, Bach thought better of the rather gratuitous sudden move to four-part texture in b.8 of the early version, and reserved that for the last four bars.

More subtle is the right-hand alteration at b.11, which undoes an exact sequence with b.12. In this radiantly consonant piece, the involution of musical argument in the move to G sharp minor introduces diminished-7th sonorities from b.8. It looks as if Bach wanted to shade away from this by keeping a dominant minor 9th at b.11 before the very easygoing sequence moves back to the radiance of E major.

In common with early versions of preludes in Book I, this is structured on harmonic proportions, clearly marked by perfect cadences, with the half-way point at b.10 and a one-third point at b.6. Bach avoids clear divisions in the second half by having 7ths in the resolution chords of cadences at b.13 and b.15. And, as ever, he finds many felicities in the manipulation of a single *figura*, particularly in the varied subdominant reprise, where the alto line of bb.3–4 is recast in the cantus at bb.14–15 to include the inversion of the main motif.

FUGUE Given the affinity between this and the G sharp minor pair, and the seemingly irregular answers in both fugues, it is tempting to look for a verset prototype here also. The subject is, however, unusual, and not in the tradition of modal versets, in having a perfect cadence on the dominant after the first three notes. This dominant accent requires a balancing tonic accent in the answer. A real answer would give a cadence on the dominant of the dominant immediately after the very strong tonic cadence at the end of the subject. Such a remote effect would be unthinkably awkward at the beginning of the fugue. A point of contact with the G sharp minor is the strong cadentiality of the subject, in this case with a typical tenor pattern of notes 2–1 of the scale; in the G sharp minor with the bass pattern of notes 5–1.[110]

The subject is very neatly balanced, with the leap down to the dominant followed by a rising scale up to e'♮ which swings back to the tonic. It thus conforms to the common shape of head, tail, and cadence. The scale segments which permeate the triple counterpoint of the exposition, based on euphonious 3rds and 6ths, aptly continue both the materials and the mood of the prelude: Tovey thought this the only pair in *The Well-tempered Clavier* for which more than a casual thematic resemblance between prelude and fugue could plausibly be argued. The scale is the predominant feature of the first countersubject, where it fills a gap in the subject in the most serene and natural way, quite different from the energetic effect of the same device in the triple counterpoint of the first Allegro of the B minor Sonata for obbligato harpsichord and violin BWV 1014. The development of scale segments, and their relation to the head of the subject, provides the motivic argument of the fugue.[111]

Like the prelude, the fugue is structured on harmonic proportions, with a full close in the dominant at the half-way point (b.18). Each half is subdivided at the quarter mark (b.9, b.26) into a complete four-voice exposition followed by a section with two entries separated by episodes. The function of the second section is to have a tonic entry in the tenor at bb.11–13 to provide a harmonic conclusion to the exposition, which had ended on the dominant as is usual in a four-voice fugue. The episode then allows the final entry of the section (alto b.16) to be the real answer in the dominant which we could not have at b.3, and which neatly brings us to the midpoint of the fugue.

The episode material is contained in the bass from bb.9–11 and makes a continuous line out of shapes from the head and tail of the subject. The line is repeated in the tenor at bb.14–16, and again in the bass at bb.26–8, before the final two entries. Each of these appearances thus prefaces an important structural entry. The pattern of semiquavers at the beginning of this line (b.9) suggests an inversion of the head of the subject, which is realized in the complete inversion of the subject in the soprano and alto entries (b.18, b.20) of the highly developmental second exposition. After a normal tonic bass entry (b.21) this is completed by a very oblique tenor entry (b.24), cadencing in C sharp minor. The main cadencing points of the second half of the fugue (F sharp, C sharp, B) thus provide a reversion of the main notes of the head of the subject (b, c'♯, f♯) and pin down its inherent instability.

Prelude and Fugue in B minor BWV 869

PRELUDE The key of B minor completes the chromatic scale and seems to have several definite associations for Bach. One is with chromaticism itself, and its possibility for expressing the fullness of human suffering. This Bach seems to have associated particularly with the suffering of Christ, and pieces in this key tend to feature the device of chiasmus, or a cross shape, noted already in the first subject of the C sharp minor fugue (see also Chapter Five section 2). The same outline is in this prelude (notes 3–6 in the alto part), and is a strong feature of the fugue subject.

A second association is with yearning, perhaps because this tonic sits on the leading note of C, the central key of the tonal system. This is inherent in the opening Kyrie fugue of the B minor Mass, setting the ancient Greek prayer for freedom from sin, and the expressive association can be traced back to the opening Sinfonia and chorus of what is perhaps Bach's earliest sacred vocal work, the cantata 'Nach dir, Herr, verlanget mich' BWV 150.[112] Also in B minor, this uses the falling chromatic tetrachord (the so-called *lamento* bass), in a texture similar to this prelude's, to express the emotion of yearning ('verlangen'). As Hugo Riemann points out, the atmosphere of the B minor prelude is very different from the clear and firm effect of the same material in the second section of the prelude in E flat major (1890 I p.156).

Having said all this, and there is a great deal more one can say of the fugue in this vein, it has to be admitted that there is just a possibility that this prelude and fugue may have originated in G minor. Dürr notes a number of missing G sharps and superfluous G naturals, suggesting a Dorian signature, and the fugue avoids c'''♯ (b.36, last beat; b.63, second beat). He nonetheless finds these hints insufficient as firm evidence and there is no denying Bach's deeply symbolic use of B minor in his music generally, and in this prelude and fugue particularly.[113]

Assuming that Bach was aiming to demonstrate the different subtypes of the genre prelude, this belongs to the type of preludio with which Corelli opened his chamber sonatas. The only piece of Corelli's which Bach seems definitely to have known is the trio Op.3 No.4 from which he took the subject of the organ fugue BWV 579 (VBN II/C/1). But there are also possible connexions between the C major and A major fugues and Corelli's spectacular trio Op.3 No.12, and it is difficult to imagine that somebody as eager to know about music as Bach, and in such a cosmopolitan environment, could have avoided at least some contact with the music of the most celebrated and influential composer of Italian instrumental music of his day.[114] In any case the manner was well known from keyboard works of J.G. Walther and others. As was his usual method of operating, Bach took a set of ingredients of a style and exploited them a great deal more rigorously than was done in the prototype, a trait of German composers in dealing with Italian styles which one may also observe in Georg Muffat's Corellian orchestral works (1682, 1701). The Corelli movement most similar to Bach's prelude is the Preludio of Op.4 No.2 in G minor (Ex.7.31).

The essence is to have sequences of serenely floating suspensions over, as it were, a third-species bass. This is another version of the *durezze e ligature* principle and, quite apart from Corelli, was a favourite texture in *stile antico* Catholic church music, a manner which Bach again carried to its ultimate of sophistication in the Confiteor of the B minor Mass. The point of the rising-4th figure is to get a climbing sequence (Ex.7.31 bb.11f) out of suspensions which must of their nature resolve downwards (bb.7ff). But where Corelli merely hints at ideas, Bach takes these old contrapuntal gambits and develops them to the hilt: after the double bar the principal idea, a traditional canzona shape, is in diminution and very close imitation involving the bass, similar to the treatment of the same idea in the D major fugue of Book II; the alto from b.32½ has an extension of the idea; and it is syncopated from b.42 (Riemann 1890 I p.155). Corelli's customary chromatic inflexion towards the final cadence is exaggerated to such a degree that many have seen the last bars as preparing the total chromaticism of the fugue subject.

There have been various speculations about this prelude. One, based on the fact that one of the sources of Book I closest to Bach (P 401, copied by an unknown pupil of Bach's known as Anon.5 in 1722–3, probably from a draft for P 415) includes also the first 14 bars of the B minor Praeludium BWV 923,

Ex.7.31 Corelli: Preludio grave from Op.4 No.2, bars 7–17.

is that Bach may have been undecided about which prelude to use.[115] BWV 923 in turn appears in a number of late sources coupled with the later version of the fugue on a theme of Albinoni BWV 951, which has some similarities to the B minor fugue. Given the closely organized nature of the Book I preludes, and the intention to demonstrate composition technique, it is unlikely that Bach would have wished to conclude the collection with such a loose, improvisatory arpeggiando prelude. That style had already been demonstrated in a more organized context in the concert endings added to the preludes in C minor and D major. Another suggestion is that the B minor prelude originally consisted only of bb.1–16. It is the only binary prelude in Book I; the first section does not modulate but has a Phrygian cadence added to a perfect cadence in the tonic; and the texture suddenly becomes very much denser after the double bar (Hermelink 1976 p.66, Bergner 1986 pp.48–51). A third suggestion is that the ending, from the interrupted cadence at the second half of b.42 to the second half of b.46, which so clearly prefigures the 'sigh' figures of the fugue subject, is an addition to the original concept (AB I p.162). While it is interesting to speculate, there is no hard evidence for any of these suggestions. On the same level one might equally point to the often remarked foreshadowing of the main episode material of the fugue in bb.24–5 of the prelude, and that this in turn is in embryo in bb.2–3, as it is in bb.14–16 of Ex.7.31.

Both prelude and fugue have rare uses of tempo words in *The Well-tempered Clavier*. Bach normally adds these only if there is some doubt about the genre. In this case, Corelli uses this manner in movements marked anything from Adagio to Presto and it may have been in response to enquiry that Bach added Andante in P 415, possibly in 1722, possibly later (KB V/6.1 p.299). While this can be equivalent to Moderato (a term Bach used only once, see Marshall 1985 p.268) the evidence of the sonatas with obbligato harpsichord is that Bach used Andante for a gentler type of slow movement than Adagio. This is borne out by J.G. Walther's description of the term, which seems to be describing just this type of movement, with all notes played equally and evenly, and each clearly distinguished from the other.[116]

FUGUE The subject of this fugue, and the working out of the fugue itself, so beautifully fits its position as the finale of the book that it is very difficult to imagine that it could have been originally conceived for any other purpose. The fact that its subject includes all 12 semitones, and b♯ as well as c♮, can only be meant to embody the word 'wohltemperirt' and the intention of going 'durch alle *Tone* und *Semitonia*'. Bach has built on traditional ingredients to construct a subject which is in itself a musical labyrinth, the antithesis of the C major's hexachord.

It is possible to see in background repertory elements of the subject as it may have been built up. The B minor Fuga 39 of the Langloz *partimento* versets, representing traditional subject types, has the ingredients of a falling triad, a leap to the minor 6th and step down, and a chromatic descent from the upper tonic (Ex.7.32a). The Albinoni theme is more sophisticated, beginning off the beat, again on the 5th degree, and covering a 10th (Ex.7.32b).

Ex.7.32 (a) Langloz MS: Fuga 39, bars 1–5; (b) Albinoni: subject of BWV 951.

Bach's fugue on this (BWV 951), fine though it is as a concerto-style fugue and with a great deal more musical substance than its early version BWV 951a, is diffuse in comparison with BWV 869/2, and the chromatic effects are more standard and direct. Bach in *The Well-tempered Clavier* aimed to demonstrate the possibilities of thematic concentration and balanced structure, and that is what he has provided here. One might compare the motif of the falling triad in semiquavers which permeates BWV 951 with the very economical and telling use of the same shape in BWV 869/2 b.65.

Expressively the subject is also much stronger than Albinoni's. Instead of the traditional chromatic tetrachord Bach experiments with other possibilities of dissonant steps and leaps (*passus/saltus duriusculi*), finding powerful and novel effects here and in cantata movements such as the opening aria (also in B minor) of BWV 154 (1724, perhaps earlier). Bach has greatly increased the effect of this harshness by setting it off with serenely diatonic episode material. The episode figure can be traced to trio sonata figurations, but it also occurred to other composers for the same purpose of relaxation, from Frescobaldi's harshest and most mannered contrapuntal piece, the *Capriccio cromatico con ligature al contrario* (1626), to the fugue of Beethoven's Op.106. Kirnberger, equating progression by small intervals with doubt and sorrow, cites this subject as a good example of the expression of despair (1782 p.2; Dok.III p.361). Whether or not we agree with that precise emotional shade, this is surely Bach's most elaborate use of the device of chiasmus, with every four quavers of the 'sigh' motif forming the cross shape, all framed by the tonic and dominant triads.[117]

Since the subject is not only very expressively chromatic but also modulates to the dominant, the answer will need to be carefully handled, and Bach changed his mind about this several times. The problem is that the subject moves up a 5th from B to F sharp, but the answer will have to start on F sharp and move up a 4th to B. In order to keep its profile it will have to shift into E minor after the opening triad: the question is, at what precise point (compare the answer in b.4 with the E minor entry in the tenor at b.30; the details of Bach's alterations are clearly explained in AB I p.163). At one stage he decided to stay in F sharp up to the fifth note of the subject, which he therefore changed to c'♯, with a corresponding c"♯ as the last semiquaver in the countersubject. This keeps the same number of 'sigh' figures and is smoother, but also blander, than his first and final thoughts. Changing to E minor on the fifth note (b) is not only more subtle but also gives a strong expressive dissonance with the c"♮ in the alto. There was also a moment when the subject in the second beat of b.5 read f'♯ e'♯, not f'♮ e'♮, with the equivalent in b.14, but this was clearly a mistake since by that point there is no question about the key of the subject. Kirnberger tells us that this fugue enjoyed a certain notoriety on account of its tortuous chromatic nature, which he says seemed insoluble even to experts of the time, and he (or J.A.P. Schulz) in 1773 proposes a rather elaborate harmonic analysis of it in terms of the figured bass, one of the earliest examples of such analysis.[118] But Bach himself has typically kept a balance by combining the subject with a countersubject of the utmost clarity, stepping down five notes of a scale in crotchets. This anchors the waywardness of the subject, even at its most intricate, as in the fourth entry, from b.13.

Structurally also Bach plays on the modulating nature of the subject. The fourth entry (bb.13–15) should start on the dominant and return to the tonic. But he avoids the tonic cadence (b.16), and uses his favourite device in four-voice fugues of having an episode before a fifth entry (in the tonic), thus integrating the exposition into the body of the fugue. In this case he has some delightful dallying, with a false entry at b.19, before the expected tonic entry (b.21). This tonic-to-dominant entry is balanced by a subdominant-to-tonic entry (b.30), and in fact much of the central part of the fugue is in the tonic key. Two half-entries (bb.34, 35) express the dominant-to-tonic relation, a feature he will exploit further, and the exact midpoint of the fugue (b.38) is marked by a complete tonic entry. The half-entries of bb.34–5 now come into their own, with a series of rising 4ths from B minor (b.41), E minor (b.42), A major (b.43), culminating in a complete entry with its answer in D major (bb.44–50). The return to the tonic (b.60) is prepared by dominant (b.53) and subdominant (b.57) entries, after which Bach mirrors the opening events of the fugue by repeating the first episode (bb.65ff) and balancing the exposition, with its inherent swing to the dominant, by a pair of entries in subdominant and tonic (from b.70).

The direction Largo goes back at least to the stage just before Bach compiled P 415 (Dürr 1984 p.55). According to Walther (1732) some writers use it for a somewhat quicker tempo than Adagio, and this seems right here, countering the temptation to take this densely chromatic piece too slowly. The first Kyrie of the B minor Mass is also Largo and **c**, and a similar tempo would be in order here.

CHAPTER EIGHT

Book II

Prelude and Fugue in C major BWV 870

PRELUDE Bach seems initially to have been undecided about which C major prelude to use to open the second collection. He used the C major prelude BWV 872a in the second (advanced-key) group of entries to the London autograph (*c.*1740–1), but transposed into C sharp major. He may well have thought it too similar to the opening prelude of Book I to use here, and have wished to demonstrate alternative possibilities for keys. It serves its purpose very well in C sharp precisely because it is such a typical C major prelude, and so embodies the desirability of being able to play as readily in C sharp as in C, and also perhaps the doctrine of equal temperament. The actual C major prelude, BWV 870, was not entered until the final phase (*c.*1742), in which Bach adapted it and the A flat major fugue from earlier pieces.

This prelude has a unique interest in the 48 in that we have it in no less than four states, two of which are in the London autograph where we can see Bach's revision in progress. All four are given in NBA V/6.2: (1) an early version of 17 bars which dates back at least to the early 1720s (BWV 870a/1, NBA V/6.2 p.307, PF p.1); J.C. Vogler's copy of this version, with ornaments and fingerings, is in NBA V/6.2 p.310, PF pp.4–5 (for comment see Chapter Six section 3); (2) the version entered in the London autograph, in which Bach seems to have revised and expanded the early version as he entered it (BWV 870b, NBA V/6.2 p.342, PF pp.34–5, reconstructed by Alfred Dürr);[1] (3) Bach's substantial revision of bb.14¾–19 of this version, entered by him at the end of the London autograph version, after crossing out his first thoughts for these bars (NBA V/6.2 p.2, and facsimile on pp.X-XI); (4) the final version in the MSS of Johann Christoph Altnickol and dependent sources (BWV 870/1, NBA V/6.2 p.156).

In choosing this prelude Bach reached back to a praeludial manner with its roots deep in the tradition, and which he had used in Book I only in the conservative E flat major prelude. Various prototypes by Fischer and others have been proposed,[2] but the manner is so much part of the keyboard tradition of the time that these could be multiplied at will. Perhaps the most significant for the initial version are the C major Praeludium and Fuga of Fischer's *Ariadne Musica* (1702), a collection with many echoes in the 48. Fischer's C major prelude has not the same harmony in detail as Bach's, but the principle of suspended harmonies over pedal points, the suspensions decorated by three-semiquaver upbeat figures which migrate between the parts and maintain a constant semiquaver impetus, is the essence of the genre. Fischer's fugue subject also is comparable to Bach's (see the discussion of the fugue below). A more instructive comparison for the final version is with the C major Praeludium IV of Fischer's *Pieces de Clavessin* (1696). This is another example of Fischer using disparate elements in a tonal structure: pedal points, demisemiquaver *roulades*, and semiquaver motifs treated imitatively. In the C major prelude Bach uses similar elements, but integrates them into a single composite texture. In the same way he had unified disparate elements similar to those in Fischer's Praeludium VI of the *Pieces de clavessin* in the B flat major prelude of Book I (see the commentary).

Fischer's Praeludium IV also shows the ambiguity of keyboard idiom common to many of the 1696 Praeludia, which could work on either stringed keyboards or organ. This ambivalence of instrumental idiom is characteristic of a number of preludes from Book II. The genre from which Bach's C major prelude develops is most typically found in organ verset collections. The early version (BWV 870a/1) is full of typical organ figurations, even though it would not work well for the organ *pedaliter*.[3] As this prelude developed, and particularly in the final version, it seems an example of Bach evoking on one instrument the style of another, as he commonly does in Book II (see Chapter Three section 9), the evocation being in some ways more powerful than the real thing.

As a manner for an initial organ piece, the texture of manual figurations over a pedal point is archetypal, used by Bach in one of his earliest organ pieces, the Praeludium BWV 545a/1, and in the Fantasia on 'Komm, heiliger Geist' BWV 651 which opens his last big chorale collection, the so-called 'Eighteen' chorales, Weimar works revised at the same time he was putting together Book II. The difference between Bach's organ style and its evocation on the harpsichord is clearly demonstrated by comparing the C major prelude with BWV 545a/1. The opening harmonic formula, also used in BWV 870/1 (and in the little C major prelude BWV 939), is a standard one for a pedal point. In its subdominant emphasis there may be a relic of the transposition of Mode VII (Mixolydian) on to C with a one-flat signature (see Georg Muffat's *Toccata septima* from the *Apparatus musico-organisticus*, 1690). But with Bach the formula is by no means wedded to C major: he shows how it can be patterned out in a single part in the Prelude of the E flat cello suite BWV 1010, and in two parts in the B flat Invention BWV 785. Two things are evident in comparing the early version of the C major prelude BWV 870a with the first layer of the London autograph version BWV 870b. One is that Bach in the early version seems to have aimed at diversity of figuration (compare the semiquaver patterns in the second halves of bb.1, 3, 5, and the first half of b.8 in BWV 870a), whereas in BWV 870b he was aiming at motivic unity. Paradoxically, by conforming all these places to the b.8 figuration he increased the similarity to the organ prelude BWV 545a, while at the same time taking the instrumental style further in the direction of the harpsichord. A further link with BWV 545a is the sequence in the bridge he added to the subdominant reprise in the first layer of BWV 870b (compare the bass part in bb.15–18 of that version with the pedal part of BWV 545a bb.4–6; Ex.8.1). The organ pedal part is strongly profiled as a dominating feature of the texture, while in BWV 870b the bass line is closely woven in with the rhythmic texture of the other parts.[4]

Ex.8.1 (a) Praeludium in C major BWV 545a/1, bars 1–6.

Ex.8.1(a) (Continued)

Ex.8.1(b) Prelude in C major BWV 870b, bars 13–19.

13 b)

15

17

19

In the discussion of the C major prelude of Book I it was noted that standard ingredients of the improvised keyboard prelude are pedal points and descending scale patterns in the bass. In the Book I C major prelude, written in a style associated with stringed keyboards, Bach has the scale first and the pedal point second; in Book II, in an organ-based idiom, it is the other way round, with the pedal in bb.1–3 and the descending bass scale outline from bb.3–5. The improvised nature of the genre is very evident in the early version (BWV 870a) which, after the initial sentence in the tonic (bb.1–5), positively avoids the establishment of any subsidiary key centres. This feature has been related to the seventeenth-century Italian *toccata di durezze e ligature* tradition (Keller 1950 p.222 and others). But the true continuation of that style is rather in prelude-type pieces in the French *livre d'orgue* tradition than here. The style of the C major prelude is one of freely figural keyboard improvisation in *stile moderno* rather than of mannered dissonance applied to learned *stile antico* counterpoint and notated in open score. In adapting the slender prelude BWV 870a to make a fitting opening to such a monumental work, Bach neatly solved the problems of brevity and shapelessness by reprising the tonally diffuse section from the second half of b.5 to the beginning of b.14 in the subdominant at bb.20–8. In order to do this he added a bridge from the end of b.14 to b.19, providing an involution of textural and chromatic density at the midpoint of the piece. His first thoughts for b.15 (Ex.8.1b) have the obvious failing that the note d" is struck five times from this bar to the beginning of b.16. The revision replaces this static moment with a much more directional effect that continues a descent of principal pitches in the cantus from the f" in b.13. Bach was particularly concerned to increase the density of this passage, as can be seen in successive revisions of bb.18–19. The second layer of BWV 870b breaks up the smooth tenor line and adds strong, dissonant chromatic steps to the alto; the final version replaces the bland circle-of-5ths outline in the bass with jagged, dissonant leaps. After these choppy waters we sail into the serene reprise at b.20.

At the end of the prelude Bach recalls this bridge from the end of b.28 to b.30, and expands the original ending to include a tonic pedal on the same harmonic formula as the opening. Typically, he wasted nothing of his original prelude BWV 870a, every bar of which is used in the expanded scheme. These elements of repetition, together with the new densely woven textures, give the prelude a weight and breadth which well fit it for its place in the collection. The final touches in Altnickol's version, notably the demisemiquavers, a feature Bach also added to the expanded version of the D minor prelude, give a concertante brilliance to the harpsichord sound and imply a more majestic movement than that of the original little organ-style prelude.

FUGUE Klaus Hofmann, discussing the little collection of five preludes and fughettas (NBA V/6.2 pp.307–39; PF), suggests that they belong to the south-

German tradition of verset cycles (see Chapter Three section 1). It is possible that they may be an extension of this in a general way but, although the pieces in C major and D minor do seem to have been possibly intended for organ *manualiter* (the D minor prelude BWV 899 in particular seems an organ working of the *inventio* of the three-part Sinfonia in the same key BWV 790), the pieces in E minor, F major, and G major seem much more suited for clavier. None of the fugues seems on the face of it to be based on verset-type subjects. Yet a closer look at the C major fughetta BWV 870a/2 shows Bach giving something of the same treatment to a verset subject as he did in the G minor fugue of Book I to a subject of Fischer's, and in the D major fugue of Book II to a subject from the *Wegweiser*. In each of these cases he took a continuous subject and split it into two halves, giving it more character, and making much more point of the stretti for which it is suited. In the case of the C major, stretto is not the point, nor any aspect of learned counterpoint in this very straightforward fugue,[5] but the principle of creating a more galant and characterful subject by separating the head and tail of a traditional one is equally in operation. The subject of Fischer's C major *Ariadne* Fuga has a head that goes from the 5th to 6th degrees of the scale, and a tail of a descending semiquaver pattern (Ex.8.2).

Ex.8.2 J.C.F. Fischer: C major Fuga from *Ariadne Musica*, bars 1–3.

If Bach was indeed thinking of Fischer's Fuga he has in this case jettisoned rather than enhanced the learned element, since Fischer from the very beginning has the subject answered in stretto at the 5th below. But the subject is archetypal and there need be no particular prototype.

In adapting the fughetta for Book II, Bach changed the time signature from ¢ with four crotchets in the bar to $\frac{2}{4}$. This is a very necessary change since ¢-time puts the most emphatic note of the subject (a' with its mordent) in the middle of the bar.[6] The purpose of ¢ was to imply a quick tempo, notionally twice as fast as the c of the G minor fugue of Book I. The new $\frac{2}{4}$ signature gives a livelier effect, and suits the subject much better, with its features of a certain type of galant $\frac{2}{4}$ movement of the 1720s and 30s.[7] This signature could have a great variety of characters: Ex.8.3 by Quantz is typical of this particular one. Its

Ex.8.3 Quantz: flute sonata in G major, QV I:113/III, Vivace, bars 1–5.

features are the bar of quavers, the bar of two crotchets with a strong leap, and semiquavers. Bach used this rhythmic type many times, notably in the first movement of the Italian Concerto. It may be related to the polonaise: the aria 'Nur ein Wink von seinen Händen' in Part VI of the *Christmas Oratorio* (1734–5, based on a lost earlier cantata), a true polonaise, also features the two crotchets in its characteristic hemiola opening. They are marked with dots (meaning separated and with equal emphasis rather than staccato). In his explanation of time signatures Hotteterre (1719 p.60) describes $\frac{2}{4}$ as suitable for 'Airs legers et piqués', also implying this separation, as would be suitable for the Quantz (Ex.8.3).[8] It would therefore seem that the two crotchets in the C major fugue subject should be emphatic and separated, rather than phrased off as would be suitable for the more reflective G minor fugue of Book I.

The early fughetta ended with a perfect cadence at bb.67–8. Bach, wishing to make the fugue into something more substantial, composed an additional 'concert ending' into the London autograph. If the fingerings in J.C. Vogler's version are anything to go by, the fughetta was conceived in terms of a conservative keyboard technique (for comments see Chapter Six section 3). In the new ending Bach shows a concern to demonstrate up-to-date keyboard effects, a concern evident also in other pieces in Book II, and in the Goldberg Variations, composed around the same time. The coda of the C major fugue is based on the so-called reversed-hand technique, where the left hand pivots over the thumb in expanding intervals over an octave. This was explained by Rameau in the *Méthode pour la mechanique des doigts* which he included in his *Pieces de clavessin* (1724) and demonstrated in the piece *Les Cyclopes*. Rameau claimed to have invented it but, like many such 'inventions', it was becoming a fashionable effect at the time. It was used by A.B. della Ciaia in his *Sonate per cembalo* Op.4, published in Rome in 1727 but some possibly composed as early as 1713; by Domenico Scarlatti; and, most relevant to Bach, by the well-travelled Hamburg organist C.F. Hurlebusch, copies of whose *Compositioni musicali per il cembalo* Bach stocked for sale in 1735–6 (Dok.II p.356). Bach seems to have been irritated into several projects by Hurlebusch, who is mentioned in various contemporary lists of the great keyboard players of the time along with him and Handel. It was perhaps the aridly technical *Minuetta con variazioni*, to which Bach listened politely when Hurlebusch visited him (Dok.III p.443, NBR p.408), that spurred him into the extraordinary technical achievements of the Goldberg Variations; and Hurlebusch seems to have been in the background to the conception of *Clavier-Übung* III around the mid 1730s (Butler 1990, Chapter I).

Bach probably did not need Hurlebusch to tell him about this, and may well have had an aversion to such Rameau-esque 'ballet on the keyboard' effects. Hurlebusch himself uses the reversed-hand pattern in an inorganic and inconsequential way for some bars of his E minor Toccata. Bach was not interested in using such effects for their own sake and his use of it in the C major fugue is strongly integrated and purposeful. His first thoughts, erased in the London autograph, are relatively straightforward (Ex.8.4).[9]

Ex.8.4 C major fugue, bars 76–83 before correction.

As usual with Bach's corrections, we can see him building up an idea into something much more cogent than the original thought. The emphasis on bottom C is structurally important for the balance of the fugue since the tessitura of most of it is rather high and reaches down to D only in b.49. This makes the fugue a good contrast to the bass-heavy prelude, but rather lightweight in itself. In the early fughetta the D was taken down to C only in the final chord (presumably the bottom note of the then keyboard, as in Book I). The multiple percussions of C in the new coda provide the necessary balance of bass pitches, and bring this fugue into line with the sophisticated structural use of pitch levels observed in Book I.

Prelude and Fugue in C minor BWV 871

PRELUDE If the C major pair were some of the last pieces to be entered into Book II, the C minor were some of the first, copied by Anna Magdalena Bach in the first layer of the London autograph *c.*1739–40. Despite the superficial similarity of her handwriting to Bach's, for which it has often been mistaken, close examination shows a very different mind, with the fluctuating density of line of an unskilful copyist, and with frequent lapses of attention indicated by corrections (Tomita 1990 p.222). She made what was intended as a fair copy from a (now lost) autograph source, and that source was also used by Altnickol in 1744.

Some commentators have exercised ingenuity in tracing motivic links between the opening bar of the prelude and the fugue subject (J.N. David 1962 p.19, Keller 1976 p.138, etc.) but in view of the fact that only the fugue exists in an early version it is unlikely that they originated together. Both nonetheless show evidence, in missing A naturals and redundant A flats, of having been copied from a source with the Dorian two-flat key signature, so it is unlikely that the prelude is a work of the late 1730s. David Schulenberg has pointed to more striking motivic similarities between this prelude and the unfinished fugue BWV 906/2, and suggests that Bach may at some stage have been deciding between it, with the C minor Fantasia BWV 906/1, and the present pair as candidates for Book II (1992 p.120). If this was so, Bach may ultimately have decided that the Fantasia is too overtly a display piece to fit into the educational programme of *The Well-tempered Clavier*, and that formally the B flat major prelude does the same thing with more subtlety (see the commentary). The C minor prelude fits its place very well, having the educative manner of the invention, with its twin aspects of finger exercise and demonstration of composition, cast in the binary galant sonata structure and so in accord with the programme of Book II.

The initial motif has the appearance of a finger *évolution* similar to that of the F sharp minor prelude of Book I. This is worked out in the manner of an invention, but with the freedoms of toccata-type migration of semiquaver scales between parts (bb.5–6) and expansion of texture at the main cadences. The sonata structure is based on the aria ritornello shape (see Chapter Three section 6). Thus, there is a closed harmonic period in the tonic to b.5, whose climbing scale is matched by the second idea's descent into E flat major, reached at b.8. The repeated a'♭s of the closing idea (bb.7–8) neatly emphasise the dominant 7th of the new key when the descending bass scale arrives at its goal note of B♭, after which there is the conventional cadence. Into this sonata format Bach has added the invention principle of having inversions of the opening double counterpoint at the main key centres. The simplicity and logic of the scheme makes it an admirable demonstration of integrated composition.

Some have classified this prelude as an allemande (Keller 1976 p.138, Bergner 1986 p.79). But it can hardly pass as even the most sonatafied allemande since it lacks the defining upbeat opening. The invention-type counterpoint also removes it from the dance model. It belongs more to the tradition, to which Bach was a particularly brilliant contributor, of the moto perpetuo chorale prelude which continuously develops a few shapes in semiquavers, such as 'Wo soll ich fliehen hin' BWV 646 from the Schübler chorales, or 'Nun freut euch, lieben Christen g'mein' BWV 734. It does nonetheless have the dance feature of inverting the principal motif after the double bar, as do the binary preludes in D major, E minor, and A minor. In the case of the C minor it is a kind of pseudo-inversion which builds on the *évolution* principle by expanding the intervals between the main notes and the auxiliary figure. As in the technical-exercise preludes in Book I, the development of the musical material is inseparable from the development of the relation of the hand to the keyboard. The second half of the prelude generally goes on developing the basic material without any exact reprise, even at the return of the second idea at bb.23–4. But there are neat structural links, notably between the climbing chromatic bass in b.4, the descending one at bb.17–18, and the final climbing one at b.27.

FUGUE This fugue is one of four of which we have early versions copied by Bach's pupil J.F. Agricola probably around 1738–9 (P 595; see AB II p.203), a source which reflects the early stages of the preparation of Book II. The fugues are in the key sequence C major, C minor, D major, D minor: in Book II the C major was transposed into C sharp and much expanded, and the D major was transposed into E flat. All four fugues have in common strong links with the verset tradition. The subject type of the C minor fugue is generic: notable examples are in Frescobaldi's *Fiori musicali* (VBN I/F/2) and Ex.8.5 by Kerll, one of the composers whose works Bach secretly copied as a child in his brother's house (VBN I/K/4).[10] Bach's version has the second half of the subject inverted, which gives a better balance without undermining its possibilities, but the stepping crotchet countersubject is the same. Kerll's short verset plays with stretto and double counterpoint at the 10th, but has nothing of the densely argued inversion and augmentation of the second half of Bach's fugue. Organic conflation of motivic shapes is nonetheless the common objective of the genre.

Within the verset tradition, the first half of the C minor fugue has in addition features of a *partimento* fugue, such as were used for practising fugal improvisation. Most of the subject entries are in the lowest sounding part; the inner part can be sketchy (bb.5–6); and connecting passages are made up of standard continuo progressions, patterned out in keyboard *style brisé* (bb.8–9). In spite of its denser contrapuntal argument, the second half could equally be expressed as a *partimento*, and in fact the combination of the subject with itself in augmenta-

Ex.8.5 J.C. Kerll: Magnificat septimi toni, Versus Quia respexit, bars 1–2.

tion shows an improvisatory casualness in having a very exposed direct octave (b.14, beats 3–4). Handel's notable example of a *partimento* double fugue in which the second subject is the augmentation of the first is more accomplished than this.[11] The essence of this improvised type of fugue lies in broad effect rather than closely worked detail, and there is no denying the expressive strength and rhetorical effectiveness of Bach's fugue, particularly in the purposeful use in the second half of what had started as conventional *brisé* figurations, and in the dramatic placing of the final stretti (bb.23–6). The making of dramatic effect out of contrapuntal devices is the point of this fugue, for which it may be usefully compared with the D sharp minor fugue of Book I.

The connexion with the verset tradition raises the question of instrument, since this fugue has similarities with the organ fugue in C major BWV 547/2 (Spitta III pp.189–90, often repeated), notably in the fact that in both fugues the bass is reserved for an augmentation entry two thirds of the way through. The comparison only points up how unlike Bach's mature *pedaliter* organ style the C minor fugue in fact is, particularly in the first half with its wide, thin spacing and sketchy counterpoint. The seeming pedal notes towards the end (bb.24–5) are more typical of Bach's early pedal-clavier pieces than of his organ works. The London autograph has an arpeggiation sign for the final right-hand chord, implying a clavier rather than organ intention.[12] It would be entirely in keeping with the character of Book II for this to be an evocation of organ style on the harpsichord, as was the case in the C major prelude.

Prelude and Fugue in C sharp major BWV 872

PRELUDE As in the case of the C minor pair, there is no evidence that this prelude and fugue originated together. The C sharp major prelude exists in three states. (1) An early version in a copy made by Anna Magdalena Bach probably around 1738, when materials were being collected for Book II, since it is on the same paper as Bach's fair copy in the London autograph (P 226). This source also has the D minor pair in a version close to Anna Magdalena's copy in the London autograph, but the C sharp major prelude is in a very much more primitive form, in C major, with plain five-part minim chords marked 'arpeggio' in the first section (NBA V/6.2 p.344, PF p.36). (2) Bach seems then to have made a draft copy (now lost), presumably in C sharp, realizing the chords in an elaborate arpeggiation pattern. From this he made the fair copy in the London autograph (NBA V/6.2 p.12). (3) At some later stage he made, in the lost draft, various improvements to the tenor line of the chordal pattern, and this improved version is what Altnickol used for his 1744 copy (NBA V/6.2 p.164). There is no doubt that this version represents Bach's final and best thoughts. Comparison of versions 2 and 3 is easily made in Kroll's BG edition, which prints the main variants side by side.

If there is no necessary connexion between this prelude and fugue, there most definitely is a connexion between the first, chordal, section of the prelude and the little fugato which ends it. This prelude belongs with the keyboard-technical preludes of Book I, and much of what was said of the C major prelude there (which also has an early version notated largely as five-part minim chords) could apply here, particularly with regard to chord shapes and harpsichord touch. What this prelude adds is the second section. This sectional structure has generally been related to Niedt's (1706) prescriptions for improvising preludes, and Kuhnau in his *Clavier-Übungen* (1689, 1692) provides examples of preludes with a chordal first section and a fugato conclusion. The educational objective of Niedt is certainly in the background here, but what Bach is doing relates also to another strand of tradition, reflected, for example, in the *Conclave thesauri magnis artis musicae* (Prague, 1719), a treatise on music theory and organ building by Mauritius Vogt (1669–1730), a German Cistercian. The *Conclave* is a very useful compendium dealing with many aspects of composition. It is organized in sections ('Tractatus'), the third of which deals with scales, voices, instruments, and *figurae*. In Chapter 5 of this section, 'De affectione, themate, capriccio, et psychosymphoniae', Vogt gives a demonstration of how to work a simple idea ('Phantasia simplex', Ex.8.6a) into a fugal texture ('Daraus konstruirte Fuge'; Ex.8.6b).[13] In the 6th chapter ('De phantasia, et inventionibus') he then lists a collection of these basic contrapuntal clichés, including Ex.8.6c (p.156).

Ex.8.6 M. Vogt: (a) plain idea; (b) fugal version; (c) second phantasia; (d) Bach: BWV 872a/1, contrapuntal outlines of bars 1–6; (e) the same worked fugally in bars 25–30.

There is no knowing if Bach knew Vogt's book, but it hardly matters since the technique of decorating basic contrapuntal formulas with motivic figurations is the essence of teaching fugal improvisation.[14] Looking at the early version of this prelude, it is clear that an equally standard contrapuntal cliché underlies the first section, which decorates it chordally (Ex.8.6d), and the second section, which decorates it fugally (Ex.8.6e). This adds a further layer of educational demonstration to that of the C major prelude of Book I.

Seeing these standard contrapuntal shapes behind the prelude shows the basic identity of the arpeggiated style of the stringed clavier and the legato ('gebunden') style of the organ, with its long lines moulded by the tension and release of suspended dissonances and the avoidance of defining cadences, such as in Praeludium VII of Fischer's *Blumen-Strauß*. It may be that a white-note, polyphonic interpretation is what Kittel had in mind when he made his curious recommendation of this and the C major prelude of Book I for the organ (see Chapter One section 5). The C major of Book I has more clearly defined shapes than this, and also a simpler arpeggiation pattern. The C major BWV 872a/1 has a somewhat different agenda, with less clearly defined shapes, and this may be why Bach chose a more elaborate arpeggiation pattern. In this a comparison with preludes of Fischer is again instructive. If the C major prelude from Book I may be compared with the C major Praeludium harpeggiato ('Clio') from Fischer's *Musicalischer Parnassus* (see Ex.7.1), this may be compared with the D major Harpeggio ('Polymnia'; Ex.8.7).

Where 'Clio' had only two layers of legatissimo (crotchets in the left hand and semiquavers in the right), 'Polymnia' is more sophisticated in having three (dotted minims and crotchets in the left hand and semiquavers in the right). Playing Bach's C major version with bass minims, repeated quavers in the tenor, and his final pattern in the right hand gives the same multi-layered effect, and this may have been the sort of way he told his students to play the plain minim chords originally. Fischer then follows the normal agenda for this type of prelude, which is to wander around setting up luscious suspended dissonances, notably the 9/7 double suspension which he puts in a rich, low tessitura towards the end, and with a minor tinge at the final cadence. Bach takes the same features and much enhances and intensifies them. More so than Fischer he reserves the most densely dissonant passage as a climax towards the end (bb.14–19), and he has chosen the harshest version of the 9/7, the one on a leading note (b.16, first chord). Some editors (including Forkel, Kroll, and Dehnhard) found this dissonance too much and 'corrected' the bass note from e♯ to the blander d♯ (KB V/6.2 p.215). Bach has also greatly heightened the final minor tinge (bb.21–3). Whether he knew 'Polymnia' or not, the comparison with Fischer's prelude illuminates the quality and richness of Bach's musical mind.

When the arpeggiation pattern came to be written out, it was obvious that things that would pass muster when semi-improvised would no longer do in

Ex.8.7 Fischer: Harpeggio from 'Polymnia', bb.1–9.

written form. It is worth remembering, too, that one of the functions of writing out keyboard music was to refine improvisation skills. Looking through the tenor line of the London autograph version, we can see that Bach generally changed it from being the usual groups of four repeated quavers when that entailed the tenor doubling the main note in the right-hand part. Thus in b.1 he changed g♯ to e♯ in the second beat to avoid doubling the right-hand g'♯; similarly at b.3, and so on. There is also the consideration that in this texture the tenor, with its insistent quavers, is effectively the most prominent part, so benefits from a more interesting profile. Equally it is the main vehicle for the legatissimo touch, similar to the bass in the D minor prelude of Book I. This consideration led Bach to make further changes in the final version, allowing further refinements of sonority, and also structural linking. The final version of b.1 gives the tenor a rounded shape for the first phrase (bb.1–3); the substitution of d♯ for g♯ in the fourth beat of b.4 not only avoids doubling the right-hand g'♯, but also emphasizes the fact that the g♯ is a 7th at the beginning of b.5; the turning figure at the beginning of b.6 marks the arrival on the dominant at the end of the second phrase, and makes an equivalent structural point at the arrival on the tonic in b.20; the arpeggio figure at b.7 and elsewhere is a stronger shape than what it replaces.

The one substantial alteration to the Allegro (b.34) is designed to avoid having all three parts jumping upwards simultaneously, a fault of counterpoint. In this section Arnold Dolmetsch suggests that the grace notes (written as hooks in P 226 and the London autograph) should be played as quavers to give the most satisfactory effect in b.30 (1946 p.117).

FUGUE This fugue is perhaps the prime example of how Bach's brilliance at developing ingredients of the tradition he came from ended by killing that tradition itself. He was hardly dead when Marpurg produced his *Abhandlung von der Fuge* (1753, 1754), inaugurating the long series of textbooks on fugue in which principles of what a fugue is were deduced from Bach's normal practice. These principles were then applied back on to Bach's own works, and anomalies identified in terms of them, such as the 'irregular' order of entries in the C major fugue of Book I. Similarly here, a lack of perspective on the tradition has led to a misapprehension of the genre. One writer finds that it is not a fugue at all (Bullivant 1960 p.19); others puzzle about the identity of the subject, whether it is the first four notes (Iliffe), the first six (Riemann), or the first bar and a half (Tovey).

As with many of the Book II fugues, the C sharp major derives from the verset tradition. Since it survives in four separate stages of elaboration, it is possible to trace its development from very unpretentious origins. The subject type is of a short quaver upbeat figure to a downbeat crotchet, such as may be found in versets or canzona sections. The shortest possible has a single quaver, the type developed in the E major fugue of Book I (for prototypes, see the commentary on that fugue). This one is of three quavers, and workings of it can be found by Speer (1697), and Murschhauser (1703). The example closest to Bach is again in the *Wegweiser* (Ex.8.8).

Seen against this background, the earliest version of Bach's fugue (NBA V/6.2 p.358, PF p.52), far from being primitive, is in fact quite a sophisticated working. Shortening the crotchets into quavers with quaver rests gives more character, and there is a clear tonal structure, with cadences on the dominant (b.4) and the tonic (b.11). The verset principle of motivic integration is carried further, with much witty play on inversion and diminution. It is this principle which Bach greatly extends in the later versions, contriving a motivic web of extraordinary wit and density, and at the same time abandoning the strict three-part texture at b.30 and running into toccata-type demisemiquavers of pure *joie de vivre* for the ending. As with the D major fugue of Book II, also on

Ex.8.8 Anon.: *Wegweiser*, Versus 20 p.15.

a *Wegweiser*-type subject, one wonders how anybody afterwards could have felt like addressing these traditional materials again.

Since the four versions of this fugue give perhaps the most rewarding insight into the workings of Bach's composing mind, they are presented in parallel in Ex.8.9 (in Appendix A). As usual, in expanding it Bach hardly wasted a note of the early versions, and the final fugue is built up entirely by addition to, and elaboration of, the piece as it lay before him. The versions are: (1) A copy of the earliest version, 19 bars in C major BWV 872a/2, by C.P.E. Bach's Hamburg copyist Michel (P 563; NBA V/6.2 p.358, PF p.52), made after Emanuel's move to Hamburg in 1768; since this is the only surviving copy there is no clue about the original date of the piece, but like the early fughettas generally it probably originated in Bach's keyboard and composition teaching at Weimar or Cöthen; Michel pairs it with the little prelude BWV 993, but this is not necessarily significant since Michel gives BWV 993 without the fughetta in P 672. (2) A copy made by J.F. Agricola around 1738 (P 595; NBA V/6.2 p.352, PF p.44) of a much expanded version, 30 bars in C major. P 595 is the source that has early versions of the fugues in C minor, D minor, and E flat major (in D major), all with strong verset links; it seems that Bach kept a stock of these for teaching and revised them periodically until the final revision when he put most of them into Book II. (3) Bach's revising score, made from Agricola's copy, in the second layer of entries to the London autograph around 1740 when he turned to the advanced keys; 35 bars in C sharp major. Initially he kept close to version 2, but added bb.25–9 which are important structurally for their two bars of dominant pedal, and an extra two bars of tonic pedal at the end; Bach composed bb.25–9 directly into this source; and they are heavily corrected. Yo Tomita suggests that the idea of augmentation was an afterthought which probably occurred to Bach after he had entered the outer parts of b.25;[15] in making this version Bach first extended demisemiquaver movement back into the second half of b.30 and the first half of b.31, then went back and added equivalent demisemiquavers at bb.8–10, 17–18, 24, 28–9, and the first half of 30. This leaves the initial two exposition phrases (to the tonic cadence at b.4, and the dominant cadence at b.7) as they were, and adds motivic point to the new semiquaver idea introduced at b.8; it also increases the buildup of rhythmic excitement, which is then released in the cadenza-like ending. (4) Bach added further demisemiquavers, and also new corrections to bb.25–9, in another copy which he kept with the draft scores (now lost), and which is reflected in Altnickol's 1744 version (in the alternative bars of Ex.8.9c).

Prelude and Fugue in C sharp minor BWV 873

PRELUDE This is the first piece so far in Book II for which there is no sign of an earlier version. In scale, structure, and style, it seems to represent Bach's composition in the late 1730s and so may have been composed specially for Book II rather than worked up from an existing piece. It is therefore surprising that there are faint indications in Altnickol's 1744 copy, in terms of missing A sharps and superfluous A naturals, that it may have originated in C minor with a Dorian key signature (KB V/6.2 p.268). It has often been compared with the E flat Sinfonia BWV 791, of which there is a highly ornamented version in the 1723 autograph. That is a relatively modest piece, but the sonatas for obbligato harpsichord and violin show that Bach was writing movements as large and as galant as the C sharp minor prelude during his Cöthen years. The full battery of Bach's galant effects in the mid to late 1730s is best represented in the *pedaliter* prelude on 'Vater unser im Himmelreich' BWV 682 in *Clavier-Übung* III, in comparison to which the C sharp minor prelude is restrained. Very little definite can be said, though, since the leaf with this prelude and fugue is missing from the London autograph. The copy made by the reliable copyist known as Anon.12 (P 416) has it headed Prelude rather than Praeludium, so it presumably belonged to the second layer of entries to the London autograph, around 1740–1, which addressed the advanced keys and was probably, like the extant items in this layer, in the hand of Bach himself.

A comparison of the control editions quickly shows the main problem caused by the lack of an autograph copy, which is the notation of ornaments. Copyists generally were careless about them and, to add to the confusion, Bach was at this stage partly using his old system of ornaments, with the traditional hook sign (ᶜ) for the appoggiatura and the wavy line (~) for the trill, as he had in the 1720 table of ornaments in Wilhelm Friedemann's *Clavier-Büchlein*; and partly the more up-to-date system of a small note for the appoggiatura and a *tr* sign for the trill. He seems to have used the older signs in the London autograph; the others are used in Altnickol's copies. Copyists unfamiliar with the little hook sign were prone to put the appoggiatura at the wrong pitch, or misread it as a slur. Dürr has therefore opted to give his version representing the London autograph tradition (his 'Fassung A') from a relatively secondary source which seems to give the hook signs accurately (P 587); an editor aiming to make a single 'definitive' version will have a lot of decisions to make. It is well worth studying the two versions given by Dürr (NBA V/6.2 pp.16, 168) and the lists of variants in the critical report. In this instance it is the sources in the London autograph tradition that generally give the maturer version of the piece, as can easily be seen in Kroll's BG edition where the main Altnickol variants are given beside the main text.

The next question is how the appoggiaturas are to be performed, and here again a comparative study of variants is illuminating. Bach sometimes gave very precise indications about this. In the Sarabande of the G major Partita BWV 829 the first four bars have four speeds of appoggiatura, carefully differentiated in the notation: small semiquavers, small quavers, full dotted quaver, and full crotchet. In typical eighteenth-century fashion, after this very exact indication in the first four-bar phrase, Bach leaves it to the player to continue in the same vein. Some variants in the C sharp minor prelude imply that small notes were intended to be played as quavers (b.49, b.61), but others imply a longer interpretation. It is possible that the version of the cadence in b.4 in sources of the London autograph tradition is a fuller representation of how the simpler Altnickol version should be played. In this case the small note could be the length of a whole dotted crotchet. Other possibilities are in b.36 of the Altnickol version, where the appoggiatura is a full quaver (slurred) in the cantus first beat, a small note in the alto second beat, and a full crotchet (slurred) in the cantus third beat. Clearly, as in the G major sarabande, variety is the essence. Part of the art of harpsichord playing is to give the effect of shading off appoggiaturas by playing them rubato rather than strictly rhythmically, and this could well be the best way to treat many of those written with ornament signs rather than full notes. It is worth noting, in the London autograph tradition, that the alto appoggiatura in the first beat of b.6, liked by Kroll though not given in BG, is very bland compared with the last-inversion 7th and augmented 2nd of the Altnickol version; and the cantus appoggiatura in the last beat of b.12 gives parallel octaves with the bass if played as a quaver: it is erased in P 416 and replaced by a mordent sign (⁎) (BG XIV p.222).

Formally the prelude is in a very much expanded version of the form noted in the preludes in E major and F sharp major of Book I. This expanded form is very characteristic of Book II, used also in the large preludes in F major, F sharp major and minor, and A flat major, representing all three layers of the London autograph.

FUGUE The source situation for the fugue is similar to that for the prelude, except that this fugue was, with the C major, one of two published by Muzio Clementi in *The Second Part of Clementi's Introduction to the Art of Playing on the Piano Forte* (London, *c.*1820–1). Since Clementi had probably acquired the London autograph in 1804, and the C major fugue is edited from the version there, it seems reasonable to suppose that his edition of the C sharp minor fugue was also made from the now missing autograph. The readings he gives, though, make this unlikely. Dürr suggests that he may have made a number of alterations, which are unique to his version, to clarify the counterpoint (KB V/6.2 p.180); Tomita, on the basis of a close examination of variants, finds it not closely related to any of the sources derived from the autograph, but closest to Nägeli's edition and to a Viennese MS copied from a heavily edited source of the second half of the eighteenth century.[16] Either way, Clementi's print frustratingly does not give us the readings of the missing autograph. This, however, is not so much a loss as the autograph of the prelude since the fugue is considerably less problematical in the details of its notation. Most of the main variants are given by Kroll parallel to the text, and all the main ones are discussed by Jones (AB II pp.164–5). Of particular interest is the right-hand variant at b.26 (not given by Kroll; see AB II p.164), which shows Bach grappling with the awkwardness of the inverted subject. What used to be thought an early version in C minor in the Kellner-circle MS P 804 (which otherwise does contain some early versions) was in fact transposed from Altnickol's 1744 copy (P 430) after it had been corrected by Bach (Tomita 1995 p.147).[17]

The fugues so far in Book II have derived from the canzona/verset tradition; the C sharp minor is the first to use an overtly dance metre and, as with other dance-based fugues such as the F major in Book I, part of the fascination of the piece is the manner in which the genres are blended. In blending styles and genres Bach was a composer of his time, but he above all others did it with endless resource and subtlety. The $\frac{12}{16}$ signature is for a particularly lively type of gigue, as in the G major French suite and, more intricately, in the D minor English suite. In this case Bach has taken over from the dance a predominance of regular rhythmic units, noted by Hermann Keller as a feature in common with the A minor fugue BWV 894/2, also $\frac{12}{16}$, dating from before 1725 (1976 p.145). Keller sees this as evidence of an early date (he thought the C minor version in P 804 was earlier) but the complexity of the C sharp minor and the compactness of its working put it on a different level from the diffuse A minor. A further element of the gigue, perceptively noted by Riemann (1890 II pp.28–9), is the importance of inversion, since gigues frequently are in fugal texture with the main idea inverted after the double bar, as indeed is so in the two gigues mentioned above.

Kirnberger, in discussing this time signature, makes a number of points specifically in relation to this fugue.[18] He strongly differentiates $\frac{12}{16}$ from $\frac{12}{8}$ on account of its greater lightness ('wegen der größern Leichtigkeit seines Vortrags weit unterschieden'), and cites as examples of the contrast this fugue for $\frac{12}{16}$ and the C minor fughetta BWV 961 for $\frac{12}{8}$.[19] His main point is that, while $\frac{12}{8}$ denotes a slower tempo and a more emphatic manner ('eine langsamere Bewegung und einen nackdrücklichen Vortrag'), and can take subdivision into semiquaver movement, the semiquavers of $\frac{12}{16}$ are to be played flowingly and smoothly, without any emphasis ('flüßig und rund, ohne allen Druck') and cannot take subdivision into shorter note values. This is obviously in contrast to $\frac{6}{16}$, as in the final fugal section of the D major Toccata BWV 912 or the F major fugue of Book II, which subdivide into demisemiquavers at the end.

In addition to Bach, Kirnberger mentions Handel and François Couperin as others who used $\frac{12}{16}$. Handel uses it for the briskest type of 'Jigg' in the second D minor suite of his 1733 collection, as does Bach in the gigues mentioned above. But Couperin uses it with typical subtlety ('d'une légérté tendre') for *La Florentine* from the second *Ordre* (1713). 'Léger' means light, but not necessarily very quick: Saint Lambert puts it in his scale of tempo words between *gravement* and *gayement*.[20] All these pieces have in common lightness of texture. Kirnberger was clearly generalising from two particular Bach pieces, as well as referring to a tradition. Perhaps a better comparison in terms of the tradition would be the two fugal sections of Buxtehude's G minor Praeludium BuxWV 163, the first in $\frac{12}{8}$ and the second in $\frac{12}{16}$. The second is in a very simple texture, in the manner of an improvisation that decorates continuo clichés. In view of the density of Bach's texture in the C sharp minor fugue one wonders if Kirnberger's comments should not be qualified with reference to it. In an earlier volume of *Die Kunst des reinen Satzes in der Musik*, Kirnberger talks of density of dissonance in contrapuntal works, which may make quick movements sound confused.[21] He singles out Bach's contrapuntal works as notable in this respect, saying that they require a special style of performance of their own ('einen ganz besondern Vortrag'). In the C sharp minor fugue this must mean a style that will preserve the lightness and vitality of the dance, but allow the complexity of the contrapuntal argument to be comprehensible to the listener.

In addition to the dance element, this fugue belongs to the genre of fugue *a due soggetti*, the second subject entering in the cantus at the exact mid-point (b.35). Again Bach shows great variety and resource in the handling of this genre. In some earlier fugues, such as the A minor fugue BWV 904/2, the way in which the second subject is introduced is crudely direct.[22] The handling in the C sharp minor could hardly be more sophisticated. The first exposition keeps to a diatonic interpretation of the subject. As Cecil Gray neatly observes, Bach plays on the lively character by having the answer in b.2 'tread on the tail' of the subject (1938 p.91). This means that the answer enters as the 5th of the tonic, then moves to the dominant, and, since Bach never wastes anything, this

5th interpretation of the opening of the subject is vital to the later development of the fugue. The tail of the subject is extended sequentially in b.4, and then again to form a long sequence moving to E major at b.13. Since this sequence has the relaxing effect of the falling circle of 5ths, a lively new, upward leaping figure enters at the E major cadence, and leads to a second tonic exposition from b.16. It is at the third (bass) entry of this exposition (b.20) that Bach starts to adumbrate his second subject in the chromatic steps of the cantus. Another falling sequence takes us to an inversion exposition from b.24, which extends and plays on these chromatic steps, notably in b.27. The full second subject enters at b.35 and is given a quasi-exposition in all parts to b.38. The oblique way in which it is introduced, over the continuing flow of semiquavers, and the rhythmic irregularity of the entries, make this a masterpiece of subtle integration. There is no doubt about the identity of the second subject since the rest of the fugue is concerned with combining it in double counterpoint at the 12th with the first, starting at b.48. This is where the interpretation of the first note of the subject as the 5th of a chord comes into its own. The alternative effect, where both subjects begin on the same note rather than a 5th apart, may be seen in the permutation at b.55. As Bach shows here and in the fugues in G minor and B major, it is the harmonic reinterpretation of themes which gives double counterpoint at intervals other than the octave its charm. As a final *jeu d'esprit* Bach has both subjects treading on each other's tails in all three parts at bb.66–8.

Prelude and Fugue in D major BWV 874

PRELUDE As with the C sharp minor prelude, the lack of an autograph for the D major deprives us of crucial evidence for performance. There are two main performance issues, one of which is relatively clear-cut, the other less so. Both problems derive from the double time signature ¢$\frac{12}{8}$, and the fact that some elements are notated in simple, and some in compound time.

The first is whether the dotted quavers and semiquavers should be assimilated to the quaver triplets (¢ ♪.♬ to $\frac{12}{8}$ ♪♪♪). Most commentators are agreed that they should be, though Landowska preferred to double-dot the dotted quavers in order to evoke 'drum beats and festivity' (1965 p.198); and Tovey liked sometimes to play the ¢-time semiquaver with the last $\frac{12}{8}$-time semiquaver, in the interests of harmony (AB II p.166). He also points out that Bach was quite capable of notating the rhythm as ♩♪ rather than ♪.♬ when it was more convenient, as at bb.34–5. Bach was usually careful to notate what he wanted in terms of the alignment of notes, and Dürr finds that, even though there is no autograph, all the main sources unambiguously align the ¢-time semiquaver with the third $\frac{12}{8}$-time quaver (KB V/6.2 p.224). The best evidence is therefore for assimilation.

Less easily resolved is the second question, whether or not the quavers in b.2 etc. should also be played as triplets. Here most commentators think that they should not.[23] Documentary evidence in favour of a triplet interpretation is in the many French treatises from Bach's lifetime that specify unequal quavers in ¢ time; and Marpurg, who met Bach probably in the late 1740s, explains that, when simple and compound time signatures are used simultaneously, the simple is to be assimilated to the compound (1765 p.24 and Tab.I Figs. 42–3), i.e. in Ex.8.10, Fig.42a and b are to be played as Fig.43.

Ex.8.10 Marpurg: notation (42a and b) and performance (43) of simultaneous simple and compound time.

As far as the notation goes the evidence is not so clear-cut as for the first question. One source in the London autograph tradition (*D-Dl* 2405 T 7) gives the quavers in b.42 in the form ♪. ♬ ♪. ♬, and a group in the Kirnberger tradition do the same at b.4. Since this rhythm elsewhere in the piece seems intended to be assimilated to the triplet quavers, this is another argument for the same at b.2 etc. Actual triplets are given only in Nägeli's edition (1801) and a couple of peripheral MS sources of the later 18th-century (♩. ♩. ♩♪ ♩♪ at b.2 and equivalent places; Tomita 1995 pp.175–202). The only place where both ¢ and values appear simultaneously is at b.18. The argument from parallel 5ths is inconclusive since both ways of playing the quavers give them. The most convincing notational evidence is in P 416 (Anon.12), characterized by Jones as 'a direct copy of [the London autograph] that reproduces its minutest idiosyncracies' (AB II p.165). Here the quavers are aligned with the 1st, 4th, 7th and 10th semiquavers (as they are in all the control editions), implying even performance.[24]

In performance decisions of this sort it is important to be sensitive to the evolution of Bach's style. In the chorale prelude 'Herr Gott nun schleuß den Himmel auf' BWV 617 from the *Orgel-Büchlein* Bach uses the time signatures $\mathbf{c}\frac{24}{16}$ for the manuals and $\mathbf{c}\,\frac{12}{8}$ for the pedal, the right hand having the chorale and an accompanying part in crotchets, and evenly notated quavers against the compound time of the left hand and pedal. In the autograph (P 283) the right-hand quavers seem aligned to assimilate to compound time. Stinson has dated this prelude 1715–16 (1996 pp.17, 128). By the 1720s there is no doubt about combinations of two and three in, for example, the first movements of the Fifth Brandenburg Concerto (1719?) or the B minor sonata for obbligato harpsichord and flute BWV 1030 (c.1726). More sophisticated is Bach's liking for layered textures, part of his fascination with complex combinations of styles and genres. The Adagio of the C minor sonata for obbligato harpsichord and violin BWV 1017 (before 1725) has three separate rhythmic strands which combine magically if played as written, with the violin adding a slightly overdotted lilt to its dotted quavers; it is difficult to believe here that the very dull effect of assimilation is what Bach intended. Complex rhythmic juxtapositions are a feature of late Baroque/galant style, particularly in the Adagio.

By 1740–1, when Bach evidently prepared the London autograph copy of the D major pair since it belongs to the 'Prelude' group, the immediate contrast of character at the beginning of a movement, with which we are most familiar from Mozart (the opening of this prelude has often been compared with that of the Jupiter Symphony), was already established in instrumental music, probably as a development of the type of Baroque aria with two conflicting emotions in one section.[25] In 1751 J.-J. Rousseau performed in Paris 'une symphonie brillante et douce alternativement', but the manner was known in Germany before this in the works of Johann Stamitz (Cucuel 1913 p.123), and adumbrations of it are already in orchestral sinfonias written by Johann Adolph Scheibe in Leipzig in the 1730s, with strong ideas for trumpets contrasting with languishing ideas for flutes.[26] Where Mozart liked to play with characters by turning them into their opposites, Bach liked to combine them, as he does to brilliant effect in b.18 of this prelude. The quavers in b.2 and elsewhere therefore seem to want to contrast with the dynamic arpeggio by being languishing: as Quantz says, the first and third a little longer and stronger, but not as much as if they were dotted (1752 Chapter xi para.12); assimilation to the rhythm of the arpeggio undermines this all-important contrast.

The fact that this manner of contrast subsequently became such a hallmark of the Classical period has misled people into trying to see too much of Classical sonata form in this piece. Keller found 'no second subject' (1976 p.146); Tovey found a 'second subject' at bb.13–16 (AB II p.166). This is in fact a large-scale version of the galant sonata-type structure based on the aria ritornello shape described in Chapter Three section 6. It has the usual elements of a square, closed four-bar phrase at the opening; an open-ended, sequential phrase that modulates to the dominant (bb.5–12); and a closing theme and cadence (bb.13–16). After the double bar the same ideas are run back to the tonic, but all is inverted, and also combined, enhanced, and developed, with a climax of semiquaver movement at bb.27–9. The closing theme in particular, which starts after the cadence in the relative minor usual at this stage, is particularly expanded (bb.33–40) in order to make a dramatic point of the return at b.41. This reverses, rather than inverts, the events of the first, closed, phrase (the 6ths now come before the 3rds), and Bach makes his favourite harmonic balance by arranging this phrase to move to the subdominant, so that the modulating phrase can move up a 5th to the tonic, as it had originally moved up a 5th from the tonic to the dominant. In comparing the whole structure to that of the Book I E major prelude of twenty years before the main difference, and one which does show a move towards Classical structures, is in the fact that the third main section (from b.41) now begins in the tonic, with a special point made of the return to that key.

In the build-up to the return, the Altnickol sources' reading of the bass in the last beat of b.36 (NBA V/6.2 p.178; BG XIV *ossia*; see AB II p.165) seems much more dynamic and suitable than the rather bland London autograph-tradition alternative (NBA V/6.2 p.26; BG XIV main text), even though it looks as if the latter was Bach's final thought.

FUGUE The combination of very 'modern' prelude and very traditional fugue is entirely typical of Bach in the 1730s. Hermann Keller compares this pair to the opening two movements of the *Ratswahlkantate* BWV 29 (1731), also in D major, where an organ concerto movement, better known as the Preludio of the E major Partita for unaccompanied violin BWV 1006, is followed by a *stile antico* chorus, better known as the Gratias agimus/Dona nobis pacem of the B minor Mass (Keller 1976 p.148). In the case of the D major prelude and fugue the modernity of the first item has been enhanced.

Riemann perceptively compares this fugue to the G minor of Book I, and indeed Bach is treating traditional materials in a very similar way in both pieces (Riemann 1890 II p.35). In the G minor Bach took a subject from Fischer in which two elements are designed to combine in stretti, and by separating the elements with a caesura makes more dramatic point of the stretti. As in the G minor, each element of the D major subject ends with a pair of crotchets, though here they are differentiated in that the second crotchet of the first pair is part of a syncopation. It may have been to partly ensure that the offbeat crotchets are unaccented that Bach changed the time signature from **c**, which it was in the lost draft according to sources of the Altnickol tradition, to ¢ (Tomita 1990 p.233). **c** was the normal signature for canzonas and versets using this type of material based on black notes; ¢ was for *stile antico* ricercars etc. based on white notes. The fact that Bach could use the same signature for this fugue as for the ricercar-type fugues in E flat major and E major shows how categories had weakened, mainly under the influence of French dance music, by the early eighteenth century. The use of ¢ must have been motivated not by considerations of style or genre, but of performance, to avoid a plodding tempo. It also gives subtlety to the metre in that all three repeated quavers are now in themselves an upbeat to an upbeat.

The fact that this black-note, canzona-type fugue comes in close proximity to the E major ricercar type suggests that Bach may have intended a demonstration pair; or, perhaps more likely, a pair of this and the E flat major fugue, which was originally in D major, and whose subject has a similar intervallic structure (Ellis 1980 p.164). Whether or not this is so, there is no doubt that in this D major, as in the C sharp major fugue, Bach is taking the most basic elements of the verset tradition and exploiting them to exhaustion. The ingredients here are perhaps the commonest of all: the typical canzona repeated notes, and the archetypal canzona motif of a rising 4th followed by steps down. In Fischer's *Blumen-Strauß* versets (Augsburg 1732), for example, all six of the Mode III fugues are based either on the repeated-note or the canzona-motif shape. In Mode IV, Fuga III has a subject in two units, the first of which is the canzona motif recto and the second the same motif inverso. Closest to Bach's concept among Fischer's fugues is the A minor Fuga from *Ariadne Musica*, which has the repeated-note head and a different tail, both designed to combine together in stretti, again like the Fischer E flat major Fuga which had provided the material for the G minor fugue of Book I. The same principle, in operation with the actual materials of the D major fugue, may be seen in the *Wegweiser* (Ex.8.11), which we have also seen providing an example of the subject type of the C sharp major fugue.

Ex.8.11 Anon.: *Wegweiser* No.47, Mode VI Versus 6.

A further aspect of the verset tradition is the use, unusual in the 48, of modal ambitus for the main, marker cadences: the 1st degree (b.16), the 5th degree (b.20), and the 3rd degree (b.27; see Ex.4.1).[27] Bach was of course expert in seventeenth–eighteenth-century modal harmony (see Burns 1995) and this fugue, far from being the 'dry and scholastic' thing that Busoni found it, is full of connoisseur's touches. The form of the subject, jumping from the tonic to the 5th below, is tonally ambiguous, seeming to be in G major in tonal terms or, specially with a subject with these associations, giving a typical outline of the plagal version of the Mixolydian mode (Mode VIII). Only subsequently does the tonality become clear. Mattheson discusses this effect in *Der vollkommene Capellmeister* with reference to a subject of Handel's (from the B minor clavier fugue HWV 608), and he congratulates Handel as an experienced composer ('einem geübten Setzer') who knows how to give the necessary notes to define the key soon after the opening (1739 Part III Chapter 20 paras.23–5). On the same page he discusses two Bach fugue subjects from the unaccompanied violin sonatas BWV 1003 and 1005. In view of Bach's apparent interest in *Der vollkommene Capellmeister* when he was putting together Book II it is possible that here is another impetus to his thought (see Chapter Four section 8). Marpurg, in the first part of his *Abhandlung von der Fuge*, refers to Mattheson's discussion and makes the connexion between Handel's subject and that of the D major fugue, attributing the unorthodox opening to Bach's originality.[28] In fact, great originality in the handling of very traditional materials is the overriding impression given by this fugue. It is a tour de force in weaving a continuum of a single predominant note value, with extraordinary motivic concentration (Tovey calculates that the canzona-motif tail of the subject accounts for three-quarters of the total notes of the fugue), yet without the faintest monotony. This is achieved by the skilful moulding of a rich mixture of ingredients: traditional Italian contrapuntal material with luxuriant French harmonic language, a traditional key scheme worked in terms of 'modern' tonality, and elaborate contrapuntal combinations given maximum dramatic point by expert manipulation of textures and spacing.[29]

The continuum is also given variety by the clarity of its organization into sections, each of which has a characteristic contribution to make to the total design in terms of contrapuntal argument, harmony, and texture. The first (to b.10), after the four-part exposition, ends with the effect of overlapping entries of the tail of the subject, essentially a falling effect here. It is worth noting that the unorthodox opening of the subject yields a leading-note 7th on the syncopated note (b.3, third beat; b.6, first beat), a favourite chord of galant-style composers. The second section (bb.10–16) opens with a rich reharmonization of the subject, in which the syncopated note now forms a dominant minor 9th (b.11, first beat). It also introduces a second effect for the tail of the subject: a climbing sequential repetition (alto b.11). The possibilities of this effect for building up a climax traditionally made this figure a favourite as the final point in canzonas.[30] The second section ends with the first of a series of two-part stretti (this one at the 4th; bb.14–15), harmonized in the bass by the falling 5ths from the beginning of the subject. Section three (bb.20–27) explores the sequential climbing effect introduced in section two. Section four has the second two-part stretto (at the 5th; bb.22–3) and forms the moment of involution of the piece at the halfway point, with the densest harmony and the tightest spacing. This sets up the gloriously open two-part stretto at the octave (bb.27–9) which starts the long final section. A three-part stretto at the 6th (bb.33ff) is followed by powerful exploitation of both effects using the tail of the subject in turn: the overlapping imitations, now over a chromatically rising bass (bb.35–6), leading to the climbing sequential repetition, its climaxing effect carried much further than it ever was by the composers of the late Renaissance, with a triple repetition in the bass followed by a two-octave descending scale (bb.37–40). The contrapuntal climax is in the four-part stretto in descending 3rds at bb.44ff. Here, the chromatically altered version of the subject in the bass at b.43, with a diminished 5th and diminished 3rd, strengthens the case for g♯ in the tenor in the third beat of b.45, evidently not originally in the London autograph, but added to Altnickol's 1744 copy as a correction (Tomita 1995 p.220; AB II p.166).

The fugue winds down using the falling effect from the end of section one, now with the tail rhythmically relocated *per arsin et thesin* between bass and tenor so that it steps out the falling 5th till it reaches the subdominant at b.49. All this is done with rich, satiated harmony, the leading-note 7th at the beginning of b.48 capped by the double 9/7 suspension at the beginning of b.49. Nothing could better exemplify Bach's aim to update and revivify traditional materials and techniques with the full resources of 'modern' harmony, dramatic control of keyboard texture, and large-scale structural plan. He left very little for others who might wish to try doing it again.

Prelude and Fugue in D minor BWV 875

PRELUDE Like the C major prelude, the D minor exists in four main states and gives further insight into Bach's technique of elaboration and improvement. (1) The earliest version (BWV 875a; NBA V/6.2 p.346, PF p.38) is of 43 bars only, and is in the same source copied by J.C. Vogler as the earliest version of the C major prelude and fugue (P 1089). This copy was made between 1727 and 1731, though the original that Vogler copied from could date from any time before that. The D minor prelude probably does not belong with the other pieces in this fascicle (BWV 899, 900, 870a, 901, and 527; see NBA V/6.2, *Fünf Praeludien und Fughetten*) which already contains a

D minor pair BWV 899. (2) At some stage Bach made a revised copy (now lost), including insertions which brought the piece up to 53 bars. Around 1739–40, in the first stage of assembling Book II, Anna Magdalena Bach copied this version into P 226 and the London autograph (NBA V/6.2 p.348, PF p.40). (3) In 1742–4 Bach substantially revised the piece again, making it up to its present 61 bars. He then went back to the lost copy and entered these new revisions, but making further revisions as he went, and this was what Altnickol used for his 1744 copy (NBA V/6.2 p.182 is a composite reconstruction of this phase). (4) He then made further, less extensive, revisions to the London autograph after Altnickol had made his 1744 copy (NBA II p.30). In spite of all this complexity, one can see essentially three phases of the piece in the London autograph (facsimile in NBA V/6.2 pp.XII–XIII).[31]

The key to this prelude is in the early version, BWV 875a (version 1 above). Technically it comes between the little preludes in the *Clavier-Büchlein* for Wilhelm Friedemann Bach and the smaller preludes of Book I, at the level of two-part Inventions such as the F major. Like the C sharp major prelude of Book I it seems to have been popular among Bach's pupils, judging by the number of copies, no doubt because it makes a brilliant effect without being technically difficult. In this case the brilliance comes from concertante figurations, and these are the educational point of the piece. The pattern at bb.30–33 of BWV 875a (Ex.8.12a) is one associated more with continuo playing than with solo keyboard music.

Ex.8.12 (a) BWV 875a bars 30–33; (b) London autograph ante corr. bars 39–43; (c) BWV 875/1 bars 47–51.

Ex.8.12 (Continued)

Heinichen gives patterns of this sort for dealing with rapid repeated notes in the bass, so as not to give a constant clatter ('ein beständiges Gehacke'), as in Ex.8.13.[32]

According to Mattheson, this effect is suitable for fully scored concertos, orchestral pieces and choruses, where excitement and noise are a priority, and C.P.E. Bach tells us that such patterns are a good way of avoiding stiffness in the hands and wrists from playing too many rapid repeated notes.[33] Continuo patterns can come into pieces for various reasons. One is that they were the stock-in-trade for improvisation, and Bach's early keyboard toccatas have many such passages. Working up decorative chord patterns from continuo progressions was taught by Niedt (1700) as the basis of improvisation, and this lies behind the chord-pattern preludes of Book I. In the context of the 48 their

Ex.8.13 J.D. Heinichen: continuo patterns for dealing with repeated bass notes.

purpose is educational: as C.P.E. Bach says, in order to become skilled enough to play continuo the pupil must spend a considerable amount of time on good solo pieces ('Handsachen'; 1762 Einleitung para.12). It is possible that the germ of the piece was an improvisation based on this effect, in which case the concertante version of it at bb.8–11 of 875a, with interlocked hands akin to one of Rameau's *batteries*, came later (Ex.8.14a).

Alternatively, the *batterie* may have come first, and the version in Ex.8.12a may simply have doubled the speed of the left-hand figuration since it is now lower in pitch and without the interlock. Either way, this type of figuration is associated with concerto style. The very Vivaldian D minor concerto of Prince Johann Ernst of Sachsen-Weimar, which Bach arranged for harpsichord as BWV 987, has similar effects. The descending scale at the opening of the prelude is a notably lively feature of Vivaldi's G minor concerto Op.3 No.2, though this is not one of the concertos arranged by Bach. It is also worth

Ex.8.14 Prelude in D minor, bb. 18–23: (a) in the second version; (b) in the final version.

Ex.8.14 (Continued)

noting that Bach made his final version of his own D minor harpsichord concerto BWV 1052 around 1738. BWV 875a cannot date from later than around 1730, but as an instructional piece, probably based on demonstration improvisation, it could date back to Weimar days.

Formally BWV 875a is in line with the two-part Inventions. An opening harmonic formula in double counterpoint (bb.1–5) is followed by a sequential modulation to the dominant (bb.7–15) when the opening formula comes in again with the counterpoint inverted (bb.16–19). The B flat major Invention works the same scheme with a virtually identical harmonic formula. The midpoint (bb.20–26) has the densest harmony, and the final section (from b.26) functions as a developmental reprise. In version 2 Bach was concerned initially to improve the weak transition in bb.5–6 of version 1, and generally round out the formal scheme. He therefore cut b.6, and added six bars which invert the opening double counterpoint in the tonic, and have a more satisfactory sequential transition to the interlocking figure. Having done that, he added the equivalent inversion after the dominant entry of the double counterpoint (after b.19 of version 1). The continuo pattern of Ex.8.12a was obviously too unsophisticated for a 'Handsache', so he recast the harmony to be more significant motivically, and added a bar that points up the reprise nature of this passage (Ex.8.12b). He also added mordent signs to the top of the opening left-hand arpeggios, and equivalent places. It was typical of the best figural composers from Monteverdi onwards to integrate surface ornament into the motivic argument, and Bach was no exception. Ex.8.12b already shows how this is beginning to happen here.

We can see Bach in the act of transforming version 2 into version 3 in the London autograph and, although these additions fit easily on a single system added at the bottom of the page, they are what transform the piece into something much weightier than one could have expected from version 1. After the tonic inversion of the double counterpoint, he scrubbed out his new two-bar transition and added a new four-bar one with more harmonic variety by using the circle of 5ths (bb.10–12 of the final version). But the most significant addition is the new development in bb.13–17 which picks up this transition and moulds elements of what has gone before so that they gradually assume the shape of the interlocking figure which we now do not reach until b.18. The scales from b.9 develop an *échappée* of a 3rd in b.13, a 5th in b.15, and a 6th in b.17, which prepares the concertante figure at b.18. Now, instead of two disparate ideas with a perfunctory transition as in version 1, we have continuous transformation and development as well as variety and contrast. The effect of the interlocking figure now is of having reached a plateau after an arduous ascent, and the arrival of the dominant in b.26 is the fulfilment of an eventful journey. All these additions had pushed the point of involution to two-thirds of the way through the piece, and it was now inadequate for its structural function. Bach therefore added bb.37–8, which invert the previous two bars and add considerably more harmonic asperity to this moment. He also added further energy and significance to the bass at bb.47–51 (Ex.8.12c). In all, these alterations considerably raise the keyboard-technical level of the piece.

Bach's final adjustments to the London autograph further enhanced both the motivic significance of the mordent figure and the concertante nature of the piece (Ex.8.14b). The mordent shape added in the right hand at bb.18ff emphasises the change of note at the beginning of each bar, and therefore the rising scale inherent in bb.18–26, originally bland. The demisemiquavers in b.21 add concerto brilliance, reminiscent of the D minor concerto BWV 1052, or of Prince Johann Ernst's D minor concerto in BWV 987. It was with reference to this prelude that Forkel, who in the same instant was making an extraordinarily imperceptive judgment of the revisions in the C and C sharp major preludes of Book I, justly found 'surprise and delight at the means which [Bach] employed to make, little by little, the faulty good, the good better, and the better perfect' (1802 p.63; NBR pp.474–5).

FUGUE This is one of the four fughettas copied by J.F. Agricola in 1738/9 as part of the preparation for Book II (P 595; NBA V/6.2 pp.352–7). They seem to have originated at widely different times since what became the C sharp major fugue is clearly much earlier and went through numerous revisions, while the C minor, although it went into Book II with very little change, shows signs of having originally had the old Dorian key signature. The D minor seems the most recent of the four. Unlike the prelude there are no earlier versions, and the fughetta shows no signs of ever having had a Dorian signature (KB V/6.2 p.380). Stylistically also it seems to have moved on from the very traditional verset origins of the other three.

The stylistic surface is, however, misleading, since underneath the decoration there lies a traditional subject type, in two halves, the first of which is designed to combine in stretti with the second. This type of subject can take various forms, as we have now seen in numerous examples from Fischer, Bach and others. The version behind the D minor subject outlines a triad in the first half and has a descending chromatic scale segment in the second. A traditional example is in the Langloz *partimenti* (Ex.7.32a).

Its ultimate origin is unclear, but it appears in later seventeenth-century Italian instrumental music: examples are in Legrenzi's *Sonate* Op.2 (1655) and Albinoni's *Suonate* Op.1 (1694), from which Bach made two workings of a subject of this type (BWV 951, 951a; see Ex.7.32b; also P. Williams 1997 p.94). The subject of the *Musical Offering* is a very elaborate version of the same type. The *partimento* example implies an improvised type of fugue, and the D minor fugue has something of the contrapuntal looseness of an improvisation, with moments of *style brisé* chord sequences (bb.11–12, 15–16) such as were noted in the C minor fugue. Similarities between the D minor fugue and the three-part Ricercar from the *Musical Offering* have often been noted, and the Ricercar is thought to have been what Bach improvised, possibly on a pianoforte, for Frederick II of Prussia during his visit to Potsdam in 1747.[34] Apart from similarities of melodic motifs, the Ricercar and this fugue share the rhythmic feature of triplets against duplets, a sophisticated mixing of note values cultivated in the galant style, and which no doubt was intended to please the Potsdam audience. There can be no doubt that the rhythms are intended to be played as written.[35] A revealing comparison is with the canons of *The Art of Fugue*, which seem designed by Bach to be a systematic demonstration of, among other things, possible rhythmic notations. The canon at the octave has the signature $\frac{9}{16}$ with the notation one would expect. The canon at the 10th has the double signature **c**$\frac{12}{8}$ with the same implication of assimilating ♪. ♬ to ♩ ♪ as in the D major prelude. The canon at the 12th has the ¢ time signature, with quaver sextuplets marked as such, and which are clearly meant to contrast with the even quavers. The **c** time signature of the D minor fugue, with semiquavers and semiquaver triplets marked as such, is the equivalent of this.[36]

Bach here has yet again taken very ordinary material from the tradition and refreshed it with charm and interest. His principle is to take a selection of features from a genre and make them the basis for the character of a fugue. Just as in the D major fugue of Book I he took features from the first section of the French overture, so here he has taken the contrast of note values of the galant sonata. In the mid- to late 1730s Bach had a special interest in combining this with traditional techniques, and with these sort of materials, as in the *Clavier-Übung* III manual chorale preludes on 'Allein Gott in der Höh' sei Ehr' BWV 675 (probably 1735–6) and 'Jesus Christus unser Heiland' BWV 689 (probably late 1738, with similar episode material, notably in bb.27–35).[37]

The rhythmic distinction of subject and countersubject neatly masks their fundamental identity (both based on rising 4ths) and makes a virtue of what could have been a weakness. As Cecil Gray points out, this is the first of the Book II fugues to have a regular countersubject throughout (1938 p.97), and Marpurg accordingly gives it a detailed motivic analysis in his section on double fugue.[38] Marpurg nonetheless manages to miss the overall contrapuntal plan of the piece, which is that the second half of the fugue has a stretto recto (b.14f), a stretto inverso (b.17f) and a three-part stretto recto and inverso at the end (b.25f), of which only the last entry is complete. Otherwise Marpurg is sound, if pedestrian, in his observations. The little link at b.5 introduces the principle of inversion. This is taken up in stretto at b.10, where the imitation is at the quarter bar ('in Arsi', as Marpurg puts it). In the rhetorical theory of fugue, the imitation *per contrario tempore* represents conflict, in this case heightened by inversion (as in b.17; Butler 1977 pp.90–2). The fugue therefore has a well graded build-up to the half-way point, after which this effect is explored and developed until the final series of entries at b.25.

There is only one major revision in this piece, and that is the change of octave in the cantus in b.13 with a link to the cantus stretto entry in b.14, a revision made in the London autograph. Opinions differ as to the virtues of this. The higher pitch duplicates the cantus pitch level in b.12 and bb.14–15, and the stretto entry in b.14 is obscured. But ultimately it has to be an improvement since this is the moment of involution at the midpoint of the piece. It heightens the pitch level, together with the expressive effect of distance from the other parts, of the same material in b.8, and it also intensifies the density of texture which had been introduced at b.10. Bach did not like gaps and sudden thinness of texture this late in his career, as has been noted in the discussion of the C sharp minor fugue.

A few fingerings of uncertain origin are in Anna Magdalena Bach's copy in P 226. They are basically concerned with taking over the alto part in the left hand, and underline the similarity of b.8 and b.13 in the corrected version (given in KB V/6.2 p.229).

Prelude and Fugue in E flat major BWV 876

PRELUDE This is a pair that can with certainty be said not to have originated together since the fugue has an early version (in D major) in J.F. Agricola's fughetta collection, while we can see Bach virtually in the act of composing the prelude into the London autograph in *c.*1739–40. It has every appearance of having been worked up from improvisation, and there is what looks like a sketch for the first six bars copied into P 416 (facsimile in NBA V/6.2 p.XIV).[39] There are therefore three main versions of the piece: the sketch in

P 416; the London autograph, which underwent at least two layers of revision; and Altnickol's version.

Many commentators have been struck by the similarity of this piece to the 'Prelude pour la Luth. ò Cembal.', as Bach headed it, BWV 998, and have related it to Bach's known interest in the lute and lute-harpsichord around 1740.[40] J.F. Agricola tells us that around that year he saw a 'Lauten-clavicymbel' designed by Bach and built by Zacharias Hildebrandt (NBR p.366; see Chapter One section 6). This seems to link to the report of a visit to Bach in 1739 by the distinguished Dresden lutenists Sylvius Leopold Weiss and Johann Kropffgans, during which much fine music was made (NBR p.204). Both Weiss and Bach were specially noted improvisers, and according to J.F. Reichardt, whose father was one of the last generation of outstanding German lutenists and who himself played the lute, Weiss and Bach on occasion improvised and played fugues in competition with each other (Hoffmann-Erbrecht 1987 p.20). It is difficult to see how this could have been a worthwhile competition if Bach had used the full resources of the clavier against the limited technical possibilities of the lute. It would make more sense if Bach had imitated lute style on the Lautenwerk, and BWV 998 would make excellent sense as a souvenir of such an occasion. The prelude has an idiomatic lute texture, also found in Weiss preludes, of sonorous low notes on the diapason courses struck with the right-hand thumb, and an arpeggiated upper part for the other fingers. The very straightforward structure of the piece, with a common opening formula that reappears four times in different keys, and a single modulating pattern that equally recurs, points to a written-out improvisation. The fugue subject also, beginning with even slow notes, is in the manner of Weiss.

The E flat prelude has obvious similarities to this in its time signature, general movement, and much of the texture. This was originally rather sparer than it later became, with only two parts (cantus and tenor) in bb.6–8 and 13–16, the bass pedal notes and chords being added later.[41] Even so the piece has a keyboard, rather than a lute, texture; the sonorous diapason notes, the most idiomatic lute feature of BWV 998, are missing; and Bach's lute-harpsichord does not seem to have gone beyond g'' in the treble, so this piece would not have been suitable for it. Bach seems here yet again to be evoking one medium in terms of another, just as the C major prelude evokes the organ and the D major the orchestra. None of these preludes would be suitable for the medium referred to, but that is their nature and their charm. Bach did not write character pieces as such, but just as François Couperin invented a novel harpsichord texture to evoke budding *fleurs-de-lis* in *Les lis naissans* (1722), so in the highly unusual texture of the E flat prelude it is as if Bach was seeing what could be done in purely clavier terms with the quasi-lute textures of the lute-harpsichord.

The similarity with BWV 998 can also shed some light on the performance of this prelude. The quick, gigue character felt by Riemann (1890 II p.46) and F. Neumann (1983 p.152) is foreign to the improvised character of the lute prelude. Given this rapid tempo, Neumann recommends playing the appoggiaturas in bb.2, 4 and 62 as semiquavers. This is to get over what some people have thought to be a problem, that the appoggiatura if played as a crotchet gives parallel 4ths with the bass. But parallels between simultaneous ornamental notes are so common in highly ornamented music that it cannot have been objected to, and Tovey has some very sensible and eloquent comments to make about this (AB II p.169). One solution, to play the appoggiatura as a dotted crotchet and resolve it in the following rest, a manner of performing appoggiaturas in compound time suggested by Quantz, is recommended by Dolmetsch (1946 p.108) and Kreutz (1952 p.364) among others, but it is difficult to make this effective as an appoggiatura on the harpsichord. Dannreuther's suggestion of duplet quavers, thereby putting the appoggiatura in a rubato relation to the metre of the piece, is good from this point of view (1893 p.179; recommended also by Tovey). In BWV 998 there are two appoggiaturas written in normal note values (b.40 and the last bar), and they are both crotchets (♩‿♪).

Formally, this prelude belongs with the most mature pieces in Book II. It uses the expanded aria ritornello form in its sonata guise, but with great flexibility and subtlety. The opening section (bb.1–12) has the usual elements of closed four-bar phrase, sequential modulation to the dominant, and a sort of closing theme (bb.10–11). The dominant phase, however, merely alludes to this; the elements appear only in oblique form, and all is much expanded. The opening idea does not reappear until b.61, and then in an abbreviated and developmental form. The prelude is a study of developing variation of the opening section, not only in the piece as we finally have it, but in the successive alterations which we can see Bach making in the course of entering the piece into the London autograph. The original rising 2nds in the bass at b.34 became falling 7ths in b.37 and rising 9ths in b.39. While this has an understandable logic, the rising 2nds are tame, and the change to falling 7ths adds strength and character, particularly since Bach in changing the 2nds to 7ths in b.34 added a c'♭ in the right-hand last beat.

FUGUE Of the four fughettas in J.F. Agricola's collection, this one (which is in D major there; NBA V/6.2 p.354, PF p.48) represents the strict ('gebunden') style. Somebody, or perhaps two different people, later pencilled in pedal indications for the subject entries in bb.1, 31 and 60. Bach's original organ fugues virtually never begin with the pedals (with the possible exception of BWV 549a), and the bass line from b.39 to b.58, even of the early version, is either impossible because of range, or very unidiomatic in terms of Bach's usual pedal writing, and is even more so in the final version. The style is nonetheless associated with the organ and so this fugue makes an excellent complement to the prelude, with its exclusive reference to plucked strings.

The original **c** time signature and the predominance of white note values place this fugue in the keyboard ricercar tradition, similar in subject and note values to Ricercar IV (Mode VIII) of Froberger's 1656 book. The change of time signature to ¢ in the E flat version was probably made for the same sort of performance considerations as in the D major fugue. Commentators have noted such features of strict style as Zarlino's 'modo di fuggir le cadenze' by bringing an entry during the cadence (b.30; Dehn 1858 p.12), and Berardi's 'motivo di cadenza', of avoiding a cadence by having a suspended 7th in the resolution, as at bb.46ff (Seidel 1986 p.142). The subject, with a rising 5th, a move further to the 6th degree, then a sequential descent to the tonic, is longer than is usual in ricercars and is similar to the one Bach used in the early Canzona in D minor BWV 588, which some have derived from the 'Canzon dopo la Pistola' in the *Messa della Madonna* of Frescobaldi's *Fiori musicali* (P. Williams 1980 I p.272). He also used it in the D sharp minor fugue of Book I. The virtue of the sequential tail of the subject is its potential for section building. In this case it is based on another of the simple, *stile antico* contrapuntal formulas noted in the discussion of the C sharp major prelude, and which is designed for stretto imitations (Ex.8.15, compare Ex.8.6).

The exposition avoids the suggestion of stretto and harmonises the subject in the robust tonal style of a quodlibet.[42] Antiphonal pairs of voices in stretto enter at b.30 (tenor and bass), and b.37 (alto and soprano) with the counterpoint inverted. Bar 59 has a repetition of the b.30 stretto in the outer parts. The early version has all entries of the subject beginning with a semibreve. In the stretto at b.30 this gives a very crude effect of parallel octaves, and also obscures the entry of the stretto since the octaves sound like note doubling rather than contrapuntal parts. In the London autograph this bar is divided over the end of a line, so it is possible that Bach, having divided the tenor semibreve into two minims, forgot to add the tie (which was added at some later stage to

Ex.8.15 Fugue in E flat major, formula behind the early version (in D major): (a) plain outline; (b) the same worked fugally.

Altnickol's 1744 copy, and is in some other sources; KB V/6.2 p.230, AB II p.169). But it is difficult to believe that he could have allowed the very obvious weakness of part writing to stand, or that the startling improvement in the dramatic effect of the first stretto entries, when the first note of the subject is curtailed to a minim, did not occur to him.

Bach made only one important revision to this fugue when including it in Book II. In the bass from b.47 to b.53 he replaced references to the subject with running quavers. This is a substantial improvement since it develops and gives point to the turning figure of four quavers introduced in the alto at the end of b.45, and which itself is a development of the pairs of quavers in the subject. It also takes this episode away from the subject material, which then can enter with more dramatic point in the reharmonised tenor entry from b.53, with the quavers continuing in the bass until they form a complete E flat scale at bb.57–8.

Prelude and Fugue in D sharp minor BWV 877

PRELUDE The advanced-key pieces which form the second layer of entries to the London autograph are generally substantial works which seem mostly to have been composed roughly at the same time (*c.*1740–41) and with a certain family resemblance between them. Only the C sharp major pair has early versions, and there the fugue was so recomposed and expanded as to be fully able to take its place beside the others. Two of the preludes are two-part inventions (D sharp minor and E minor), but of a novel sort, and without the abstruse speculations of the Duetti published in *Clavier-Übung* III in 1739 and probably composed in that year (Butler 1990 p.19, who suggests they may be for Lautenwerk). These preludes differ from the Inventions of *c.*1720 in being large-scale binary pieces in an expansive sonata structure. They also have galant stylistic features: the D sharp minor prelude uses (bb.6–8 etc.) a kind of Alberti pattern for the right hand which figures prominently also in the preludes in F sharp major and B major (see Chapter Three section 9). But the main distinguishing feature of this invention type is that, rather than restricting the motivic material to a single unit of double counterpoint, these two invention preludes aim for more variety by combining the initial figure with successively different counterpoints of contrasting character. The D sharp minor prelude has no less than five different counterpoints (bb.2, 9, 10, 17 and 28) with variations of two of them (b.12, bb.34–5).

Various features of the earlier Inventions remain. The opening idea has the appearance of a finger *évolution* such as was used in the C major Invention. The fact that it is now in an advanced key brings this forward to the level of Book II (C.P.E. Bach gives fingering patterns for broken 3rds in advanced keys, 1753

Chapter I paras.69–70). The whole-bar inversion pattern changes to a half-bar inversion pattern from b.3, when the harmonic rhythm also changes, a union of surface pattern with harmonic structure cultivated also in the Inventions. This principle can be seen in operation in a larger structural context in bb.3–9, which moves from the tonic to the relative major by means of a descending scale in the bass from f♯ to F♯, the essential notes of the top line moving in 10ths with the bass. This scale is divided into two tetrachords, the upper of which is in D sharp minor and the lower in F sharp major. The structure is therefore reflected on the surface of the music by the busy pattern of half-bar inversions changing at b.6 to a more relaxed pattern of broken chords. A further developmental feature of the old Inventions is sequential repetition of the opening idea, either whole (bb.10–11) or in part (bb.13–14). The virtue of this is that it yields progressions (in this case of 3rds) which can be used for section building and modulation.

Bach now builds these principles from the Inventions into a galant sonata structure, again on the old aria ritornello plan. In minor-key movements of this sort Bach normally has a move through the relative key on the way to the dominant (see Chapter Three section 6). Here this is at b.9, where the main idea enters, is answered in b.10, and uses a sequential repetition to move up a third to the dominant at b.12. A busy sequence of half-bar units with simultaneous semiquavers leads to a closing idea of contrasting character (b.15). It is worth noting that the rich variety of this movement, in comparison with the earlier Inventions, is not bought at the price of unity, but is the fruit of a much more sophisticated variation technique. The demisemiquavers of the closing idea were already in b.12, where they were part of a variation of the very first of the varied counterpoints, at b.2. More subtly, the descending scale of b.1 provides, as we have seen, the structure for the whole first section (bb.3–9), but is also the fundamental shape of which the closing idea (bb.15–16) is a new and highly decorated variation, extended to cover two octaves (a″♯ to a♯). As usual with this type of binary piece, the second half runs the events of the first from the dominant back to the tonic, with extensions and further variations. Here the second half opens by combining the opposites of the opening and closing ideas, represented by the demisemiquavers of yet another counterpoint.

It is worth noting that the final appoggiaturas of each half are written as small notes (♪‿♩) in the London autograph, but as quavers (♫) in Altnickol's version, which probably represents Bach's later thought (AB II p.170). There is a very tenuous possibility that this prelude may have originally been in E minor or D minor, but the evidence for this is tiny and there are rather more indications of this possibility in the fugue (KB V/6.2 pp.231, 282).

FUGUE This is one of the ripest fugues of Book II. To get a perspective on it, one may compare the freedom of motivic working and expressive manipulation of texture here with the logical contrapuntal scheme of the D sharp minor fugue of Book I. Its subject is of a type with pauses, which Bach had used with grand objectivity in the 'Dorian' fugue for organ BWV 538/2, and with great maturity of subjective expression in the F sharp minor fugue of Book I. But the development of the Book II D sharp minor has a looseness and freedom which reaches far beyond that. It is linked in the rhythm of its subject, and the relation of subject to countersubject, with the F sharp minor fugue of Book II (Ellis 1980 p.115), a link that may provide a key to Bach's intention.

As in the D major fugue, the canzona rhythm at the opening of the subject suggests a traditional prototype, which Bach was seeking to develop and reconcile with the expressive style of the 1730s. In this case the prototype seems to be the freely contrapuntal technique of Froberger's capriccios. In Capriccio II (Mode II) of Froberger's *Libro* of 1656, for example, the first section has successive expositions on the principle of fugal inversion, with the subject presented in different harmonic contexts; a hint of stretto in the second exposition; and freely developed groups of semiquavers, justified by a pair of semiquavers in the subject, which are then used for a rhetorical climax at the end of the section. Bach has taken ingredients of this sort and given them a personal expressivity quite foreign to the prototype. The repeated notes at the opening of the subject are now an expression of melancholy and meditation, with the restriction of pitch giving an effect of depressive concentration, an expressive effect used in vocal music from Caccini to Schumann. Riemann has very perceptively observed that this sombre mood is enhanced by the prominence of subject leads in the alto part (bb.1, 17, 23, 30). This mood is then explored in the varying harmonic contexts in which the subject appears.

After this formulaic, but newly expressive, opening the subject steps down a minor 2nd. In Froberger's capriccio it continues in the *lamento* pattern of descending semitones. Bach, instead of this cliché, has a subject that climbs up the first five notes of the scale, with expressive pauses in the manner of the F sharp minor fugue of Book I. But whereas there the countersubject is a contrasting but expressively complementary figure, here it is another version of the same shape as the subject, again giving a concentration of mood, as in the F sharp minor fugue of Book II. Subject and countersubject thus form a continuous line which can be developed. The alto from b.1 to b.5 climbs up a minor 7th, as does the bass in the inversion of the counterpoint from b.7 to b.11. Since this is the end of the first exposition the scale is then extended up to the octave d'♯ at b.13, before running on fluidly into the next section. A similar pitch strategy may be seen in the bass from b.19, which runs from D♯ up to g♯ in b.23. The principle is given powerful rhetorical expansion as the fugue develops, with the three top parts rising to a pitch peak at b.38 before descending for the final climax. It thus reconciles the optimistic 'Dorian' subject which sails up to the top of the octave, with the subjective Book I F sharp minor fugue, which gets no further than the 5th of the scale before falling back, and is accompanied by a sobbing, falling countersubject.

The overtly rhetorical ending suggests that rhetoric is the key to this fugue. The peroration at bb.40–2 uses a rhetorical effect, rather than the contrapuntal density of the Book I D sharp minor fugue. There are two reasons for Bach to have been particularly interested in demonstrating learned rhetoric in music in the late 1730s. One is the importance attributed to it in Mattheson's *Der vollkommene Capellmeister*, which includes a detailed section on rhetoric in music. Far from music artificially imitating verbal rhetoric, for Mattheson rhetorical figures are so natural in music that it almost seems as if it was from music that the old Greek rhetoricians developed their categories (1739 Part II chap.xiv para.46). This was by no means a personal view of his, but is supported by a long literary tradition going back to the Renaissance.[43] Bach also seems to have been keen to show his learning in this matter after the criticisms of his supposed lack of knowledge of rhetoric, and therefore ability to communicate, made by Scheibe in 1737–8 (NBR pp.337–53; see Chapter Four section 4).

This criticism is magnificently refuted in the D sharp minor fugue. It takes a traditional manner of fugal writing, of the type represented by Froberger's capriccios, and employs well-known rhetorical effects, but all in a loosely poetical way of great maturity that contrasts strongly with the remorselessly logical contrapuntal schemes of earlier fugues such as the D sharp minor and A minor of Book I. It is not necessary to know the technical rhetorical terms to feel the effects, but for the sake of demonstration it is worth identifying them. The pauses in the subject represent the *suspiratio* (from the Latin *suspirare*, to sigh), traditionally expressive of love and yearning. The combination of subject and countersubject, which reinforce each other, uses the device of *climax* or gradation, in which a word at the end of one part of a sentence is taken up at the beginning of the next and given extra meaning. The standard example, given by Kircher and others, is from Psalm 42: 'Like as the hart *desireth* the water-brooks: so *longeth* my soul after thee, O God.' Sentences can be built using this device many times successively, each repetition of a word being a step on the way to the climax. J.G. Walther (1732) gives a more straightforward example: 'Jauchzet und singet, singet und rühmet, rühmet und lobet.' The musical equivalent is a type of figure common in Monteverdi and hence in the seventeenth-century concertato style (Ex.8.16).

The argument of the fugue is not ostensibly contrapuntal, apart from the stretto at bb.23–6, since much of it depends on the free, expressive development of the semiquaver figure that enters at b.6, but rhetorical in that it consists of presenting the subject in different harmonic contexts. Initially the subject begins on the tonic note but, after the exposition, the four entries in bb.15–21

Ex.8.16 Monteverdi: from the motet Exulta filia, showing the rhetorical device of gradation.

have its first notes as the 5th of the chord, the first three entries giving the head of the subject in the form of a pseudo-tonal answer. The alto entry in b.23 has its first notes as the 3rd of a galant-style augmented 6th chord, and in b.30 as the 7th of a dominant 7th. This technique of giving an idea new meanings by making small alterations and presenting it in new contexts is known in rhetoric as *paronomasia* (Greek term for allusion). Finally there is the peroration (from b.40), defined by Forkel as 'the ultimate, strongest repetition of such phrases as constitute, as it were, a consequence of the preceding proofs, refutations, dissections and confirmations' (Butler 1977 p.97). This takes two forms. The first (bb.40–2) is rhetorical, using the device of *tmesis* (making insertions into a word or phrase), which is related to the subject's *suspiratio* in that the pauses are now filled with a complementary idea, and which is equally associated with sighing and longing. The second (bb.43–5) is contrapuntal in that it presents the subject simultaneously with its inversion.

Devices of this kind are very characteristic of the larger fugues of Book II, notably those in G minor and B flat minor. The wonder is, not that Bach knew all about them and made use of them in his music, but that he managed to make such powerful effects with them. Few of his contemporaries could have used them to such 'moving and expressive' effect, and it is typical of him to have answered criticism in such a magnificently positive way rather than trifling with words.

The galant augmented 6th chord is a feature of this fugue. It comes at the end of b.23 and again at the end of b.32. It is therefore most likely that Bach meant the b' (last alto note of b.45) to be natural, since he entered a cautionary ♮ as a correction in the London autograph. It is natural in most of the sources of the London autograph and Kirnberger traditions, but sharp in most of those of the Altnickol tradition (Tomita 1993 p.62, 1995 p.324). Curiously, Dürr omits the natural in his Version A without comment in his report (NBA V/6.2 p.47), though he refers to it later as Version A while proposing b'♯ as perhaps Bach's final thought (KB V/6.2 p.286). The b'♮ gives the effect of the last inversion of a German 6th. In the late 1740s Bach used this chord in the very beautiful ending of the Crucifixus of the B minor Mass, where it swings the harmony from E minor into G major at the words 'passus et sepultus est'. The combination of this chord and the tierce de Picardie give the end of the D sharp minor fugue something of the same effect.

Prelude and Fugue in E major BWV 878

PRELUDE Since the fugue that goes with this is derived without a doubt from Fischer's *Ariadne Musica*, it is natural to look there for a prototype for the prelude. As in the case of the fugue, the type is a common one, but in the case of the prelude there does not seem to be a particular example which Bach used. The type where parts unfold with suspended dissonances over pedal notes is a commonplace, with numerous examples in the keyboard works of Fischer and Pachelbel (see Pachelbel's G minor Fantasia, ed. Seiffert p.29), and back to Frescobaldi's *Fiori musicali* (Toccata per l'elevatione from *Messa della Madonna*). Bach provided several versions of it in pieces in the background of Book II such as the D minor Praeludium BWV 899/1 and the G major Praeludium BWV 902/1. The D minor is close to Fischer's examples in having an opening tonic pedal, followed by a repetition of the opening material on a dominant pedal. The G major is a much more sophisticated working of the same ingredients in the galant binary sonata idiom, with a substantial modulatory phrase before the dominant repetition, and much concertante writing, including galant triplets. The galant sonata manner is particularly marked after the double bar. This is a piece that Bach could well have used in Book II.

The E major prelude equally uses the galant binary sonata form, but more clearly derived from the aria ritornello (Chapter Three section 6). Of the four ingredients customary in the first section, the second begins at b.9; the closing idea, in this case with a pedal, at b.18; and an extended cadence from b.21. Unlike the G major Praeludium BWV 902/1, but like Fischer's preludes, this moves straight to the dominant (b.5) and so has to have some other harmonic argument for the remainder of the section. It therefore moves around F sharp minor (bb.10ff), with prominent diminished 7ths, before clearing into the closing pedal at b.18. The second half runs the material from the dominant back to the tonic with variations and expansions, and also uses a more keyboard-sonata style, as did the G major Praeludium BWV 902/1. The little E minor Praeludium BWV 900/1 is short and yet diffuse by comparison.

The manner of the opening of this prelude invites comparison with that of the G major Praeludium BWV 902/1 which, in a copy by J.G. Preller, has many added ornaments (NBA V/6.2 p.334, PF p.28). Paul Badura-Skoda has therefore suggested ornaments for the E major (1993 pp.481–2). It has to be said that Preller's ornaments seem excessive and undisciplined in comparison with genuine Bach ornamentations such as in the E flat minor prelude of Book I. It should be noted that the appoggiatura in b.43 of the E major prelude is written as a quaver in b.21 in all three traditions.

This prelude has a notable crux of four possible readings in the bass of b.50, first beat, about which there appears to be no firm consensus. They are as follows: (1) b a g♯ (London autograph before correction); (2) g♯ f♯ e(London autograph after correction); (3) c'♯ b a (Kirnberger); (4) b g♯ e (Altnickol).

They are discussed in detail by Steglich (1954) who finds (3) the best motivically (cf bb.1–2), but (4) probably Bach's last thought, since it resolves the prominent D♯–a diminished 5th in the bar before. Dürr tentatively suggests that (3) was the original, mistakenly copied by Anna Magdalena Bach as (1), which was later unauthentically altered to (2); (4) was then a different tradition (KB V/6.2 pp.233–4). He and others have noted Dehnhard's suggestion that this and other mistaken pitches, as well as single instead of double accidentals, would be explained if Anna Magdalena Bach had copied from an original in D major. Jones thinks that the alteration from (1) to (2) is authentic, done at the third stage of revision to the London autograph; that (3) is a conjectural correction of Anna Magdalena Bach's error by Kirnberger; and (4), being non-thematic, is the original reading (AB II p.172). Tomita considers (3) most likely to be original since it is motivic, and therefore most probably Bach's first thought (1993 p.65). In deciding, it does not seem necessary to have to resolve the D♯–a diminished 5th from b.49 in this figure since the notes are amply resolved elsewhere in bb.50–51. Also the embargo on consecutive octaves a'–g'♯ (cantus bb.49–50 first beats) and a–g♯ (bass b.49 last beat, b.50 first beat, in version (2)), mentioned by some commentators, seems somewhat pedantic in the free, toccata texture of these bars. Version (4) seems to be an effort to get round the various difficulties. This is certainly a place where players are as well able as anybody to decide. For those most sensitive to harmony, perhaps (2) is best; for motifs, perhaps (3).

FUGUE There is no evidence for an earlier version of this fugue, and it fits in very well with Bach's preoccupation with the *stile antico* in the 1730s and 40s, culminating in *Clavier-Übung* III (1739) and the B minor Mass (*stile antico* items of the 1740s), and including his adding parts for cornetts, trombones and continuo to Palestrina's six-part *Missa sine nomine* (after *c*.1742).[44] In fact, though, the role model is not so much the style of Palestrina as that of learned seventeenth-century keyboard counterpoint in the Frescobaldi tradition. In the fugues in C sharp minor and B flat minor of Book I this was explicit in the mannered dissonances of their subjects; the E major of Book II uses one of a number of standard subjects which are designed to combine in stretto with themselves at three bars, two bars, and one bar's distance (in $\frac{2}{2}$ barring), a requirement that accounts for the small number of such subjects. The subject of the so-called 'St Anne' fugue in E flat major BWV 552/2, which concludes *Clavier-Übung* III, is another of them.[45] The subject also has a very standard shape in strict counterpoint, which one might call the cambiata figure, made explicit in the demonstration fugues using this subject in Fux's *Gradus ad Parnassum* (1725), of which Bach possessed a copy, and which seems to have had a certain influence on his fugal writing in the 1730s (see Chapter Four section 6). Of the various possible prototypes, Fux is probably the best place to start.

Fux gives six demonstration fugues using this subject in two different modes: in two parts, three parts, four parts, and a double fugue in four parts (see Mann 1958 Exx.48, 53, 65, 69, 71, 83). The basic concepts are explained in relation to two-part fugue and concern the answer, modal ambitus and the structure of fugue, and stretto. The recipe is to have a minimum of three sections, the first of which cadences on the 5th of the mode, the second on the 3rd, and the last on the tonic or final of the mode. Each section has a successively closer stretto than the one before, which accounts for the nature of the subject (Mann 1958 pp.83–90, see Ex.4.1). Fux was inventing nothing here, but explaining a common tradition of teaching and composition. These elements are clearly visible in the E major fugue. Of five main cadences, the first is on the 5th degree (b.9), the second last is on the 3rd degree (b.35), and the last on the tonic. To this Bach has added a cadence on the 6th degree (one step above the 5th, b.16), and a cadence on the 2nd degree (one step below the 3rd, b.23). Other common features of *stile antico* are the standard shapes for groups of crotchets in strict counterpoint, and the tendency for the last phrase to end with a descending scale pattern decorated with suspensions. In fact, much of the motivic currency of the E major fugue is to be found in this section of Fux's *Gradus*.

Various other prototypes for the E major fugue have been proposed from the repertory of seventeenth-century learned keyboard counterpoint, notably Froberger's Fantasia II (1649). A stronger case for similarity could be made for his Ricercar IV (1658), since that is in a major mode (Mode V) while Fantasia II is Phrygian (Mode IV). Another use of this very standard subject is in Frescobaldi's Fantasia ottava on three subjects (1608). However, the points one might make about the shape of figurations, the gradual build-up of faster note values, and the layout of sections apply generally to this type of piece no matter what the particular subject is.[46] Similarities are therefore likely to be generic rather than particular. That Bach considered this subject as archetypal of the old tradition of musical craftsmanship is clear from the riddle canon BWV 1076, which he holds in the Haussmann portrait. In it this subject is combined with another archetypal element, the first eight notes of the bass of the Goldberg Variations.

A much stronger case for direct influence can be made from the E major fugue of Fischer's *Ariadne Musica.* The key of E major is unusual for a fugue of this type, and both composers interpret the traditional modal subject tonally: Froberger's Fantasia and Ricercar both begin on the 5th of their respective modes (as do Fux's examples); Bach's and Fischer's fugues begin on the tonic.[47]

The relation of the two fugues in fact goes much deeper than mere identity of subject and key.[48] The exposition of Bach's fugue is very similar in layout to Fischer's, and Bach (b.37) builds up to the same high-pitch, climactic treble entry as Fischer (b.32), followed by a prominent dominant entry in the bass. After the exposition, Fischer's brief fugue has a section with stretti of the countersubject, and a final section with stretti of the subject, an agenda typical of this genre, though without the clear section-defining cadences normal with Frescobaldi and Froberger. Bach also has clear cadences, and each section has a distinct contrapuntal agenda, greatly expanding on Fischer's limited objectives. The second section (bb.9–15) has stretti of subject and countersubject; the third (bb.16–22) introduces two new subjects in double counterpoint; the fourth (bb.23–34) starts with two pairs of stretti in a low tessitura and close spacing (treble and alto at b.23, bass and tenor at b.25) which introduce passing crotchets into the subject, a development powerfully exploited in this and the final sections: it opens out in b.27 into a brilliantly spaced stretto of the subject in diminution and inversion; the final section (bb.35–43) is a reprise of the stretto at bb.9ff, but with diminution inversions of the subject. This is the fulfilment of the gradual fusing of the subject with its countersubject, which began with the introduction of crotchets into the main subject at b.23. Fluid remoulding of materials is a traditional feature of seventeenth-century learned keyboard counterpoint, and is its main developmental interest. But such a consistently logical and dramatic exploitation of it brings the technique into the style of the late Baroque. This updating is matched in details such as second-practice (by leap) resolution of suspensions in the tenor at b.39 and the alto at bb.11–12, growing from the leaping quavers of the countersubject, a freedom that is carried further in the galant-style final cadence.

This fugue shows a different possibility for combinatorial development of the subject by variation from that exploited in the D sharp minor fugue of Book I. As in other fugues linked to the verset tradition, such as the G minor from Book I and the D major from Book II, Bach has taken standard ingredients and made something much stronger from them than did his prototypes. He fully exploits each element of the subject. The rising nature of the head of the subject is emphasised in the double counterpoint he adds in the lower parts from b.16 by rising chromatic steps in the bass; and the falling steps of the end of the subject are magnificently developed in the final section, culminating in stretto descending scales between bass and treble from b.40 which cover the whole octave.

In the London autograph it is evident that Bach's ¢ with breve bars caused Anna Magdalena difficulty in aligning parts in the very long bars, and quarter-stave dividers were added later in some bars. The semibreve bars used by Fischer and Fux avoid the problem, but chop the contrapuntal lines up into pairs of minims. Seventeenth-century usage was by no means uniform with regard to breve or semibreve bars, and Fischer attempted a compromise by adding the words 'Alla breve'. Bach may have started with semibreve bars, but changed his mind (Jones 1991 p.607). The longer, breve bars more clearly distinguish this fugue as *stile antico*, as they do in the E flat organ fugue BWV 552, and Bach seems to have preferred them for allowing the characteristic plasticity of line of the genre to be more visible, an important consideration in view of the use he has made of that plasticity.

A manuscript deriving from Kirnberger's personal manuscript copy adds the word 'Pedal' to the bass entries at bb.1, 10, 36 and 40.[49] There is no other evidence that this fugue was conceived for an instrument with pedals. It may be significant that the cognate fugues in C sharp minor from Book I and E flat major from Book II, associated with the clavier, begin with entries from the bass up, while the organ fugue in E flat major BWV 552 begins with the lowest manual part (the tenor), and reserves the pedal for the final entry of the exposition in the bass. This is typical of Bach's dramatic and structural organ pedal strategy, which is not so evident in the E major fugue. In it the downward transposition of an octave of the subject in the tenor at the end of b.37 implies that playability on the clavier was Bach's concern. For the difficult issue of ornamentation in this type of fugue, see Chapter Four section 6.

Prelude and Fugue in E minor BWV 879

PRELUDE This is one of four binary inventions in Book II, three of which are strictly in two parts (D sharp minor, A minor, and this) and one not so strictly (C minor).[50] Of the four, the E minor prelude comes closest in its techniques and features to the 1723 Inventions. It has the long trills of the E minor Invention, and the section-ending idea of expanding leaps of the G minor. But the most important similarity is in the technique of developing sequences by putting all or some of the opening *inventio* end to end with itself, of which the C major Invention is the classic demonstration. In his discussion of double counterpoint in *Die Kunst des reinen Satzes in der Musik* Kirnberger cites bb.5–10 of the E minor prelude, and the inversion at bb.53–4, as examples of just this technique of melodic extension by joining small motifs together,[51] and in fact most of the prelude is based on this principle. It seems that Bach was intending here to update some of the demonstrative intentions of the 1723 Inventions by incorporating them into the binary sonata mould.

This prelude is from the first layer of the London autograph (1739–40). There are no known early versions, and various features apart from its binary structure point to its being a late work. Its particular qualities become evident if one compares it with a piece using an ordinary version of the opening material, such as the Schübler chorale prelude 'Wo soll ich fliehen hin' BWV 646, also in E minor. Here the opening semiquaver motif is regularly accompanied by a 7–6 suspension or its inversion. The motif is presented recto and inverso in the first two bars, before running into the sequence, closing pattern, and cadence formula of the normal aria ritornello shape (Ex.8.17).

The very neat balance of recto and inverso presentations of the opening motif in the chorale prelude is greatly condensed in the E minor prelude by having them end to end with each other in the very opening idea ('zusammengesetzt' as Kirnberger says). Bach then uses this double idea to spin out further sequences, showing how it can be made to go up in 3rds (bb.5–10), or down in 3rds (bb.13–22). Within this he develops a concept of the invention, seemingly typical of Book II and already observed in the D sharp minor prelude, in which the *inventio*, rather than being regularly accompanied in a

Ex.8.17 Chorale prelude 'Wo soll ich fliehen hin' BWV 646, bars 1–6.

standard formula, is constantly combined with fresh counterthemes. There are no less than six of these in the first 22 bars: a bare octave at b.1, then ever new thoughts in bars 3, 5, 11, 17 and 21. In addition to this heightening of inventiveness, Bach has given his wealth of counterthemes the strong characterisation of the galant style, particularly those in bb.3–4 and 18–20.[52]

In this sort of binary sonata movement one expects the events of the first half to be run from the dominant back to the tonic in the second half, with extensions and developments. The formal correspondence of the two halves is neatly pointed up in the London autograph where they are on facing pages. Although the second half is ten bars longer than the first, Bach seems to have thought of them as 'around the same length' since he does not start taking account of remaining space till after system 5 of the right-hand page. The layout makes the formal plan of the prelude very clear, since corresponding events are on corresponding systems. The second half begins with further ingenious demonstrations of melody extension through sequential repetition, using the inversion of the opening motif, and again with ever fresh accompaniments featuring galant ornaments such as the tied trill (b.51) and turn (bb.57ff; Bach's own copy in the London autograph has the most authoritative scheme of ornaments). After this development bb.81 to the end are a tonic reprise of bb.23–48.

Older commentators (Tovey 1924, Emery 1953, Landowska 1965, O'Donnell 1974) preferred chromatic (i.e. semitone) auxiliaries for all the long trills. More recent ones (Schulenberg 1992, P. Badura-Skoda 1993, Jones in AB II) agree with Kroll that they should be diatonic, i.e. a semitone for the dominant notes at bb.29 and 86, and a whole tone for the tonic notes at bb.33 and 89. It is not just a matter of a preferable sonority: the diatonic interpretation has the great merit of giving variety to, and also differentiating the structural functions of, the otherwise identical bs at bb.33 and 86.

FUGUE The subject of this fugue uses a greater variety of note values than any other in the 48 (the E minor of Book I uses the least variety; Ellis 1980 p.235) and this, together with the staccato markings and strong suggestion of dance metre, make it the most highly characterised and galant fugue in the collection. Its freedom of treatment of motifs and its putting sonority and playability before rigorous counterpoint contrast with the exhaustive motivic working of the prelude. It was no doubt to point up its nature as a brilliant 'concert' fugue that Bach cut the original final cadence at bb.70–1 (as in the London autograph) and added 17 new bars in the manner of a cadenza, complete with dramatic pauses (as in Altnickol's 1744 copy; Bach had made the addition in the lost draft version). In this it makes a useful comparison with the G major 'concert' fugue of Book I, and shows Bach moving on from the Vivaldian concerto style and structure to those of the galant sonata.

The variety of note values is to a certain extent for the eye rather than the ear in that the dotted quavers and semiquavers should almost certainly be assimilated to the triplet rhythm. Whatever the views of Quantz and C.P.E. Bach, there is no doubt that Bach intended this in, for example, the opening chorus of 'Unser Mund sei voll Lachens' BWV 110 (an arrangement of the D major Overture BWV 1069/1) where the voice parts have two-note simplified versions of the orchestral triplets (Pirro 1907 p.119). In the London autograph fair copy of the E minor fugue Bach has aligned the semiquavers with the third triplet. This feature of dance metre reinforces the similarity of this fugue to the Tempo di Gavotta and Gigue of the E minor clavier Partita BWV 830. The six-bar E minor fugue subject is the same length as the opening phrase of the sonatafied Tempo di Gavotta (not a typical dance phrase), and the fugue's episodes share its technique of sequential extension. The concluding ten bars of the fugue use similar figurations to those at the end of the Gigue, and also to that of the E major Sinfonia BWV 792 (in $\frac{9}{8}$-time). A favourite rhythmic feature shared by the fugue and the two Partita movements is mixing duple semiquavers with triplet quavers. Variety of rhythms and note values is a characteristic of the galant style. Even with a triplet interpretation of the Partita movements they seem inevitable in the Tempo di Gavotta b.7 (second crotchet) and similar places, and in the Gigue b.11 (first crotchet).

This connexion with sonatafied dance may explain the curious, not to say experimental, structure of the fugue in its earlier version. After the tonic exposition (bb.1–18) Bach follows his usual tonal scheme for the first half of a binary movement in a minor key by passing through the relative major (from the end of b.23, with its dominant answer from the end of b.29) to the dominant (from the end of b.41). He then seems to have envisaged a balanced scheme of tonic entry (end of b.49) with a dominant one before it (end of b.41) and a subdominant one after (end of b.59), as a final exposition (with entries bass-middle-cantus) to balance the first exposition (with entries cantus-middle-bass). In this form Bach, in making the copy in the London autograph, needed only to draw an extra system at the bottom of the sheet for the fugue to be conveniently accommodated on one opening. Ultimately, though, he must have felt this scheme unsatisfactory, not only because it lacked a final tonic entry of the subject, but also because the timid spacing and pitch levels of the original ending made a poor conclusion for such a brilliant piece. The new ending gives a strong tonic entry (b.71) in the lowest register of the bass, corresponding to the treble entry at the beginning of the fugue, and combines it with the widest spacing between the hands. As with extensions of pieces in Book I, Bach has developed potentialities from the material he was extending. The dominant pedal, decorated with an A sharp (bb.68–70), is picked up again in b.78, decorated now with D sharp (b.82), C natural (originally; b.83), and with the A sharp–B step twice more repeated (bb.83–4 and 85) before the final cadence. It may have been the large number of A sharps from b.77 that made

Bach change the diminished 7th in b.83, with c in the bass, to a dominant 7th with A natural in the bass. This very prominent A natural, being the 7th, has to be dragged up to B, giving a much stronger dramatic point to the final A sharps.

That sonority and playability are paramount is clear from the free treatment of the countersubject (cantus bb.7–8), which is subsequently divided between two parts (bb.13–14 etc.), or has its intervals changed (bass bb.30–1, and specially cantus bb.72–3). This is the sort of freedom one expects in the fugal sonatas of Domenico Scarlatti, and is further evidence that style and character are the main considerations here.

As John Butt points out, the staccato marks undermine the strong beats throughout the subject, giving it a great part of its character (1990 p.166). It may have been to make the first downbeat clear, thereby allowing the subsequent rhythmic irregularity to make its effect, that Bach added a mordent to the third note of the subject in bb.1 and 7 of Altnickol's 1744 copy (P 430). The word Adagio at the fermata in b.83 is in P 430 and so is well attested. The subsequent Allegro at the end of b.83 is only in a couple of Dresden copies and the early editions.

Prelude and Fugue in F major BWV 880

PRELUDE This prelude is a further example of Bach's ability to create magnificently novel and evocative textures on the keyboard, as he does in the C major and E flat major preludes. The ancestry of the texture is complex, but deeply embedded in repertories of harpsichord and organ. A remote ancestor is the Italian organ toccata with dissonances and suspensions (*durezze e ligature*), notated in the predominantly white note values of the *stile antico*. This was developed in the classical French organ tradition into *plein jeu* and *grand plein jeu* pieces which add decorative quaver movement. Leading features of the genre are the avoidance of definite cadence, and so of the establishment of secondary key centres, and having at least one suspended dissonance on the first beat of most bars. The D minor prelude BWV 539/1 (perhaps mid 1720s and seemingly for organ without pedals) is a development from this type (P. Williams 1980 I pp.97–8, who cites a movement from Grigny's 1699 *Livre d'orgue*, of which Bach made a copy, for comparison). As with most of Bach's pieces that allude to a French style, he makes much more consistent and motivic use of quaver figurations than does Grigny, and out of French ingredients creates the moto perpetuo of a single note value more typical of the Italian style than the pure French. Grigny's relatively few quavers are no more motivic than those of the typical Lullian entrée or overture. In Bach's immediate environment the texture is used in the Pachelbel tradition by, for example, Buttstett in his Praeludium III in C major (*Clavier-Kunst*, 1713). Buttstett uses it as one element among several. Bach's novelty is to construct a large, continuous piece using it exclusively.

A further related piece is the A minor Fantasia BWV 904/1 (perhaps from the late 1720s or 1730s). This could conceivably be for organ with pedals, since the bass entries are structural (they support entries of a ritornello) and there is nothing in them that is unidiomatic to Bach's pedal writing, were it not that the main source (J.P. Kellner) has it unambiguously marked 'pro Cembalo' (Stinson 1990 p.103). Both this and the D minor prelude let chords build up from tied notes in quaver figurations, but neither uses the French *tenue* slur for held notes.

The slurs in b.1 and elsewhere in the London autograph are a later addition, possibly by Bach during teaching, since they do not appear in copies made from the London autograph before 1742 (Tomita 1990 p.255). Interpretations of them vary. Peter Williams (1983 p.240) suggests that they are to clarify the *figura*: to show that the quaver figurations are to be slurred in fours within the beat (♩♩♩♩) rather than across the beat (𝄾♩♩♩♪), as might seem to be the case in b.2. This would relate also to the seventeenth-century usage of, for example, Froberger and Fischer of notating longer scales, in the days before they were pivoted over the thumb, in groups of four notes alternating between the hands. The slur therefore has the hand-shape implication of using four consecutive fingers, thus negating the usual paired fingerings.

The French *tenue* slur is best explained by Saint Lambert (1702 Chapter vii). It is typical of the unmeasured prelude and shows that chord notes under the slur, or the initial note of stepwise figurations, are to be held beyond their value. C.P.E. Bach mentions this use of the slur in several places and gives a similar example to Saint Lambert's chordal one (1753 Chapter iii para.18). J.S. Bach certainly used the slur for this purpose in harpsichord works such as the Largo of the C minor sonata for harpsichord and violin BWV 1017, and possibly also in organ works such as the chorale prelude on 'Ich ruf' zu dir' BWV 639 (Butt 1990 p.185). This use of the slur is also found in some secondary sources of the D major prelude of Book II (AB II p.166). It certainly seems very appropriate to the F major prelude.

The question of organ intention, proposed with great assurance by Riemann (1890 II p.185) and others, is not possible to resolve with certainty. The 'Giant fugue' bass minims from bb.6–8 may look suitable for pedals, but the prevalence of running bass quavers make this prelude far less suitable for performance with pedals than the Fantasia 'pro Cembalo' BWV 904/1. As a manual piece there can be no more inherent objection to organ performance than in the case of the fantasia or the prelude BWV 539/1. It also sounds magical on a harpsichord with *peau de buffle* (introduced in Paris and London in the late 1760s). Looking at Book II as a whole, and given the F major prelude's richly mixed antecedents, it seems more likely to be another case of Bach suggesting styles and sonorities on the harpsichord, the suggestion being in some ways more potent than the real thing.

Formally this prelude belongs to the group based on the aria ritornello pattern in its sonata guise, with a modulation in its second element (see Chapter Three section 6). Bach seems to have been particularly concerned with expanding and updating this model in Book II. The crotchet figure in the treble at bb.13–14 and 69–70 has the effect of a closing idea. Main cadences confirm modulations and initiate new starts, in the dominant (b.16), the relative minor (b.33), and the tonic (b.57). There are thus four sections rather than Bach's more usual three for pieces using this structure. The third section is unusual in that it modulates, via a majestic rising sequence (bb.41–7) and rising crotchet scales (bb.49–51) that balance the falling quaver patterns trailing their chords, to A minor rather than back to the tonic. The little three-quaver transition back to F in the bass at the end of b.56 gives the tonic reprise, now adjusted not to modulate, the feeling of a da capo. Within this structure Bach again favours harmonic proportions (2–2–3–2) between sections. If the French prototype avoided cadences, Bach equally avoids them within sections. He also builds up the very rich French 9/7 chord with augmented 5th (beginning of b.49, end of b.54), using it with telling structural effect at the climax of the involution of the piece, just before the return.

FUGUE The free, insouciant, quality of this fugue is not only in its metre, but in its structure and freedom of voicing (bb.85–7) as well. The order of entries from the cantus down, with an extra 'false' bass entry at b.21, and episodes made from bass-led sequences (bb.38–44, 45–52) are characteristic of *partimento* fugues and so part of the improvised tradition of fugue (Schulenberg 1995 p.6). As in the E minor fugue there are no learned devices, and in this case no retained countersubject. The argument of the fugue is in the *joie de vivre* of spinning episodes out of elements of the subject, and the *jeu d'esprit* in the second half of introducing the subject in oblique harmonic contexts. The middle-voice entry at b.52 begins in D minor, but ends with the D triad as part of an interrupted cadence in F (b.56), which in turn switches to being the dominant of B flat. After the delay of the tonic return from b.76, and the implication of F minor, the long-expected tonic entry at bb.85–9, far from being in the expected F major, very wittily swings the subject yet further in the minor direction with a much stronger reharmonization to an emphatic B flat minor, entailing a chromatic change to the subject's second quaver. The final, humorous, bass entry (b.89) extends the head of the subject to bring it up the scale from B flat to F.

The figure in b.4 of the subject, which provides most of the material for the episodes, is also used in the Prelude of the A major English Suite BWV 806.

It is a commonplace of gigues, with examples by Dieupart, Le Roux, and Marchand among others (Landowska 1965 pp.201–2). However, the $\frac{6}{16}$ time signature implies a more fluent movement than either $\frac{6}{8}$ or other gigue signatures based on quavers. In François Couperin's *Les papillons* (second *Ordre*, 1713) it is marked 'très légèrement'. Kirnberger (1776) gives a detailed description of this time signature:

> The signature $\frac{2}{8}$ would be suitable only for short, comical ('lustigen') dances on account of the quickness of its movement and its extreme fluency ('Leichtigkeit') of performance. But it is not in use and I have introduced it only because $\frac{6}{16}$ time, which derives from it, is used in many pieces where its fleeting movement ('Flüchtigkeit') and lightness of performance distinguish it sharply from $\frac{6}{8}$ time. It was not without reason that J.S. Bach and Couperin wrote some of their pieces in $\frac{6}{16}$. [Kirnberger here quotes the subject of the F major fugue.] Put this subject in $\frac{6}{8}$ time and instantly the movement is changed: the pace is heavier ('schwerfälliger'); each note, specially passing notes, is given too much weight; and the character ('Ausdruck') of the piece suffers and is no longer what Bach intended. To play this fugue properly on the clavier, the notes must be struck in a light and fleeting movement, without the least emphasis . . .. On the violin, pieces in this and similar light metres should be played only with the tip of the bow, whereas in heavier metres a longer bowstroke and more pressure are required.[53]

The feel of this time signature is best caught in the concluding fugue of the early D major toccata BWV 912, which also runs into demisemiquavers at the end. The F major fugue is rhythmically more complex: part of its wit is the metrical ambiguity of the opening where, as in the E minor fugue, staccato marks undermine the downbeat.

Prelude and Fugue in F minor BWV 881

PRELUDE The complex source transmission of this pair is set out by Richard Jones in a special note (AB II p.207). The leaf is missing from the London autograph, and that version, with its various stages of revision, has to be reconstructed from copies. Bach's final thoughts are largely represented in Altnickol's 1744 copy (P 430); Kirnberger's personal copy (Am.B.57(2)) gives an earlier version.

Of all the preludes in Book II this comes closest to the galant sonata style of Bach's eldest sons. As well as features such as the appoggiaturas of the opening and the written-out *Anschlag* of b.58, the four-bar phraseology, and the principle of having two contrasted characters sharing the first eight bars, are all part of the mid-century style. This principle of contrast has already been observed in the D major prelude, with its reference to orchestral sinfonias of the 1730s. Stylistically advanced composers of the 1720s and 1730s, such as Telemann in his fantasias and Leclair and Domenico Scarlatti in their sonatas, tended to have a succession of character ideas rather than continuous motivic growth. Bach knew the manner, yet never abandoned his highly integrative thought processes. This prelude is as economical in its material as any other, and develops entirely from the two ideas at its opening. They alternate up to b.20, then a closing phrase combines their elements: right-hand semiquavers, walking crotchets in the bass, and from b.24 the falling steps of the opening appoggiaturas in bass and tenor. The second section explores new developments of these elements till the very expressive condensed reprise at b.56. The prelude is thus another amalgamation of the invention principle and the binary sonata.

It is tempting to see this expressive, appoggiatura-rich style as suitable for the pianoforte, particularly since the same appoggiatura figure is used in the three-part Ricercar from the *Musical Offering* which Bach may have improvised on one of Frederick II of Prussia's Silbermann pianofortes at Potsdam in 1747. But it equally appears in the E flat major fugue BWV 998/2 'pour la Luth. ò Cembal.' (dating from the early to mid 1740s), and in the fragmentary C minor fugue BWV 906/2 whose autograph fair copy dates from *c.*1738, but which is paired with a Fantasia that first survives in an autograph of *c.*1726–31. This gentle, moderato type of movement with appoggiaturas in 3rds, not to be confused with the slow Lamento of the early Capriccio BWV 992/3 or the Adagio of the B minor sonata for obbligato harpsichord and violin BWV 1014/1, seems to have been a favourite with Bach, going back at least to the A major prelude of Book I (see Chapter One section 7).

The semiquaver figure of bb.5–8 is similar to the technical innovations claimed by Rameau in his harpsichord *Methode* of 1724. While Rameau used this sort of *batterie* with wit and strong musical purpose, others such as C.F. Hurlebusch used such things for fashionable effect and in a less musically directed way. Bach's use of this 'modern' feature, as of the hand-crossing in the B flat prelude, is delightfully understated, and he works it into a cogent musical scheme of the ultimate integration of opposites. There is no need to think of manual changes to differentiate the characters, still less of a *pièce croisée* (Landowska 1965 p.202). Bach indicated manual changes where he wanted them in the G sharp minor prelude, and the essence of the semiquaver figure is the intimacy of the hands. Bach's scheme is better served by the player's art on a single manual.

FUGUE In his mature works Bach shows great resource in his melodic use of the diminished 7th, demonstrating in many ways how it can still be used expressively, without clichéd, melodramatic effect (see the commentary on the

D minor fugue of Book I). In the F minor fugue Bach repeats what he had done in the F major fugue of Book I, which is to take a traditional subject and recreate it in a dance metre, in this case a bourrée (Jenne 1974). The transformation is not quite so thoroughgoing in the F minor since it has no retained countersubject to form the consequent phrase of a dance section. Nonetheless the regular periodicity of the dance predominates, typically in phrases of 2+2+4 bars (bb.17–24, etc.). In addition to metre and phraseology, the overall structure of the fugue is also that of the binary dance/sonata in its minor-key form. It visits the relative major (bb.24–31) on the way to the dominant, in which it has a firm, section-ending cadence at the half-way point (b.40), the only one in the piece other than at the end.

Much of the argument of the second half is bass-led, as in the F major fugue. The semiquaver tail of the tonic entry from b.40 is greatly extended up to the highest textures in the piece (bb.46–7), and ends with a witty demonstration of how to do a dominant pedal in this style (bb.50–3; another is at bb.80–3). This is a kind of inversion of the episode from bb.17 to 24, and it is inverted again at bb.66–71. Another bass phrase from the second half of b.55 extends the head of the subject in the subdominant, answered from b.61 by an equivalent phrase in the tonic. The final entries balance subdominant (cantus b.71) with tonic (middle b.74).

In spite of Bach's deliciously light and inventive treatment of an old warhorse idea, the decline of connoisseurship of genre and metre in the later eighteenth century, lamented by Kirnberger, led people, perhaps intentionally, to replace it with subjective, *empfindsam* emotion. J.F. Reichardt (1782) found in this fugue 'the deepest and sweetest feelings of grief', and compared it to Goethe's description of Strasbourg Cathedral (Dok.III p.359; M. Zenck 1982 pp.11–14); and much later A. Knab (1914) still found in the subject a development of the 'sobbing' motif of the prelude. Reichardt was, however, right in saying that this fugue, in its expressive melody and clarity of layout, gives the lie to the common late-eighteenth-century view that keyboard fugues are for the eye not the ear, and sound to the listener no better than thoroughbass exercises (Pasquali *c.*1758 pp.21–3). One of Bach's objectives was no doubt to confound this opinion in this combination of fugue, sonata, dance and character piece (see Chapter Four section 5).

Prelude and Fugue in F sharp major BWV 882

PRELUDE The mindset that sees French overtures in every dotted rhythm will not comprehend the subtle blend of styles and manners that contribute to this piece. The similarity of the opening to that of the E flat major organ prelude BWV 552/1 (*Clavier-Übung* III), implying an overdotted manner of performance, is misleading. The appoggiatura to the right-hand second beat in b.1, added at an early stage to Altnickol's 1744 copy (probably by Bach; Tomita 1995 p.504), suggests a gentler character than the straight tirata that opens the E flat prelude. Bach was very careful in the notation of rhythms in this piece, changing ♩. ♪ to ♩. 𝄿 𝅘𝅥𝅯 in beats 2–3 of b.1 and elsewhere (NBA V/6.2 p.X). He neglected to do so in bb.44 and 67, but it is clear that these conventional anticipations after cadential trills are meant to be played as semiquavers since in the London autograph he has been careful to align them with the bass semiquavers. Throughout the piece he has aligned semiquavers after dotted notes with the fourth of the groups of four semiquavers, and in the first beats of b.1 and equivalent places the first left-hand semiquaver with the second last right-hand demisemiquaver. The elaborate demisemiquavers at b.57 imply a measured performance of this note value throughout.[54]

There is thus no need for the dotted rhythms to be overdotted. In this prelude Bach has combined them with a constant stream of semiquavers, as he does also in the A flat major prelude. The feel of the dotted rhythms in the F sharp major prelude is light, tripping, and dance-like, as for example in the accompanying parts of the Hornpipe of Handel's concerto Op.6 No.7. The semiquaver patterns particularly suggest this lightness (see Chapter Three section 9). This concertante element has a built-in rhythmic flexibility and a capability for motivic development that sets it apart from mere harmonic wash. It combines lightness and cogency and contributes substantially to the richness and brilliance which Bach is able to conjure from only two parts, rightly noted by Cecil Gray as one of the principal charms of this piece (1938 p.113).

This is another of Bach's large-scale expansions of the format of several sections based on the aria ritornello shape, used also in the preludes in F major, F sharp minor and A flat major. It is also one of the preludes that introduce two contrasting ideas at the opening, and then subtly explore their fundamental relationship (see Chapter Three section 9). The opening three bars introduce decorated, dotted right-hand character figures in bb.1–2 and a plain dotted rhythm in the bass. Bar 3 shows that the continuous semiquavers introduced at b.4, seemingly a new and contrasting idea, are in reality another decoration growing out of the dotted rhythm. All the materials of the prelude are therefore closely linked. The opening period is of 8 bars, but divided irregularly 3+5. A modulating phrase combines all three figures (bb.8–14), followed by a closing phrase and cadence in the dominant (bb.15–17). Bach subsequently treats the sequence of these elements with great freedom. There is a large expansion of the section shape from the dominant (b.17) to the relative minor (b.45). The reprise (from b.57) switches the order of events, reserving the third element (bb.4–6) for a final coda (from b.68). It uses the favoured scheme, noted also in the D major prelude, of beginning the modulating phase on the subdominant (b.61) so that it now modulates back to the tonic (b.68). The flourish in the last three bars, like that at the end of the A flat major prelude, pulls back the impetus by means of a large-scale hemiola (three minim beats in bb.73–4).

This prelude's sense of expansive well-being, with joyful trills that have been likened to the fife trills in the chorus 'Jauchzet, frohlocket' that opens the *Christmas Oratorio* (Kluge-Kahn 1985 p.63), has nothing of the thorny implications for F sharp major of François Couperin's *L'épineuse* (26th *Ordre*, 1730). Whether Couperin intended some tuning effect, or merely that the F sharp major key signature resembles a thorn bush, Bach's prelude is in line with other advanced-key pieces of Book II, such as the C sharp major and G sharp minor preludes. These seem to take the characters of their natural equivalents, rather than having any special character of their own, unlike Book I where advanced-key pieces tend to have decidedly strong and individual characters.

FUGUE This continues the series of galant-style fugues in dance rhythms. The dance in this case is the gavotte, with its characteristic two minims in the bar, beginning on the second minim; minim harmonic rhythm; and offbeat phrase endings provided by the appoggiaturas of the countersubject (Jenne 1974c p.4). The phrase structure of the gavotte is kept in the predominantly four- or two-bar units (reflected in the four-, eight-, and twelve-bar periods listed in the plan given below) but, unlike previous examples, there is little left of the binary structure. A remarkable feature of this fugue is its seamlessness: there is a complete lack of intermediate structural cadences in the course of its 84 bars.

Of numerous witty and felicitous features, the most striking is beginning the subject with a cadential trill. There is nothing in itself unusual in beginning a fugue with a trill since it was normal practice to put an ornament on the first notes of *stile antico* fantasias (see Chapter Four section 6). There is also precedent in the verset tradition where virtually any insignificant idea will do as the subject of a fughetta, as in the first verset of Kerll's fifth-mode Magnificat (1686; Ex.8.18).

Bach's trill is novel in that it starts the subject on the 7th degree of the scale. This allows the very neat answer (noted by Marpurg, 1753 p.54, Dok.III pp.30–1) to turn the tonic f♯ into a dominant 7th in C sharp and so tee off the series of appoggiaturas in the countersubject. Since the trill echoes the cadential trill at the end of the prelude it is similar in intention and effect to those minuets of Haydn and Mozart which have sections that begin with a closing gesture such as a cadence. Opinions differ on how to play the trill. Since it is a closing feature it would seem most effective to make it sound as much like a cadential trill as possible, and to play it in the way normal for that, beginning with an upper auxiliary. This also sets off the play Bach makes on it later in the piece. In the cantus at b.20 he converts it into a turn, beginning on the main

Ex.8.18 J.C. Kerll: Magnificat quinti toni, Versus Quia respexit, bars 1–6.

note because it continues a rising scale. Bach never wastes a detail like this. In b.70 he teases the listener by putting the trill in the bass, when it is the turn version in the middle part that begins the subject. Then in b.72 he puts the turn version in the bass, where it is not on a semitone and introduces nothing. To make the two ornaments uniform would undermine these touches.

A notable galant feature is the flattened 7th degree in b.2 of the subject, an effect beloved by Telemann, who may have got it from Polish music with a Mixolydian tinge; it is also used by C.P.E. Bach at the opening of his second 'Prussian' sonata (1742) and in the subject of W.F. Bach's D major fugue (F.31). Galant also are the prevalent appoggiaturas. Here Spitta's observation that the countersubject and the episodes derived from it resemble the duet 'Nun verschwinden alle Plagen' from BWV 32 (1726) is particularly apt. The duet celebrates the disappearance of troubles ('Plagen') with sighing appoggiaturas and snaking chromatic melismas, worked in the lightest gavotte rhythm in D major. The F sharp major fugue has just the same light-hearted treatment of appoggiaturas and *lamento* falling chromatic steps in the countersubject.

Formally the fugue has more in common with the Vivaldi concerto model than with the binary dance/sonata:

bb.1–12 Exposition: the middle part from b.8 will not work as a bass, so there is only one retained countersubject.

bb.12–20 Episode 1: based on a block of triple counterpoint (end of b.12 to beginning of b.14), which includes in the middle part the three rising notes (6–7–8 of the scale) from the end of the countersubject, and in the bass a figure used notably in the pedals in the C major organ prelude BWV 545/1, which we have also seen in the C major prelude of Book II.

bb.20–24 A further tonic entry in the treble. This reflects Vivaldi's practice in Op.3 of repeating all or part of the opening ritornello in the tonic after the first episode, a practice frequently adopted by Bach (see the discussion of the G major fugue of Book I).

bb.24–32 Episode 2: based on the countersubject's appoggiaturas, worked in trio-sonata style.

bb.32–44 Middle exposition, with entries in the dominant (b.32), tonic (b.36), and relative minor (b.40). This covers the same tonal ground as the part of a binary movement after the double bar, moving from the dominant through the tonic to the relative minor, but since it forms a block of entries in the centre of the fugue it has more the effect of a central ritornello. From here on, the sequence of events up till now is repeated:

bb.44–52 Episode 1.

bb.52–56 Subdominant entry.

bb.56–64 Episode 2.

bb.64–84 Final exposition. The first two entries (b.64, b.70) are extended to six bars each, using the appoggiatura episode material; the final tonic entry (b.76) is extended to a full eight-bar gavotte phrase.

Prelude and Fugue in F sharp minor BWV 883

PRELUDE This piece has been compared to various other Bach slow movements. The comparison with the middle movement of the *Italian Concerto* has the merit of suggesting the tempo as Andante, rather than the Adagio of the C major organ toccata BWV 564. The Benedictus of the B minor Mass is a more useful comparison because of its mixture of triplets with other note values, and the (probably flute) solo is suggestive for the projection of the soloistically conceived treble line in the F sharp minor prelude. A closer comparison than any of these is with the Allemande of the D major clavier Partita BWV 828 (1728), and this reveals the subtle blend of prototypes that goes into the prelude.

The D major Allemande is a synthesis of the traditional keyboard allemande with the galant-style binary sonata. For the allemande, the texture of elaborately decorated right-hand melody, which stands away in pitch from two left-hand accompanying parts, was standard in French-style keyboard dance music from the early seventeenth century (Ledbetter 1987 pp.54–6). Movement is divided between the two left-hand parts to preserve a quaver impetus, and one of them is usually a well-developed tenor line which may take part in motivic imitations. This layout allows great freedom of expressive and structural moulding through increasing or lessening the number of parts in chords and the density of movement.

For the galant style, features are the rhythmic subtlety of the solo line, reflected in diversity of note values, and the sonata version of the aria ritornello shape. In the D major Allemande, a binary piece, this is treated very expansively over an extended first section. The F sharp minor prelude is another example of Bach's favoured use of the shape for preludes of Book II, running it several times from one key centre to another with constant free remoulding and development of elements. It thus has main cadences and new starts in the dominant (b.12), the relative major (b.21), and the tonic (b.30). The freedom of the form and Bach's great resourcefulness mean that each of the preludes of this type has a unique structure and expression. This one builds up to the most impassioned climax in its third section (from b.21), culminating in a dramatic fermata, before sinking back into the drooping intervals of the reprise.

Bach seems to have associated this key with a mood of wistful melancholy, present also in the F sharp minor canon of the sonata for harpsichord and violin BWV 1015. Galant-style triplets in slow movements seem not to have been slurred but articulated separately, if the staccato dots carefully notated by Bach throughout the chorale prelude on 'Vater unser im Himmelreich' BWV 682 from *Clavier-Übung* III are anything to go by.[55] The dots are probably a warning not to play the triplets too glibly, as in a gigue. Altnickol has triplets in the first beats of b.7 and b.8. These were replaced by demisemiquavers in the London autograph, which seems to represent Bach's final thoughts for this piece and has generally more precise and more carefully differentiated rhythmic notation (AB II p.180). It is unlikely that he meant anything other than what he wrote. In his later works he tended to notate performance details exactly, and the essence of this style of slow movement is variety rather than assimilation.

FUGUE After the run of light, character fugues from E minor to F sharp major, the F sharp minor returns to the genre of learned fugue. It is on three subjects, and it seems to demonstrate one of the traditional genera of counterpoint (*oblighi*). It is characteristic of Bach's maturity that he could write such a learned piece, but with a clarity of design and texture which makes it one of the most satisfying fugues in the collection.

Of fugues with three subjects, the F sharp minor is the most systematically laid out in that each subject has a separate exposition of its own subject before being combined with the preceding ones (see Chapter Four section 7). The first subject is built on a common traditional outline of notes 5654321 of the scale. A notable example is the fugue subject of Georg Böhm's G minor Prelude, Fugue and Postlude (in the Andreas Bach Book). From this common outline Bach has devised a subject with gaps, which can be filled by figures taken from the subject itself. Bach, around 1740, was interested in writing demonstrations of traditional contrapuntal techniques (*oblighi*), as he did in *The Art of Fugue* and in some of the fugues of Book II (see Chapter Four section 8). The *obligo* in the F sharp minor fugue is related to the technique of *contrapunto fugato* (Butler 1983 pp.298–9). This is described by Mattheson (1739 III Chapter 22 para.25), who based his description on Berardi's *Documenti armonici* (1687 pp.20–1). In this *obligo*, a melodic figure is repeated over and over again at various pitches (Ex.8.19).

Bach's demonstration is not so straightforward here as in the case of other *oblighi* since in Berardi's and Mattheson's examples the figure is set against a cantus firmus in long note values. But, although they do not say so, the shape of the added figure is derived from the cantus (or subject), and it is this feature which Bach has adopted. The steps and leaps in the subject are echoed in the countersubject (bb.4–6) and fill its gaps. For this the possibilities of the ordinary subject outline are much enriched by the galant-style resolution of the second suspension in b.2 (via an upward leap to another harmony note), a style

Ex.8.19 J. Mattheson: example of *contrapunto fugato*.

of resolution suggested for a similar descending scale by Quantz (1752 Chapter xiii para.28; see Ex.7.18). This enables much witty play, such as the imitations in b.7 and the *style brisé* version in b.8.

In the first exposition (bb.1–20) it is remarkable with what ease Bach develops the shapes of the subject. In particular the falling triad of the opening is treated to imitation recto (bb.9–10), inverso (bb.10–12) and both (bb.13–15), before being converted into a seemingly innocuous continuo bass pattern (bb.16–20). In performance, the second subject (from the second half of b.20) is much improved by the addition of the trill on the dotted quaver added in Altnickol's copy, if not by Bach then almost certainly at his instigation (Dürr 1998 p.351). It is added to all dotted quavers in bb.20–23 regardless of whether the subject is complete or not, and with the clear implication that it should be added subsequently where playable. As often with Bach, the precise nature of this subject is undefined: when it first appears in all three voices (bb.20–3, also bb.30–1) it seems to include the *inganno* of flattening the leading note (Mann 1958 p.91). Bach reserves the normal upward progression of the leading note for the eventual combination of all three subjects (bb.55–7 etc.).

The tonal scheme is as usual for a minor-key piece, the main key centres coinciding with the main contrapuntal events. The second exposition begins after a cadence in the relative major (b.20); the third, over a cadence in the dominant (b.36). A subdominant entry of the original subject and countersubject (bb.51–4) ushers in a final exposition giving three permutations of all three subjects, in the tonic (b.55), dominant (b.60), and tonic (b.66). These are separated by trio-sonata style episodes in which the upper parts give many variants of the first three quavers of the subject.

One important variant in Altnickol's copy is the bass note G♯ (rather than B) on the first beat of b.23. Opinions differ about this: Jones thinks B the authentic reading since it is more obvious (AB II p.180); Tomita thinks G♯ more likely to be a correction because it is less obvious (1995 p.565). On purely musical grounds, it is most unlike Bach at this stage to have such a definite perfect cadence near the beginning of an exposition, and particularly in the course of a subject entry. The G♯ not only avoids this, but it also gives a logical bass outline from the end of b.22 of F♯ | G♯ A | a | a b | c'♯.

Prelude and Fugue in G major BWV 884

PRELUDE Three preludes have at different times been associated with this G major fugue. Probably the earliest is BWV 902/1a, plainly a teaching piece based on a finger-exercise pattern and not unlike the little preludes in Wilhelm Friedemann Bach's *Clavier-Büchlein*.[56] By 1729 Bach had replaced this with the much grander prelude BWV 902/1, as we can see from a copy made that year by J.C. Vogler (see Chapter Three section 8). Bach finally jettisoned BWV 902/1 for the purposes of Book II. This was possibly because it was 'too important' for the fugue (Spitta III p.184), although Bach had been perfectly happy with contrast of scale and weight in the E flat major and A minor pairs of Book I. He may have wanted to keep BWV 902/1 for some other purpose (Dürr 1998 p.356), or thought that Book II already had a prelude (the E major) with a similar opening and structure, and wanted to preserve the principle of variety which is characteristic of his collections. Whatever his reason, the prelude he finally chose forms a very good foil to the fugue for contrasted articulation of lively semiquavers.

In another late manuscript (*c.*1760s) an early version of BWV 884/1 appears alongside the early version of the D minor prelude, suggesting a common origin in the 1720s.[57] The G major belongs, together with the D minor prelude of Book II and the C sharp major prelude of Book I, with pieces obviously written for students, which make a brilliant effect without being particularly technically demanding. It is notable for its very regular overall design, of 48 bars with a section end at b.16 and a main subdominant cadence at b.32, which yet creates an impression of fluidity by means of irregular phrase lengths, such as the three-bar phrases at section openings, and the general lack of internal cadences. In this it contrasts with the, otherwise similar, Allemande from the G major French Suite which also has a sonata layout. Both pieces share the minor-key tinge at section ends, a feature of Corellian harmony emphasised and extended at this later stage of sonata development (see Chapter Three section 6).

FUGUE If Bach did not have to make many alterations to the early version of the prelude, the fugue needed quite a lot of recasting to make it suitable. Structurally it did not need the extensive new composition such as he added in stages to the C sharp major fugue: in the G major he recast bb.53 to the end to include a dominant pedal and some cadenza-like flourishes in the spirit of the 'concert' endings added to some of the preludes in the first half of Book I. What the early version did need was conversion from a very freely conceived piece to a fugue in three obbligato voices (the early version, BWV 902/2, is in NBA V/6.2 pp.332–3 and PF pp.26–7). Dürr considers that the early version may go back as far as Arnstadt *c.*1707 or earlier (1998 p.359) and it shares with early pieces such as the A minor fugue BWV 947, and the fugal sections of early clavier toccatas, the technique of making episodes out of what are essentially continuo progressions, where the action is in the bass and the right hand has continuo-player's free-voiced chords. This and the sequence of entries from the treble down, so that the subject is always in the bass, make the G major in origin the closest in the 48 to *partimento* fugue (Schulenberg 1992 pp.219–20).

In its final version it is still technically undemanding, yet a very attractive and effective piece, probably the reason why Bach ultimately combined it with a prelude of similar technical and emotional level. It was clearly popular as a student's piece, judging by the number of manuscript copies with fingerings in the Kirnberger group of sources. One reason for its value as a learner's piece is the necessity for articulating the continuous semiquavers of the subject to bring out its rhythmic shape. H.C. Wolff's awful idea that the highest and lowest notes of the subject should be accented is exactly what is not required.[58] Articulation on the harpsichord must be done with slurring and separation. The first bar is essentially an upbeat so should be separate, while the subsequent downbeats need to be slurred. This makes the shift of the highest note from the third beat (b.1) to the first beat (b.3) a delightfully subtle and witty touch. Similar articulation is needed in the Courante of the G major Partita BWV 829 and No.19 of the Goldberg Variations.

This fugue is in line with the series of light, lively sonata fugues (*Spielfugen*). The seeming counterpoint at bb.17–19 is simply figuring out the right-hand chords of the early version, an effect of counterpoint designed for playability already noted in the E minor fugue. Kirnberger's fingerings for bb.62–4, as in other similar flourishes in the 48, divide the scales between the hands on the seventeenth-century *roulade* principle (Ex.8.20).[59]

Ex.8.20 Fugue in G major, bars 62–4 with Kirnberger's fingerings.

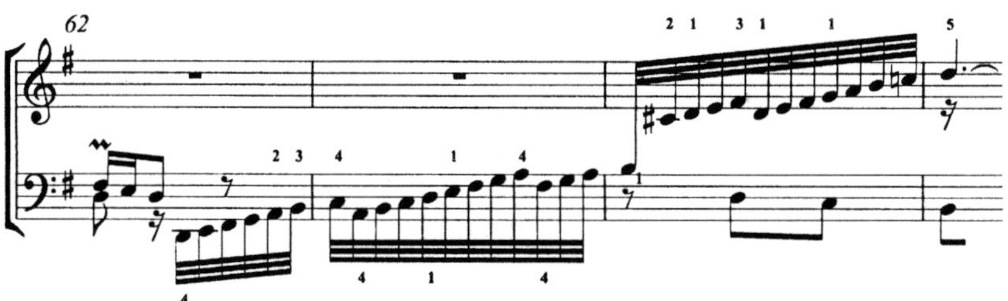

Marpurg's helpful stemming to show the division between the hands for the middle-part entry in bb.67–9 is given by Kroll and Jones, but not in NBA (Marpurg 1765 Tab.VII/32).

Prelude and Fugue in G minor BWV 885

PRELUDE Tempo words in the 48 are important for defining genre, and are used only if there are several possibilities. Without any indication to the contrary a piece of this character in **c** time with dotted semiquavers would normally be classed as an Adagio, as in the opening movement of Handel's F minor harpsichord suite (1720). The word Largo is obviously meant to modify that, but the question is whether Largo is slower or quicker than Adagio. This issue has been clouded by Brossard's (1705) description of Largo as very slow, repeated by J.G. Walther (1732). But Brossard is describing a particular situation in Italian recitatives where the tempo becomes free so that the actor can project the emotions of the words. Walther broadens the definition by adding that some composers use Largo as a 'somewhat faster' movement than Adagio. This is borne out by Telemann's (1725) sequence of words for slow tempi, of adagio–largo–affettuoso. Bach's practice seems to have matched this since he normally intensifies the word adagio (adagio molto, etc.) but moderates the word largo (ma non tanto, etc.), just as, at the opposite end of the spectrum, he intensifies presto (prestissimo etc.) but moderates allegro (ma non presto, etc.; Marshall 1985 p.271). The movement of this piece is therefore not the Adagio of the C major organ toccata BWV 564, but the more going, processional pace of the opening chorus of the *Trauerode* BWV 198.

This is another piece in dotted rhythm where the model of the French overture has been misapplied (see the discussion of the F sharp major prelude). The overture is based on dotted quavers, not semiquavers, and where semiquavers occur in an overture they are either after dotted quavers, or in short groups, when Bach sometimes marks them with dots over the notes, not after them, indicating that they are to be played equally, as in No.16 of the Goldberg Variations. The dotted semiquavers in the G minor prelude are of the type used in minor-key arias, classically for the expression of cruelty and pride (for examples see Fuller 1985). Bach has applied this manner to the same kind of descendant of the toccata *di durezze e ligature* as the F major prelude, thereby giving it a very different expressive effect. The G minor prelude is less clearly structured than the F major and, like the C major prelude, seems to grow out of praeludial improvisation. This impression comes from the large proportion of bass pedal notes and the fact that, where the bass does move, it is only for a few scale steps in crotchets. Half way through b.7 a common organ improvisation effect is introduced in which a bass pedal note becomes the 7th of a last-inversion dominant 7th (4#/2 chord). The tension of this chord is then released in the falling bass dotted semiquavers in the second half of b.7. This moment provides the shape of the whole of the second half of the prelude (from b.11). Half way through b.11 the 7th chord is the harsh dissonance of A flat major over G. Bass scale steps upward from b.12 are interrupted by the 4#/2 chords at bb.13½ and 14½, which drive them down for a moment, until the peak is reached at b.15. The 4#/2 at the beginning of b.16 is released into falling bass semiquavers, the fall now continued in the first half of b.18. Bach has thus taken a formula of improvisation and made it the basis for a logical and dramatic structure.

The mood of high tragedy derives from the rhythm and the key, but also from the preponderance of diminished-7th sonorities and the constant suspended dissonances. Those cadences which have no suspensions in the goal chord (C minor at b.5, G minor at b.11) are the main structural ones. Expressively the falling bass at b.7½ is important, particularly since it leads to a b♭ going 'the wrong way' (upwards), followed by a b♮ going 'the wrong way' (downwards) in b.8; the effect is repeated at the end of b.18. This way of expressing the idea of death in music is at least as old as Monteverdi, and used by Bach throughout his career as a composer of vocal music, from the *Actus Tragicus* BWV 106 ('sterben') to the Credo of the B minor Mass ('mortuorum').

The question of whether or not the semiquavers after dotted quavers (♪. ♬) should be synchronized with the demisemiquavers after dotted semiquavers (♬. ♬) is best answered in terms of style. A close examination of the alignment of notes in Bach's fair copy in the London autograph does not yield a firm conclusion (Dürr in KB V/6.2 p.245 carefully assesses each instance). The comparison with Contrapunctus 6 'in stile francese' in *The Art of Fugue* is misleading, since there a complex scheme of thematic diminution is being worked out. There is no such scheme of rigorous motivic working in the G minor prelude, nor is it in French style. Bach has taken a character texture from a particular type of Italianate aria. To differentiate the two notations in performance would be pedantic and would lend the dotted-quaver version a thematic weight it is not intended to bear. Bach himself went some way towards clarifying the notation by replacing the 𝄿 ♪ ♪. ♬ rhythm given by Altnickol in the second beat of b.1 and equivalent places by 𝄿𝅀 ♬ ♬. ♬ in the London autograph.

FUGUE The highly profiled subject of this fugue is strongly expressive, though opinions differ as to what precisely it expresses. The emphatic opening with a single note, as an exclamation or command, is similar to the A major fugue of Book I, though in the G minor it comes on a weak beat, giving the whole subject a rhythmic subtlety which contributes much to its character. Pirro, in a survey of expressive figures in Bach's texted works, finds in the repeated notes affirmation (citing the chorus 'Das ist je gewißlich wahr' from BWV 141, then thought to be by Bach, now known to be by Telemann), and, by analogy, certain knowledge (as in the ten commandments of BWV 679), decision, fidelity, and submission to the divine will (1907 pp.42–3). Later, however, he cites a similar subject in a vocal piece by Fischer where the rests go with the word 'sighs' ('Seufzer'; p.116). Others have proposed more subjective interpretations. The rhythm of a short note and two long ones, so prominently featured, does strongly suggest a reference to Mattheson's bacchius metre, though the expressive associations of that, as listed by Mattheson, are unlikely for this fugue (see Chapter Four section 5 and Ex.4.3). There is nonetheless an impression of learnedness in Bach's use of this metre, though what he intended may not now be recoverable. The fugue itself is certainly a very learned presentation of double counterpoint at the octave, 10th and 12th, though with expressive character very strongly in the foreground, and fugal technique as a means of achieving it. The contrapuntal density of the fugue gives a strong concentration to its character.

As generally in Bach's most brilliant combinations, there is a fundamental simplicity in the nature of the counterpoint. Here as in other places in Book II, Bach seems to be recreating Fuxian counterpoint in a 'modern' idiom (see Chapter Four section 7). Fux (1725) sets out the rule for counterpoint at the 12th in the traditional way. In double counterpoint at the 12th the intervals to look out for are consonances that invert as dissonances and therefore need special treatment. The main rule for this type of counterpoint *in stile antico* is that the 6th should be avoided since it inverts as a 7th. Bach knew this very well, but in his counterpoint has actually concentrated on the forbidden interval of the 6th since it is perfectly possible to handle the resulting 7th in the inversion *in stile moderno*. The various inversions of the subject and countersubject are given in Ex.8.21 (in Appendix A). The subject (like that of the F sharp minor fugue) outlines a scale descending from the 6th degree, which can be harmonized as a circle of 5ths with a 7th in every other chord. Thus, the 6ths in b.6 etc. invert at the 12th as 7ths in b.29 etc., turning what is a weakness *in stile antico* into the tonally strongest inversion. The modern, second-practice nature of the material is enhanced by the 7th resolving by leap. Since 7th chords are made up of accumulated 3ds, the material will work also in inversion at the 10th as well as at the octave. Bach was not the first to perceive the possibilities of this fundamentally simple idea: it was there in the tradition for him to use, as the *partimento* shows (Ex.8.22a).[60]

To invert this at the 12th means transferring the countersubject in bb.3–4 from the 3rd above the subject to the 3rd below, as in Ex.8.22b. The harmonic transformation emerging from this was what interested Bach most, as may be seen also in the B major fugue.

Further elements of the tradition contribute to this richly allusive fugue. Counterpoint at the 10th, where one part is doubled at the 3rd, was a traditional way of gaining four parts from the triple invertible counterpoint of the trio sonata. As such it is much used by, for example, Purcell in the four-part texture of his orchestral writing. The technique of making a four-part piece out of a bicinium has a German tradition going back through Werckmeister and Buxtehude to Theile and Christoph Bernhard in the mid seventeenth century, and to Zarlino and even Arnold Schlick in the early sixteenth century.[61] Basically it means doubling two canonic lines at the 3rd to make four parts. As Marpurg points out, the G minor fugue could itself be called a

Ex.8.22 (a) Anon.: Langloz MS, Fuga 12, bars 1–4; (b) bars 10–12, with countersubject inverted at the 12th.

canonic double fugue since the countersubject grows out of the subject and forms a continuous line with it (1753 pp.140–1, Dok III pp.37–8). As the fugue progresses this aspect of the tradition comes more and more to the fore (bb.45ff, 51ff) until it is fully unveiled at b.59. The dramatic possibilities of this texture are richly exploited by Bach from here to the end of the fugue. The inversion at the 12th at b.67 is joined by the octave and 10th at b.67, followed by non-contrapuntal but rhetorical chords and pauses. This is the most striking example of the more dramatic approach to fugal writing in Book II, where the climax is intensified by rhetorical, rather than contrapuntal, effects, a feature already noted in the D sharp minor fugue.

Prelude and Fugue in A flat major BWV 886

PRELUDE This is the largest, and possibly the latest, prelude in Book II. The London autograph has the earliest known version of the piece, entered in a late layer (*c*.1741). Judging by the number of corrections Bach made as he wrote it, he was at least partly composing as he wrote, or writing after improvisation (Tomita 1990 p.269). Thereafter a fair copy was made, now lost, with a number of significant alterations which are reflected in Altnickol's copy. Dürr points out that the notation of demisemiquavers as , rather than as in the F sharp major prelude, is in line with Bach's later trend to more exact notation, continued in *The Art of Fugue* in the early 1740s (1998 p.370). There is therefore not necessarily any performance implication in this change of notation.

This prelude is yet another example of Bach's seemingly inexhaustible ability to invent novel and sonorous keyboard textures while drawing elements from many directions, as we have seen particularly in the preludes in E flat major, F major and F sharp major. It also further demonstrates the infinite possibilities of the aria ritornello model in its sonata guise for flexible development. The opening section is subsequently re-run with variations and developments from the usual main key centres for a major-key piece: the dominant (b.17), the relative minor (b.34) and the subdominant (b.50). In this prelude there is no tonic reprise of the opening, but a tonic coda begins in b.64 after a strong marker cadence.

The opening section follows the usual phases of the sonata first half. As elsewhere in Book II Bach favours an irregular opening period, in this case of seven bars. The first bars provide the main materials of the piece: the chords and bass pattern of b.1 and the semiquavers of b.2. Both of these patterns are obviously based on keyboard hand-shapes and an improvised origin can be assumed. Development starts immediately after the alternating patterns of the first four bars, with the delightful C.P.E. Bach-style arpeggios with staccato dots in bb.5 and 6. The modulating phase, beginning at b.7, outlines a pattern of falling 3rds in both hands, answered by rising 3rds in bb.11–14. This climaxes on a last-inversion dominant 7th (4♮/2; b.15), which is released into a closing idea and cadence at b.16. The 4♮/2 chord, as in the G minor prelude, plays an important marking role in the piece as a whole, coming in the equivalent place in the 3rd section (b.48), and with an enhanced effect in the dramatic concluding chords (b.75). The closing idea also plays an important role in marking section ends at bb.33, 49 and 62.

The main sections of the prelude alternate in shape, just as the first two bars alternate in pattern. The second section (from b.17), unlike section 1, has the outlines of rising and falling 3rds in contrary motion (bb.23–32) and a majestic chordal version of the dotted quaver-semiquaver rhythm (from b.24). Section 3 (from b.34) corresponds to section 1 in that it goes through the same patterns of similar-motion falling and rising 3rds, though now adapted to modulate from F minor to D flat major. As one expects in the minor phase, there is a peak of density of movement in bb.38–9. Given the correspondence of section 3 to section 1, it is perhaps curious that the right-hand arpeggio in b.39 has no staccato dot in any source. Section 4, as section 2, has contrary motion patterns of 3rds (bb.53–5, and through most of the coda). The prelude ends with a strong Neapolitan harmony in b.74, which may well be intended to match the equivalent effect at the end of the fugue. Like the F sharp major prelude, the

A flat ends with a large-scale hemiola (three minim beats in bb.75–6), and very similar chording.

The similarities with the F sharp major prelude are sufficient to make one suspect that Bach in both pieces was working at a particular effect. The stiffness of the French overture is quite foreign to the character of these two pieces. It seems more likely that he was interested in the simultaneous projection of the fleetness of dotted rhythms and the flexibility of continuous semiquavers, an effect of combining rhythmic freedoms analagous to that observed in the C sharp minor prelude of Book I.

FUGUE The origin of this fugue is in the series of preludes and fughettas dating from the 1720s, perhaps even before the genesis of Book I, from which Bach also developed the C major pair and the G major fugue. The main source is the copy by J.C. Vogler (P 1089) made *c.*1727–31, though the pieces may date from quite a lot earlier than that. The fughetta is in F major (BWV 901/2; NBA V/6.2 pp.326–7, PF pp.20–1). As Hermann Keller points out, Bach had only to change the right-hand clef from C1 to G2 and add the A flat major key signature to effect the transposition (1976 p.179). Of all the triple counterpoints that include the *lamento* bass which Bach used in his keyboard works, this the most ordinary. His originality in treating standard materials, and his ability to give them fresh expressive force, can be seen elsewhere in his treatment of this standard element in triple counterpoint in the F minor three-part Sinfonia BWV 795 and the A major prelude of Book I (see the commentary).

Each strand of the triple counterpoint of the F major fughetta is a standard figure. Pirro's observation (1907 p.430) that the main subject is similar to the opening theme of the Allemande of François Couperin's G major *Concert Royal* (1722) has been repeated by various writers, and has led to this fugue being misconstrued as in a dance genre (Kunze 1969 p.88). This is a common misunderstanding of the mixture of French dance and Italian sonata, begun by Italian composers of the mid-seventeenth century, with the sonata element finally predominating even in French music in Couperin's last decade. Bach's theme is more akin to that of the first Allegro of Corelli's sonata Op.5 No.3, perhaps Couperin's model, and which points to its trio-sonata origin. Since its pattern outlines a circle-of-5ths progression, it goes back to the beginning of sonata composition based on tonal structures in the mid-seventeenth century, when the circle of 5ths began to be used for the sequential continuation of themes. A prototype in Bach's environment (also in F major) is the fugue from the *Sonata terza* of Kuhnau's *Frische Clavier-Früchte* (1696). Bach is playing here with standard material, and the charm of it is that it puts the *lamento* pattern into a major-mode context. This mixture of modes was also a feature of pre-Corelli sonata composers as can be seen in the subject by G.M. Bononcini given in Ex.3.1 as an early example of the aria ritornello shape. Bononcini also uses the *lamento* in a major-mode context (Op.6 No.5, Venice 1672; Klenz 1962 p.161). The circle-of-5ths pattern is very common,[62] and often subjected to stiff, workaday treatment as in the E minor fugue BWV 956 (possibly by J.P. Kellner; Stinson 1990 p.130). Bach's three well-contrasted themes in the F major fughetta BWV 901/2, with its attractive modal ambiguity, compare very favourably with this.

The fughetta is in a trio-sonata style, beginning with upper-part entries, such as would be doubled by the keyboard continuo until well into the 18th century. There is a triple-invertible episode (bb.10–13), and it is effectively in three parts until the final entry at bb.22–4. Nonetheless, the main subject also has roots in the verset tradition, such as the canzona-type subject of Froberger's Capriccio I (1656) and thence in versets by Kerll (1686, Magnificat Sexti Toni, Versus Deposuit potentes) and Pachelbel (Magnificat Sexti Toni, *c.*1701–5; ed. Zászkaliczky VIII p.35). It may be significant that these last two examples are in Mode VI, or effectively F major. If Bach was contemplating another update of the verset, as he plainly was in Book I, he may here have been wishing to reinterpret traditional organist's elements in 'modern' trio-sonata style, such as a capellmeister might use, applied to the keyboard.

When Bach came to preparing the A flat major fugue, he seems to have worked from the F major version up to b.24, and then from a draft of the continuation (Tomita 1990 pp.271–3). The London autograph version of this piece is datable precisely to 1742, and is one of the last things Bach did to complete Book II. He also made another copy at around the same time (P 274) which has interesting variants, though not as significant as those for the prelude. Altnickol's copy has further emendations (AB II p.185). The final product is an excellent demonstration of the contrast between Bach's early exploration of strictly schematic plans, and his late, much freer but also more organic and searching, exploration of the nature of musical materials, a contrast of early and late already noticed in the two D sharp minor fugues of the 48.

Bach took the early fughetta into the later fugue with only minor alterations. Yet even here small changes make for more significant development, and link to the continuation. The conversion of the original crotchet b'♮ (in F major) to two quavers d''♮ d''♭ (in A flat) in the cantus of the episode (last beat of b.10; with equivalent in the alto in the second beat of b.12) allows a more thematically cogent alto part from bb.10–11, but it also links the ordinary leading-note-to-tonic progression at the end of the *lamento* subject (alto bb.4–5) to the *inganno* of the flattened leading note in the second exposition (cantus b.20, alto b.21), a feature which develops the *lamento* figure. The shape of the fughetta is straightforward, with a standard series of entries in the sequence tonic–dominant–tonic–dominant (bb.1–10), and a corresponding sequence tonic–dominant–tonic–tonic (bb.13–24), so as to end in the tonic. After the first entry in the second sequence there is a strong cadence in F minor at b.16, providing the only tonal contrast in the fughetta. This gives Bach his cue for the continuation at b.24, where he picks up the F minor with an entry in that key, and continues in a now much larger major-key scheme, with a cadence in the relative-minor dominant at b.27, strengthening the relative-minor phase.

Bach richly exploited the chromatic tetrachord in his last decade (P. Williams 1997 pp.100–3). In this fugue he takes its minor-key, flattening, effect and develops these aspects massively in the continuation of the fugue. Already in b.26 the idea of organic growth is present in the way this episode develops naturally out of the F minor entry. The episode from b.27 revolves the permutations of the bb.10–13 episode, with a logical sequence of entries of the semiquaver figure, in the cantus at b.27, the alto at b.29, and the bass at b.30. Thereafter the flattening, minor-key nature of the *lamento* subject is much accentuated by entries in E flat minor (b.32) and B flat minor (b.35). The sharp dissonance of the last inversion of a major 7th (beginning of b.37) sets off an entry in D flat major (the subdominant) in the bass (*per arsin et thesin* in Marpurg's sense). After this involution of very flat-key entries, there are two bright and clear tonic and dominant entries at bb.41–3. But b.44 again picks up the flattening tendency, and brings it to a rhetorical climax on the flattest chord in the key, the Neapolitan B𝄫 major. This dramatic tendency for the close of Book II fugues has already been noted in the fugues in D sharp minor and G minor. The rhetorical gesture is then capped by the final entry in a climactic richness of texture and harmony (bb.48–50).

In a copy made for Padre Martini (DD 70), Wilhelm Friedemann Bach added an *Accent steigend* (i.e. appoggiatura) to the subject on the second beat of b.2 and equivalent places. Since it is lacking in all other sources this seems to be his own addition (KB V/6.2 p.249).

Prelude and Fugue in G sharp minor BWV 887

PRELUDE This is the third of the group of four advanced-key preludes from the second layer of entries to the London autograph (*c.*1740–1) which feature 'modern' keyboard figurations. The group is in related keys: F sharp major and B major, and their relatives D sharp minor and G sharp minor. It has been noted with the D sharp minor and F sharp major preludes that advanced keys seem to have less bearing on character than they do in preludes of Book I, perhaps indicating changing attitudes to keyboard temperament as part of style. Several writers have remarked on the G minor character of this piece, and there is some evidence for transposition from G minor in the treatment of accidentals in the principal sources (KB V/6.2 pp. 250, 320).

As in the D major and F minor preludes, Bach is again addressing the principle of contrast in the opening material and, as in those preludes, the argument of the piece lies in the development and integration of opposites. In this case two somewhat facile ingredients are used: the left-hand figuration in b.2, and the echo principle of repeating an entire unit at a different dynamic. The seemingly opposite materials are the articulate, contrapuntally devised *inventio* in the right hand of b.1, and the prattling accompanying figure in the left hand of b.2. These are in fact two versions of the same shape in that both outline the 5th G sharp to D sharp at both beats 1–2 and beats 1–4 of b.1, with a dip to F double-sharp in the middle. Unity of materials is underlined by the fact that the right-hand figure runs into the left hand at the end of b.1. The offbeat appoggiaturas in the right hand at b.2 may be regarded as a variation of the onbeat chords in the left hand at b.1. The repetition of these two bars *piano* as a block emphasises their identity as a microcosm of materials and styles.

Formally this prelude is unusual in that it does not relate directly to the aria ritornello model. There is an initial four-bar shape, followed by a phase that modulates to the dominant (bb.5–8), but thereafter events are unpredictable. A long period of motivic working (bb.8–15) takes us to a dominant reprise which lasts, with developments, from b.16 to the double bar. In this development the initially contrasted ideas are brought together with felicities of motivic working too numerous to detail. One may just notice that the double counterpoint from b.8 unites the contrapuntal semiquavers of b.1 with the sighing appoggiaturas of b.2 not only by putting them end to end (right-hand b.8 second beat to b.9 first beat), but also in the downward stepping quavers in the bass of b.8, a variation of appoggiaturas used for the same purpose in the F minor prelude. This passage is given coherent shape by the bass stepping down a chromatic octave, from the d♯ at the beginning of b.8 to the D♯ half way through b.11, a relation of surface features to fundamental structures typical of Bach. The three-semiquaver upbeat figure from the end of b.1 is richly used here, and in the following episode (bb.11–15) it is combined with the prattling bass figure in the manner of a violin sonata, matching recreative manipulation of shapes to iridescent changes of manner.

The 'invention' element of this prelude uses a technique similar to that of the other large binary invention preludes in Book II (in D sharp minor and E minor) of combining the opening idea with ever new counterthemes. This happens at b.16, and is the main argument after the double bar. A reprise at b.31 starts with the very subdominant colouring of the Neapolitan key, after which the original order of events (bb.8–15) is reversed, with the rising violin-sonata manner first (bb.34–5), so that the inversion of the double counterpoint can step down its chromatic scale to the tonic reprise at b.41. The final tour de force is an inversion at bb.47–9 of the original galant right-hand-plus-accompaniment (bb.5–7), with strong, close-spaced dissonances in the left hand. On the face of it this is one of Bach's more galant-style preludes, but one has only to look at the treatment of similar ingredients in, for example, the first movement of the second of C.P.E. Bach's Württemberg Sonatas (1744) to see the real gulf of style and objectives that separates father and son.

That the appoggiaturas are to be interpreted as quavers is clear from the first halves of b.44 and b.45. Bach in his autograph fair copy does not use small notes for appoggiaturas but the hooks for the *Accent* of his table of ornaments in Wilhelm Friedemann Bach's *Clavier-Büchlein*. These would not make the necessary accidentals clear in these bars.

The *piano* and *forte* markings in b.3 and b.5 probably imply a two-manual harpsichord: the other clavier works which use them are *Clavier-Übungen* II and IV ('Clavicymbel mit zweyen Manualen'). Otherwise most indications of this sort are in the organ works (Marshall 1985 p.267). The fact that they are notated here does not rule out the possibility of manual changes for contrasted ideas at the openings of the D major and F minor preludes, though with the agenda in those pieces of uniting contrasted ingredients the change is not logical. In keeping with the flexibility implied by the word clavier, Bach did not use these indications in the 48 other than in the G sharp minor prelude, where dynamic or colour contrast at the opening is a structural necessity. They need not, of course, rule out the clavichord which, as C.P.E. Bach says, can express both detailed and larger nuances just as well as many other instruments (1753 Chapter iii para.29).

FUGUE Subjects on a single note value are part of the verset and *partimento* traditions, particularly in the case of gigue rhythm. If Bach had a campaign of concert/sonata fugues in various rhythmic characters from E minor to F sharp major, it may be that this fugue belongs to that series. It certainly provides the opposite pole from the variety of the E minor subject. Conversely, if Bach intended to demonstrate some of the rhythmic characters described by Mattheson, as he seems to have wished to demonstrate genera of counterpoint in Book II and in *The Art of Fugue*, then this example of the tribrach (three short syllables) could go with the bacchius of the G minor fugue, which comes next to it in Mattheson's list (see Ex.4.3a). Mattheson describes the tribrach as in the 'modern' fashion, used mainly in gigues, though it may also figure in more serious pieces (1739 II Chapter 6 paras.27–8).[63] For the contemplative and intricate character of this fugue it is worth bearing in mind Kirnberger's remarks on the difference between $\frac{6}{8}$ and $\frac{6}{16}$, cited in the discussion of the F major fugue: the pace is much weightier ('weit schwerfälliger') in $\frac{6}{8}$.

As a fugue on two subjects, this has a more spaciously articulated plan than the C sharp minor fugue, and in plan is similar to the F sharp minor, with separate expositions for each subject (bb.1–61 and bb.61–97) and a final section combining both as a double fugue (bb.97–143). Within this scheme Bach was concerned, as in the invention-type preludes in Book II, with combining his subjects with ever new counterpoints. Out of this constant free remoulding of motifs the final section, where both themes are constant companions, emerges. The countersubject at b.5 grows neatly from the subject so that the treble line from b.1 to b.9 covers a rising 5th g'♯ to d"♯, as does the opening of the prelude. Yet in the first section only the entries at b.5 and b.19 actually use it. The entry at b.55 uses an inversion of the counterpoints at b.13: the remaining entries develop other shapes in their counterpoints. The five-note scale is nonetheless an important shaping element. At bb.17–19 it leads the cantus down from d"♯ to g'♯ to give the alto the pitch of its entry, an important pointer since this is the concluding entry of the first exposition. Further uses of this shape are in the bass at bb.23–5, and the cantus at bb.40–2, which takes the treble up from a'♯ to d"♯ where it lingers before having the highest entry in pitch at b.45. Such shaping elements are important in a piece that is so understated in rhythmic profile. Shapes dependent on pitch levels and texture become larger and more dramatic in the second section, culminating in the long and wide-ranging bass line from b.81 to b.95, which emphasises the rising phase of the second subject and prepares the final section, with its combination of both subjects.

The pitch levels of subject entries are planned with particular care for structural shaping, binding the fugue together in an overarching scheme. The structure of the first section is related to the principle of fugal inversion, with two expositions: the first having the sequence of entries tonic–dominant–tonic–tonic and concluding with a marker Phrygian cadence (bb.30–1); the second having the sequence dominant–dominant–tonic, and concluding with a matching Phrygian cadence (bb.60–1). Within this, the pitch levels of entries are carefully planned to open out from the octave g'♯ to g♯ in the first exposition to the highest entry at b.45 answered by the lowest at b.55 in the second. The fact that the bass from b.61 continues to extend the pitch downwards till b.68, thereby making this trend of the first section flow into the second, neatly makes an organic link over the join. The final section then runs these pitch levels in reverse, starting with the lowest entry at b.97, answered by the highest at b.103. The E major entry (b.111, the only one in the fugue not in the tonic or dominant) and the final two tonic entries (b.125, b.135) return to the original g♯–g'♯ octave.

Altogether this is a subtle example of Bach's later fugal writing, organically developmental rather than schematic in its combinations, with subjects having a simple clarity of outline and cast in two-bar galant phraseology.

Prelude and Fugue in A major BWV 888

PRELUDE Opinions have differed as to the character of this prelude. The similarity of the basic motif (cantus in the first half of b.1), particularly in its inversion from b.9, to that of the second section of the Prelude of the A major English Suite has led some commentators to see it as a gigue character. The pattern of a free opening section followed by a gigue-like second section, as in the A major English Suite, is found in French harpsichord preludes such as that of Rameau's A minor Suite (1706). The English Suite motif is a commonplace of French allemandes and gigues, used notably in the Gigue of Dieupart's A major suite for harpsichord (1701), which Bach copied out around 1709–12.[64] The motif is similar, and the technique of developing it by extension and inversion is common to both preludes yet, despite the similarities, many have felt the A major prelude to have the character of a pastorale rather than the robust movement of a gigue. In this case it may be compared to the Pastorale for organ BWV 590, a genre of pastorale in $\frac{12}{8}$-time without the dotted siciliano rhythm, apparently modelled on a concerto pastorale of Locatelli's (from Op.1 No.8, copied out by Bach in 1734; Stinson 1989 p.113).

A further genre with which this prelude invites comparison is the three-part sinfonia. But again, in spite of the ingenious motivic working, the texture is more akin to an instrumental trio: Dürr has noted the freedom of motivic treatment and the amount of the bass line that has continuo, rather than contrapuntal, function (1998 p.391). The A major prelude's motif of a rising triad with triplet decoration is in fact a different commonplace motif from the gigue one. It is worked in a trio for oboe d'amore, viola da gamba, and continuo in the aria 'Liebt, ihr Christen' from the second part of BWV 76 (1724), which more aptly than the gigue model suggests the gentle movement of this prelude. The prelude seems yet another example of Bach's liking in Book II for referring on the keyboard to other instrumental sonorities.

The contrapuntal argument of the prelude is a demonstration of how to develop the motif by extension and inversion, with inverso entries in the E major section from b.9. It plays with various combinations until the systematic series of alternating recto and inverso entries over the concluding pedal in bb.30–2. Formally the prelude belongs to the more sophisticated treatment of the head–continuation–cadence shape characteristic of Book II (there is no early version of this prelude). Comparison with the E major prelude of Book I points up the more subtle formal articulation of the A major prelude, and the more inventive and developmental use of a subdominant reprise. The opening section moves up to the dominant (b.9). The second section moves to the relative minor (b.16), and the third to the subdominant reprise (b.22), introduced by a feinted tonic reprise at b.20. The reprise is a fairly close adaptation of the opening section, moving up from subdominant to tonic, but with the upper two parts exchanged, a feature which reinforces the impression of a trio for two solo instruments and continuo. The climax of the first section is provided by the bass extending the rising 3rds of the basic motif to cover 1½ octaves from e–a' at bb.6–8. This pattern is masked in the reprise (bb.27–9) by the bass having to break back an octave, but Bach once more makes a virtue of necessity by saving a straight series of rising 3rds as his conclusion in the treble (from d'–a") in bb.32–3.

FUGUE Various attempts have been made to discern chorale melody outlines behind themes in Bach's secular works.[65] Some identifications are plainly wrong, as when the mode of a chorale melody is mistaken, and most are open to the objection that chorale melodies are based on commonplace melodic gambits such as are bound to lie behind much tonal music. The subject of this fugue is the only one in the 48 which strongly suggests a chorale origin. A glance at the incipits in the Schmieder catalogue (p.938) of organ chorale paraphrases of the melody of the German Gloria in excelsis ('Allein Gott in der Höh sei Ehr', Ex.8.23a) shows how close the subject of this fugue is to a family of subjects based on this chorale. The closest is BWV 664 (Ex.8.23b), a Weimar setting which Bach later included in the manuscript of the 'Eighteen' chorale preludes around 1746–7 (Wollny 1999 p.xv). If this chorale was indeed in Bach's mind, there may be a Christmas association of pastoral prelude and Gloria fugue (shepherds and angels). Here again, as with the prelude, there is a possible comparison with the C major organ Prelude and Fugue BWV 547, in that the C major fugue has a close relation to the second *manualiter* setting of 'Allein Gott' in *Clavier-Übung* III, BWV 677.[66] The low A' in the bass at b.16 of the A major fugue rules out organ performance, but this note was evidently not in the (lost) composing score, nor originally in Altnickol's version. Associations of this kind should not be too glibly made, however. This chorale outline has been suggested for far less likely candidates such as Ex.8.23c (Tröster 1984 p.38).

Even if Bach did consciously choose to use it, the main interest for him was not that in itself but the rhythmic disjunction in the middle of the subject which is so suggestive of contrapuntal development. Bach plays with the syncopation in the second half of b.1, originally written ♫♩. ♬ ♪, by giving its complementary rhythm in two parts at b.3, and subsequently with the rhythm ♩. ♪ from b.5, the bass enhancing the harmonic cliché by jumping octaves.

It is by no means certain that the chorale reference is intentional. One would in any case expect a chorale fughetta to incorporate successive phrases of the chorale melody and not be entirely based on the first. Yet the lack of contrapuntal devices, together with the freedom of motivic working, suggest at least the technique of the chorale fughetta. In addition, there is a suggestion of chorale improvisation in that the fugue is based on two clichés of continuo harmony. One is the rising 5–6 progression in the second half of b.5; the other is the falling circle of 5ths with 6/5 chords at bb.8–9. The manipulation of these two elements, inherent in the subject, constitutes the argument of the fugue. A further suggestion of improvisation is in the second half of b.16,

Ex.8.23 (a) Chorale melody 'Allein Gott in der Höh' sei Ehr', first phrase; (b) Organ trio BWV 664, bars 1–3; (c) Presto of the A major Sonata for harpsichord and violin BWV 1015, bars 1–5.

where the very playable right-hand hand-shapes suggest in the last quaver a highly dissonant chord with augmented 5th and major 7th. In terms of pure line this would be difficult to arrive at, but it is perfectly standard as a continuo-player's progression.

As in the prelude, a feature of this fugue is the lack of marked cadences. In this case the strong cadence at the half-way point (bb.15–16) is particularly telling, all the more so in the London autograph for the bass descending to A', exceeding the usual range for *The Well-tempered Clavier.* The first half of the fugue follows Bach's usual practice in three-part expositions of having an extra entry in the dominant (bass b.7). In this case the dominant entry neatly paves the way for the relative minor (b.9½) and its dominant (b.12). The second half gives an exposition of tonic (bass b.16), subdominant (cantus b.20), and dominant (middle b.23½), with the chromatic element in the rising 5–6 steps enhanced until it infects the subject itself (b.23 last beat). The scheme of enhancing the chromatic element was not part of the original conception of the piece (which was mainly concerned with the rhythm of the subject) but occurred to Bach as he wrote out and later revised the London autograph copy.

The ending of the fugue is characteristically neat. If the dominant entry in the bass at b.7, which seems to belong to the exposition, really leads into the main argument of the fugue, the final tonic entry (b.27) reprises the tonic cantus entry that in fact completes the exposition (bb.5–6), and makes it more final with expansion of texture and some decorations in the bass.

Prelude and Fugue in A minor BWV 889

PRELUDE Much has been made of the rigorously chromatic nature of this prelude and the schematic exactness of its construction. It has been seen as an exercise in mathematics, and even as anticipating Schoenberg's disintegration of tonality.[67] In fact it lacks the starkly speculative character of other chromatic writing of Bach's around this time, such as in the first two Duetti (1739) or some of the canons in *The Art of Fugue* (*c*.1742–6). It equally lacks the intensely expressive use of chromaticism of Variation 25 of the Goldberg Variations. Bach is not interested here in the expressive possibilities of the *lamento* bass but, in keeping with the demonstrative and speculative functions of the 48, with its possibilities as a standard building block. This accounts for the relentless continuity of line, without a single expressive *sospiro* other than the rest that begins each half.

The strict scheme of the prelude, with melodic inversion of themes after the double bar, recalls the equally strict binary scheme of the E minor fugue of Book I. Generally speaking, schematic strictness seems an earlier characteristic, as we have seen in comparing the D sharp minor fugues of Books I and II. In the case of the A minor prelude and fugue there are some slight hints of a possibly earlier origin, such as the use of the term Fughetta in the Altnickol sources of the fugue, the term used in early versions such as BWV 870a etc. (Dürr 1998 p.396). Bach did nonetheless return in his later works to very schematic plans, represented most notably in his fascination with canon in the 1740s, so there is no stylistic reason to suggest an early origin.

The strictness of the scheme, and the seeming complexity of the chromatic language, should not blind us to the underlying straightforwardness of the basic material. Kirnberger (or his pupil J.A.P. Schulz) gave this prelude as an easier option for analysis in terms of the fundamental bass than the B minor fugue of Book I.[68] Although Kirnberger had the rationalist aim of finding fundamental simplicity behind complexity, the analysis is in fact a good example of how fundamental-bass analysis can make harmony look more complex than it actually is. It is an abstraction and ignores the physical feel of the progressions on the keyboard, a prime consideration for Bach. The A minor prelude is based on two standard formulas of continuo harmony. One is the *lamento* bass harmonised with 7–6 suspensions (Ex.8.24a), which may also be expressed as a circle-of-5ths progression (Ex.8.24b), as in the A flat major fugue of Book II (see also Ex.7.26). The other is the chromatically decorated cadence formula Ex.8.24c, with its inversion, which also involves a falling chromatic line.

Ex.8.24 (a) *Lamento* bass with 7–6 suspensions; (b) with a circle-of-5ths progression; (c) invertible chromatic cadence formula.

Bach has simply filled in any whole-tone steps with semitones, and decorated the resolutions of the 7ths with a chromatic lower auxiliary, a galant trait also found in the F minor three-part Sinfonia and the A major prelude of Book I. The material of the prelude is therefore a chromatic elaboration of a common formula, just as the six-part Ricercar from the *Musical Offering* (1747) uses in its episodes a chromatic elaboration of the rising scale formula which opens the second (*Gravement*) section of the early G major *Pièce d'orgue* BWV 572 (before *c.*1712). Such formulas are the basis of improvisation. Tomita suggests that what looks like a fair copy of the A minor prelude in the London autograph may in fact be a 'mature record' of improvisation, with at most a brief draft to precede it (1990 p.277; 1993 p.119). The purpose of the prelude is then to demonstrate the possibilities of developing this formula.

FUGUE Bach was infinitely resourceful in subtly outlining the diminished 7th in a rhetorical way. The crudely direct version in the portentous cliché that opens the A minor fugue can only be intended in the spirit of parody, inviting playful treatment from Bach here as from Haydn in the finale of his F minor quartet from Op.20.[69] Bach parodies the cliché by adding an extended continuation based on its main features of a falling 3rd and 7th, which yield a subject of all leaps (*di salto*) as opposed to the chromatic steps of the prelude (*alla diritta*; P.Williams 1997 pp.93–4). Bach gives these intervals first in plain staccato quavers (bb.2–3), then decorated with demisemiquavers (bb.3–4). The designation Fughetta given by Altnickol implies lightness of treatment and, in common with other light-hearted fugues such as the E major from Book I, Bach leaves the end of the subject vague so that it can freely merge into a variety of subsequent events.

The immoderate sequential extension characteristic of the subject applies equally to the main events of the fugue. In bb.16–18 the demisemiquavers are made to run down from b''♭ to E. The rising trill from the end of b.4, a figure of comedy here as in the F sharp major fugue, is then made to climb from E up to b'♭. Finally the demisemiquavers run all the way down from b'' (b.25), migrating between parts and turning into staccato quavers, to bottom AA in the last bar. This exceptionally low note for the 48 was not originally in Altnickol's copy. It may be that Bach decided to use it having put the demisemiquavers in b.15 down an octave in the London autograph version, so making the bass go down to the second lowest note of the piece (D) at the halfway point, and thus providing a logical and dramatic pitch strategy for the whole fugue. On the other hand, the extra-elaborate version of the bass trill given by Altnickol in the last bar gives just the right touch of Schlendrian pomposity to the conclusion of this tour of the keyboard.

In spite of its character as fughetta this fugue is notable for its level of intellectual control. In the triple counterpoint at bb.6–7, of which, as Tovey notes, Bach uses four of the possible six permutations, each of the strands is made out of the falling intervals of the subject and its continuations. Bach also plays with the modulating nature of the subject, making it move in bb.10–13 from C major to E minor by inserting an extra 1½ bars of triple counterpoint in bb.11–12½, and from E minor to D minor at bb.13–15. The A minor entry in the middle voice at b.17 is really the answer in D minor, in which key the subject proper enters at b.21.

Prelude and Fugue in B flat major BWV 890

PRELUDE Bach showed an interest in the brilliant use of hand-crossing in the later 1720s, in the Gigue of the B flat Partita (published 1726) and the C minor Fantasia BWV 906 (in an autograph of *c.*1726–31). He seems to have come back to it in the late 1730s, when there is another autograph of the C minor Fantasia (*c.*1735–40). In the later stages of assembling Book II Bach evidently took up aspects which he wanted to explore more rigorously and systematically than he had been able to do there, thanks to the anthology nature of the collection, and developed them elsewhere: keyboard technique in the Goldberg Variations (1741) and devices of fugue in *The Art of Fugue* (early 1740s). In Book II Bach seems concerned with styles and techniques of composition rather than keyboard effects in themselves. They come into it, but in ways which show how they can be a cogent part of a musical argument, rather than elements of display for their own sake. They therefore tend to be rather understated in effect.[70]

Comparison with the Gigue of the B flat Partita, with its headlong movement and open arpeggiated texture, emphasizes the relatively relaxed character of the B flat prelude, with its intricate motivic working in three parts. Dürr points out that the subdominant emphasis in b.2 also implies a relatively relaxed mood. However, he also points out that Altnickol originally had a time signature of $^{12}_{8}$, perhaps reflecting an earlier version, which Bach then corrected to $^{12}_{16}$. If this is so, the change to the lighter, more fluent signature implies a warning against too deliberate a tempo. This may have been necessary in view of the fact that the opening gambit of descending scales over a pedal is a common improvisation formula in organ preludes: a scheme very similar to the opening of the B flat prelude is used by Fischer in the G major Praeludium No.13 of *Ariadne Musica* (Ex.8.25).

Ex.8.25 Fischer: Praeludium 13 from *Ariadne Musica*, bars 1–5.

In line with his policy for the 48, Bach here again takes a traditional ingredient and updates it, in this case making it the basis for a galant binary sonata movement. The principle of the genre is to have a number of ideas that run from tonic to dominant in the first half, and to run the same ideas back from dominant back to tonic, generally with some development, in the second half (see Chapter Three section 6). The essence is that the ideas should contrast. In the case of Domenico Scarlatti there is a great deal of development of ideas, and he likes to shuffle them into different sequences in the second half. Contrast of successive ideas is rarely Bach's objective. Where it exists initially, as in the D major and F minor preludes, the rest of the piece is generally devoted to fusing the ideas together. The B flat major prelude has virtually no contrast, being on the invention principle of developing everything from the opening. But the patterns that evolve may nonetheless be divided into motivic areas, and Bach thus fuses the principles of thematically unified invention, and galant sonata with a succession of contrasting ideas. If the principle of non-integrative contrast did not appeal to Bach, the possibilities arising from changing the sequence of events in the second half, and of combining the scheme with a tonic reprise, obviously fascinated him. A comparison with other large-scale binary sonata movements reveals the B flat prelude as his most complex exploration of these possibilities.

The D major prelude has a simple scheme, based on a series of three motivic areas, or phases, which are run three times, with developments; the final series being the tonic reprise:

1 2 3 :|: 1 2 3; 1 2 3 :|

The C minor Fantasia BWV 906 is more elaborate, with a series of four motivic areas in the first half, and a more subtle plan after the double bar in that the elements are shuffled in the second series, and one (2) is omitted, being reserved for the third series (the tonic reprise; X in the second series is a new figuration, which grows out of previous ones):

1 2 3 4 :|: 1 4 3 X; 1 2 |:

The B flat prelude has a much more complex version of this scheme, with a series of no less than seven motivic areas before the double bar. Of these, the first gives its material in two forms: 1a in bb.1–2, and inverted as 1b in bb.3–4. The following table identifies the sequence of events:

first series	:|:	middle series	;	reprise	:|
1ab	bb.1–8	7	bb.33–6	1a	bb.49–52
2	bb.9–12	3	bb.37–42	2	bb.53–6
3	bb.13–16	6	bb.43–4	4	bb.57–64½
4	bb.17–20	5	bb.45–8	1b	bb. 64½–69
5	bb.21–3			X	bb.70–82
6	bb.24–7			7	bb.83–7
7	bb.28–32				

The feature, also in Fischer's G major prelude, of the opening idea (1a) being immediately presented in inversion (1b) pre-empts Bach's usual practice of inverting the opening material after the double bar, as he does in the D major prelude. But, as usual with Bach, the problem is the grit in the oyster, stimulating him to make strength out of potential weakness. In this case he solves the problem of beginning the second half by picking up the closing idea of the first half (7). He then gives a very satisfactory overall shape to the second half by reserving its next appearance to the very end. But Bach goes further in exploiting the problem in that it gives him the opportunity for extra development in the reprise. In the C minor Fantasia the reprise was brief, since only one element had been omitted from the middle series and was therefore available for use. The reprise in the B flat prelude is much more substantial. It has three elements which have been omitted from the middle series (1, 2 and 4), and also has substantial new development (X), here rather than in the middle series. But the main point is the way in which Bach capitalises on the two forms (1a and 1b) of the opening gambit. By separating them, and inserting ideas 2 and 4 between them, he achieves a formal subtlety which makes a virtue of the initial problem. The elaborateness of this formal scheme has led analysts to argue about the location of the reprise, or to doubt if there is a reprise at all. Seen in terms of Bach's formal prototypes, and the nature of the material, the plan and solution are clear.

FUGUE Like the A minor fugue, this conceals considerable contrapuntal art beneath a highly characterized surface and a general freedom of treatment. It belongs with those fugues that take a traditional subject and reinterpret it in the spirit of a galant dance, in this case the minuet. The traditional outline is in the subject of the B flat major fugue of Fischer's *Ariadne Musica* (Ex.8.26a); another version appears in the B flat three-part Sinfonia BWV 800 (Ex.8.26b).

There is no necessary connexion with B flat since the outline is also a commonplace of allemandes and gigues, and is used in D major in the character of a gigue in the last movement of the Fifth Brandenburg Concerto.

Traditional subjects were often too brief for Bach's purposes in the 48. In the G minor fugue of Book I and the D major fugue of Book II he split subjects into two elements, making a dramatic point of the contrast between these elements. In the B flat major fugue he has added two bars of a climbing figure (bb.3–4), which contrasts both in melodic direction and in articulation with the opening two bars. The slurred pairs of quavers have nothing to do

Ex.8.26 (a) Fischer: Fuga 17 from *Ariadne Musica*, bars 1–2; (b) three-part Sinfonia in B flat BWV 800, bars 1–2.

with grief-laden figures in the cantatas. Pirro characterises this subject rather as expressive of lassitude (1907 p.388); the paired quavers complement the opening while contributing to a sense of ease and gracefulness that matches the prelude.

Looking at other keyboard counterpoint of around this time, Peter Williams feels this fugue to belong with the *manualiter* preludes of *Clavier-Übung* III, particularly the first Kyrie BWV 672 (1980 II pp.179, 193). In fact a comparison with this points up the entirely secular feeling of this fugue. There is a delightful sense of freedom about the subject. Albrechtsberger and others have noted that it begins on an unorthodox degree of the scale (1790; Dok.III p.484), but too much should not be made of this since the first note is merely an auxiliary to the tonic. It would be much more surprising for the subject of a *stile antico* fugue, consisting of fundamental note values, to begin on the supertonic. This subject consists entirely of one decorative note value, and the fact that it begins with an unessential note after a quaver rest gives us the feeling of being drawn *in medias res*, just as the indefinite opening of a Schumann song draws us into its expressive world. A more striking irregularity, and one which equally contributes to the sense of freedom and gracefulness, is that the subject, in the character of a minuet, constitutes a five-bar phrase.

The minuet character is not just in the surface movement, but also in the fundamentally binary structure of the fugue. In a typical Bach sonata-dance one expects some regular phrases in the tonic to begin; then a sequence modulating to the dominant; then a closing idea with either a pedal effect or a chromatic twist. So here, the exposition ends with a cadence in the tonic (b.19); then there is a phrase that moves to the dominant (bb.20–8); followed by a closing idea with a chromatic twist, and a cadence (bb.29–32).[71] Within this there are several neat touches. The exposition ends with a long-held tonic b'♭ in the middle part (bb.14–16), answered in the modulating section by a long-held dominant f'' in the cantus (bb.22–4). The chromatic step at the end of the cantus answer in b.9 is taken up and extended in the middle part in bb.25–7, and then provides the chromatic tinge in the bass closing idea at bb.29–30.

The second 'half' covers the usual tonal ground for a binary piece. It starts in the dominant (b.32) and moves through the relative minor (bb.44ff) to the subdominant (b.54), the importance of this key centre being marked by a formal cadence, and thence back to the tonic, represented by the answer (bb.78ff). This 'half' then ends again with the closing idea before the double bar.

A particular feature of this fugue is that the first 'half' (to b.32) is relatively artless contrapuntally, whereas the second explores abstruse possibilities of a harmonic formula in triple counterpoint that works variously in permutations at the octave, 10th, and 12th. Ex.8.27 gives the permutations used in basic outline, all in B flat.

Ex.8.27 Permutations of triple counterpoint in the B flat major fugue: (a) basic counterpoint, bar 33; (b) inversion at the 10th and 12th, bar 41; (c) inversion at the octave and 12th, bar 49; (d) the same inverted at the octave, bar 56; (e) the basic counterpoint inverted at the octave, bar 63.

(a) gives the initial form. In (b) the crotchet parts are inverted at the 12th, the dotted minims at the 10th: this permutation is harmonically vague at the end, so Bach runs it on into G minor (b.44); (c) has the crotchet parts inverted at the octave and the dotted minims at the 12th: this is the weakest permutation in sonority, so Bach puts a firm cadence at the beginning (bb.48–9) and uses only the second half of it; (d) is a stronger version of the same permutation, with strongly dissonant 2nds between the lower parts: the beginning is nonetheless weak, so Bach does something else in b.55; (e) returns to the initial version, with the crotchet parts inverted at the octave.

The version of the formula from b.80 is not quite the same since the dotted minims enter a bar later: Bach clearly wanted to exploit the cumulative effect of putting the dotted-minim cadence in sequence. It is typical of him to construct this contrapuntal complexity from a common formula which, no matter how abstruse the counterpoints, ensures that the result will sound natural.

The written-out chord spread in b.88 (a three-part chord with arpeggiation sign in the London autograph) is a device Bach also used at the end of the E minor fugue of Book I to preserve the integrity of part-writing.

Prelude and Fugue in B flat minor BWV 891

PRELUDE It is difficult to find a parallel for this piece in Bach's works. On the face of it, it looks like a three-part Sinfonia or a movement from one of the sonatas for harpsichord and violin. Yet, in spite of its strict three-part texture, it is unique in having a non-thematic first entry of the treble part (b.3), and a bass that is thematic only twice in the entire piece (b.25, b.42). This is another example of the non-specific title Prelude allowing freedom and experimentation in the treatment of material. Given the continuo character of the bass, this seems an evocation of an instrumental trio on the keyboard, to go with the preludes in C sharp minor and A major.

The argument of the prelude is to take a long subject consisting of two elements, and combine it with motivically related figurations. Since the subject consists of two elements, one might expect these to be divided at some stage between parts, and this indeed happens in the middle section of the prelude, forming a telling structural pattern. The first element of the subject, similar in outline to that of the B flat major fugue, is in the middle part in bb.1–3½. Its falling pattern contrasts with the rising shape with repeated notes of the second element in bb.3½–5 whose ending, as often with Bach, is indefinite. This second element has often been seen as similar to the opening of the prelude in the same key in Book I. One expects its sequential shape to be used later for modulations, which indeed happens in the middle section.

The initial statement of the subject (bb.1–5) is surrounded by patterns of four quavers, falling or rising. The objective of surrounding it with these explains the unorthodox first cantus entry, which also obscures the precise nature of the subject on its first entry. From the dominant entry in the cantus at b.8, and for rest of the prelude, the figurations are dominated by the shape of the middle-part quaver figure at b.7. An episode based on this (bb.16–24) leads to entries in the tonic (b.25) and relative major (b.31). Bach here is not using his customary harmonic scheme for a binary movement, which would move from tonic to dominant via the relative major before the double bar, and in fact this prelude is better regarded as a ternary scheme.

The first section is bb.1–41, closing with a cadence in A flat major (the fact that this is the key of the answer for the relative major carries the logic of the first section on into the middle section). The middle section presents oblique settings of the subject, with its two elements migrating between parts. The A flat entry in the bass (b.42) is on the wrong degree of the scale (root, not 3rd), and the second element migrates to the middle voice (b.44) and modulates to G flat major, relative major of the subdominant. The middle voice then runs from the second element to the first when it reaches G flat (b.48), thus reversing the order of elements. The second element now migrates to the cantus (b.50) and runs on into E flat minor, subdominant and an important key centre, where there is a complete statement of both elements (b.55). This all makes a very satisfactory pattern for the middle section, i.e. element 1 in the bass, elements 2 and 1 in the middle voice, and elements 2, 1, and 2 in the treble, the treble providing a neat *enjambement* from middle section to reprise, just as the A flat entry had carried the logic of the first section into the middle section.

From b.55 Bach has his favourite plan of a subdominant reprise whose answer is in the tonic (b.62). The third section is in fact a freely condensed version of the first: bb.55–69 are a transposition of bb.1–15 with the upper parts inverted; bb.70–2 are based on bb.20ff; bb.78–81 transpose bb.37–40.

FUGUE This is one of the grandest, most ingenious, but also one of the most expressive of Bach's fugues. In contrast to those fugues of Book I that follow a similarly strict contrapuntal scheme (in D sharp minor and A minor) this fugue makes much more expressive and rhetorical point of its devices. One factor contributing to this is the number of expressive rests (*sospiri*) in the subject and its two countersubjects, which not only contribute to the expression of the subject but also aerate the texture of the fugue so that the devices can make a dramatic effect. Given the dense contrapuntal argument, the key of B flat minor contributes to the expressive ethos of weighty intellectual brooding, as in the equivalent fugue from Book I.

By writing this fugue originally in $\frac{3}{4}$ time Bach may have intended a *stile moderno* counterpart to the *alla breve* equivalent fugue in Book I. The harmonic subtlety of its 'modern' chromatic language contributes strongly to its expressive power. Bach works systematically through a similar scheme to that of the A minor fugue of Book I, of exposition of subject and two countersubjects; exposition in stretto recto (bb.27–37); exposition of the inverted subject (bb.42–63); exposition in stretto inverso (bb.80–93); and finally what amounts to a fifth exposition in stretto inverso in counterpoint at the 10th (bb.96–101). But now, unlike the A minor fugue of Book I, Bach does not proceed doggedly, without a break, from one exposition to the next. He separates them with episodes whose sequential nature gives a feeling of relaxation, and which allow each successive stage of the argument to make its own dramatic entrance.

Both of the writers on fugue who knew Bach personally give special attention to this fugue. Kirnberger comments on Bach's ability to devise material which is so rich in possibilities of permutation that he can in fact use only a small proportion of them in order to construct an artistic piece, and Kirnberger gives a dozen further combinations over and above those used by Bach (Dok.III pp.228–9). These are of interest in that they show that Bach, in the fourth exposition of the fugue where the subject is in inversion stretto (*al contrario riverso*; b.80, b.89), out of all the possibilities has chosen permutations where the second voice enters on the interval of a tritone, and which are therefore the most harmonically directional. As far as the ordinary stretto recto is concerned, the imitation at the 2nd and 7th may seem abstruse, but in fact the principle here has the same fundamental simplicity as in the A minor fugue of Book I. The subjects of both fugues outline an ascending scale. In imitation at two notes' distance the second part can enter on the tonic (as in the A minor fugue), but in imitation at one note's distance the second part must enter on the 7th degree. The objective in each case is to get into a sequence of parallel 3rds or 6ths.

Marpurg points out that the 7th degree is important for inversion imitation (*fuga contraria riversa*) in a minor key in that, to work out the imitation, an ascending scale beginning on the tonic is set against a descending scale beginning on the 7th degree as follows (in A minor):

a b c d e f g a
g f e d c b a g (1753 I p.6; Mann 1958 p.148)

This was a traditional explanation: the same example of contrary motion scales is given by Walther in his 'Praecepta' (1708 p.364).

Marpurg posits the central idea of this fugue as a demonstration of double counterpoint at the inversion, with imitations *per arsin et thesin* (i.e. with the onbeats and offbeats reversed). To these traditional skills we might add counterpoint at the 10th, used here, as in the G minor fugue, with superb dramatic effect. Demonstrations of this trick for making four parts out of two go back in Germany to the seventeenth-century *Kunstbuch* tradition (see the commentary on the G minor fugue). In fact the B flat minor fugue, very intriguingly, looks forward to Bach's own *Kunstbuch*, *The Art of Fugue*, in its use of traditional genera of counterpoint. It is as if the first four fugues of *The Art of Fugue* extract and systematically explore devices of counterpoint that are used only fleetingly here. Contrapunctus 1 uses for episodes the kind of interlocking figures that the B flat minor uses at bb.77½–79; Contrapunctus 2 uses rhythmic displacement of the subject (*per arsin et thesin*); Contrapunctus 3 features chromatic steps, as does the first countersubject of the B flat minor (*alla diritta*; what

Berardi might have called *di grado cromatico per semituono maggiore, e minore*); Contrapunctus 4 features a very similar figure of *contrapunto ostinato* (a figure constantly repeated) to that in the bass of the B flat minor at bb.67–8.

Within all this contrapuntal artifice Bach as usual shows masterly control of keyboard texture in order to make events clear. This is partly thanks to the very varied figurations in the two countersubjects, and partly to the way the main events are introduced. At the first stretto recto (b.27) the texture is reduced to a very aerated three parts. At the first inversion entry (b.42) the fact of the inversion is underscored by the descending chromatic scale of the inverted first countersubject, emphasised by being doubled in 6ths. The inverted exposition (b.67) is introduced by a rising sequence, and enters over a high pedal note whose decoration gives a very spacious hemiola rhythm; and the final peroration is strongly introduced after a dominant pedal (bb.94–5), over an interrupted cadence from which the bass runs down completely naturally into the inversion of the subject.

Prelude and Fugue in B major BWV 892

PRELUDE Judging by its broken-triad figurations, this prelude belongs in a group with the preludes in D sharp minor and the F sharp major, in which case they may be regarded as a Book II group, using similar material in different formal contexts: the D sharp minor in a binary sonata movement; the F sharp major in Bach's favourite structure of a series of presentations of the aria ritornello shape; and the B major in the more virtuoso style of a concerto. It concentrates on keyboard effects and textures, and for that reason is one of the most enjoyable of the Book II preludes from the purely playing point of view. Its nearest companion in Bach's other keyboard works is the Praeambulum of the G major Partita BWV 829 (1730) which equally presents a series of keyboard-technical ideas.

In the B major prelude and fugue Bach seems, as so often in the 48, to be setting out to combine old and new. In the prelude the combination is of old and new keyboard techniques, based on two forms of the scale. The first is the 'modern' one pivoted over the thumb: the opening bar looks like the demonstration of the B major scale in C.P.E. Bach's *Versuch*, which points out that it can be fingered in only one way (1753 Chap.1 para.56). This contrasts with the right-hand motif at the beginning of the B major prelude of Book I, which looks like an *évolution* for the three middle fingers. The second is the old manner of playing scales, alternating between the hands (from b.17). Although much used by keyboard composers up to the middle of the eighteenth century, this technique dates back to the *roulade* pattern of seventeenth-century composers such as Pachelbel (P. Williams 1994).

In spite of its free, toccata-like appearance this prelude has a similar logical agenda to the preludes in D major, F minor, and F sharp major, which present two contrasting ideas at the beginning and subsequently amalgamate them in various ways. The B major presents the scale (bb.1–2), then the contrasting broken-triad figure (bb.3ff) which is used for the modulation to the dominant (b.12). During the course of this modulation the broken triad merges back into the scale (from b.7½). Then there are two sections that systematically alternate two effects. The first has a trio-sonata texture with a scalic bass (from b.12), followed by a passage of *roulades* (from b.17). The second has a trio-sonata texture with a broken-triad bass (from b.23), followed by *roulades* (from b.29). The broken-triad figure dominates the lead-back (from b.33) to the reprise (b.37) which, freely recast, concentrates on the scale figure. It is a remarkable demonstration of how tight intellectual control can make the materials of virtuosity, which can be vapid and pointless, significant. This control greatly enhances the *joie de vivre* of the prelude.

FUGUE The short chord at the end of the prelude recalls the rhetorical device of *peroratio ex abrupto* (Meister 1993), and fittingly sets up the 'honourable and grave' sustained notes of the fugue's subject (see the discussion of Ex.4.2). Like the prelude, this fugue is also concerned with combining old and new. Here the combination is of a subject and its countersubjects, which show the same interest in combining traditional materials and techniques with the most recent galant trends. The ¢ time signature (used in the London autograph fair copy)[72] in itself combines old and modern styles in that either it can indicate the old-style *alla breve*, as in the E major fugue, or it can simply mean two minims in the bar, as in French dance music and fugues in 'modern' style such as those in E minor and F sharp major. The principal subject, moving exclusively in minims, is in the manner of seventeenth-century learned keyboard counterpoint. While in the 17th century this type of subject often included some mannered feature such as chromatic steps, here the type is brought up to date by having a decisively tonal outline: its essentially harmonic, rather than linear nature, outlines the standard tonal progression of the circle of 3rds (see Chapter Three section 5). It therefore consists almost entirely of leaps, rather than the traditional balance of leaps and steps. The leaps in themselves, though, as well as outlining tonal harmony, may also reflect the old *obligo di non uscir di grado*.[73] The cantus firmus character of the subject invites generic counterpoints, and Butler has seen in the regular syncopation of the first countersubject Berardi's *contrapunto alla zoppa* (limping counterpoint; 1983 p.297), though it could equally well be an example of *contrapunto perfidiato* with a regular rhythmic pattern (Berardi 1687 pp.18–20). The layout of the exposition is also old-style in that it has entries from the bass up, as in the chorus 'Sicut locutus est' from the Magnificat BWV 243 where this layout is explicitly designed to represent old traditions.

An instructive comparison is with the F sharp minor Ricercare of Pachelbel (ed. Seiffert p.30). Pachelbel's mannered element here is the rare key. His Ricercare is an inversion fugue, so he has an extra agenda not present in Bach's, but the overall scheme is similar. The initial expositions feature free counterpoints that contrast with the even notes of the subject in their dactylic rhythm (Ex.8.28a). After a cadence in the dominant a new subject is introduced, characterized by more quaver movement (Ex.8.28b), and this subject is retained, dominating the rest of the fugue in double counterpoint with the first subject at the octave and 12th.

Pachelbel's Ricercare has a series of eight expositions, presenting different combinations involving its two subjects, its counterpoints having the free plasticity of the seventeenth century, and it makes little drama of its restricted tonal scheme. The comparison with Bach's fugue reveals the extraordinary integrative quality of Bach's mind. The B major fugue is in three broad sections

Ex.8.28 J. Pachelbel: Ricercare in F sharp minor: (a) first subject and opening counterpoint; (b) second subject.

(bb.1–27 with a cadence in the dominant, 27–60 with a cadence in the subdominant, and 60–104) and is more tightly constructed in that the new subject introduced at b.28, and which dominates the remainder of the fugue, does not receive a separate exposition. Bach in general does not stop to give new subjects separate expositions, in the manner of the chorale fughetta, and in this respect the B major fugue is similar in plan to the A major fugue of Book I. A further comparison is with the B flat major fugue, which uses a binary dance structure and introduces a new countersubject after the dominant cadence, as it were the double bar. The B major fugue may be seen as a very much expanded working of this shape.

Within this broad structure Bach pursues two closely related 'modern' agendas. One is to explore the harmonic nature of the subject; the other is to explore the harmonic effect of double counterpoint at the 12th. The scheme of the fugue is therefore highly integrated, in spite of its seeming sectionality, in that both overall structure and motivic detail spring from the nature of the basic materials. The 3rd-based main subject outlines a typically galant chord, the leading-note 7th in a major key, one of the strikingly galant features of the final aria of BWV 209.[74] The outline is clear if the subject is written as a series of 3rds (Ex.8.29a). The first countersubject also outlines 7th chords: first a major 7th (b.6), then the leading-note 7th (b.7). The new subject, from b.28, also outlines a 7th chord (Ex.8.29b). Apart from forming 7th chords, the 3rds of the subject also generate most of the motivic material in quavers, notably the group of four quavers imitated between tenor and bass in bb.9–10, which decorates the interval of a 3rd and provides the material for the new subject introduced at b.28.

The first section presents the subject and two countersubjects in triple counterpoint. In the second section the material of the two countersubjects is

Ex.8.29 Fugue in B major: (a) the subject expressed as a series of 3rds, bars 2–3; (b) the first and second subjects as falling 3rds, giving a 7th outline, bars 28–9; (c) inversion at the 12th, making the subject modulate down a 3rd, bars 43–4.

subsumed into the new subject, which works in double counterpoint at the 12th with the original one. There is no doubt of this being a second subject, rather than a countersubject, since it dominates the rest of the fugue. To give it a separate exposition in the manner of Pachelbel would be superfluous to the argument of an already long piece. As with other contrapuntal tours de force in the 48, the principle of the counterpoint at the 12th is simple, i.e. to transpose what was a 3rd above the subject (Ex.8.29b) to a 3rd below it (Ex.8.29c). Not only is this in keeping with the 3rd-based nature of this fugue, but it also swings the tonality of the subject down a 3rd to its relative minor, giving a decidedly new harmonic colour to the inversion (bb.42–5, 53–6). The point of the third section is to balance this falling-3rd tendency with a rising-3rd one. The entry at b.60, which opens the third section, is placed on the 3rd of E major, and therefore its cadence (bb.62–3) is up a 3rd in G sharp minor. A similar entry at b.85 takes the subject strategically from D sharp minor up to the dominant, F sharp major.

After the entry at b.60 there follows a long episode before the final series of tonic and dominant entries begins at b.75. In keeping with the large-scale dramatic projection of many of the Book II fugues, this episode (bb.63–74) takes the top three parts high up the keyboard, thereby making a special dramatic point of the tonic return in the bass at b.75. A similar effect on a smaller scale is in the second section at bb.45ff. Here the very prominent bass entry at b.48 is followed by a tenor one at b.53 which is extremely difficult to make clear on the harpsichord. Nonetheless the placing of the first note of the tenor entry on the last note of a two-bar bass sequence, and the fact that the tenor entry answers in a fashion the very prominent bass one, makes the ear expect it. This mastery of keyboard sonority is as much part of Bach's achievement as any ingenuity of contrapuntal working. Sonority is important too in those larger fugues of Book II whose climax is a rhetorical rather than a contrapuntal one. Counterpoint is the essence of fugue, but its traditional nature is also as a dimension of wit. Bach takes the little auxiliary figure at the end of the first section (alto at the end of bb.22 and 24, bass at the end of b.23), surely the most unconsidered trifle in all the grand argument of this fugue, and makes it the basis for his final rhetorical peroration at bb.88–9, at the same time giving it the neat structural function of the closing idea in the binary sonata.

Prelude and Fugue in B minor BWV 893

PRELUDE This prelude was originally in **c** time with bars twice as long as in the final ¢ version (in the London autograph; the **c**-time version is reflected in sources of the Altnickol group other than Altnickol's 1744 copy, see NBA

V/6.2 pp.298–300). The c-time version has note values half the length of the ¢ version, and its predominance of semiquavers and demisemiquavers gives it a visual similarity to the final state of the C major prelude, and also to the preludes in F sharp major and A flat major. Galant features of these last two preludes have already been noted. The B minor adds an unusually high number of these in performance indications: turns, staccatos, slurred 'sighs', reinforcing its galant nature.

Bach's reason for changing the time signature remains a matter of conjecture. Kroll, Bischoff and others have surmised that it was for convenience of notation. But the labour of writing beams does not seem to have deterred Bach in, for example, the B flat major two-part Invention or in the other Book II preludes which share these note values. It is more likely that Bach intended some subtle adjustment of rhythmic projection, along the lines that Kirnberger suggested for the F major fugue (Dok.III pp.233–4, trans. Beach and Thym pp.387–8). Notated in semiquavers, the opening *soggetto* in the treble looks superficially like the concertante, harmonic-wash type of figuration used in the preludes in D sharp minor, F sharp major, and B major. This is misleading since the figure, although triad-based, is the fundamental *inventio* of the piece. The ¢-time notation removes the impression of too fleeting a metre and, since the ¢ time signature can apply to either fast or slow tempi Bach, who generally adds tempo words only in cases where there is an ambiguity, has added the word Allegro in the London autograph.

The difference of time signature is, however, a subtle one. In c time, quavers are a fundamental note value but semiquavers are decorative and therefore candidates for freer performance. Demisemiquavers are an extra decorative level of note value, with the implication of yet more freedom of shaping. Most of the demisemiquavers form the ornament of the turn, written as such with an ornament sign at b.32 in the London autograph and b.53 in the Altnickol sources. Since Bach is treating this ornament motivically he has not generally used an ornament sign, which could sometimes be ambiguous, but written out exactly the notes he wants. Nonetheless, in terms of c time the semiquavers and demisemiquavers can on no account be played with the strict rhythm of fundamental note values. This is a further significance of the direction Allegro, to clarify that the quavers in ¢ time are decorative, not fundamental, note values.

Formally this prelude is yet another variant of the type in a number of sections based on the aria ritornello shape in its sonata guise, which Bach particularly favours in Book II. In texture and motivic working it belongs with the invention types in Book II, such as the D sharp minor and E minor preludes, with which it shares the technique of combining ever new counterthemes with the main subject. This seems to be Bach's way of reconciling the galant sonata principle, with its succession of different ideas, with his urge to extract the maximum development from a single idea. The ordering of the counterthemes then determines the formal structure of the piece.

The prelude is in three sections, each of which runs through the phases of the sonata structure. It begins with a closed period of two four-bar phrases, the second of which inverts the opening material. This is followed by a sequential passage (bb.9–12) and a closing idea (bb.13–16). Rather than taking us to the dominant, as in a binary movement, this takes us to the relative major, which introduces yet another (and even more galant) countertheme (bb.21–4). The middle section has two statements of the main theme, with yet a new countertheme in bb.25–8, then an inverted reprise of the version at bb.5–8. This is followed by the sequential passage, now with the leading part in the bass and a new counterpoint in the treble (bb.33–6) followed by a more relaxed bridge which takes us to one of Bach's most freely treated subdominant reprises (from b.41). This has a version of the original eight-bar opening period, now compressed into four bars (bb.41–4, with the contrapuntal exchange after two bars); then the sequential passage (bb.45–8) and the closing idea (bb.49–52). The rest is a free extension of the basic materials, with a rhetorical pause to dramatize the tonic return. The fact that this uses the final new countertheme (bb.21–4, cf. bb.59–60) gives an ambiguity of binary, with the same theme closing each section, and ternary, based on successive workings of the aria ritornello shape: a subtle combination of formal types typical of Bach. This scheme has been worked a number of times in Book II, but always in a new, original, yet seemingly inevitable way.

FUGUE The use of passepied metre in this fugue makes one suspect that here, as in the F major fugue of Book I, Bach may be updating a generic type of subject. In the case of the F major fugue the relationship to a particular fugue from Fischer's *Ariadne Musica* is close. If the B minor has no obvious particular prototype, a subject featuring octave leaps is nonetheless a standard type in verset fugues.[75] Otherwise they are unusual in keyboard music, though common enough in orchestral string music where clarity of texture and playability are not such a problem. Whether Bach was consciously referring to either of these types or not, the octave leaps are the prominent feature of the subject, and one of the sources of wit in this sparkling piece.

Although the passepied metre is clear, the B minor fugue does not make the thoroughgoing use of dance phraseology that the F major fugue of Book I does. Bach seems to have wanted to make a freer and more flexible use of the dance type here. There is a striking lack of structural marker cadences, the only one being the dominant cadence at bb.27–8, and even this important punctuation mark is elided by coming in the middle of a subject entry. On the smaller scale, the subject's two-bar units correspond to the passepied dance steps, with the performance implication that there should be a slight accent, or 'touching down', at the at the beginning of every dance-step pattern, that is on the even-numbered bars. Quavers should be light, without heavy articulation, and semiquavers even lighter to create the feeling of delicacy suggested by the tiny steps of the dance (Little 1975 pp.122–3). It may be that the leaps featured in this fugue, starting with the subject, have an element of satire on this.

Many have commented on Bach's finishing Book II with such a light-hearted piece, lacking in contrapuntal artifice. The equivalent fugue in Book I treats B minor in the very serious character of the key that completes the chromatic octave and is therefore expressive of the fullness of human suffering, with elaborate chromaticism and chiastic outlines. The Book II fugue relates to a different association of the key, with galant French dance music and particularly the flute, of which it is one of the home keys, as in the B minor Overture BWV 1067. Book II was clearly intended to complement Book I rather than replicate it, and Bach chose a different character for this fugue just as he chose a different type of C major prelude, transposing the available broken-chord pattern one to C sharp where it could make a different point.[76]

Wit and freedom are the main characteristics of this fugue, and Bach's ability to make positive capital out of what are potential flaws in his material. He combines the awkward octave leaps of the subject initially with contrasting, smooth-stepping figurations (bb.9–10), but then introduces a new countersubject which itself features leaps (bb.29ff), and he spends much of the rest of the fugue finding playable patterns for permutations of this and the subject. The first countersubject has what would normally be considered a flaw in a countersubject in that it implies a stretto with the subject (bb.7–8), thus pre-empting the effect of a real stretto later in the fugue. Bach plays on this very wittily in two parts at bb.69ff, where it is not clear until b.73 which part has the subject and which the countersubject; and he finishes the fugue, from b.97, by playing on it in three parts, with middle, bass, and cantus versions of the subject's opening figure. In common with Bach's lighter keyboard fugues, there is freedom in the treatment of parts. In the London autograph version of b.16 the countersubject semiquavers migrate from the cantus to the middle part at the end of the bar, emphasising the stretto in the countersubject.[77] This is a small effect here, but it is made the basis of a whole episode in bb.60ff. The general high spirits are much enhanced by the prevalence of trills chasing each other, an effect of *joie de vivre* as much here as in the fugues in F sharp major and A minor.

Ellis, in his computer analysis of the subjects of the 48 fugues, leaves his reader with an intriguing 'final thought' by juxtaposing this subject with that of *The Art of Fugue* (1980 p.424). The resemblance is no doubt entirely accidental, yet the mastery shown in the B minor fugue is no less than in Bach's later, more overt demonstrations.

Appendix A

Examples 7.30, 8.9 and 8.21

Ex.7.30 (a) *Wegweiser*: Tastata; (b) Murschhauser: *Arpeggiata overo Toccata secundi toni* (1703), bars 1–4; (c) Fischer: Tastada from 'Terpsichore' suite (1738), bars 1–4.

Ex.8.9 Fugue in C sharp major; four versions in parallel: (a) 19-bar version; (b) 30-bar version; (c) 35-bar version, with final revisions on extra staves.

Ex.8.9 (Continued)

Ex.8.9 (Continued)

Ex.8.9 (Continued)

Ex.8.9 (Continued)

23

Ex.8.9 (Continued)

Ex.8.9 (Continued)

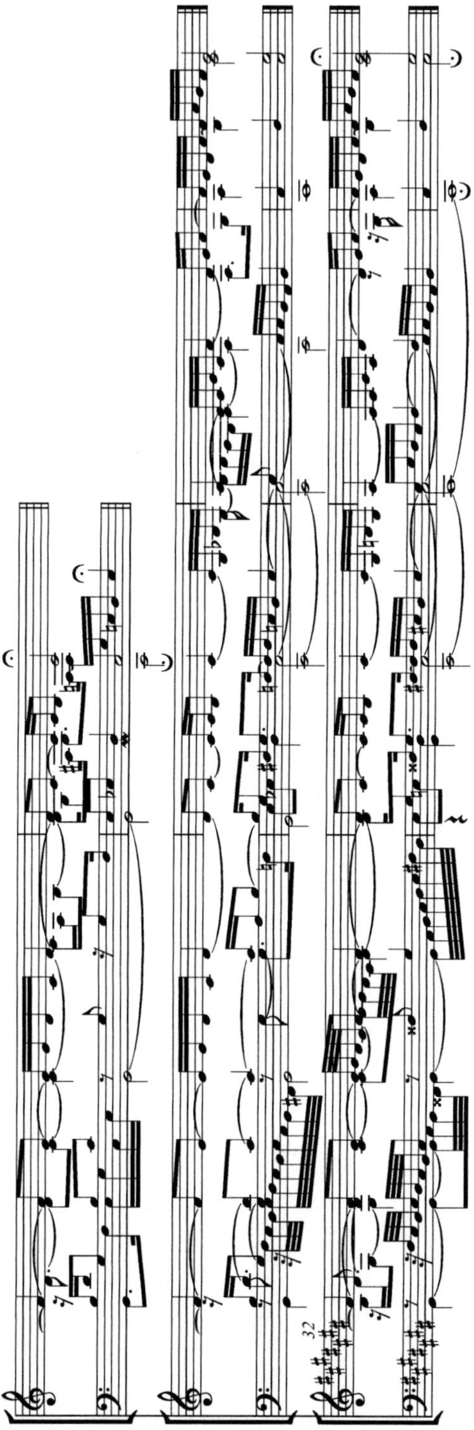

Ex.8.21 Fugue in G minor, inversions of subject and countersubject: (a) basic block; (b) inverted at the octave; (c) inverted at the 10th; (d) inverted at the 12th; (e) inverted at the 10th and 12th; (f) simultaneous possibilities.

Appendix B

The problem of temperament

The harmonic series

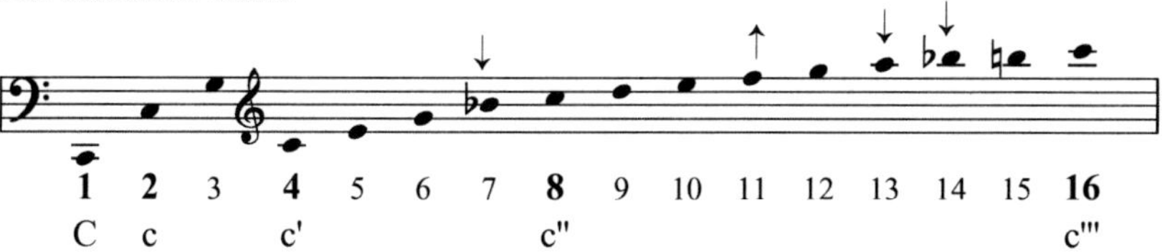

1. Proportions of intervals are:
   2:1 = octave
   3:2 = 5th
   4:3 = 4th
   5:4 = major 3rd
   6:5 = minor 3rd

2. The problem of tuning is that:
   3 pure major 3rds (5:4 × 5:4 × 5:4 = **125**:64)
   do not equal a pure octave (2:1 or **128**:64)
   the difference (128:125) is called a **diesis** (*c.*41 cents)[1]

   4 pure 5ths (c–g g–d' d'–a' a'–e''
   3:2 × 3:2 × 3:2 × 3:2 = **81**:16)
   do not equal two octaves plus a major 3rd
   (c–c' c'–c'' c''–e''
   2:1 × 2:1 × 5:4 = 20:4 or **80**:16)
   the difference (81:80) is called the **syntonic comma** (*c.*22 cents)

   12 pure 5ths (**531441**:4096)
   do not equal 7 octaves (128:1 or **524288**:4096)
   the difference (531441:524288) is called the **ditonic comma** (*c.*24 cents)

Therefore, in tuning, if you have pure 5ths, the major 3rds will be wide; if you have pure major 3rds, the 5ths will be narrow.

Pure major 3rds are noticeably lower than those tuned in equal temperament.

3. In **Medieval** music, Nos.1–4 of the series were perceived as perfect consonances; tuning was **Pythagorean** with pure 5ths, and the wide major 3rds (Pythagorean 3rds) were only semi-consonant.

In the **Renaissance** (from *c.*1400) Nos.1–6 came to be perceived as perfect consonances; tuning was **meantone**, with pure major 3rds and narrow 5ths.

In the early **eighteenth century**, Rameau (1720s) considered Nos.1–8 as fundamental, to explain the materials of tonal harmony, which consists of 7th chords as well as triads.

Tuning became either a subtle compromise or **equal temperament** (all 5ths 1⁄12 ditonic comma narrow; all major 3rds ⅔ syntonic comma wide).

1 A cent is 1% of an equal-tempered semitone.

Notes

Introduction

1 Thus the title-page of Salomon Franck's (Weimar 1718) publication of cantata texts reads (1) Epistolisches Andachts-Opffer (2) In Geistlichen CANTATEN (3) über Die Sonn- und Fest-Tages Episteln durch das ganze Jahr (4) Angezündet von Salomon Francken (5) Fürstl. Sächsis. Gesamten Ober-*Consistorial-Secretario* in Weimar (6) Weimar und Jena bey Johann Felix Bielcken 1718 (reproduced in Hamel 1951); Bach's theological library offers many similar examples (see Leaver 1983).

2 The abbreviation *p.t.* is normally taken to stand for *pro tempore*, i.e. Bach still held this post but was already scheduled to move to Leipzig. Bach's appointment in Leipzig was not, however, confirmed until April 1723; the date 1722 is an addition to the title-page, and may correct an earlier date (KB V/6.1 p.21). Peter Williams has suggested that the abbreviation stands for *pleno titulo*, i.e. full title (1980 II p.3), but this would not make sense on other title-pages.

3 Dok.III p.476, NBR p.322; Stephen Daw questions whether Bach played through the whole Book at a sitting, or bit by bit on a number of occasions (Butt 1997 p.197).

4 '. . . più per fuggir l'otio, che per altro fine' (ed. Butler p.X).

5 A clear and detailed account of the sources is given by Richard Jones in the Critical Notes of AB I; more detail is given by Alfred Dürr in KB V/6.1, with a concise summary in Dürr 1998 pp.68–70.

6 Facsimile edition, introduced by H. Pischner and K.-H. Köhler (Leipzig: VEB Deutscher Verlag für Musik, 1971).

7 KB V/6.1 p.91; facsimile edition, introduced by R. Kirkpatrick (New Haven: Yale University Press, 1959); ed. W. Plath in NBA V/5.

8 The last owner of the MS was Franz Konwitschny, director of the Gewandhaus Orchestra; the microfilm is in the Bach-Archiv, Leipzig.

9 See Dürr 1984 pp.60–7 for a full discussion of possibilities.

10 Dadelsen 1958 p.35; it was not until 1732 that he started to use the double-sharp sign 𝄪.

11 Buttstett's wife (Martha Lämmerhirt) came from the same family as Bach's mother.

12 '[J.M.] Bachs [Sonata? now lost] *Revange* wird doch wohl der klare Kern seyn. Ey! hätte doch der Lully *redivivus* lieber seine Marsch-*Testes sub lit H.* weggelassen/ und uns ein paar *testiculi* von dieser raren *Revange* (unsere Frantzosen schreiben es: *Revanche* oder *Revenche*) mitgetheilet/ daß man hätte sehen können/ was es für ein Wunder-Thier sey/ und ob mit ihm auszukommen!' (Mattheson 1717 pp.222-3).

Mattheson must have further irritated Bach in 1725 by publishing a mocking criticism of his word setting in BWV 21 (Dok.II pp.153–4, NBR p.325); for an assessment of Bach's relation to Mattheson, see Stauffer 1983.

13 Breitkopf later sold MS copies for five thalers; Bach's most elaborate printed keyboard publication (*Clavier-Übung* III, 1739) went on sale for the expensive price of three thalers.

14 Breckoff 1965 p.4.

15 The title of these, *Die wohlklingende Fingersprache*, may be a comment on Bach's *Das wohltemperirte Clavier*, emphasising ingratiating eloquence over traditional technicalities.

16 Details are in the Critical Notes of AB II; more detail is in KB V/6.2 and a summary in Dürr 1998 pp.70–3; see also Breckoff 1965, Brokaw 1986, Franklin 1989a, and Tomita 1990, 1993, 1995.

17 *GB-Lbl* MS Add. 35021; facsimile edition, introduced by D. Franklin and S. Daw (London: The British Library, 1980); edited by A. Dürr in NBA V/6.2 (Fassung A).

18 For the Bärenreiter offprint (BA II) Dürr has avoided concocting a hybrid and given what seems to be the latest version of each piece, and revived the good old system of Kroll and Bischoff of giving significant variants in the margin so that players can make their own decisions.

19 Early versions are edited in NBA V/6.2 Anhang, reprinted in PF.

20 NBA V/6.2 p.XVI: this title-page is pasted over the original one; Alfred Dürr asked for it to be lifted but the curators were unwilling to interfere with the MS.

Chapter One: Clavier

1 Kirkpatrick 1981 p.302. Landowska 1965 Plate 9 shows her playing a seventeenth-century fretted clavichord in her own collection, and has an amalgam of her writings on this issue on pp.139–50.

2 For Dolmetsch's recording of the 48 see Campbell 1975 Chapter XX; Elizabeth Goble (1977) describes her clavichord lessons with him; Kirkpatrick (1981) gives a good impression of Dolmetsch's personality and playing, as well as an account of his own recordings. Dolmetsch's recordings for Columbia have been reissued by The Dolmetsch Foundation (ARCT 1017); Kirkpatrick's 1959 and 1967 recordings have been reissued by DGG Archiv (463 601–2 and 463 623–2).

3 *Manuductio ad organum* (Salzburg).

4 Early uses of clavier to mean clavichord are Valentin Trichter's 1742 *Lexicon* for elegant young men; the 1751 edition of Marpurg's *Die Kunst das Clavier zu spielen* (a German rewriting of François Couperin's *L'art de toucher le clavecin*) uses clavier for clavichord as opposed to *Spinett* or *Flügel* (p.6); the 1757 edition of Barthold Fritz's *Anweisung* (Vorbericht); numerous uses in the later eighteenth century are cited by Auerbach (1930 pp.44–62).

5 For example: Krieger 1699, where large *pedaliter* pieces imply the organ; Sorge *c.*1739, for organ, harpsichord and clavichord (see Auerbach 1930 p.4). In many collections for clavier (e.g. Kuhnau's) one might see a distinction of repertory, with French dances more suited to stringed keyboards, and large preludes and fugues at their best on the organ.

6 None concern his playing the harpsichord, but to maintenance of instruments (Dok.II pp.41, 70, 86) or collecting a new instrument from Berlin (p.73).

7 For detailed surveys of Bach's harpsichords, see Stauffer 1995 and Koster 1999.

8 Berlin, Musikinstrumenten-Museum des Staatlichen Instituts für Musikforschung Preussischer Kulturbesitz, Kielflügel No.316.

9 Ernst showed that the keyboard, soundboard, and much of the rest could not date from before 1850 (pp.28–9).

10 A Breitenbach instrument with precisely this disposition is described by Adlung (1768 p.110, written in the late 1720s).

11 Krickeberg and Rase 1987. Liebermann (1990) thinks it questionable that the J.H. Harrass who died in 1714 was the same as the instrument maker, but found two more harpsichord-making members of the Harrass family in the Grossbreitenbach church records: Johann Mathias (1671–1746) and his son Johann Heinrich (1707–78). If Bach owned this instrument, Krickeberg and Rase wonder, did he order it with this disposition, or was he given it?

12 Germann 1985 p.134; Krickeberg and Rase 1987 pp.305–10; Koster 1996 p.71; Ahrens 1998 p.57.

13 1802 Vorrede p.v, NBR p.419; see Schrade 1937 for essential background to interpreting Forkel and Rochlitz.

14 See Henkel 1991 for keyboard instruments in Leipzig households in Bach's time.

15 They are first illustrated by C.P.E. Bach (1753 Chapter 3 paras 19 and 20, see Cooper 1971 p.36); Thielo (1753 p.55) also describes, but does not notate, *Bebung*.

16 Forkel MS pp.72–3. A similar list is in Forkel 1782 p.10, describing things the harpsichord cannot do.

17 See the quotation from J.F. Reichardt given on p.36 of Mitchell's translation of C.P.E. Bach's *Versuch*; C.P.E. Bach was dissatisfied with clavichords of Fritz and Hass, preferring those of Friederici and Silbermann (Ottenberg 1987 pp.168–9). According to Adlung, 'Ein Clavichord soll stark klingen, jedoch aber nicht pochend, sondern lieblich, auf Harfenart' (1768 II p.152). Reichardt (1776) praised Silbermann's clavichords for their loudness, and C.P.E. Bach gave his to a Lithuanian nobleman who was hard of hearing (Cooper 1971 p.173).

18 Baffert (1988 p.191) cites the following, from a review published in 1780 by the Abbé Grosier of La Borde's *Essai sur la musique ancienne et moderne*, and which is not in Dok.III: 'Un célèbre Compositeur d'Italie vint en Allemagne, prévenu contre le Clavicorde, qu'il regardoit comme un instrument imparfait que l'on conservoit encore par habitude. Un de ses Compatriotes qui habitoit ce pays depuis long-temps, le conduisit chez un grand Maître, (*Sébast. Bach*, père de tous les *Bachs*, autant que je puis me rappeller). Déjà étonné par les préludes de cet habile Professeur sur le Clavicorde, il fut attendri aux larmes par un *adagio* qui les suivit, attendit à peine la fin du morceau pour se jetter au cou de l'Artiste, & s'écria: *c'est le Roi des instruments. . . .*' The status of this reminiscence is uncertain, and no year or other corroborating evidence is given; the preludes were probably improvisations, and the Adagio may have been something like the E flat minor prelude of Book I.

19 Mrs Delany's brother Bernard Granville was given by Handel a copy of Johann Krieger's *Anmuthige Clavier-Übung* (Nuremberg 1699), about which Handel said that he had 'in his youth formed himself upon his plan, and said that Krieger was one of the best of his time for the organ, and to form a good player, but the clavichord must be made use of by beginners instead of the organ or harpsichord' (Burrows 1994 p.8).

20 It was published in the same year in London by J.D. Fletcher whose English preface mentions only the harpsichord, and that the pieces were 'peculiarly adapted to that Instrument'. Mattheson tells us that clavichords were rare in England, and disliked by English harpsichordists (1725 pp.150–1).

21 This instrument is discussed and illustrated by Brauchli (1998 p.148); the date 1716 has more recently been confirmed by Siegbert Rampe. Of the others, one is by Johann Christoph Fleischer (1723) at the Drottningholm Theatre (Boalch 1995 p.316). This is in many ways an exceptional instrument, with a most unusual

compass for its date (FF–d') and very elaborate and expensive decoration. Significantly, it is made on the key rack of a fretted clavichord with the normal C/E–c' compass, and with a few notes added at either end (Whitehead 1999). The other is by H.A. Haas (Hamburg 1732; Whitehead and Nex 2000 pp.156–9, 170–1). There are no further German unfretted clavichords that can be securely dated before 1742. An instrument formerly thought to be by Gottfried Silbermann (1723) at Markneukirchen (Boalch 1995 p.627) is now known not to be by Silbermann, and is thought to be Saxon or Bohemian from *c.*1740–50. There seems to have been something of a prior vogue for unfretted clavichords in Sweden, since there are unfretted instruments by Johan Petter Roos (1726; Jakobstads Museum, Finland) and by Daniel Stråle (1738; Nordiske Museet, Stockholm). Both of these have the same feature as the Fleischer of being made on the key rack for a fretted instrument, showing that unfretted instruments were unusual. These makers did not think it worth setting up a whole new keyboard design for an order that might not be repeated (Helenius-Öberg 1986 pp.118, 124, 146; Barnes 1991 p.200). It is difficult to know what to make of J.G. Walther's (1732) article 'Faber (Daniel Tobias)', often cited as the first German reference to an unfretted clavichord. Faber invented it, but the fact that it was 'durchgehends Bundfrey' was only one novel feature, others being three special-effect stops. Walther's article 'Bundfrey' shows that he meant genuinely unfretted, rather than double-fretted as the term usually meant at this time, in that he says the chromatic semitones should have separate choirs of strings as well as the diatonic ones.

22 Speth submitted this publication to the Augsburg Cathedral authorities anonymously as the work of Italian organists, even though he probably was himself the composer (see T. Fedke, preface to the Bärenreiter edition). The unfretted clavichord may have been another aspect of the Italian dimension, emphasising the modernity of his tonal language. Seventeenth-century Italian clavichords were usually fretted, but Mersenne illustrates one which is unfretted up to the top octave (c'–c"; 1636, Livre troisiesme des instrumens à chordes, pp.114–15).

23 It is difficult to measure exactly the tuning of tangents, but given a rough value for the diesis of 41 cents, one would expect a range of around 80 cents for the chromatic semitone to 120 for the diatonic semitone (the equal-tempered semitone being 100 cents). Henkel (1981) gives values for 11 German fretted clavichords from the second half of the seventeenth to the second third of the eighteenth centuries, and it is remarkable how often this range is exceeded, particularly in the direction of narrowing the chromatic semitone.

24 The clavichord by Johann Jacob Donat (Leipzig 1700; see Henkel 1981 p.37), which might on the face of it seem an ideal candidate for Book I of the 48, with its fully chromatic C–c''' compass and double fretting, is in fact untypical of this period both in its compass and in its lavish and expensive decoration, including a painted soundboard. It is for a wealthy amateur rather than a student professional.

25 See Brauchli 1998 pp.98–9 for fretting patterns of surviving instruments.

26 Meer 1975 p.103; Henkel 1981 p.17; Brauchli 1998 p.97, p.100 Nos.12–17.

27 For spinets in Leipzig households in Bach's time see Henkel 1991 p.58.

28 A typical example is No.49 in Henkel 1979, which obviously survived on account of its unusual painted decoration.

29 Adlung began the manuscript of *Musica mechanica organoedi* in 1726 and constantly added to it thereafter. According to Marpurg he wrote it while a student at Jena (1723–7; see Mahrenholz, *Nachwort* to the facsimile edition).

30 Except for two notes in *La bandoline*: FF (as an alternative) and BB♭.

31 Dok.II p.504; Buchmayer 1908 p.76; Kinsky 1936 p.161.

32 The valuers do not seem to have seen the instruments involved since Johann

Christian had them 'bey sich' (English translation in Spitta III pp.358–9).

33 Played in this manner the C sharp major prelude might have a similar effect to the organ prelude on 'Ich ruf zu dir' BWV 639; for further organ performance of pieces from the 48 in the 19th century see Busch 2000.

34 Krasske (1695 p.11) describes the fully chromatic C–c''' keyboards of the organ of the Oberkirche at Frankfurt an der Oder as the up-to-date compass; Bach's console at Arnstadt is more typical in lacking the low C♯; Walter Emery's reference to house organs with low C♯ (1970 p.167) is probably to English organs, albeit by makers of German origin.

35 For house organs in Leipzig households in Bach's day see Henkel 1991 p.58.

36 See Schünemann 1933 p.88.

37 The version of BWV 870a/1 in N.10490 has fewer ties than those in P 804 and P 1089. Yo Tomita thinks that this is probably for harpsichord effectiveness (1990 p.24).

38 Werner Breig notes that building fugue entries up from the bottom voice is typical of the 48, but not of Bach's organ works (1995 p.27).

39 Such as the E major prelude and fugue of Book II, which are close in style to the verset tradition and in one source have pedal indications (P 1182, in the Kirnberger tradition; this source dates from the second half of the eighteenth century, but not after *c.*1780; the 'Ped.' indications were added to the bass line in a different coloured ink after the MS had been finished).

40 Also Lauten-Clavessin, Lautenclavicymbel: the terminology is very varied; the term Lautenwerk points to the fact that most were made by organ builders.

41 Bunge 1905 p.29, Flade 1950 p.408; more recently André Burguète checked the Cöthen inventories for this document but was unable to find it (Henning and Richter 1982 p.477).

42 The organ builder Anton Berger mentioned in his application for citizenship there his 'newly invented' instrument that gives the sound of the lute with gut strings and a keyboard (Henning 1993 p.20).

43 The fullest account of the documentary evidence is in Henning and Richter 1982 and 1988.

44 A careful presentation of the documentary evidence is in Ferguson 1967; see also 'Lute-harpsichord' in *New Grove 2*.

45 Only one 14-course instrument by Hoffmann survives (in the Leipzig Musikinstrumenten-Museum); 14 courses were rare, 13 courses were more normal; the Hoffmann instrument has other peculiarities.

46 Other than the Gigue Double of the C minor suite BWV 997 which goes to c'''. This double does not figure in the only tablature source of the piece, and all other sources give it as for clavier or harpsichord.

47 For a description of the Potsdam pianofortes see P. Badura-Skoda 1993 pp.163–6.

48 A much later account given by Frederick II to Baron van Swieten is plainly inaccurate (Dok.III p.276, NBR pp.366–7). It is not known if C.P.E. Bach or Agricola were present at this event: C.P.E. Bach had been in Frederick's employment since 1738, and Agricola was at the time Composer to the Prussian Court. The reason for J.S. Bach's visit was an invitation from Frederick (Ottenberg 1987 p.50).

49 Engel 1879 p.468, P. Badura-Skoda 1993 p.159; various proposals have been made for the new type of 'Clavicymbel' other than the pianoforte, including the Lautenwerk (Stauffer 1995 p.299) and the Hammerpantaleon (Koster 1996 p.78).

50 Koster 1996 pp.77–8; by 1743 Bach had written all his clavier works other than parts of *The Art of Fugue*, and the *Musical Offering*.

51 Müller 1982 p.39, C. Wolff 1987 p.205, E. Badura-Skoda 1991 p.161.

Chapter Two: Well-tempered

1 1776 pp.2–3. Marpurg was probably quoting from memory and associating it with *The Art of Fugue*, for which he wrote a preface to the second printing in 1752, after Bach's death.

2 See 'Temperament' and 'Well-tempered clavier' in *New Grove 2*; Klop 1974 and Clayson and Garrett 1980 for the mathematical proportions; see Appendix B for a simple explanation of the problem of temperament.

3 1928 p.139.

4 Billeter 1970 p.73.

5 1985a, German version 1987b.

6 For a detailed account of tuning in German organs from Praetorius 1619 to Werckmeister, see H. Vogel 1986.

7 For the immediate background to Werckmeister, see Friedrich 1989 p.13, and Beckmann 1990.

8 *Subsemitonia* were never popular among seventeenth-century German organ builders and players (H. Vogel 1986 pp.240f); Werckmeister admits to not having tried them in 1687 (p.120). The words 'schöne Veränderungen' are specifically applied to enharmonic possibilities of the tritone in 1691 (p.61, the section explaining Temperament III).

9 Rasch 1983 p.7.

10 The French acoustician Sauveur (1707 p.119) says that this was the tuning used by the best makers and musicians in Paris at that time, and that they absolutely rejected equal temperament. He himself recommended the –⅕-comma option (see Rasch 1984 p.197). In Germany ⅙-comma meantone is mentioned by Sorge (1744), who later strongly criticised Gottfried Silbermann's use of it. Silbermann was trained in Alsace.

11 1707 p.111.

12 See Rasch 1983 p.34.

13 'Temperament' in *New Grove 2*.

14 1697 p.34. This canzona is now lost. It cannot be the *Phantasia supra ut, re, mi, fa, sol, la, clavicymbalis accommodata* printed by Kircher (1650 pp.466–75), which transposes the hexachord into four different modes and has a version with chromatic steps. Werckmeister is quite clear that the canzona he knows goes systematically round the circle of 5ths. It may have been modelled on John Bull's famous chromatic *Ut, re, mi, fa, sol, la* (MB XIV No.17), which was known in Austria, copied out by Poglietti and even published under his name (Riedel 1980 p.157). Part of a fantasia for viols by Alfonso Ferrabosco the younger, in which the hexachord is transposed around the entire circle of 5ths, was published by Angelo Berardi (Bologna 1690) as an example of equal temperament (Field 1996 p.26).

15 I Kings 7, in particular the 12 oxen that supported the molten sea, the twelve 5ths of equal temperament each being narrowed by 1⁄12 comma.

16 It was perhaps for this reason that Werckmeister ended by attributing a kind of moral virtue to the proportions of equal temperament ('Welches dann ein Vorbild seyn kan/ wie alle fromme/ und wohl *temperirte* Menschen/ mit Gott in stets währender gleicher/ und ewiger *Harmonia* leben/ und *jubiliren* werden.' 1707 p.110). The numerological approach to temperaments has been revivified in our own day notably by Herbert Kellner, who was inspired by Harry Hahn's numerological interpretation of *The Well-tempered Clavier* to devise a tuning for it.

17 Neidhardt 1706 p.41.

18 Others who made calculations for equal temperament around this time, apart from

Neidhardt and Sinn, were the Wernigerode theologian Heinrich Georg Neuss (1654–1716), inventor of the pitch pipe and clavier tuner, who took lessons by post in matters musical from J.G. Walther's friend Heinrich Bokemeyer; the Ansbach capellmeister Georg Heinrich Bümler (1669–1745), whose system was published by Mattheson (1722 Pt.I pp.ii, 52), and who later became a founder-member of Mizler's Corresponding Society of Musical Sciences, of which Bach was to be the 14th member in 1747; and a certain Henfling, reported by Bümler (1722) to have calculated equal temperament *c.*1702 more completely than Neidhardt in 1706; others reported in Meckenheuser 1727 are engineer Faulhaber in Ulm, who calculated it in 1652 (p.9), and the Hamburg geometrician Heinrich Meissner in 1692 (p.10).

19 Adlung 1768 II p.54; although not published till after Adlung's death this book was complete in MS by 1729.

20 Adlung 1758 p.312. Meckenheuser spent three days trying to get it right, till his organ builder finally got fed up and walked out.

21 There are obvious difficulties in tuning an organ pipe to a string. 'Ein geübter lässet den Monochord weg, und kömmt viel leichter und richtiger davon' (Adlung 1758 p.310). Adlung had been a student of J.N. Bach in the early 1720s and must have had the story from him. For connexions between J.N. Bach, Jena and J.S. Bach, see Fritz Stein, *MGG* (1957) art. 'Jena', Sp.1859.

22 This recipe is given by Sorge (1744 p.30 and 1758 p.10) and Marpurg (1754b p.34 and 1764 p.135), who attributes it to Sorge. Barthold Fritz (1756 p.15) preferred the more normal method of tuning by 5ths (as given in Werckmeister 1698/1715, Neidhardt 1706, Adlung 1758 etc.). In all these instructions one must allow for the fact that higher-pitched intervals beat faster than lower ones.

23 'Es fehlet (heisset es) ihren *Tertiis maioribus* an der Abwechselung der Schwebungen, und folglich mehrerer Gemüths-Bewegungen' (1732 p.40).

24 Details of Neidhardt's and Sorge's calculations are in Lindley 1985a and 1987b.

25 See Lange 1972–3 pp.653–4 for an assessment of Sorge's musical and mathematical skills.

26 C.P.E. Bach writing to Forkel *c.*1774 (Dok.III p.285; translation from NBR p.396).

27 C.P.E. Bach's obituary for his father (1754; Dok.III p.89; translation from NBR p.307); Wöhlke notes that whereas other members of Mizler's Corresponding Society of Musical Sciences such as Bümler, Lingke, Schröter, Sorge and Telemann, argued about the most practical way of tuning equal temperament, Bach is pictured in the Haussmann portrait (presented to the Society on his joining) holding an extraordinarily ingenious canon as his comment on the relationship of music to mathematics (1940 p.47); see also Mizler 1746 p.470.

28 Forkel in 1772, probably on the basis of information from W.F. or C.P.E. Bach (Dok.III p.240). Other citations to this effect are assembled in Lindley 1985a and 1987b.

29 Kirnberger's tunings cannot logically be ascribed to Bach for reasons which will be discussed below in section 3.

30 These are the only tunings discussed in the literature in Bach's area *c.*1670–1720, and are those discussed in the books listed by Bach's predecessor at St Blasius, Mühlhausen, Johann Georg Ahle (1704 p.47). Ahle mentions Trost 1677 and Christian Förner (something like Werckmeister III), Praetorius 1619 and Printz 1696 (¼-comma meantone), Vockerodt 1698 (⅓-comma, equal temperament, ¼-comma meantone), Werckmeister 1691 and 1698a (Werckmeister III and equal temperament mainly).

31 Snyder 1987 pp.84–5; H.Vogel 1989 p.131.

32 Snyder 1986 p.677; 1987 p.105.

33 Terry 1928 p.41. The list does not specify which works.

34 P. Williams 1984 pp.140ff; also 1985a.

35 Mattheson 1740 p.388.

36 The addition of one more tempered 5th greatly increases the possibilities for using triads as tonics, as shown by Kellner (1977 etc.) and Barnes (1979). Barnes's proposed tuning is good, but his method of arriving at it, based on a statistical analysis of the use of major thirds in preludes of both Books of the 48, is questionable since it assumes a single tuning for pieces which originated at widely different stages of Bach's career.

37 Mark Lindley (1985a; 1987b) notes these and other features of the early keyboard toccatas which benefit from an unequal temperament.

38 Reported to Marpurg by Bach's pupil Kirnberger (Marpurg 1776, Dok.III p.304, NBR p.368).

39 C.P.E. Bach 1753, Einleitung §4.

40 Lindley (1987b p.411) suggests that Mizler had this opinion from Bach. Mizler reprinted it in 1739 (fascicle for 1737) along with a number of thoroughbass tutors, at the time when he was publishing his own *Anfangsgründe des Generalbasses* (Leipzig 1739). For details of this tuning in English, see Arnold 1931 p.204.

41 Dok.I p.159, NBR pp.74ff.

42 Sinn 1717 p.116. Sinn does not mention the number of the Werckmeister temperament, but it must be this, as the circulating temperament of 1691.

43 In a letter to Mattheson dated 8 December 1717, printed in Mattheson 1725 p.236.

44 Heinichen 1711 p.261. In the expanded version of 1728 the circle is the same, but goes up clockwise rather than anti-clockwise, and he has corrected a few errors. See Lester 1989 p.108 (1711) and Rasch 1983 (1728).

45 KB V/6.1 p.187.

46 KB V/6.1 pp.116, 187–8.

47 Lindley (1985a and 1987b) mentions further instances.

48 KB V/6.1 pp.134–5.

49 KB V/6.1 p.188, where the possibility of an E minor original for the E flat minor Prelude is raised; pp.189, 134: there are evidences for an original Dorian key signature for the G sharp minor Prelude and Fugue, implying a G minor original. Dürr is, however, cautious: 'Sie führen jedoch über den Grad einer bloßen Vermutung nicht hinaus.'

50 See Introduction, section 2; possible connexions are explored by Stauffer (1983) and Butler (1983).

51 Dok.II p.220. Bach is not known to have possessed any works of Mattheson (VBN).

52 See his letter to Fux of 18 December 1717 (English version in Lester 1977 p.46).

53 1719 p.66. The tuning is given in Lester 1989, Appendix 2.

54 'Geometrae sind gute Leute, sie reichen aber mit ihrem Circul nicht bis an die Ohren und Seelen-Kräffte. Dass die 12 *hemitonia* gleich gross seyn sollen ist der Music Zweck keineswegs; sondern dass sie alle rein und lieblich klingen sollen/ sie mögen gross oder klein seyn/ solches muss der *Scopus* bleiben. Sie klingen aber alle falsch wenn man sie gleicher Grösse macht/ wozu denn die Mühe?' (1719 p.111).

55 'Kömmt denn nun auf den neuesten and reinesten Clavicymbeln die Temperatur und Stimmung nicht eben gantz genau mit obigen *scalis & calculis* überein, sondern ist bereits um ein merckliches accurater und besser, so hindert doch solches am veritablen Unterscheid [sic] der Tone gar nicht; sondern es quadriret vielmehr die aus solcher feinem *diversité* fliessende, vergnügliche Abwechselung desto genauer mit zärtlichen, verständigen, empfindlichen Ohren und Seelen' (p.112).

56 Neidhardt already in 1706 found Werckmeister III at fault for its Pythagorean (whole-comma) major 3rds, a view repeated by Sorge (1744 p.26). Neidhardt later (1732 p.36) disliked even $+\frac{11}{12}$–comma major 3rds. Telemann had to move house to

get away from a carillon with Pythagorean 3rds (Marpurg 1776 pp.213ff). Marpurg says that Bach would have found the Pythagorean 3rd 'ein abscheuliches Intervall' (1776 p.213, Dok.III p.304). Martin Jira (2000) proposes Werckmeister's sixth temperament of 1691 as that used by Bach up to *c*.1722 on the grounds that it has no major 3rds a whole comma wide, and that it was mentioned by J.G. Walther in 1708 (Jira p.32). Werckmeister in his sixth and last temperament builds a speculative tuning system on the number 7 because of its symbolic importance (the completion of the week, etc.). In fact Walther does not mention this temperament specifically, but merely the paradox of the 7th harmonic being out of tune when the in-tune Nos.1–6 add up to 21, which is 3 × 7 (ed. Benary p.83). Werckmeister's description of the temperament is full of errors (1691 pp.72–3); it has a very narrow 5th G–D (more than –3/5 comma) and a larger than 1-comma-wide major 3rd D–F sharp (see Lindley 1987a pp.261–2).

57 Stölzel shared Bach's interest in learned counterpoint, reflected in his *Anleitung zur musicalischen Setzkunst* (*D-B* Mus.Ms.830); Bach included a suite of his in Friedemann's *Clavier-Büchlein*, adding a trio of his own to the Minuet.

58 Full details are in Friedrich 1989 pp.49–52.

59 Friedrich 1989 p.72.

60 Lindley 1988 p.118, from which this translation is taken.

61 Dähnert 1962 pp.139–40.

62 Dok.III p.88, BR p.224. Although Bach joined relatively late (his membership number 14 may be significant), his contact with members such as Schröter, Telemann, and Stölzel went back for many years beforehand. For Bach's involvement in Mizler's society, see Wöhlke 1940 pp.115ff.

63 VBN I/F/4.

64 Mizler 1742 p.53; see also Federhofer 1988 p.11.

65 See 'Schröter, Christoph Gottlieb' in *New Grove 2*; also Lindley 1987a p.277.

66 Butler 1990 pp.4–8; see also the commentary on the C major fugue in Chapter Eight.

67 Dok.II p.384; 'Hille, Johann Georg' in *New Grove 2*.

68 Dok.III pp.412–13, NBR p.335. Marpurg, who was critical of Sorge's discussion of dissonance in his composition tutor (*Vorgemach der musicalischen Composition*, 1745, see Dok.III p.171), reported in a letter to J.G. Hoffmann in 1759 that Bach thought Telemann had written the *Vorgemach*, implying a rather low opinion of Sorge on Bach's part (Dok.III p.127). On the strength of this, Spitta (III p.255) assumes a positively dismissive attitude on Bach's part. As the editors of BR point out, if this is true Sorge cannot have been that much put out, since the *Gespräch* of 1748 has his usual reverential attitude and also the Bach citations.

69 For an assessment of Bach's relations with Silbermann, see Flade 1953.

70 Dok.III p.88, NBR p.307.

71 Kirnberger 1771 p.10; translated by Beach and Thym p.19.

72 See footnote 38.

73 Kirnberger 1771 p.11, Beach and Thym p.19.

74 Notably H. Kelletat and M. Vogel.

Chapter Three: Preludes

1 Hofmann 1988a p.228; also in the *Wegweiser*: 'den in der *Music* unterweisenden Meistern und lehrende [!]' (4/1708); others are cited at the beginning of Chapter Six.

2 A partial edition of the Andreas Bach Book and the Möller MS is in Hill 1991; for

Eckelt see C. Wolff 1986; for a full discussion of other sources from Bach's environment see Hill 1987 Chapter V.

3 See the Introduction to Poulin and Taylor's translation p.xviii; possible connexions between Niedt and Bach are considered by John Butt in a review of this translation (*Journal of the Royal Musical Association* cxv/2 (1990) pp.264–5); the introduction to thoroughbass attributed to Bach (1738) is a paraphrase of Chapters I–IX of Niedt's Part I (English translation in Spitta III pp.315ff; facsimile with translation in Poulin 1994).

4 Using a succession of set textures over a given bass was a standard part of seventeenth-century improvisation technique, explained in terms of the bass viol by Christopher Simpson in *The Division Violist* (London 1659).

5 See LV 56 and 58 in H. Lohmann's edition.

6 Fischer's *Musicalischer Parnassus* was not published until 1738, but the suites, while slightly later in style than those of *Les pièces de clavessin* of 1696, are certainly not in the style of the late 1730s and were probably written considerably earlier than their publication date.

7 Ed. Benary p.151; P. Williams 1983 pp.332–9.

8 Keyboard versions by Kenneth Gilbert 1997, 1998.

9 This instruction was repeated by various seventeenth-century writers: see Hogwood 1976, Tagliavini 1983 and Coelho 1987.

10 For Forkel's definition of the invention principle, see section 7 below.

11 Bach returned to the term Fantasia for an Invention-type opening movement (in two parts) of the A minor Partita BWV 827 (1727), originally called Prelude in the 1725 album of Anna Magdalena Bach; Mattheson also used the term fantasia for a two-part invention type (P. Williams 1986 p.273).

12 The effect of a flattening, minor inflexion at cadences in major keys was already a feature of Cavalli's harmony (Glover 1978 p.97), analogous to the Neapolitan effect in minor keys beloved of other mid-seventeenth-century composers such as Carissimi.

13 The fundamental discussion of this is by Wilhelm Fischer in an essay on the background to the Viennese Classical style (1915); Fischer used the terms *Vordersatz*, *Fortspinnung*, and *Nachsatz* for elements 1–3; see Lee 1993 for an exhaustive discussion of Bach's treatment.

14 A full discussion of Bach's procedures in enlarging these preludes is in Bergner 1986.

15 For details of possible influences of Fischer on Bach see Oppel 1910 and Sumikura 1977.

16 1802 p.54, NBR p.467; the ramifications of this fundamental principle in Bach's composition are explored in Dreyfus 1996.

17 For Bach's facility in score reading on the clavier, even from separate part books laid side by side, see Forkel 1802 pp.16–17 (NBR p.435).

18 In his *MGG* article on Bach (1949–51), Friedrich Blume claims that Bach demonstrably used *L'art de toucher le clavecin*, but produces no evidence (Sp.1021). Its possible relation to Bach's teaching method will be discussed in Chapter 6. It is certain that C.P.E. Bach knew and admired it (1753 Chapter I para.88), and the francophile Marpurg, who knew both Bachs, said they both admired Couperin (Dok.III p.4). All that can be said with reasonable certainty is that Bach knew at least Couperin's second book (1717) since both Anna Magdalena and Wilhelm Friedemann copied pieces from it, either directly or indirectly (VBN I/C/3 and II/C/2–3).

19 It has been suggested that Bach may have known Domenico Scarlatti's *Essercizi* (London 1738/9) and that this may account for his use of this device in the Goldberg Variations (1741; Boyd 1986 p.209, Marshall 1989 pp.46–7). There is a possible link

in the Dresden lutenist Silvius Leopold Weiss, who had known Scarlatti in Rome around 1710, and who was also well known to Bach and paid him at least one visit, in Leipzig, in 1739. But the device was a commonplace by that stage, and Bach had already used it in the 1720s in the Gigue of the B flat major Partita BWV 825 (1726) and the Fantasia in C minor BWV 906 (*c.*1726–31).

Chapter Four: Fugues

1 With the move from the 1720s to purify the German language of foreign words, Bach may later have gone over to the terms *Führer* and *Gefährte*, used by Mattheson in 1739, or *Leiter* and *Gefährte*, used by Marpurg in 1753. The terms do not occur in Mizler's translation of Fux's *Gradus* (1742), part of whose function was to provide German terminology for Fux's Latin (canon became 'Cirkelgesang' and so on). Bach probably kept to the old terms, judging by the macaronic nature of his own writings and the fact that he used traditional terminology in *The Art of Fugue* (mixed Latin and Italian in the manuscript, Latin only in the print).

2 Marpurg dedicated his *Abhandlung* to Telemann who, he said, showed how fugue could be adapted to modern taste (1753, dedicatory letter).

3 The fundamental discussion of rhetoric and fugue is Butler 1977; for particular application to Bach see Walker 1999.

4 See the Introduction to Marco and Palisca 1968.

5 Bach certainly knew Schmidt's cantata 'Auf Gott hoffe ich' since he made a copy of it at Weimar in 1714–16 (VBN I/S/1), and he may have known a couple of others of Schmidt's works. Schmidt was a respected composer, as Dresden capellmeister and as Marpurg's list of distinguished fuguists shows.

6 The literature on Bach and rhetoric is very extensive; for a basic discussion see Forchert 1987.

7 Eggebrecht (1959) describes such chromatic figures in the works of Schütz, the prime examplar of German word setting in Bach's tradition.

8 For a general survey see Mather and Karns 1987, and for Bach's use of dance rhythms see Little and Jenne 1991, though this does not discuss dance features in non-dance genres such as fugues; for possible influence of Kuhnau's use of rhythmopoeia on Bach, see Serauky 1955.

9 Part II Chapter 6 para.6.

10 Part II Chapter 6 para.21.

11 If we accept Mattheson's characterisations we would have to feel satire and sarcasm in these anapaests (1739 Part II Chapter 6 para.25); as with his key characters, his rhythmic characters may be very relevant to his own operatic compositions, or Handel's, but can hardly be applied wholesale to Bach.

12 Vornemlich ist es unmöglich, eine Fuge gut zu komponiren oder zu executiren, wenn man nicht alle verschiednen Rhythmen kent; und eben daher, weil heut zu Tage dieses Studium versäumt wird, ist die Musik von ihrer alten Würde herabgesunken, und kann keine Fugen mehr aushalten, weil sie, durch die elende Execution die weder Einschnitt noch Accente bezeichnet, ein blosses Chaos von Tönen geworden sind (1777b Vorrede p.2).

13 The entry in VBN (I/F/2) makes it look as if the entire work was copied by Bach. Bach wrote no more than his name and date on the title-page (see Spitta I pp.420–1, and VBN pp.56–7). Both Kirnberger and C.P.E. Bach copied ricercars from the *Fiori musicali* (Riedel 1987 p.220).

14 For example, Murschhauser, in his very conservative and modal *Academia musico-poetica* (1721 p.142; Bach may have owned a copy of this work, VBN II/M/3), gives

this outline for the subject (*subjectum*) of a *Fuga primi toni*, with an answer (*resolutio*) similar to Bach's.

15 Dreyfus uses Mattheson's term *fuga mixta* for this mix of genres (1996 p.144).

16 Edited by T. Dart and D. Moroney in *John Blow's Anthology*, pp.27–9.

17 See Walker 1995 for the concept of the countersubject in Bach's background.

18 The term *soggetto* was also used by Calvisius (1592) to label thematic material (Walker 1999 p.161).

19 There is no direct evidence that Bach knew Battiferri's ricercars: Walther 1732 mentions only vocal works of his. But they enjoyed prestige as models of counterpoint, were copied out by Fux (Apel 1972 p.689), are mentioned by Marpurg and Kirnberger, both of whom discussed fugue with Bach (Dok.III pp.46, 158, 223), and a copy in the hand of W.F. Bach suggests that Bach may have used them in teaching (Riedel 1963 pp.302–3, 1968 p.22).

20 Walther's examples are considerably less polished technically than Fux's, and for that reason point up Bach's ability to make strong harmonic sense of these devices.

21 See the commentaries in Chapter 8 on the G minor and B flat minor fugues of Book II. Johann Theile, in his MS *Kunst-Buch* (*c.*1675–85, ed. Dahlhaus 1965) gives an extensive demonstration of how a canon in two parts (*bicinium*) may be converted into three parts (*tricinium*) and four (*quatricinium*) by the arts of double counterpoint; Theile's *Kunst-Buch* has often been proposed as the model for *The Art of Fugue* and the *Musical Offering* (see also the introduction to Chapter Six).

22 It looks as if Kirnberger was interested in demolishing old authority (Berardi, Bononcini, Fux) and establishing his own, based on the achievements of Bach; Bach's works tend to disprove his strictures.

23 In 1983 (p.296) Butler proposed the E flat fugue from *Clavier-Übung* III as exactly 'a double fugue on 3 subjects', i.e. the first of which combines with each of the others, but never with both, and suggested it may have been written as late as spring 1739, thus answering Mattheson's challenge. Butler subsequently revised this estimate to late 1735 or early 1736 (1990 p.20) on account of parallels with C.F. Hurlebusch's *Compositioni musicali* (Hamburg ?1735; VBN II/H/9).

24 Butler (1983 p.298) comments on Bach's avoidance of 'excessive stricture' by slipping in a leap at b.8. In fact this genus of counterpoint grows out of the final notes of the subject (bb.3–4) and the leap at b.8 wittily refers to this and expands it.

25 Kerll was in the Bach family tradition through Johann Pachelbel, with whom Bach's eldest brother Johann Christoph had studied in Erfurt.

26 For Bach's relation to the south German verset tradition and his use of these features in fugues see Hofmann 1991.

27 For an account of the Italian *partimento* fugue see Borgir 1987 Chapter 19; for Bach and *partimento* see Schulenberg 1995 and Renwick 2001.

28 See for example the *Ouverture* of François Couperin's *Huitième concert* (1724) and Holman 1986; a solo harpsichord piece with this effect is the Gigue from Couperin's eighth *Ordre* (1717).

29 See Mann 1987 Chapter II; a practical edition is in Ledbetter 1990.

30 1987 p.16; another Zachow pupil, Gottfried Kirchhoff (1685–1746), who succeeded Zachow at Halle in 1714 (a post declined by Bach), published a collection of *partimento* fugues in all 24 keys (*L'ABC musical*, now lost; see Marpurg 1753 pp.149–50); BWV 907 and 908 are possibly from this (see Stinson 1990 pp.127–9).

31 Edited in Renwick 2001.

32 See Siegele 1975 pp.17–22; Reinken's A minor sonata is ed. in Spitta III pp.366–84. The earliest sources of BWV 965 and 966 are in copies made by J.G. Walther dating from 1712 or later.

33 See Zehnder 1991, P. Williams 1999.

Chapter Five: All the Tones and Semitones

1 For a presentation of the complexity of the situation in the first two decades of the eighteenth century see Chafe 1991 Chapter 3, Deppert 1993 pp.187–201, and Butt 1994 pp.57–60.

2 In his personal copy of the 48 (Am.B.57) Kirnberger wrote in red ink what he imagined to be the mode of some of the fugues of Book I and all those of Book II; designations for Book I are: C, C♯ = Ionisch; c, d♯, g♯ = Aeolisch; c♯, f♯ = Dorisch; in Book II all the major-key fugues are Ionisch, except for F which is 'Ionisch und Lÿdisch vermischt', and F♯ which is 'Lÿdisch und Mixolydisch und Ionischen Tones vermischt' (see the commentary on this fugue in Chapter 8); oddly, c is also Ionisch (Aeolisch crossed out), as is d♯; c♯ and d are Dorisch; e, f, f♯, g, g♯, a, b♭, b are Aeolisch; the designations seem no more than experimental doodles since Kirnberger went through phases of preferring Dorian to Aeolian etc., and in any case, in all these authentic modes the subsidiary cadences are traditionally on the 5th and 3rd degrees, which is not the tonal ambitus normally used by Bach (see Chapter Three section 6). Werckmeister in his continuo tutor stresses the importance of knowing modal ambitus etc. for improvisation (1698b p.44), and no doubt Kirnberger was trying to relate the fugues of the 48 to this old tradition. Werckmeister had already in 1686 said that most musicians of that time understood 'modus' as meaning only two modes: 'Jonicus, mit dem Mixolydio, und Dorius mit dem Aeolio' (Deppert 1993 p.189). Bach was certainly interested in the modal tradition around the time when Kirnberger studied with him (*c.*1740), but compositions with genuinely modal elements in *Clavier-Übung* III make it clear that Bach was not interested in this topic in the 48, which was designed to demonstrate principles of tonal harmony.

3 From the title-page of P 208, by an unknown copyist in the second half of the eighteenth century.

4 Werckmeister felt it necessary to correct this common practical usage, pointing out that 'semitonia' were not properly 'black' notes, but the difference between C and C sharp, etc.; the usage nonetheless persisted: C.P.E. Bach says the 'black' notes were still called 'Halbtöne' (1753 Chapter I para.21).

5 '. . . durch alle Tone und Accorde dergestalt geführet sind/ daß in denenselben zweyen Exempeln alle Griffe/ mithin die Signaturen aller Clavium/ anbey die bequemsten Vorthel zur Faust/ gewiesen werden' (title-page; see Arnold 1931 pp.243–7, and P.Williams 1970 II p.47). Treiber had already published (Jena 1702) a similar work entitled *Sonderbare Invention: Eine Aria in einer einzigen Melodey aus allen Tonen und Accorden, auch jederley Tacten zu componiren*, covering 10 major and 10 minor keys. Treiber's terminology is common to writers on music in the Thuringian area, such as Werckmeister and Niedt, and is therefore illuminating evidence of the concepts Bach grew up with. For example, Treiber's advice to the student to avoid 'nag-octaves and horse-fifths' ('Pferde-Octaven und Roß-Quinten', 1702 Vorrede; 1704 p.6) was also used by Werckmeister (1698b p.31) who may have originated it; it chimes with Bach's judgment of an organ in Görlitz (1741) as a 'Pferdsorgel . . . weilen es eine Roßen mässige Arbeit ist droben zu spielen' (Dok.II p.389).

6 'aus den Chromatischen Clavibus' (1707 p.66). Treiber's publications relate to the tradition of *partimenti* in many keys, in itself related to versets in all modes, which reached its logical conclusion in Mattheson's *Exemplarische Organisten-Probe* (see Borgir 1987 p.142).

7 Mattheson (1717 p.93) says that he had completed his cycle of 24 pieces by 1715.

8 For Bach's use of this terminology, see Poulin 1994 pp.25–6.

9 For a survey, see Field 1996.

10 In understanding the difference between key and mode it is important to bear in mind that the modes of Gregorian chant are not merely arrangements of tones and

semitones, but that each has an inherent melodic structure with a principal centre of gravity (the tonic or final) and a number of subsidiary ones, the most important of which is the dominant. Each mode then has an authentic (or principal) version in which the tessitura of the melody lies mainly above the final; and a plagal (literally oblique) version in which the tessitura lies around the final, in which case the dominant centre of gravity is drawn down lower in the scale.

11 Nos. 9–12 of the *Apparatus* are in fact 'new' keys, though with strong modal colouring.

12 See Rasch 1992 p.129 for the use of these numbers in seventeenth-century collections. A dozen is of course the lowest convenient number for basic measurements, being divisible in whole numbers by every number from 1 to 6 except 5.

13 For a discussion of the development and characteristics of the modal system *c.*1600 see Meier 1992; for a basic description of mode and key in the seventeenth century see H.S. Powers and F. Wiering in *New Grove 2*, art. 'Mode, §III, 5 (ii)'; a much fuller discussion of the situation in Germany is in Lester 1989.

14 '. . . da er algemach das thema durch das gantze Clavier in alle 12. Claves transponiret . . . und also durch den Circul der quinten oder quarten gehet/ biß er wieder in den Clavem kömmt darinnen er angefangen hat . . .' (Werckmeister 1697 p.37); see Chapter Two section 1.

15 A copy was owned by Johann Bernhard Bach, organist at Eisenach, signed 1705 (Lester 1989 p.106; Walker 2000 p.275), and it is one of the works used by J.G. Walther (1708).

16 It is even less likely to be by Heinichen, as Spitta thought (Rasch 1990 pp.23–4).

17 '. . . wenn ein *Choral* zu Hause oder in der Kirche ohne Orgel gesungen wird/ man singe solchen aus welchen *Clave* oder *Tone* als man immer wolle/ das Haupt-Wesen als *Modus*, *Ambitus*, *Repercussio*, *Affectus* wird nicht verändert/ sondern bleibt wie es ist' (1716 p.51).

18 '. . . il n'y a que deux Tons, le majeur & le mineur . . . le plus grand agrément de la Musique, sur-tout pour peindre les sentimens, les passions, exige un fréquent entrelacement de ces différentes toniques & leur dépendances . . .' (1760 p.39).

19 '. . . weil man heutiges Tages alle Lieder aus allen clavibus spielen will' (1691 Zuschrifft).

20 For a general account of this very complex nomenclature, see Chafe 1991 Chapter 3.

21 'Angeführte 3 *modulandi genera* werden in denen heütigen *Compositionibus* nicht mehr *pur*, sondern vermischet gebrauchet . . .' (p.68).

22 '. . . vermittelst welcher das heutigen Tages bräuchliche *Genus Diatonico-Chromaticum* also eingerichtet wird/ daß alle *Intervalla*, nach gehöriger *Proportion*, einerley Schwebung überkommen/ und sich daher die *Modi regulares* in alle und iede *claves*, in einer angenehmen Gleichheit/ *transponiren* lassen' (title-page).

23 See Crussard 1945; Charpentier's list is given in Anthony 1997 p.231. Mark Lindley relates the key characters of Charpentier and Masson (1677) to the French *tempérament ordinaire* (1987a pp.227–8).

24 Mattheson's order of keys, with the modal designations when he gives them, is as follows: D.moll (*Dorio*), G.moll (*Transpositus Dorius*), A.moll (*Aeolii*), E.moll (*Phrygio*), C.dur (*Jonicus*), F.dur (*Jonicus transpositus*), D.dur, G.dur (*Hyppo Jonicus*), C.moll, F.moll, B.dur (*Lydius transpositus*) [= B flat major], Dis.dur [= E flat major], A.dur, E.dur, H.moll [= B minor], Fis.moll, H.dur.

25 George Buelow (1970) analysed the key characters in Mattheson's opera *Cleopatra* (Hamburg 1704) and found a high degree of correlation with the 1713 characters. Mattheson's characters are also interesting to apply to his friend Handel: the character for E major as the piercing grief of major-key lament is applicable, for example, to the aria 'Verdi prati' from *Alcina* (1735), but hardly to the E major pieces in the 48.

26 '. . . durchgehends einen frischen/ lebhafften und munteren Geist' (I p.76, repeated in 1731 p.276).
27 For a general survey see Steblin 1983; Wessel 1955 (pp.144–60) makes detailed comparisons of character listings.
28 See the commentary on the C sharp major prelude in Chapter Seven; the view is implicit in Treiber 1704, and is repeated by Mattheson in 1719 (II p.241; see Buys 1955 p.29).
29 pp.83–7, translated in Buelow 1986 pp.283–4; Bach acted as Leipzig agent for Heinichen 1728 (VBN II/H/8).
30 The second Passepied of the B minor French Overture BWV 831 was originally in C major.
31 See the discussion of Bach's key schemes in Chapter Three section 6; for an assessment of Corelli as an exemplar of tonality, see Barnett 1998, and Allsop 1999 pp.99–105.
32 See the Glossary for hexachords.
33 Daniel Speer in his basic tutor (1697) has three categories: natural; *dur* (or sharp); and *moll* (or flat). The terms are still used with these meanings in Friedrich Wesselius's old-fashioned little *Principia musica* (Schweinfurt 1726, 2/1747). See Butt 1994 p.58 for a summary of this usage.
34 This is the terminology used by Bach's brother Johann Christoph in the Möller MS and Andreas Bach Book (see Hill 1991 pp.xxix–xlvi) and in sources from the same area such as the so-called Mylau tablature (*c.*1700; see Shannon 1977).
35 This was the system in use throughout Bach's life, though systems with designations for flats were suggested, such as that by the Hildesheim cantor Johann Caspar Lange, who proposed 'del', 'gel', etc. for flats (1688 pp.18ff).
36 Part I was reprinted in 1695, 1710 and 1718; Part II in 1695, 1696, [1703] and 1726. The terminology persisted till the end of Bach's life: both C.P.E. Bach and Marpurg describe *The Art of Fugue* as 'aus dem D moll, oder dem D la Re über die kleine Terz' (Dok.III p.15, NBR pp.257, 376).
37 Luther, following Augustinian tradition, regarded music as having the dual function of refreshing the heart (*recreatio cordis*) and purifying the disposition (*Gemüt*). In a letter to Ludwig Senfl (4 October 1530) he expressed its function as 'das Gemüt ruhig und fröhlich zu machen, zum offenbaren Zeugnis, daß der Teufel, der Urheber der traurigen Sorgen und unruhigen Gedanken vor der Stimme der Musik fast ebenso flieht, wie vor dem Wort der Theologie' (Eggebrecht 1957 p.540).
38 For summaries of views on solmisation see Lester 1989 pp.xvii-xix, and Butt 1994 pp.58–60.
39 Leaver 1983 Nos.36 and 37; see also Hamel 1951 p.93. Hamel proposes the title-page of the third of Pfeiffer's books noted by Bach (Leaver 1983 No.39) as a sort of unexpressed programme for the French Suites.
40 See Stiller 1984 for an estimate of Bach's involvement with Lutheran practice and theology.
41 See Holman 1994 pp.7–9 for an English parallel.
42 The Sorau cantor and friend of W.F. Bach's, Johann Samuel Petri, was still sympathising with Buttstett in 1782, against Mattheson 'der sich mit allen damaligen Musikern zankte, und besonders den armen Buttstedt mit seiner Solmisation in seinem Orchestre sehr hinunter reißt. Er läßt auch in seinen übrigen Schriften, z.E. im vollkommenen Kapellmeister, *item* in seiner Organistenprobe viele Galle blikken' (p.96). Mattheson was also extremely discourteous to Fux, who entered into correspondence with him on the conservative side (see Schenkman 1978–9/1).
43 The title is often misread as 'ut re mi fa sol la', which misses the point.
44 For a survey of this tradition from the late fifteenth to the late seventeenth centuries

see Yates 1964.

45 See Yates 1964 Chapter XXII; also Huffman 1992 for a concise account of Fludd's controversies with Kepler and Mersenne.

46 For a selection of Kircher's illustrations of music see Godwin 1979 Chapter VI.

47 In his Göttingen dissertation of 1942; this wartime thesis was not published and the only copies known to me are the typewritten ones in *D-B.*

48 See C. Wolff 2000 for a full presentation of Bach's speculative interests.

49 Bach's alterations to Niedt's text are presented in detail by Blankenburg (1942 p.74) and Poulin (1994 pp.10–13).

Chapter Six: Bach as Teacher

1 Christoph Wolff has suggested that Bach provided title-pages for *The Well-tempered Clavier* (1722), the Inventions and Sinfonias (1723), and the *Orgel-Büchlein* (*c.*1722–3) for the benefit of the Leipzig authorities as part of his application for the Thomas cantorship: they demonstrate both his learning, and his methodical approach as a teacher (2000 p.227).

2 'denen *Practicirten* zur Lust; denen zarten Ohren zur Ergötzlichkeit; denen Liebhabern der Edlen *Music* zur Zeit-Verkürzung; denen *Instructoribus* zum Vortheil; denen Lernenden aber zur nutzlichen Ubung'; see also the title-page of Fischer's *Ariadne Musica* (cited in Chapter Three section 1).

3 Although he taught a substantial number of pupils in the course of his career (83 are listed in NBR pp.315–17), this is relatively few in comparison with the numbers taught by some others in his position.

4 Poulin and Taylor 1989 pp.xiv, 36; see also Chapter Three sections 2–5.

5 'den anfahenden Lehr-begierigen'; Borris 1933 p.13; Niedt 1710 n.p. 'Geneigter Leser', trans. Poulin and Taylor 1989 p.5.

6 Dok.II p.231; NBR pp.294–5; see C. Wolff 2000 Chapters 1–3 for a comprehensive survey of Bach's early training.

7 Bach learnt a high level of notational skill from Johann Christoph, as the Möller and Andreas Bach manuscripts show; his early handwriting is very similar to his brother's (Hill 1987 pp.62, 83).

8 For seventeenth-century examples see Fuller 1993; François Couperin recommends that children learn their first pieces by ear (1717 p.8); for Bach see Forkel 1802 p.38, NBR pp.453–4.

9 See Riedel 1960 p.23 for similar *Lehrgänge* in southern Germany (Spiridion, Poglietti, Justinus, and the *Wegweiser*), and Kahl 1948 for the early training of Quantz, G.H. Stölzel and J.H. Quiel.

10 See for example Kent 1992 for the alterations Bach made in his copy of Grigny's *Livre d'orgue.*

11 His earliest known pupils are Johann Martin Schubart and Johann Caspar Vogler (NBR p.315).

12 Krautwurst 1986 pp.180–1; see also Dok.II pp.46–7, NBR p.318.

13 Edited in Spitta II, Supplement VI; the exercise was written without the violin part, so was probably intended as a figured-bass exercise in the abstract (Dürr 1978b pp.14–15); E.L. Gerber says that when his father played his realisations 'the accompaniment was so beautiful that no principal voice could have added to the pleasure it gave me' (Dok.III p.476, NBR p.322).

14 NBA V/5 KB p.59; the exception is the Praeambulum No.8, added later; the incomplete chorale prelude No.5 may also be an afterthought. The fact that

Friedemann's handwriting was developing rapidly makes it possible to be fairly precise about the dates of his entries.

15 *Us-Wc* MT 224.K62 Case; see Chapter One section 5.

16 In his Introduction, however, he recommends learning the *Probe-Stücke* without the ornaments first, practising them separately, and adding them later (1753 Einleitung para.19).

17 See Butt 1994 pp.75–9 for typical examples. Beginning with pairs of notes, and building up to larger groups, is presented as Bach's system of clavichord teaching by F.C. Griepenkerl (1820), see Spányi and Collins 2000.

18 Rokseth 1930 p.364; Ammerbach 1571 ed. Jacobs 1984 pp.lxxxiiiff.

19 See below for J.C. Vogler's fingerings in BWV 870a.

20 See for example the little teaching prelude by Purcell (No.1 in Moroney 1999); also Beechey 1972, and Lindley and Boxall 1992 p.48.

21 In fingerings for ornaments it was usual for the given finger to apply to the main note, even though the ornament might begin with an auxiliary; this is clear from the final right-hand trill of the *Applicatio*, and is explained by C.P.E. Bach (1753 Chapter 1 para.98).

22 In the preface to his edition of the Chromatic Fantasia and Fugue (Peters 1820), reproduced in Kooiman 1983b p.25; English translation in Spányi and Collins 2000.

23 Similar fingerings, with the principle of thumb on raised tonics, are given by P.C. Hartung in the first German listing of fingerings for all keys (Nuremberg 1749, examples pp.4–5).

24 These fingerings are discussed by Kooiman (1983a) and Faulkner (1984), both of whom give them inaccurately, and Lindley (1985b and 1989).

25 Chapter XVII Section VI para.18; these points are omitted from the excerpt given in Dok.III p.18.

26 1753 Chapter 1 paras.14, 90; Chapter 2 Section 3 paras.8, 36.

27 1785 p.vi; English translation in Hogwood 1988.

28 Griepenkerl's (1820) additions to Forkel sound too much like a piano teacher's 'secret', and the instruction to keep the fingers 6–8 mm above the key, with crooked thumb, hardly tallies with descriptions of Bach's very economical finger movement with fingers close to the keys. For a possible nineteenth-century piano descendant of this touch see Bellman 2001, though the touch described there involves the forearm being drawn back, and the use of the sustaining pedal to connect notes (p.403).

29 Compare the chorale No.3 with François Couperin's 'Progrès de tremblemens enchainés' (1717 p.31).

30 Forkel 1802 p.14, NBR p.433; the *Clavier-Büchlein* versions of some of the preludes are not the earliest, so they are unlikely to have been composed expressly for this 'method'.

31 The G major Minuet of D'Anglebert's 1689 *Pièces de clavecin* (VBN I/A/3) has been proposed as a model for the Aria of the Goldberg Variations (Elster 1988).

32 See Stauffer 1994 for a survey of Bach's organ teaching.

33 P. Williams 1984 p.34.

34 Dok.III p.362, NBR p.320; the first part is translated by Beach and Thym (1982); see also Forkel 1802 p.41, NBR pp.456–7.

Chapter Seven: Book I

1 Thus, the copy of François Couperin's *Les bergeries* in Anna Magdalena's 1725 notebook simplifies Couperin's complex notation of *tenues* to plain semiquavers.

Bach, in music for publication, seems to have been as careful as Couperin to notate them all where necessary, for example in the Toccata of the E minor Partita BWV 830 bb.48ff.

2 For the use of 'wet' and 'dry' notation in French and French-influenced German keyboard music, see Ledbetter 1992 pp.69–71.

3 There are three phases of notation: (1) 𝅘𝅥𝅯, (2) 𝅘𝅥𝅰‿♪, (3) ♪.‿♩ (see Dürr 1984 p.15).

4 The version in W.F. Bach's *Clavier-Büchlein* is not an intermediate one, but the first version, into which Bach began to add the extra bars from the second version, but did not finish doing this; Plath's edition (NBA V/5 p.19) should be compared with the facsimile he gives (p.x).

5 This is not to say that all stations are of equal structural importance: for example, the dominant triad in b.11 is less important structurally than the tonic in b.19, but any analysis must start with the markers that Bach has clearly arranged.

6 The famous 'Schwenke bar' (a 6/4 chord on g after b.22), given by many old editions including Czerny's and Fauré's, was added at the foot of the page with an asterisk in P 203 by the Hamburg organist C.F.G. Schwenke who copied out Book I at the age of 16. His version was followed by some of the earliest editions and hence by later editors (AB I p.167). A different chord (root-position major triad on g) is given in P 1075 (by an unknown copyist, with analytical markings entered *c.*1760 by C.F. Penzel, cantor at Merseburg and possibly a pupil of Bach's; KB V/6.1 pp.43–8).

7 The background to this is well explored by H. Zenck (1959).

8 J.N. David's turgid derivation of each fugue subject from the companion prelude was parodied by R. Suthoff-Groß (1968), who derived all the Book I subjects from the C major prelude, and then from the C minor prelude as well, in an essay worthy of Ronald Knox.

9 Herbert Kellner (1980 pp.137–8, etc.) sees the total bar count of 35 as significant in that his tuning (based on trinitarian symbolism) involves tempered to pure 5ths in the ratio 5:7 (5 × 7=35); in addition, without the ties there are 551 keystrokes in the piece (i.e. 19 = tuning steps, x 29 = SDG or JSB): therefore there should be no ties in bb.33–4.

10 Dehnhard (1977 p.xvii) suggests that Bach forgot the bass tie in b.34, having just changed systems.

11 Schulenberg 1992 p.168.

12 See for example the 'Principi Del Sig.[nr] Cavaliere Alesandro Scarlatti' (*GB-Lbl* MS Add.14244) p.3.

13 Brossard 1705, art. 'USO'.

14 For the significance of the hexachord, and of the numbers 6 and 12, for Froberger and Corelli, see Rasch 1992 p.129; for the significance of the hexachord for Bach, see Marissen 1995 pp.92–5; for hexachords and tetrachords see P. Williams 2000 pp.764–9.

15 See Chapter Four section 9. Bach uses the typical black-note canzona rhythm ♩♫ only once, in the bass entry at b.17, preferring the more purposeful upbeat version right from the beginning, as he does in the similarly canzona-based D major fugue of Book II.

16 Authentic and plagal tessituras are explained in Chapter Five section 1; also Meier 1992 pp.20–5; for Schenker's views on the primacy of 3 voices, see Renwick 1995 p.111.

17 Hofmann 1991 p.71.

18 Corelli's first trio sonata was written to 'correct' the unbalanced Mixolydian structure of Cazzati's 'La Casala' from Op.35 (1665; see Allsop 1999 p.72; for 'La Casala' see Klenz 1962 pp.276–85).

19 We cannot say how much of Op.3 Bach knew, and his authorship of BWV 579 is not entirely above question (P. Williams 1980 I p.249).

20 From the 12th of Albinoni's Op.1 trio sonatas (Venice 1694); again Bach's authorship is not entirely above doubt (Schulenberg 1992 p.53).
21 Mann 1958 pp.79, 134.
22 Marpurg also saw e' as the last note of the subject (Dok.III p.25).
23 One of the terms for the inversion or permutation of counterpoint was 'Verwechselung', which in the theory of alchemy was used for transmutation. It may be that Bach here was aiming to demonstrate the fundamental unity from which all manifestations grow, which is the essence of alchemic theory (see Yearsley 1998). Johann Theile, the prime exemplar of contrapuntal art in Bach's background, was known as an esoteric in his day, and master of 'sonderbaren Kunst-Stücke und Geheimnisse, welche aus den doppelten Contrapuncten entspringen' (Dahlhaus 1965 p.VII; see also Chapter Four section 7 and Chapter Five section 4).
24 Hugo Riemann (1890) attempted to interpret the fugues in terms of eight-bar phrases and ternary structures, as precursors of Viennese Classical sonata form. This can only be done by ignoring Bach's clear cadential articulation.
25 W. Korte (1940 pp.34–7) sees 5 sections (the fifth being the final pedal bb.24ff) which he relates to Baroque concepts of Balthasar Neumann (Vierzehnheiligen) and Leibniz (basic monad to *ultima ratio rerum*); for Bach and Leibniz's monads, see Lowinsky 1969.
26 There is nothing to support Wanda Landowska's theory that the dot was not added by Bach (1914 p.53).
27 See Chapter Six section 3. Busoni suggested making it yet more useful as an étude for the modern piano by playing it in double octaves, or 6ths (1894 p.8).
28 For the possible effect of sensitivity to *figurae* on performance, see P. Williams 1983 p.335.
29 Poulin and Taylor 1989 p.xiv.
30 Suggested by C.F.A. Williams 1893 p.88.
31 See Chapter Four section 5; also the listings in the Appendix of Houle 1987.
32 Suggested by Ulrich Siegele (1986 p.129).
33 Ed. F.W. Riedel, *Die Orgel* II/3 p.21. An interim phase between this and the C minor fugue may be seen in the B flat Fuga of Fischer's *Ariadne Musica*, see Ex.8.26.
34 There does seem to be something gnomic about this subject: 'Der Zeitgenosse Liszts und Wagners sieht in der c-moll Fuge des ersten Teils einen Elfentanz' (Knab 1914 p.27).
35 Bach's fondness for Vivaldi's Op.3 No.11 is evident also in his using material from the last movement for the opening chorus of BWV 21 (see Schulze 1984 p.162 for the literature about this connexion).
36 Dramatic sonority is increased in some sources (P 203, P 208) by adding alto quavers f' and e'♭ in the third beat. Bach himself increased the number of parts for sonority's sake in the final two bars.
37 'Zwischenspiele' (Dok.III pp.144–5, NBR p.363).
38 Schenker 1926; for a critique of Schenker's analysis, see Dreyfus 1996 Chapter 6.
39 The turn and upward leap of a major 6th was used to express well-being by Wagner from the *Rienzi* overture to Isolde's *Liebestod*.
40 Bach may have been influenced by the later concertos of Albinoni in this and other respects (Butler 1995).
41 See for example the organ chorales BWV 652 and 768 (Variation 10), or the sarabande of the B minor flute Overture BWV 1067.
42 Karl Nef 1904 takes this prelude as an excellent example of texture used expressively on the harpsichord, a technique described by Quantz (1752 Chapter XVII Section VI paras.9, 14, 17). Thus in b.1 of the prelude, the melodic peak is enhanced by a chord, and so on (Nef 1904 pp.22–3).

43 *DTÖ* 27 pp.89–91, where it is attributed to Georg Reutter the elder; Strungk is one of the fuguists Bach is said to have admired (NBR pp.398, 442).
44 Seiffert 1899 p.389.
45 Theill 1985 I pp.5–8.
46 P. Williams 1980 II p.237; this chorale prelude is from Kirnberger's collection and its date is not known, but it is clearly an earlyish piece.
47 For example Torelli's Op.5 No.1 (1692), see Apel 1990 p.250.
48 See Harper 1978–9; Macey 1994; for Bach and *inganni* see Chafe 191 Chapter 2.
49 See Chapter Five section 3. For comparisons with Frescobaldi, see Koptchewski 1988; the appearance of the notes BACH is noted by Zacher (1988 p.246).
50 KB V/6.1 p.219; one other source with the instruction 'Pedale' dates from 1824 and was copied from this source. The low C♯ would not have been available on many pedal boards (see Schulenberg 1992 p.409 fn.41); see also Chapter One section 5.
51 See for example the *Wegweiser* (ed. R. Walter p.11); further examples are listed by Fuller (1985 p.112).
52 '. . . ein etwas frisches/ ermuntrendes und zugleich *elevi*rtes Wesen' (1713 p.171); the description is repeated by J.G. Walther (1732), and Scheibe (*c.*1730) has similar wording: 'sehr *patheti*sch doch dabey recht frisch und munter' (ed. Benary 1961, Anhang p.83).
53 BG XIV p.214; see Dolmetsch 1946 p.85, Donington 1974 p.449, P. Badura-Skoda 1993 p.61.
54 Dreyfus 1996 pp.150, 163; J.N. David 1962 p.26.
55 For various ways of defining tonal ambitus in Bach's time, see Seidel 1986.
56 As the C major prelude outlines Ut Mi Sol, the D minor outlines Re Fa La.
57 *The Musical Guide*, Part II Chapter VI.
58 *Exemplarische Organisten-Probe*; similarities between the first of Mattheson's D minor pieces and this prelude are noted by Schenkman (1981 p.12).
59 Lester 1992 pp.84–5.
60 '. . . les expressions de *Tristesse* ou de *Douleur*, dans les *Exclamations, &c.*' (Brossard 1705 p.128); this character was repeated by various eighteenth-century writers, see Wessel 1955 p.80.
61 Dürr gives the following arguments in favour of the authority of the anonymous part of the Breitkopf MS: it is on paper similar to that of original Bach sources; it has been transmitted as part of a composite copy, the rest of which is by Bach's pupil C.G. Meißner; and it has several unique, but musically better, readings, see for example b.43 (KB V/6.1 p.389).
62 'Das schöne majestetische *Dis* . . . Unsere *Toccaten* und *Praeludia* haben keine aus dem *Dis* bey sich . . . Unsere Orgeln und *Clavicymbeln* haben nicht alle die richtige *Temperatur*, insonderheit die ersten' (1719 I p.44).
63 The most sensible discussions of the possible date of this prelude are in Hermelink 1976 p.67 and Dürr 1988 pp.100–1.
64 'nicht Alla breve mäßig sondern wie der 1ste Tact gewesen fortgespielt'; this annotation is not legible in the facsimile. The entry must have been made before 1783, and Dürr thinks it may derive from Bach's instruction (Dürr 1988 p.97; NBA V/6.1 p.VI).
65 See Chapter Five section 2; Bach's only other keyboard piece in E flat minor (Minuet II of the keyboard suite BWV 819) has no special character.
66 Dolmetsch 1946 p.64; P. Badura-Skoda 1993 p.55.
67 The division is later joined, at bb.17–18.
68 See Hill 1991 p.198.
69 For the archetypal form of this Mode I outline, see Meier 1992 p.185.
70 A comprehensive survey of views is given by Ellis (1980 pp.80–1).

71 For Bach's obbligato style of continuo playing see Schulze 1979 p.51 and C. Wolff 1993.
72 Bach seems to have taken the bass of the organ Passacaglia BWV 582 from Raison's 1688 book (VBN II/R/1); see also Klotz 1984 p.XXIV and pp.57–8.
73 S.W. Dehn, keeper of the music collection at the Royal Library, Berlin, and author of good traditional analyses of fugues from the 48 (1858), mentions in letters to Roitzsch (1847–9) a MS collection of 72 two-part fugues by Bach in Princess Amalia's library. The MS (evidently in poor condition) seems to have been lost and Dehn's projected edition never appeared (Heller 1978 pp.217–19).
74 For further examples see Spitta II p.167. Schulenberg suggests that the octaves are part of the language of the 'rage aria', so the fugue has the added tension of a passionate affect worked in a supremely rational structure (1992 pp.181–2). Others have found it contemplative (Riemann), decided (Busoni), fiery (Tausig), capricious (Bischoff).
75 A ruse Bach also uses in the D sharp minor prelude and the B flat major fugue of Book II.
76 See also the commentary on the B flat major prelude.
77 See Mather and Karns 1987 pp.282–5.
78 This undermines Busoni's opinion that this prelude, together with the fugues in F sharp major and minor, forms part of a series of elementary studies for repeated notes (I/2 p.25).
79 1752 Tab.XIV Fig.15; trans. Reilly p.151.
80 The same figure is given by Griepenkerl (1820) as one of Bach's finger exercises (Spányi and Collins 2000 p.50).
81 The autograph version of the motif in the right hand on the third beat of b.10, with c"♯ for the 4th semiquaver instead of the a' given by a few sources and many editors after Kroll, demands the thumb on f'♯.
82 See also the subject of the F sharp minor Fuga, No.11 of *Ariadne Musica.*
83 Laurence Dreyfus (1996 pp.158–9) sees the concealment of this entry as a connoisseur's touch for its own sake, but one might equally see it as part of a progression from obscurity to clarity in the series of entries as a whole.
84 This and the other frequently cited parallel, the chorale prelude 'O Lamm Gottes unschuldig' BWV 618 in the *Orgel-Büchlein*, notate with slurs the obvious pairing of quavers in the countersubject's 'sigh' motif. Pirro (1907) lists other examples of this motif.
85 See particularly Klotz 1984 pp.146, 148, 152; Troeger 1987 pp.147–8; P. Badura-Skoda 1993 p.425; F. Neumann 1983 pp.321–2; Schulenberg 1992 p.187.
86 See Renwick 2001.
87 For the expression of joy (see Pirro 1907 pp.158, 182, 358, 369, 388; Schweitzer II pp.109–14).
88 Dürr in KB V/6.1 pp.189, 362, and 1984 p.43.
89 Bach does not use this key as a tonic in instrumental works outside the 48 (Keller 1976 p.102).
90 Candé (1984 p.291) lists various interesting correspondences between Bach and Vivaldi themes, citing an aria from *Ottone in Villa* (1713) for this prelude.
91 Suthoff-Groß (1968 p.533) remarks that only four preludes of Book I use less than 12 notes, and this is the only one to use less than 11.
92 ed. Zászkalicsky VIII p.8.
93 See Butler 1983 for possible links between Mattheson 1739 and *The Art of Fugue.*
94 Dürr 1984 p.45; later he toned down this opinion slightly with regard to the prelude, but remained convinced of a G minor origin for the fugue (KB V/6.1 pp.190, 364).
95 Spitta II pp.164–5; Tovey 1924 p.137.

96 For an example of Bach parodying a Kerll vocal work, see H.T. David 1961 and Wollny 1991.
97 See Chapter Five section 1; also Meier 1992 Part I Chapter 1.
98 See Stinson 1996 p.109 for a comparison with the *Orgel-Büchlein* prelude BWV 612 and possible expressive references.
99 See Ledbetter 1990 pp.56–61.
100 For chronology of compass in Bach's clavier works see Dürr 1978a.
101 For pedal harpsichords and clavichords in Bach's environment see P. Williams 1984 pp.194–5, and Ford 1997. Some preludes of J.C.F. Fischer's *Les pieces de clavessin* (1696) require a pedal harpsichord/clavichord.
102 A less obvious prototype for this prelude is in the practice of playing flourishes (*passaggi*) between the lines of a chorale, the *passaggi* described by Mattheson as rapid demisemiquaver runs, divided between the hands (1739 Part III Chapter 25 para.59). Hermelink compares the B flat prelude to exuberantly youthful Arnstadt chorale preludes of this type (1976 p.62).
103 Compare the beaming in bb.11–14 and b.19 with the carefully notated division between the hands in bb.3–4, b.8, and b.10. The fingerings in Kirnberger's personal copy (Am.B.57 (1); see KB V/6.1 p.87) continue to divide these scales between the hands; they also divide the *roulade* in b.33 of the D major prelude between the hands, equally unnecessarily.
104 See Hoffmann-Erbrecht 1987 p.21, who explores various possible influences of Weiss on Bach; also C. Wolff 1993.
105 Candé (1984 pp.291–2) sees a similarity to the fugue of Vivaldi's Op.3 No.11, cited above with reference to the A minor fugue. This similarity is noted by various writers, but in movement and expression Vivaldi's fugue seems remote from the B flat minor prelude.
106 Busoni also has an entertaining demonstration of how this subject works in double counterpoint with that of the C sharp minor fugue.
107 Czaczkes (1982 I p.208) has the subject end 'ohne Zweifel' at the beginning of b.3.
108 For Werckmeister the 9th signified the angel guarding the entrance to Paradise, i.e. the octave (1707 p.102), in which case the descending 9th at bb.72–3 could represent Adam's fall, and the rising one of the subject a yearning for restoration to serenity.
109 Arnold Dolmetsch used it for this purpose, though few would follow him in using only fingers 2–5 of the right hand as far as b.9 (Goble 1977 p.91).
110 Cadence patterns were categorized according to the normal movement of parts in a four-part cadence, so a cantus cadence moves from the leading note to the tonic (steps 7–1, *clausula cantizans*); an alto one has steps 5–4–3 (*altizans*, the commonest subject-ending in the 48); tenor has 2–1 (*tenorizans*, as here; six subjects end this way in Book I; only two in Book II); and bass has 5–1 (*bassizans*, only the G sharp minor of Book I has this); see Deppert 1993 pp.75–7.
111 Numerous felicitous motivic connexions are noted by Czaczkes (1982 I p.220–2).
112 Once doubted as a Bach work, but see Glöckner 1988; for expressive symbolism see Chafe 1991 pp.132–4.
113 KB V/6.1 pp.190, 382–3. Dürr notes that, on one hand, bending motifs is not rare in Bach; on the other, the bass in the earlier version of the fugue (see b.23) does not exceed E (1984 p.57); both Invention and Sinfonia in B minor descend to C♯, and the evidence of other preludes and fugues in this book shows that Bach was concerned to exploit the four-octave compass fully.
114 For the reception of Corelli's music in Germany, see Allsop 1999 Chapter 11; it looks from J.G. Walther's (1732) entry on Corelli that Walther knew only Op.5 and Op.6 at first hand (he wrote two sets of variations on movements from Op.5), and

took his information about the trio sonatas from a Roger catalogue.

115 Hermelink 1976 p.66; for the possible identity of Anon.5 see Dürr 1986 p.163.

116 '. . . denn alle Noten fein gleich und überein (ebenträchtig) *executi*rt, auch eine von der andern wohl unterschieden, und etwas geschwinder als *adagio tracti*rt werden müssen.' 1732, based on Brossard 1705.

117 See Mellers 1980 pp.244–7, who also proposes other symbolisms; see Butt 1991 pp.23, 85 for the expressive use of similar figures in the B minor Mass; Blankenburg (1950 p.66) points to the downward minor triad as expressing the words 'Et incarnatus est', as opposed to the upward major one for 'Et resurrexit', a symbolism taken from J.H. Buttstett's *Ut Mi Sol* (Erfurt 1716; see the discussion of the C major prelude with its rising triads). Given this symbolism, the whole of Book I might be seen as a circle from birth to death, with death on the leading note to C again; the Cross leading to the Resurrection.

118 Kirnberger 1773 p.53; Dok.III pp.259–60: for an assessment see Lester 1992 pp.248–9.

Chapter Eight: Book II

1 Another copy of this version, with significant differences, was sent by Wilhelm Friedemann Bach to Padre Martini in Bologna (*I-Bc* DD 70, see Jones 1991 p.442 and AB II p.159; edited in NBA V/6.2 p.6, BA II p.152); details of its readings are in Tomita 1995 pp.1ff). Dürr's seems generally the most satisfactory reconstruction; others are in Schünemann 1935 p.8 and Brokaw 1986 p.150, 1989 p.235; Tomita gives very detailed accounts of the revisions and greatly refines on previous discussions (1990 pp.208–17, 1993 pp.18–25).

2 Notably the preludes IV and V from Fischer's *Pieces de clavessin* (1696; Oppel 1910 p.67, often repeated), and preludes by Kuhnau (1689) and Johann Krieger (1699; P. Williams 1984 pp.104–5).

3 Hermann Keller (1933) published BWV 870a as an organ piece, adapting the bass for the pedals; it looks nonetheless more like a *manualiter* piece, but using typical pedal figurations: the bass line is not an idiomatic pedal part and cannot be disentangled from the tenor.

4 Peter Williams notes that Bach uses in b.19 of this version the same sequence pattern as he had in the episodes of the B minor fugue of Book I (1997 p.90).

5 Marpurg (1753) points to imitative use of the head of the subject in episodes (Dok.III p.34). This and other features have often been adduced in comparing this fugue with the C minor fugue of Book I, a comparison which only highlights its relative artlessness.

6 Of the main sources for the early version only C.P.E. Bach's copyist Michel gives **c** (*D-B* N.Mus.Ms.10490), but his copy has many mistakes (Tomita 1990 p.27, 1995 p.30).

7 See P. Williams 1993 for Bach's use of this time signature.

8 Hotteterre gives as his example a violin sonata movement by Michele Mascitti which also features separate crotchets.

9 See Tomita 1993 p.29.

10 *Fiori musicali* (Rome, 1635), Messa della Domenica, Canzon post il comune, Alio modo; Capriccio sopra la Girolmeta, Alio modo; J.C. Kerll, *Modulatio organica* (Munich, 1686); see Chapter Four section 9.

11 Ledbetter 1990 pp.60, 105; see also Kirnberger 1777 pp.173–4: the material is traditional.

12 Since the sign has a hook at the top, Dürr suggests that the arpeggiation may be intended to be downwards (NBA V/6.2 p.ix). For a discussion of this issue see the commentary on the E flat minor prelude in Book I (in Chapter Seven).

13 'Omnia verò haec themata, sive subjecta, quae sunt pro fugis, deducuntur ex phantasijs simplicibus.' (Vogt 1719 p.154; see also Unger 1941 p.39).

14 The *Wegweiser* has a fugue and two variations (4/1708, Part I pp.42–3).

15 1990 p.228; see also Tomita 1998.

16 Communication from Yo Tomita.

17 Kroll notes a number of missing A sharps, which may imply a Dorian C minor origin (BG XIV p.246).

18 Kirnberger 1776 pp.123–4, Dok.III p.224, translated Beach and Thym 1982 p.391.

19 Generally thought to be a Cöthen piece but actually undatable (Stinson 1989 p.41).

20 1702 p.25; translated Harris-Warrick 1984 p.45.

21 1771 pp.216–17, Dok.III p.220, NBR pp.367–8.

22 Dadelsen and Rönnau's dating of *c.*1715–23 (1973 Preface) seems more appropriate than Stinson's of *c.*1726–34 (1989 p.107).

23 Against assimilation are Tovey (AB II p.166), Keller (1950 p.227, 1976 p.146), F. Neumann (1966 p.459, in answer to McIntyre 1965), Finke-Hecklinger (1970 p.77), Hofmann (1988b p.52), P. Badura-Skoda (1993 pp.47–8), Schulenberg (1992 p.208); for are Emery (reported by P. Badura-Skoda above; see also Emery 1957 pp.41–2), McIntyre (1965 pp.480, 484–5), Jones (AB II p.165, a pupil of Emery's); this list is not intended to be exhaustive. The issue of seventeenth-century keyboard gigues which exist in both duple- and triple-time versions (McIntyre 1965 p.480) is not relevant to this piece since their rhythmic convention arose before the $\frac{12}{8}$ signature became current (Ledbetter 1992 pp.66–9).

24 F. Neumann 1966 gives a facsimile of the relevant page of P 416.

25 Such as the aria 'Morirò, ma vendicata' from Handel's *Teseo* (1713).

26 Stauffer (1995 p.297) suggests that some of Book II may have originated in items for the Collegium Musicum concerts.

27 Kirnberger, who regarded Bach as a great champion of modal harmony, went through his personal copy (Am.B.57) pencilling in mode names for the fugues; he designated this one Ionian ('Jonisch'). These designations have no basis in traditional theory and seem to be just doodles: he also calls the C minor and the D sharp minor 'Jonisch' (see the introduction to Chapter Five).

28 Marpurg 1753 p.41; Dok III p.28; English translation in Mann 1958 pp.168–9.

29 Bach's fascination with rich harmony may be seen by comparing any of the verset fugues mentioned above with the treatment of the same materials in the chorale prelude on 'Christum wir sollen loben schon' BWV 696 (P. Williams 1980 II p.233).

30 See for example Orlando Gibbons's Fantasia MB XX No.12.

31 For detailed accounts of the revisions, see AB II p.167, Tomita 1993 pp.41–5, Stauffer 1985 pp.189–90, Brokaw 1986 Chapter 9.

32 Heinichen 1728 pp.573–7, Buelow 1986 pp.202–5.

33 Mattheson 1731 pp.352–5, see also C.P.E. Bach 1753 Einleitung para.9, 1762 Chapter 19 para.17; and Arnold 1931 pp.774–7, P. Williams 1970 I p.36.

34 Schulenberg 1995 p.6; see the Ricercar bb.128–37; according to Picken (1950 p.51) the similarities were first noted by Sir Hubert Parry, but the subjects had long before been discussed side by side by Marpurg (1753 p.78; Dok.III pp.31–2, English translation in Mann 1958 p.173).

35 For unambiguous examples in Bach's works, see the discussion of the D major prelude; for further examples, see F. Neumann 1987.

36 The mirror fugue, Contrapunctus 13, is not comparable since the semiquavers are dotted, though inconsistently in the various versions (Fuller 1985 pp.100–1).

37 For a theory of dating items in *Clavier-Übung* III, see Butler 1990 pp.83–4.

38 1753 pp.141–3; Dok.III p.39; translation in Mann 1958 pp.196–8.

39 Jones (1991 p.442) and Tomita (1990 p.94) are agreed that this is probably a sketch; Dürr more cautiously suggests it may be just a false start at copying (KB V/6.2 p.230).

40 The autograph of BWV 998 is dated *c.*1735 or later by Kobayashi (1988 p.65).

41 It may also have been Bach who added further tenor notes in b.5 of Altnickol's copy (P 430; facsimile in NBA V/6.2 p.XIV). For a very clear presentation of Bach's successive enrichments see Tomita 1993 pp.49–54.

42 This was clearly a favourite fugue among Bach's pupils and later; it is thought to have provided Mozart with the fugal theme for the overture to *Die Zauberflöte*, plausibly enough since it is in the Masonic key of E flat (Dehn 1858 p.10; Cowgill 1998 p.213).

43 For sources see the relevant terms in Bartel 1997; Mattheson's *Kern melodischer Wissenschaft* (1737) and its expanded version in *Der vollkommene Capellmeister* (1739) may have been a stimulus to Bach's interest in fugue around the late 1730s (Butler 1983).

44 Dürr 1976 p.119; for a detailed discussion of the relation of this fugue to the *stile antico* see C. Wolff 1968.

45 For a comparison of the two fugues, see P. Williams 1980 I p.190.

46 See Marpurg's dissection of a Ricercar by Battiferri (1753 pp.124–7 and Tab.XXXIV; Mann 1958 pp.181–4).

47 The derivation from Fischer is noted in a comment in Am.B 57(2): 'Von J.C.F.Fischer entlehntes Thema'. This was probably added by F.A. Grasnick (d.1877) (communication from Yo Tomita).

48 See Bullivant 1960 p.233.

49 P 1182: by an unknown copyist before *c.*1780 (communication from Yo Tomita); the words were added in a different coloured ink after the music had been copied.

50 The term Invention is only one of several that Bach applied to this type of piece: apart from Praeludium, he called it Praeambulum in the *Clavier-Büchlein*, and Fantasia in the opening movement of the A minor Partita BWV 827.

51 'Verlängerung einer Melodie durch die Zusammensetzung solcher kleinen Sätze' (1777 pp.163–5; Dok.III p.230).

52 The addition of a demisemiquaver to the plain semiquavers in the treble of b.3 etc. seems to have been made by Bach as a late correction in Altnickol's 1744 copy; the staccato marks given by Kroll and others at bb.18 and 20 do not stem from Bach but were added after 1750 to Kirnberger's personal copy Am.B.57(2), perhaps by Kirnberger himself (AB II pp.173–4; Dürr 1998 pp.318–19).

53 Kirnberger 1776 pp.119–20, Dok.III pp.223–4, Little and Jenne 1991 p.161; Kirnberger's footnote identifying Couperin as François, *le grand*, is omitted in Dok.III.

54 According to Dürr (1998 p.370) the change from ♩. ♬♪ (here) to ♩‿♬♬ (in the A flat major prelude) is just Bach's later notational trend (see the commentary on the A flat prelude).

55 They are a feature of flute technique in the Adagio, to be tongued separately according to e.g. Michel Corrette in his flute Method (*c.*1740).

56 NBA V/6.2 pp.338–9, PF pp.32–3, for source details see Dürr 1998 pp.355–7.

57 AB II p.181; Tomita 1999 pp.60–3.

58 1940/8 p.88; this article on Bach's rhythm is a good example of wrong-headed writing about Bach on the basis of too little background knowledge: for example, he proposes that the B minor fugue of Book I is all one beat out.

59 For the identification of the fingerings in Am.B.57(2), see KB V/6.2 p.67; similar

passages are in the C minor and B flat major preludes of Book I. Kirnberger studied with Bach in 1739–41, at the time when Book II was being assembled.

60 Renwick 2001 p.46.

61 Dahlhaus 1965 p.7; Snyder 1980 pp.549–52; and see Ex.4.9.

62 For further examples see Allsop 1992 pp.297, 303.

63 Rhythmic characters, as opposed to *genera* of counterpoint, seem less explored in *The Art of Fugue*; it is noticeable, though, that the subject in Contrapunctus 1, and much of the counterpoint, uses the paean metre (one long and three short syllables), traditionally used for overtures and entrées (Mattheson 1739 II Chapter 6 para.13).

64 VBN I/D/1; see also the commentary on the F major fugue.

65 See, for example, Tröster 1984; for discussions relating specifically to *The Well-tempered Clavier* see Tolonen 1971 and Kluge-Kahn 1985.

66 See Stinson 1989 pp.465–6, also Butler 1990 p.12.

67 Alfredo Casella, cited in Damerini 1963 p.200.

68 Kirnberger 1773; see Beach and Thym 1979 p.208, and Lester 1992 p.240.

69 The diminished 7th leap in fugue subjects is a commonplace from the later seventeenth century: see Buxtehude's G minor Praeludium BuxWV 148, which first appears in a tablature of 1675 and also exists in a copy by Bach's brother Johann Christoph (Schulze 1991); for Bach's use of the diminished 7th in subjects in the 48, see the commentaries on the D minor and G minor fugues of Book I and the F minor fugue of Book II.

70 The fugue attributed to Benedetto Marcello, on which Bach seems to have based the concluding fugue in the early E minor Toccata BWV 914, contains hand-crossing which again does little for a banal piece; Bach in his reworking omitted it (see Eisert 1994 pp.172–6, 212–17).

71 For examples of a chromatic tinge before the double bar of a binary piece see the discussion of the G major prelude.

72 Bach seems originally to have used **c**; cf. the equivalent time-signature change from $\frac{3}{4}$ to $\frac{3}{2}$ in the B flat minor fugue.

73 Avoidance of steps; see the discussion of genera of counterpoint in Chapter 4 section 8.

74 Possibly written for L. Mizler in 1734 (Dürr 1995 p.1001); the harmonic point is not affected by the doubt about Bach's authorship.

75 Examples are in Fischer's *Blumen-Strauss* (1732; ed. Werra p.111) and in the Langloz *partimenti*.

76 François Couperin in his B minor 8th *Ordre* (1717) chose to finish with a small character piece (*La Morinète*) rather than the massive Passacaille.

77 Jones considers Altnickol's reading to be Bach's final thought (AB II); Tomita gives reasons for thinking the London autograph has the final reading (1993 p.142).

Glossary

These explanations are summary. More detail will be found in the *New Harvard Dictionary of Music* and *New Grove 2*.

chiasmus	from the Greek letter chi (χ); a musical figure in which, if you draw a line from the first note to the last and between the two middle notes the two lines form a cross, as they do with the notes (in German) B A C H
chromatic tetrachord	see *lamento* bass
comma	for the ditonic and syntonic commas, see Appendix B
diesis	(enharmonic) the difference between an octave and three pure major 3rds (= *c.*41 cents); see Appendix B
divisions	a technique of variation in which the beat is divided into successively smaller note values
durezze e ligature	dissonances and suspensions; in seventeenth-century Italy a toccata *di durezze e ligature* was customarily played during the Elevation of the Mass, using two 8' diapasons and tremulant
evolutio	a term used by J. Theile and others for the inversion(s) of invertible counterpoint; see Chapter 4 section 7
évolution	a term used by François Couperin (1717) for a finger exercise that systematically uses a specific interval or figuration ('petits exercices pour former les mains')
galant style	introduced by opera composers in Naples after *c.*1710; generally has straightforward harmony,

	four-bar phrases often with dance rhythms, and a mixture of note values in the solo line (triplets, lombardic rhythm ♬♩., etc.)
golden section	the division of a line into two unequal segments, the lesser segment being to the greater as the greater is to the whole line; the section point is normally expressed as × 0.618 of the line; a proportion much used in music from the sixteenth century onwards
harmonic proportions	proportions from the harmonic series (2:1, 3:2 etc.), see Appendix B
hexachord	a six-note scale devised for teaching pitch relations by Guido of Arezzo *c.*1000, based on the initial notes and syllables of each line of the plain-chant hymn 'Ut queant laxis' (for the feast of St John the Baptist, patron saint of singing since he is first mentioned in St Mark's Gospel as 'Vox clamantis in deserto'); each line begins on a successively higher note of the major scale, starting with C (Ut), and the initial syllables are Ut re mi fa sol la (see solmisation)
inganno	(1) exploiting the ambiguity of solmisation to derive new pitch material from an existing theme; or using notes that form words in solmisation (see Harper 1978–9); (2) Marpurg uses this term for flattening a leading note, thereby deflecting the effect of a perfect cadence
labyrinth	a piece that modulates systematically through all or most of the 24 keys; the maze from which Ariadne escaped the Minotaur in Greek mythology
lamento bass	a ground-bass pattern that steps down in semitones from the tonic to the dominant; the best-known example is probably Dido's Lament from Purcell's *Dido and Aeneas* (see P. Williams 1997)
partimento	a fugal movement expressed mostly as a single-line figured bass (see Renwick 2001)
per arsin et thesin	used by Marpurg (1753 etc.) for changing the onbeats into offbeats and vice versa in a fugue subject
permutation counterpoint	a complex of usually two, three, or four melodic

	strands which can be sounded simultaneously, each of which is usable as a bass so that each strand may be used in any voice; invertible counterpoint (see Chapter 4 section 7)
Pythagorean 3rd	the major 3rd which is the product of four pure 5ths; see Appendix B
roulade	a seventeenth-century method of fingering scale passages without pivoting over the thumb, in which successive groups of three or four notes are alternated between the hands
second practice	a term used by Monteverdi (*seconda pratica*, 1605) for the free, expressive treatment of dissonance, as opposed to the first practice (*stile antico*)
solmisation	the system of naming notes in the hexachord; in order to gain a seven-note scale from the six-note hexachord it is necessary to have a series of overlapping hexachords: (1) beginning on C (the natural hexachord); (2) beginning on F (the soft hexachord, so-called from the rounded shape of B♭ for the 4th degree, or Fa); and (3) beginning on G (the hard hexachord, from the square shape of B♮ for the 3rd degree, or Mi); thus a scale of C major changes to the hard hexachord after G (ut re mi fa sol re mi fa) in order to get up the octave; equally, any note can have several different syllables from different hexachords, as C sol fa ut, D la sol re, E la mi, G sol re ut, A la mi re; the fact that each note can have several different syllables gives rich possibilities for playing with ambiguity in *inganno*; Bach's name in notes (BACH) can be interpreted as fa mi fa mi, hence the special significance for him of the adage 'Mi et fa sunt tota musica' (see Agricola 1757, trans. Baird pp.53–63)
stile antico	Monteverdi's first practice (*prima pratica*); a continuation of the high Renaissance polyphonic style of Palestrina: alla breve ¢ time signature, white note values, fluid unsymmetrical lines, careful dissonance treatment, learned counterpoint; was standard for church music in Italy and the Catholic parts of Germany in the seventeenth and eighteenth centuries

versets	short organ pieces that replace alternate verses of the Mass Ordinary or Magnificat
vieil ton	the standard Renaissance lute tuning in which the six fingered courses of the lute are tuned (from the top down) g' d' a f c G (or the same intervals down from a')

Bibliography

For a comprehensive listing of Bach literature, see Yo Tomita's Bach Bibliography website (<music.qub.ac.uk/~tomita/bachbib>). Only items cited in the text of this book are listed here, if the bibliographical information given in the text needs to be supplemented.

1. Music

Ammerbach, Elias Nicolaus, *Orgel oder Instrument Tabulatur* (Leipzig, 1571), ed. C. Jacobs (Oxford: Clarendon Press, 1984)

Bach, Johann Sebastian, *Das wohltemperierte Klavier/ Le clavecin bien tempéré/ Forty-Eight Preludes and Fugues*, ed. H. Bischoff (Leipzig, 1881), ed. F.B. Busoni (Leipzig, [c.1894–9]), ed. C. Czerny (Leipzig, [1837]), ed. W. Dehnhard (Mainz/Vienna, 1977, 1983), ed. D.F. Tovey and H. Samuel (London, 1924)

Battiferri, Luigi, *Ricercari . . . opera terza* (Bologna, 1669), ed. G.G. Butler (Neuhausen-Stuttgart: American Institute of Musicology, 1981)

Buttstett, Johann Heinrich, *Musicalische Clavier-Kunst* (Leipzig, [1713])

Corelli, Arcangelo, *Sonate a violino e violone o cimbalo . . . troisième edition ou l'on joint les agréemens des adagio . . . comme il les joue* (Amsterdam, [1710])

Couperin, François, *Pieces de clavecin . . . premier livre* (Paris, 1713), *Second Livre de pieces de clavecin* (Paris, [1717]), *Troisieme livre de pieces de clavecin* (Paris, 1722), *Quatrieme livre de pieces de clavecin* (Paris, 1730), ed. K. Gilbert (Paris: Heugel, 1969–72)

D'Anglebert, Jean Henry, *Pieces de clavecin* (Paris, 1689), ed. K. Gilbert (Paris: Heugel, 1975)

Fischer, Johann Caspar Ferdinand, *Les pieces de clavessin* (Augsburg, 1696), *Musicalisches Blumen-Büschlein* (Augsburg, 1698), *Ariadne Musica* ([Schlackenwerth, 1702], Augsburg, 2/1715), *Blumen-Strauß . . . in acht tonos ecclesiasticos eingetheilet* (Augsburg, 1732), *Musicalischer Parnassus* (Augsburg, 1738), ed. E. v. Werra (Leipzig: Breitkopf & Härtel, 1901)

Frescobaldi, Girolamo, *Il primo libro delle fantasie* (Milan, 1608), *Toccate . . . libro primo* (Rome, 5/1637), *Il primo libro di capricci* (Venice, 2/1626), *Fiori musicali* (Venice, 1635)

Froberger, Johann Jakob, 'Libro secondo di toccate' (1649), 'Libro quarto di toccate' (1656), *Diverse . . . partite* (Mainz, 1693), *Dive[r]se . . . partite* (Mainz, 1696, 2/1699, 3/1714), ed. H. Schott (Paris: Heugel, 1979–92), ed. S. Rampe (Kassel: Bärenreiter, 1993)

Gorzanis, Giacomo, 'Libro de intabulatura di liuto' (1567), ed. B. Tonazzi (Milan: Suvini Zerboni, 1975)

Havingha, Gerhard, *VIII suites . . . voor de clavecÿmbal off spinet* (Amsterdam, 1725), facs. intro. C. Romijn (Utrecht: STIMU, 1990)

Kapsberger, Giovanni Girolamo, *Libro primo d'intavolatura de chitarone* (Venice, 1604), ed. K. Gilbert (Bologna: Ut Orpheus, 1998)

Kerll, Johann Caspar, *Modulatio organica* (Munich, 1686), ed. F. di Lernia (Vienna: Universal Edition, 1991)

Kirnberger, Johann, *Clavierübungen . . . vierte Sammlung* (Berlin, 1766), ed. R. Rasch (Utrecht: The Diapason Press, 1990)

——*Recueil d'airs de danse caractéristiques* (Berlin, [1777]) [1777b]

Krieger, Johann, *Anmuthige Clavier-Übung* (Nuremberg 1699), ed. S. Rampe and H. Lerch (Kassel: Bärenreiter, 1999), *Präludien und Fugen* (MS 1688), ed. F.W. Riedel (Porz am Rhein: Kistner u. Siegel, [1960])

Kuhnau, Johann, *Neüer Clavier Übung erster Theil* (Leipzig, 1689), *Andrer Theil* (Leipzig, 1692), ed. K. Päsler, H.J. Moser, DdT I/4 (Wiesbaden: Breitkopf & Härtel, 1958)

Mattheson, Johann, *Pieces de clavecin/Harmonisches Denckmahl* (London, 1714)

Muffat, Georg, *Apparatus musico-organisticus* (Salzburg, 1690)

Murschhauser, F.X. Anton, *Octi-tonium novum organicum* (Augsburg, 1696), *Prototypon longo-breve organicum* (Nuremberg, 1703, 1707)

Pachelbel, Johann, *Magnificatfugen* (MS 1701–5), ed. T. Zászkaliczky (Kassel: Bärenreiter, 1982), *Präludien . . . Choralbearbeitungen*, ed. M. Seiffert (Leipzig, 1903)

Purcell, Henry, *Twenty Keyboard Pieces*, ed. D. Moroney (London: The Associated Board of the Royal Schools of Music, 1999)

Speth, Johann, *Ars magna consoni et dissoni* (Augsburg, 1693), ed. T. Fedke (Kassel: Bärenreiter, 1973)

Wolf, Ernst Wilhelm, *Eine Sonatine . . .* (Leipzig, 1785)

2. *Literature before 1850*

Adlung, Jakob, *Anleitung zu der musikalischen Gelahrtheit* (Erfurt, 1758)

——*Musica mechanica organoedi* (Berlin, 1768), facs. intro. C. Mahrenholz (Kassel: Bärenreiter, 1961)

Agricola, Johann Friedrich, *Anleitung zur Singkunst* (Berlin, 1757), trans. J. Baird (Cambridge: Cambridge University Press, 1995)

Ahle, Johann Rudolf, *Kurze . . . Anleitung zu der . . . Singkunst* (Mühlhausen, 1690, 2/1704)

Altenburg, Johann Ernst, *Versuch einer Anleitung sur heroisch-musikalischen Trompeter- und Pauker-Kunst* (Halle, 1795), trans. E. Tarr (Nashville: The Brass Press, 1974)

Bach, Carl Philipp Emanuel, *Versuch über die wahre Art das Clavier zu spielen* (Berlin, 1753, 1762), trans. W.J. Mitchell (London: Cassel, 1947)

Banchieri, Adriano, *Cartello musicale* (Venice, 1613–14)

Bendeler, Johann Philipp, *Organopoeia* (Frankfurt, [*c*.1690])

Berardi, Angelo, *Documenti armonici* (Bologna, 1687)

——*Miscellanea musicale* (Bologna, 1689)

——*Arcana musicali* (Bologna, 1690)

Bernhard, Christoph, 'Tractatus compositionis augmentatus' [*c*.1660], ed. J. Müller-Blattau (Kassel: Bärenreiter, 2/1963)

Bononcini, Giovanni Maria, *Musico prattico* (Bologna, 1688), German trans. (Stuttgart, 1701)

Brossard, Sébastien de, *Dictionnaire de musique* (Paris, 2/1705)

Buttstett, Johann Heinrich, *Ut, mi, sol, re, fa, la, tota musica et harmonia aeterna* (Leipzig, [1716])

Cherubini, Luigi, *Cours de contrepoint et de fugue* (Paris, [c.1837]), trans. J.A. Hamilton (London: R. Cocks, 1838)

Couperin, François, *L'art de toucher le clavecin* (Paris, 2/1717)

Denis, Jean, *Traité de l'accord de l'espinette* (Paris, 1643, 2/1650), facs. intro. A. Curtis (New York: Da Capo, 1969)

Forkel, Johann Nikolaus, *Musikalischer Almanach . . . 1782* (Leipzig, 1781 etc.)

——*Über Johann Sebastian Bachs Leben, Kunst und Kunstwerke* (Leipzig, 1802), trans. NBR

——'Von der wahren Güte der Clavichorde' (MS), ed. Neupert 1955

Fritz, Barthold, *Anweisung, wie man Claviere . . . in allen zwölf Tönen gleich rein stimmen könne* (Leipzig, 1756, 2/1757)

Fux, Johann Joseph, *Gradus ad Parnassum* (Vienna, 1725), German trans. Mizler 1742

Griepenkerl, Friedrich Conrad, 'Einige Bemerkungen über den Vortrag der chromatischen Phantasie' (Leipzig, 1820), trans. Spányi and Collins 2000

Hartung, Philipp Christoph, *Deß Musici theoretici-practici zweyter Theil* (Nuremberg, 1749)

Heinichen, Johann David, *Neu erfundene . . . Anweisung . . . des General-Basses* (Hamburg, 1711)

——*Der General-Bass in der Composition* (Dresden, 1728), partial trans. Buelow 1986

Hertel, Johann Wilhelm, *Sammlung musikalischer Schriften . . . zweytes Stück* (Leipzig, 1758)

Hotteterre, Jacques, *L'art de preluder* (Paris, 1719)

Janovka, Tomáš Baltazar, *Clavis ad thesaurum magnae artis musicae* (Prague, 1701)

Kircher, Athanasius, *Musurgia universalis* (Rome, 1650), partial German trans. (Schwäbisch Hall, 1662)

Kirnberger, Johann, *Die Kunst des reinen Satzes in der Musik* (Berlin, 1771, 1776, 1777 [1777a], 1779), partial trans. D. Beach and J. Thym (New Haven: Yale University Press, 1982)

——*Die wahren Grundsätze zum Gebrauch der Harmonie* (Berlin, 1773), trans. and intro. D.W. Beach and J. Thym, *Journal of Music Theory* xxiii (1979) 163–225

——*Grundsätze des Generalbasses* (Berlin, 1781)

——*Gedanken über die verschiedenen Lehrarten in der Komposition* (Berlin, 1782), trans. R.B. Nelson and D.R. Boomgaarden, *Journal of Music Theory* xxx (1986) 71–94

Kittel, Johann Christian, *Der angehende praktische Organist, zweite Abtheilung* (Erfurt, 1803)

Kollmann, Augustus Frederic Christopher, *An Essay on Musical Harmony* (London, 1796)

——*An Essay on Practical Musical Composition* (London, 1799)

——'Of Johann Sebastian Bach, and his works', *Quarterly Musical Register* i (1/1812) 28–40

Krasske, Tobias, *Kurtze Beschreibung der neuen Orgel bey der Ober-Kirchen zu Franckfurt an der Oder* (Frankfurt a.d. Oder, 1695)

Lange, Johann Caspar, *Methodus nova . . . in artem musicam* (Hildesheim, 1688)

Lorber, Johann Christoph, *Lob der edlen Musik* (Weimar, 1696)

Marpurg, Friedrich Wilhelm, *Die Kunst das Clavier zu spielen* (Berlin, 2/1751, 3/1760)

——*Abhandlung von der Fuge* (Berlin, 1753, 1754)

——*Anleitung zum Clavierspielen* (Berlin 1755, 2/1765)

——*Anfangsgründe der theoretischen Musik* (Leipzig, 1757)

——*Kritische Briefe über die Tonkunst* III (Berlin, 1764)

——*Versuch über die musikalische Temperatur* (Breslau, 1776)

Mattheson, Johann, *Das neu-eröffnete Orchestre* (Hamburg, 1713)

——*Das beschützte Orchestre* (Hamburg, 1717)

——*Exemplarische Organisten-Probe* (Hamburg, 1719)

——*Réflexions sur l'éclaircissement d'un problème de musique pratique* (Hamburg, 1720)

——*Critica musica* (Hamburg, 1722, 1725)

——*Grosse General-Baß-Schule* (Hamburg, 1731)

——*Kern melodischer Wissenschaft* (Hamburg, 1737)
——*Der vollkommene Capellmeister* (Hamburg, 1739), trans. E.C. Harriss (Ann Arbor: UMI Research Press, 1981)
——*Grundlage einer Ehrenpforte* (Hamburg, 1740)
Meckenheuser, Johann Georg, *Die so genannte: Allerneueste musicalische Temperatur* (Quedlinburg, 1727)
Merbach, Georg Friedrich, *Clavierschule für Kinder* (Leipzig, 1782)
Mersenne, Marin, *Harmonie universelle* (Paris, 1636)
Mizler, Lorenz, *Anfangs-Gründe des General Basses* (Leipzig, [1739])
——*Gradus ad Parnassum . . . von Johann Joseph Fux . . . aus dem Lateinischen . . . übersetzt* (Leipzig, 1742)
——*Das neu eröffnete musikalische Bibliothek* (1737, 1746) (Leipzig, 1752)
Morley, Thomas, *A Plaine and Easie Introduction to Practicall Musicke* (London, 1597), ed. R.A. Harman (London: Dent, 1952)
Muffat, Georg, *Florilegium secundum* (Passau, 1698)
——*An Essay on Thoroughbass* (MS 1699 or earlier), ed. H. Federhofer (Brooklyn: American Institute of Musicology, 1961)
——*Auserlesene Instrumentalmusik* (Passau, 1701)
Murschhauser, Franz Xaver Anton, *Academia musico-poetica* (Nuremberg, 1721)
Neidhardt, Johann Georg, *Beste und leichteste Temperatur* (Jena, 1706)
——*Sectio canonis harmonici* (Königsberg, 1724)
——*Gäntzlich erschöpfte mathematische Abtheilungen des . . . Monochordi* (Königsberg, 1732)
Niedt, Friederich Erhardt, *Musicalische Handleitung* (Hamburg, 1700–17), trans. Poulin and Taylor 1989
Pasquali, Nicolo, *The Art of Fingering the Harpsichord* (Edinburgh, [c.1758])
Petri, Johann Samuel, *Anleitung zur praktischen Musik* (Lauban, 1767)
Praetorius, Michael, *Syntagmis musici . . . tomus secundus. Tomus tertius* (Wolfenbüttel, 1619)
Printz, Wolfgang Caspar, *Musica modulatoria vocalis* (Schweidnitz, 1678)
——*Phrynidis Mytilenaei oder des satyrischen Componisten dritter Theil* (Dresden, 1696)
Quantz, Johann Joachim, *Versuch einer Anweisung die Flöte traversiere zu spielen* (Berlin, 1752), trans. E.R. Reilly (London: Faber and Faber, 2/1985)
Rameau, Jean-Philippe, 'De la méchanique des doigts sur le clavessin', *Pièces de clavessin* (Paris, 1724), ed. K. Gilbert (Paris: Heugel, 1979)
——*Code de musique pratique* (Paris, 1760)
Rellstab, Johann Carl Friedrich, *Anleitung für Clavierspieler* (Berlin, 1790)
Saint-Lambert, M. de, *Les principes du clavecin* (Paris, 1702), trans. R. Harriss-Warrick (Cambridge: Cambridge University Press, 1984)
Sauveur, Joseph, 'Sur les sistemes temperés de musique' (1707), facs. ed. Rasch 1984

Scheibe, Johann Adolph, 'Compendium musices theoretico-practicum (c.1730), ed. Benary 1961

Schmidt, Johann Michael, *Musico-theologia* (Bayreuth, 1754)

Simpson, Christopher, *A Compendium of Practical Musick* (London, 1667)

Sinn, Christoph Albert, *Die aus mathematischen Gründen richtig gestellte musicalische Temperatura practica* (Wernigerode, 1717)

Sorge, Georg Andreas, *Anweisung zur Stimmung und Temperatur* (Hamburg, 1744)

——*Gespräch zwischen einem Musico theoretico und einem Studioso musices* (Lobenstein, 1748)

——*Ausführliche . . . Anweisung zur Rational-Rechnung . . . des Monochords* (Lobenstein, 1749)

——*Der in der Rechen- und Meßkunst wohlerfahrene Orgelbaumeister* (Lobenstein, 1773)

Speer, Daniel, *Grund-richtiger . . . Unterricht . . . oder . . . musicalisches Kleeblatt* (Ulm, 2/1697)

Telemann, Georg Philipp, *Der harmonische Gottesdienst. Teil I* (Hamburg, 1725), 'Telemanns Vorbericht', ed. G. Fock (Kassel: Bärenreiter, 1953)

Thielo, Carl August, *Grundregeln, wie man . . . die Fundamenta der Music und des Claviers lernen kann* (Copenhagen, 1753)

Treiber, Johann Philipp, *Sonderbare Invention: Eine Arie . . . aus allen Tonen . . . zu componiren* (Jena, 1702)

——*Der accurate Organist im General-Bass* (Jena, 1704, 2/1713)

Trost, Johann Caspar, *Ausführliche Beschreibung deß Neuen Orgelwercks auf der Augustus-Burg zu Weissenfels* (Nuremberg, 1677)

Türk, Daniel Gottlob, *Von den wichtigsten Pflichten eines Organisten* (Halle, 1787)

——*Clavierschule* (Leipzig, 1789), trans. R. Haggh (Lincoln and London: University of Nebraska Press, 1982)

Virdung, Sebastian, *Musica getutscht* (Basel, 1511), trans. B. Bullard (Cambridge: Cambridge University Press, 1993)

Vockerodt (Fokkerodt), Johann Arnold, *Gründlichen musicalischen Unterrichts erster Teil* (Mühlhausen, 1698)

Vogt, Mauritius, *Conclave thesauri magnae artis musicae* (Prague, 1719)

Walther, Johann Gottfried, 'Praecepta der musicalischen Composition' (1708), ed. P. Benary (Leipzig: Breitkopf & Härtel, 1955)

——*Musicalisches Lexicon* (Leipzig, 1732)

Werckmeister, Andreas, *Orgel-Probe* (Frankfurt, 1681)

——*Musicae mathematicae hodegus curiosus* (Frankfurt, 1687)

——*Musicalische Temperatur* (Quedlinburg, 1691), facs. intro. Rasch 1983

——*Hypomnemata musica* (Quedlinburg, 1697)

——*Erweiterte und verbesserte Orgel-Probe* (Quedlinburg, 1698) [1698a]

——*Die nothwendigsten Anmerckungen . . . wie der Bassus continuus . . . wol könne*

tractiret werden (Aschersleben, 1698, 2/1715) [1698b]
——*Harmonologia musica* (Quedlinburg, 1702)
——*Musicalische Paradoxal-Discourse* (Quedlinburg, 1707)
Zarlino, Gioseffo, *Le istitutioni harmoniche* (Venice, 1558), part three trans. G.A. Marco and C.V. Palisca (New Haven: Yale University Press, 1968)
Zedler, Johann Heinrich, *Grosses vollständiges Universal Lexicon* (Halle, 1733ff)

3. Literature after 1850

Ahrens, Christian, 'Zum Bau und zur Nutzung von 16'-Registern und von Pedalen bei Cembali und Clavichorden', *Cöthener Bach-Hefte* viii (1998) 57–71
Allsop, Peter, *The Italian 'Trio' Sonata from its Origins until Corelli* (Oxford: Clarendon Press, 1992)
——*Arcangelo Corelli* (Oxford: Clarendon Press, 1999)
Anthony, James, *French Baroque Music* (Portland: Amadeus Press, 4/1997)
Apel, Willi, *The History of Keyboard Music to 1700* (Bloomington, Indiana University Press, 1972)
——*Italian Violin Music of the Seventeenth Century* (Bloomington: Indiana University Press, 1990)
Arbogast, Jochen, *Stilistische Untersuchungen zum Klavierwerk des Thomaskantors Johann Kuhnau* (Regensburg: Bosse, 1983)
Arnold, Franck Thomas, *The Art of Accompaniment from a Thorough-Bass* (London: Oxford University Press, 1931)
Auerbach, Cornelia, *Die deutsche Clavichordkunst des 18. Jahrhunderts* (Kassel: Bärenreiter, 1930)
Badura-Skoda, Eva, 'Komponierte J.S. Bach "Hammerklavier-Konzerte"?', *Bach-Jahrbuch* (1991) 159–71
Badura-Skoda, Paul, *Interpreting Bach at the Keyboard* (Oxford: Clarendon Press, 1993)
Baffert, Jean-Marc, 'Vier unbekannte Bach-Erwähnungen in Druckschriften des 18. Jahrhunderts', *Bach-Jahrbuch* (1988) 191–3
Barbour, James Murray, *Tuning and Temperament* (East Lansing: Michigan State College Press, 1951)
Barnes, John, 'Bach's keyboard temperament: internal evidence from the *Well-tempered Clavier*', *Early Music* vii (1979) 236–49
——review of Helenius-Öberg 1986, *Galpin Society Journal* xliv (1991) 198–201
Barnett, Gregory, 'Modal theory, church keys, and the sonata at the end of the seventeenth century', *Journal of the American Musicological Society* li (1998) 245–81

Bartel, Dietrich, *Musical-Rhetorical Figures in German Baroque Music* (Lincoln and London: University of Nebraska Press, 1997)

Bartelink, Bernard, 'Das wohltemperirte Clavier op orgel uitgevoerd', *Mens en Melodie* xii (1957) 152–4

Beckmann, Klaus, 'Zur Chronologie der freien Orgelwerke Buxtehudes', *Dietrich Buxtehude und die europäische Musik seiner Zeit*, ed. A. Edler and F. Krummacher (Kassel: Bärenreiter, 1990) 224–34

Beechey, Gwylem, 'A 17th-century German organ tutor', *The Musical Times* cxiii (1972) 86–9

Bellman, Jonathan, 'Frédéric Chopin, Antoine de Kontski and the *carezzando* touch', *Early Music* xxix (2001) 398–407

Benary, Peter, *Die deutsche Kompositionslehre des 18. Jahrhunderts* (Leipzig: Breitkopf & Härtel, 1961)

Bent, Ian (ed.), *Music Analysis in the Nineteenth Century. Volume I: Fugue, Form and Style* (Cambridge: Cambridge University Press, 1994)

Bergner, Christoph, *Studien zur Form der Praeludien des Wohltemperierten Klaviers von Johann Sebastian Bach* (Neuhausen-Stuttgart: Hänssler, 1986)

Berke, Dietrich and Dorothee Hanemann (eds), *Alte Musik als ästetische Gegenwart* (Kassel: Bärenreiter, 1987)

Besseler, Heinrich, 'Charakterthema und Erlebnisform bei Bach', *Kongress-Bericht, Gesellschaft für Musikforschung, Lüneburg 1950*, ed. H. Albrecht, H. Osthoff, W. Wiora (Kassel: Bärenreiter, [1952]) 7–32

Billeter, Bernhard, 'Die Silbermann Stimmungen', *Archiv für Musikwissenschaft* xxvii (1970) 73–85

Blankenburg, Walter, 'Die innere Einheit von Bachs Werk', Dr. diss., University of Göttingen, 1942

——'Der Titel und das Titelbild von J.H. Buttstett's Schrift "Ut mi sol . . . " (1717)', *Die Musikforschung* iii (1950) 64–6

——(ed.), *Johann Sebastian Bach* (Darmstadt: Wissenschaftliche Buchgesellchaft, 1970)

Boalch, Donald H., *Makers of the Harpsichord and Clavichord 1440–1840*, rev. C. Mould (Oxford: Clarendon Press, 3/1995)

Bodky, Erwin, *The Interpretation of Bach's Keyboard Works* (Cambridge: Harvard University Press, 1960)

Borgir, Tharald, *The Performance of the Basso Continuo in Italian Baroque Music* (Ann Arbor: UMI Research Press, 1987)

Borris, Siegfried, *Kirnbergers Leben und Werk und seine Bedeutung im Berliner Musikkreis um 1750* (Kassel: Bärenreiter, 1933)

Boyd, Malcolm, *Domenico Scarlatti* (London: Weidenfeld and Nicolson, 1986)

Brauchli, Bernard, *The Clavichord* (Cambridge: Cambridge University Press, 1998)

Breckoff, Werner, *Zur Entstehungsgeschichte des zweiten Wohltemperierten Klaviers von Johann Sebastian Bach* (Tübingen: Philosophische Fakultät der Universität Tübingen, 1965)

Breig, Werner, 'Versuch einer Theorie der Bachschen Orgelfuge', *Die Musikforschung* xlviii (1995) 14–52

Brokaw, James A., 'Techniques of Expansion in the Preludes and Fugues of J.S. Bach', Ph.D. diss., University of Chicago, 1986

——'The genesis of the prelude in C major BWV 870', in Franklin (1989) 225–39

Buchmayer, Richard, 'Cembalo oder Pianoforte?', *Bach-Jahrbuch* (1908) 64–93

Buelow, George J., 'An evaluation of Johann Mattheson's opera *Cleopatra* (Hamburg, 1704)', *Studies in Eighteenth-Century Music*, ed. H.C. Robbins-Landon and R.E. Chapman (London: Allen and Unwin, 1970) 92–107

——'Johann Mattheson and the invention of the *Affektenlehre*', in Buelow and Marx (1983) 393–407

——*Thorough-Bass Accompaniment according to Johann David Heinichen* (Lincoln and London: University of Nebraska Press, 2/1986)

——and Hans Joachim Marx (eds), *New Mattheson Studies* (Cambridge: Cambridge University Press, 1983)

Bullivant, Roger, 'The Fugal Technique of J.S. Bach', D.Phil. diss., University of Oxford, 1960

Bunge, Rudolf, 'Johann Sebastian Bachs Capelle zu Cöthen und deren nachgelassene Instrumente', *Bach-Jahrbuch* (1905) 14–47

Burns, Lori, *Bach's Modal Chorales* (Stuyvesant: Pendragon Press, 1995)

Burrows, Donald, *Handel* (Oxford: Oxford University Press, 1994)

Busch, Hermann, 'Das wohltemperierte Clavier auf der Orgel: Eine Interpretationstradition des 19. Jahrhunderts', *The Organ Yearbook* xxix (2000) 127–35

Butler, Gregory B., 'Fugue and rhetoric', *Journal of Music Theory* xxi (1977) 49–109

——'*Der vollkommene Capellmeister* as a stimulus to J.S. Bach's late fugal writing', in Buelow and Marx (1983) 293–305

——*Bach's Clavier-Übung III* (Durham and London: Duke University Press, 1990)

——'J.S. Bach's reception of Tomaso Albinoni's mature concertos', *Bach Studies 2*, ed. D. Melamed (Cambridge: Cambridge University Press, 1995) 20–46

Butt, John, *Bach Interpretation* (Cambridge: Cambridge University Press, 1990)

——*Bach: Mass in B minor* (Cambridge: Cambridge University Press, 1991)

——*Music Education and the Art of Performance in the German Baroque* (Cambridge: Cambridge University Press, 1994)

——(ed.) *The Cambridge Companion to Bach* (Cambridge: Cambridge University Press, 1997)

Buys, Hans Brandts, *Het wohltemperirte Clavier van Johann Sebastian Bach* (Arnhem: Loghum Slaterus, 3/1955)

Campbell, Margaret, *Dolmetsch: The Man and his Work* (London: Hamish Hamilton, 1975)

Candé, Roland de, *Jean-Sébastien Bach* (Paris: Seuil, 1984)

Chafe, Eric, *Tonal Allegory in the Vocal Music of J.S. Bach* (Berkeley: University of California Press, 1991)

Christensen, Thomas, 'The Spanish Baroque guitar and seventeenth-century triadic theory', *Journal of Music Theory* xxxvi (1992) 1–42

Clayson, Richard, and Andrew Garrett, *Tuning Compass* (Lyminge: authors, 1980)

Coelho, Victor, 'Frescobaldi and the lute and chitarrone toccatas of "Il Tedesco della Tiorba"', in Silbiger (1987) 137–56

Cooper, Kenneth, 'The Clavichord in the Eighteenth Century', Ph.D. diss., Columbia University, 1971

Constantini, Franz Peter, 'Die Entwicklung der Versettenkomposition vom ausgehenden Mittelbarock bis zum Rokoko', Dr. diss., University of Vienna, 1967

——'Zur Typusgeschichte von J.S. Bachs Wohltemperiertem Klavier', *Bach-Jahrbuch* (1969) 31–45

Cowgill, Rachel, 'The London Apollonian recitals, 1817–32: a case-study in Bach, Mozart and Haydn reception', *Journal of the Royal Musical Association* cxxiii/2 (1998) 190–228

Crussard, Claude, 'Marc-Antoine Charpentier théoricien', *Revue de musicologie* xxiv (1945) 49–68

Cucuel, Georges, *La Pouplinière et la musique de chambre au XVIIIe siècle* (Paris: Fischbacher, 1913)

Czaczkes, Ludwig, *Analyse des Wohltemperierten Klaviers* (Vienna: Österreichischer Bundesverlag, I 1956, II 1965; 2/1982)

Dadelsen, Georg, *Beiträge zur Chronologie der Werke Johann Sebastian Bachs* (Trossingen: Hohner, 1958)

——and Klaus Röhnau (eds), *J.S. Bach: Fantasien, Präludien und Fugen* (Munich: Henle, [1973])

Dahlhaus, Carl (ed.), *Johann Theile: Musikalisches Kunst-Buch* (Kassel: Bärenreiter, 1965)

Dähnert, Ulrich, *Der Orgel- und Instrumentenbauer Zacharias Hildebrandt* (Leipzig: VEB Breitkopf & Härtel, 1962)

Damerini, Adelino, 'Valori eterni del "Clavicembalo ben temperato" di J.S. Bach', *L'approdo musicale* xvi/xvii (1963) 196–200

Dannreuther, Edward, *Musical Ornamentation (Part I)* (London: Novello, [1893])

Dart, Robert Thurston and Davitt Moroney (eds), *John Blow's Anthology*

(London: Stainer & Bell, 1978)

David, Hans T., 'A lesser secret of Bach uncovered', *Journal of the American Musicological Society* xiv (1961) 199–223

David, Johann Nepomuk, *Das wohltemperierte Klavier: Versuch einer Synopsis* (Göttingen: Vandenhoeck u. Ruprecht, 1962)

Dehn, Siegfried Wilhelm, *Analyse dreier Fugen aus dem Wohltemperierten Klavier* (Leipzig: Peters, 1858)

Deppert, Heinrich, *Kadenz und Klausel in der Musik von J.S. Bach* (Tutzing: Schneider, 1993)

Dirksen, Pieter, 'The background to Bach's Fifth Brandenburg Concerto', in Dirksen (1992) 156–85

——(ed.), *Proceedings of the International Harpsichord Symposium Utrecht 1990* (Utrecht: STIMU, 1992)

Dolmetsch, Arnold, *The Interpretation of the Music of the Seventeenth and Eighteenth Centuries* (London: Novello, 2/1946)

Donington, Robert, *The Interpretation of Early Music* (London: Faber and Faber, 2/1974)

Douglass, Fenner, Owen Jander and Barbara Owen (eds.), *Charles Brenton Fisk, Organ Builder. Volume One. Essays in his Honor* (Easthampton: The Westfield Center for Early Keyboard Studies, 1986)

Dreyfus, Laurence, *Bach and the Patterns of Invention* (Cambridge: Harvard University Press, 1996)

Durante, Sergio, 'On *artificioso* compositions at the time of Frescobaldi', in Silbiger (1987) 195–217

Dürr, Alfred, *Zur Chronologie der Leipziger Vokalwerke J.S. Bachs* (Kassel: Bärenreiter, 1976)

——'Tastenumfang und Chronologie in Bachs Klavierwerken', *Festschrift Georg von Dadelsen*, ed. T. Kohlhase and V. Schierliess (Neuhausen-Stuttgart: Hänssler, 1978) 73–88 [1978a]

——'Heinrich Nicolaus Gerber als Schüler Bachs', *Bach-Jahrbuch* (1978) 7–18 [1978b]

——*Zur Frühgeschichte des Wohltemperierten Klaviers I von Johann Sebastian Bach* (Göttingen: Vandenhoeck u. Ruprecht, 1984)

——'Überlegungen zu Johann Sebastian Bachs Klaviernotation, dargestellt am Beispiel des Autographs zum Wohltemperierten Klavier I', *Spiegelungen: Festschrift für Hermann J. Abs*, ed. W. Knopp (Mainz: v. Hase & Koehler, 1986) 205–20

——'Das Präludium Es-Dur BWV 852 aus dem *Wohltemperierten Klavier I*', *Studien zur Instrumentalmusik*, ed. A. Bingmann, K. Hortschansky, W. Kirsch (Tutzing: Schneider, 1988) 93–101

——*Die Kantaten von Johann Sebastian Bach* (Kassel: Bärenreiter, 6/1995)

——*Johann Sebastian Bach: Das wohltemperierte Klavier* (Kassel: Bärenreiter,

1998)

Eggebrecht, Hans Heinrich, 'Über Bachs geschichtlichen Ort', *Deutsche Vierteljahrsschrift für Literaturwissenschaft und Geistesgeschichte* xxxi (1957) 527–56, also in Blankenburg (1970)

——'Zum Figur-Begriff der Musica poetica', *Archiv für Musikwissenschaft* xvi (1959) 57–69

Eisert, Christian, *Die Clavier-Toccaten BWV 910–916 von Johann Sebastian Bach* (Mainz: Schott, 1994)

Ellis, Mark Richard, 'Linear Aspects of the Fugues of J.S. Bach's "The Well-tempered Clavier", a Quantitative Survey', Ph.D. diss., Nottingham University, 1980

Elster, Peter, 'Anmerkungen zur Aria der sogenannten Goldbergvariationen BWV 988: Bachs Bearbeitung eines französischen Menuetts', in Hoffmann and Schneiderheinze (1988) 259–67

Emery, Walter, *Bach's Ornaments* (London: Novello, 1953)

——*Editions and Musicians* (London: Novello, 1957)

——'The compass of Bach's organs as evidence of the date of his works', *The Organ* cxxvi (1952) 97–100, also in Blankenburg (1970)

Ernst, Friedrich, *Der Flügel Joh. Seb. Bachs* (Frankfurt: Peters, 1955)

——*Bach und das Pianoforte* (Frankfurt: Verlag Das Instrument, [1963])

Faulkner, Quentin, *J.S. Bach's Keyboard Technique: A Historical Introduction* (St. Louis: Concordia, 1984)

Federhofer, Hellmut, 'Johann Joseph Fux und die gleichschwebende Temperatur', *Die Musikforschung* xli (1988) 9–15

Felix, Werner, Winfried Hoffmann and Armin Schneiderheinze (eds), *Bericht über die Wissenschaftliche Konferenz . . . Leipzig 1975* (Leipzig: VEB Deutscher Verlag für Musik, 1977)

Ferguson, Howard, 'Bach's "Lautenwerk"', *Music & Letters* xlviii (1967) 259–64

Field, Christopher, 'Jenkins and the cosmography of harmony', *John Jenkins and his Time*, ed. A. Ashbee and P. Holman (Oxford: Clarendon Press, 1996) 1–74

Finke-Hecklinger, Doris, *Tanzcharaktere in Johann Sebastian Bachs Vokalmusik* (Trossingen: Hohner, 1970)

Fischer, Wilhelm, 'Zur Entwicklungsgeschichte des Wiener klassischen Stils', *Studien zur Musikwissenschaft* iii (1915) 24–84

Flade, Ernst, 'Bachs Stellung zum Orgel- und Cembalobau seiner Zeit', *Bericht über die Wissenschaftlische Bachtagung der Gesellschaft für Musikforschung . . . Leipzig 1950*, ed. W. Vetter and E.H. Meyer (Leipzig: Peters, 1951) 405–10

——*Gottfried Silbermann* (Leipzig: VEB Breitkopf & Härtel, 2/1953)

Forchert, Arno, 'Bach und die Tradition der Rhetorik', in Berke and Hanemann (1987) I:169–78

Ford, Karin, 'The pedal clavichord and pedal harpsichord', *Galpin Society Journal* l (1997) 161–79

Franklin, Don O., 'Articulation in the cembalo works of J.S. Bach: a notational study', in Berke and Hanemann (1987) II:452–66

——'Reconstructing the *Urpartitur* for *The Well-tempered Clavier* II: a study of the "London Autograph" (BL Add. MS 35021)', in Franklin (1989) 240–78 [1989a]

——(ed.), *Bach Studies* (Cambridge: Cambridge University Press, 1989) [1989b]

Freeman, David E., 'Johann Christian Bach and the early Classical Italian masters', *Eighteenth-Century Keyboard Music*, ed. R.L. Marshall (New York: Schirmer, 1994) 230–69

Friedrich, Felix, *Der Orgelbauer Heinrich Gottfried Trost* (Wiesbaden: Breitkopf & Härtel, 1989)

Fuchs, Josef Rainerius, *Studien zu Artikulationsangaben in Orgel- und Clavierwerken von Joh. Seb. Bach* (Neuhausen-Stuttgart: Hänssler, 1985)

Fuller, David, 'The "dotted style" in Bach, Handel, and Scarlatti', in P. Williams (1985b) 99–117

——'"Sous les doits de Chambonniere"', *Early Music* xxi (1993) 191–202

Gehrmann, Hermann (ed.), *Jan Pieterszoon Sweelinck werke deel 10* 'De Compositions-Regeln' (s'Gravenhage: M. Nijhoff, 1901)

Geiringer, Karl and Irene, *Johann Sebastian Bach* (London: Allen and Unwin, 1967)

Germann, Sheridan, 'The Mietkes, the Margrave and Bach', in P. Williams (1985b) 119–48

Glöckner, Andreas, 'Zur Echtheit und Datierung der Kantate BWV 150 "Nach dir, Herr, verlanget mich"', *Bach-Jahrbuch* (1988) 195–203

Glover, Jane, *Cavalli* (London: Batsford, 1978)

Goble, Elizabeth, 'Keyboard lessons with Arnold Dolmetsch', *Early Music* v (1977) 89–91

Godwin, Joscelin, *Athanasius Kircher: A Renaissance Man and the Quest for Lost Knowledge* (London: Thames & Hudson, 1979)

Gray, Cecil, *The Forty-Eight Preludes and Fugues of J.S. Bach* (London: Oxford University Press, 1938)

Hahn, Harry, *Symbol und Glaube im I. Teil des Wohltemperierten Klaviers von Joh. Seb. Bach* (Wiesbaden: Breitkopf & Härtel, 1973)

Hamel, Fred, *Johann Sebastian Bach* (Göttingen: Vandenhoeck u. Ruprecht, 1951)

Harper, John, 'Frescobaldi's early *inganni* and their background', *Proceedings of the Royal Musical Association* cv (1978–9) 1–12

Harrison, Daniel, 'Rhetoric and fugue: an analytical application', *Music Theory Spectrum* xii (1990) 1–42

Helenius-Öberg, Eva, *Svenskt klavikordbygge 1720–1820* (Stockholm: Almqvist & Wiksell, 1986)

Heller, Karl, 'Friedrich Konrad Griepenkerl. Aus unveröffentlichten Briefen des Bach-Sammlers und -Editors', *Bach-Jahrbuch* (1978) 211–28

——'Norddeutsche Musikkultur als Traditionsraum des Jungen Bach', *Bach-Jahrbuch* (1989) 7–19

Hellwig, Friedemann, 'Historische musikalische Temperaturen und ihre Einstimmung', *Der klangliche Aspekt beim Restaurierung von Seitenklavieren*, ed. V. Schwarz (Graz: Akademische Druck und Verlagsanstalt, 1973) 57–67

Henkel, Hubert, 'Der Cembalobau der Bachzeit im sächsisch-thüringischen und im Berliner Raum', in Felix, Hoffmann, Schneiderheinze (1977) 99–110

——*Musikinstrumenten-Museum der Universität Leipzig. Katalog Band 2. Kiel-Instrumente; Band 4 Clavichorde* (Leipzig: VEB Deutscher Verlag für Musik, 1979, 1981)

——'Identifikation eines frühen deutschen Cembalos?', *Das Musikinstrument* xxxviii (1989) 34–40

——'Musikinstrumente im Nachlass Leipziger Bürger', *Bach-Studien 10*, ed. R. Szeskus (Wiesbaden: Breitkopf & Härtel, 1991) 56–67

Henning, Uta, 'A present to the greatest monarchs: About the reconstruction of Johann Christoph Fleischers theorbo-harpsichord (1718) by Rudolf Richter (1986)', *The Consort* xli (1993) 20–9

——and Rudolf Richter, 'The most beautiful among the claviers', *Early Music* x (1982) 477–86

——and Rudolf Richter, 'Die Laute auf dem Claviere: Zur Rekonstruktion des Theorbenflügels nach Johann Cristoph Fleischer (1718) durch Rudolf Richter (1986)', *Basler Jahrbuch für historische Musikpraxis*', xii (1988) 109–22

Hermelink, Siegfried, 'Das Präludium in Bachs Klaviermusik', *Jahrbuch des staatlichen Instituts für Musikforschung Preußisches Kulturbesitz* (1976) 7–80

Herz, Gerhard, *Essays on Bach* (Ann Arbor: UMI Research Press, 1985)

Heyde-Dohrn, Elinor v.d., 'Joh. Seb. Bachs "Wohltemperiertes Klavier" aus der Sicht des Organisten', *Heinrich Sievers zum 70. Geburtstag* (Tutzing: Schneider, 1978) 39–72

Hill, Robert, 'The Möller Manuscript and the Andreas Bach Book: Two Keyboard Anthologies from the Circle of the Young Johann Sebastian Bach', Ph.D. diss., Harvard University, 1987

——(ed.), *Keyboard Music from the Andreas Bach Book and the Möller Manuscript* (Cambridge, MA: Harvard University Press, 1991)

Hoffmann, Winfried and Armin Schneiderheinze (eds), *Bericht über die Wissenschaftliche Konferenz zum V. Internationalen Bachfest der DDR . . . Leipzig 1985* (Leipzig: VEB Deutscher Verlag für Musik, 1988)

Hoffmann-Erbrecht, Lothar, 'Der Lautenist Sylvius Leopold Weiß und Johann Sebastian Bach', *Gitarre und Laute* (11–12/1987) 19–23

Hofmann, Klaus, '"Fünf Präludien und fünf Fugen": Über ein unbeachtetes Sammelwerk Johann Sebastian Bachs', in Hoffmann and Schneiderheinze (1988) 227–35 [1988a]

——'Über Themenbildung und thematische Arbeit in einigen zweiteiligen Präludien des Wohltemperierten Klaviers II', *Johann Sebastian Bachs Spätwerk und dessen Umfeld*, ed. C. Wolff (Kassel: Bärenreiter, 1988) 48–57 [1988b]

——'Johann Sebastian Bach und der deutsche Süden. Eine Bestandaufnahme', *Johann Sebastian Bach und der süddeutsche Raum*, ed. H.-J. Schulze and C. Wolff (Regensburg: Bosse, 1991) 61–77

Hogwood, Christopher, 'Frescobaldi on performance', *Italian Music and the Fitzwilliam*, ed. C. Cudworth (Cambridge: Fitzwilliam Museum, 1976) 14–22

——'A Supplement to C.P.E. Bach's *Versuch*: E.W. Wolf's *Anleitung* of 1785', *C.P.E. Bach Studies*, ed. S.L. Clark (Oxford: Clarendon Press, 1988) 133–57

Holman, Peter, 'An orchestral suite by François Couperin', *Early Music* xiv (1986) 71–6

——*Henry Purcell* (Oxford: Oxford University Press, 1994)

Houle, George, *Meter in Music 1600–1800* (Bloomington: Indiana University Press, 1987)

Howell, Almonte C., 'French Baroque organ music and the eight church tones', *Journal of the American Musicological Society* xi (1958) 106–18

Huffman, William H., *Robert Fludd: Essential Readings* (London: The Aquarian Press, 1992)

Iliffe, Frederick, *The Forty-Eight Preludes and Fugues of John Sebastian Bach Analysed for the Use of Students* (London: Novello, 1897)

Jenne, Natalie, 'Bach's use of dance rhythms in fugues', *Bach* v/2 (4/1974) 3–7

Jira, Martin, *Musikalische Temperaturen und musikalischer Satz in der Klaviermusik von J.S. Bach* (Tutzing: Schneider, 2000)

Jones, Richard, 'Stages in the development of Bach's *The Well-tempered Clavier II*', *The Musical Times* cxxxii (1991) 441–6; 'Further observations on the development of *The Well-tempered Clavier II*', 607–9

Kahl, Willi, *Selbstbiographien deutscher Musiker des 18. Jahrhunderts* (Cologne: Staufen Verlag, 1948)

Keller, Hermann, *Die Klavierwerke Bachs* (Leipzig: Peters, 4/1950)

——*The Well-tempered Clavier by Johann Sebastian Bach* (London: Allen and Unwin, 1976)

Kelletat, Herbert, *Zur musikalischen Temperatur insbesondere bei Johann Sebastian Bach* (Kassel: Oncken, 1960; Berlin: Merseburger, 2/1981)

Kellner, Herbert, 'Betrachtungen zur Stimmung Werckmeister III von 1691', *Das Musikinstrument* xxvi (1977) 995–6

——'Das wohltemperirte Clavier: tuning and musical structure', *The English Harpsichord Magazine* iii (1980) 137–40

Kent, Christopher, 'J.S. Bach and the Livre d'orgue of Nicolas de Grigny', *Aspects of Keyboard Music*, ed. R. Judd (Oxford: Positif Press, 2/1992) 45–59

Kinsky, Georg, 'Pedalklavier oder Orgel bei Bach', *Acta musicologica* viii (1936) 158–61

Kirkpatrick, Ralph, 'On playing the clavichord', *Early Music* x (1981) 293–305

Klenz, William, *Giovanni Bononcini of Modena* (Durham: Duke University Press, 1962)

Klop, G., *Harpsichord Tuning* (Garderen: Werkplaats voor clavicimbelbouw, 1974)

Klotz, Hans, *Die Ornamentik der Klavier- und Orgelwerke von Johann Sebastian Bach* (Kassel: Bärenreiter, 1984)

Kluge-Kahn, Hertha, *Johann Sebastian Bach: Die verschlüsselten theologischen Aussagen in seinem Spätwerk* (Wolfenbüttel: Möseler, 1985)

Knab, Armin, 'Joh. Seb. Bachs Wohltemperiertes Klavier', *Die Musik* xiii (1914) 26–31, and Beilage

Kobayashi, Yoshitake, 'Zur Chronologie der Spätwerke Johann Sebastian Bachs', *Bach-Jahrbuch* (1988) 7–72

Kooiman, Ewald, 'Bachs Klaviertechniek', *Het Orgel* lxxix (1983) 2–15 [1983a]

——'Eine Quelle zu Bachs Klaviertechnik', *Ars organi* xxxi (1983) 21–6 [1983b]

Koptchewski, Nikolai, 'Stilistische Parallelen zwischen dem Klavierwerk Frescobaldis und dem Spätwerk Bachs', in Hoffmann and Schneiderheinze (1988) 437–47

Korte, Werner, 'Johann Sebastian Bach', (1940) in Blankenburg (1970) 23–42

Koster, John, 'The quest for Bach's *Clavier*: An historical interpretation', *Early Keyboard Journal* (1996) 65–84

——'The harpsichord culture in Bach's environs', in Schulenberg (1999) 57–77

Krautwurst, Franz, 'Anmerkung zu den Augsburger Bach-Dokumenten', in Sachs (1986) 176–84

Kreutz, Alfred, 'Ornamentation in J.S. Bach's keyboard works', *Music Book Volume VII*, ed. M. Hinrichsen (London: Hinrichen, 1952) 358–79

Krickeberg, Dieter, 'Michael Mietke – ein Cembalobauer aus dem Umkreis von Johann Sebastian Bach', *Cöthener Bach-Hefte 3*, ed. G. Hoppe (Köthen: Historisches Museum, 1985) 47–56

——and Horst Rase, 'Beiträge zur Kenntnis des mittel- und norddeutschen Cembalobaus um 1700', *Studia organologica: Festschrift für John Henry van der Meer*, ed. F. Hellwig (Tutzing: Schneider, 1987) 285–310

Kunze, Stefan, 'Gattungen der fuge in Bachs Wohltemperierten Klavier', *Bach-*

Interpretationen, ed. Martin Geck (Göttingen: Vandenhoeck u. Ruprecht, 1969) 74–93

Landowska, Wanda, 'Les oeuvres de clavecin de J.S. Bach', *Musica* vi (10/1907) 156–7

——'Für welches Instrument hat Bach ein "Wohltemperiertes Klavier" geschrieben?', *Neue Zeitschrift für Musik* lxxviii (1911) 308–10

——'Über die C dur-Fuge aus dem I. Teil des Wohltemperierten Klaviers', *Bach-Jahrbuch* (1914) 53–8

——*Landowska on Music*, ed. D. Restout and R. Hawkins (London: Secker and Warburg, 1965)

Landshoff, Ludwig, *Joh. Seb. Bach. Die 15 zweistimmigen Inventionen . . . Revisionsbericht* (Leipzig: Peters, 1933)

Lange, Helmut, K.H., 'Gottfried Silbermann's organ tuning', *ISO Information* viii (1972) 543–56; ix, x (1973) 647–58, 721–30

Leaver, Robin A., *Bachs theologische Bibliothek* (Neuhausen-Stuttgart: Hänssler, 1983)

Ledbetter, David, *Harpsichord and Lute Music in 17th-Century France* (London: Macmillan, 1987)

——*Continuo Playing According to Handel* (Oxford: Clarendon Press, 1990)

——'What the lute sources tell us about the performance of French harpsichord music', in Dirksen (1992) 59–85

Lee, Hio-Ihm, *Die Form der Ritornelle bei Johann Sebastian Bach* (Pfaffenweiler: Centaurus, 1993)

Lester, Joel, 'The Fux-Mattheson correspondence: an annotated translation', *Current Musicology* xxiv (1977) 37–62

——*Between Modes and Keys: German Theory 1592–1802* (Stuyvesant: Pendragon Press, 1989)

——*Compositional Theory in the Eighteenth Century* (Cambridge, MA: Harvard University Press, 1992)

Liebermann, H., 'Zum 325. Geburtstagsjubiläum Johann Heinrich Harraß (1665–1714)', *Bräetmicher Heimat Echo* (9/1990) 8–10

Lindley, Mark, *Lutes, Viols & Temperaments* (Cambridge: Cambridge University Press, 1984)

——'J.S. Bach's tunings', *The Musical Times* cxxvi (1985) 721–6 [1985a]

——'Keyboard technique and articulation', in P. Williams (1985b) 207–43 [1985b]

——'Stimmung und Temperatur', *Geschichte der Musiktheorie Band 6*, ed. F. Zaminer (Darmstadt: Wissenschaftliche Buchgesellschaft, 1987) 109–331 [1987a]

——'J.S. Bachs Klavier Stimmung,' in Berke and Hanemann (1987) 409–21 [1987b]

——'A suggested improvement for the Fisk organ at Stanford', *Performance*

Practice Review i (1988) 107–32

——'Early fingering: some editing problems and some new readings for J.S. Bach and John Bull', *Early Music* xvii (1989) 60–9

——and Maria Boxall, *Early Keyboard Fingerings: An Anthology* (London: Schott, 2/1992)

Little, Meredith, 'The contribution of dance steps to musical analysis and performance: *La Bourgogne*', *Journal of the American Musicological Society* xxviii (1975) 112–24

——and Natalie Jenne, *Dance and the Music of J.S. Bach* (Bloomington: Indiana University Press, 1991)

Loucks, Richard, 'Was the *Well-tempered Clavier* performable on a fretted clavichord?', *Performance Practice Review* v (1992) 44–89

Lowinsky, Edward, 'Taste, style, and ideology in eighteenth-century music', *Aspects of the Eighteenth Century*, ed. E.R. Wasserman (Baltimore: The Johns Hopkins Press, 1969) 163–205

Macey, Patrick, 'Frescobaldi's musical tributes to Ferrara', *The Organist as Scholar*, ed. K.J. Snyder (Stuyvesant: Pendragon Press, 1994) 197–231

McIntyre, Ray, 'On the interpretation of Bach's gigues', *The Musical Quarterly* li (1965) 478–92

Mann, Alfred, *The Study of Fugue* (London: Faber and Faber, 1958)

——*Theory and Practice* (New York: Norton, 1987)

Marissen, Michael, *The Social and Musical Designs of Bach's Brandenburg Concertos* (Princeton: Princeton University Press, 1995)

Marshall, Robert L., *The Compositional Process of J.S. Bach* (Princeton: Princeton University Press, 1972)

——'Tempo and dynamic indications in the Bach sources', in P. Williams (1985b) 255–69

——'Organ or "Klavier"? Instrumental prescriptions in the sources of Bach's keyboard works', *J.S. Bach as Organist*, ed. G. Stauffer and E. May (London: Batsford, 1986) 212–39, also in Marshall (1989)

——*The Music of Johann Sebastian Bach* (New York: Schirmer, 1989)

Mather, Betty Bang and Dean M. Karns, *Dance Rhythms of the French Baroque* (Bloomington: Indiana University Press, 1987)

Mattax, Charlotte, *Accompaniment on the Theorbo and Harpsichord* (Bloomington: Indiana University Press, 1991)

Meer, John Henry van der, 'The dating of German clavichords', *The Organ Yearbook* vi (1975) 100–13

Meier, Bernhard, *Alte Tonarten, dargestellt an der Instrumentalmusik des 16. und 17. Jahrhunderts* (Kassel: Bärenreiter, 1992)

Meister, Hubert, 'Die musikalische Rhetorik und ihre Bedeutung für das Verständnis barocker Musik', *Musica sacra* cxiii (1993) 291–300, 382–8, 479–86

Mellers, Wilfred, *Bach and the Dance of God* (London: Faber and Faber, 1980)
Müller, Werner, *Gottfried Silbermann* (Frankfurt: Verlag Das Instrument, 1982)
Nef, Karl, 'Clavicymbel und Clavichord', *Jahrbuch der Musikbibliothek Peters für 1903*, ed. R. Schwartz (Leipzig: Peters, 1904) 15–30
——'J.S. Bachs Verhältnis zu den Klavierinstrumenten', *Bach-Jahrbuch* (1909) 12–26
Neumann, Frederick, 'External evidence for uneven notes', *The Musical Quarterly* lii (1966) 448–64
——*Ornamentation in Baroque and Post-Baroque Music* (Princeton: Princeton University Press, 3/1983)
——'Conflicting binary and ternary rhythms', *The Music Forum* vi (1987) 93–127
Neumann, Werner, *J.S. Bachs Chorfuge* (Leipzig: Kistner u. Siegel, 1938)
Neupert, Hanns, *Das Klavichord* (Kassel: Bärenreiter, 2/1955)
Newcomb, Anthony, 'The anonymous ricercars of the Bourdeney Codex', in Silbiger (1987) 97–123
O'Donnell, John, 'Bach's trills: some historical and contextual considerations', *Musicology . . . Australia* iv (1974) 14–24
Oppel, Reinhard, 'Über Joh. Kasp. Ferd. Fischers Einfluß auf Joh. Seb. Bach', *Bach-Jahrbuch* (1910) 63–9
Ottenberg, Hans-Günther, *Carl Philipp Emanuel Bach* (Oxford: Oxford University Press, 1987)
Picken, Laurence E.R., 'A keyboard fugue by "Bach"', *Proceedings of the Royal Musical Association* lxxvi (1949–50) 47–57
Pirro, André, *L'esthétique de Jean-Sébastien Bach* (Paris: Fischbacher, 1907)
Poulin, Pamela L., *J.S. Bach's Precepts and Principles for playing the Thorough-Bass . . . 1738* (Oxford: Clarendon Press, 1994)
——and Irmgard C. Taylor, *Friederich Erhardt Niedt: The Musical Guide* (Oxford: Oxford University Press, 1989)
Rasch, Rudolf (ed.), *Andreas Werckmeister: Musicalische Temperatur* (Utrecht: The Diapason Press, 1983)
——(ed.), *Joseph Sauveur: Collected Writings on Musical Acoustics* (Utrecht: The Diapason Press, 1984)
——'Does "well-tempered" mean "equal-tempered"?', in P. Williams (1985b) 293–310
——(ed.), *Friedrich Suppig: Labyrinthus musicus* (Utrecht: The Diapason Press, 1990)
——'Johann Jakob Froberger and the Netherlands', in Dirksen (1992) 121–41
Renwick, William, *Analyzing Fugue: A Schenkerian Approach* (Stuyvesant: Pendragon Press, 1995)
——*The Langloz Manuscript* (New York: Oxford University Press, 2001)
Riedel, Friedrich Wilhelm, *Quellenkundliche Beiträge zur Geschichte der Musik für*

Tasteninstrumente in der zweiten Hälfte des 17. Jahrhunderts (Kassel: Bärenreiter, 1960)

——'Musikgeschichtliche Beziehungen zwischen Johann Joseph Fux und Johann Sebastian Bach', *Festschrift Friedrich Blume*, ed. A.A. Abert and W. Pfannkuch (Kassel: Bärenreiter, 1963) 290–304

——'Der Einfluß der italienischen Klaviermusik des 17. Jahrhunderts auf die Entwicklung der Musik für Tasteninstrumente in Deutschland während der ersten Hälfte des 18. Jahrhunderts', *Studien zur italienisch-deutschen Musikgeschichte V*, ed. F. Lippmann (Cologne: Böhlau, 1968) 18–33

——'Die zyklische Fugen-Komposition von Froberger bis Albrechtsberger', *Die süddeutsch-österreichiche Orgelmusik im 17. und 18. Jahrhundert*, ed. W. Salmen (Innsbruck: Helbling, 1980) 154–67

——'The influence and tradition of Frescobaldi's works in the transalpine countries', in Silbiger (1987) 218–32

Riemann, Hugo, *Catechismus der Fugencomposition* (parts 1–2) *Analyse des Wohltemperierten Klaviers* (1890ff), trans. J.S. Shedlock (London: Augener, [n.d.])

Rokseth, Yvonne, *La musique d'orgue au XVe siècle et au début du XVIe* (Paris: Droz, 1930)

Rubbra, Edmund, *Counterpoint* (London: Hutchinson University Library, 1960)

Sachs, Klaus-Jürgen (ed.), *Festschrift Martin Ruhnke zum 65. Geburtstag* (Neuhausen-Stuttgart: Hänssler, 1986)

Schenker, Heinrich, 'Das Organische der Fuge', *Das Meiterwerk in der Musik* ii (Munich: Drei Masken Verlag, 1926), trans. H. Siegel (Cambridge: Cambridge University Press, 1996)

Schenkman, Walter, 'Portrait of Mattheson the editor, together with his correspondents', *Bach* ix/4 (10/1978) 2–10, x/1 (1/1979) 3–12

——'Mattheson's "Forty-Eight" and their commentaries', *The Music Review* xlii (1981) 9–21

Schleuning, Peter, *The Fantasia* (Cologne: A.Volk, 1971)

Schott, Howard, 'From harpsichord to pianoforte', *Early Music* xiii (1985) 28–38

Schrade, Leo, 'Johann Sebastian Bach und die deutsche Nation', *Deutsche Vierteljahrsschrift für Literaturwissenschaft und Geistesgeschichte* xv (1937) 220–52

Schulenberg, David, *The Keyboard Music of J.S. Bach* (New York: Schirmer, 1992)

——'Composition and improvisation in the school of J.S. Bach', in Stinson (1995b) 1–42

——(ed.), *Bach Perspectives Volume Four* (Lincoln and London: University of Nebraska Press, 1999)

Schulze, Hans-Joachim, 'Cembaloimprovisation bei Johann Sebastian Bach',

Zu Fragen der Improvisation in der Instrumentalmusik der ersten Hälfte des 18. Jahrhunderts, Heft 10, ed. E. Thom (Blankenburg/Harz: [Institut für Aufführungspraxis], 1979) 50–7

——*Studien zur Bach-Überlieferung im 18. Jahrhundert* (Leipzig: Peters, 1984)

——'Bach und Buxtehude. Eine wenig beachtete Quelle in der Carnegie Library zu Pittsburgh/PA', *Bach-Jahrbuch* (1991) 177–81

Schünemann, Georg, 'J.G. Walther und H. Bokemeyer. Eine Musikfreundschaft um Sebastian Bach', *Bach-Jahrbuch* (1933) 86–118

——'Bachs Verbesserungen und Entwürfe', *Bach-Jahrbuch* (1935) 1–32

Seidel, Elmar, 'Über eine besondere Art Bachs, die Tonart der IV Stufe zu verwenden', *Musiktheorie* i/2 (5/1986) 139–52

Seiffert, Max, *Geschichte der Klaviermusik* (Leipzig: Breitkopf & Härtel, 1899)

Serauky, Walter, 'Die Affekten-Metrik des Isaac Vossius in ihrem Einfluß auf Johann Kuhnau und Johann Sebastian Bach', *Festschrift Max Schneider*, ed. W. Vetter (Leipzig: VEB Deutscher Verlag für Musik, 1955) 105–13

Shannon, John R. (ed.), *The Mylau Tabulaturbuch* (Neuhausen-Stuttgart: American Institute of Musicology, 1977)

Shedlock, John South, 'Das wohltemperierte Klavier', *The Musical Times* xxiv (1883) 533–5, 594–6

Siegele, Ulrich, 'Von Bachschen Modellen und Zeitarten', *Festschrift Walter Gerstenberg*, ed. G. v. Dadelsen and A. Holschneider (Wolfenbüttel: Möseler, 1964) 162–5

——*Kompositionsweise und Bearbeitungstechnik in der Instrumentalmusik Johann Sebastian Bachs* (Stuttgart-Neuhausen: Hänssler, 1975)

——'Zur Analyse der Fuge c-moll aus dem ersten Teil des Wohltemperierten Klaviers', *Köthener Bach-Hefte 4*, ed. G. Hoppe (Köthen: Historisches Museum, 1986) 101–36, trans. in Franklin (1989b)

Silbiger, Alexander (ed.), *Frescobaldi Studies* (Durham, NC: Duke University Press, 1987)

Smend, Friedrich, 'Luther und Bach' (1947), *Bach-Studien*, ed. C. Wolff (Kassel: Bärenreiter, 1969) 152–75

Snyder, Kerala J., 'To Lübeck in the steps of J.S. Bach', *The Musical Times* cxxvii (1986) 672–7

——*Dietrich Buxtehude* (London: Collier Macmillan, 1987)

Spányi, Miklós and John Collins, 'Johann Sebastian Bach's clavichord technique described by Griepenkerl', *Clavichord International* iv/2 (11/2000) 47–52

Spring, Matthew (ed.), *John Wilson: Thirty Preludes in all (24) Keys for Lute* (Utrecht: The Diapason Press, 1992)

Stauffer, George B., *The Organ Preludes of Johann Sebastian Bach* (Ann Arbor: UMI Research Press, 1980)

——'Johann Mattheson und J.S. Bach: The Hamburg Connection', in Buelow and Marx (1983) 353–68

——'Bach as reviser of his own keyboard works', *Early Music* xiii (1985) 185–98

——'J.S. Bach as organ pedagogue', *The Organist as Scholar: Essays in Honor of Russell Saunders*, ed. K.J. Snyder (Stuyvesant: Pendragon Press, 1994) 15–44

——'J.S. Bach's harpsichords', *Festa musicologica: Essays in Honor of George J. Buelow*, ed. T.J. Mathiesen and B.V. Rivera (Stuyvesant: Pendragon Press, 1995) 289–318

Steblin, Rita, *A History of Key Characteristics in the Eighteenth and Early Nineteenth Centuries* (Ann Arbor: UMI Research Press, 1983)

Steglich, Rudolf, 'Kleiner Beitrag zur Bach-Interpretation', *Die Musikforschung* vii (1954) 459–60

Stiller, Günther, *Johann Sebastian Bach and Liturgical Life in Leipzig*, trans. H.J.A. Bouman et al. (St Louis: Concordia, 1984)

Stinson, Russell, 'Towards a chronology of Bach's instrumental music: Observations on three keyboard works', *The Journal of Musicology* vii (1989) 440–70

——*The Bach Manuscripts of Johann Peter Kellner and his Circle* (Durham, NC: Duke University Press, 1990)

——'The compositional history of Bach's *Orgelbüchlein* reconsidered', in Stinson (1995) 43–78 [1995a]

——(ed.), *Bach Perspectives Volume One* (Lincoln and London: University of Nebraska Press, 1995) [1995b]

——*Bach: The Orgelbüchlein* (New York: Schirmer, 1996)

Sumikura, Ichiro, 'Johann Sebastian Bach and Johann Kaspar Ferdinand Fischer', in Felix, Hoffmann, Schneiderheinze (1977) 233–8

Suthoff-Groß, Rudolf, '"Das wohltemperierte Klavier" von J.S. Bach: Die totale Synopsis', *Neue Zeitschrift für Musik* cxxix (1968) 529–36

Tagliavini, Luigi, 'The art of "not leaving the instrument empty"', *Early Music* xi (1983) 299–308

Terry, Charles Sanford, *Bach: A Biography* (London: Oxford University Press, 1928)

Theill, Gustav Adolf, *Beiträge zur Symbolsprache Johann Sebastian Bachs* (Bonn: Brockhaus, 1985)

Toch, Ernst, 'Unklarheiten im Schriftbild der cis-moll-Fuge des "Wohltemperierten Klaviers"', *Bach-Jahrbuch* (1940–48) 122–5

Tolonen, Youko, *Protestanttinen koraali ja Bachin fuugatemat teoksessa Das wohltemperierte Klavier I* (Helsinki: Soumen Musikkitierteellinen Seura, 1971)

Tomita, Yo, 'J.S. Bach's Well-tempered Clavier, Book II: A Study of its Aim, Historical Significance, and Compiling Process', Ph.D. diss., Leeds University, 1990

——*J.S. Bach's 'Das wohltemperierte Clavier II': A Critical Commentary* (Leeds:

Household World, 1993)

——*J.S. Bach's 'Das wohltemperierte Clavier II': A Critical Commentary . . . Volume II* (Leeds: Household World, 1995)

——'Through a glass darkly: Analysing Bach's ink', *The Musical Times* cxxxix (1998) 37–42

——'Bach and his early drafts: Some observations on little known early versions of *Well-tempered Clavier* II and the Goldberg Variations from the Manfred Gorke collection', *Bach* xxx/2 (1999) 49–72

Tovey, Donald Francis, *A Companion to 'The Art of Fugue'* (London: Oxford University Press, 1931)

Trautmann, Christoph, '"Calovii Schrifften. 3 Bände" aus Johann Sebastian Bachs Nachlaß und ihre Bedeutung für das Bild des lutherischen Kantors Bach', *Musik und Kirche* xxxix (1969) 145–60

Troeger, Richard, *Technique and Performance on the Harpsichord and Clavichord* (Bloomington: Indiana University Press, 1987)

Tröster, Immanuel, *Joh. Seb. Bach* (Iserlohn: Karthause, 1984)

Unger, Hans-Heinrich, *Die Beziehungen zwischen Musik und Rhetorik im 16. bis 18. Jahrhundert* (Würzburg: Triltsch, 1941)

Vogel, Harald, 'Tuning and temperament in the north German school of the seventeenth and eighteenth centuries', in Douglass, Jander and Owen (1986) 237–65

——'Mitteltönig – wohltemperiert. Der Wandel der Stimmungsästhetik im norddeutschen Orgelbau und Orgelrepertoire des 17. und 18. Jahrhunderts', *Jahrbuch alte Musik* I (1989) 119–51

Vogel, Martin, 'Die Kirnberger-Stimmung vor und nach Kirnberger', *Colloquium amicorum: Joseph Schmidt-Görg zum 70. Geburtstag*, ed. C. Kross and H. Schmidt (Bonn: Beethovenhaus, 1967) 441–9

Walker, Paul, 'Fingering, Bach and the *Wegweiser*', *Early Keyboard Studies Newsletter* i/3 (6/1985) 1–5

——'From Renaissance *fuga* to Baroque fugue: The role of the Sweelinck theory manuscripts', *Schütz-Jahrbuch* vii/viii (1985/86) 93–104

——'Die Entstehung der Permutationsfuge', *Bach-Jahrbuch* (1989) 21–41

——'Zur Geschichte des Kontrasubjekts und zu seinem Gebrauch in den frühesten Klavier- und Orgel-Fugen Johann Sebastian Bachs', *Das Frühwerk Bachs. Kolloquium . . . Rostock . . . 1990*, ed. K. Heller and H.-J. Schulze (Cologne: Schewe, 1995)

——'Fugue and the musical-rhetorical analogy and rhetoric in the development of fugue', in Schulenberg (1999) 159–79

——*Theories of Fugue from the Age of Josquin to the Age of Bach* (Rochester: University of Rochester Press, 2000)

Werker, Wilhelm, *Studien über die Symmetrie im Bau der Fugen und die motivische Zusammengehörigkeit der Präludien und Fugen des 'Wohltemperierten Klaviers' von*

Johann Sebastian Bach (Leipzig: Breitkopf & Härtel, 1922)

Wessel, Frederick T. 'The Affektenlehre in the Eighteenth Century', Ph.D. diss., Indiana University, 1955

Westphal, Rudolf, 'Die C-Takt-Fugen des Wohltemperierten Claviers', *Musikalisches Wochenblatt* xiv (1883) 237–8, 253–4, 265–7, 278–80, 289–91, 301–3, 313–15, 323–6

——'Die Aristoxenische Rhythmuslehre', *Vierteljahrschrift für Musikwissenschaft* vii (1891) 74–107

Whitehead, Lance, 'The clavichords of Johann Fleischer the younger', *Clavichord International* iii/1 (5/1999) 4–11

——and Jenny Nex, 'The three unique models of Hass clavichords', *Early Keyboard Journal* xviii (2000) 155–74

Williams, Charles Francis Abdy, 'the rhythmical construction of Bach's 'Forty-Eight' fugues', *Proceedings of the Royal Musical Association* xix (1892–3) 73–93

Williams, Peter, *Figured Bass Accompaniment* (Edinburgh: Edinburgh University Press, 1970)

——*The Organ Music of J.S. Bach* (Cambridge: Cambridge University Press, 1980, 1984)

——'J.S. Bach's *Well-tempered Clavier*: A new approach', *Early Music* xi (1983) 46–52, 332–9

——'Was Johann Sebastian Bach an organ expert or an acquisitive reader of Andreas Werckmeister?', *Journal of the American Musical Instrument Society* xi (1985) 38–54 [1985a]

——(ed.), *Bach, Handel, Scarlatti Tercentenary Essays* (Cambridge: Cambridge University Press, 1985) [1985b]

——'The acquisitive minds of Handel & Bach', in Douglass, Jander and Owen (1986) 267–81

——'Two case studies in performance practice and the details of notation: 1: J.S. Bach and 2/4 time', *Early Music* xxi (1993) 613–22; '2: J.S. Bach and left-hand – right-hand distribution', xxii (1994) 101–13

——*The Chromatic Fourth during Four Centuries of Music* (Oxford: Clarendon Press, 1997)

——'Some thoughts on Italian elements in certain music of Johann Sebastian Bach', *Recercare* xi (1999) 185–94

——'Witting and unwitting allusion in certain keyboard music of J.S. Bach', *The Musical Quarterly* lxxxiv (2000) 756–75

Wöhlke, Franz, *Lorenz Christoph Mizler* (Würzburg: Triltsch, 1940)

Wolff, Christoph, *Der stile antico in der Musik Johann Sebastian Bachs* (Wiesbaden: F. Steiner, 1968)

——'Johann Valentin Eckelts Tabulaturbuch von 1692', in Sachs (1986) 374–86

——'Bach und das Pianoforte', *Bach und die italienische Musik*, ed. W. Osthoff and R.Wiesend (Venice: Centro Tedesco di Studi Veneziani, 1987) 197–209

——*Bach: Essays on his Life and Music* (Cambridge, MA: Harvard University Press, 1991)

——'Das Trio in A-Dur BWV 1025', *Bach-Jahrbuch* (1993) 47–67

——*Johann Sebastian Bach, the Learned Musician* (Oxford: Oxford University Press, 2000)

Wolff, Hellmuth Christian, 'Der Rhythmus bei Bach', *Bach-Jahrbuch* (1940/48) 83–121

Wollny, Peter, 'Bach's Sanctus BWV 241 and Kerll's "Missa superba"', *Bach-Jahrbuch* (1991) 173–6

——(ed.), *Johann Sebastian Bach: Die Achtzehn Grossen Orgelchoräle . . . Faksimile der Originalhandschrift* (Laaber: Laaber, 1999)

Wustmann, Rudolf, 'Tonartensymbolik zu Bachs Zeit', *Bach-Jahrbuch* (1911) 60–74

Yates, Frances A., *Giordano Bruno and the Hermetic Tradition* (London: Routledge and Kegan Paul, 1964)

Yearsley, David, 'Alchemy and counterpoint in an age of reason', *Journal of the American Musicological Society* li (1998) 201–43

Zacher, Gerd, 'Befreundete bei Bach. Die Unterschrift in der cis-moll-Fuge des Wohltemperierten Claviers I', *Musiktheorie* iii (1998) 243–7

Zehnder, Jean-Claude, 'Giuseppe Torelli und Johann Sebastian Bach', *Bach-Jahrbuch* (1991) 33–95

Zenck, Hermann, 'J.S. Bachs Wohltemperiertes Klavier', *Numerus und Affectus*, ed. W. Gerstenberg (Kassel: Bärenreiter, 1959) 67–85, also in Blankenburg (1970)

Zenck, Martin, 'Stadien der Bach-Deutung in der Musikkritik, Musikästhetik und Musikgeschichtsschreibung zwischen 1750 und 1800', *Bach-Jahrbuch* (1982) 7–32

Index

References to music examples are in **bold**; references to Notes are *italic*.